OPERATIONS AND PROCESS MANAGEMENT

You will find a CD contained within your copy of *Operations and Process Management* featuring a range of additional resources. Each chapter contains the following resources which allow you to consolidate understanding and put the core principles into practice:

- **Video of the author** giving further guidance on key concepts and questions.
- **Active case** – allows you to work through the decision making process, analyzing issues, listening to different perspectives and answering questions in relation to a real organizational situation.
- **Study guide** provides practical guidance on core concepts and issues discussed in the text. This features animated diagrams, further examples, Excel spreadsheets and practice notes.
- **Self-test material** provides the opportunity to test your understanding and assess progress.
- **Hints** on how to tackle the 'Applying the principles' examples in the text.
- **Summary checklist** – a downloadable list of the summary checklist found at the end of each chapter.
- **Operations principles** – a downloadable list of all the operations principles from each chapter.
- **Flashcards** for you to test your knowledge of key terms and phrases.

 A CD icon in the left hand margin of this book signals when you should refer to your CD for additional resources.

Further information about the CD can be found in the CD guided tour following the Preface and Book guided tour.

PEARSON
Education

We work with leading authors to develop the strongest educational materials in business, bringing cutting-edge thinking and best learning practice to a global market.

Under a range of well-known imprints, including Financial Times Prentice Hall, we craft high quality print and electronic publications which help readers to understand and apply their content, whether studying or at work.

To find out more about the complete range of our publishing, please visit us on the World Wide Web at:
www.pearsoned.co.uk

OPERATIONS AND PROCESS MANAGEMENT

Principles and practice for strategic impact

Nigel Slack
Stuart Chambers
Robert Johnston
Alan Betts

 Prentice Hall
FINANCIAL TIMES

An imprint of **Pearson Education**
Harlow, England • London • New York • Boston • San Francisco • Toronto
Sydney • Tokyo • Singapore • Hong Kong • Seoul • Taipei • New Delhi
Cape Town • Madrid • Mexico City • Amsterdam • Munich • Paris • Milan

Pearson Education Limited

Edinburgh Gate
Harlow
Essex CM20 2JE
England

and Associated Companies throughout the world

Visit us on the World Wide Web at:
www.pearsoned.co.uk

First published 2006

© Pearson Education Limited 2006

ISBN-13: 978-0-273-68426-8
ISBN-10: 0-273-68426-4

British Library Cataloguing-in-Publication Data
A catalogue record for this book is available from the British Library

Library of Congress Cataloging-in-Publication Data
A catalog record for this book is available from the Library of Congress

10 9 8 7 6 5 4 3 2 1
11 10 09 08 07 06

Typeset in 9/12.5 pt Stone Serif by 71
Printed and bound by Mateu-Cromo Artes Graficas, Spain

The publisher's policy is to use paper manufactured from sustainable forests.

Brief contents

Contents

Guide to case studies in the book and on CD

p. 27	Case study from book	💿	Case study from CD

Chapter	Location	Company name and description	Region	Manufac-turing/ Service	Company size	Techniques/topics
Chapter 1 Operations and processes	p. 27	**AAF Rotterdam:** hires out and sells theatrical equipment and offers production services	The Netherlands	M, S	Small to medium	Strategic impact of processes Process differences and similarities Evaluating processes
	💿	**EleXon Computers:** sells computers and IT solutions	Europe	S	Medium	Process design Organizational structure
Chapter 2 Operations strategy	p. 58	**Dresding Wilson:** provides technical solutions to health-care industries	Europe, Singapore, and USA	M, S	Medium to large	Operations strategy Market requirements Operations capability Operations focus
	💿	**Long Ridge Gliding Club:** provides gliding facilities for club members and holiday courses	UK	S	Small	Operations strategy Performance objectives Trade-offs
Chapter 3 Supply network design	p. 88	**Delta Synthetic Fibres:** a company in the man-made fibre industry	Global	M	Medium	Capacity planning Lead and lag strategies Financial impact of operations
	💿	**Freeman Biotest:** supplies the food processing industry	UK	M	Medium	Capacity expansion Technology choice Breakeven analysis
Chapter 4 Process design 1 – positioning	p. 125	**North West Constructive Bank – The New Mortgage Centre (1):** a large retail banking group	UK	S	Medium to large	Operations reorganization Volume / variety analysis Process flow Job design
	💿	**McPherson Charles Solicitors:** firm of solicitors (lawyers)	UK	S	Medium	Volume-variety positioning Layout Technology Job design
Chapter 5 Process design 2 – analysis	p. 159	**North West Constructive Bank – The New Mortgage Centre (2):** a large retail banking group	UK	S	Medium to large	Process mapping Process balancing Process variability
	💿	**Action Response:** charity who provides financial help quickly in urgent situations	International	S	Small to medium	Process analysis Process bottlenecks Process capacity
Chapter 6 Product and service design processes	p. 200	**Developing 'Savory Rosti-crisps' at Dreddo Dan's:** provides 'healthy snacks'	USA	M, S	Large	Managing development processes Time to market Design as a process
	💿	**Getting Customer #1:** precision die-casting company faced with the task of developing a new component for a target customer	Germany	M	Large	Product design Outsourcing Organization Risk
Chapter 7 Supply chain management	p. 232	**Supplying Fast Fashion (Benetton, H&M, Zara):** alternative supply chain strategies in fashion garment retailing	Europe, Italy, Sweden, Spain	M, S	Large	Supply chain configuration Supply chain integration Outsourcing Design processes
	💿	**NK Fleet Management:** a company responsible for managing and servicing car fleets	Sweden	S	Medium	Supply chain relationships Partnerships Service level agreements
Chapter 8 Capacity management	p. 264	**Blackberry Hill Farm:** a commercial enterprise at a working farm	UK	M, S	Small	Assessing capacity Understanding demand-capacity mismatches Controlling capacity
	💿	**Fresh Salads Ltd: The Iceberg Lettuce Harvest:** specializes in vegetable growing and distribution	UK	M	Medium	Measuring capacity Coping with demand-capacity mismatches

Chapter	Location	Company name and description	Region	Manufac-turing/Service	Company size	Techniques/topics
Chapter 9 Inventory management	p. 298	**supplies4medics.com:** European internet supplier of medical hardware by direct mail	Belgium, Europe	S	Medium	Inventory strategies Ordering using EOQ ABC analysis
		Rotterdam Serum: suppliers of antibody and other serum to the animal-care sector	The Netherlands	M	Large	Inventory management Customer service Capacity loading Job scheduling
Chapter 10 Resource and planning control	p. 327	**SubText Studios, Singapore:** Computer Generated Imaging (CGI) company	Singapore	S	Small	Basic scheduling Time estimation Customer interface
		Coburn Finnegan Accountants: a small accountancy practice	Ireland	S	Small	Capacity loading Job scheduling
Chapter 11 Lean synchron-ization	p. 368	**Boys and Boden (B&B):** privately-owned timber and building materials merchant	UK	M	Medium	JIT Cell layout Fast response Waste elimination
		Treating Ann: self-employed painter and decorator's experience with the health care system	UK and Belgium	S	Large	Process flow Waste elimination
Chapter 12 Quality management	p. 396	**Turnround at the Preston plant:** produces precision coated papers for ink-jet printers	Canada	M	Medium	SPC Quality improvement Downsizing Process knowledge and learning
		'You have eight messages': high quality hotel	The Netherlands	S	Medium	Quality management
Chapter 13 Improvement	p. 446	**Geneva Construction and Risk (GCR):** insurance company for building and construction industries	Switzerland and worldwide	S	Large	TQM 6 sigma Improvement strategy
		Ferndale Sands Conference Centre: conference centre which prides itself on offering 'the executive retreat'	Australia, Europe	S	Small	Improvement activities Prioritizing improvement
Chapter 14 Risk and resilience	p. 480	**The Chernobyl failure:** the worst accident in the history of commercial nuclear power generation	Ukraine	N/A	Ex-company	Errors and violations Failure planning Human factors in safety Disaster recovery
		Paterford Elevators: services and maintains elevators and elevator systems	USA	S	Medium	Failure Maintenance Service
Chapter 15 Project management	p. 512	**United Photonics Malaysia Sdn Bhd:** subsidiary that produces high precision specialty lenses	Malaysia	S, M	Subsidiary of large firm	Network planning Time estimation Stakeholder management Project risk
		National Trust: new project needing support of National Trust stakeholders	UK	S	Large	Stakeholder identification Stakeholder management

Supporting resources

Visit **www.pearsoned.co.uk/slack** to find valuable online resources.

For instructors

- Instructor's Manual featuring:
  - Teaching notes for all chapters
  - Guided solutions for all case studies in the book
  - Guided solutions for Active cases on the CD and ideas for teaching with them
  - Guide notes for teaching with the CD.

- PPTs of all the figures and illustrations from the main text.

For more information please contact your local Pearson Education sales representative or visit **www.pearsoned.co.uk/slack.**

Preface

Why operations and process management?

Operations management is changing. It has always been exciting, it has always been challenging, but now it has acquired a much more prominent profile. There are several reasons for this.

It is seen as being more important. Of course it has always been important, but increasingly managers in all types of enterprise are accepting that operations management can make or break their businesses. Effective operations management can keep costs down, enhance the potential to improve revenue, promote an appropriate allocation of capital resources, and most important, develop the capabilities that provide for future competitive advantage.

It can have a real strategic impact. Operations are not always operational. The operations function also has a vital strategic dimension, and operations management is now expected to play a part in shaping strategic direction, not just responding to it.

It matters to all sectors of the economy. At one time operations management was seen as being of most relevance to manufacturing and a few types of mass service businesses. Now its lessons are seen as applying to all types of enterprise; all types of service and manufacturing, large or small organisations, public or private, for-profit or not-for-profit.

It is of interest to all managers. Perhaps most importantly, because operations management is accepted as being founded on the idea of managing processes, and because managers in all functions of the business are now accepting that they spend much of their time managing processes, it is clear that, to some extent, all managers are operations managers. The principles and practice of operations management are relevant to every manager.

Its scope has extended. The obvious unit of analysis of operations management is the operations function itself – the collection of resources that produce products and services. But, if managers from other functions are to be included, operations management must also address itself to process management at a more generic level. Also, no operation can consider itself in isolation from its customers, suppliers, collaborators and competitors. It must see itself as part of the extended supply network. Operations management increasingly needs to work at all three levels of analysis – the individual process, the operation itself, and the supply network.

All this has implications for the way operations management is studied, especially at post experience and post graduate levels, and the way operations management is practised. It has also very much shaped the way this book has been structured. In addition to covering all the important topics that make the subject so powerful, it places particular emphasis on the following.

- **Principles** – that is, the core ideas that describe how operations behave, how they can be managed, and how they can be improved. They are not immutable laws or prescriptions that dictate how operations *should* be managed, nor are they descriptions that simply explain or categorize issues.
- **Diagnosis** – an approach that questions and explores the fundamental drivers of operations performance. Aims to uncover or 'diagnose' the underlying trade-offs which operations

need to overcome and the implications and consequences of the courses of action that could be taken.

- **Practice** – anyone with managerial experience, or who is approaching career choices, understands the importance of developing practical knowledge and skills that can be applied in practice. This requires an approach, as well as frameworks and techniques, which can be adapted to take account of the complexity and ambiguity of operations, yet give guidance to identifying and implementing potential solutions.

Who should use this book?

This book is intended to provide an introduction to operations and process management for everyone who wishes to understand the nature, principles and practice of the subject. It is aimed primarily at those who have some management experience (although no prior academic knowledge of the area is assumed), or who are about to embark on a career in management. For example:

- *MBA students* should find that its practical discussions of operations management activities enhance their own experience.
- *Postgraduate students* on other specialist masters degrees should find that it provides them with a well-grounded and, at times, critical approach to the subject.
- *Executives* should find its diagnostic structure helps to provide an understandable route through the subject.

Distinctive features

Clear structure

The book is structured on a model of operations management that distinguishes between activities that contribute to the direction, design, delivery, and development of operations and processes.

CD and website resources

Significant supplementary material is fully integrated with the text in order to help 'time poor' experienced students customise their learning to their own needs. This combination of text and integrated supporting material will help to fulfil readers' demanding requirements. The CD resources include:

- video based introduction to each chapter
- active cases that allow the testing and exploration of principles in realistic contexts
- study guides that follow the flow of each chapter and include further examples and animated diagrams
- excel spreadsheets and examples
- practice notes that provide a step-by-step guide to operations techniques
- hints an how to tackle the 'applying the principles' examples in the text
- 'test yourself' multiple choice questions
- flashcards for you to test your knowledge of key terms and phrases.

Diagnostic logic chains

Every chapter follows a series of questions that form a 'diagnostic logic' for the topic. These are the questions that anyone can ask to reveal the underlying state of their, or any other, operations. The questions provide an aid to diagnosing where and how an operation can be improved.

Illustrations-based

Operations management is a practical subject and cannot be taught satisfactorily in a purely theoretical manner. Because of this each chapter starts with two real life examples of how the topic is treated in practice.

Operations principles

Whenever a core idea of operations and process management is described in the text, a brief 'operations principle' summary is included in the margin. This helps to distil those essential points of the topic.

Critical commentaries

Not everyone agrees about what is the best approach to the various topics and issues within the subject. This is why we have, at the end of each chapter, included a 'critical commentary'. These are alternative views to the one being expressed in the main flow of the text. They do not necessarily represent our view, but they are worth debating.

Summary checklists

Each chapter is summarized in the form of a list of checklist questions. These cover the essential questions that anyone should ask if they wish to understand the way their own or any other operation works. More importantly, they can also act as prompts for operations and process improvement.

Case studies

Every chapter includes a case study, relating real or realistic situations that require analysis, decision, or both. The cases have sufficient content to serve as the basis of case sessions in class, but are short enough to serve as illustrations for the less formal reader. As mentioned, further 'active cases' are offered on the CD accompanying the book.

Applying the principles

Selected problems, short exercises and activities are included at the end of each chapter. These provide an opportunity to test out your understanding of the principles covered in the chapter.

Taking it further

A short annotated list of further reading and useful websites is provided which takes the topics covered in the chapter further, or treats some important related issues.

Instructor's manual and PowerPoint slides

Visit **www.pearsoned.co.uk/slack** to find valuable online resources. A dedicated new Web-based instructor's manual is available to lecturers adopting this textbook. It includes teaching notes for all chapters, guided solutions for all case studies in the book, guided solutions for Active cases on the CD and ideas for teaching with them. A set of PowerPoint slides featuring figures and illustrations from the main text is also available.

Book guided tour

Integration with student CD – CD icons clearly indicate where additional resources can be found on the CD accompanying this book. Please see page *xx* for further details of the CD resources.

Diagnostic logic chain – every chapter is organized around a series of questions that form a 'diagnostic logic' for the topic. This 'diagnostic' or problem-solving approach equips you with the questions to effectively assess the operations and processes in your company and 'diagnose' how they can be improved.

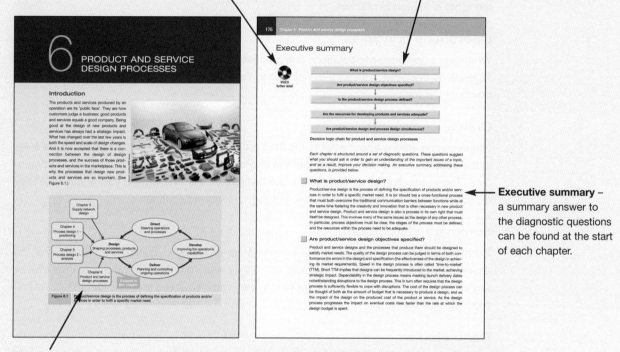

Executive summary – a summary answer to the diagnostic questions can be found at the start of each chapter.

Clear structure – the book is structured on a model of operations management that distinguishes between activities that contribute to the *direction*, *design*, *delivery*, and *development* of operations and processes.

Examples – each chapter opens with two examples. A balance of service and manufacturing examples gives you a practical and wide-ranging understanding of operations and process management.

Figures and diagrams are featured throughout the text to highlight key points and clarify topics discussed.

Operations principles – key concepts are distilled and presented in the margin of the text as a useful reference and reminder.

Critical commentaries provide an alternative viewpoint to the perspective presented in the main text.

Summary checklists present the essential questions that anyone should ask if they wish to understand how an operation works. They are located at the end of each chapter and are downloadable from the CD.

Case studies with questions which depict various-sized organizations in different sectors and locations, from both service and manufacturing backgrounds, are included at the end of every chapter. Apply your understanding of concepts and techniques by addressing operations-related problems in a real business context.

Applying the principles contain selected problems, short exercises and activities to test your understanding of the principles covered in each chapter.

Supplements covering quantitative topics appear at the end of relevant chapters.

CD guided tour

You will find a CD contained within your copy of *Operations and Process Management* featuring a range of additional resources to help you with your studies. These include video, active cases, self-test material and a study guide featuring animated diagrams, further examples, Excel spreadsheets and practice notes. These interactive features provide the opportunity to consolidate your understanding and to put the principles and concepts into practice.

Once you have loaded your CD, you will be greeted with a home page. The home page lists all the chapters from the main text and a selection of specific resources. Click on a chapter title to access the resources for that chapter.

FT Prentice Hall
FINANCIAL TIMES

Operations and Process Management:
Principles and Practice for Strategic Impact
Nigel Slack, Stuart Chambers, Robert Johnston & Alan Betts

Main Menu

Welcome to the CD accompanying Operations and Process Management: Principles and Practice for Strategic Impact. This CD features a range of additional resources to help you with your studies. These include video, active cases, self-test material and a study guide featuring animated diagrams, further examples, excel spreadsheets and practice notes.

These interactive features provide the opportunity to consolidate your understanding and to put the principles and concepts into practice. A CD icon in the main text signals when you should refer to your CD to find specific extra material and guidance.

Choose a chapter below, or if you know which resource you want to use, go to the lists on the right for direct access:

- 1. Operations and Processes
- 2. Operations Strategy
- 3. Supply Network Design
- 4. Process Design 1 - Positioning
- 5. Process Design 2 - Analysis
- 6. Product and Service Design Processes
- 7. Supply Chain Management
- 8. Capacity Management
- 9. Inventory Management
- 10. Resource Planning and Control
- 11. Lean Synchronization
- 12. Quality Management
- 13. Improvement
- 14. Risk and Resilience
- 15. Project Management

Operations Principles
The principles of how to understand, manage and improve operations and processes

Practice Notes
Balancing Cycle — Provide a step-by-step guide to operations techniques

Excel Sheets
Allows you to put into practice important quantitative techniques

Applying Principles: Hints
Suggestions and ideas on how you can apply the principles introduced within an organisational context

Summary Checklists
A checklist of key questions that you can put into practice when addressing operations and process related challenges in your own organization

Note: This CD should be used with your monitor set to 800x600 resolution. View the Readme document for further information.

A CD icon 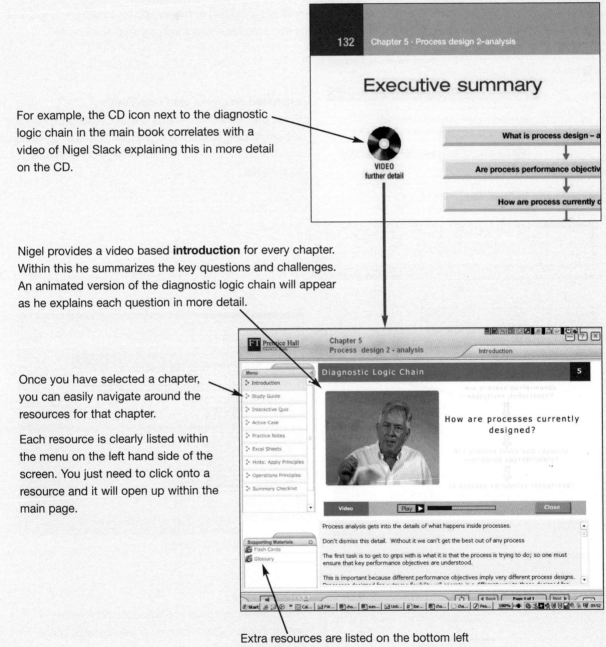 in the main text signals when you should refer to your CD to find extra resources.

For example, the CD icon next to the diagnostic logic chain in the main book correlates with a video of Nigel Slack explaining this in more detail on the CD.

Nigel provides a video based **introduction** for every chapter. Within this he summarizes the key questions and challenges. An animated version of the diagnostic logic chain will appear as he explains each question in more detail.

Once you have selected a chapter, you can easily navigate around the resources for that chapter.

Each resource is clearly listed within the menu on the left hand side of the screen. You just need to click onto a resource and it will open up within the main page.

Extra resources are listed on the bottom left of the home page.

CD guided tour *continued*

STUDY GUIDE

On the CD you will find an interactive study guide. This provides practical guidance on core concepts and issues discussed in the text and allows *you* to put the principles into practice.

Within the study guide you will find a range of interactive features including further examples to provide a real world context as well as animated diagrams, Excel spreadsheets and practice notes which are explained below.

Animated diagrams with commentary

Press play to hear an alternative and applied explanation of important diagrams. The diagram animates to co-ordinate with the commentary to reinforce key concepts and techniques.

Excel spreadsheets

Within the study guide, you will find links to Excel spreadsheets. These allow you to put important quantitative techniques into practice.

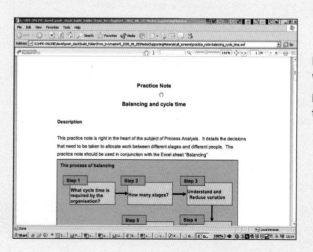

Practice notes

Within the study guide you will also find links to practice notes. These provide a step-by-step guide to operations techniques.

ACTIVE CASES

On the CD you will also find an active case for each chapter as well as self test questions and hints on 'applying the principles' questions raised at the end of each chapter in the book. These resources are explained below.

The **active case study** allows you to work through the decision making process, analyze issues and answer questions in relation to a real organizational situation.

Listen to the perspective of different people within an organization to build up your understanding of the issues.

Answer questions about the decisions that you would take and receive feedback specific to your choices.

ASSESSMENTS

Multiple choice questions provide the opportunity to test your understanding of the subject matter and assess your progress.

Hints on 'applying the principles' give suggestions and ideas on how you can apply the principles introduced within an organizational context.

About the authors

NIGEL SLACK is Professor of Operations Management and Strategy at Warwick University. Previously he was Professor of Manufacturing Strategy and Lucas Professor of Manufacturing Systems Engineering at Brunel University, University Lecturer in Management Studies at Oxford University and Fellow in Operations Management at Templeton College, Oxford.

He worked initially as an industrial apprentice in the hand-tool industry and then as a production engineer and production manager in light engineering. He is a chartered engineer, and the author of numerous publications in the operations management area including books, academic papers and chapters in books. Most recently, in 2004, *Operations Management*, 5th edition (with Stuart Chambers and Robert Johnston), and in 2003, *Cases in Operations Management*, 3rd edition (with Robert Johnston, Alan Harrison, Stuart Chambers and Christine Harland), both published by Financial Times Prentice Hall. Also, *The Blackwell Encyclopedic Dictionary of Operations Management*, 2nd edition, published by Blackwell in 2005; *Operations Strategy*, published by Financial Times Prentice Hall in 2003, and *Perspectives in Operations Management* (Volumes I to IV), published by Routledge in 2003, all with Michael Lewis. He also acts as a consultant to many international companies around the world in many sectors, especially financial services, transport, leisure and manufacturing. His research is in the process management and operations strategy areas.

STUART CHAMBERS is a Principal Teaching Fellow at Warwick Business School. He began his career as an undergraduate apprentice at Rolls Royce Aerospace, graduating in mechanical engineering, and then worked in production and general management with companies including Tube Investments and the Marley Tile Company. In his mid-thirties and seeking a career change, he studied for an MBA, and then took up a three-year contract as a researcher in manufacturing strategy. This work enabled him to help executives develop the analyses, concepts and practical solutions required for them to develop manufacturing strategies. Several of the case studies prepared from this work have been published in an American textbook on manufacturing strategy.

In addition to lecturing on a range of operations courses at the Business School and in industry, Stuart is continuing his research in the manufacturing strategy field. His research interests also include service quality management in leisure and catering businesses. He undertakes consultancy in a diverse range of industries and is co-author of several operations management books.

ROBERT JOHNSTON is Professor of Operations Management at Warwick Business School and Associate Dean, responsible for finance and resources. He is the founding editor of the *International Journal of Service Industry Management* and he also serves on the editorial board of the *Journal of Operations Management* and the *International Journal of Tourism and Hospitality Research*. Before moving to academia Dr Johnston held several line management and senior management posts in a number of service organizations in both the public and private sectors. He continues to maintain close and active links with many large and small organizations through his research, management training and consultancy activities. As a specialist in service operations, his research interests include service design, service recovery, performance measurement and service quality. He is the author of *Service Operations Management,* 2nd edition, with Graham Clark, published by Financial Times Prentice Hall in 2005, and numerous other publications in the service and general operations management area.

ALAN BETTS is a freelance consultant and trainer working, primarily, with executives of service organizations to apply the principles of operations and process management. Following a career in financial services, Alan completed Institute of Personnel and Development qualifications and an MA in Human Resource Management and moved to the Operations Management group at Warwick Business School as a Senior Research Fellow. His chief interests are the development of innovative approaches to e-learning and m-learning, together with the coaching and development of managers and executives. Alan is a director of Bedford Falls Learning Limited, HT2 Limited and Capability Development Limited. He is a visiting Professor at the University of San Diego and is a Fellow of the Royal Society of Arts.

Also, Ben Betts of Rare Studios, who masterminded and executed much of the e-learning and support material.

Acknowledgements

In preparing this book, the authors, as usual, unashamedly exploited their friends and colleagues. In particular we had invaluable help from a great and distinguished reviewer team. For their help we are particularly grateful to:

Pär Åhlström, Chalmers University, Sweden
Malcolm Afferson, Sheffield Hallam University, UK
Stephen Disney, Cardiff University, UK
John Maguire, Sunderland University, UK
Andrea Masini, London Business School, UK
Alison Smart, Manchester Business School, University of Manchester, UK

We would also like to thank the numerous reviewers who have provided valuable feedback on various aspects of the project.

David Bamford, Manchester Business School, University of Manchester, UK
Des Doran, Kingston University, UK
Paul Forrester, Birmingham University UK
Gino Franco, Derby University, UK
Roger Hall, Huddersfield University, UK
Ingjaldur Hannibalsson, University of Iceland, Iceland
Koos Krabbendam, University of Twente, The Netherlands
Michael Lewis, Bath University
Bob Lowson, University of East Anglia, UK
Harvey Maylor, University of Bath, UK
Ronnie Mcmillan, University of Strathclyde, UK
Phil Morgan, Oxford Brookes University, UK
Venu Venugopal, Nyenrode University, The Netherlands
Jan de Vries, University of Groningen, The Netherlands
Graham Walker, Wolverhampton University, UK
Richard Wright, Gloucestershire University, UK

Our academic colleagues in the Operations Management Group at Warwick Business School also helped, both by contributing ideas and by creating a lively and stimulating work environment. Our thanks go to Jannis Angellis, Hilary Bates, Alistair Brandon-Jones, Simon Croom, Mike Giannakis, Nick Parks, Zoe Radnor, Michael Shulver, Rhian Silvestro and Paul Walley.

We are also grateful to many friends, colleagues and company contacts. In particular thanks for help with this edition goes to Philip Godfrey and Cormac Campbell and his expert colleagues at OEE, David Garman and Caro Burnett of TDG, Hans Mayer and Tyko Persson of Nestlé, Peter Norris and Mark Fisher of the Royal Bank of Scotland, John Tyley of Lloyds TSB, Joanne Chung of Godfrey Hall, BMW, Karen Earp of Four Seasons Hotel Group, Johan Linden of SVT, John Matthew of HSPG, Dan McHugh of Credit Swiss First Boston, Jenny Ireland of Morgan Stanley, Leigh Rix of The National Trust, and Simon Topman of Acme Whistles.

Mary Walton is coordinator to our group at Warwick Business School. Her continued efforts at keeping us organized (or as organized as we are capable of being) are always appreciated, but never more so than when we were engaged on 'the book'.

The prerequisite for any book of this type is that it serves a real market need. We were privileged to receive advice from some of the most insightful salespeople in business education publishing. These were, Clare Audet, who guided the marketing effort, with help from Oli Adams (Marketing Executive) and a great team of sales representatives: Jordon Beevers, Mike Done, Alex Gay, John Henderson, Ster Hutten, Winek Kosior, Penny Lane, Richard Puttock, Vicky Rudd and Wendy Vessis.

We were also lucky to receive continuing professional and friendly assistance from a great publishing team. Thanks to Amanda McPartlin (Acquisitions Editor), Jacqueline Senior, (Publisher), Karen Mclaren (Senior Editor), Amanda Thomas (Project Control Team Leader), Kay Holman (Senior Project Controller), Colin Reed (Senior Designer – text), Michelle Morgan (Senior Designer – cover), Sue Williams (freelance picture researcher), Robert Chaundy (freelance copy-editor), Jonathon Price (freelance proof-reader), Annette Musker (freelance indexer), and a big thank you to David Harrison (Media Development Editor) for all of his work on the CD. Our particular thanks go to Janey Webb (Development Editor) at Pearson Education. Without her considerable effort, enthusiasm, common sense, and professional dedication, this project would have been very significantly impaired.

Finally, the manuscript, and much more besides was organized and put together by Angela Slack. It was another heroic effort, which she undertook with (relatively) little complaint. To Angela – our thanks.

1 OPERATIONS AND PROCESSES

Introduction

Operations and process management is about how organizations produce goods and services. Everything you wear, eat, use, or read comes to you courtesy of the operations managers who organized its production, as does every bank transaction, hospital visit, and hotel stay. The people who produced them may not always be called operations managers, but that is what they really are. Within the operations function of any enterprise, operations managers look after the processes that produce products and services. But managers in other functions, such as Marketing, Sales and Finance, *also* manage processes. These processes often supply internal 'customers' with services such as marketing plans, sales forecasts, budgets, and so on. In fact parts of all organizations are made up

of processes. That is what this book is about – the tasks, issues and decisions that are necessary to manage processes effectively, both within the operations function, and in other parts of the business where effective process management is equally important. This is an introductory chapter, so we will examine some of the basic principles of operations and process management. The model that is developed to explain the subject is shown in Figure 1.1.

Figure 1.1   Operations and process management is about how organizations produce goods and services

Executive summary

VIDEO
further detail

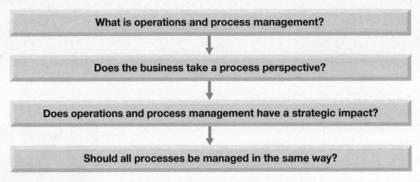

Decision logic chain for operations and processes

Each chapter is structured around a set of diagnostic questions. These questions suggest what you should ask in order to gain an understanding of the important issues of a topic, and as a result, improve your decision making. An executive summary, addressing these questions, is provided below.

What is operations and process management?

The operations function is the part of the organization that produces products or services. Every organization has an operations function because every organization produces some mixture of products and services. 'Operations' is not always called by that name, but whatever its name, it is always concerned with managing the core purpose of the business– producing some mix of products and services. Processes also produce products and services, but on a smaller scale. They are the component parts of operations. But, other functions also have processes that need managing. In fact *every* part of *any* business is concerned with managing processes. All managers have something to learn from studying operations and process management, because the subject encompasses the management of all types of operation, no matter in what sector or industry, and all processes, no matter in which function.

Does the business take a process perspective?

A 'process perspective' means understanding businesses in terms of all their individual processes. It is only one way of modelling organizations, but it is a particularly useful one. Operations and process management uses the process perspective to analyze businesses at three levels: the operations function of the business; the higher and more strategic level of the supply network; and a lower, more operational, level of individual processes. Within the business, processes are only what they are defined as being. The boundaries of each process can be drawn as thought appropriate. Sometimes this involves radically reshaping the way processes are organized, for example to form end-to-end processes that fulfil customer needs.

Does operations and process management have a strategic impact?

Operations and process management can make or break a business. When they are well managed, operations and processes can contribute to the strategic impact of the business in four ways: cost, revenue, investment and capabilities. Because the operations function has responsibility for much of a business's cost base, its first imperative is to keep costs under control. But also, through the way it provides service and quality, it should be looking to enhance the business's ability to generate revenue. Also, because operations are often the source of much investment, it should be aiming to get the best possible return on that investment. Finally, the operations function should be laying down the capabilities that will form the long-term basis for future competitiveness.

Should all processes be managed in the same way?

Not necessarily. Processes differ, particularly in what are known as the four Vs: volume, variety, variation and visibility. High volume processes can exploit economies of scale and be systematized. High variety processes require enough inbuilt flexibility to cope with the wide variety of activities expected of them. High variation processes must be able to change their output levels to cope with highly variable and/or unpredictable levels of demand. High visibility processes add value while the customer is 'present' in some way and therefore must be able to manage customers' perceptions of their activities. Generally high volume together with low variety, variation and visibility facilitate low cost processes, while low volume together with high levels of variety, variation and visibility all increase process costs. Yet in spite of these differences, operations managers use a common set of decisions and activities to manage them. These activities can be clustered under four groupings: directing the overall strategy of the operation, designing the operation's products, services and processes, planning and controlling process delivery, and developing process performance.

What is operations and process management?

Operations and process management is the activity of managing the resources and processes that produce products and services. The core body of knowledge for the subject comes from 'operations management', which examines how the 'operations function' of a business produces products and services for external customers. We also use the shorter terms 'the operation' or 'operations', interchangeably with the 'operations function'. In some organizations an operations manager could be called by some other name, for example a 'fleet manager' in a logistics company, an 'administrative manager' in a hospital, or a 'store manager' in a supermarket.

All business have 'operations', because all businesses produce products, services, or some mixture of both. If you think that you don't have an operations function, you are wrong. If you think that your operations function is not important, you are also wrong. Look at the six businesses illustrated in Figure 1.2. There are two financial service companies, two manufacturing companies, and two hotels. All of them have *operations functions* that produce the things that their customers are willing to pay for. Hotels produce accommodation services, financial services invest, store, move or sell us money and investment opportunities, and manufacturing businesses physically change the shape and the nature of materials to produce products. These businesses are from different sectors (banking, hospitality, manufacturing, etc.), but the main differences between their operations activities are not necessarily what one expects. There are often bigger differences *within* economic sectors than *between* them. All the three operations in the left-hand column of the figure provide value-for-money products and services and compete largely on cost. The three in the right-hand column provide more 'up-market' products and services that are more expensive to produce and compete on some combination of high specification and customization. The implication of this is important. It means that the surface appearance of a business and its economic sector are less important to the way its operations should be managed than its intrinsic characteristics, such as the volume of its output, the variety of different products and services it needs to produce, and, above all, how it is trying to compete in its market.

Operations principle
All organizations have 'operations' that produce some mix of products and services.

Operations principle
The economic sector of an operation is less important in determining how it should be managed than its intrinsic characteristics.

Operations *and process* management

Within the operations shown in Figure 1.2, resources such as people, computer systems, buildings, and equipment will be organized into several individual 'processes'. A 'process' is an arrangement of resources that transforms inputs into outputs that satisfy (internal or external) customer needs. So, amongst other processes, banking operations contain account management processes, hotel operations contain room cleaning processes, furniture manufacturing operations contain assembly processes, and so on. The difference between *operations* and *processes* is one of scale, and therefore complexity. Both transform

Financial services

An account
management
centre at a large
retail bank

Investment banks
advise large clients
on aspects of their
financial strategy

Source: Courtesy Arup

Furniture manufacturing

Mass production
of kitchen units

Craft production
of reproduction
'antique' furniture

Hotels

Value-for-money
hotel

Lobby of an
international
luxury hotel

Source: Sue Williams

Source: Courtesy Stewart Linford Chairmaker
Limited, photo: Richard Shymansky

Figure 1.2   All types of business have 'operations' because all businesses produce some mix of products and services. And the differences in the operations within a category of business are often greater than the differences between businesses

inputs into outputs, but processes are the smaller version. They are the component parts of operations, so the total operations function is made up of individual processes. But, within any business, the production of products and services is not confined to the operations function. For example, the marketing function 'produces' marketing plans and sales forecasts, the accounting function 'produces' budgets, the human resources function 'produces' development and recruitment plans, and so on. In fact *every* part of *any* business is concerned with managing processes. And operations and process management is the term we use to encompass the management of all types of operation, no matter in what sector or industry, and all processes, no matter in which function of the business. The general truth is that processes are everywhere, and all types of manager have something to learn from studying operations and process management.

From 'production', to 'operations', to 'operations and process' management

Figure 1.3 illustrates how the scope of this subject has expanded. Originally, operations management was seen as very much associated with the manufacturing sector.

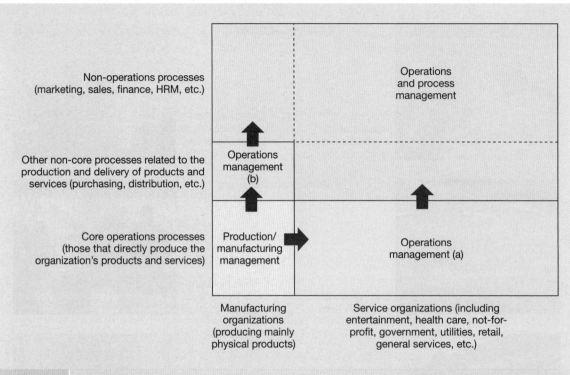

Non-operations processes
(marketing, sales, finance, HRM, etc.)

Operations
and process
management

Other non-core processes related to the
production and delivery of products and
services (purchasing, distribution, etc.)

Operations
management
(b)

Core operations processes
(those that directly produce the
organization's products and services)

Production/
manufacturing
management

Operations
management (a)

Manufacturing
organizations
(producing mainly
physical products)

Service organizations (including
entertainment, health care, not-for-
profit, government, utilities, retail,
general services, etc.)

Figure 1.3   Operations management has expanded from treating only the core production processes in manufacturing organizations to include service organizations, non-core operations processes, and processes in other functions such as marketing, finance and HRM

In fact it would have been called 'production' or 'manufacturing' management, and was concerned exclusively with the core business of producing physical products. Starting in the 1970s and 1980s, the term *operations management* became more common. It was used to reflect two trends. First, and most importantly, it was used to imply that many of the ideas, approaches and techniques traditionally used in the manufacturing sector could be equally applicable in the production of services. The second use of the term was to expand the scope of 'production' in manufacturing companies to include not just the core processes that directly produce products, but also the non-core production-related processes that contribute to the production and delivery of products. This would include such processes as purchasing, physical distribution, after-sales service, and so on. More recently the term *operations and process management* (or sometimes just process management) has been used to denote the shift in the scope of the subject to include the whole organization. It is a far wider term than operations management because it applies to all parts of the organization. This is very much how we treat the subject in this book. That is why it is called 'Operations and *Process* Management'. It includes the examination of the operations function in both manufacturing and service sectors and also the management of processes in non-operations functions.

Towards the beginning of all chapters we present two examples of individual businesses, or types of business, that illustrate the topic being examined in the chapter. Here we look at two businesses – one service company and one manufacturing company–which have succeeded partly because of their creative approach to operations and process management.

Example   IKEA[1]

With over 100 giant stores operating throughout the world, IKEA has managed to develop its own special way of selling furniture. Customers often spend around two hours in the store – far longer than in rival furniture retailers, because of the way IKEA organizes its store operations. IKEA's philosophy goes back to the original business, started in the 1950s in southern Sweden by Ingvar Kamprad. Because customers wanted to see some of his furniture, he built a showroom, not in the centre of Stockholm where land was expensive, but on the outskirts of town. Instead of buying expensive display stands, he simply set the furniture out as it would be in a domestic setting. Also, instead of moving the furniture from the warehouse to the showroom area, he asked customers to

pick the furniture up themselves from the warehouse, an approach that is still the basis of IKEA's process today.

The stores are all designed to facilitate the smooth flow of customers, from parking, moving through the store itself, to ordering and picking up goods. At the entrance to each store large notice-boards provide advice to shoppers who have not used the store before. For young children, there is a supervised children's play area, a small cinema, a parent and baby room and toilets, so parents can leave their children in the supervised play area for a time. Parents are recalled via the loudspeaker system if the child has any problems. Customers may also borrow pushchairs to keep their children with them. IKEA like to allow customers to make up their minds in their own time. If advice is needed, 'information points' have staff who can help. Every piece of furniture carries a ticket with a code number which indicates the location in the warehouse from where it can be collected. (For larger items customers go to the information desks for assistance.) There is also an area where smaller items are displayed, and can be picked directly. Customers then pass through the self-service warehouse where they can pick up the items viewed in the showroom. Finally, the customers pay at the checkouts, where a ramped conveyor belt moves purchases up to the checkout staff. The exit area has service points, and a loading area that allows customers to bring their cars from the car park and load their purchases.

Example   Dell[2]

Dell started as a method of cutting out the 'middle man' and delivering quality computers direct to the customer without having to pay retail mark-ups. But using its direct selling methods, Dell went on to become the number one computer supplier in the business. Founded in 1984, the company introduced its first computer system to its own design a year later, after which growth was rapid. Dell's first international expansion began with the opening of its UK subsidiary in 1987. Now from

its corporate headquarters in Austin, Texas, the company controls regional sales and service subsidiaries and manufacturing plants around the world.

One reason for the company's success was the realization that, because its sales operations had direct contact with customers it could realize other significant benefits. For example, it could find out what customers were thinking without the information being passed back up the supply chain, and it could allow customers to 'design their own' computer, at least to the extent of deciding the specification of key components. Clever product design allowed Dell to offer a very wide variety of products by combining a far smaller number of standard modules. Through the company's website, or by calling its sales representative, customers can be guided through a step-by-step 'design' process which specifies the computer's speed, storage, type of monitor, etc. This information is passed directly to a Dell factory that 'kits' the order (that is, collects the specific modules which will go into that computer) and makes the computer 'to order'. Fast assembly and delivery times ensure that a computer specified by a customer and made specifically for that customer is delivered fast and efficiently. Relationships with suppliers are similarly close. Dell says that they regard their suppliers as partners in creating value for customers. *'When we launch a new product'*, says Michael Dell, *'suppliers' engineers are stationed right in our plants. If a customer calls up with a problem, we'll stop shipping product while they fix design flaws in real time.'*

What do these two examples have in common?

All the operations managers in IKEA and Dell will be concerned with the same basic task – managing the processes that produce their products and services. And many, if not most, of the managers in each company who are called by some other title will be concerned with managing their own processes that contribute to the success of their business. Although there will be differences between each company's operations and processes, such as the type of services they provide, the resources they use, and so on, the managers in each company will be making the same *type* of decisions, even if *what* they actually decide is different. The fact that both companies are successful because of their innovative and effective operations also implies further commonality. First, it means that they both understand the importance of taking a 'process perspective' in understanding their supply networks, running their operations, and managing all their individual processes. Without this they could not have sustained their strategic impact in the face of stiff market competition. Second, both businesses will expect their operations to make a contribution to their overall competitive strategy. And third, in achieving a strategic impact, both will have come to understand the importance of managing *all* their individual processes throughout the business so that they too can all contribute to the businesses success.

DIAGNOSTIC QUESTION

Does the business take a process perspective?

If a business takes a process perspective, it understands that all parts of the business can be seen as processes, and that all processes can be managed using operations management principles. But it is also important to understand that a process perspective is not the only way of describing businesses, or any type of organization. One could represent an organization as a conventional 'organizational structure' that shows the reporting relationships between various departments or groups of resources. But even a little experience in any organization shows that rarely, if ever, does this fully represent the organization. Alternatively one could describe an organization through the way it makes decisions – how it balances conflicting criteria, weighs up risks, decides on actions and learns from its mistakes. Or one could describe the organization's culture – its shared values, ideology, pattern of thinking and day-to-day rituals, or its power relationships – how it is governed, seeks consensus (or at least reconciliation) and so on. Or one can represent the organization as a collection of processes, interconnecting and (hopefully) all contributing to fulfilling its strategic aims. This is the perspective that we emphasize throughout this book. As we define it here, the process perspective analyses businesses as a collection of interrelated processes. Many of these processes will be within the operations function, and will contribute directly to the production of its products and services. Other processes will be in the other functions of the business, but will still need managing using similar principles to those within the operations function. None of these individual perspectives gives a total picture of real organizations, but nor are they necessarily mutually exclusive. A process perspective does not preclude understanding the influence of power relationships on how processes work, and so on. Each perspective adds something to our ability to understand and therefore more effectively manage a business.

We use the process perspective here, not because it is the only useful and informative way of understanding businesses, but because it is the perspective that directly links the way we manage resources in a business with its strategic impact. Without effective process management, the best strategic plan can never become reality. The most appealing promises made to clients or customers will never be fulfilled. Also the process perspective has traditionally been undervalued. The subject of operations and process management has only recently come to be seen as universally applicable and, more importantly, universally valuable.

So, operations and process management is relevant to all parts of the business

If processes exist everywhere in the organization, operations and process management will be a common responsibility of all managers irrespective of which function they are

> **Operations principle**
> All parts of the business manage processes so all parts of the business have an operations role and need to understand operations management.

in. Each function will have its 'technical' knowledge, of course. In Marketing this includes the market expertise needed for designing and shaping marketing plans; in Finance it includes the technical knowledge of financial reporting conventions. Yet each will also have an *operations* role that entails using its processes to produce plans, policies, reports and services. For example, the marketing function has processes with inputs of market information, staff, computers, and so on. Its staff transform the information into outputs such as marketing plans, advertising campaigns and sales force organizations. In this sense all functions are operations with their own collection of processes.

The implications of this are very important. Because every manager in all parts of an organization is, to some extent, an operations manager, they should all want to give good service to their customers, and they will all want to do this efficiently. So, operations management must be relevant for all functions, units and groups within the organization. And the concepts, approaches and techniques of operations management can help to improve any process in any part of the organization.

The 'input–transformation–output' model

> **Operations principle**
> All processes have inputs of transforming and transformed resources that they use to create products and services.

Central to understanding the processes perspective is the idea that all processes transform *inputs* into *outputs*. Figure 1.4 shows the *general transformation process model* that is used to describe the nature of processes. Put simply, processes take in a set of input resources, some of which are transformed into outputs of products and/or services and some of which do the transforming.

> **Operations principle**
> Transformed resource inputs to a process are materials, information, or customers.

Process inputs

Transformed resource inputs are the resources that are changed in some way within a process. They are usually materials, information or customers. For example, one process in a bank prints statements of accounts for its customers. In doing so, it is processing materials. In the bank's branches, customers are processed by giving them advice regarding their financial affairs, cashing their cheques, etc. However, behind the scenes, most of the bank's processes are concerned with processing information about its customers' financial affairs. In fact, for the bank's operations function as a whole, its information transforming processes are probably the most important. As customers, we may be unhappy with badly printed statements and we may even be unhappy if we are not

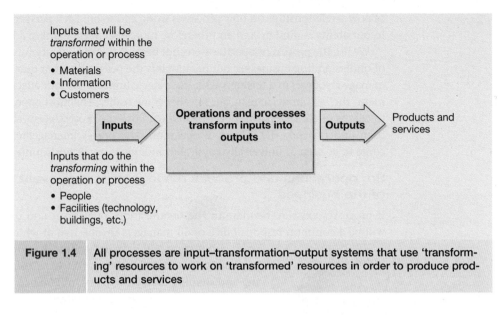

Figure 1.4 All processes are input–transformation–output systems that use 'transforming' resources to work on 'transformed' resources in order to produce products and services

treated appropriately in the bank. But if the bank makes errors in our financial transactions, we suffer in a far more fundamental way.

Operations principle
All processes have transforming resources of facilities and people.

There are two types of *transforming* resource that form the 'building blocks' of all processes. They are *facilities* – the buildings, equipment, plant and process technology of the operation, and *people* – who operate, maintain, plan and manage the operation.

The exact nature of both facilities and people will differ between processes. In a five-star hotel, the facilities consist mainly of buildings, furniture and fittings. In a nuclear-powered aircraft carrier, the facilities are the nuclear generator, turbines, and sophisticated electronic detection equipment. Although one operation is relatively 'low-technology' and the other 'high-technology', their processes all require effective, well-maintained facilities. People also differ between processes. Most staff employed in a domestic appliance assembly process may not need a very high level of technical skill, whereas most staff employed by an accounting firm in an audit process are highly skilled in their own particular 'technical' skill (accounting). Yet although skills vary, all staff have a contribution to make to the effectiveness of their operation. An assembly worker who consistently misassembles refrigerators will dissatisfy customers and increase costs just as surely as an accountant who cannot add up.

Process outputs

All processes produce products and services, and although products and services are different, the distinction can be subtle. Perhaps the most obvious difference is in their respective tangibility. Products are usually tangible (you can physically touch a television set or a newspaper) whereas services are usually intangible (you cannot touch consultancy advice or a haircut, although you may be able to see or feel the results). Also, services may have a shorter stored life. Products can usually be stored for a time – some food products only for a few days, and some buildings for hundreds of years. But the life of a service is often much shorter. For example, the service of 'accommodation in a hotel room for tonight' will 'perish' if it is not sold before tonight – accommodation in the same room tomorrow is a different service.

Figure 1.5 — Operations at the level of the

Analysis at the level of the *supply network*–a supply network is an arrangement of operations

Need to know–the role of each operation in the network and the relationship between them

Strategic analysis

Analysis at the level of the *operation*–an operation is an arrangement of processes

Need to know–the role of each process in the operation and the relationship between them

Analysis at the level of the *process*–a process is an arrangement of resources

Need to know–the role of each unit of resource in the process and the relationship between them

Operational analysis

Flow between operations

Flow between processes

Flow between resources (people and facilities)

Figure 1.5   Operations and process management requires analysis at three levels: the supply network, the operation, and the process

The three levels of analysis

Operations and process management uses the process perspective to analyze businesses at three levels. The most obvious level is that of the business itself, or more specifically the operations function of the business. The other functions of the business could also be treated at this level, but that would be beyond the scope of this book. And, while analyz-ing the business at the level of the operation is important, for a more comprehensive assessment we also need to analyze the con-tribution of operations and process management at a higher and more strategic level (the level of its supply network) and at a lower, more operational level (the level of the individual processes). These three levels of operations analysis are shown in Figure 1.5.

> **Operations principle**
> A process perspective can be used at three levels: the level of the operation itself, the level of the supply network, and the level of individual processes.

The process perspective at the level of the operation

The operations part of a business is itself an input–transformation–output system, which transforms various inputs to produce (usually) a range of different products and services. Table 1.1 shows some operations described in terms of their main inputs, the purpose of their operations, and their outputs. Note how some of the inputs to the operation are transformed in some way while other inputs do the transforming. For example, an air-line's aircraft, pilots, air crew, and ground crew are brought into the operation in order to act on passengers and cargo and change (transform) their location. Note also how in some operations customers themselves are inputs. (The airline, department store and police department are all like this.) This illustrates an important distinction between operations

Table 1.1	Some operations described in terms of their inputs, purpose and outputs		
Type of operation	What are the operation's inputs?*	What does the operation do?	What are the operation's outputs?
Airline	Aircraft Pilots and air crew Ground crew *Passengers* *Cargo*	Move passengers and freight around the world	Transported passengers and freight
Department store	*Goods for sale* Staff sales Computerized registers *Customers*	Display goods Give sales advice Sell goods	Customers and goods 'assembled' together
Police department	Police officers Computer systems *Information* *Public (law-abiding and criminal)*	Prevent crime Solve crime Apprehend criminals	Lawful society Public with feeling of security
Frozen food manufacturer	*Fresh food* Operators Food-processing equipment Freezers	Food preparation Freeze	Frozen food

*Input resources that are transformed are printed in *italics*.

whose customers receive their outputs without seeing inside the operation, and those whose customers are inputs to the operation and therefore have some visibility of the operation's processes. Managing high-visibility operations where the customer is inside the operation usually involves a different set of requirements and skills from those whose customers never see inside the operation. (We will discuss this issue of visibility later in this chapter.)

Most operations produce both products and services

Some operations produce just products and others just services, but most operations produce a mixture of the two. Figure 1.6 shows a number of operations positioned in a spectrum from almost 'pure' goods producers to almost 'pure' service producers. Crude oil producers are concerned almost exclusively with the product that comes from their oil wells. So are aluminium smelters, but they might also produce some services such as technical advice. To an even greater extent, machine tool manufacturers produce services such as technical advice and applications engineering services as well as products. The services produced by restaurants are an essential part of what the customer is paying for. They both manufacture food and provide service. A computer systems services company may produce software 'products', but more so, it is providing an advice and customization service to its customers. A management consultancy, although producing reports and documents, would see itself largely as a service provider. Finally, some pure services do not produce products at all. A psychotherapy clinic, for example, provides therapeutic treatment for its customers without any physical product.

Operations principle
Most operations produce a mixture of tangible products and intangible services.

Services and products are merging

Increasingly the distinction between services and products is both difficult to define and not particularly useful. Even the official statistics compiled by governments have difficulty

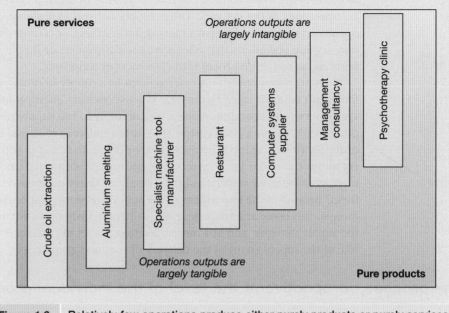

Figure 1.6 Relatively few operations produce either purely products or purely services. Most types of operation produce a mixture of goods and services

FURTHER EXAMPLE

in separating products and services. Software sold on a disk is classified as a product. The same software sold over the Internet is a service. Some authorities see the essential purpose of all businesses, and therefore all operations, as being to 'serve customers'. Therefore, they argue, all operations are service providers who may (or may not) produce products as a means of serving their customers. Our approach in this book is close to this. We treat operations and process management as being important for all organizations. Whether they see themselves as manufacturers or service providers is very much a secondary issue.

The process perspective at the level of the supply network

Any operation can be viewed as part of a greater network of operations. It will have operations that supply it with the products and services it needs to make its own products and services. And unless it deals directly with the end consumer, it will supply customers who themselves may go on to supply their own customers. Moreover, any operation could have several suppliers and/or several customers and may be in competition with other operations producing similar services to those it produces itself. This collection of operations is called the supply network.

There are three important issues to understand about any operation's supply network. First, it can be complex. Operations may have a large number of customers and suppliers who themselves have large numbers of customers and suppliers. Also, the relationships between operations in the supply network can be subtle. One operation may be in direct competition with another in some markets while at the same time acting as collaborators or suppliers to each other in others. Second, theoretically the boundaries of any operation's supply chain can be very wide indeed. They could go back to the operation that digs raw material out of the ground and go forward to the ultimate reuse and/or disposal of a product. Sometimes it is necessary to do this (for example, when considering the environmental sustainability of products), but generally some kind of boundary to the network needs to be set so that more attention can be given to the most immediate operations in the network. Third, supply networks are always changing. Not only do operations sometimes lose customers and win others, or change their suppliers, they also may acquire operations that once were their customers or suppliers, or sell parts of their business, so converting them into customers or suppliers.

Thinking about operations management in a supply network context is a particularly important issue for most businesses. The overarching question for any operations manager is 'Does my operation make a contribution to the supply network as a whole?'. In other words, are we a good customer to our suppliers in the sense that the long-term cost of supply to us is reduced because we are easy to do business with? Are we good suppliers to our customers in the sense that, because of our understanding of the supply network as a whole, we understand their needs and have developed the capability to satisfy them? Because of the importance of the supply network perspective, we deal with it twice more in this book: at a strategic level in Chapter 3 where we discuss the overall design of the supply network, and at a more operational level in Chapter 7 where we examine the role of the supply chain in the delivery of products and services.

The process perspective at the level of the individual process

Because processes are smaller versions of operations, they have customers and suppliers in the same way as whole operations. So we can view any operation as a network of individual processes that interact with each other, with each process being, at the same time, an internal supplier and an internal customer for other processes. This 'internal customer' concept provides a model to analyze the internal activities of an operation. If the whole operation is not working as it should, we may be able to trace the problem back along this internal network of customers and suppliers. It can also be a useful reminder to all parts of the operation that, by treating their internal customers with the same degree of care that they exercise on their external customers, the effectiveness of the whole operation can be improved.

Many of the examples used in our treatment of operations and process management are 'operations processes' in that they are part of the operations function. But some are

Table 1.2	Some examples of processes in non-operations functions		
Organizational function	Some of its processes	Outputs from its process	Customer(s) for its outputs
Marketing and sales	Planning process Forecasting process Order taking process	Marketing plans Sales forecasts Confirmed orders	Senior management Sales staff, planners, operations Operations, finance
Finance and accounting	Budgeting process Capital approval processes Invoicing processes	Budget Capital request evaluations Invoices	Everyone Senior management, requestees External customers
Human resources management	Payroll processes Recruitment processes Training processes	Salary statements New hires Trained employees	Employees All other processes All other processes
Information technology	Systems review process Help desk process System implementation project processes	System evaluation Advice Implemented working systems and aftercare	All other processes All other processes All other processes

'non-operations processes' and are part of some other function. And it is worth emphasizing again that these processes also need managing, using the same principles. Table 1.2 illustrates just some of the processes that are contained within some of the more common non-operations functions, the outputs from these processes and their 'customers'.

'End-to-end' business processes

There is one particularly important thing to understand about processes – we can define them in any way we want. The boundaries between processes, the activities that they perform, and the resources that they use, are all there because they have been designed in that way. It is common in organizations to find processes defined by the type of activity they engage in, for example invoicing processes, product design processes, sales processes, warehousing processes, assembly processes, painting processes, etc. This can be convenient because it groups similar resources together. But it is only one way of drawing the boundaries between processes. Theoretically, in large organizations there must be almost an infinite number of ways that activities and resources could be collected together as distinct processes. One way of redefining the boundaries and responsibilities of

> **Operations principle**
> Processes are defined by how the organization chooses to draw process boundaries.

processes is to consider the 'end-to-end' set of activities that satisfy defined customer needs. Think about the various ways in which a business satisfies its customers. Many different activities and resources will probably contribute to 'producing' each of its products and services. Some authorities recommend grouping the activities and resources together in an end-to-end manner to satisfy each defined customer need. This approach is closely identified with the 'business process engineering' (or re-engineering) movement (examined in Chapter 13). It calls for a radical rethink of process design that will probably involve taking activities and resources out of different functions and placing them together to meet customer needs. Remember, though, that designing processes around end-to-end customer needs is only one way (although often the sensible one) of designing processes.

FURTHER EXAMPLE

Example | ## The Programme and Video Division (PVD)

A broadcasting company has several divisions including several television and radio channels (entertainment and news), a 'general services' division that includes a specialist design workshop, and the 'Programme and Video Division' (PVD) that makes programmes and videos for a number of clients including the television and radio channels that are part of the same company. The original ideas for these programmes and videos usually come from the clients who commission them, although PVD itself does share in the creative input. The business is described at the three levels of analysis in Figure 1.7.

At the level of the operation

The division produces products in the form of tapes, discs and media files, but its real 'product' is the creativity and 'artistry' that is captured in the programmes. *'We provide a service',* says the division's boss, *'that interprets the client's needs (and sometimes their ideas), and transforms them into appealing and appropriate shows. We can do this because of the skills, experience and creativity of our staff, and our state-of-the-art technology.'*

At the level of the supply network

The division has positioned itself to specialize in certain types of product, including children's programmes, wildlife programmes and music videos. *'We did this so that we could develop a high level of expertise in a few relatively high margin areas. It also reduces our dependence on our own broadcasting channels. Having specialized in this way we are better positioned to partner and do*

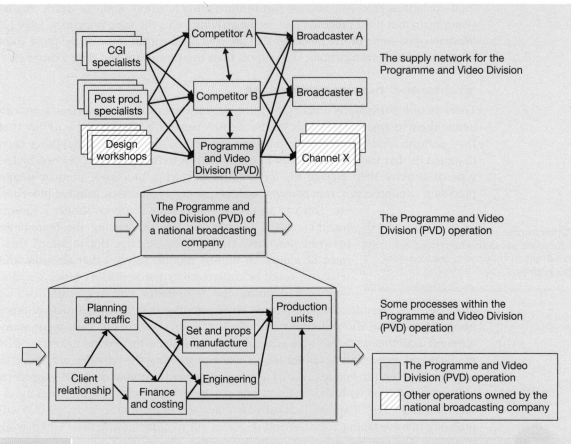

Figure 1.7   Operations and process management analysis for the Programme and Video Division (PVD) of a national broadcasting company at three levels: the supply network, the operation, and individual processes

work for other programme makers who are our competitors in some other markets. Specialization has also allowed us to outsource some activities such as computer graphic imaging (CGI) and post-production that are no longer worth keeping in-house. However, our design workshop became so successful that they were "spun out" as a division in their own right and now work for other companies as well as ourselves.'

At the level of individual processes

Many smaller processes contribute directly or indirectly to the production of programmes and videos, including the following:

- The planning and traffic department that acts as the operations management for the whole operation, drawing up schedules, allocating resources and 'project managing' each job through to completion
- Workshops that manufacture some of the sets, scenery and props for the productions
- Client liaison staff who liaise with potential customers, test out programme ideas and give information and advice to programme makers
- An engineering department that cares for, modifies and designs technical equipment
- Production units that organize and shoot the programmes and videos
- The finance and costing department that estimates the likely cost of future projects, controls operational budgets, pays bills and invoices customers.

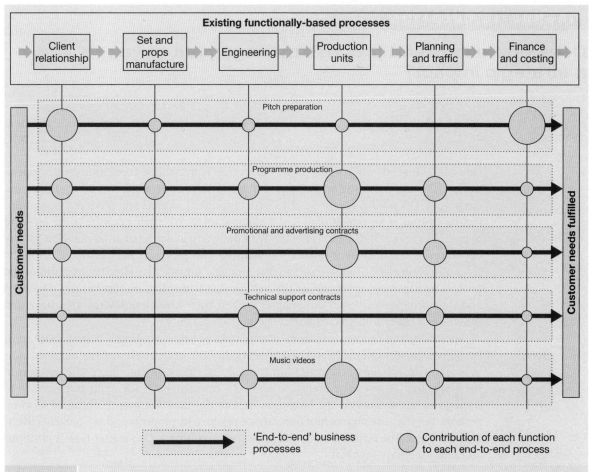

Figure 1.8   An example of how processes in the Programme and Video Division (PVD) could be reorganized around end-to-end business processes that fulfil defined customer needs

Creating end-to-end processes

PVD produces several products and services that fulfil customer needs. Each of these, to differ-ent extents, involves several of the existing departments within the company. For example, preparing a 'pitch' (a sales presentation that includes estimates of the time and cost involved in potential projects) needs contributions mainly from Client Relations and the Finance and Costing departments, but also needs smaller contributions from other departments. Figure 1.8 illustrates the contribution of each department to each product or service. (No particular sequence is implied by Figure 1.8.) The contributions of each department may not all occur in the same order. Currently, all the division's processes are clustered into conventional departments defined by the type of activity they perform: engineering, client relationship, etc. A radical redesign of the operation could involve regrouping activities and resources into five 'business' processes that fulfil each of the five defined customer needs. This is shown diagrammatically by the dotted lines in Figure 1.8. It would involve the physical movement of resources (people and facilities) out of the current functional processes into the new end-to-end business processes. This is an example of how processes can be designed in ways that do not necessarily reflect conventional functional groupings.

Does operations and process management have a strategic impact?

One of the biggest mistakes a business can make is to confuse 'operations' with 'operational'. Operational is the opposite of strategic; it means detailed, localized, short-term, day-to-day. Operations are the resources that produce products and services.[3] Operations can be treated at an operational *and a strategic* level. We shall examine some views of operations strategy in the next chapter. For now, we treat a fundamental question for any operation – does the way we manage operations and processes have a strategic impact? If a business does not fully appreciate the strategic impact that effective operations and process management can have, at the very least it is missing an opportunity. The IKEA and Dell examples earlier in this chapter are just two of many businesses that have harnessed their operations to create strategic impact.

Operations and process management can make or break a business. Although for most businesses, the operations function represents the bulk of its assets and the majority of its people, the true value of the operation is more than 'bulk'. It can 'make' the business in the sense that it gives the ability to compete through both the short-term ability to respond to customers and the long-term capabilities that will keep it ahead of its competitors. But if an operations function cannot produce its products and services effectively, it could 'break' the business by handicapping its performance no matter how it positions and sells itself in its markets.

Cost, revenue, investment and capability

The strategic importance of operations and process management is being increasingly recognized. It attracts far more attention than it did a few years ago and, according to some reports, accounts for the largest share of all the money spent by businesses on consultancy advice.[4] Partly this may be because the area has been neglected in the past. But it also denotes an acceptance that it can have both short-term and long-term impact. This can be seen in the impact that operations and process management can have on the costs, revenues, investment, and capabilities of businesses.

- It can reduce the **costs** of producing products and services by being efficient. The more productive the operation is at transforming inputs into outputs, the lower will be the cost of producing a unit of output. Cost is never totally unimportant for any business, but generally the higher the cost of a product or service when compared to the price it commands in the market, the more important cost reduction will be as an operations objective. Even so, cost reduction is almost always treated as an important contribution that operations can make to the success of any business.
- It can increase **revenue** by increasing customer satisfaction through quality, service and innovation. Existing customers are more likely to be retained and new customers are more likely to be attracted to products and services if they are error-free and appropriately designed, if the operation is fast and responsive in meeting their needs and keeping its delivery promises, and if the operation can be flexible, both in customizing its products and services and in introducing new ones. It is operations that directly

influence the quality, speed, dependability and flexibility of the business, all of which have a major impact on a company's ability to maximize its revenue.

- It can ensure **effective investment** (called *capital employed*) to produce its products and services. Eventually all businesses in the commercial world are judged by the return that they produce for their investors. This is a function of profit (the difference between costs and revenues) and the amount of money invested in the business's operations resources. We have already established that effective and efficient operations can reduce costs and increase revenue, but what is sometimes overlooked is their role in reducing the investment required per unit of output. Operations and process management does this by increasing the effective capacity of the operation and by being innovative in how it uses its physical resources.

> **Operations principle**
> All operations should be expected to contribute to their business by controlling costs, increasing revenue, making investment more effective and growing long-term capabilities.

- It can **build capabilities** that will form the basis for *future* innovation by building a solid base of operations skills and knowledge within the business. Every time an operation produces a product or a service, it has the opportunity to accumulate knowledge about how that product or service is best produced. This accumulation of knowledge should be used as a basis for learning and improvement. If so, in the long term, capabilities can be built that will allow the operation to respond to future market challenges. Conversely, if an operations function is simply seen as the mechanical and routine fulfilment of customer requests, then it is difficult to build the knowledge base that will allow future innovation.

FURTHER EXAMPLE

Example | The Programme and Video Division (PVD) continued

The PVD, described earlier, should be able to identify all four ways in which its operations and processes can have a strategic impact. The division is expected to generate reasonable returns by controlling its costs and being able to command relatively high fees. *'Sure, we need to keep our costs down. We always review our budgets for bought-in materials and services. Just as important, we measure the efficiency of all our processes, and we expect annual improvements in process efficiency to compensate for any increases in input costs.* (Reducing costs) *Our services are in demand by customers because we are good to work with'*, says the division's Managing Director. *'We have the technical resources to do a really great job and we always give good service. Projects are completed on time and within budget. More importantly, our clients know that we can work with them to ensure a high level of programme creativity. That is why we can command reasonably high prices.'* (Increasing revenue) The division also has to justify its annual spend on equipment to its main board. *'We try and keep up to date with the new technology that can really make an impact on our programme making, but we always have to demonstrate how it will improve profitability.* (Effective investment) *We also try to adapt new technology and integrate it into our creative processes in some way so that gives us some kind of advantage over our competitors.'* (Build capabilities)

Operations management in not-for-profit organizations

Terms such as *competitive advantage, markets* and *business* that are used in this book are usually associated with companies in the for-profit sector. Yet operations management is also relevant to organizations whose purpose is not primarily to earn profits. Managing operations in an animal welfare charity, hospital, research organization or government department is essentially the same as in commercial organizations. However, the strategic objectives of not-for-profit organizations may be more complex and involve a mixture of political, economic, social and/or environmental objectives. Consequently, there may be a greater chance of operations decisions being made under conditions of conflicting objectives. So, for example, it is the operations staff in a children's welfare department who have to face the conflict between the cost of providing extra social workers and the risk of a child not receiving adequate protection.

FURTHER EXAMPLE

Should all processes be managed in the same way?

All processes differ in some way, so, to some extent, all processes need to be managed differently. Some of the differences between processes are 'technical' in the sense that different products and services require different skills and technologies to produce them. However, processes also differ in terms of the nature of demand for their products or services. Four characteristics of demand in particular have a significant effect on how processes need to be managed:

> **Operations principle**
> The way in which processes need to be managed is influenced by volume, variety, variation and visibility.

- The volume of the products and services produced
- The variety of the different products and services produced
- The variation in the demand for products and services
- The degree of visibility that customers have of the production of products and services.

The 'four Vs' of processes

Volume

Processes with a high volume of output will have a high degree of repeatability, and because tasks are repeated frequently it often makes sense for staff to specialize in the tasks they perform. This allows the systemization of activities, where standard procedures may be codified and set down in a manual with instructions on how each part of the job should be performed. Also, because tasks are systemized and repeated, it is often worth developing specialized technology that gives higher processing efficiencies. By contrast, low-volume processes with less repetition cannot specialize to the same degree. Staff are likely to perform a wide range of tasks, and while this may be more rewarding, it is less open to systemization. Nor is it likely that efficient, high-throughput technology could be used. The implications of this are that high-volume processes have more opportunities to produce products or services at low-unit cost. So, for example, the volume and standardization of large fast-food restaurant chains such as McDonald's or KFC enables them to produce with greater efficiency than a small, local cafeteria or diner.

Variety

Processes that produce a high variety of products and services must engage in a wide range of different activities, changing relatively frequently between each activity. They must also contain a wide range of skills and technology sufficiently 'general purpose' to cope with the range of activities and sufficiently flexible to change between them. A high level of variety may also imply a relatively wide range of inputs to the process and the additional complexity of matching customer requirements to appropriate products or services. So, high-variety processes are invariably more complex and costly than low-variety ones. For example, a taxi company is usually prepared to pick up and drive customers almost anywhere (at a price); they may even take you by the route of your choice. There are an infinite number of potential routes (products) that it offers. But its cost per kilometre travelled will be higher than for a less customized form of transport such as a bus service.

Variation

Processes are generally easier to manage when they only have to cope with predictably constant demand. Resources can be geared to a level that is just capable of meeting demand. All activities can be planned in advance. By contrast, when demand is variable and/or unpredictable, resources will have to be adjusted over time. Worse still, when demand is unpredictable, extra resources will have to be designed into the process to provide a 'capacity cushion' that can absorb unexpected demand. So, for example, processes that manufacture high-fashion garments will have to cope with the general seasonality of the garment market together with the uncertainty of whether particular styles may or may not prove popular. Operations that make conventional business suits are likely to have less fluctuation in demand over time, and be less prone to unexpected fluctuations. Because processes with lower variation do not need any extra safety capacity and can be planned in advance, they generally have lower costs than those with higher variation.

Visibility

Process visibility is a slightly more difficult concept to envisage. It indicates how much of the processes are 'experienced' directly by customers, or how much the process is 'exposed' to its customers. Generally processes that act directly on customers (such as retail or healthcare processes) will have more of their activities visible to their customers than those that act on materials and information. However, even material and information transforming processes may provide a degree of visibility to the customers. For example, parcel distribution operations provide Internet-based 'track and trace' facilities to enable their customers to have visibility of where their packages are at any time. Low-visibility processes, if they communicate with their customers at all, do so using less immediate channels such as the telephone or the Internet. Much of the process can be more 'factory-like'. The time lag between customer request and response could be measured in days rather than the near-immediate response expected from high-visibility processes. This lag allows the activities in a low-visibility process to be performed when it is convenient to the operation, so achieving high utilization. Also, because the customer interface needs managing, staff in high-visibility processes need customer contact skills that shape the customer's perception of process performance. For all these reasons high–visibility processes tend to have higher costs than low-visibility processes.

Many operations have both high- and low-visibility processes. This serves to emphasize the difference that the degree of visibility makes. For example, in an airport some of its processes are relatively visible to its customers (check-in desks, information desks, restaurants, passport control, security staff, etc.). These staff operate in a high-visibility 'front-office' environment. Other processes in the airport have relatively little, if any, customer visibility (baggage handling, overnight freight operations, loading meals on to the aircraft, cleaning, etc.). We rarely see these processes but they perform the vital but low-visibility tasks in the 'back-office' part of the operation.

The implications of the four Vs of processes

All four dimensions have implications for processing costs. Put simply, high volume, low variety, low variation and low visibility all help to keep processing costs down. Conversely, low volume, high variety, high variation and high customer contact generally carry some kind of cost penalty for the process. This is why the volume dimension is drawn with its 'low' end at the left, unlike the other dimensions, to keep all the 'low cost' implications on the right. Figure 1.9 summarizes the implications of such positioning.

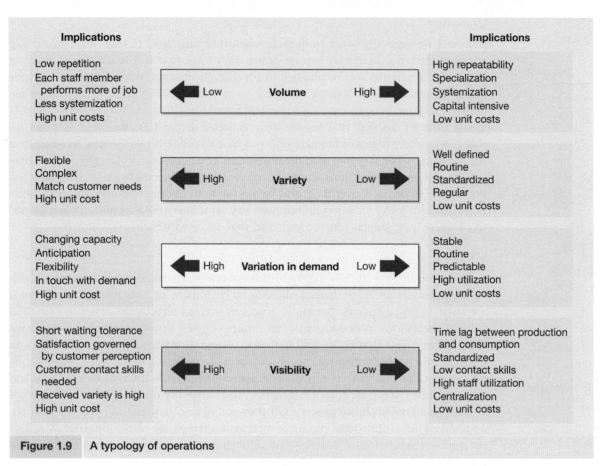

Implications   **Implications**

Low repetition   High repeatability
Each staff member   Low   **Volume**   High   Specialization
  performs more of job   Systemization
Less systemization   Capital intensive
High unit costs   Low unit costs

Flexible   Well defined
Complex   High **Variety**   Low   Routine
Match customer needs   Standardized
High unit cost   Regular
                                                                    Low unit costs

Changing capacity   Stable
Anticipation   Routine
Flexibility   High **Variation in demand** Low Predictable
In touch with demand   High utilization
High unit cost   Low unit costs

Short waiting tolerance   Time lag between production
Satisfaction governed   and consumption
  by customer perception   Standardized
Customer contact skills   High **Visibility**   Low   Low contact skills
  needed   High staff utilization
Received variety is high   Centralization
High unit cost   Low unit costs

Figure 1.9   A typology of operations

Charting processes using the four Vs

In almost any operation, processes can be identified that have different positions on the four dimensions, and which therefore have different objectives and will need managing in different ways. To a large extent the position of a process on the four dimensions is determined by the demand of the market it is serving. However, most processes have some discretion in moving themselves on the dimensions. Look at the different positions on the visibility dimension that retail banks have adopted. At one time, using branch tellers was the only way customers could contact a bank. Now access to the bank's services could be through (in decreasing order of visibility) a personal banker, who visits your home or office, a conversation with a branch manager, the teller at the window, telephone contact through a call centre, Internet banking services, or an ATM cash machine. These other processes offer services that have been developed by banks to serve different market needs.

Figure 1.10 illustrates the different positions on the four Vs for some retail banking processes. Note that the personal banking/advice service is positioned at the high-cost end of the four Vs. For this reason such services are often only offered to relatively wealthy customers that represent high profit opportunities for the bank. Note also that the more recent developments in retail banking such as call centres, Internet banking and ATMs all represent a shift towards the low-cost end of the four Vs. New processes that exploit new technologies can often have a profound impact on the implications of each dimension. For example, Internet banking, when compared with an ATM cash machine, offers a far higher variety of options for customers, but because the process is automated through its information technology, the cost of offering this variety is less than at a conventional branch or even a call centre.

PRACTICE NOTE

Figure 1.10   Four Vs analysis for some retail banking processes

A model of operations and process management

Managing operations and processes involves a whole range of separate decisions that will determine their overall purpose, structure and operating practices. These decisions can be grouped together in various ways. Look at other books on operations management and you will find many different ways of structuring operations decisions and therefore the subject as a whole. Here we have chosen to classify activities into four broad groups, relating to four broad activities. Although there are some overlaps between these four categories, they more or less follow a sequence that corresponds to the life cycle of operations and processes.

- **Directing** the overall strategy of the operation. A general understanding of operations and processes and their strategic purpose, together with an appreciation of how strategic purpose is translated into reality (direct), is a prerequisite to the detailed design of operations and process.
- **Designing** the operation's products, services and processes. Design is the activity of determining the physical form, shape and composition of operations and processes together with the products and services that they produce.
- Planning and control process **delivery**. After being designed, the delivery of products and services from suppliers and through the total operation to customers must be planned and controlled.
- **Developing** process performance. Increasingly it is recognized that operations and process managers cannot simply routinely deliver products and services in the same way that they have always done. They have a responsibility to develop the capabilities of their processes to improve process performance.

We can now combine two ideas to develop the model of operations and process management that will be used throughout this book. The first is the idea that *operations* and the *processes* that make up both the operations and other business functions are transformation systems that take in inputs and use process resources to transform them into outputs. The second idea is that the resources both in an organization's operations as a

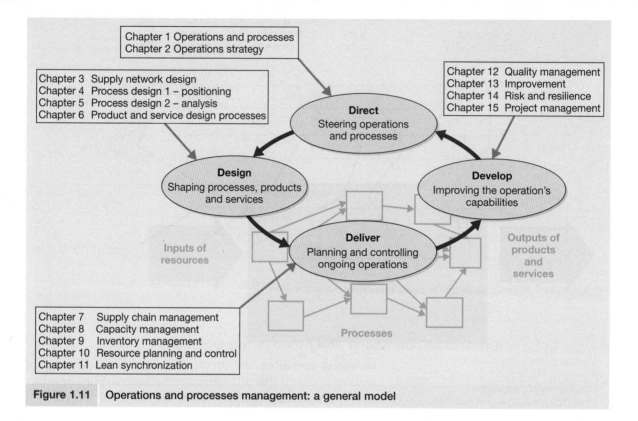

Figure 1.11   Operations and processes management: a general model

whole and in its individual processes need to be managed in terms of how they are *direct-ed*, how they are *designed*, how *delivery* is planned and controlled, and how they are *developed* and improved. Figure 1.11 shows how these two ideas go together. This book will use this model to examine the more important decisions that should be of interest to all managers of operations and processes.

Critical commentary

Each chapter contains a short critical commentary on the main ideas covered in the chapter. Its purpose is not to undermine the issues discussed in the chapter, but to emphasize that, although we present a relatively orthodox view of operation, there are other perspectives.

■ The central idea in this introductory chapter is that all organizations have operations (and other functions) that have processes that produce products and services, and that all these processes are essentially similar. However, some believe that by even trying to characterize organizations in this way (perhaps even by calling them 'processes') one loses or distorts their nature and depersonalizes or takes the 'humanity' out of the way in which we think of the organization. This point is often raised in not-for-profit organizations, especially by 'professional' staff. For example the head of one European 'Medical Association' (a doctors' Trade Union) criticized hospital authorities for expecting a 'sausage factory service based on productivity targets'. No matter how similar they appear on paper, it is argued, a hospital can never be viewed in the same way as a factory. Even in commercial businesses, professionals, such as creative staff, often express discomfort at their expertise being described as a 'process'.

■ To some extent these criticisms of taking such a process perspective are valid. How we describe organizations does say much about our underlying assumptions of what an 'organization' is and how it is supposed to work. Notwithstanding the point we made earlier about how a purely process view can misleadingly imply that organizations are neat and controllable with unambiguous boundaries and lines of accountability, a process perspective can risk depicting the messy reality of organizations in a naive manner. Yet, in our view it is a risk well worth taking.

Summary checklist

DOWNLOADABLE

This checklist comprises questions that can be usefully applied to any type of operations and reflect the major diagnostic questions used within the chapter.

☐ Is the operations function of the business clearly defined?

☐ Do operations managers realize that they are operations managers even if they are called by some other title?

☐ Do the non-operations functions within the business realize that they manage processes?

☐ Does everyone understand the inputs, activities and outputs of the processes of which they are part?

☐ Is the balance between products and services produced by the operations function well understood?

☐ Are future changes that may occur in the balance between products and services produced by the operation understood?

☐ What contribution is operations making towards reducing the cost of products and services?

☐ What contribution is operations making towards increasing the revenue from products and services?

☐ What contribution is operations making towards better use of capital employed?

☐ How is operations developing its capability for future innovation?

☐ Does the operation understand its position in the overall supply network?

☐ Does the operation contribute to the overall supply network?

☐ Are the individual processes that comprise the operations function defined and understood?

☐ Are individual processes aware of the internal customer and supplier concept?

☐ Do they use the internal customer and supplier concept to increase their contribution to the business as a whole?

☐ Do they use the ideas and principles of operations management to improve the performance of their processes?

☐ Has the concept of end-to-end business processes been examined and considered?

☐ Are the differences (in terms of volume, variety, variation and visibility) between processes understood?

☐ Are the volume, variety, variation and visibility characteristics of processes reflected in the way they are managed?

Case study   AAF Rotterdam

'Our growth over the last two or three years has just been amazing. We have clients all over Europe and although many of the jobs we are now doing are more challenging they are far more interesting. We are also now making a good operating profit, even if almost all of it is being swallowed up to fund our growth. Our biggest problem is now adapting ourselves in a way that is appropriate for a larger company. We aren't just a group of friends having a good time anymore; we need to become a profession-al business.' The speaker was Marco Van Hopen, one of the three directors of AAF, a theatrical services company, based just outside Rotterdam in The Netherlands. He had founded the company with two friends in 1999 when they decided to make a busi-ness out of their interest in theatrical and stage design. 'It's the combination of skill and adrenalin that I like', said Marco. 'Because most events are live there is no chance for a second take; all the equipment must work first time, on time, and every time. Also, there has recently been a dramatic increase in the sophistication of the technology we use, such as programmable automated lighting units.'

Background

From the original three founders of the company, AAF had now grown to employ 16 full-time employees together with over 20 freelance crew, who were hired as and when necessary. In the previous year the company's revenue had been slightly over €3,000,000 and its operating profit slightly under €200,000. It was located on an industrial estate that provided good access to the main European road network. The majority of the company's 2000 square metre building was devoted to a combined storage area and workshop. Also within the site were the administrative and technical offices and a design studio.

The company had started by hiring and selling stage equipment (mainly lighting, sound and staging equipment) to clients that ranged from small local theatrical groups through to very large production and conference compa-nies. Then it had moved into offering 'production services' that included designing, constructing and installing entire sets, particularly for conferences but also for shows and theatrical events. The majority of the company's 'produc-tion services' clients were production companies that contracted AAF as a 'second tier' supplier on behalf of the main client, that was usually a corporation putting on its own event (for example, a sales conference). The events organized for the main client could be anywhere in the world, although AAF confined itself to European locations. As Marco Van Hopen says, 'We have succeeded in differ-entiating ourselves through offering a complete "design, build and install" service that is creative, dependable and sufficiently flexible to incorporate last-minute changes. The key skill is to articulate client requirements and trans-late these into a workable set design. This means working closely with clients. It also requires a sound technical understanding of equipment capabilities. Most important, every project is different, that's what makes it so exciting.'

Although both parts of the business were growing, it was the production services business that was growing particularly quickly. In the previous year around 60 per cent of the company's revenue had come from hiring and selling equipment, with the remainder coming from pro-duction services. However, production services were far more profitable. 'The large production jobs may be 40 per cent of our revenue but last year they accounted for almost 80 per cent of our profits. Some people ask me why we don't focus on production services, but we will *never get out of hiring and sales. Partly this is because we have over €1,000,000 invested in the equipment, partly it is because it provides us with a steady and relatively predictable stream of income, but mostly it is because we need access to the latest equipment in order to win production services contracts. However, in the near future our own production services work could be the biggest "customer" for our hire and sales business.'* (Van Hopen)

The workshop and store

The combined workshop and storage area was seen as the heart of the company's operations. Equipment was stored on high-level racks in predetermined locations. A team of eight technicians prepared hire equipment for customers, delivered it to customer sites (about 80 per cent of all orders were delivered, the rest being collected from the AAF site by customers themselves). About 30 per cent of customers, usually the smaller ones, also required the equipment to be installed. The technicians also checked the equipment on return from the customer, and carried out any repairs or maintenance that was required. As the equipment had become more sophisticated, the job of preparing, installing and maintaining hire equipment had also become far more technically demanding. These technicians used the workshop area, adjacent to the storage area, to calibrate equipment, pre-programme lighting sequences and carry out any repairs. The workshop, which had recently been re-equipped with new wood and metal-working equipment, was also used to construct the sets used for production services' clients. Two employees worked almost full-time on this, but equipment technicians could also be used for set construction if it was required. If workshop facilities were needed by both equipment hire and production services at the same time, usually production services were given priority, an arrangement that was not always to the liking of the equipment hire technicians.

Design studio

The design studio used computer-aided design equipment and simulations that could predict the effects of different lighting configurations. Although Marco Van Hopen was involved in the design process for many jobs, the company now also employed one full-time and one part-time designer: *'We often bring clients to the design studio to test various ideas on them using our simulation and projection facilities. It is a great way to get clients to visualize the set design and "bring them into" the design process.'*

Administrative and crew offices

The administration office received orders from hire and sales customers as well as providing the first point of contact for production services' clients. Three full-time employees organized the company's operations, sched-

uled work for the workshop and crew, sent out invoices and generally managed the business. In addition two part-time account assistants were employed to do cost estimates for the more complex 'production services' jobs. Adjacent to the administrative office was the 'crew office', an area for the production crew to plan the logistics required to ensure efficient installation of sets. *'The crew office is the nerve centre of all the project management that goes into a good service. It is a focal point for designers, workshop people and crew to come together.'* (Van Hopen)

Problems

Although excited by the recent growth of the company and its future prospects, Van Hopen was also concerned that the company should be able to improve its profitability: *'There's no point in growing and doing exciting things if we can't also make money out of it. I realize that, by its nature, growth is expensive. However, I think maybe that we have let our costs slip out of control. We need to be able to get more out of what we already have, and the best way to do this is to get ourselves organized. The main problem is that our activities are getting less predictable. The hire and sales business is basically routine, and although some of our clients can be late in placing their orders, it is largely predictable. Not only do we have a wide range of equipment, we also have excellent relationships with other sound and lighting companies; so that, if we can only partially fulfil a customer's order, we can hire any other equipment we need from our competitors. This may reduce our profits slightly, but we keep the client happy. The irony is that we don't seem to be able to achieve similar levels of flexibility within our own company. This is important now that production services are growing quickly. We have fewer production services contracts (48 last year, compared with almost 3000 hire contracts) but they are complex and you cannot always predict exactly what you will need to complete them. We have succeeded in growing the production services business partly because of the quality of our designs where we put a lot of time and effort into working closely with the client before we submit a final design, but also because we have built up a reputation for dependability. Clients trust us to be totally reliable. This means that sometimes our crews have be flexible and sometimes work through the night in order to get things ready on time. But we are paying for this flexibility in terms of excessive hours worked. What we perhaps should consider is improving the agility with which we move people out of the store and workshop area and on to fulfilling production services contracts when necessary. I don't know how it would work yet, I just feel that by working together more we could increase our ability to take on more work without increasing our cost base.'*

QUESTIONS

1 Do you think Marco Van Hopen understands the importance of operations to his business?

2 What contribution does he seem to expect from his operations?

3 Sketch out how you see the supply network for AAF and AAF's position within it.

4 What are the major processes within AAF, and how do they relate to each other?

5 Evaluate Van Hopen's idea of increasing the flexibility with which the different parts of the company work with each other.

Active case study   EleXon Computers

ACTIVE CASE

Since their inception 17 years ago, EleXon computers have grown and diversified from a small unit assembling and selling computers primarily within the UK, into a much larger international company serving a much wider and more diverse market. Despite its growth, the underlying organization of the company has not changed. The inadequacy of existent systems and processes has become increasingly obvious and increasingly a source of tension within and between departments.

● How would you re-organize the operations and processes to satisfy their differing perspectives and demands?

Please refer to the Active case on the CD accompanying this book to listen to the frustrations of each department.

Applying the principles

HINTS

Some of these exercises can be answered by reading the chapter. Others will require some general knowledge of business activity and some might require an element of investigation. All have hints on how they can be answered on the CD accompanying this book.

1 Quentin Cakes make about 20,000 cakes per year in two sizes, both based on the same recipe. Sales peak at Christmas time when demand is about 50 per cent higher than in the quieter summer period. Their customers (the stores that stock their products) order their cakes in advance through a simple Internet-based ordering system. Knowing that they have some surplus capacity, one of their customers has approached them with two potential new orders.

(a) The *Custom Cake* option – this would involve making cakes in different sizes where consumers could specify a message or greeting to be 'iced' on top of the cake. The consumer would give the inscription to the store who would e-mail it through to the factory. The customer thought that demand would be around 1000 cakes per year, mostly at celebration times such as St Valentine's Day and Christmas.

(b) The *Individual Cake* option – this option involves Quentin Cakes introducing a new line of very small cakes intended for individual consumption. Demand for this individual-sized cake was forecast to be around 4000 per year, with demand likely to be more evenly distributed throughout the year than their existing products.

The total revenue from both options is likely to be roughly the same and the company has the capacity to adopt only one of the two ideas. But which one should it be?

2 Described as having *'revolutionized the concept of sandwich making and eating'*, Prêt A Manger opened their first shop in the mid-1980s, in London. Now they have over 130 shops in the UK, New York, Hong Kong and Tokyo. They say that their secret is to focus continually on quality, in all their activities. *'Many food retailers focus on extending the shelf life of their food, but that's of no interest to us. We maintain our edge by selling food that simply can't be beaten for freshness. At the end of the day, we give whatever we haven't sold to charity to help feed those who would otherwise go hungry.'* The first Prêt A Manger shop had its own kitchen where fresh ingredients were delivered first thing every morning, and food was prepared throughout the day. Every Prêt shop since has followed this model. The team members serving on the tills at lunchtime will have been making sandwiches in the kitchen that morning. They rejected the idea of a huge centralized sandwich factory even though it could significantly reduce costs. Prêt also own and manage all their shops directly so that they can ensure consistently high standards. *'We are determined never to forget that our hardworking people make all the difference. They are our heart and soul. When they care, our business is sound. If they cease to care, our business goes down the drain. We work hard at building great teams. We take our reward schemes and career opportunities very seriously. We don't work nights (generally), we wear jeans, we party!'*

- Do you think Prêt A Manger fully understand the importance of their operations management?
- What evidence is there for this?
- What kind of operations management activities at Prêt A Manger might come under the four headings of direct, design, deliver and develop?

3 Visit a furniture store (other than IKEA). Observe how the shop operates, for example, where customers go, how staff interact with them, how big it is, how the shop has chosen to use its space, what variety of products it offers, and so on. Talk with the staff and managers if you can. Think about how the shop that you have visited is different from IKEA. Then consider the question:

- What implications do the differences between IKEA and the shop you visited have for their operations management?

4 Write down five services that you have 'consumed' in the last week. Try and make these as varied as possible. Examples could include public transport, a bank, any shop or supermarket, attendance at an education course, a cinema, a restaurant, etc. For each of these services, ask yourself the following questions.

- Did the service meet your expectations? Is so what did the management of the service have to do well in order to satisfy your expectations? If not, where did they fail? Why might they have failed?
- If you were in charge of managing the delivery of these services, what would you do to improve the service?
- If they wanted to, how could the service be delivered at a lower cost so that the service could reduce its prices?
- How do you think that the service copes when something goes wrong (such as a piece of technology breaking down)?
- Which other organizations might supply the service with products and services? (In other words, they are your 'supplier', but who are *their* suppliers?)
- How do you think the service copes with fluctuation of demand over the day, week, month or year?

These questions are just some of the issues which the operations managers in these services have to deal with. Think about the other issues they will have to manage in order to deliver the service effectively.

5 Find a copy of a financial newspaper (*Financial Times, Wall Street Journal, Economist,* etc.) and identify one company that is described in the paper that day.

- What do you think would be the main operations issues for that company?

Notes on chapter

1 Thanks to Mike Shulver and Paul Walley for this information.
2 Sources include Dell, M. (1999) *Direct from Dell,* Harper Business, New York.
3 Slack, N. and Lewis, M.A. (2002) *Operations Strategy,* Financial Times Prentice Hall, Harlow, UK.
4 Source: *The Economist,* 22 March 1997.

Taking it further

Chase, R.B., Aquilano, N.J. and Jacobs, F.R. (2001) *Production and Operations Management: Manufacturing and services* (9th edn), Unwin/McGraw-Hill. There are many good general textbooks on operations management. This was one of the first and is still one of the best, though written very much for an American audience.

Hammer, M. and Stanton, S. (1999) *How Process Enterprises Really Work,* Harvard Business Review, Nov.-Dec. Hammer is one of the gurus of process design. This paper is typical of his approach.

Heizer, J. and Render, B. (1999) *Operations Management* (5th edn), Prentice Hall, New Jersey. Another good US-authored general text on the subject.

Johnston, R., Chambers, S., Harland, C., Harrison, A. and Slack, N. (2003) *Cases in Operations Management* (3rd edn), Financial Times Prentice Hall, Harlow, UK. Many great examples of real operations management issues. Not surprisingly, based around a similar structure as this book.

Johnston, R. and Clark, E. (2005) *Service Operations Management,* Financial Times Prentice Hall, Harlow, UK. What can we say! A great treatment of service operations from the same stable as this textbook.

Keen, P.G.W. (1997) *The Process Edge: Creating value where it counts,* Harvard Business School Press. Operations management as 'process' management.

Slack, N. and Lewis, M. (eds) (2005) *The Blackwell Encyclopedic Dictionary of Operations Management* (2nd edn), Blackwell Business, Oxford. For those who like technical descriptions and definitions.

Useful websites

www.iomnet.org The Institute of Operations Management site. One of the main professional bodies for the subject.

www.poms.org A US academic society for production and operations management. Academic, but some useful material, including a link to an encyclopedia of operations management terms.

www.sussex.ac.uk/users/dt31/TOMI One of the longest-established portals for the subject. Useful for academics and students alike.

www.ft.com Useful for researching topics and companies.

FURTHER RESOURCES

For further resources including examples, animated diagrams, self test questions, excel spreadsheets, active case studies and video materials please explore the CD accompanying this book.

Introduction

In the long-term, the major (and some would say, only) objective for operations and processes is to provide a business with some form of strategic advantage. That is why the management of a business's processes and operations and its intended overall strategy must be logically connected. Without this connection, operations and processes will be without a coherent direction and they may finish up making internal decisions that either do not reflect the business's strategy, or conflict with each other, or both. So a clear operations strategy is vital. And, although operations and process management is largely 'operational', it also has a strategic dimension that is vital if operations is to fulfil its potential to contribute to com-

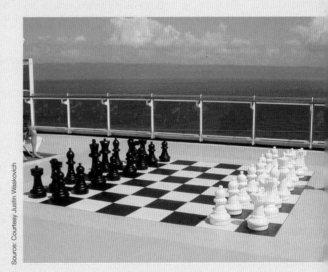

Source: Courtesy Justin Waskovich

petitiveness. Figure 2.1 shows the position of the ideas described in this chapter in the general model of operations management.

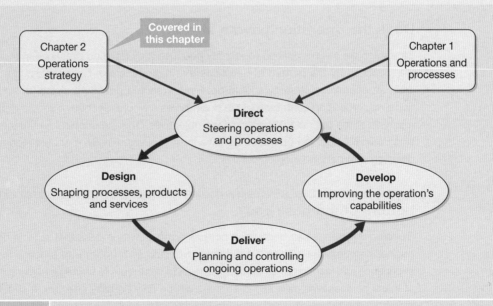

| Figure 2.1 | Operations strategy is the pattern of decisions and actions that shape the long-term vision, objectives and capabilities of the operation and its contribution to overall strategy |

Executive summary

VIDEO
further detail

Decision logic chain for operations strategy

Each chapter is structured around a set of diagnostic questions. These questions suggest what you should ask in order to gain an understanding of the important issues of a topic, and as a result, improve your decision making. An executive summary, addressing these questions, is provided below.

What is operations strategy?

Operations strategy is the pattern of decisions and actions that shape the long-term vision, objectives, and capabilities of the operation and its contribution to overall strategy. It is the way in which operations resources are developed over the long term to create sustainable competitive advantage for the business. Increasingly, many businesses are seeing their operations strategy as one of the best ways to differentiate themselves from competitors. Even in those companies that are marketing led (such as fast-moving consumer goods), an effective operations strategy can add value by allowing the exploitation of market positioning.

Does the operation have a strategy?

Strategies are always difficult to identify because they have no presence in themselves, but are identified by the pattern of decisions that they generate. Nevertheless one can identify what an operations strategy should do. First, it should provide a vision for how the operation's resources can contribute to the business as a whole. Second, it should define the exact meaning of the operation's performance objectives. Third, it should identify the broad decisions that will help the operation achieve its objectives. Finally, it should reconcile strategic decision with performance objectives.

Does operations strategy make sense from the top and the bottom of the business?

Operations strategy can been seen both as a top-down process that reflects corporate and business strategy through to a functional level, and as a bottom-up process that allows the experience and learning at an operational level to contribute to strategic thinking. Without both of these perspectives, operations strategy will be only partially effective. It should communicate both top to bottom *and* bottom to top throughout the hierarchical levels of the business.

Does operations strategy align market requirements with operations resources?

The most important short-term objective of operations strategy is to ensure that operations resources can satisfy market requirements. But this is not the only objective. In the longer term, operations strategy must build the capabilities within its resources that will allow the business to provide something to the market that its competitors find difficult to imitate or match. These two objectives are called the market requirements perspective and the operations resource capability perspective. The latter is very much influenced by the resource-based view (RBV) of the firm. The objective of operations strategy can be seen as achieving 'fit' between these two perspectives.

Does operations strategy set an improvement path?

The purpose of operations strategy is to improve the business's performance relative to those of its competitors in the long term. It therefore must provide an indication of how this improvement is to take place. This is best addressed by considering the trade-offs between performance objectives in terms of the 'efficient frontier' model. This describes operations strategy as a combination of repositioning performance along an existing efficient frontier, and increasing overall operations effectiveness by overcoming trade-offs to expand the efficient frontier.

DIAGNOSTIC QUESTION

What is operations strategy?

Operations strategy is the pattern of decisions and actions that shape the long-term vision, objectives and capabilities of the operation and its contribution to the overall strategy of the business.[1] The term 'operations strategy' sounds at first like a contradiction. How can 'operations', a subject that is generally concerned with the day-to-day creation and delivery of goods and services, be strategic? 'Strategy' is usually regarded as the opposite of those day-to-day routine activities. But, as we indicated in the previous chapter, *'operations'* is not the same as *'operational'*. 'Operations' are the resources that create products and services. 'Operational' is the opposite of strategic, meaning day-to-day and detailed.

Perhaps more significantly, many of the businesses that seem to be especially competitively successful, and that appear to be sustaining their success into the longer term, have a clear and often inventive operations strategy. Just look at some of the high-profile companies quoted in this book, or that feature in the business press. From Tesco to Wal-Mart, from Ryanair to Southwest Airlines, it is not just that their operations strategy provides these companies with adequate support; it is their operations strategy that is the pivotal reason for their competitive superiority. Yet not all businesses compete so directly through their operations. Some are more marketing led. Consumer product companies like Coca Cola or Heinz are more marketing driven. But even these types of business need a strong operations strategy. Their brand position may be shaped in the consumer's mind by their promotional activities, but it would soon erode if they could not deliver products on time, or if their quality was sub-standard, or if they could not introduce new products in response to market trends. With this type of business, operations strategy may not be the pre-eminent factor in driving their strategy, but it is still important, and without it their marketing efforts would come to almost nothing.

Look at these two examples of businesses with operations strategies that are clear and explicit and have contributed to their competitive success.

Example | ## Flextronics[2]

Behind every well-known brand name in consumer electronics, much of the high-tech manufacturing which forms the heart of the product is probably done by companies few of us have heard of. Companies such as Ericsson and IBM are increasingly using Electronic Manufacturing Services (EMS) companies which specialize in providing the outsourced design, engineering, manufacturing and logistics operations for big brand names. Flextronics is one of the leading EMS providers

One of Flextronic's industrial parks

in providing 'operational services' to technology companies. With over 70,000 employees spread throughout its facilities in 28 countries, it has a global presence that allows it the flexibility to serve customers in all the key markets throughout the world.

Flextronics manufacturing locations have to balance their customers' need for low costs (electronic goods are often sold in a fiercely competitive market) with their need for responsive and flexible service (electronics markets can also be volatile). Flextronics could have set up manufacturing plants close to its main customers in North America and Western Europe. This would certainly facilitate fast response and great service to customers; unfortunately these markets also tend to have high manufacturing costs. Flextronics' operations strategy must therefore achieve a balance between low costs and high levels of service. One way Flextronics achieves this is through its strategic location and supply network decisions, adopting what it calls its 'Industrial Park Strategy'. This involves finding locations that have relatively low manufacturing costs but are close to its major markets. It has established Industrial Parks in places such as Hungary, Poland, Brazil and Mexico. Flextronics' own suppliers also are encouraged to locate within the Park to provide stability and further reduce response times.

Example	## Southwest Airlines[3]

Southwest Airlines is the only airline that has been consistently profitable every year for over 30 years. It is also now one of the largest airlines in the world by value. Yet back in 1971 it was an upstart three-jet airline operating from Dallas, Texas (still its headquarters). The strategy of the company has been consistent since it was founded, to get its passengers to their destinations when they want to get there, on time, at the lowest possible fares, and to make sure that they have a good time doing it. Its success in achieving this is down to clever management, a relaxed and employee-centred

Source: © Southwest Airlines

corporate style, and what was then a unique way of organizing its operations. For over 30 years it has introduced a series of cost-saving innovations. Unlike most airlines it provided simple snacks (originally only peanuts) instead of full meals. This not only reduced costs but also reduced turnaround time at airports. Because there are no meals there is less mess to clear up and also less time is needed to prepare the galley and load up the aircraft with supplies. Passengers were sold tickets without a seat allocation (simpler and faster) and expected to seat themselves (faster). Originally boarding passes were plastic and reusable and the company was one of the first to use electronic tickets. It was also early in its adoption of the Internet to sell tickets directly to passengers. Although most airlines at the time used a range of different aircraft for different purposes, Southwest has consistently stuck with Boeing 737s since it started. This significantly reduces maintenance costs, reduces the number of spare parts needed and makes it easier for pilots to fly any aircraft. Southwest's employee involvement practices are designed to empower employees to take responsibility for maintaining high efficiency and high quality of service, with profit sharing plans for almost all employees and innovative stock options plans for its pilots. The result has been what some claim to be the most productive workforce in the airline industry.

What do Flextronics and Southwest Airlines have in common?

Neither of these companies suffered from any lack of clarity regarding what they wanted to do in the market. They are clear about what they are offering their customers (and they document it explicitly on their websites). They are also both equally clear in spelling out their operations strategy. Flextronics is willing to relocate whole operations in its commitment to responsive but low-cost customer service. Southwest Airlines redefined the airline market with its (at that time) novel, no-frills service. Without a 'top–down' strategic clarity it is difficult to achieve clarity in the way individual processes should be managed. But both these companies are also known for the way they have perfected the operational-level processes to the extent that their learned expertise contributes to strategy in a 'bottom–up' manner. Also in both these cases the requirements of their markets are clearly reflected in their operations' performance objectives (responsiveness and cost for Flextronics, and low cost with friendly but well-defined levels of service for Southwest Airlines). Similarly, both businesses have defined the way in which they achieve these objectives by strategically directing their operations resources (through the type of aircraft that Southwest Airlines buys and through their location and supply chain decisions in the case of Flextronics). In other words, both have reconciled their market requirements with their operations resource capabilities. These are the issues that we shall address in this chapter.

DIAGNOSTIC QUESTION

Does the operation have a strategy?

There are some problems in asking this apparently simple question. In most operations management decisions you can see what you are dealing with. You can touch inventory, talk to people, programme machines, and so on. But strategy is different. You cannot see a strategy, feel it, or touch it. Also, whereas the effects of most operations management decisions become evident relatively fast, it may be years before an operations strategy decision can be judged to be a success or not. Moreover any 'strategy' is always more than a single decision. Operations strategy will be revealed in the total *pattern* of decisions that a business takes in developing its operations in the long term. Nevertheless, the question is an obvious starting point and one that must be addressed by all operations.

So, what should an operations strategy do? First, it should articulate a vision of how the business's operations and processes can contribute to its overall strategy. This is something beyond the individual collection of decisions that will actually constitute the strategy. Second, it should translate market requirements into a message that will have some meaning within its operations. This means describing what customers want in terms of a clear and prioritized set of operations' *performance objectives*. Third, it should identify the broad decisions that will shape the operation's capabilities, and allow their long-term development so that they will provide the basis for the business's sustainable advantage. Finally, it should explain how its intended market requirements and its strategic operations decisions are to be reconciled.

> **Operations principle**
> Operations strategy should articulate a 'vision' for the operations function's contribution to overall strategy.

An operations strategy should articulate a vision for the operations contribution

The 'vision' for an operation is a clear statement of how operations intend to contribute value for the business. It is not a statement of what the operation wants to *achieve* (those are its objectives), but rather an idea of what it must *become* and what contribution it should make. A common approach to summarizing operations contribution is the Hayes and Wheelwright Four-Stage Model.[4] The model traces the progression of the operations function from what is the largely negative role of 'stage 1' operations to becoming the central element of competitive strategy in excellent 'stage 4' operations. Figure 2.2 illustrates the four steps involved in moving from stage 1 to stage 4.

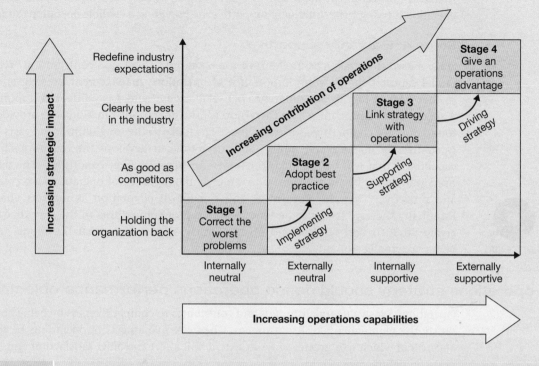

Figure 2.2 Hayes and Wheelwright's four-stage model of operations contribution sees operations as moving from implementation of strategy, through to supporting strategy, and finally driving strategy

Stage 1: Internal neutrality

This is the very poorest level of contribution by the operations function. The other functions regard it as holding them back from competing effectively. The operations function is inward-looking and at best reactive with very little positive to contribute towards competitive success. Its goal is to be ignored. At least then it isn't holding the company back in any way. Certainly the rest of the organization would not look to operations as the source of any originality, flair or competitive drive. Its vision is to be 'internally neutral', a position it attempts to achieve not by anything positive but by avoiding the bigger mistakes.

Stage 2: External neutrality

The first step of breaking out of stage 1 is for the operations function to begin comparing itself with similar companies or organizations in the outside market. This may not immediately take it to the 'first division' of companies in the market, but at least it is measuring itself against its competitors' performance and trying to be 'appropriate', by adopting 'best practice' from them. Its vision is to become 'up to speed' or 'externally neutral' with similar businesses in its industry by adopting 'best practice' ideas and norms of performance from others.

Stage 3: Internally supportive

Stage 3 operations have probably reached the 'first division' in their market. They may not be better than their competitors on every aspect of operations performance but they are broadly up with the best. Yet, the vision of stage 3 operations is to be clearly and unambiguously the very best in the market. They may try to achieve this by gaining a clear view of the company's competitive or strategic goals and developing 'appropriate' operations resources to excel in the areas in which the company needs to compete effectively. The operation is trying to be 'internally supportive' by providing a credible operations strategy.

Stage 4: Externally supportive

Stage 3 used to be taken as the limit of the operations function's contribution. Yet the model captures the growing importance of operations management by suggesting a further stage – stage 4. The difference between stages 3 and 4 is subtle, but important. A stage 4 company is one where the vision for the operations function is to provide *the* foundation for competitive success. Operations looks to the long term. It forecasts likely changes in markets and supply, and, over time, it develops the operations-based capabilities that will be required to compete in future market conditions. The operations function is becoming central to strategy-making. Stage 4 operations are creative and proactive. They are innovative and capable of adaptation as markets change. Essentially they are trying to be 'one step ahead' of competitors in the way that they create products and services and organize their operations – what the model terms being 'externally supportive'.

PRACTICE NOTE

An operations strategy should define operations performance objectives

Operations adds value for customers and contributes to competitiveness by being able to satisfy the requirements of its customers. There are five aspects of operations performance, all of which to a greater or lesser extent will affect customer satisfaction and business competitiveness.

- **Quality** – doing things right, providing error-free goods and services that are 'fit for their purpose'.
- **Speed** – doing things fast, minimizing the time between a customer asking for goods and services and the customer receiving them in full.
- **Dependability** – doing things on-time, keeping the delivery promises that have been made to customers.
- **Flexibility** – changing what you do or how you do it, the ability to vary or adapt the operation's activities to cope with unexpected circumstances or to give customers individual treatment, or to introduce new products or services.
- **Cost** – doing things cheaply, producing goods and services at a cost that enables them to be priced appropriately for the market while still allowing a return to the organization (or, in a not-for-profit organization, that give good value to the taxpayers or whoever is funding the operation).

The exact meaning of performance objectives is different in different operations

Different operations will have different views of what each of the performance objectives actually means. Table 2.1 looks at how two operations, an insurance company and a steel plant, define each performance objective. For example, the insurance company sees quality as being at least as much about the manner in which their customers relate to their service as it does about the absence of technical errors. The steel plant, on the other hand, while not ignoring quality of service, emphasizes primarily product-related technical issues. Although they are selecting from the same pool of factors that together constitute the generic performance objective, they emphasize different elements.

> **Operations principle**
> Operations performance objectives can be grouped together as quality, speed, dependability, flexibility and cost.

Table 2.1   Aspects of each performance objective for two operations

Insurance company	Performance	Steel plant
Aspects of each performance objective include . . .	objectives	Aspects of each performance objective include . . .
• Professionalism of staff • Friendliness of staff • Accuracy of information • Ability to change details in future	**Quality**	• Percentage of products conforming to their specification • Absolute specification of products • Usefulness of technical advice
• Time for call centre to respond • Prompt advice response • Fast quotation decisions • Fast response to claims	**Speed**	• Lead-time from enquiry to quotation • Lead-time from order to delivery • Lead-time for technical advice
• Reliability of original promise date • Customers kept informed	**Dependability**	• Percentage of deliveries 'on-time, in-full' • Customers kept informed of delivery dates
• Customization of terms of insurance cover • Ability to cope with changes in circumstances, such as level of demand • Ability to handle wide variety of risks	**Flexibility**	• Range of sizes, gauges, coatings, etc. possible • Rate of new product introduction • Ability to change quantity, composition and timing of an order
• Premium charged • Arrangement charges • 'No-claims' deals • 'Excess' charges	**Cost**	• Price of products • Price of technical advice • Discounts available • Payment terms

Sometimes operations may choose to re-bundle elements using slightly different headings. For example, it is not uncommon in some service operations to refer to 'quality of service' as representing all the competitive factors we have listed under quality *and* speed *and* dependability (and sometimes aspects of flexibility). For example, information network operations use the term 'Quality of Service' (QoS) to describe their goal of providing guarantees on the ability of a network to deliver predictable results. This is often specified as including uptime (dependability), bandwidth provision (dependability and flexibility), latency or delay (speed of throughput), and error rate (quality). In practice, the issue is not so much one of universal definition but rather consistency within an operation or a group of operations. At the very least it is important that individual companies are clear in their own minds how each performance objective is to be defined.

Operations principle
The interpretation of the five performance objectives will differ between different operations.

The relative priority of performance objectives differs between businesses

Not every operation will apply the same priorities to its performance objectives. Businesses that compete in different ways should want different things from their operations functions. In fact, there should be a clear logical connection between the competitive stance of a business and its operations objectives. So, a business that competes primarily on low prices and 'value for money' should be placing emphasis on operations objectives such as cost, productivity and efficiency, one that competes on a high degree of customization of its services or products should be placing an emphasis on flexibility, and so on. Many successful companies understand the

Operations principle
The relative importance of the five performance objectives depends on how the business competes in its market.

importance of making this connection between their message to customers and the operations performance objectives that they emphasize, for example:[5]

> *'Our management principle is the commitment to quality and reliability . . . to deliver safe and innovative products and services . . . and to improve the quality and reliability of our businesses.' (Komatsu)*

> *'The management team will . . . develop high quality, strongly differentiated consumer brands and service standards . . . use the benefits of the global nature and scale economies of the business to operate a highly efficient support infrastructure . . . [with] high quality and service standards which deliver an excellent guest experience . . .' (InterContinental Hotels Group)*

> *'A level of quality, durability and value that's truly superior in the market place . . . the principle that what is best for the customer is also best for the company . . . [our] customers have learnt to expect a high level of service at all times – from initiating the order, to receiving help and advice, to speedy shipping and further follow-up where necessary . . . [our] employees "go that extra mile".' (Lands' End)*

An operations strategy should identify the broad decisions that will help the operation achieve its objectives

Few businesses have the resources to pursue every single action that might improve their operations performance. So an operations strategy should indicate broadly how the operation might best achieve its performance objectives. For example, a business might specify that it will attempt to reduce its costs by aggressive outsourcing of its non-core business processes and by investing in more efficient technology. Or, it may declare that it intends to offer a more customized set of products or services through adopting a modular approach to its product or service design. The balance here is between a strategy that is overly restrictive in specifying how performance objectives are to be achieved, and one that is so open that it gives little guidance as to what ideas should be pursued.

There are several categorizations of operations strategy decisions. Any of them are valid if they capture the key decisions. Here we categorize operations strategy decisions in the same way we categorize operations management decisions, as applying to the activities of design, delivery, and development. Table 2.2 illustrates some of the broad operations strategy decisions that fall within each category.

An operations strategy should reconcile strategic decisions to objectives

Operations principle
An operation's strategy should articulate the relationship between operations objectives and the means of achieving them.

PRACTICE NOTE

FURTHER EXAMPLE

We can now bring together two sets of ideas and, in doing so, we also bring together the two perspectives of (a) market requirements and (b) operations resources to form the two dimensions of a matrix. This *operations strategy* matrix is shown in Figure 2.3. It describes operations strategy as the intersection of a company's performance objectives and the strategic decisions that it makes. In fact there are several intersections between each performance objective and each decision area (however one wishes to define them). If a business thinks that it has an operations strategy, then it should have a coherent explanation for each of the cells in the matrix. That is, it should be able to explain and reconcile the intended links between each performance objective and each decision area. The process of reconciliation takes place between *what* is required from the operations function (performance objectives), and *how* the operation tries to achieve this through the set of choices made (and the capabilities that have been developed) in each decision area.

Table 2.2	Some strategic decisions that may need to be addressed in an operations strategy
Strategic decisions concerned with the *design* of operations and processes	• How should the operation decide which products or services to develop and how to manage the development process? • Should the operation develop its products or services in-house or outsource the designs? • Should the operation outsource some of its activities, or take more activities in-house? • Should the operation expand by acquiring its suppliers or its customers? If so, which ones should it acquire? • How many geographically separate sites should the operation have? • Where should operations sites be located? • What activities and capacity should be allocated to each site? • What broad types of technology should the operation be using? • How should the operation be developing its people? • What role should the people who staff the operation play in its management?
Strategic decisions concerned with planning and controlling the *delivery* of products and services	• How should the operation forecast and monitor the demand for its products and services? • How should the operation adjust its activity levels in response to demand fluctuations? • How should the operation monitor and develop its relationship with its suppliers? • How much inventory should the operation have and where should it be located? • What approach and system should the operation use to plan its activities?
Strategic decisions concerned with the *development* of operations performance	• How should the operation's performance be measured and reported? • How should the operation ensure that its performance is reflected in its improvement priorities? • Who should be involved in the improvement process? • How fast should improvement in performance be? • How should the improvement process be managed? • How should the operation maintain its resources so as to prevent failure? • How should the operation ensure continuity if a failure occurs?

| Figure 2.3 | The operations strategy matrix defines operations strategy by the intersections of performance objectives and operations decisions |

Does operations strategy make sense from the top and the bottom of the business?

The traditional view of operations strategy is that it is one of several *functional strategies* that are governed by decisions taken at the top of the organizational tree. In this view operations strategy, together with marketing, human resource, and other functional strategies, take their lead exclusively from the needs of the business as a whole. This is often called a 'top-down' perspective on operations strategy. An alternative view is that operations strategies emerge over time from the operational level, as the business learns from the day-to-day experience of running processes (both operations and other processes). This is known as the 'emergent' or 'bottom-up' perspective on operations strategy. An operations strategy should reflect both of these perspectives. Any functional strategy, especially operations strategy, cannot afford to be in conflict with the business's overall strategy. Yet at the same time, any operation will be strongly influenced by its day-to-day experiences. Not only will operational issues set practical constraints on strategic direction, but more significantly, day-to-day experiences can be exploited to provide an important contribution to strategic thinking. This is illustrated in Figure 2.4.

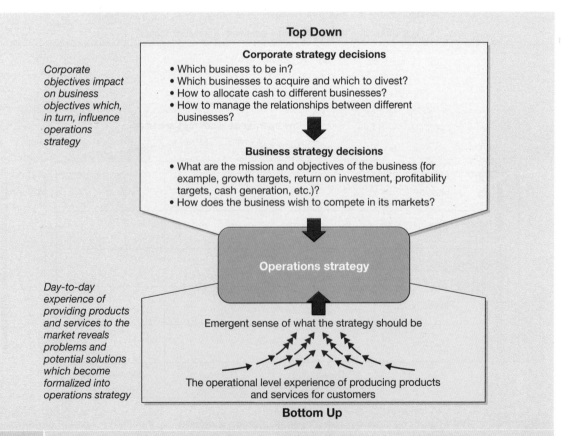

Figure 2.4 Top-down and bottom-up perspectives of operations strategy

Top-down–operations strategy should reflect the needs of the whole business

A top-down perspective often identifies three levels of strategy: corporate, business and functional. A corporate strategy should position the corporation in its global, economic, political and social environment. This will consist of decisions about what types of business the group wants to be in, what parts of the world it wants to operate in, how to allocate its cash between its various businesses, and so on. Each business unit within the corporate group will also need to put together its own business strategy that sets out its individual mission and objectives. This business strategy guides the business in relation to its customers, markets and competitors, and also defines its role within the corporate group of which it is a part. Similarly, within the business, functional strategies need to consider what part each function should play in contributing to the strategic objectives of the business. The operations, marketing, product/service development and other functions will all need to consider how best they should organize themselves to support the business's objectives.

> **Operations principle**
> Operations strategies should reflect top-down corporate and/or business objectives.

Bottom-up–operations strategy should reflect operational reality

Although it is a convenient way of thinking about strategy, the top-down hierarchical model does not represent the way strategies are always formulated in practice. When any group is reviewing its corporate strategy, it will also take into account the circumstances, experiences and capabilities of the various businesses that form the group. Similarly, businesses, when reviewing their strategies, will consult the individual functions within the business about their constraints and capabilities. They may also incorporate the ideas that come from each function's day-to-day experience. In fact many strategic ideas emerge over time from operational experience rather than being originated exclusively at a senior level. Sometimes companies move in a particular strategic direction because the ongoing experience of providing products and services to customers at an operational level convinces them that it is the right thing to do. There may be no formal high-level decision-making that examines alternative strategic options and chooses the one that provides the best way forward. Instead, a general consensus emerges from the operational experience. The 'high level' strategic decision-making, if it occurs at all, may simply confirm the consensus and provide the resources to make it happen effectively. This is sometimes called the concept of emergent strategies.[6] It sees strategies as often being formed in a relatively unstructured and fragmented manner to reflect the fact that the future is at least partially unknown and unpredictable. The bottom part of Figure 2.4 illustrates this.

> **Operations principle**
> Operations strategy should reflect bottom-up experience of operational reality.

This view of operations strategy reflects how things often happen, but at first glance it seems less useful in providing a guide for specific decision-making. Yet while emergent strategies are less easy to categorize, the principle governing a bottom-up perspective is clear: an operation's objectives and actions should be shaped at least partly by the knowledge it gains from its day-to-day activities. The key virtues required for shaping strategy from the bottom up are an ability to learn from experience and a philosophy of continual and incremental improvement.

| Example | Flexibility in innovation |

A metrology systems company develops integrated systems for large international clients in several industries. It is part of a group that includes several high-tech companies. It competes through a strategy of technical excellence and innovation together with an ability to advise and customize its systems to clients' needs. As part of this strategy it attempts to be the first in the market with every available technical innovation. From a top-down perspective, its operations function, therefore, needs to be capable of coping with the changes that constant innovation will bring. It must develop processes that are flexible enough to develop and assemble novel components and systems. It must organize and train its staff to understand the way technology is developing so that they can put in place the necessary changes to the operation. It must develop relationships with its suppliers that will help them to respond quickly when supplying new components. Everything about the operation, its processes, staff, and its systems and procedures, must, in the short term, do nothing to inhibit, and in the long term actively develop, the company's competitive strategy of innovation.

However, over time, as its operations strategy develops, the business discovers that continual product and system innovation is having the effect of dramatically increasing its costs. And, although it does not compete on low prices, its rising costs were impacting profitability. Also there was some evidence that continual changes were confusing some customers. Partially in response to customer requests, the company's system designers started to work out a way of 'modularizing' their system and product designs. This allowed one part of the system to be updated for those customers who valued the functionality the innovation could bring, without interfering with the overall design of the main body of the system. Over time, this approach became standard design practice within the company. Customers appreciated the extra customization, and modularization reduced operations costs. Note that this strategy emerged from the company's experience. No top-level board decision was ever taken to confirm this practice, but nevertheless it emerged as the way in which the company organizes its design activity. Figure 2.5 illustrates these top–down and bottom–up influences for the business.

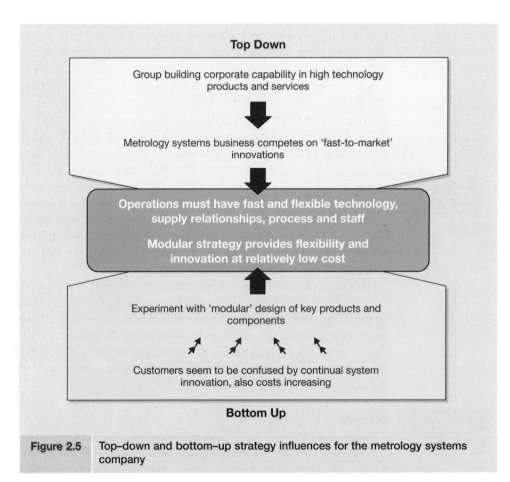

Top Down

Group building corporate capability in high technology products and services

Metrology systems business competes on 'fast-to-market' innovations

Operations must have fast and flexible technology, supply relationships, process and staff

Modular strategy provides flexibility and innovation at relatively low cost

Experiment with 'modular' design of key products and components

Customers seem to be confused by continual system innovation, also costs increasing

Bottom Up

Figure 2.5   Top–down and bottom–up strategy influences for the metrology systems company

Does operations strategy align market requirements with operations resources?

Any operations strategy should reflect the intended market position of the business. Companies compete in different ways: some compete primarily on cost, others on the excellence of their products or services, others on high levels of customer service, and so on. The operations function must respond to this by providing the ability to perform in a manner that is appropriate for the intended market position. This is a market perspective on operations strategy. But operations strategy must do more than simply meet the short-term needs of the market (important though this is). The processes and resources within operations also need to be developed in the long term to provide the business with a set of competencies or capabilities (we use the two words interchangeably). Capabilities in this context are the 'know-how' that is embedded within the business's resources and processes. These capabilities may be built up over time as the result of the experiences of the operation, or they may be bought in or acquired. If they are refined and integrated they can form the basis of the business's ability to offer unique and 'difficult to imitate' products and services to its customers. This idea of the basis of long-term competitive capabilities deriving from the operation's resources and processes is called the resource perspective on operations strategy.[7]

Operations strategy should reflect market requirements

A particularly useful way of determining the relative importance of competitive factors is to distinguish between what Professor Terry Hill has termed 'order-winners' and 'qualifiers'.[8] Figure 2.6 shows the difference between order-winning and qualifying objectives in terms of their utility, or worth, to the competitiveness of the organization. The curves illustrate the relative amount of competitiveness (or attractiveness to customers) as the operation's performance varies.

> **Operations principle**
> Operations strategy should reflect the requirements of the business's markets.

Figure 2.6   Order-winners and qualifiers. Order-winners gain more business the better they are. Qualifiers are the 'givens' of doing business

- **Order-winners** are those things that directly and significantly contribute to winning business. They are regarded by customers as key reasons for purchasing the product or service. Raising performance in an order-winner will either result in more business or improve the chances of gaining more business. Order-winners show a steady and significant increase in their contribution to competitiveness as the operation gets better at providing them.
- **Qualifiers** may not be the major competitive determinants of success, but are important in another way. They are those aspects of competitiveness where the operation's performance has to be above a particular level just to be considered by the customer. Performance below this 'qualifying' level of performance may disqualify the operation from being considered by customers. But any further improvement above the qualifying level is unlikely to gain the company much competitive benefit. Qualifiers are those things that are generally expected by customers. Being great at them is unlikely to excite customers, but being bad at them can disadvantage the competitive position of the operation.

Different customer needs imply different objectives

Operations principle
Different customer needs imply different priorities of performance objectives.

If, as is likely, an operation produces goods or services for more than one customer group, it will need to determine the order-winners and qualifiers for each group. For example, Table 2.3 shows two 'product' groups in the banking industry. Here the distinction is drawn between the customers who are looking for

Table 2.3	Different banking services require different performance objectives	
	Retail banking	*Corporate banking*
Products	Personal financial services such as loans and credit cards	Special services for corporate customers
Customers	Individuals	Businesses
Product range	Medium but standardized, little need for special terms	Very wide range, many need to be customized
Design changes	Occasional	Continual
Delivery	Fast decisions	Dependable service
Quality	Means error-free transactions	Means close relationships
Volume per service type	Most service are high volume	Most services are low volume
Profit margins	Most are low to medium, some high	Medium to high
Order-winners	Price Accessibility Speed	Customization Quality of service Reliability
Qualifiers	Quality Range	Speed Price
Performance objectives emphasized within the processes that produce each service	Cost Speed Quality	Flexibility Quality Dependability

FURTHER EXAMPLE

banking services for their private and domestic needs and the corporate customers who need banking services for their (often large) businesses.

The product/service life cycle influence on performance objectives

One way of generalizing the market requirements that operations need to fulfil is to link it to the life cycle of the products or services that the operation is producing. The exact form of product/service life cycles will vary, but generally they are shown as the sales volume passing through four stages – introduction, growth, maturity and decline. The important implication of this for operations management is that products and services will require operations strategies in each stage of their life cycle (see Figure 2.7).

- **Introduction stage.** When a product or service is first introduced, it is likely to be offering something new in terms of its design or performance. Few competitors will be offering the same product or service, and because the needs of customers are not perfectly understood, the design of the product or service could frequently change. Given the market uncertainty, the operations management of the company needs

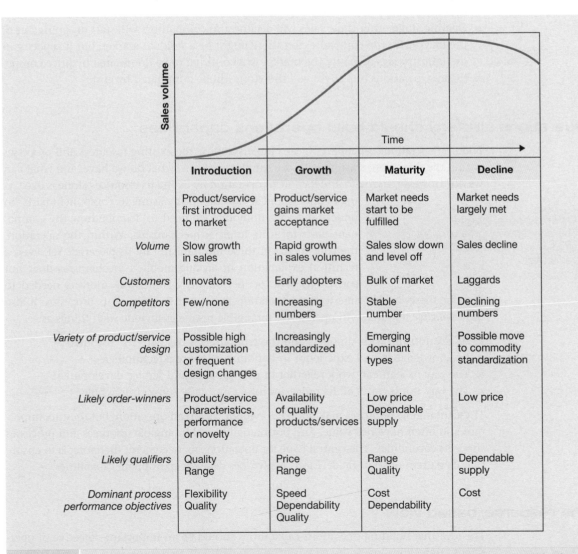

	Introduction	Growth	Maturity	Decline
	Product/service first introduced to market	Product/service gains market acceptance	Market needs start to be fulfilled	Market needs largely met
Volume	Slow growth in sales	Rapid growth in sales volumes	Sales slow down and level off	Sales decline
Customers	Innovators	Early adopters	Bulk of market	Laggards
Competitors	Few/none	Increasing numbers	Stable number	Declining numbers
Variety of product/service design	Possible high customization or frequent design changes	Increasingly standardized	Emerging dominant types	Possible move to commodity standardization
Likely order-winners	Product/service characteristics, performance or novelty	Availability of quality products/services	Low price Dependable supply	Low price
Likely qualifiers	Quality Range	Price Range	Range Quality	Dependable supply
Dominant process performance objectives	Flexibility Quality	Speed Dependability Quality	Cost Dependability	Cost

Figure 2.7   The effects of the product/service life cycle on the operation and its process performance objectives

to develop the flexibility to cope with these changes and the quality to maintain product/service performance.

- **Growth stage**. As the volume of products or services grows, competitors start to develop their own products and services. In the growing market, standardized designs emerge. Standardization is helpful in that it allows the operation to supply the rapidly growing market. Keeping up with demand could prove to be the main operations preoccupation. Rapid and dependable response to demand will help to keep demand buoyant while ensuring that the company keeps its share of the market as competition starts to increase. Also, increasing competition means that quality levels must be maintained.

- **Maturity stage**. Eventually demand starts to level off. Some early competitors will have left the market and the industry will probably be dominated by a few larger companies. The designs of the products or services will be standardized and competition will probably emphasize price or value for money, although individual companies might try to prevent this by attempting to differentiate themselves in some way. So operations will be expected to get the costs down in order to maintain profits or to allow price cutting, or both. Because of this, cost and productivity issues, together with dependable supply, are likely to be the operation's main concerns.

- **Decline stage**. After time, sales will decline and competitors will start dropping out of the market. To the companies left there might be a residual market, but if capacity in the industry lags demand, the market will continue to be dominated by price competition. Operations objectives will therefore still be dominated by cost.

Operations strategy should build operations capabilities

Building operations capabilities means understanding the existing resources and processes within the operation, starting with the simple questions, what do we have, and what can we do? However, trying to understand an operation by listing its resources alone is like trying to understand an automobile by listing its component parts. To understand an automobile we need to describe how the component parts form its internal mechanisms. Within the operation, the equivalents of these mechanisms are its *processes*. Yet, even a technical explanation of an automobile's mechanisms does not convey its style or 'personality'. Something more is needed to describe these. In the same way, an operation is not just the sum of its processes. It also has *intangible* resources. An operation's intangible resources include such things as:

> **Operations principle**
> The long-term objective of operation strategy is to build operations-based capabilities.

- Its relationship with suppliers and the reputation it has with its customers
- Its knowledge of and experience in handling its process technologies
- The way its staff can work together in new product and service development
- The way it integrates all its processes into a mutually supporting whole.

These intangible resources may not be as evident within an operation, but they are important and often have real value. And both tangible and intangible resources and processes shape its capabilities. The central issue for operations management, therefore, is to ensure that its pattern of strategic decisions really does develop appropriate capabilities.

The resource-based view

The idea that building operations capabilities should be an important objective of operations strategy is closely linked with the popularity of an approach to business strategy called the resource-based view (RBV) of the firm.[9] This holds that businesses with an 'above average' strategic performance are likely to have gained their sustainable competitive advantage because of their core competencies (or capabilities). This means that the way an organization inherits, or acquires, or develops its operations resources will, over the long term, have a significant impact on its strategic success. The RBV differs in its approach from the more traditional view of strategy which sees companies as seeking to protect their competitive advantage through their control of the market, for example by creating *barriers to entry* through product differentiation, or making it difficult for customers to switch to competitors, or controlling access to distribution channels (a major barrier to entry in gasoline retailing, for example, where oil companies own their own retail stations). By contrast, the RBV sees firms being able to protect their competitive advantage through *barriers to imitation,* that is by building up 'difficult-to-imitate' resources. Certain of these resources are particularly important, and can be classified as 'strategic' if they exhibit the following properties:

- *They are scarce.* Scarce resources, such as specialized production facilities, experienced engineers, proprietary software, etc., can underpin competitive advantage.
- *They are imperfectly mobile.* Some resources are difficult to move out of a firm. For example, resources that were developed in-house, or are based on the experience of the company's staff, or are interconnected with the other resources in the firm, cannot be traded easily.
- *They are imperfectly imitable and imperfectly substitutable.* It is not enough only to have resources that are unique and immobile. If a competitor can copy these resources, or replace them with alternative resources, then their value will quickly deteriorate. The more the resources are connected with process knowledge embedded deep within the firm, the more difficult they are for competitors to understand and to copy.

FURTHER EXAMPLE

Reconciling market requirements and operations resource capabilities

The market requirements and the operations resource perspectives on operations strategy represent two sides of a strategic equation that all operations managers have to reconcile. On one hand, the operation must be able to meet the requirements of the market. On the other hand, it also needs to develop operations capabilities that make it able to do the things that customers find valuable but competitors find difficult to imitate. And ideally, there should be a reasonable degree of alignment or 'fit' between the requirements of the market and the capabilities of operations resources. Figure 2.8 illustrates the concept of fit diagrammatically. The vertical dimension represents the nature of market requirements

Figure 2.8   Operations strategy must attempt to achieve 'fit' between market requirements and operations resource capabilities

either because they reflect the intrinsic needs of customers or because their expectations have been shaped by the firm's marketing activity. This includes such factors as the strength of the brand or reputation, the degree of differentiation, and the extent of market promises. Movement along the dimension indicates a broadly enhanced level of market 'performance'. The horizontal scale represents the nature of the firm's operations resources and processes. This includes such things as the performance of the operation in terms of its ability to achieve competitive objectives, the efficiency with which it uses its resources, and the ability of the firm's resources to underpin its business processes. Movement along the dimension broadly indicates an enhanced level of 'operations capability'.

If market requirements and operations capability of an operation are aligned, it would diagrammatically be positioned on the 'line of fit' in Figure 2.8. 'Fit' is to achieve an approximate balance between 'market requirements' and 'operations capability'. So when fit is achieved, firms' customers do not need, or expect, levels of operations capability that cannot be supplied. Nor does the operation have strengths either that are inappropriate for market needs or that remain unexploited in the market.[10]

An operation that has position A in Figure 2.8 has achieved 'fit' in so much as its operations capabilities are aligned with its market requirements, yet both are at a relatively low level. In other words, the market does not want much from the business, which is just as well because its operation is not capable of achieving much. An operation with position B has also achieved 'fit', but at a higher level. Other things being equal, this will be a more profitable position that position A. Positions C and D are out of alignment. Position C denotes an operation that does not have sufficient operations capability to satisfy what the market wants. Position D indicates an operation that has more operations capability than it is able to exploit in its markets. Generally, operations at C and D would wish to improve their operations capability (C) or reposition themselves in their market (D) in order to get back into a position of fit.

DIAGNOSTIC QUESTION

Does operations strategy set an improvement path?

An operations strategy is the starting point for operations improvement. It sets the direction in which the operation will change over time. It is implicit that the business will want operations to change for the better. Therefore, unless an operations strategy gives some idea as to how improvement will happen, it is not fulfilling its main purpose. This is best thought about in terms of how performance objectives, both in themselves and relative to each other, will change over time. To do this, we need to understand the concept of, and the arguments concerning, the trade-offs between performance objectives.

An operations strategy should guide the trade-offs between performance objectives

An operations strategy should address the relative priority of operation's performance objectives ('for us, speed of response is more important than cost efficiency, quality is more important than variety', and so on). To do this it must consider the possibility of improving its performance in one objective by sacrificing performance in another. So, for example, an operation might wish to improve its cost efficiencies by reducing the variety of products or services that it offers to its customers. Taken to its extreme, this 'trade-off' principle implies that improvement in one performance objective can *only* be gained at the expense of another. 'There is no such thing as a free lunch' could be taken as a summary of this approach to managing. Probably the best-known summary of the trade-off idea comes from Professor Wickham Skinner, the most influential of the originators of the strategic approach to operations, who said:[11]

> . . . most managers will readily admit that there are compromises or trade-offs to be made in designing an airplane or truck. In the case of an airplane, trade-offs would involve matters such as cruising speed, take-off and landing distances, initial cost, maintenance, fuel consumption, passenger comfort and cargo or passenger capacity. For instance, no one today can design a 500-passenger plane that can land on an aircraft carrier and also break the sound barrier. Much the same thing is true in . . . [operations].

> **Operations principle**
> In the short term, operations cannot achieve outstanding performance in all its operations objectives simultaneously.

But there is another view of the trade-offs between performance objectives. This sees the very idea of trade-offs as the enemy of operations improvement, and regards the acceptance that one type of performance can only be achieved at the expense of another as both limiting and unambitious. For any real improvement of total performance, it holds, the effect of trade-offs must be overcome in some way. In fact, overcoming trade-offs must be seen as the central objective of strategic operations improvement.

> **Operations principle**
> In the long term, a key objective of operations strategy is to improve all aspects of operations performance.

These two approaches to managing trade-offs result in two approaches to operations improvement. The first emphasizes 'repositioning' performance objectives by trading off improvements in some objectives for a reduction in performance in other. The other emphasizes increasing the 'effectiveness' of the operation by overcoming trade-offs so that improvements in one or more aspects of performance can be achieved without any reduction in the performance of others. Most businesses at some time or other will adopt both approaches. This is best illustrated through the concept of the 'efficient frontier' of operations performance.

FURTHER EXAMPLE

Trade-offs and the efficient frontier

Figure 2.9(a) shows the relative performance of several companies in the same industry in terms of their cost efficiency and the variety of products or services that they offer to their customers. Presumably all the operations would ideally like to be able to offer very high variety while still having very high levels of cost efficiency. However, the increased complexity that a high variety of product or service offerings brings will generally reduce the operation's ability to operate efficiently. Conversely, one way of improving cost efficiency is to severely limit the variety on offer to customers. The spread of results in Figure 2.9(a) is typical of an exercise such as this. Operations A, B, C and D have all chosen a different balance between variety and cost efficiency. But none is dominated by any other operation in the sense that another operation necessarily has 'superior' performance. Operation X, however, has an inferior performance because operation A is able to offer higher variety at the same level of cost efficiency and operation C offers the same variety but with better cost efficiency. The convex line on which operations A, B, C and D lie is known as the 'efficient frontier'. They may choose to position themselves differently (presumably because of different market strategies) but they cannot be criticized for being ineffective. Of course any of these operations that lie on the efficient frontier may come to believe that the balance they have chosen between variety and cost efficiency is inappropriate. In these circumstances they may choose to reposition themselves at some other point along the efficient frontier. By contrast, operation X has also chosen to balance variety and cost

> **Operations principle**
> Operations that lie on the 'efficient frontier' have performance levels that dominate those which do not.

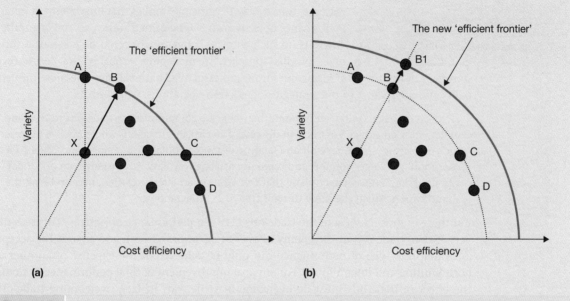

Figure 2.9   If the performance of a group of operations is compared, some will lie on the efficient frontier

efficiency in a particular way but is not doing so effectively. Operation B has the same ratio between the two performance objectives but is achieving them more effectively. Operation X will generally have a strategy that emphasizes increasing its effectiveness before considering any repositioning.

However, a strategy that emphasizes increasing effectiveness is not confined to those operations that are dominated, such as operation X. Those with a position on the efficient frontier will generally also want to improve their operations effectiveness by overcoming the trade-off that is implicit in the efficient frontier curve. For example, suppose operation B in Figure 2.9(b) is the metrology systems company described earlier in this chapter. By adopting a modular product design strategy it improved both its variety and its cost efficiency simultaneously (and moved to position B1). What has happened is that operation B has adopted a particular operations practice (modular design) that has pushed out the efficient frontier. This distinction between positioning on the efficient frontier and increasing operations effectiveness to reach the frontier is an important one. Any operations strategy must make clear the extent to which it is expecting the operation to reposition itself in terms of its performance objectives and the extent to which it is expecting the operation to improve its effectiveness.

Improving operations effectiveness by using trade-offs

Improving the effectiveness of an operation by pushing out the efficient frontier requires different approaches depending on the original position of the operation on the frontier.[12] For example, in Figure 2.10 operation P has an original position that offers a high level of variety at the expense of low cost efficiency. It has probably reached this position by adopting a series of operations practices that enable it to offer the variety even if these practices are intrinsically expensive. For example, it may have invested in general-purpose technology and recruited employees with a wide range of skills. Improving variety even further may mean adopting even more extreme operations practices that emphasize variety. For example, it may reorganize its processes so that each of its larger customers has a dedicated set of resources that understands the specific requirements of that customer and can organize itself to totally customize every product and service it produces. This will

Figure 2.10 Operations 'focus' and the 'plant-within-a-plant' concept illustrated using the efficient frontier model

probably mean a further sacrifice of cost efficiency, but it allows an ever greater variety of products or services to be produced (P1). Similarly, operation Q may increase the effectiveness of its cost efficiency, by becoming even less able to offer any kind of variety (Q1). For both operations P and Q effectiveness is being improved through increasing the focus of the operation on one (or a very narrow set of) performance objectives and accepting an even further reduction in other aspects of performance.

The same principle of focus also applies to organizational units smaller than a whole operation. For example, individual processes may choose to position themselves on a highly focused set of performance objectives that match the market requirements of their own customers. So, for example, a business that manufactures paint for interior decoration may serve two quite distinct markets. Some of its products are intended for domestic customers who are price sensitive but demand only a limited variety of colours and sizes. The other market is professional interior decorators who demand a very wide variety of colours and sizes but are less price sensitive. The business may choose to move from a position where all types of paint are made on the same processes (position X in Figure 2.10(b)) to one where it has two separate sets of processes (Y and Z): one that makes paint only for the domestic market and the other that makes paint only for the professional market. In effect, the business has segmented its operations processes to match the segmentation of the market. This is sometimes called the 'plant-within-a-plant' concept.

Improving operations effectiveness by overcoming trade-offs

This concept of highly focused operations is not universally seen as appropriate. Many companies attempt to give 'the best of both worlds' to their customers. At one time, for example, a high-quality, reliable and error-free automobile was inevitably an expensive automobile. Now, with few exceptions, we expect even budget-priced automobiles to be reliable and almost free of any defects. Auto manufacturers found that not only could they reduce the number of defects on their vehicles without necessarily incurring extra costs, but they could actually reduce costs by reducing errors in manufacture. If auto manufacturers had adopted

> **Operations principle**
> An operation's strategic improvement path can be described in terms of repositioning and/or overcoming its performance trade-offs.

a purely focused-based approach to improvement over the years, we may now only be able to purchase either very cheap low quality automobiles or very expensive high quality automobiles. So a permanent expansion of the efficient frontier is best achieved by overcoming trade-offs through improvements in operations practice.

Even trade-offs that seem to be inevitable can be reduced to some extent. For example, one of the decisions that any supermarket manager has to make is how many checkout positions to open at any time. If too many checkouts are opened then there will be times when the checkout staff do not have any customers to serve and will be idle. The customers, however, will have excellent service in terms of little or no waiting time. Conversely, if too few checkouts are opened, the staff will be working all the time but customers will have to wait in long queues. There seems to be a direct trade-off between staff utilization (and therefore cost) and customer waiting time (speed of service). Yet even the supermarket manager deciding how many checkouts to open can go some way to affecting the trade-off between customer waiting time and staff utilization. The manager might, for example, allocate a number of 'core' staff to operate the checkouts but also arrange for those other staff who are performing other jobs in the supermarket to be trained and 'on-call' should demand suddenly increase. If the manager on duty sees a build-up of customers at the checkouts, these other staff could quickly be used to staff checkouts. By devising a flexible system of staff allocation, the manager can both improve customer service and keep staff utilization high.

Critical commentary

Each chapter contains a short critical commentary on the main ideas covered in the chapter. Its purpose is not to undermine the issues discussed in the chapter, but to emphasize that, although we present a relatively orthodox view of operation, there are other perspectives.

■ The ideas that operations strategy could ever become the driver of a business's overall strategy, and the associated concept of the resource-based view of the firm, are both problematic to some theorists. Business strategy, and functional strategies, were for many years seen as, first, market driven and second, planned in a systematic and deliberative manner. So, it became almost axiomatic to see strategy as starting from a full understanding of market positioning. In fact, the main source of sustainable competitive advantage was seen as unambiguously associated with how a business positioned itself in its markets. Get the market proposition right and customers would respond by giving you business. Get it wrong and they would go to the competitors with a better offering. Strategy was seen as aligning the whole organization to the market position that could achieve long-term profitable differentiation when compared to competitors. Functional strategies were simply a more detailed interpretation of this overall imperative. Furthermore, strategy must be something that could be planned and directed. If managers could not influence strategy, then how could business be anything other than a lottery?

■ The idea that sustainable competitive advantage could come from the capabilities of one's resources was a clear threat to the established position. Furthermore, the idea that strategies emerged, sometimes haphazardly and unpredictably, over time rather than were deliberate decisions taken by senior managers, was also seemingly counter-intuitive. Yet there is now considerable research evidence to support both of these, once outrageous, propositions. The position we have taken in this chapter is one of blending some aspects of the traditional view with the more recent ideas. Nevertheless, it is important to understand that there are still different views on the very nature of strategic management.

Summary checklist

This checklist comprises questions that can be usefully applied to any type of operations and reflect the major diagnostic questions used within the chapter.

☐ Does the operation have a fully articulated operations strategy?

☐ Does it include a vision for the role and contribution of the operations function?

☐ What position on the Hayes and Wheelwright stage 1 to 4 model are your operations?

☐ Are the operation's performance objectives fully articulated?

☐ Are the main strategic decisions that shape operations resources fully identified?

☐ Are the logical links established between what the market requires (in terms of performance objectives) and what capabilities an operations possesses (in terms of the major strategic decision areas)?

☐ What is the balance between top–down direction and bottom–up learning in formulating operations strategy?

☐ Is there a recognized process for both top–down and bottom–up communication on strategic issues?

☐ Are performance objectives understood in terms of whether they are order-winners or qualifiers?

☐ Have different parts of the operation (probably producing different products or services) their own relative priority of performance objectives that reflect their possibly different competitive positions?

☐ Is the idea of operations-based capabilities fully understood?

☐ What capabilities does the operation currently possess?

☐ Are these operations and/or resources scarce, imperfectly mobile, imperfectly imitable, or imperfectly substitutable?

☐ If none of the above, are they really useful in terms of their strategic impact?

☐ Where would you put the operation in terms of Figure 2.8 that describes the broad fit between market requirements and operations resource capabilities?

☐ Have the key trade-offs for the operation been identified?

☐ What combination of repositioning in order to change the nature of trade-offs, and overcoming the trade-offs themselves, is going to be used to improve overall operations performance?

Case study   Dresding Wilson

'The last four years have been characterized by many challenges, many opportunities grasped, many lessons learnt and many reasons to feel confident of our continued success.' (Press release from Dresding Wilson, January 2004) In fact, the quote had been lifted directly from the opening address that Dr Laura Dresding had given to the Dresding Wilson senior management conference a month earlier. What had not made it into the press release was her following comments. *'OK, so we have also made many mistakes. But that is part of growing up, and grown up is what we should start considering ourselves. We need to get more professional in everything that we do. We have entered markets that either are, or will become, more and more competitive. This means that we will need to shift the way we do things. We have grown by "letting many flowers bloom". That is fine when you are a small and ambitious player in an emerging market. Now we must get more integrated in the way we move forward and we must focus ruthlessly on the needs of our customers. Whatever customers find important is what we should find important.'*

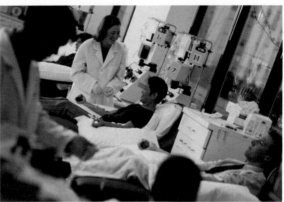

Source: © Getty Images

Company history

The company, originally called Dresding Medical, was founded in 1991 by Dr Laura Dresding, a clinician who had also acted as a clinical adviser to several medical equipment companies. It supplied cardiovascular and heart function monitoring devices, most of which it manufactured in a relatively small factory/laboratory in Bracknell in the south of England. Within three years it had dropped other manufacturers' products to concentrate on sales of its own expanding product range. Originally owning 100 per cent of the company, by 2004 Dr Dresding's share had dropped to 60 per cent, the rest being owned by three venture capital companies. One of the company's earliest decisions was to remain highly vertically integrated. *'We don't have any objection in principle to outsourcing; in fact we are now outsourcing around 30 per cent of our total production. But we do most of our own work simply because it ensures our control over quality. It has also helped us to convince our customers and the industry standards authorities of our commitment to quality.'* (James Key, MD, Manufacturing Division) Sales, at first relatively slow, started to expand significantly during the mid-1990s, and in 1995 the company bought a Danish medical equipment company that produced neurological stimulators. Although the market for neurological products was growing relatively slowly, the Danish plant was also used to produce components for Dresding's own range of products.

The Technology Development Division

Since 1993, Dresding had also been offering technology consulting advice as well as taking on some development work for other original equipment manufacturers (OEMs). In late 1997 it was decided to split off this activity and form a separate 'Technology solutions' division both to develop new in-house products and to develop and license 'technology solutions' to other OEMs. The new division was moved to a separate building on the Bracknell site and Bob Anderson, then the company's chief engineer, was made its first director. In his words, *'At that time we only had 12 full development engineers and five technicians, together with two development engineers in the Danish plant. But although we were small we were a tightly knit team and highly motivated to make a success of the new division. Within nine months we had issued our first technology licence and within 18 months we had grown our revenues by 350 per cent. We quickly discovered that we were in the service business. By 1998 we had over 20 key clients and had started developing several new initiatives for in-house use.'*

The most significant development to come out of the technology division in 1998 was the 'Insight' monitoring system. This was a method of allowing centralized patient monitoring and surveillance in specific care areas. The system allowed hospitals to avoid transferring patients to high-cost intensive care units and facilitated a better patient to medical staff ratio. It also enabled comprehensive vital signs surveillance both at the bedside and at a central monitoring station. *'We were tremendously excited by the development because it posed a number of challenges, most notably the integration of software development, diagnostic software, new on-patient modules and wireless communication systems. We launched in early 1999 and immediately we were overwhelmed by clients expressing interest. With hindsight, that was where we made our biggest mistake. We expanded too fast, took on too many new staff, did not sufficiently test some of the subcomponents of the system, especially in the areas that were new to us such as diagnostic software. Worst of all, we made promises to the market without being able to fulfil them. In the end it took us two years to get over the problems and convince the market that we really did have a system that they could trust. If it was not for the intrinsic merit of the system, we could have been in real trouble. As it was, we came out of it stronger and with a better grip on our development procedures.'* (Bob Anderson, MD, Technology Division)

The 'Dresding Assurance' initiative

Meanwhile the rest of the company had been developing with less drama. In 1997 a new plant in Winchester, also in the south of England, had been opened and a two-year programme to further embed quality procedures in the company's three manufacturing units (Denmark, Bracknell and Winchester) had been started. *'Our idea was twofold. First we wanted to learn as much as we could from the experiences (and mistakes) of other businesses by examining how they approached quality. Second, we wanted to establish an absolutely impeccable set of standards and build a reputation that we could use in the marketplace. We organized a series of factory tours for all our managers and team leaders in all three plants and visited non-competitor businesses in our own and similar industries. This was a fantastic exercise, it stimulated debate but it also bonded the management teams from all three locations. On the basis of what we had learnt, over a two-year period we got ourselves the highest level of certification from all the major assurance and quality institutions in all our major markets, including, vitally, the FDA in America and several US military certifications.'* (James Key, MD, Manufacturing Division)

By the end of 1999 the company felt sufficiently confident to launch 'Dresding Assurance', a brand building initiative that emphasized the quality of its products, in all major markets. The initiative was generally successful, no more so than in the Asian markets where sales growth increased almost 70 per cent between 1999 and 2000. In fact, by the end of 1999 Dresding had to open a technical support facility in Singapore. One year later the Singapore technical support office was upgraded to become the 'Singapore development centre' within the technical division of the company.

The financial year 2000/01 saw the fastest growth in the company's revenues. This was partly because of very healthy sales growth from the manufacturing division, and partly because the technology division had overcome some of its problems of two years earlier. However, notwithstanding the revenue growth, the company's profitability shrank by almost 40 per cent in the same year. This was largely because of increased manufacturing costs. *'Although we were running a tight ship in manufacturing, we were offering an increasingly wide range of products and systems that had increased the complexity of our manufacturing processes. To try and overcome this we decided to adopt the same approach that we had used in improving our quality systems. We visited high-variety manufacturers, this time usually in unrelated industries. We were trying to pick up hints on how to use modular design principles and flexible manufacturing cells to reduce the effective cost of variety. Again, it proved a great experience. Adopting more flexible manufacturing cells gave immediate benefits, but redesigning products took far longer.'* (James Key, MD, Manufacturing Division)

The Medical Services Division and the Ryder Wilson merger

In September 2002 the company made its biggest acquisition to date when it took control of Ryder Wilson, a US manufacturer of monitoring systems that also had a clinical management activity. *'Suddenly we had a "Medical service division" that was a significant player in the market. It was at this point that we decided to rename the company Dresding Wilson and position ourselves clearly as an innovation-based provider of technical solutions to the medical equipment and direct health care industries, with three mutually supportive and integrated divisions.'* (Ruth Zimmerman, MD, Medical Service Division).

Recent developments

'The integration of the Ryder Wilson manufacturing facility went very smoothly. Their manufacturing facility and ours were both world class so we were not coping with

ongoing problems at the time of the merger. We had similar manufacturing policies and were reading the industry
in the same way – a market that is demanding more customization and constant reassurance over quality. Ryder
Wilson also had a great reputation. They were slightly less
innovative but this is not too much of a disadvantage.'
(James Key, MD, Manufacturing Division)

'Our focus has shifted from being primarily a product
innovator to being a systems innovator. This is partly
because there are fewer "breakthroughs" in product technology compared with when we started the division in
1996. Licence revenue from OEMs has levelled off, but the
importance of our support role, especially to the service
division, is likely to grow. An interesting part of this role is
an increasing involvement with educating customers
regarding the technical possibilities and choices that they
face as well as training customers' in-house technicians. I
can see consultancy and customer training becoming a
significant part of our revenue in the next few years.' (Bob
Anderson, MD, Technology Division)

'The service and management division is not yet two
years old and we are still the baby of the business, but we
have by far the greatest potential for growth. Hospitals
and clinics all over the world are moving towards outsourcing a greater proportion of their activities. Deploying
our undoubted technical expertise should allow us to capitalize on opportunities for designing, installing and running monitoring units. However, I have to admit that we
have had some problems. I guess the merger with Ryder
Wilson created a lot of publicity just at the time when outsourcing, monitoring and surveillance activities were all
hot topics in hospital management. We found ourselves
not only designing and installing systems, but also arranging leasing agreements, providing agency staff and training

programmes where we had little or no experience. At the
same time we were coping with a certain amount of reorganization after the merger. The result was a number of
customers who were not too pleased with us and one law-
suit from a Californian clinic (now settled). We are fixing
our problems, but there have been some hard lessons,
especially in terms of understanding the risks involved in
becoming service providers in this kind of market. We are
also competing with existing in-house teams as well as
other clinical service companies. Unless we can significantly undercut the cost of service provided by the resi-
dent teams, we cannot win the business. Of course our
technology helps us to provide a low cost service, but we
can't afford to make any mistakes in how we deliver service. The challenge is to integrate the various service
processes that we have, much in the same way as we
have integrated the physical systems within our products.'
(Ruth Zimmerman, MD, Medical Service Division)

QUESTIONS

1   What are the significant strategic events in the history of
the company from its foundation to the present day?

2   What do you see as the operation's strategies for each
of the three divisions of the company?

3   How has each division's operations resource capability
developed in relation to the requirements of its market
over time?

4   What do you see as the strengths and weaknesses of
the company's approach to developing its operations
strategy?

5   What challenges does the move to becoming a 'service provider' pose for the company?

Active case study   Long Ridge Gliding Club

**ACTIVE
CASE**

Long Ridge Gliding Club is based in the UK on the crest of a ridge overlooking spectacular scenery. The
club services two broad types of customer: club members and casual flyers that come for one-off trial
flights, holiday courses and corporate events. However, complaints from all types of customer are increasing and the chairman faces a decision.

● Based on your judgement of their operations strategy and performance, how would you advise the
chairman?

*Please refer to the Active case on the CD accompanying this book to find out more about the club, its
services and what seems to be going wrong.*

Applying the principles

Some of these exercises can be answered by reading the chapter. Others will require some general knowledge of business activity and some might require an element of investigation. All have hints on how they can be answered on the CD accompanying this book.

HINTS

1 The environmental services department of a city has two recycling services – newspaper collection (NC) and general recycling (GR). The NC service is a door-to-door collection service which, at a fixed time every week, collects old newspapers that householders have placed in reusable plastic bags at their gate. An empty bag is left for the householders to use for the next collection. The value of the newspapers collected is relatively small and the service is offered mainly for reasons of environmental responsibility. By contrast the GR service is more commercial. Companies and private individuals can request a collection of materials to be disposed of, using either the telephone or the Internet. The GR service guarantees to collect the material within 24 hours unless the customer prefers to specify a more convenient time. Any kind of material can be collected and a charge is made depending on the volume of material. This service makes a small profit because the revenue both from customer charges and from some of the more valuable recycled materials exceeds the operation's running costs.

- How would you describe the differences between the performance objectives of the two services?

2 *'It is about four years now since we specialized in the small to medium firms market. Before that we also used to provide legal services for anyone who walked in the door. So now we have built up our legal skills in many areas of corporate and business law. However, within the firm, I think we could focus our activities even more. There seem to be two types of assignment that we are given. About 40 per cent of our work is relatively routine. Typically these assignments are to do with things like property purchase and debt collection. Both these activities involve a relatively standard set of steps which can be automated or carried out by staff without full legal qualifications. Of course, a fully qualified lawyer is needed to make some decisions; however, most work is fairly routine. Customers expect us to be relatively inexpensive and fast in delivering the service. Nor do they expect us to make simple errors in our documentation; in fact if we did this too often we would lose business. Fortunately our customers know that they are buying a standard service and don't expect it to be customized in any way. The problem here is that specialist agencies have been emerging over the last few years and they are starting to undercut us on price. Yet I still feel that we can operate profitably in this market and anyway, we still need these capabilities to serve our other clients. The other 60 per cent of our work is for clients who require far more specialist services, such as assignments involving company merger deals or major company restructuring. These assignments are complex, large, take longer, and require significant legal skill and judgment. It is vital that clients respect and trust the advice we give them across a wide range of legal specialisms. Of course they assume that we will not be slow or unreliable in preparing advice, but mainly it's trust in our legal judgment which is important to the client. This is popular work with our lawyers. It is both interesting and very profitable.'*

'The help I need from you is in deciding whether to create two separate parts to our business: one to deal with routine services and the other to deal with specialist services. What I may do is appoint a senior 'Operations Partner' to manage each part of the business, but if I do, what aspects of operations performance should they be aiming to excel at?' (Managing Partner, Branton Legal Services)

3 Revisit the description of Southwest Airlines. Think about the following issues:
- How is Southwest Airlines different from a 'full service' airline such as British Airways or KLM?
- What seem to be the major reasons why Southwest Airlines is so successful?
- What threats to its success could Southwest Airlines face in the future?

4 Search the Internet site of Intel, the best known microchip manufacturer, and identify what appear to be its main elements in its operations strategy.

5   McDonald's has come to epitomize the 'fast food' industry. When the company started in the 1950s it was the first to establish itself in the market. Now there are hundreds of 'fast food' brands in the market competing in different ways. Some of the differences between these fast food chains are obvious. For example, some specialize in chicken products, others in pizza and so on. However, some differences are less obvious. Originally, McDonald's competed on low price, fast service and a totally standardized service offering. They also offered a very narrow range of items on their menu. Visit a McDonald's restaurant and deduce what you believe to be its most important performance objectives. Then try and identify two other chains which appear to compete in a slightly different way. Then try to identify how these differences in the relative importance of competitive objectives must influence the structural and infrastructural decisions of each chain's operations strategy.

Notes on chapter

1   For a more thorough explanation, see Slack, N. and Lewis, M. (2002) *Operations Strategy,* Financial Times Prentice Hall, Harlow, UK.

2   Source: company website (www.flextronics.com), and press releases.

3   Source: company website (www.southwest.com) and Freiberg, C. and Freiberg, J. (1998) *NUTS! Southwest Airline's Crazy Recipe for Commercial and Personal Success,* Broadway Books, New York.

4   Hayes, R.H. and Wheelwright, S.C. (1984) *Restoring our Competitive Edge,* John Wiley.

5   All quotes taken from each company's website.

6   Mintzberg, H. and Waters, J.A. (1995) 'Of strategies: deliberate and emergent', *Strategic Management Journal,* July/Sept.

7   For a full explanation of this concept, see Slack and Lewis, *op. cit.*

8   Hill, T. (1993) *Manufacturing Strategy* (2nd edn), Macmillan.

9   There is a vast literature which describes the resource-based view of the firm. For example, see Barney, J. (1991) 'The resource-based model of the firm: origins, implications and prospect', *Journal of Management,* Vol. 17, No. 1; or Teece, D.J. and Pisano, G. (1994) 'The dynamic capabilities of firms: an introduction', *Industrial and Corporate Change,* Vol. 3, No. 3.

10 See Slack and Lewis, *op. cit.*

11 A point made initially by Skinner. Skinner, W. (1985) *Manufacturing: The formidable competitive weapon,* John Wiley.

12 Hayes, R.H. and G.P. Pisano (1996) 'Manufacturing strategy at the intersection of two paradigm shifts', *Production and Operations Management,* Vol. 5, No. 1.

Taking it further

There are many good books on strategy. For example, see **Johnson, G. and Scholes, K.** (1998) *Exploring Business Strategy* (4th edn), Prentice Hall; also see **deWit, B. and Meyer, R.** (1998) *Strategy: Process, content, and context,* International Thomson Business Press.

Hamel, G. and Prahalad, C.K. (1993) 'Strategy as stretch and leverage', *Harvard Business Review,* Vol. 71, Nos 2 & 3. This article is typical of some of the (relatively) recent ideas influencing operations strategy.

Hayes, R.H. and Pisano, G.P. (1994) 'Beyond world class: the new manufacturing strategy', *Harvard Business Review,* Vol. 72, No. 1. Same as above.

Hayes, R.H. and Wheelwright, S.C. (1984) *Restoring our Competitive Edge*, John Wiley. This book is all about manufacturing rather than operations generally. However, it was one of the first books on the subject and had a big impact.

Hayes, R.H., Wheelwright, S.C. and Clark, K.B. (1988) *Dynamic Manufacturing,* Free Press, New York. The successor volume to the Hayes and Wheelwright book above. The same comments apply.

Hill, T. (1993) *Manufacturing Strategy* (2nd edn), Macmillan. The first non-US author to have a real impact in the area. As was common at the time, the book concentrates on manufacturing alone.

Prahalad, C.K. and Hamel, G. (1990) 'The core competence of the corporation', *Harvard Business Review,* Vol. 68, No. 3. An easy explanation of the resource-based view of strategy.

Slack, N. and Lewis, M. (2002) *Operations Strategy,* Financial Times Prentice Hall. What can we say – just brilliant!

Useful websites

www.aom.pac.edu/bps/ General strategy site of the American Academy of Management.

www.cranfield.ac.uk/som Look for the 'Best factory awards' link. Manufacturing, but interesting.

www.worldbank.org Global issues. Useful for international operations strategy research.

www.weforum.org Global issues, including some operations strategy ones.

www.ft.com Great for industry and company examples.

FURTHER RESOURCES

For further resources including examples, animated diagrams, self test questions, excel spreadsheets, active case studies and video materials please explore the CD accompanying this book.

3 SUPPLY NETWORK DESIGN

Introduction

Every business or organization is part of a larger and interconnected network of other businesses and organizations. This is the supply network. It includes suppliers and customers, suppliers' suppliers and customers' customers, and so on. At a strategic level, operations managers are involved in influencing the nature or 'design' of the network, and the role of their operation in it. This chapter treats some of these strategic design decisions in the context of supply networks. It forms the context for 'supply chain management', the more operational aspects managing the individual 'trends' or chains through the supply network. We shall discuss supply chain management in Chapter 7. Because many supply network decisions require an estimate of future demand, this chapter includes a supplement on forecasting. (See Figure 3.1.)

Source: © Getty Images

Figure 3.1 Supply network design involves configuring the shape and capabilities of the supply network

Executive summary

| What is supply network design? |
| How should the supply network be configured? |
| Where should operations be located? |
| How much capacity should each operation in the supply network have? |

Decision logic chain for supply network design

Each chapter is structured around a set of diagnostic questions. These questions suggest what you should ask in order to gain an understanding of the important issues of a topic, and as a result, improve your decision making. An executive summary, addressing these questions, is provided below.

What is supply network design?

Supply network design involves configuring the shape and capabilities of the supply network. The supply network includes the chains of suppliers providing inputs to the operation, the chain of customers who receive outputs from the operation, and sometimes other operations that may at times compete and other times cooperate. It is a complex task that differs from 'design' in its conventional sense, because one does not necessarily own the assets being 'designed'. It consists of three interrelated activities – shaping the network (including how much of the network to own), influencing the location of operations in the network, and planning the long-term capacity strategy for each part of the network.

How should the supply network be configured?

A number of trends are reshaping networks in many industries. These include reducing the number of individual suppliers, the disintermediation of some parts of the network, and a greater tolerance of other operations being both competitors and complementors at different times. The vertical integration, outsourcing, or 'do or buy' decision also shapes supply networks. The decision to own less of the supply network (to outsource) has also been a trend in recent years. The extent of outsourcing should depend on the effect it has on operations performance and the long-term strategic positioning of the business's capabilities.

Where should operations be located?

Location means the geographical positioning of an operation. It is important because it can affect costs, revenues, customer service and capital investment. Many businesses never consider relocation, but even those that see no immediate need to relocate may find benefits from relocation. Those businesses that actively investigate relocation often do so because of either changes in demand or changes in supply. The process of evaluating alternative locations involves identifying alternative location options, usually reduced to a list of representative locations, and evaluating each option against a set of (hopefully) rational criteria, usually involving consideration of capital requirements, market factors, cost factors, future flexibility, and risk.

How much capacity should each operation in the supply network have?

This will depend on demand at any point in time. Capacity will need to be changed in the long term, as long-term demand changes, either in advance of demand changes (capacity leading) or after demand changes (capacity lagging). However, the concept of economy of scale will always be important. Economies of scale derive from both capital and operating efficiencies that derive from large-scale processes. However, after a certain level of capacity, most operations start to suffer diseconomies of scale. The economy of scale curves for operations of different size, put together, give an idea of the optimal capacity size for a particular type of operation. However, this is only an indication. In reality, economy of scale will depend on factors that include risk and strategic positioning.

What is supply network design?

Supply network design involves configuring the shape and capabilities of one's own and other operations with which the business interacts. These include all suppliers and their suppliers, and all customers and their customers. It may also include other businesses that could be competitors under some circumstances. It is the most strategic of all the design activities and in many ways is not the same type of activity as smaller-scale design. In process design, decisions can be made with a high degree of confidence that they will be enacted as intended. In supply network design not only is the task intrinsically more complex, but there is a further crucial difference: most of the network that is being 'designed' may not be under the direct control of the 'designers'. Suppliers, customers and others in the network are independent operations. They will naturally pursue what they see as their own best interests, which may not coincide with one's own. The 'design' in supply network design is being used to mean 'influencing' and 'negotiating' rather than design in its conventional sense. However, design is a useful perspective on the tasks involved in the strategic configuration of supply networks because it conveys the idea of understanding the individual components in the network, their characteristics, and the relationships between them.

Terminology is important when describing supply networks. On the 'supply side' of the 'focal' operation (the operation from whose perspective the network is being drawn) is a group of operations that directly supply the operation; these are often called first-tier suppliers. They are supplied by second-tier suppliers. However, some second-tier suppliers may also supply an operation directly, thus missing out a link in the network. Similarly, on the demand side of the network, 'first-tier' customers are the main customer group for the operation. These in turn supply 'second-tier' customers, although again the operation may at times supply second-tier customers directly. The suppliers and customers who have direct contact with an operation are called its immediate supply network. Figure 3.2 illustrates this.

Flow through the network

Materials, parts, information, ideas and sometimes people all flow through the network of customer–supplier relationships formed by all these operations. Also along with the forward flow of transformed resources (materials, information and customers) in the network, each customer–supplier linkage will feed back orders and information. For example, when stocks run low, retailers place orders with distributors who likewise place orders with the manufacturer, who will in turn place orders with its suppliers, who will replenish their own stocks from their own suppliers. So flow is a two-way process with items flowing one way and information flowing the other.

It is not only manufacturers who are part of a supply network. The flow of physical materials may be easier to visualize, but service operations also have suppliers and customers who themselves have their own suppliers and customers. One way to visualize the supply networks of some service operations is to consider the downstream flow of information that passes between operations. Most financial service supply networks can be

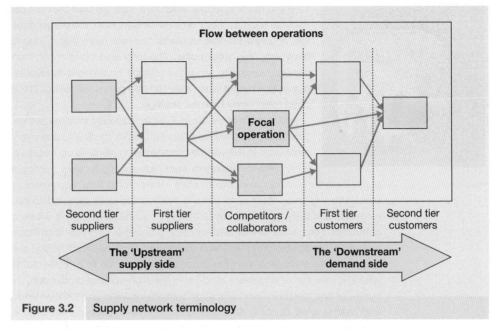

Figure 3.2 | Supply network terminology

thought about like this. However, not all service supply networks deal primarily in information. For example, property companies that own and/or run shopping malls have suppliers who provided security services, cleaning services, maintenance services, and so on. These first-tier suppliers will themselves receive service from recruitment agencies, consultants, etc. First-tier customers of the shopping mall are the retailers who lease retail space within the mall, who themselves serve retail customers. This is a supply network like any other. What is being exchanged between operations is the quality, speed, dependability, flexibility and cost of the services each operation supplies to its customers. In other words, there is a flow of 'operations performance' through the network. And although visualizing the flow of 'performance' through supply networks is an abstract approach to visualizing supply networks, it is a unifying concept. Broadly speaking, all types of supply network exist to facilitate the flow of 'operations performance'.

Note that this chapter deals exclusively with decision at the level of the supply network rather than at the level of 'the operation' or 'the process'. Yet networks of processes exist within operations, and networks of resources exist within processes. The issues of network configuration, location and capacity at these more operational levels are discussed in Chapters 4 and 5 (for layout and flow) and Chapter 8 (for capacity management).

Here are two examples of organizations that have made clear 'design' decisions concerning their supply networks.

Example | ### Intel inside[1]

Intel is probably the best-known microprocessor manufacturer in the world. It has 11 fabrication plants (known as fabs) located at sites throughout the world. These are hugely complex operations that can cost over $2 billion each in capital investment. Intel's selection of new sites on which to build its fabs involves a comprehensive evaluation of the location, including the land's physical characteristics, local infrastructure and transportation, the capability of the potential technical workforce, as well as local economic and social factors. Evaluation is performed by sending a team of Intel's experts to meet with a variety of people throughout the community.

Microprocessor fabs use a complex and demanding process involving more than 300 process stages, and Intel's fabs are approximately twice as large as the industry's average-sized factory. Because of the volatility in the demand for microprocessors, Intel has to plan its capacity with great

Source: © Getty Images/Digital Vision

care and make sure that when new fabs are built they are capable of working effectively as soon as they come on-stream. Also, the demand for chips can change rapidly, and new fabrication plants can take more than a year to build and, when built, have very high fixed costs. The long lead times mean that it is difficult to adjust capacity smoothly as prices change or demand fluctuates. Most operations turn down their output when demand and prices are falling. This is why Intel have developed their 'Copy Exactly' strategy.

Intel says that its 'Copy Exactly' capacity strategy solves the problem of getting production facilities up to speed quickly by duplicating everything from the development plant to the volume-manufacturing plant. To do that, as a new process technology is created, managers from high-volume facilities participate at the development plant. Everything at the development plant – the process flow, equipment set, suppliers, plumbing, manufacturing clean room, and training methodologies–is selected to meet high volume needs, recorded, and then copied exactly to the high-volume plant. This is different from most other semiconductor companies where development processes can vary significantly from those used in high-volume manufacturing. At some companies, each new technology is developed by a team of specialist engineers, and then the process is transferred to a high-volume manufacturing facility where a new set of engineers modifies it for high-volume production. This delays the process ramp-up, and results in hundreds of differences between one location and another. 'Copy Exactly' also creates great flexibility for Intel's factory network. Because each fab is nearly identical, products can be partially completed in one fab and finished in another as if the product were built in only one factory. No other semiconductor manufacturer can do this. Moreover, by creating a global virtual fab network, Intel limits impact from natural or man-made disasters. If an event occurs in one part of the world, Intel manufacturing does not come to a halt. The rest of the fab network is able to continue production and continue shipping product to customers.

Example | The BBC outsources its Technology Division[2]

The British Broadcasting Corporation (BBC) is one of the world's best-known and most respected broadcasting organizations. The public face of the BBC is its broadcast output listened to and

Source: Ryan McVay/Getty Images

watched by millions all over the world. But behind the scenes it depends on its ability to create, manage and distribute broadcast 'content'. A pivotal part of this capability is BBC Technology, a division of the corporation that provides technology services, not just for the BBC, but also for other broadcasters, platform owners, content owners and government organizations. So, when John Varney, Chief Technology Officer at the BBC, announced that it would 'outsource' much of its technology infrastructure to a subsidiary of Germany's Siemens Company in a massive £2 billion 10-year deal, he caused some surprise among his global broadcasting peers. *'It's a revolutionary deal for this industry'*, said Mitchell Linden, head of what used to be the BBC Technology North America unit in San Francisco. *'Now everyone is intensely curious. We have US broadcasters, media companies and multimedia suppliers like Apple all wanting to find out what we did, why we did it and what we are going to do in the future.'*

What the BBC did is significant. Encouraged by pressure from the British government to cut costs and divest, it conducted an internal strategic review of the Corporation's technology requirements that identified potential annual savings for the BBC of around £30m if its technology services were outsourced. After evaluating possible candidates, it signed the Technology Framework Contract, which gives Siemens' Business Services full responsibility for maintaining and developing the BBC's UK Information technology (IT) infrastructure–including networks, servers, desktops, telephones, broadcasting systems, channel platforms and distribution, support for 53 overseas news bureaux, and its website. But the £30 million annual cost savings isn't the only reason for outsourcing to Siemens, says John Varney. Because Siemens, with revenues of over £20bn globally, is one of the world's largest IT and business services providers, it will be able to help move away from tape storage towards making programmes digitally on desktop PCs, something Varney believes will *'revolutionize the use of technology in making and distributing programmes'*. This would make the company's content accessible on everything from the Web to mobile phones, a challenge that faces everyone in the broadcasting industry.

According to Adrian Corcoran, managing director of BBC Technology, *'This is exciting news for our staff and our customers. Being part of a large, global organization gives us the resources, opportunities and investment that just weren't available as part of the BBC, whose focus quite rightly is content, not technology investment.'* But not everyone was happy with the deal. Some BBC staff affiliated with the Broadcasting Entertainment Cinematograph and Theatre Union (BECTU) disputed the BBC's claim that the deal would save £30m per year and voted in favour of industrial action in reaction to the agreement. *'This isn't just the BBC selling off one of its Crown Jewels, it's a case of handing its central nervous system over to the private sector'*, said Gerry Morrissey, Assistant General Secretary of the union.

What do these two examples have in common?

At first glance they seem to be about different things. Intel has developed a clear strategy for selecting new locations and introducing new capacity into its global network of fabs. The BBC, a public corporation, has chosen to give responsibility for running its technology division to a private company. Yet both organizations are making decisions that will shape their supply network in some way. Intel's fab plants remain under its own ownership and control (unlike many microprocessor companies–the so-called 'fabless' businesses that have outsourced, or never had, manufacturing capability). By contrast, the BBC has moved to reduce its ownership of its network by contracting with Siemens. Between them the two examples cover the main issues in the strategic decision of supply networks.

- How should the network be shaped? Both in terms of ordering the relationships between operations in the network, and in terms of how much of the network the operation should own.
- Where should each part of the network owned by the company be located?
- What capacity should each part of the network owned by the company have at any point in time?

Note that all three of these decisions rely on assumptions regarding the level of future demand. The supplement to this chapter explores forecasting in more detail. In Chapter 7, we will cover the more operational day-to-day issues of managing operations networks.

DIAGNOSTIC QUESTION

How should the supply network be configured?

An operation may want to use its influence to manage network behaviour by reconfiguring the network so as to change the scope of the activities performed in each operation and the nature of the relationships between them. The most common example of network reconfiguration has come in the attempts made over the last few years by many companies to reduce the number of suppliers with whom they have direct contact. The complexity of dealing with many hundreds of suppliers may both be expensive for an operation and (sometimes more important) prevent the operation from developing close relationships with suppliers. It is not easy to be close to hundreds of different suppliers. This has led many companies to reconfigure their supply-side network to make it simpler and more orderly. It has also meant that some suppliers have become increasingly important to their customers.

For example, take the front part of a car, the bit with the bumper, radiator grill, fog lights, side-lights, badge and so on.[3] At one time each of these components came from different specialist suppliers. Now the whole of this 'module' may come from one 'system supplier'. Traditional car makers are getting smaller and are relying on systems suppliers such as TRW in the US, Bosch in Germany, and Magna in Canada to provide them with whole chunks of car. Some of these system suppliers are global players that rival the car makers themselves in scope and reach. Cost pressures have forced car makers to let their suppliers take more responsibility for engineering and pre-assembly. This also means that they work with fewer suppliers. For example, Ford Europe's old Escort model took parts from around 700 direct suppliers, while the replacement Focus model used only 210. Future models may have fewer than 100 direct suppliers. This can also make joint development easier. For example, Volvo paired up with one supplier (Autoliv) to develop safety systems incorporating side air bags. In return, Volvo got exclusive rights to use the systems for the first year. A smaller number of system suppliers also makes it easier to update components. While a car maker may not find it economic to change its seating systems more than once every seven or eight years, a specialist supplier could have several alternative types of seat in parallel development at any one time.

Disintermediation

Another trend in some supply networks is that of companies within a network bypassing customers or suppliers to make contact directly with customers' customers or suppliers' suppliers. 'Cutting out the middle men' in this way is called *disintermediation*. An obvious example of this is the way the Internet has allowed some suppliers to 'disintermediate' traditional retailers in supplying goods and services to consumers. So, for example, many services in the travel industry that used to be sold through retail outlets (travel agents) are now also available direct from the suppliers. The option of purchasing the individual components of a vacation through the websites of the airline, hotel, car-hire company, etc., is now easier for consumers. Of course, they may still wish to purchase an 'assembled' product from retail travel agents which can have the advantage of convenience. Nevertheless the process of disintermediation has developed new linkages in the supply network.

FURTHER EXAMPLE

Coopetition

One approach to thinking about supply networks is called the 'value net' for a company. It sees any business as being surrounded by four types of players: suppliers, customers, competitors and complementors. Complementors enable one's products or services to be valued more by customers because they can also have the complementor's products or services, as opposed to having yours alone. Competitors are the opposite: they make customers value your product or service less when they can have their product or service, rather than yours alone. Competitors can also be complementors and vice versa. For example, adjacent restaurants may see themselves as competitors for customers' business. A customer standing outside and wanting a meal will choose between the two of them.

Yet in another way they are complementors. Would that customer have come to this part of town unless there was more than one restaurant to choose from? Restaurants, theatres, art galleries, tourist attractions generally, all cluster together in a form of cooperation to increase the total size of their joint market. It is important to distinguish between the way companies cooperate in increasing the total size of a market and the way in which they then compete for a share of that market.

Customers and suppliers have 'symmetric' roles. Historically, insufficient emphasis has been put on the role of the supplier. Harnessing the value of suppliers is just as important as listening to the needs of customers. Destroying value in a supplier in order to create it in a customer does not increase the value of the network as a whole. For example, pressurizing suppliers because customers are pressurizing you will not add long-term value. In the long term it creates value for the total network to find ways of increasing value for suppliers and well as customers. All the players in the network, whether they be customers, suppliers, competitors or complementors, can be both friends and enemies at different times. This is not 'unusual' or 'aberrant' behaviour. It is the way things are. The term used to capture this idea is 'coopetition'.[4]

Insource or outsource? Do or buy? The vertical integration decision

No single business does everything that is required to produce its products and services. Bakers do not grow wheat or even mill it into flour. Banks do not usually do their own credit checking – they retain the services of specialist credit checking agencies that have the specialized information systems and expertise to do it better. This process is called outsourcing and has become an important issue for most businesses. This is because, although most companies have always outsourced some of their activities, a larger proportion of direct activities are now being bought from suppliers. Also many indirect processes are now being outsourced. This is often referred to as business process outsourcing (BPO). Financial service companies in particular are starting to outsource some of their more routine back-office processes. In a similar way many processes within the Human Resource function, from simply payroll services through to more complex training and development processes, are being outsourced to specialist companies. The processes may still be physically located where they were before, but the staff and technology are managed by the outsourcing service provider. The reason for doing this is often primarily to reduce cost. However, there can sometimes also be significant gains in the quality and flexibility of service offered. *'People talk a lot about looking beyond cost cutting when it comes to outsourcing companies' human resource functions'*, says Jim Madden, CEO of Exult, the California-based specialist outsourcing company. *'I don't believe any company will sign up for this (outsourcing) without cost reduction being part of it, but for the clients whose human resource functions we manage, such as BP, and Bank of America, it is not just about saving money'*.

The outsourcing debate is just part of a far larger issue which will shape the fundamental nature of any business. Namely, what should the scope of the business be? In other words, what should it do itself and what should it buy in? This is often referred to as the 'do or buy decision' when individual components or activities are being considered, or 'vertical integration' when it is the ownership of whole operations that is being decided. Vertical integration is the extent to which an organization owns the network of which it is a part. It usually involves an organization assessing the wisdom of acquiring suppliers or customers. Vertical integration can be defined in terms of three factors (Figure 3.3):[5]

● **Direction.** Should an operation expand by buying one of its suppliers or by buying one of its customers? The strategy of expanding on the supply side of the network is

Figure 3.3   The direction, extent and balance of vertical integration

sometimes called backward or upstream vertical integration, and expanding on the demand side is sometimes called forward or downstream vertical integration.

- **Extent.** How far should an operation take the extent of its vertical integration? Some organizations deliberately choose not to integrate far, if at all, from their original part of the network. Alternatively, some organizations choose to become very vertically integrated.

- **Balance among stages.** This is not strictly about the ownership of the network, but rather the exclusivity of the relationship between operations. A totally balanced network relationship is one where one operation produces only for the next stage in the network and totally satisfies its requirements. Less than full balance allows each operation to sell its output to other companies or to buy in some of its supplies from other companies. Fully balanced networks have the virtue of simplicity and also allow each operation to focus on the requirements of the next stage along in the network. Having to supply other organizations, perhaps with slightly different requirements, might serve to distract from what is needed by their (owned) primary customer. However, a totally self-sufficient network is sometimes not feasible, nor is it necessarily desirable.

Making the outsourcing/vertical integration decision

Whether it is referred to as do or buy, vertical integration or no vertical integration, in-house or outsourced supply, the choice facing operations is rarely simple. Organizations in different circumstances with different objectives are likely to take different decisions. Yet the question itself is relatively simple, even if the decision itself is not: 'Does in-house or outsourced supply in a particular set of circumstances give the appropriate perform-

Operations principle
Assessing the advisability of outsourcing should include how it impacts on relevant performance objectives.

ance objectives that it requires to compete more effectively in its markets?' For example, if the main performance objectives for an operation are dependable delivery and meeting short-term changes in customers' delivery requirements, the key question should be: 'How does in-house or outsourcing give better dependability and deliver flexible performance?' This means

judging two sets of opposing factors – those that give the potential to improve performance, and those that work against this potential being realized. Table 3.1 summarizes some arguments for in-house supply and outsourcing in terms of each performance objective.

Table 3.1 How in-house and outsourced supply may affect an operation's performance objectives

Performance objective	'Do it yourself': in-house supply	'Buy it in': outsourced supply
Quality	The origins of any quality problems are usually easier to trace in-house and improvement can be more immediate, but there can be some risk of complacency.	Supplier may have specialized knowledge and more experience, also may be motivated through market pressures, but communication of quality problems more difficult.
Speed	Can mean closer synchronization of schedules which speeds up the throughput of materials and information, but if the operation also has external customers, internal customers may receive low priority.	Speed of response can be built into the supply contract where commercial pressures will encourage good performance, but there may be significant transport/delivery delays.
Dependability	Easier communications internally can help dependable delivery, which also may help when internal customers need to be informed of potential delays, but as with speed, if the operation also has external customers, internal customers may receive low priority.	Late delivery penalties in the supply contract can encourage good delivery performance, but distance and organizational barriers may inhibit communication.
Flexibility	Closeness to the real needs of a business can alert the in-house operation that some kind of change is required in its operations, but the ability to respond may be limited by the scale and scope of internal operations.	Outsource suppliers are likely to be larger and have wider capabilities than in-house suppliers. This gives them more ability to respond to changes, but they can only respond when asked to do so by the customer and they may have to balance the conflicting needs of different customers.
Cost	In-house operations give the potential for sharing some costs such as research and development, or logistics. More significantly, in-house operations do not have to make the margin required by outside suppliers, so the business can capture the profits that would otherwise be given to the supplier, but relatively low volumes may mean that it is difficult to gain economies of scale or the benefits of process innovation.	Probably the main reason why outsourcing is so popular. Outsourced companies can achieve economies of scale and they are motivated to reduce their own costs because it directly impacts on their profits, but extra costs of communication and coordination with an external supplier need to be taken into account.

Deciding whether to outsource

Although the effect of outsourcing on the operation's performance objective is important, there are other factors that companies take into account when deciding whether outsourcing an activity is a sensible option. For example, if an activity has long-term strategic importance to a company, it is unlikely to outsource it. A retailer might choose to keep the design and development of its website in-house even though specialists could perform the activity at less cost, because it plans to move into Web-based retailing at some point

Figure 3.4   The decision logic of outsourcing

Operations principle
Assessing the advisability of outsourcing should include consideration of the strategic importance of the activity and the operation's relative performance.

in the future. Nor would a company usually outsource an activity where it had specialized skills or knowledge. For example, a company making laser printers may have built up specialized knowledge in the production of sophisticated laser drives. This capability may allow it to introduce product or process innovations in the future. It would be foolish to 'give away' such capability. After these two more strategic factors have been considered, the company's operations performance can be taken into account. Obviously, if its operations performance is already superior to that of any potential supplier, it would be unlikely to outsource the activity. But also, even if its performance was currently below that of potential suppliers, it may not outsource the activity if it feels that it could significantly improve its performance. Figure 3.4 illustrates this decision logic.

FURTHER EXAMPLE

DIAGNOSTIC QUESTION

Where should operations be located?

Location is the geographical positioning of an operation. It can be an important decision because it usually has an effect on an operation's costs as well as its ability to serve its customers (and therefore its revenues). So getting location wrong can have a significant impact on profits. In retailing, a difference in location of a few metres can make the difference between profit and loss. Mislocating a fire service station can slow down the average journey time of the fire crews in getting to the fires. Locating a factory where there is difficulty attracting labour with appropriate skills may damage the effectiveness of the factory's operations, and so on. The other reason why location decisions are important is that, once taken, they are difficult to undo. The costs of moving an operation from one site to another can be hugely expensive and the risks of inconveniencing customers very high. No operation wants to move very often.

Why relocate?

Not all operations can logically justify their location. Some are where they are for historical reasons. Yet even the operations that are 'there because they're there' are implicitly making a decision not to move. Presumably their assumption is that the cost and disruption involved in changing location would outweigh any potential benefits of a new location. Two stimuli often cause organizations to make location decisions: changes in demand for goods and services, and changes in supply of inputs to the operation.

Changes in demand

A change in location may be prompted by customer demand shifting. For example, as garment manufacture moved to Asia, suppliers of zips, threads, etc. started to follow them. Changes in the volume of demand can also prompt relocation. To meet higher demand, an operation could expand its existing site, or choose a larger site in another location, or keep its existing location and find a second location for an additional operation; the last two options will involve a location decision. High-visibility operations may not have the choice of expanding on the same site to meet rising demand. A dry-cleaning service may attract only marginally more business by expanding an existing site because it offers a local, and therefore convenient, service. Finding a new location for an additional operation is probably its only option for expansion.

Changes in supply

The other stimulus for relocation is changes in the cost, or availability, of the supply of inputs to the operation. For example, a mining or oil company will need to relocate as the minerals it is extracting become depleted. A manufacturing company might choose to relocate its operations to a part of the world where labour costs are low, because the equivalent resources (people) in its original location have become relatively expensive. Sometimes a business might choose to relocate to release funds if the value of the land it occupies is worth more than an alternative, equally good, location.

Evaluating potential changes in location

Evaluating possible locations is almost always a complex task because the number of location options, the criteria against which they could be evaluated, and the comparative rarity of a single location that clearly dominates all others, make the decision strategically sensitive. Furthermore, the decision often involves high levels of uncertainty. Neither the relocation activity itself nor the operating characteristics of the new site could be as assumed when the decision was originally made. Because of this, it is useful to be systematic in terms of (a) identifying alternative options, and (b) evaluating each option against a set of rational criteria.

Identify alternative location options

The first relocation option to consider is not to relocate at all. Sometimes relocation is inevitable, but often staying put is a viable option. Even if seeking a new location seems the obvious way forward, it is worth evaluating the 'do nothing' option, if only to provide a 'base case' against which to compare other options. But in addition to the 'do nothing' option there should be a number of alternative location options. It is a mistake to consider only one location, but seeking out possible locations can be a time-consuming activity. Increasingly, for larger companies, the whole world offers possible locations.

While it has always been possible to manufacture in one part of the world in order to sell in another, until recently non-manufacturing operations were assumed to be confined to their home market. But no longer: the operational skills (as well as the brand image) of many service operations are transferable across national boundaries. Hotels, fast food, retailers and professional services all make location decisions on an international stage. Similarly, information-processing operations can now locate outside their immediate home base, thanks to virtually seamless telecommunications networks. If a financial services, or any other, business sees a cost advantage in locating part of its back-office operations in a part of the world where the 'cost per transaction' is lower, it can do so.

The implication of the globalization of the location decision is to increase both the number of options and the degree of uncertainty in their relative merits. The sheer number of possibilities makes the location decision impossible to 'optimize'. Unless every single option is explored, no one best choice is possible. Rather, the process of identifying location options usually involves selecting a limited number of sites that represent different attributes. For example, a distribution centre, while always needing to be close to transport links, could be located in any of several regions and could be either close to population centres or in a more rural location. The options may be chosen to reflect a range of both these factors. However, this assumes that the 'supply' of location options is relatively large, which is not always the case. For example, in many retail location decisions, there are a limited number of High Street locations that become available at any point in time. Often, a retailer will wait until a feasible location becomes available and then decide whether to either take up that option or wait and take the chance that a better location becomes available soon. In effect, the location decision here is a sequence of 'take or wait' decisions. Nevertheless, in making the decision to take or wait, a similar set of criteria to the more common location problem may be appropriate.

Set location evaluation criteria

Although the criteria against which alternative locations can be evaluated will depend on circumstances, those illustrated in Figure 3.5 are typical. They fall into five broad categories.

Capital requirements The capital or leasing cost of a site is usually a significant factor. This will probably be a function of the location of the site and its characteristics. For example, the shape of the site and its soil composition can limit the nature of any buildings erected there. Access to the site is also likely to be important, as are the availability of utilities, etc. In addition the cost of the move itself may depend on which site is eventually chosen.

Market factors Location can affect how the market, either in general or as individual customers, perceives an operation. Locating a general hospital in the middle of the countryside may have many advantages for its staff, but it clearly would be very inconvenient for its customers. Likewise, restaurants, stores, banks, petrol filling stations and many other high visibility operations must all evaluate how alternative locations will determine their image and the level of service they can give. The same arguments apply to labour markets. Location may affect the attractiveness of the operation in terms of staff recruitment and retention. For example, 'science parks' are usually located close to universities because they hope to attract companies that are interested in using the skills available at the university.

Cost factors Two major categories of cost are affected by location. The first is the cost of producing products or services. For example, labour costs can vary between different areas in any country, but are likely to be a far more significant factor when international

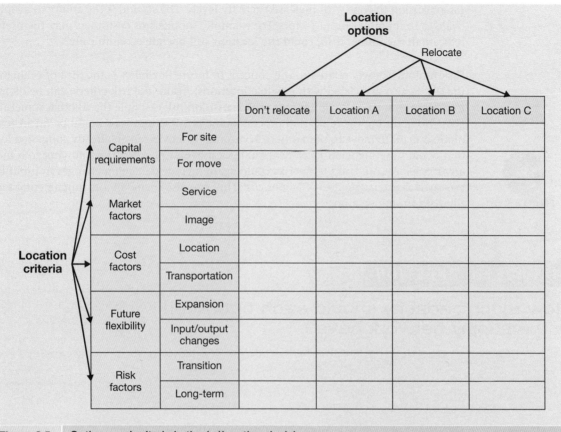

Figure 3.5   Options and criteria in the (re)location decision

comparisons are made, when they can exert a major influence on the location decision, especially in some industries such as clothing, where labour costs as a proportion of total costs are relatively high. Other cost factors, known as community factors, derive from the social, political and economic environment of its site. These include such factors as local tax rates, capital movement restrictions, government financial assistance, political stability, local attitudes to 'inward investment', language, local amenities (schools, theatres, shops, etc.), the availability of support services, the history of labour relations and behaviour, environmental restrictions and planning procedures. The second category of costs relates to both the cost of transporting inputs from their source to the location of the operation and the cost of transporting products and services from the location to customers. Whereas almost all operations are concerned to some extent with the former, not all operations are concerned with the latter, either because customers come to them (for example, hotels), or because their services can be 'transported' at virtually no cost (for example, some technology help desks). For supply networks that process physical items, however, transportation costs can be very significant.

Future flexibility   Because operations rarely change their location, any new location must be capable of being acceptable, not only under current circumstances but also under possible future circumstances. The problem is that no one knows exactly what the future holds. Nevertheless, especially in uncertain environments, any evaluation of alternative locations should include some kind of scenario planning that considers the robustness of each in coping with a range of possible futures. Two types of the flexibility of any location could be evaluated. The most common is to consider the potential of the location for expansion to cope with increased activity levels. The second is the ability to adapt to changes in input or output factors. For example, suppliers or customers may themselves relocate in the future. If so, could the location still operate economically?

Risk factors Closely related to the concept of future flexibility is the idea of evaluating the risk factors associated with possible locations. Again, the risk criteria can be divided into 'transition risk' and 'long-term risk'. Transition risk is simple the risk that something goes wrong during the relocation process. Some possible locations might be intrinsically more difficult to move to than others. For example, moving to an already congested location could pose higher risks to being able to move as planned than moving to a more accessible location. Long-term risks could again include damaging changes in input factors such as exchange rates or labour costs, but can also include more fundamental security risks to staff or property.

PRACTICE NOTE

DIAGNOSTIC QUESTION

How much capacity should each operation in the supply network have?

The design of supply networks also includes defining the capacity of each operation in the network. Unless the capacity of individual operations reflects the needs of the network as a whole, it will either limit flow through the network or be the cause of capacity underutilization, both of which will in the long term reduce the effectiveness of the network as a whole. Here we shall treat capacity in a general long-term sense. Shorter-term aspects of capacity management are treated in Chapter 8. But whether over the short or long term, demand forecasts are one of the main inputs to capacity management, which is why forecasting is treated in the supplement to this chapter.

The optimum capacity level

Most organizations need to decide on the size (in terms of capacity) of each of their facilities. A chain of truck service centres, for example, might operate centres that have various capacities. The effective cost of running each centre will depend on the average service bay occupancy. Low occupancy because of few customers will result in a high cost per customer served because the fixed costs of the operation are being shared between few customers. As demand, and therefore service bay occupancy, increases the cost per customer will reduce. However, operating at very high levels of capacity utilization (occupancy levels close to capacity) can mean longer customer waiting times and reduced customer service. This effect is described in more detail in Chapter 5. There may also be less obvious cost penalties of operating centres at levels close to their nominal capacity. For example, long periods of overtime may reduce productivity levels as well as costing more in extra payments to staff; utilizing bays at very high utilization levels reduces maintenance and cleaning time that may increase breakdowns, reduce effective life, and so on. This usually means that average costs start to increase after a point that will often be lower than the theoretical capacity of the operation.

Figure 3.6 Unit cost curves for individual truck service centres of varying capacities

Operations principle
All types of operation exhibit economy of scale effects where operating costs reduce as the scale of capacity increases.

The blue curves in Figure 3.6 show this effect for the service centres of 5, 10, and 15-bay capacity. As the nominal capacity of the centres increases, the lowest cost point at first reduces. This is because the fixed costs of any operation do not increase proportionately as its capacity increases. A 10-bay centre has less than twice the fixed costs of a 5-bay centre. Also the capital costs of constructing the operations do not increase proportionately to their capacity. A 10-bay centre costs less to build than twice the cost of a 5-bay centre. These two factors, taken together, are often referred to as economies of scale. However, above a certain size, the lowest cost point may increase. This occurs because of what are called diseconomies of scale, two of which are particularly important. First, complexity costs increase as size increases. The communications and coordination effort necessary to manage an operation tends to increase faster than capacity. Although not seen as a direct cost, this can nevertheless be very significant. Second, a larger centre is more likely to be partially underutilized because demand within a fixed location will be limited. The equivalent in operations that process physical items is transportation costs. For example, if a manufacturer supplies the whole of its European market from one major plant in Denmark, all supplies may have to be brought in from several countries to the single plant and all products shipped from there throughout Europe.

Operations principle
Diseconomies of scale increase operating costs above a certain level of capacity resulting in a minimum cost level of capacity.

Scale of capacity and the demand–capacity balance

Large units of capacity also have some disadvantages when the capacity of the operation is being changed to match changing demand. For example, suppose that a manufacturer forecasts demand to increase over the next three years, as shown in Figure 3.7, levelling off at around 2400 units a week. If the company seeks to satisfy all demand by building three plants as demand builds up, each of 800 units capacity, the company will have substantial amounts of overcapacity for much of the period when demand is increasing. Overcapacity means low capacity utilization, which in turn means higher unit costs. If the company builds smaller plants, say 400-unit plants, there will still be overcapacity but to a lesser extent, which means higher capacity utilization and possibly lower costs.

Operations principle
Changing capacity in large units of capacity reduces the chance of achieving demand – capacity balance.

| **Figure 3.7** | The scale of capacity increments affects the utilization of capacity |

The timing of capacity change

Changing the capacity of an operation is not just a matter of deciding on the best size of a capacity increment. The operation also needs to decide when to bring new capacity 'on stream'. Continuing the above example, Figure 3.8 shows the forecast demand for the new manufacturing operation. The company has decided to build 400-unit-per-week plants in order to meet the growth in demand for its new product. In deciding when the new plants are to be introduced, the company must choose a position somewhere between two extreme strategies:[5]

> **Operations principle**
> Capacity leading strategies increase opportunities to meet demand.

- Capacity leads demand – timing the introduction of capacity in such a way that there is always sufficient capacity to meet forecast demand
- Capacity lags demand – timing the introduction of capacity so that demand is always equal to or greater than capacity.

Figure 3.8 shows these two extreme strategies, although in practice the company is likely to choose a position somewhere between the two. Each strategy has its own advantages and disadvantages. These are shown in Table 3.2. The actual approach taken by any company will depend on how it views these advantages and disadvantages. For example, if the company's access to funds for capital expenditure is limited, it is likely to find the delayed capital expenditure requirement of the capacity-lagging strategy relatively attractive.

> **Operations principle**
> Capacity lagging strategies increase capacity utilization.

'Smoothing' with inventory

> **Operations principle**
> Using inventory to overcome demand – capacity imbalance tends to increase working capital requirements.

The strategy on the continuum between pure leading and pure lagging strategies can be implemented so that no inventories are accumulated. All demand in one period is satisfied (or not) by the activity of the operation in the same period. Indeed, for customer-processing operations there is no alternative to this. A hotel cannot satisfy demand in one year by using rooms which were vacant

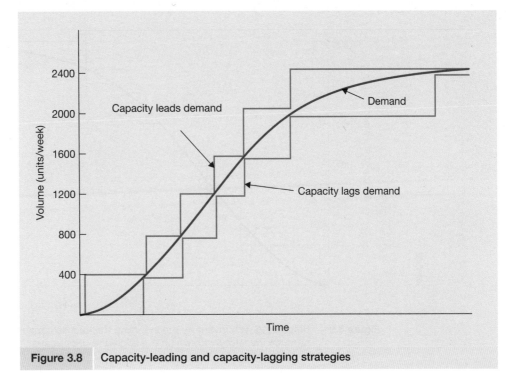

Figure 3.8   Capacity-leading and capacity-lagging strategies

the previous year. For some materials- and information-processing operations, however, the output from the operation which is not required in one period can be stored for use in the next period. The economies of using inventories are fully explored in Chapter 10. Here we confine ourselves to noting that inventories can be used to obtain the advantages of both capacity leading and capacity lagging. Figure 3.9 shows how this can be done.

Table 3.2	The arguments for and against pure leading and pure lagging strategies of capacity timing	
Advantages		**Disadvantages**
Capacity-leading strategies		
Always sufficient capacity to meet demand, therefore revenue is maximized and customers are satisfied		Utilization of the plants is always relatively low, therefore costs will be high
Most of the time there is a 'capacity cushion' which can absorb extra demand levels if forecasts are pessimistic		Risk of even greater (or even permanent) over-capacity if demand does not reach forecast levels
Any critical start-up problems with new plants are less likely to affect supply to customers		Capital spending on plant early
Capacity-lagging strategies		
Always sufficient demand to keep the plants working at full capacity, therefore unit costs are minimized		Insufficient capacity to meet demand fully, therefore reduced revenue and dissatisfied customers
Overcapacity problems are minimized if forecasts are optimistic		No ability to exploit short-term increases in demand
Capital spending on the plants is delayed		Under-supply position even worse if there are start-up problems with the new plants

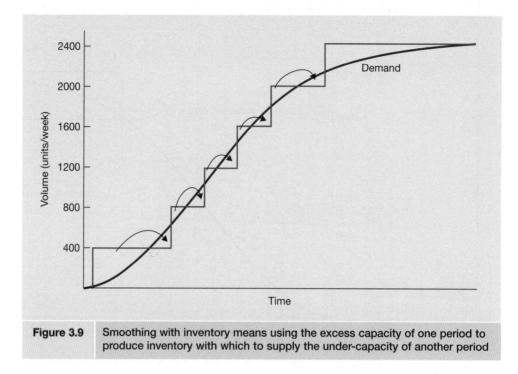

Figure 3.9 | Smoothing with inventory means using the excess capacity of one period to produce inventory with which to supply the under-capacity of another period

Capacity is introduced such that demand can always be met by a combination of production and inventories, and capacity is, with the occasional exception, fully utilized.

This may seem like an ideal state. Demand is always met and so revenue is maximized. Capacity is usually fully utilized and so costs are minimized. There is a price to pay, however, and that is the cost of carrying the inventories. Not only will these have to be funded but the risks of obsolescence and deterioration of stock are introduced (see Chapter 9). Table 3.3 summarizes the advantages and disadvantages of the 'smoothing-with-inventory' strategy.

Break-even analysis of capacity expansion

Excel

An alternative view of capacity expansion can be gained by examining the cost implications of adding increments of capacity on a break-even basis. Figure 3.10 shows how increasing capacity can move an operation from profitability to loss. Each additional

Table 3.3 | The advantages and disadvantages of a smoothing-with-inventory strategy

Advantages	*Disadvantages*
All demand is satisfied, therefore customers are satisfied and revenue is maximized	The cost of inventories in terms of working capital requirements can be high. This is especially serious at a time when the company requires funds for its capital expansion
Utilization of capacity is high and therefore costs are low	Risk of product deterioration and obsolescence
Very short-term surges in demand can be met from inventories	

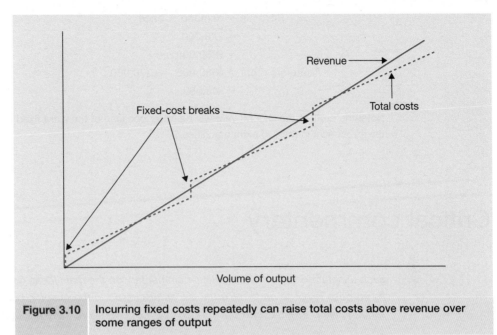

Figure 3.10   Incurring fixed costs repeatedly can raise total costs above revenue over some ranges of output

PRACTICE NOTE

unit of capacity results in a fixed-cost break, which is a further lump of expenditure that will have to be incurred before any further activity can be undertaken in the operation.

The operation is therefore unlikely to be profitable at very low levels of output. Eventually, assuming that prices are greater than marginal costs, revenue will exceed total costs. However, the level of profitability at the point where the output level is equal to the capacity of the operation may not be sufficient to absorb all the extra fixed costs of a further increment in capacity. This could make the operation unprofitable in some stages of its expansion.

Worked example

A specialist graphics company is investing in new systems that will enable it to make high-quality images for its clients. Demand for these images is forecast to be around 100,000 images in year 1 and 220,000 images in year 2. The maximum capacity of each system is 100,000 images per year. They have a fixed cost of €200,000 per year and a variable cost of processing of €1 per image. The company believes they will be able to charge an average of €4 per image. What profit are they likely to make in the first and second years?

$$\text{Year 1 demand} = 100,000 \text{ images; therefore company will need one machine}$$

$$\text{Cost of producing images} = \text{fixed cost for one machine} + (\text{variable cost} \times 100,000)$$

$$= €200,000 + (€1 \times 100,000)$$

$$= €300,000$$

$$\text{Revenue} = \text{demand} \times \text{price}$$

$$= 100,000 \times €4$$

$$= €400,000$$

$$\text{Therefore profit} = €400,000 - €300,000$$

$$= €100,000$$

$$\text{Year 2 demand} = 220,000 \text{ units; therefore company will need three machines}$$

$$\text{Cost of producing images} = \text{fixed cost for three machines} + (\text{variable cost} \times 220,000)$$

$$= (3 \times €200,000) + (€1 \times 220,000)$$

$$= €820,000$$

$$\text{Revenue} = \text{demand} \times \text{price}$$
$$= 220{,}000 \times €4$$
$$= €880{,}000$$
$$\text{Therefore profit} = €880{,}000 - €820{,}000$$
$$= €60{,}000$$

Note: the profit in the second year will be lower because of the extra fixed costs associated with the investment in the two extra machines.

Critical commentary

Each chapter contains a short critical commentary on the main ideas covered in the chapter. Its purpose is not to undermine the issues discussed in the chapter, but to emphasize that, although we present a relatively orthodox view of operation, there are other perspectives.

■ Probably the most controversial issue in supply network design is that of outsourcing. In many instances there has been fierce opposition to companies outsourcing some of their processes. Trade Unions often point out that the only reason that outsourcing companies can do the job at lower cost is that they either reduce salaries, reduce working conditions, or both. Furthermore, they say, flexibility is only achieved by reducing job security. Employees who were once part of a large and secure corporation could find themselves as far less secure employees of a less benevolent employer with a philosophy of permanent cost cutting. Even some proponents of outsourcing are quick to point out the problems. There can be significant obstacles, including understandable resistance from staff who find themselves 'outsourced'. Some companies have also been guilty of 'outsourcing a problem'. In other words, having failed to manage a process well themselves, they ship it out rather than face up to why the process was problematic in the first place. There is also evidence that, although long-term costs can be brought down when a process is outsourced, there may be an initial period when costs rise as both sides learn how to manage the new arrangement.

Summary checklist

DOWNLOADABLE

This checklist comprises questions that can be usefully applied to any type of operations and reflect the major diagnostic questions used within the chapter.

☐ Is the operation fully aware of all its first- and second-tier suppliers' and customers' capabilities and requirements?

☐ Are capabilities of suppliers and requirements of customers understood in terms of all aspects of operations performance?

☐ Does the operation have a view on how it would like to see its supply network develop over time?

☐ Have the benefits of reducing the number of individual suppliers been explored?

☐ Are any parts of the supply network likely to become disintermediated, and have the implications of this been considered?

☐ Does the operation have an approach to how it treats others in the supply network who might be both complementors and competitors?

☐ Is the vertical integration/outsourcing issue always under review for possible benefits?

☐ Is outsourcing (or bringing back in-house) evaluated in terms of all the operation's performance objectives?

☐ Is there a rational set of criteria used for deciding whether to outsource?

☐ Is the relocation decision ever considered?

☐ Have factors such as changes in demand or supply that may prompt a relocation been considered?

☐ If considering a relocation, are alternative locations always evaluated against each other and against a 'do nothing' option?

☐ Are sufficient location options being considered?

☐ Do location evaluation criteria include capital, market, cost, flexibility, and risk factors?

☐ Is the optimum economy of scale for the different types of operation with the business periodically assessed?

☐ Are the various strategies for timing changes in capacity always evaluated in terms of their advantages and disadvantages?

☐ Are the fixed-cost breaks of capacity increase understood, and are they taken into account when increasing or decreasing capacity?

Case study   Delta Synthetic Fibres

DSF is a small but technically successful company in the man-made fibre industry. The company is heavily dependent on the sales of Britlene, a product it developed itself, which accounted in 1996 for some 95 per cent of total sales. Britlene is used mainly in heavy-duty clothing, although small quantities are used to produce industrial goods such as tyre cord and industrial belting. Its main properties are very high wear resistance, thermal and electrical insulation.

In 1996 the company developed a new product, Britlon. Britlon had all the properties of Britlene but was superior in its heat-resistant qualities. It was hoped that this additional property would open up new clothing uses (e.g. a substitute for mineral wool clothing, added to nightwear to improve its inflammability) and new industrial uses in thermal and electrical insulation. By late 1996 the major technical and engineering problems associated with bulk production of Britlon seemed to have been solved and the company set up a working party to put forward proposals on how the new product should be phased into the company's activities.

The basic production method of Britlene and Britlon is similar to that of most man-made fibres. To make a man-made fibre, an oil-based organic chemical is polymerized (a process of joining several molecules into a long chain) in conditions of intense pressure and heat, often by the addition of a suitable catalyst. This polymerization takes place in large autoclaves (industrial pressure cookers). The polymer is then extruded (forced through a nozzle like the rose of a garden watering can), rapidly cooled and then either spun onto cones or collected in bales.

The raw materials for Britlene and Britlon are produced at Teesside in the UK.

Britlene facilities

Britlene is produced at three factories in the UK: Teesside, Bradford and Dumfries. The largest site is at Teesside with three plants. There is one plant at each of the other two sites. All five production plants have a design capacity of 5.5 million kg per year of Britlene. However, after allowing for maintenance and an annual shutdown, expected output is 5 million kg per year. Each plant operates on a 24-hours-per-day, seven-days-per-week basis.

Source: © Corbis

Proposed Britlon facilities

Britlon's production process is very similar to that used for Britlene, but a totally new type of polymerization unit is needed prior to the extrusion stage. DSF approached Alpen Engineering Company, an international chemical plant construction company, for help on a large-scale plant design of the new unit. Together they produced and tested an acceptable design.

Acquiring Britlon capacity

There are two ways of acquiring Britlon capacity. DSF could convert a Britlene plant, or it could construct an entirely new plant.

For a conversion, the new polymer unit would need to be constructed first. When complete it would be connected to the extrusion unit which would require minor conversion. At least two years would be needed either to build a new Britlon plant or to convert an old Britlene plant to Britlon production.

The company's Chief Executive Officer was quoted as saying: '*The creation of an entirely new site would increase the complexities of multi-site operation to an unacceptable level. Conversely, the complete closure of one of the three existing sites is, I consider, a waste of the manpower and physical resources that we have invested in that location. I believe expansion could take place at one, two or all of the existing sites.*'

Only on Teesside is there higher than average general unemployment, but the unemployment rate for skilled and semi-skilled workers is quite low at all sites. Demand for skilled labour on Teesside is from two giant companies, both of whom are expanding in that area; at Dumfries and Bradford there is little or no competition.

Table 3.4	Forecast sales for Britlene and Britlon (millions of kg per year)	
Potential sales	*Britlene*	*Britlon*
1996 (actual)	24.7	–
1997	22	–
1998	20	–
1999	17	3 (assuming availability)
2000	13	16
2001	11	27
2002	10	29

Demand

Demand forecasts for the two products are shown in Table 3.4. They show that, although Britlene sales will probably fall rapidly once Britlon is introduced, there is likely to be a residual level of sales of the older product.

QUESTIONS

1 What order schedule would you propose for conversions and new plant?

2 In which locations would you make these capacity changes?

3 What criteria have you used to make your recommendations?

4 What do you see as the main dangers facing DSF as it changes its capacity over the next five or six years?

Active case study   Freeman Biotest

ACTIVE CASE

Freeman Biotest, a large company who supply the food-processing industry, is having problems with one of their process lines, a 'Brayford line'. They are uncertain about whether to replace it with a new 'Brayford line' or to commission a completely new type of process line. Representatives from the marketing, technology, operations and finance teams express their opinions and raise a number of concerns about the implications of each line.

● How would you recommend Freeman Biotest address their need for extra capacity and their problematic process line?

Please refer to the Active case on the CD accompanying this book to listen to the views of those involved.

Applying the principles

HINTS

Some of these exercises can be answered by reading the chapter. Others will require some general knowledge of business activity and some might require an element of investigation. All have hints on how they can be answered on the CD accompanying this book.

---

1 For the Walt Disney Corporation, the decision to invest in Disneyland Paris was one of the most important location decisions it had ever made. The decision was in two parts. First, should Disney open one of its famous theme parks in Europe at all? Second, if so, where in Europe should it be located? The decision to locate in Europe was influenced partly by its experiences at Tokyo Disneyland, which had been a tremendous success. In Europe, however, there was already a well-established market in holidays to Disney in Florida. For holiday-makers in the UK especially, Florida was only slightly more expensive than travelling to what was then called Euro Disney, with the added benefit of better weather. Also, said some critics, *'Why build a fake castle on a continent full of real castles? Why build a theme*

park on a continent which is already a theme park?' If any doubts troubled Disney, it overcame them. At least two sites were considered – one in Spain and one in France. The advantage of France was that the demography of Europe means that by locating its theme park 30 kilometres east of Paris, it is within relatively easy travelling distance of millions of potential customers. Spain is geographically less convenient. There was also an existing transport infrastructure in this part of France, which was made even better by the French government as an inducement. The French government also offered Disney numerous other financial inducements. Spain, geographically more isolated and reputedly unable to match the French government's inducements, had the critical advantage, however, of better and more predictable weather. What perhaps was not forecast at the time was the initial hostility of the French media to what some regarded as cultural imperialism. Also, initially not all the European (largely French) staff were as amenable to the strict dress and behaviour codes as were their equivalents in Disney's US locations.

- Summarize what you see as the major factors influencing the Walt Disney Corporation's decision to locate near Paris.
- What difficulties do you think the Disney Corporation must have faced in the early days of running Disneyland Paris?
- When transferring a service operation of this type between national or regional cultures, how might the design of the operation need to change?

2 Visit sites on the Internet that offer (legal) downloadable music using MP3 or other compression formats. Consider the music business supply chain, (a) for the recordings of a well-known popular music artist, and (b) for a less well-known (or even largely unknown) artist struggling to gain recognition.

- How might the transmission of music over the Internet affect each of these artists' sales?
- What implications does electronic music transmission have for record shops?

3 Visit the websites of companies that are in the paper manufacturing/pulp production/packaging industries. Assess the extent to which the companies you have investigated are vertically integrated in the paper supply chain that stretches from foresting through to the production of packaging materials.

4 Many developing nations are challenging the dominance of more traditional Western locations, notably Silicon Valley, for high-tech research and manufacturing. Two examples are Bangalore in India and Shanghai in China. Make a list of all the factors you would recommend a multinational corporation to take into account in assessing the advantages and disadvantages and risks of locating in developing countries. Use this list to compare Bangalore and China for a multinational computer corporation,

(a) siting its research and development facility;
(b) siting a new manufacturing facility.

5 Tesco.com is now the world's largest and by far the most profitable online grocery retailer. In 1996 Tesco.com was alone in developing a 'store-based' supply network strategy. This means that it used its existing stores to assemble customer orders which were placed online. Tesco staff would simply be given printouts of customer orders and then walk round the store picking items off the shelves. The groceries would then be delivered by a local fleet of Tesco vans to customers. By contrast, many new e-grocery entrants and some existing supermarkets pursued a 'warehouse' supply network strategy of building new, large, totally automated and dedicated regional warehouses. Because forecasts for online demand were so high, they believed that the economies of scale of dedicated warehouses would be worth the investment. In the late 1990s Tesco came under criticism for being over-cautious and in 1999 it reviewed its strategy. Tesco concluded that its store-based strategy was correct and persevered. The most famous of the pure e-grocery companies was called WebVan. At the height of the dot-com phenomenon WebVan Group went public with a first-day market capitalization of $7.6 billion. By 2001, having burnt its way through $1.2 billion in capital before filing for bankruptcy, WebVan Group went bust, letting go all of its workers and auctioning off everything from warehouse equipment to software.

- Draw the different supply network strategies for Tesco and companies like WebVan.
- What do you think the economy of scale curves for the Tesco operation and the WebVan operation would look like relative to each other?
- Why do you think WebVan went bust and Tesco was so successful?

Notes on chapter

1 Source: company website (www.intel.com).
2 Source: BBC news site at www.bbc.co.uk.
3 Source: Zwick, S. (1999) 'World cars', *Time Magazine,* 22 Feb.
4 Brandenburger, A.M. and Nalebuff, B. (1996) *Coopetition,* Doubleday, New York.
5 Hayes, R.H. and Wheelwright, S.C. (1994) *Restoring our Competitive Edge,* John Wiley.

Taking it further

Bartlett, C. and Ghoshal, S. (1989) *Managing Across Borders,* Harvard Business School Press. A great introduction to understanding the background to managing international supply networks.

Chopra, S. and Meindl, P. (2000) *Supply Chain Management: Strategy, planning and operations,* Prentice Hall, New Jersey. A good textbook that covers both strategic and operational issues.

Dell, M. (with Catherine Fredman) (1999) *Direct from Dell: Strategies that revolutionized an industry,* Harper Business. Michael Dell explains how his supply network strategy (and other decisions) had such an impact on the industry. Interesting and readable, but not a critical analysis!

Ferdows, K. (1997) 'Making the most of foreign factories', *Harvard Business Review,* March–April. An articulate exposition of why factories that start out as foreign subsidiaries can end up by becoming pivotal to a multinational's success.

Quinn, J.B. (1999) 'Strategic outsourcing: leveraging knowledge capabilities', *Sloan Management Review, Summer*. A bit academic but a good discussion on the importance of 'knowledge' in the outsourcing decision.

Schniederjans, M.J. (1998) *International Facility Location and Acquisition Analysis,* Quorum Books, New York. Very much one for the technically minded.

Useful websites

www.locationstrategies.com Exactly what the title implies. Good industry discussion.

www.conway.com American location selection site. You can get a flavour of how location decisions are made.

www.transparency.org A leading site for international business (inducing location) that fights corruption.

www.intel.com More details on Intel's 'Copy Exactly' strategy and other capacity strategy issues.

www.outsourcing.com Site of the Institute of Outsourcing. Some good case studies.

www.bath.ac.uk/crisps A centre for research in strategic purchasing and supply. Some interesting papers.

www.outsourcing.co.uk Site of the UK National Outsourcing Association. Some interesting reports, news items, etc.

FURTHER RESOURCES

For further resources including examples, animated diagrams, self test questions, excel spreadsheets, active case studies and video materials please explore the CD accompanying this book.

Supplement to Chapter 3
Forecasting

Introduction

Some forecasts are accurate. We know exactly what time the sun will rise at any given place on earth tomorrow or one day next month or even next year. Forecasting in a business context, however, is much more difficult and therefore prone to error. We do not know precisely how many orders we will receive or how many customers will walk through the door tomorrow, next month, or next year. Such forecasts, however, are necessary to help managers make decisions about resourcing the organization for the future.

Forecasting – knowing the options

Simply knowing that demand for your goods or services is rising or falling is not enough in itself. Knowing the rate of change is likely to be vital to business planning. A firm of lawyers may have to decide the point at which, in their growing business, they will have to take on another partner. Hiring a new partner could take months, so they need to be able to forecast when they expect to reach that point and then when they need to start their recruitment drive. The same applies to a plant manager who will need to purchase new plant to deal with rising demand. She may not want to commit to buying an expensive piece of machinery until absolutely necessary but in enough time to order the machine and have it built, delivered, installed and tested. The same is so for governments, whether planning new airports or runway capacity or deciding where and how many primary schools to build.

The first question is to know how far you need to look ahead. This will depend on the options and decisions available to you. Take the example of a local government district where the number of primary-age children (5–11 year olds) is increasing in some areas and declining in other areas within its boundaries. The council is legally obliged to provide school places for all such children. Government officials will have a number of options open to them and they may each have different lead times associated with them. One key step in forecasting is to know the possible options and the lead times required to bring them about (see Table 3.5).

Table 3.5	Options available and lead-time required for dealing with changes in numbers of school children
Options available	Lead time required
Hire short-term teachers	Hours
Hire staff	
Build temporary classrooms	
Amend school catchment areas	
Build new classrooms	
Build new schools	Years

Individual schools can hire (or lay off) short-term (supply) teachers from a pool, not only to cover for absent teachers but also to provide short-term capacity while more teachers are hired to deal with increases in demand. Acquiring (or dismissing) such temporary cover may require only a few hours' notice. (This is often referred to as short-term capacity management.)

Hiring new (or laying off existing) staff is another option, but both of these may take months to complete (medium-term capacity management).

A shortage of accommodation may be fixed in the short to medium term by hiring or buying temporary classrooms. It may take only a couple of weeks to hire such a building and equip it ready for use.

It may be possible to amend catchment areas between schools to try to balance an increasing population in one area against a declining population in another. Such changes may require lengthy consultation processes.

In the longer term, new classrooms or even new schools may have to be built. The planning, consultation, approval, commissioning, tendering, building and equipping process may take up to five years depending on the scale of the new build.

Knowing the range of options, managers can then decide the time scale for their forecasts; indeed several forecasts might be needed for the short term, medium term and long term.

In essence forecasting is simple

In essence forecasting is easy. To know how many children may turn up at a local school tomorrow, you can use the number that turned up today. In the long term, in order to forecast how many primary-age children will expect to attend a school in five years' time, one need simply look at the birth statistics for the current year for the school's catchment area – see Figure 3.11.

However, such simple extrapolation techniques are prone to error and indeed such approaches have resulted in some local government authorities committing themselves to building schools which five or six years later, when complete, had few children, while other schools were bursting at the seams with temporary classrooms and temporary teachers, often resulting in falling morale and declining educational standards. The reason why such simple approaches are prone to problems is that there are many contextual variables (see Figure 3.12) that will have a potentially significant impact on, for example, the school population five years hence. For example, one minor factor in developed countries, though a major factor in developing countries, might be the death rate in children between birth and five years of age. This may depend upon location, with a slightly higher mortality rate in poorer areas than in more affluent areas. Another more significant factor is immigration and emigration as people move into or out of the local area. This will be affected by housing stock and housing developments, the ebb and flow of jobs and the changing economic prosperity in the area.

One key factor which has an impact on the local birth rate is the amount and type of the housing stock. City centre tenement buildings tend to have a higher proportion of

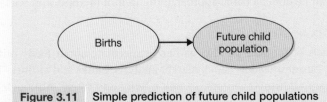

Figure 3.11   Simple prediction of future child populations

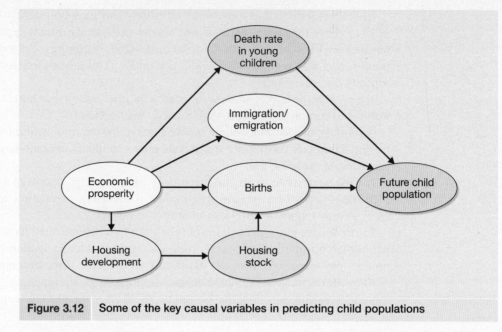

Figure 3.12   Some of the key causal variables in predicting child populations

children per dwelling, for example, than suburban semi-detached houses. So not only will existing housing stock have an impact on the child population but so also will the type of housing developments under construction, planned and proposed.

Approaches to forecasting

There are two main approaches to forecasting. Managers sometimes use qualitative methods based on opinions, past experience and even best guesses. There is also a range of qualitative forecasting techniques available to help managers evaluate trends and causal relationships and make predictions about the future. Also quantitative forecasting techniques can be used to model data. Although no approach or technique will necessarily result in an accurate forecast, a combination of qualitative and quantitative approaches can be used to great effect by bringing together expert judgements and predictive models.

Qualitative methods

Imagine you were asked to forecast the outcome of a forthcoming football match. Simply looking at the teams' performance over the last few weeks and extrapolating it is unlikely to yield the right result. Like many business decisions the outcome will depend on many other factors. In this case the strength of the opposition, their recent form, injuries to players on both sides, the match location and even the weather will influence the outcome. A qualitative approach involves collecting and appraising judgements, options, even best guesses as well as past performance from 'experts' to make a prediction. There are several ways this can be done: a panel approach, the Delphi method, and scenario planning.

Panel approach

Just as panels of football pundits gather to speculate about likely outcomes, so too do politicians, business leaders, stock market analysts, banks and airlines. The panel acts like a focus group allowing everyone to talk openly and freely. Although there is the great advantage of several brains being better than one, it can be difficult to reach a consensus, or sometimes the views of the loudest or highest status may emerge (the bandwagon effect). Although more reliable than one person's views, the panel approach still has the weakness that everybody, even the experts, can get it wrong.

Delphi method

Perhaps the best-known approach to generating forecasts using experts is the Delphi method.[1] This is a more formal method that attempts to reduce the influences from procedures of face-to-face meetings. It employs a questionnaire, emailed or posted to the experts. The replies are analyzed and summarized and returned, anonymously, to all the experts. The experts are then asked to reconsider their original response in the light of the replies and arguments put forward by the other experts. This process is repeated several times to conclude either with a consensus or at least with a narrower range of decisions. One refinement of this approach is to allocate weights to the individuals and their suggestions based on, for example, their experience, their past success in forecasting, or other people's views of their abilities. The obvious problems associated with this method include constructing an appropriate questionnaire, selecting an appropriate panel of experts and trying to deal with their inherent biases.

Scenario planning

One method for dealing with situations of even greater uncertainty is scenario planning. This is usually applied to long-range forecasting, again using a panel. The panel members are usually asked to devise a range of future scenarios. Each scenario can then be discussed and the inherent risks considered. Unlike the Delphi method, scenario planning is not necessarily concerned with arriving at a consensus but with looking at the possible range of options and putting plans in place to try to avoid the ones that are least desired and to take action to follow the most desired.

Quantitative methods

There are two main approaches to quantitative forecasting: time series analysis and causal modelling techniques. Time series analysis examines the pattern of past behaviour of a single phenomenon over time, taking into account reasons for variation in the trend in order to use the analysis to forecast the phenomenon's future behaviour. Causal modelling is an approach that describes and evaluates the complex cause and effect relationships between the key variables (such as in Figure 3.12).

Excel

Time series analysis

Simple time series plot a variable over time, then by removing underlying variations with assignable causes use extrapolation techniques to predict future behaviour. The key weakness with this approach is that it simply looks at past behaviour to predict the future, ignoring causal variables that are taken into account in other methods such as causal modelling or qualitative techniques. For example, suppose a company is attempting to predict the future sales of a product. The past three years' sales, quarter by quarter, are shown in Figure 3.13(a). This series of past sales may be analyzed to indicate future sales. For instance, underlying the series might be a linear upward trend in sales. If this is taken out of the data, as in Figure 3.13(b), we are left with a cyclical seasonal variation. The mean deviation of each quarter from the trend line can now be taken out, to give the average seasonality deviation. What remains is the random variation about the trends and seasonality lines, Figure 3.13(c). Future sales may now be predicted as lying within a band about a projection of the trend, plus the seasonality. The width of the band will be a function of the degree of random variation.

Figure 3.13   Time series analysis with (a) trend, (b) seasonality and (c) random variation

Forecasting unassignable variations The random variations that remain after taking out trend and seasonal effects are without any known or assignable cause. This does not mean that they do not have a cause, but just that we do not know what it is. Nevertheless, some attempt can be made to forecast it, if only on the basis that future events will, in some way, be based on past events. We will examine two of the more common approaches to forecasting that are based on projecting forward from past behaviour. These are:

● Moving-average forecasting
● Exponentially smoothed forecasting.

The moving-average approach to forecasting takes the previous *n* periods' actual demand figures, calculates the average demand over the *n* periods, and uses this average as a forecast for the next period's demand. Any data older than the *n* periods plays no part in the next period's forecast. The value of *n* can be set at any level, but is usually in the range 4 to 7.

Example   Eurospeed parcels using moving-average

Table 3.6 shows the weekly demand for Eurospeed, a European-wide parcel delivery company. It measures demand, on a weekly basis, in terms of the number of parcels that it is given to deliver (irrespective of the size of each parcel). Each week, the next week's demand is forecast by taking the moving average of the previous four weeks' actual demand. Thus if the forecast demand for week *t* is F_t and the actual demand for week *t* is A_t, then:

$$F_t = \tfrac{1}{4}(A_{t-4} + A_{t-3} + A_{t-2} + A_{t-1})$$

Table 3.6	Actual demand and moving-average forecast (thousands) calculated over a four-week period	
Week (t)	Actual demand (A)	Forecast demand (F)
20	63.3	
21	62.5	
22	67.8	
23	66.0	
24	67.2	64.9
25	69.9	65.9
26	65.6	67.7
27	71.1	66.3
28	68.8	67.3
29	68.4	68.9
30	70.3	68.5
31	72.5	69.7
32	66.7	70.0
33	68.3	69.5
34	67.0	69.5
35		68.6

For example, the forecast for week 35:

$$F_{35} = (72.5 + 66.7 + 68.3 + 67.0)/4$$
$$= 68.8$$

Exponential smoothing There are two significant drawbacks to the moving-average approach to forecasting. First, in its basic form, it gives equal weight to all the previous n periods which are used in the calculations (although this can be overcome by assigning different weights to each of the n periods). Second, and more important, it does not use data from beyond the n periods over which the moving average is calculated. Both these problems are overcome by exponential smoothing, which is also somewhat easier to calculate. The exponential-smoothing approach forecasts demand in the next period by taking into account the actual demand in the current period and the forecast that was previously made for the current period. It does so according to the formula:

$$F_t = \alpha A_{t-1} + (1 - x)F_{t-1}$$

where α = the smoothing constant.

The smoothing constant α is, in effect, the weight that is given to the last (and therefore assumed to be most important) piece of information available to the forecaster. However, the other expression in the formula includes the forecast for the current period which included the previous period's actual demand, and so on. In this way all previous data has a (diminishing) effect on the next forecast.

Example   Eurospeed parcels using exponential smoothing

Table 3.7 shows the data for Eurospeed's parcels forecasts using this exponential-smoothing method, where $\alpha = 0.2$. For example, the forecast for week 35 is:

$$F_{35} = (0.2 \times 67.0) + (0.8 \times 68.3) = 68.04$$

Table 3.7	Actual demand and exponentially smoothed forecast (thousands) calculated with smoothing constant $\alpha = 0.2$	
Week (t)	**Actual demand (A)**	**Forecast demand (F)**
20	63.3	60.00
21	62.5	60.66
22	67.8	60.03
23	66.0	61.58
24	67.2	62.83
25	69.9	63.70
26	65.6	64.94
27	71.1	65.07
28	68.8	66.28
29	68.4	66.78
30	70.3	67.12
31	72.5	67.75
32	66.7	68.70
33	68.3	68.30
34	67.0	68.30
35		68.04

The value of α governs the balance between the responsiveness of the forecasts to changes in demand, and the stability of the forecasts. The closer α is to 0 the more forecasts will be dampened by previous forecasts (not very sensitive but stable). Figure 3.14 shows the Eurospeed volume data plotted for a four-week moving average, exponential smoothing with $\alpha = 0.2$ and exponential smoothing with $\alpha = 0.3$.

Figure 3.14   A comparison of a moving-average forecast and exponential smoothing with the smoothing constant $\alpha = 0.2$ and 0.3

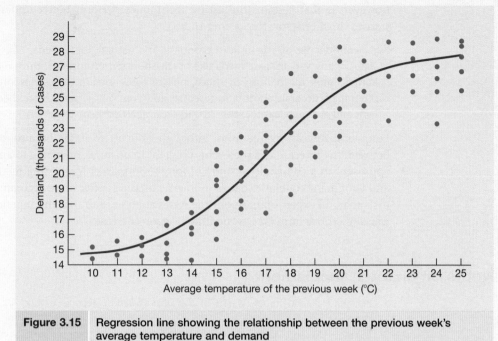

Figure 3.15   Regression line showing the relationship between the previous week's average temperature and demand

Causal models

Causal models often employ complex techniques to understand the strength of relationships between the network of variables and the impact they have on each other. Simple regression models try to determine the 'best fit' expression between two variables. For example, suppose an ice-cream company is trying to forecast its future sales. After examining previous demand, it figures that the main influence on demand at the factory is the average temperature of the previous week. To understand this relationship, the company plots demand against the previous week's temperatures. This is shown in Figure 3.15. Using this graph, the company can make a reasonable prediction of demand, once the average temperature is known, provided that the other conditions prevailing in the market are reasonably stable. If they are not, then these other factors that influence demand will need to be included in the regression model, which becomes increasingly complex.

These more complex networks comprise many variables and relationships each with its own set of assumptions and limitations. While developing such models and assessing the importance of each of the factors and understanding the network of interrelationships is beyond the scope of this text, many techniques are available to help managers undertake this more complex modelling and also feed data back into the model to further refine and develop it, in particular structural equation modelling.

The performance of forecasting models

Forecasting models are widely used in management decision-making, and indeed most decisions require a forecast of some kind, yet the performance of this type of model is far from impressive. Hogarth and Makridakis,[2] in a comprehensive review of the applied management and finance literature, show that the record of forecasters using both judgement and sophisticated mathematical methods is not good. What they do suggest, however, is that certain forecasting techniques perform better under certain circumstances. In short-term forecasting there is:

> . . . considerable inertia in most economic and natural phenomena. Thus the present states of any variables are predictive of the short-term future (i.e. three months or less). Rather simple mechanistic methods, such as those used in time series forecasts, can often make accurate short-term forecasts and even out-perform more theoretically elegant and elaborate approaches used in econometric forecasting.[3]

Long-term forecasting methods, although difficult to judge because of the time lapse between the forecast and the event, do seem to be more amenable to an objective causal approach. In a comparative study of long-term market forecasting methods, Armstrong and Grohman[4] conclude that econometric methods offer more accurate long-range forecasts than do expert opinion or time series analysis, and that the superiority of objective causal methods improves as the time horizon increases.

Notes on chapter supplement

1 Linstone, H.A. and Turoof, M. (1975) *The Delphi Method: Techniques and Applications,* Addison-Wesley.
2 Hogarth, R.M. and Makridakis, S. (1981) 'Forecasting and planning: an evaluation', *Management Science,* Vol. 27, pp. 115–38.
3 Hogarth and Makridakis, *op. cit.*
4 Armstrong, J.S. and Grohman, M.C. (1972) 'A comparative study of methods for long-range market forecasting', *Management Science,* Vol. 19, No. 2, pp. 211–21.

Taking it further

Hoyle, R.H. (ed.) (1995) *Structural Equation Modeling,* Sage, Thousand Oaks, CA. For the specialist.

Maruyama, G.M. (1997) *Basics of Structural Equation Modeling,* Sage, Thousand Oaks, CA. For the specialist.

4 PROCESS DESIGN 1 – POSITIONING

Introduction

Processes are everywhere. They are the building blocks of all operations, and their design will affect the performance of the whole operation and, eventually, the contribution it makes to its supply network. No one, in any function or part of the business, can fully contribute to its competitiveness if the processes in which they work are poorly designed. It is not surprising then that process design has become such a popular topic in the management press and among consultants. This chapter is the first of two that examine the design of processes. This first one is primarily concerned with how

processes and the resources they contain must reflect the volume and variety requirements placed on them (see Figure 4.1). The next chapter examines the more detailed and analytical aspects of process analysis.

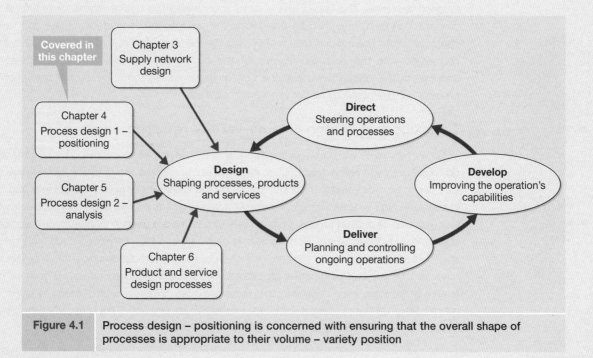

| Figure 4.1 | Process design – positioning is concerned with ensuring that the overall shape of processes is appropriate to their volume – variety position |

Executive summary

VIDEO
further detail

Decision logic chain for process design–positioning

Each chapter is structured around a set of diagnostic questions. These questions suggest what you should ask in order to gain an understanding of the important issues of a topic, and as a result, improve your decision making. An executive summary, addressing these questions, is provided below.

What is process design–positioning?

Process design is concerned with conceiving the overall shape of processes and their detailed workings. The first of these tasks (conceiving the overall shape or nature of the process) can be approached by positioning the process in terms of its volume and variety characteristics. The second task (conceiving the detailed workings of the process) is more concerned with the detailed analysis of the objectives, capacity and variability of the process. In this chapter we treat the first of these issues: how the overall nature of the process is determined by its volume–variety position.

Do processes match volume–variety requirements?

Volume and variety are particularly influential in the design of processes. They also tend to go together in an inverse relationship. High-variety processes are normally low-volume and vice versa. So processes can be positioned on the spectrum between low volume and high variety, and high volume and low variety. At different points on this spectrum processes can be described as distinct process 'types'. Different terms are used in manufacturing and services to identify these types. Working from low volume and high variety towards high volume and low variety, the process types are project processes, jobbing processes, batch processes, mass processes, and continuous processes. The same sequence is characterized as professional services, service shops, and mass services. Whatever terminology is used, the overall design of the process must fit its volume–variety position. This is usually summarized in the form of the 'product–process' matrix.

Are process layouts appropriate?

There are different ways in which the different resources within a process (people and technology) can be arranged relative to each other. But however this is done, it should reflect the process's volume–variety position. Again, there are pure 'types' of layout that correspond with the different volume–variety positions. These are fixed position layout, functional layout, cell layout, and product layout. Many layouts are hybrids of these pure types, but the type chosen is influenced by the volume and variety characteristics of the process.

Is process technology appropriate?

Process technologies are the machines, equipment and devices that help processes transform materials and information and customers. Process technology is different from the product technology that is embedded with the product or service itself. Again, process technology should reflect volume and variety. In particular, the degree of automation in the technology, the scale and/or scalability of the technology, and the coupling and/or connectivity of the technology, should all be appropriate to volume and variety. Generally, low volume and high variety requires relatively unautomated, general purpose, small-scale and flexible technologies. By contrast, high volume and low variety processes require automated, dedicated, large-scale technologies that are sometimes relatively inflexible.

Are job designs appropriate?

Job design is about how people carry out their tasks within a process. It is particularly important because it governs people's expectations and perceptions of their contribution to the organization as well as being a major factor in shaping the culture of the organization. Some aspects of job design are common to all processes irrespective of their volume and variety position. These are such things as ensuring the safety of everyone affected by the process, ensuring a firm ethical stance, and upholding an appropriate work/life balance. However, other aspects of job design are influenced by volume and variety, in particular the extent of division of labour, the degree to which jobs are defined, and the way in which job commitment is encouraged. Broadly, high variety and low volume processes require broad, relatively undefined jobs with decision-making discretion. Such jobs tend to have intrinsic job commitment. By contrast, high volume and low variety processes tend to require jobs that are relatively narrow in scope and closely defined with relatively little decision-making discretion. This means some deliberative action is needed in the design of the job (such as job enrichment) in order to help maintain commitment to the job.

DIAGNOSTIC QUESTION

What is process design–positioning?

To 'design' is to conceive the looks, arrangement and workings of something *before it is constructed*. In that sense it is a conceptual exercise. Yet it is one which must deliver a solution that will work in practice. Design is also an activity that can be approached at different levels of detail. One may envisage the general shape and intention of something before getting down to defining its details. However, it is often only through getting to grips with the detail of a design that the feasibility of its overall shape can be assessed. So it is with designing processes. First, one must consider the overall shape and nature of the process. The most common way of doing this is by positioning it according to its volume and variety characteristics. Second, one must analyze the details of the process in order to ensure that it fulfils its objectives effectively. But don't think of this as a simple sequential process. There may be aspects concerned with the broad positioning of the process that will need to be modified following its more detailed analysis.

In this chapter we discuss the more general approach to process design by showing how a process's position on the volume–variety scale will influence its layout and technology, and the design of its jobs. In the next chapter we will discuss the more detailed aspects of process design, in particular its objectives, current configuration, capacity and variability. This is illustrated in Figure 4.2.

Example   Supermarket processes[1]

Supermarkets don't just stack things at random; they know that the design of their stores has a huge impact on profitability. They must maximize their revenue per square metre and minimize the costs of operating the store. At a basic level, supermarkets have to get the amount of space allocated to

Figure 4.2   Process design is treated in two parts: Positioning, that sets the broad characteristics of the design; and Analysis, that refines the details of the design

Source: J. Sainsbury plc

the different areas right. For example, stores where there is a large peak of sales, say in the early evening, tend to have more space devoted to check-outs to avoid long queues at peak times. After that, the question is, 'How can store layout make customers buy more?' The circulation must be right. Supermarkets often put their entrance on the left-hand side of a building with a layout designed to take customers in a clockwise direction around the store. Aisles between the shelves should be wide enough to ensure a relatively slow flow of trolleys so that customers pay more attention to the products on display (and buy more). However, wide aisles can come at the expense of reduced shelf space that would allow a wider range of products to be stocked.

The actual location of all the products is a critical decision, directly affecting the convenience to cus-tomers, their level of spontaneous purchase, and the cost of filling the shelves. Although the majority of supermarket sales are packaged tinned or frozen goods, the displays of fruit and vegetables are usually located adjacent to the main entrance, as a signal of freshness and wholesomeness, provid-ing an attractive and welcoming point of entry. Basic products that figure on most people's shopping lists, such as flour, sugar and bread, are often located at the back of the store and apart from each other so that customers have to pass higher-margin items as they search. High-margin items are usu-ally put at eye level on shelves (where they are more likely to be seen) and low-margin products lower down or higher up. Some customers also go a few paces up an aisle before they start looking for what they need. Some supermarkets call the shelves occupying the first metre of an aisle 'dead space', not a place to put impulse-bought goods. But the prime site in a supermarket is the 'gondola-end', the shelves at the end of the aisle. Moving products to this location can increase sales 200 or 300 per cent. It is not surprising that suppliers are willing to pay for their products to be located here.

| Example | Chocolate and visitors are processed by Cadbury's |

Flow of chocolate

In the Cadbury's chocolate factory, on the outskirts of Birmingham, UK, chocolate products are manufactured to a high degree of consistency and efficiency. Production processes use specialist technology to meet the technical and capacity requirements of each stage of the process. In the production of Cadbury's Dairy Milk bars, the liquid chocolate is prepared from cocoa beans, fresh milk and sugar using equipment that is connected together with pipes and conveyors. These processes operate continuously, day and night, to ensure consistency of both the chocolate itself and the rate of output. The liquid chocolate is pumped through heated pipework to the moulding section, where it is dispensed into a moving line of precision-made plastic moulds that form the chocolate bars and vibrate them to remove any trapped air bubbles. The moulds are continuously

Nuts destined for chocolate products being processed

Customers being processed

Source: Courtesy Cadbury Trebor Bassett

conveyed into a large refrigerator, allowing sufficient time for the chocolate to harden. The next stage inverts the moulds and shakes out the bars. These then pass directly to a set of automated wrapping and packing machines, from where they go to the warehouse.

Flow of customers

Cadbury also have a large visitor centre called 'Cadbury World' alongside the factory (linked to a viewing area which looks onto the packaging area described above). It is a permanent exhibition devoted entirely to chocolate and the part Cadbury has played in its history. The design of the visitor centre uses a single route for all customers. The main exhibition and demonstration areas allow a smooth flow of visitors, avoiding bottlenecks and delays. Entry to the Exhibition Area is by timed ticket, to ensure a constant flow of visitors, who are free to walk around at their preferred speed, but are constrained to keep to the single track through the sequence of displays. On leaving this section, they are directed upstairs to the Chocolate Packaging Plant, where a guide escorts batches of visitors to where they can see the packing processes. The groups are then led down to and around the Demonstration Area, where skilled employees demonstrate small-scale production of handmade chocolates.

What do these two examples have in common?

All three operations described in these two examples operate with relatively high volume of demand. The chocolate factory produces identical products flowing using identical processes round the clock. It may make several products but variety is relatively low. The visitor centre, located next door, also has a high volume of visitors, but, unlike chocolate, they have a mind of their own. Yet, the process is designed to constrain the route that visitors take and therefore the variety of their experiences. Even more problematic is the plight of the supermarket, again with high volume, but what of its variety? Looked at one way, every customer is different and therefore variety will be extremely high. Yet, because of the way the process is designed, partly to encourage similarity of flow and partly by making customers 'customize' their own service, variety is made to seem very low. For example, checkout processes deal with only two 'products': customers with baskets and customers with trolleys. The important point is that in all three cases the volume and variety of demand (or how it is interpreted by the operation) has a profound effect on the design of the processes. Just think about the design of a small convenience store, or a small artisan chocolate manufacturer, or even a small visitor experience. Because they have different volume–variety characteristics, they would be designed in very different ways.

Do processes match volume–variety requirements?

Two factors are particularly important in process design: these are the *volume* and *variety* of the products and services that it processes. Moreover volume and variety are related in so much as low-volume operations processes often have a high variety of products and services, and high-volume operations processes often have a narrow variety of products and services. So, we can *position* processes on a continuum from those that operate under

Operations principle
The design of any process should be governed by the volume and variety it is required to produce.

conditions of low volume and high variety, through to those that operate under conditions of high volume and low variety. The volume–variety position of a process influences almost every aspect of its design. Processes with different volume–variety positions will be arranged in different ways, have different flow characteristics, and have different technology and jobs. So, the first steps in process design are to understand how volume and variety shape process characteristics, and to check whether processes have been configured in a manner that is appropriate for their volume–variety position. Think about the volume–variety characteristics of the following examples.

The 'product–process' matrix

The most common method of illustrating the relationship between a process's volume–variety position and its design characteristics is shown in Figure 4.3. Often called the 'product–process' matrix, it can in fact be used for any type of process, whether producing products or services. Its underlying idea of the product–process matrix is that many of the more important elements of process design are strongly related to the volume–variety position of the process. So, for any process, the tasks that it undertakes, the flow of items through the process, the layout of its resources, the technology it uses, and the design of jobs, are all strongly influenced by its volume–variety position. This means that most processes should lie close to the diagonal of the matrix that represents the 'fit' between the process and its volume–variety position. This is called the 'natural' diagonal.[2]

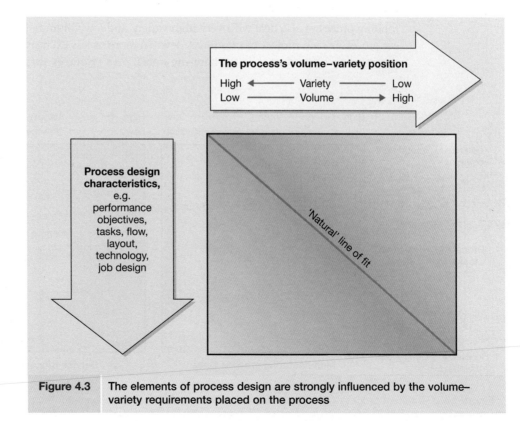

Figure 4.3   The elements of process design are strongly influenced by the volume–variety requirements placed on the process

Process types

Processes that inhabit different points on the diagonal of the product–process matrix are sometimes referred to as 'process types'. Each process type implies differences in the set of tasks performed by the process and in the way materials or information or customers flow through the process. Different terms are sometimes used to identify process types depending on whether they are predominantly manufacturing or service processes and there is some variation in how the names are used. This is especially so in service process types. It is not uncommon to find manufacturing terms used also to describe service processes. Perhaps most importantly, there is some degree of overlap between process types. The different process types are shown in Figure 4.4.

> **Operations principle**
> Process types indicate the position of processes on the volume–variety spectrum.

Project processes

Project processes are those that deal with discrete, usually highly customized products. Often the time scale of making the product is relatively long, as is the interval between the completions of each product. The activities involved in the process may be ill-defined and uncertain, sometimes changing during the process itself. Examples include advertising agencies, shipbuilding, most construction companies· and movie production companies, drilling oil wells and installing computer systems. Any process map for project processes will almost certainly be complex, partly because each unit of output is usually large with many activities occurring at the same time and partly because the activities often involve significant discretion to act according to professional judgement. In fact a process map for a whole project would be extremely complex, so rarely would a project be mapped, but small parts may be.

Jobbing processes

Jobbing processes also deal with very high variety and low volumes, but whereas in project processes each project has resources devoted more or less exclusively to it, in jobbing processes each 'product' has to share the operation's resources with many others. The

Figure 4.4   Different process types imply different volume–variety characteristics for the process

process will work on a series of products but, although all the products will require the same kind of attention, each will differ in its exact needs. Examples of jobbing processes include many precision engineers such as specialist toolmakers, furniture restorers, 'make-to-measure' tailors, and the printer who produces tickets for the local social event. Jobbing processes produce more and usually smaller items than project processes but, like project processes, the degree of repetition is low. Many jobs could be 'one-offs'. Again, any process map for a jobbing process could be relatively complex for similar reasons to project processes. Although jobbing processes sometimes involve considerable skill, they are usually more predictable than project processes.

Batch processes

Batch processes can look like jobbing processes, but without the degree of variety normally associated with jobbing. As the name implies, batch processes usually produce more than one 'product' at a time. So each part of the operation has periods when it is repeating itself, at least while the 'batch' is being processed. The size of the batch could be just two or three, in which case the batch process would differ little from jobbing, especially if each batch is a totally novel product. Conversely, if the batches are large, and especially if the products are familiar to the operation, batch processes can be fairly repetitive. Because of this, the batch type of process can be found over a wider range of volume and variety levels than other process types. Examples of batch processes include machine tool manufacturing, the production of some special gourmet frozen foods, the manufacture of most of the component parts that go into mass-produced assemblies such as automobiles, and the production of most clothing. Batch process maps may look straightforward, especially if different products take similar routes through the process with relatively standard activities being performed at each stage.

Mass processes

Mass processes produce in high volume, usually with narrow effective variety. An automobile plant, for example, might produce several thousand variants of car if every option of engine size, colour and equipment is taken into account. Yet its effective variety is low because the different variants do not affect the basic process of production. The activities in the automobile plant, like all mass processes, are essentially repetitive and largely predictable. In addition to the automobile plant, examples of mass processes include consumer durable manufacturers, most food processes such as a frozen pizza manufacturer, beer bottling plants and CD production. Process maps for this type of process will be straightforward sequences of activities.

Continuous processes

Continuous processes are one step beyond mass processes in so much as they operate at even higher volume and often have even lower variety. Sometimes they are literally continuous in that their products are inseparable, being produced in an endless flow. Continuous processes are often associated with relatively inflexible, capital-intensive technologies with highly predictable flow. Examples of continuous processes include petrochemical refineries, electricity utilities, steelmaking and Internet server firms. Like mass processes, process maps will show few elements of discretion, and although products may be stored during the process, the predominant characteristic of most continuous processes is of smooth flow from one part of the process to another.

Professional services

Professional services are high-variety, low-volume processes, where customers may spend a considerable time in the service process. Such services usually provide high levels of customization, so contact staff are given considerable discretion. They tend to be people-based rather than equipment-based, with emphasis placed on the process (how the service is delivered) as much as the 'product' (what is delivered). Examples include management consultants, lawyers' practices, architects, doctors' surgeries, auditors, health and safety inspectors and some computer field service operations. Where process maps are used they are likely to be drawn predominantly at a high level. Consultants, for example, frequently use a predetermined set of broad stages, starting with understanding the real nature of the problem through to the implementation of their recommended solutions. This high-level process map guides the nature and sequence of the consultants' activities.

Service shops

Service shops are characterized by levels of customer contact, customization, volume of customers and staff discretion that position them between the extremes of professional and mass services (see next paragraph). Service is provided via a mix of front- and back-office activities. Service shops include banks, high street shops, holiday tour operators, car rental companies, schools, most restaurants, hotels and travel agents. For example, an equipment hire and sales organization may have a range of equipment displayed in front-office outlets, while back-office operations look after purchasing and administration. The front-office staff have some technical training and can advise customers during the process of selling the product. Essentially the customer is buying a fairly standardized 'product' but will be influenced by the process of the sale which is customized to the individual customer's needs.

Mass services

Mass services have many customer transactions and little customization. Such services are often predominantly equipment-based and 'product' oriented, with most value added in the back-office, sometimes with comparatively little judgement needed by front-office staff who may have a closely defined job and follow set procedures. Mass services include supermarkets, a national rail network, airports, and many call centres. For example, airlines move a large number of passengers on their networks. Passengers pick a journey from the range offered. The airline can advise passengers on the quickest or cheapest way to get from A to B, but they cannot 'customize' the service by putting on special flights for them.

Moving off the natural diagonal

A process lying on the natural diagonal of the matrix shown in Figure 4.3 will normally have lower operating costs than one with the same volume–variety position that lies off the diagonal. This is because the diagonal represents the most appropriate process design for any volume–variety position. Processes that are on the right of the 'natural' diagonal would normally be associated with lower volumes and higher variety. This means that they are likely to be more flexible than seems to be warranted by their actual volume–variety position. That is, they are not taking advantage of their ability to standardize their activities. Because of this, their costs are likely to be higher than they would be with a process that was closer to the diagonal. Conversely, processes that are on the left of the diagonal have adopted a position that would normally be used for higher volume and lower variety processes. Processes will therefore be 'over-standardized' and probably too inflexible for their volume–variety position. This lack of flexibility can also lead to high costs because the process will not be able to change from one activity to another as readily as a more flexible process. One note of caution regarding this idea: although logically coherent, it is a conceptual model rather than something that can be 'scaled'. Although it is intuitively

> **Operations principle**
> Moving off the 'natural diagonal' of the product–process matrix will incur excess cost.

obvious that deviating from the diagonal increases costs, the precise amount by which costs will increase is very difficult to determine. Nevertheless, a first step in examining the design of an existing process is to check whether it is on the natural diagonal of the product–process matrix. The volume–variety position of the process may have changed without any corresponding change in its design. Alternatively, design changes may have been introduced without considering their suitability for the process's volume–variety position.

FURTHER EXAMPLE

Example

Meter installation[3]

The 'meter installation' unit of a water utility company installed and repaired water meters. The nature of each installation job could vary significantly because the metering requirements of each customer varied and because meters had to be fitted into various different water pipe systems. When a customer requested an installation or repair a supervisor would survey the customer's water system and transfer the results of the survey to the installation team of skilled plumbers. An appointment would then be made for a plumber to visit the customer's location and install or repair the meter on the agreed appointment date. The company decided to install free of charge a new 'standard' remote-reading meter that would replace the wide range of existing meters and could be read automatically using the customer's telephone line. This would save meter reading costs. It also meant a significant increase in work for the unit and more skilled plumbing staff were recruited. The new meter was designed to make installation easier by including universal quick-fit joints that reduced pipe cutting and jointing during installation. As a pilot, it was also decided to prioritize those customers with the oldest meters and conduct trials of how the new meter worked in practice. All other aspects of the installation process were left as they were.

The pilot was not a success. Customers with older meters were distributed throughout the company's area, so staff could not service several customers in one area and had to travel relatively long distances between customers. Also, because customers had not initiated the visit themselves, they were more likely to have forgotten the appointment, in which case plumbers had to return to their base and try to find other work to do. The costs of installation were proving to be far higher than forecast and the plumbers were frustrated at the waste of their time and the now relatively standardized installation job. The company decided to change its process. Rather than replace the oldest meters which were spread around its region, it targeted smaller geographic areas to limit travelling time. It also cut out the survey stage of the process because, using the new meter, 98 per cent of installations could be fitted in one visit, minimizing disruption to the customer and the number of missed appointments. Just as significantly, fully qualified plumbers were often not needed, so installation could be performed by less expensive labour.

This example is illustrated in Figure 4.5. The initial position of the installation process is at point A. The installation unit was required to repair and install a wide variety of meters into a very wide variety of water systems. This needed a survey stage to assess the nature of the job and the use of skilled labour to cope with the complex tasks. The installation of the new type of meter changed the volume–variety position for the process by reducing the variety of jobs tackled by the process and increasing the volume it had to cope with. However, the process was not changed. By choosing a wide geographic area to service, retaining the unnecessary survey stage and hiring over-skilled staff, the company was still defining itself as a high-variety, low-volume 'jobbing' process. The design of the process was appropriate for its old volume–variety position, but not the new one. In effect it had moved to point B in Figure 4.5. It was off the diagonal, with unnecessary flexibility and high operating costs. Redesigning the process to take advantage of the reduced variety and complexity of the job (position C on Figure 4.5) allowed installation to be performed far more efficiently.

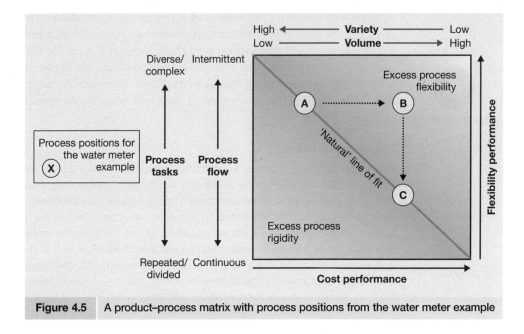

Figure 4.5   A product–process matrix with process positions from the water meter example

Layout, technology and design

If movement down the natural diagonal of the product–process matrix changes the nature of a process, then the key elements of its design will also change. At this broad level, these 'key elements' of the design are the two 'ingredients' that make up processes, technology and people, and the way in which these ingredients are arranged within the process relative to each other. This latter aspect is usually called *layout*. In the remainder of the chapter, we start by discussing layout and then the design decisions that relate to process technology and the jobs that the people within the process undertake.

DIAGNOSTIC QUESTION

Are process layouts appropriate?

There is little point in having a well-sequenced process if in reality its activities are physically located in a way that involves excessive movement of materials, information or customers. Usually the objective of the layout decision is to minimize movement, but, especially in information transforming process where distance is largely irrelevant, other criteria may dominate. For example, it may be more important to lay out processes such that similar activities or resources are grouped together. So, an international bank may group its foreign exchange dealers together to encourage communication and discussion between them, even though the 'trades' they make are processed in an entirely different location. Some high visibility processes may fix their layout to emphasize the behaviour of the customers who are being processed.

Layout should reflect volume and variety

Again, the layout of a process is determined partly by its volume and variety characteristics. When volume is very low and variety is relatively high, 'flow' may not be a major issue. For example, in telecommunications satellite manufacture each product is different, and because products 'flow' through the operation very infrequently, it is not worth arranging facilities to minimize the flow of parts through the operation. With higher volume and lower variety, flow becomes a far more important issue. If variety is still high, however, an entirely flow-dominated arrangement is difficult because there will be different flow patterns. For example, a library will arrange its different categories of books and its other services partly to minimize the average distance its customers have to 'flow' through the operation. But, because its customers' needs vary, it will arrange its layout to satisfy the majority of its customers (but perhaps inconvenience a minority). When the variety of products or services reduces to the point where a distinct 'category' with similar requirements becomes evident but variety is still not small, appropriate resources could be grouped into a separate cell. When variety is relatively small and volume is high, flow can become regularized and resources can be positioned to address the (similar) needs of the products or services, as in a classic flow line.

> **Operations principle**
> Resources in low volume-high variety processes should be arranged to cope with irregular flow.

> **Operations principle**
> Resources in high volume-low variety processes should be arranged to cope with smooth, regular flow.

Most practical layouts are derived from only four *basic layout types* that correspond to different positions on the volume–variety spectrum. These are illustrated diagrammatically in Figure 4.6 and are as follows.

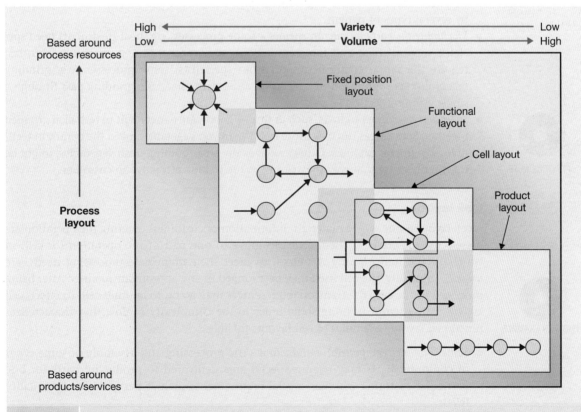

Figure 4.6   Different process layouts are appropriate for different volume–variety combinations

Fixed-position layout

Fixed-position layout is in some ways a contradiction in terms, since the transformed resources do not move between the transforming resources. Instead of materials, information or customers flowing through an operation, the recipient of the processing is stationary and the equipment, machinery, plant and people who do the processing move as necessary. This could be because the product or the recipient of the service is too large to be moved conveniently, or it might be too delicate to move, or perhaps it could object to being moved; for example:

- *Power generator construction* – the product is too large to move.
- *Open-heart surgery* – patients are too delicate to move.
- *High-class restaurant* – customers would object to being moved to where food is prepared.

Functional layout

Functional layout is so called because the functional needs and convenience of the transforming resources that constitute the processes dominate the layout decision. (Confusingly, functional layout can also be called 'process layout'.) In functional layout, similar activities or resources (or those with similar needs) are located together. This may be because it is convenient to group them together, or that their utilization can be improved. It means that when materials, information or customers flow through the operation, they will take a route from activity to activity according to their needs. Usually this makes the flow pattern in the operation complex. Examples of process layouts include:

- *Hospital* – some processes (e.g. radiography equipment and laboratories) are required by several types of patient.
- *Machining the parts for aircraft engines* – some processes (e.g. heat treatment) need specialist support (heat and fume extraction); some processes (e.g. machining centres) require the same technical support from specialists; some processes (e.g. grinding machines) get high machine utilization as all parts that need grinding pass through a single grinding section.
- *Supermarket* – some products, such as tinned goods, are convenient to restock if grouped together. Some areas, such as those holding frozen vegetables, need the common technology of freezer cabinets. Others, such as the areas holding fresh vegetables, might be together because that way they can be made to look attractive to customers.

PRACTICE NOTE

Cell layout

FURTHER EXAMPLE

A cell layout is one where materials, information or customers entering the operation are preselected (or preselect themselves) to move to one part of the operation (or cell) in which all the transforming resources, to meet their immediate processing needs, are located. Internally, the cell itself may be arranged in any appropriate manner. After being processed in the cell, the transformed resources may go on to another cell. In effect, cell layout is an attempt to bring some order to the complexity of flow that characterizes functional layout. Examples of cell layouts include:

- *Some computer component manufacture* – the processing and assembly of some types of computer parts may need a special area dedicated to producing parts for one particular customer who has special requirements such as particularly high quality levels.

- *'Lunch' products area in a supermarket* – some customers use the supermarket just to purchase sandwiches, savoury snacks, cool drinks, etc. for their lunch. These products are often located close together in a 'cell' for the convenience of these customers.
- *Maternity unit in a hospital* – customers needing maternity attention are a well-defined group who can be treated together and who are unlikely to need the other facilities of the hospital at the same time that they need the maternity unit.

Product layout

Product layout involves locating people and equipment entirely for the convenience of the transformed resources. Each product, piece of information or customer follows a pre-arranged route in which the sequence of required activities corresponds to the sequence in which the processes have been located. The transformed resources 'flow' along a 'line'. This is why this type of layout is sometimes called flow or line layout. Flow is clear, predictable and therefore relatively easy to control. It is the high volume and standardized requirements of the product or service that allows product layouts. Examples of product layout include:

- *Automobile assembly* – almost all variants of the same model require the same sequence of processes.
- *Self-service cafeteria* – generally the sequence of customer requirements (starter, main course, dessert, drink) is common to all customers, but layout also helps control customer flow.

Layout selection

Getting the process layout right is important, if only because of the cost, difficulty and disruption of making any layout change. It is not an activity many businesses would want to repeat very often. Also, an inappropriate layout could mean that extra cost is incurred *every time* an item is processed. But more than this, an effective layout gives clarity and transparency to the flow of items through a process. There is no better way of emphasizing that everyone's activities are really part of an overall process than by making the flow between activities evident to everyone.

One of the main influences on which type of layout will be appropriate is the nature of the process itself, as summarized in its 'process type'. There is often some confusion between process types and layout types. Layout types are not the same as process types. Process types were described earlier in the chapter and indicate a broad approach to the organization and operation of a process. Layout is a narrower concept but is very clearly linked to process type. Just as process type is governed by volume and variety, so is layout. But for any given process type there are usually at least two alternative layouts. Table 4.1 summarizes the alternative layouts for particular process types. Which of these is selected, or whether some hybrid layout is chosen, depends on the relative importance of the performance objectives of the process, especially cost and flexibility. Table 4.2 summarizes.

Table 4.1   Alternative layout types for each process type

Manufacturing process type	Potential layout types		Service process type
Project	Fixed position layout Functional layout	Fixed position layout Functional layout Cell layout	Professional service
Jobbing	Functional layout Cell layout		
Batch	Functional layout Cell layout	Functional layout Cell layout	Service shop
Mass	Cell layout Product layout		
Continuous	Product layout	Cell layout Product layout	Mass service

Table 4.2   The advantages and disadvantages of the basic layout types

	Advantages	Disadvantages
Fixed-position	Very high mix and product flexibility Product or customer not moved or disturbed High variety of tasks for staff	High unit costs Scheduling of space and activities can be difficult Can mean much movement of plant and staff
Functional	High mix and product flexibility Relatively robust if in the case of disruptions Relatively easy supervision of equipment or plant	Low facilities utilization Can have very high work-in-progress or customer queuing Complex flow can be difficult to control
Cell	Can give a good compromise between cost and flexibility for relatively high-variety operations Fast throughput Group work can result in good motivation	Can be costly to rearrange existing layout Can need more plant and equipment Can give lower plant utilization
Product	Low unit costs for high volume Gives opportunities for specialization of equipment Materials or customer movement is convenient	Can have low mix flexibility Not very robust if there is disruption Work can be very repetitive

Is process technology appropriate?

Process technologies are the machines, equipment and devices that help processes 'transform' materials and information and customers. This is a particularly important issue because few operations have been unaffected by the advances in process technology over the last two decades. And the pace of technological development is not slowing down. But it is important to distinguish between *process technology* (the machines and devices that help to *create* products and services) and *product technology* (the technology that is embedded within the product or service and creates its specification or functionality). Some process technology, although not used for the actual creation of goods and services, nonetheless plays a key role in *facilitating* their creation. For example, the information technology systems that run planning and control activities can be used to help managers and operators run the processes. Sometimes this type of technology is called *indirect* process technology, and it is becoming increasingly important. Many businesses spend more on the computer systems that run their processes than they do on the direct process technology that creates their products and services.

Process technology should reflect volume and variety

Again, different process technologies will be appropriate for different parts of the volume–variety continuum. High variety–low volume processes generally require process technology that is *general purpose,* because it can perform the wide range of processing activities that high variety demands. High volume–low variety processes can use technology that is more *dedicated* to its narrower range of processing requirements. Within the spectrum from general purpose to dedicated process technologies, three dimensions in particular tend to vary with volume and variety. The first is the extent to which the process technology carries out activities or makes decisions for itself, that is, its degree of 'automation'. The second is the capacity of the technology to process work, that is, its 'scale' or 'scalability'. The third is the extent to which it is integrated with other technologies; that is, its degree of 'coupling' or 'connectivity'. Figure 4.7 illustrates these three dimensions of process technology.[4]

> **Operations principle**
> Process technology in high volume, low variety processes is relatively automated, large-scale and closely coupled when compared to that in low volume, high variety processes.

The degree of automation of the technology

To some extent, all technology needs human intervention. It may be minimal, for example the interventions for periodic maintenance in a petrochemical refinery. Conversely, the person who operates the technology may be the entire 'brains' of the process, for example the surgeon using keyhole surgery techniques. Generally, processes that have high variety and low volume employ process technology with lower degrees of automation than those with higher volume and lower variety. For example, investment banks trade in highly complex and sophisticated financial 'derivatives', often customized to the needs of individual clients, and each may be worth millions of dollars. The back-office of

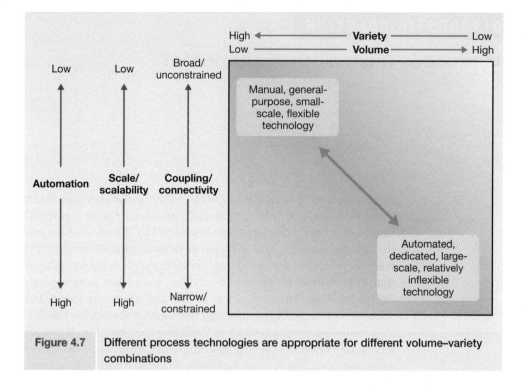

Figure 4.7   Different process technologies are appropriate for different volume–variety combinations

the bank has to process these deals to make sure that payments are made on time, documents are exchanged, and so on. Much of this processing will be done using relatively general-purpose technology such as spreadsheets. Skilled back-office staff are making the decisions rather than the technology. Contrast this with higher-volume, low variety financial products, such as straightforward equity (stock) trades. Most of these products are simple and straightforward and are processed in very high volume of several thousand per day by 'automated' technology.

FURTHER EXAMPLE

The scale/scalability of the technology

There is usually some discretion as to the scale of individual units of technology. For example, the duplicating department of a large office complex may decide to invest in a single, very large, fast copier, or alternatively in several smaller, slower copiers distributed around the operation's various processes. An airline may purchase one or two wide-bodied aircraft or a larger number of smaller aircraft. The advantage of large-scale technologies is that they can usually process items more cheaply than small-scale technologies, but usually need high volume and can cope only with low variety. By contrast, the virtues of smaller-scale technology are often the nimbleness and flexibility that is suited to high-variety, lower-volume processing. For example, four small machines can between them produce four different products simultaneously (albeit slowly), whereas a single large machine with four times the output can produce only one product at a time (albeit faster). Small-scale technologies are also more robust. Suppose the choice is between three small machines and one larger one. In the first case, if one machine breaks down, a third of the capacity is lost, but in the second, capacity is reduced to zero.

The equivalent to scale for some types of information processing technology is *scalability*. By scalability we mean the ability to shift to a different level of useful capacity quickly and cost-effectively. Scalability is similar to absolute scale in so much as it is influenced by the same volume–variety characteristics. IT scalability relies on consistent

IT platform architecture and the high process standardization that is usually associated with high-volume and low-variety operations.

The coupling/connectivity of the technology

Coupling means the linking together of separate activities within a single piece of process technology to form an interconnected processing system. Tight coupling usually gives fast process throughput. For example, in an automated manufacturing system products flow quickly without delays between stages, and inventory will be lower–it can't accumulate when there are no 'gaps' between activities. Tight coupling also means that flow is simple and predictable, making it easier to keep track of parts when they pass through fewer stages, or information when it is automatically distributed to all parts of an information network. However, closely coupled technology can be both expensive (each connection may require capital costs) and vulnerable (a failure in one part of an interconnected system can affect the whole system). The fully integrated manufacturing system constrains parts to flow in a predetermined manner, making it difficult to accommodate products with very different processing requirements. So, coupling is generally more suited to relatively low variety and high volume. Higher-variety processing generally requires a more open and unconstrained level of coupling because different products and services will require a wider range of processing activities.

DIAGNOSTIC QUESTION

Are job designs appropriate?

Job design is about how people carry out their tasks within a process. It defines the way they go about their working lives. It positions the expectations of what is required of them, and it influences their perceptions of how they contribute to the organization. It also defines their activities in relation to their work colleagues and it channels the flows of communication between different parts of the operation. But, of most importance, it helps to develop the culture of the organization – its shared values, beliefs and assumptions. Inappropriately designed jobs can destroy the potential of a process to fulfil its objectives, no matter how appropriate its layout or process technology. So jobs must be designed to fit the nature of the process. However, before considering this, it is important to accept that some aspects of job design are common to all processes, irrespective of what they do or how they do it. Consider the following.

- *Safety.* The primary and universal objective of job design is to ensure that all staff performing any task within a process are protected against the possibility of physical or mental harm.
- *Ethical issues.* No individual should be asked to perform any task that either is illegal or (within limits) conflicts with strongly held ethical beliefs.
- *Work/life balance.* All jobs should be structured so as to promote a healthy balance between time spent at work and time away from work.

Note that all these objectives of job design are also likely to improve overall process performance. However, the imperative to follow such objectives for their own sake transcends conventional criteria.

Job design should reflect volume and variety

As with other aspects of process design, the nature and challenges of job design are governed largely by the volume–variety characteristics of a process. An architect designing major construction projects will perform a wide range of very different, often creative and complex tasks, many of which are not defined at the start of the process, and most of which have the potential to give the architect significant job satisfaction. By contrast, someone in the architect's accounts office keying in invoice details has a job that is repetitive, has little variation, is tightly defined and that cannot rely on the intrinsic interest of the task itself to maintain job commitment. These two jobs will have different characteristics because they are part of processes with different volume and variety positions. Three aspects of job design in particular are affected by the volume–variety characteristics of a process: how tasks are to be allocated to each person in the process, the degree of job definition, and the methods used to maintain job commitment. Figure 4.8 illustrates this.

> **Operations principle**
> Job designs in high volume, low variety processes are relatively closely defined with little decision-making discretion and needing action to help commitment when compared to those in low volume, high variety processes.

How should tasks be allocated? – the division of labour

The most obvious aspect of any individual's job is how big it is, that is how many of the tasks within any process are allocated to an individual. Should a single individual perform

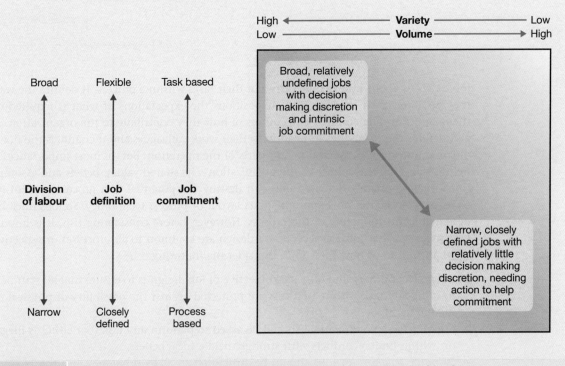

Figure 4.8   Different job designs are appropriate for different volume–variety combinations

the whole of the process? Alternatively, should separate individuals or teams perform each task? Separating tasks into smaller parts between individuals is called the *division of labour*. Perhaps its epitome is the assembly line, where products move along a single path and are built up by operators continually repeating a single task. This is the predominant model of job design in most high volume–low variety processes. For such processes there are some *real advantages* in division-of-labour principles:

- *They promote faster learning*. It is obviously easier to learn how to do a relatively short and simple task than a long and complex one, so new members of staff can be quickly trained and assigned to their tasks.
- *Automation becomes easier*. Substituting technology for labour is considerably easier for short and simple tasks than for long and complex ones.
- *Non-productive work is reduced*. In large, complex tasks the proportion of time between individual value-adding elements can be very high, for example in manufacturing, picking up tools and materials, putting them down again and generally searching and positioning.

There are also *serious drawbacks* to highly divided jobs:

- *The work is monotonous*. Repeating the same task for eight hours a day and five days a week is not fulfilling. This may lead to an increased likelihood of absenteeism, staff turnover and error rates.
- *It can cause physical injury*. The continued repetition of a very narrow range of movements can, in extreme cases, lead to physical injury. The over-use of some parts of the body (especially the arms, hands and wrists) can result in pain and a reduction in physical capability, called repetitive strain injury (RSI).
- *It can mean low flexibility*. Dividing a task into many small parts often gives the job design a rigidity that is difficult to change under changing circumstances. For example, if an assembly line has been designed to make one particular product but then has to change to manufacture a quite different product, the whole line will need redesigning. This will probably involve changing every operator's set of tasks.
- *It can mean poor robustness*. Highly divided jobs imply items passing between several stages. If one of these stages is not working correctly, for example because some equipment is faulty, the whole operation is affected. On the other hand, if each person is performing the whole of the job, any problems will affect only that one person's output.

To what degree should jobs be defined?

Jobs in high-variety processes are difficult to define in anything but the most general terms. Such jobs may require tacit knowledge gained over time and through experience and often require individuals to exercise significant discretion in what they do and how they do it. Some degree of job definition is usually possible and advisable, but it may be stated in terms of the 'outcome' from the task rather than in terms of the activities within the task. For example, the architect's job may be defined in terms of *'achieving overall coordination, taking responsibility for articulating the overall vision of the project, ensuring stakeholders are comfortable with the process, etc.'* By contrast, a process with less variety and higher volume is likely to be defined more closely, with the exact nature of each activity defined and individual staff trained to follow a job step-by-step.

How should job commitment be encouraged?

Many factors may influence job commitment. An individual's job history and expectations, relationships with co-workers and personal circumstances can all be important.

So are the volume and variety characteristics of the process by defining the possible ways in which commitment can be enhanced. In high-variety processes, especially those with a high degree of staff discretion, job commitment is likely to come from the *intrinsic nature of the task* itself. Exercising skill and decision making, for example, can bring their own satisfaction. Of course, commitment can be enhanced through extra responsibility, flexibility in working times and so on, but the main motivator is the job itself. By contrast, low variety–high volume jobs, especially those designed with a high division of labour and little discretion, can be highly alienating. Such jobs have relatively little intrinsic task satisfaction. It has to be *'designed into' the process* by emphasizing the satisfaction to be gained from the performance of the process as a whole. A number of job design approaches have been suggested for achieving this in processes involving relatively repetitive work.

- **Job enlargement** involves allocating a larger number of tasks to individuals, usually by combining tasks that are broadly of the same type as those in the original job. This may not involve more demanding or fulfilling tasks, but it may provide a more complete and therefore slightly more meaningful job. If nothing else, people performing an enlarged job will not repeat themselves as often. For example, suppose that the manufacture of a product has traditionally been split up on an assembly-line basis into 10 equal and sequential jobs. If that job is then redesigned so as to form two parallel assembly lines of five people, each operator would have twice the number of tasks to perform.

- **Job enrichment** like job enlargement, increases the number of tasks in a job, but also implies allocating tasks that involve more decision-making, or greater autonomy, and therefore greater control over the job. These could include the maintenance of, and adjustments to, any process technology used, the planning and control of activities within the job, or the monitoring of quality levels. The effect is both to reduce repetition in the job *and* to increase personal development opportunities. So, in the assembly-line example, each operator could also be allocated responsibility for carrying out routine maintenance and such tasks as record-keeping and managing the supply of materials.

- **Job rotation** means moving individuals periodically between different sets of tasks to provide some variety in their activities. When successful, job rotation can increase skill flexibility and make a small contribution to reducing monotony. However, it is not always viewed as beneficial either by management (because it can disrupt the smooth flow of work) or by the people performing the jobs (because it can interfere with their rhythm of work).

- **Empowerment** means enhancing individuals' ability, and sometimes authority, to change how they do their jobs. Some technologically constrained processes, such as those in chemical plants, may limit the extent to which staff can dilute their highly standardized task methods without consultation. Other less defined processes to empowerment may go much further.

- **Team-working** is closely linked to empowerment. Team-based work organization (sometimes called self-managed work teams) is where staff, often with overlapping skills, collectively perform a defined task and have some discretion over how they perform the task. The team may control such things as task allocation between members, scheduling work, quality measurement and improvement, and sometimes even the hiring of staff. Groups are described as 'teams' when the virtues of working together are being emphasized and a shared set of objectives and responsibilities is assumed.

PRACTICE NOTE

Critical commentary

Each chapter contains a short critical commentary on the main ideas covered in the chapter. Its purpose is not to undermine the issues discussed in the chapter, but to emphasize that, although we present a relatively orthodox view of operation, there are other perspectives.

■ Three sets of criticisms could be prompted by the material covered in this chapter. The first relates to the separation of process design into two parts – positioning and analysis. It can reasonably be argued that this separation is artificial in so much as (as is admitted at the beginning of this chapter) the two approaches are very much interrelated. An alternative way of thinking about the topic would be to consider all aspects of the arrangement of resources together. This would include the issues of layout that have been discussed in this chapter together with the more detailed process mapping issues to be described in Chapter 5. The second criticism would challenge the core assumption of the chapter – that many significant process design decisions are influenced primarily by volume and variety. Whereas it is conventional to relate layout and (to a slightly lesser extent) process technology to volume–variety positioning, it is less conventional to do so for issues of job design. Some would argue that the vast majority of job design decisions will not vary significantly with volume and variety. The final criticism is also related to job design. Some academics would argue that our treatment of job design is too influenced by the discredited (in their eyes) principles of the 'scientific' management movement that grew into 'work study' and 'time and motion' management.

Summary checklist

This checklist comprises questions that can be usefully applied to any type of operations and reflect the major diagnostic questions used within the chapter.

☐ Do processes match volume–variety requirements?

☐ Are 'process types' understood and do they match volume–variety requirements?

☐ Can processes be positioned on the 'diagonal' of the product–process matrix?

☐ Are the consequences of moving away from the 'diagonal' of the product–process matrix understood?

☐ Are the implications of choosing an appropriate layout, especially the balance between process flexibility and low processing costs, understood?

☐ Are the process layouts appropriate?

☐ Which of the four basic layout types that correspond to different positions on the volume–variety spectrum is appropriate for each process?

☐ Is process technology appropriate?

☐ Is the effect of the three dimensions of process technology (the degree of automation, the scale/scalability, and the coupling/connectivity of the technology) understood?

☐ Are job designs appropriate?

☐ Does job design ensure the imperative to design jobs that are safe and ethical, and promote adequate work/life balance?

☐ Is the extent of division of labour in each process appropriate for its volume–variety characteristics?

☐ Is the extent of job definition in each process appropriate for its volume–variety characteristics?

☐ Are job commitment mechanisms in each process appropriate for its volume–variety characteristics?

North West Constructive Bank – The New Mortgage Centre 1

It had been a long day for Andy Curtis when he emerged from the meeting. In spite of the early May sunshine he looked pale when he gathered his team around him. *'It was terrible in there. The Marketing people gave me a really tough time when I reported our current average turnaround times. They were quite happy to remind me that I had told them our "discount rate" product was killing us operationally and that we had to pull it if we were to survive the reorganization. I've been made to look stupid because now, four weeks after reorganization **and** after the product has been pulled, our turnaround times are even worse. I think they **are** right, we really are a shambles.'* Mary Godfrey, his deputy, was protective of her staff and offended that Marketing was calling her team a shambles. *'It's no use blaming us, the staff are working flat out but we can't seem to make any inroads to the piles of work.'*

Andy Curtis was the Mortgage Operations Manager for North West Constructive Bank (NWCB), a large retail banking group with a mid-sized mortgage business. His main responsibility was running the new applications process in the bank's new mortgage centre. For twelve months Andy had led a project team that had been planning the consolidation of the bank's original three mortgage processing centres into one new site. Prior to the consolidation, the bank's mortgage business had been divided into three regions: 'Northern', 'Southern', and 'Western' applications. *'The driver for the consolidation was to achieve economies of scale. There is no reason why a processing centre need be located close to its market and we could make significant savings by giving up our city centre leases on the three old sites, consolidating all our operations on a single floor of the bank's main headquarters building. We also felt that there would be room to develop more flexibility between the three regions when demand varied.'*

Andy and his team had always known that the merger of the three centres could be difficult; that is why they had planned it for early February, before the spring peak in applications. It was also why they had decided to (at least initially) keep the three regional sets of processing cells located close to each other. Figure 4.9 shows the current layout of the new mortgage floor.

Seven months ago, about halfway through the team's planning process, it became clear that the bank's port-

Source: Courtesy Leeds Building Society

folio of mortgage products would be changing. It was accepted that the bank's marketing strategy had been excessively reactive to competitor activity. *'Every time one of our competitors introduced a new mortgage product, we tried to copy them. Sometimes this worked, sometimes it didn't. But we were left with a confusing and incoherent legacy of products that neither our agents nor our branches fully understood. Also, we felt that there was considerable opportunity to develop products that satisfied specific market segments but could fit into a relatively standard back office process. For example, we will introduce "The Flexible Mortgage", targeted at people with fluctuating incomes, but as far as our back-office is concerned, it will require almost the same processing steps as a normal mortgage.'* (Parminder Singh, Mortgage Product Manager) The introduction of the new product portfolio was scheduled to start in June.

Andy's team planning the reorganization of the back office was delighted by the idea of a simplified product portfolio: *'It would make life a lot simpler for us. We can see two operational advantages coming together. First, by consolidating all three centres into one we can get greater economies of scale. Second, the new product portfolio could considerably reduce the variety, and hopefully complexity, of our processing. In hindsight, I am really happy that both the consolidation and the product changes did not happen together. The disruption of the reorganization has been bad enough without having to cope with different products at the same time.'*

Figure 4.9   Floor plan for new mortgage processing centre

Demand

Applications for new mortgages could arrive through three main channels. Twenty per cent were 'further advances'. These were from existing customers who wanted to extend their borrowing. This type of application came to the new applications process direct from the mortgage businesses sales. The remaining 80 per cent of applications were split evenly between those coming via the branches of the bank and those coming from independent sales agents who usually acted as mortgage brokers for their clients. Demand fluctuated according to the time of year and specific offers. Demand from agents in particular was more volatile as they usually chased the best deals for their clients. The discounted rate product had been seen as very attractive by the market, and the bank's Marketing Department had been delighted at its take-up. Although always intended as a short-term offer, Marketing had wanted the product to continue for another one or two months, but Andy persuaded the board to pull it as originally planned in January. His reasons were largely concerned with reducing the demand on the new applications process during the reorganization. *'The discounted rate product was **too** successful as far as we were concerned. Demand on all three centres had been around 15 per cent higher during the last quarter of the year and I didn't want this to continue into the reorganization*

period. I know it sounds crazy to want less business, but Marketing accepted that it was of marginal profitability and the effect on the processing centres had been disruptive. Our "service level agreement" promise to our agents of achieving an average processing time of 15 days had already slipped to 20 days, and the 17-day promise to our own branches has slipped to 22 days!'

Unfortunately, when the news of the imminent demise of the discounted rate product hit the agents there was a final surge as they persuaded clients to make a fast decision to obtain the discounted rate. To some extent Andy and his team had anticipated some of this surge and had warned of some slippage in turnaround times, but the short-term increase in demand had been larger than expected and now, four weeks later, they certainly hadn't expected things to be getting worse.

The new applications process

The new consolidated site was relatively close to the old southern area centre. Therefore, slightly over 80 per cent of the southern area staff had transferred from the old centres. By contrast, only around 10 per cent in the other teams had worked in the old processing centres. Most of the new staff had experience in financial services operations but were new to mortgage processing.

The processing of a mortgage application involves four sets of activities:

- 'Input' where applications are received and keyed into the computer and initial checks about accompanying evidence are carried out.
- 'Underwriting' where the decision to lend is made.
- 'Offer' where the team liaises with surveyors to obtain surveys.
- 'Completion' where sanction letters are sent to solicitors.

When the processes were moved to the new centre, the only significant change from the old way of working was the grouping together of all the 'keying in' activities associated with the input stage. This was felt to be a fairly risk-free move because all three centres were already using a standardized 'preliminary information screen'. *'Input is a fairly simple activity and there is relatively little difference between different types of product, therefore it makes sense to put them all together. In fact it has worked very well. Bringing the teams together has already allowed us to examine the marginal differences between the ways we used to do it and adopt a method of working that combines different elements of best practice. We have twelve staff in the input section, that is a reduction of seven staff compared to the combined data input staff that were needed in the three separate centres. It has also allowed staff to specialize to some extent, which can be useful at times.'*

The numbers of staff in each team were as follows:

	Northern area	Southern area	Western area
Underwriting	19	22	5
Offer	28	28	12
Completion	14	15	5

All teams had to process a range of products. Every staff member was trained to deal with standard mortgages, but more experienced staff were used for more 'specialist' mortgages such as 'Buy to Let'. There was an ongoing training programme to train all staff to deal with all types of mortgage, but with staff turnover at 11 per cent there would always be some staff who were able to do only the basic work.

Problems with the new process

In spite of his irritation at the recent meeting, Andy Curtis was broadly optimistic about his team's ability to get over their problems. *'Our problem is in fact three sets of problems, all of which have hit us at the same time. First, there is the move itself. That was bound to cause some disruption but I don't think that it has thrown up any particular problems that we were not aware of. It's just that it has created an uncertain and unstable environment in which to cope with our other problems. Second, there is the last-minute rush by agents to take advantage of our discounted rate product before it was withdrawn. This meant an extra load above what we expected and hit us just at the wrong time. I'm not sure who should carry the blame for this. It's probably not useful to even try and allocate blame. I know that Marketing should have forecast the extent of the short-term surge in demand, but there again, there is no reason why we could not have forecast it ourselves. The third problem is probably the most important. Although we have only been operating with the new process and layout for four weeks, it is already clear that it isn't working as well as it should. Or perhaps it would be more accurate to say that we have failed to capitalize on the potential for redesigning the total process that bringing together the three centres has given us.'*

Andy confided his feeling that the underlying process could be improved to his senior team. Together they put together a list of the key problems with the process as they saw them. The main points to emerge from this list were as follows:

- Staff were having to move about more than at the old centres. There, the information was within easy reach of all staff. Now, the files had been consolidated to avoid duplication, so the filing room was further away for most staff.
- This led to another problem. Because of the effort in retrieving a file, staff were developing a habit of keeping it out of the filing system for longer than necessary. They were keeping it on their desk 'in case it was required again'. This made it unavailable to any other member of staff who could need it.
- All the fax machines were located together in one location. This helped to maintain a high utilization of the machines, but again meant that staff had further to walk. Even the Southern Area team, for whom the fax machines are most convenient, resented the other teams constantly walking through their area.
- There was no clarity of flow. The high level of in-process inventory of partially processed applications (both physical files and virtual files on the IT system) resulted in the 'black hole syndrome', with applications disappearing into people's in-trays.
- There was a significant amount of rework required within the system. Putting together the data from the three old centres for the previous year showed that 22.5 per cent of all offers made were either returning to the process for adjustment, or recycled in some way within the process, sometimes more than once. This problem seemed to be continuing at the same rate in the new centre.

'I think our problems come down to two major issues', Andy told his group. *'First there is the question of getting*

the flow through our process right. One thing that has become clear is that processing a mortgage is a relatively standard task irrespective of whether the customer is from the north or south or west region. The only activity where specialized knowledge matters is at the offer stage where knowledge of the region is required. Nor should the different sales channels matter. We promise a faster turnround time to the agents than to our own branches because, as independents, we need to keep the agents happy. But, if our processing was right, we should be able to offer the same fast throughput time to both the brokers and the branches. We have already put all the input activities together and that has worked well. I don't see why we can't have work flowing from the input section to underwriting, then to offer and then to completion just like a smooth-running assembly line. The existing teams organize themselves so that applications flow from an underwriting stage to an offer stage, then to a completion stage, so why can't

we simply do that for the whole operation? At the same time we have to solve the recycling problem. This must be the root cause of a lot of our problems. Ideally, no application should progress beyond the input stage without it being capable of moving smoothly through the rest of the process. One idea may be to put an extra step in the process for agents where we phone the customer to check details at the input stage.'

QUESTIONS

1 Is Andy right that Marketing should have forecast the last-minute surge in demand for the 'discounted rate' product?

2 What appears to be the volume–variety position of the new centre? Is it different from the old centres?

3 How would you recommend that Andy sets about improving the performance of his processes?

This case study is concluded in Chapter 5.

Active case study   McPherson Charles Solicitors

ACTIVE CASE

McPherson Charles, based in Bristol, UK, has rapidly grown to be one of the biggest law firms in the region. The company is embarking upon a 'plans for the future' programme aiming to improve the effectiveness of their operations. Three of the partners, each responsible for a different area (property law, family law, litigation), meet to discuss this but clearly have different ideas about where the priorities of the firm should lie.

● How would you evaluate the existing processes and operations and what would be your recommendation to each partner to ensure future growth for the firm as a whole?

Please refer to the Active case on the CD to listen to the different perspectives and learn more about the operations for which each partner is responsible.

Applying the principles

HINTS

Some of these exercises can be answered by reading the chapter. Others will require some general knowledge of business activity and some might require an element of investigation. All have hints on how they can be answered on the CD accompanying this book.

1 Visit a branch of a retail bank and consider the following questions:
● What categories of service does the bank seem to offer?
● To what extent does the bank design separate processes for each of its types of service?
● What are the different process design objectives for each category of service?

2   Revisit the example at the beginning of this chapter that examines some of the principles behind supermarket layout. Then visit a supermarket and observe people's behaviour. You may wish to try and observe which areas they
move slowly past and which areas they seem to move past without paying attention to the products. (You may
have to exercise some discretion when doing this; people generally don't like to be stalked round the supermarket too obviously.) Try and verify, as far as you can, some of the principles that were outlined in the example.

- If you were to redesign the supermarket, what would you recommend? What do you think, therefore, are the
main criteria to be considered in the design of a supermarket layout?
- What competitive or environmental changes may result in the need to change store layouts in the future?
- Will these apply to all supermarkets, or only certain ones, such as town centre stores?

3   Consider a retail bank. It has many services that it could offer through its branch network, using telephone-based
call centres, or using an Internet-based service. Choose a service that (like the bank's services) could be delivered
in different ways. For example, you could choose education courses (that can be delivered full-time, part-time, by
distance learning, by e-learning, etc.), or a library (using a fixed facility, a mobile service, an Internet-based service, etc.), or any other similar service. Evaluate each alternative delivery process in terms of its effect on its customers' experiences.

4   Many universities and colleges around the world are under increasing pressure to reduce the cost per student of
their activities. How do you think technology could help operations such as universities to keep their costs down
but their quality of education high?

5   Robot-type technology is starting to play a part in some medical surgical procedures. What would it take before
you were willing to subject yourself to a robot doctor?

6   Security devices are becoming increasingly high-tech. Most offices and similar buildings have simple security
devices such as 'swipe cards' that admit only authorized people to the premises. Other technologies are becoming more common (although perhaps more in movies than in reality) such as fingerprint, iris and face scanning.
Explore websites that deal with advanced security technology and gain some understanding of their state of development, advantages and disadvantages. Use this understanding to design a security system for an office building
with which you are familiar. Remember that any system must allow access to legitimate users of the building (at
least to obtain information for which they have clearance) and yet provide maximum security against any unau-
thorized access to areas and/or information.

Notes on chapter

1   Sources: Paul Walley, our colleague in the Operations Management Group at Warwick Business
School; Martin, P. (2000) 'How supermarkets make a meal of you', *Sunday Times,* 4 Nov.

2   Hayes, R.H. and Wheelwright, S.C. (1984) *Restoring our Competitive Edge,* John Wiley.

3   Example provided by Professor Michael Lewis, Bath University, UK.

4   Typology derived from Slack, N. and Lewis, M.A. (2001) *Operations Strategy,* Financial Times
Prentice Hall, Harlow, UK.

Taking it further

Anupindi, R., Chopra, S., Deshmukh, S.D., Van Mieghem, J.A. and Zemel, E. (1999) *Managing
Business Process Flows,* Prentice Hall, New Jersey. An excellent, although mathematical, approach
to process design in general.

Hammer, M. (1990) 'Reengineering work: don't automate, obliterate', *Harvard Business Review,*
July–August. This is the paper that launched the whole idea of business processes and process management in general to a wider managerial audience. Slightly dated but worth reading.

Hopp, W.J. and Spearman, M.L. (2001) *Factory Physics* (2nd edn), McGraw-Hill. Very technical so don't bother with it if you aren't prepared to get into the maths. However, some fascinating analysis, especially concerning Little's Law.

Ramaswamy, R. (1996) *Design and Management of Service Processes,* Addison-Wesley Longman. A relatively technical approach to process design in a service environment.

Shostack, G.L. (1982) 'How to design a service', *European Journal of Marketing,* Vol. 16, No. 1. A far less technical and more experiential approach to design of service processes.

Useful websites

www.bpmi.org Site of the Business Process Management Initiative. Some good resources including papers and articles.

www.bptrends.com News site for trends in business process management generally. Some interesting articles.

www.bls.gov/oes US Department of Labor employment statistics.

www.fedee.com/hrtrends Federation of European Employers' guide to employment and job trends in Europe.

www.iienet.org The American Institute of Industrial Engineers' site. They are an important professional body for process design and related topics.

www.waria.com A Workflow and Reengineering Association website. Some useful topics.

FURTHER RESOURCES

For further resources including examples, animated diagrams, self test questions, excel spreadsheets, active case studies and video materials please explore the CD accompanying this book.

PROCESS DESIGN 2 – ANALYSIS

Introduction

The previous chapter set the broad parameters for process design; in particular it showed how volume and variety shape the positioning of the process in terms of layout, process technology and the design of jobs. But this is only the beginning of process design. Within these broad parameters there are many, more detailed decisions to be made that will dictate the way materials, information and customers flow through the process. Do not dismiss these detailed design decisions as merely the 'technicalities' of process design. They are important because they determine the actual performance of the process in practice and eventually its contribution to the performance of the whole business. (See Figure 5.1.)

Source: Courtesy AstraZeneca plc

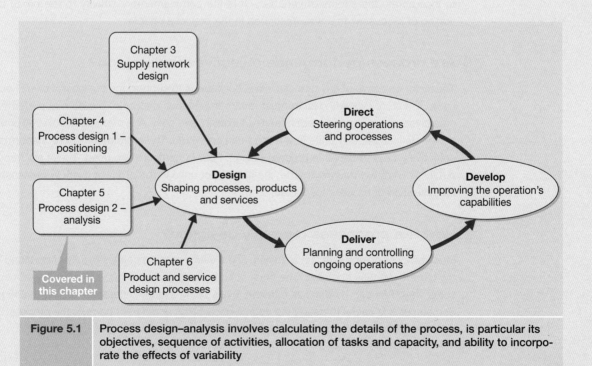

Figure 5.1   Process design–analysis involves calculating the details of the process, is particular its objectives, sequence of activities, allocation of tasks and capacity, and ability to incorporate the effects of variability

Executive summary

Decision logic chain for process design–analysis

Each chapter is structured around a set of diagnostic questions. These questions suggest what you should ask in order to gain an understanding of the important issues of a topic, and as a result, improve your decision making. An executive summary, addressing these questions, is provided below.

What is process design–analysis?

The analysis stage of process design involves calculating the details of the process, in particular its objectives, sequence of activities, allocation of tasks and capacity, and its ability to incorporate the effects of variability. It is the complementary activity to the broad positioning of processes that was described in the previous chapter.

Are process performance objectives understood?

The major objective of any process in the business is to support the business's overall objectives. Therefore process design must reflect the relative priority of the normal performance objectives: quality, speed, dependability, flexibility and cost. At a more detailed level, process design defines the way units flow through an operation. Therefore more 'micro' performance objectives are also useful in process design. Four in particular are used. These are throughput (or flow) rate, throughput time, the number of units in the process (work in process) and the utilization of process resources.

How are processes currently designed?

Much process design is in fact redesign, and a useful starting point is to fully understand how the current process operates. The most effective way of doing this is to map the process in some way. This can be done at different levels using slightly different mapping techniques. Sometimes it is useful to define the degree of visibility for different parts of the process, indicating how much of the process is transparent to customers.

Are process tasks and capacity configured appropriately?

This is a complex question with several distinct parts. First, it is necessary to understand the task precedence to be incorporated in the process. This defines what activities must occur before others. Second, it is necessary to examine how alternative process design options can incorporate series and parallel configuration. These are sometimes called 'long-thin' and 'short-fat' arrangements. Third, cycle time and process capacity must be calculated. This can help to allocate work evenly between the stages of the process (called balancing). Fourth, the relationship between throughput, cycle time and work in process must be established. This is done using a simple but extremely powerful relationship known as Little's law (throughput time = work in process $\times$ cycle time).

Is process variability recognized?

In reality, processes have to cope with variability, in terms of both time and the tasks that are performed within the process. This variability can have very significant effects on process behaviour, usually to reduce process efficiency. Queuing theory can be used to understand this effect. In particular, it is important to understand the relationship between process utilization and the number of units waiting to be processed (or throughput time).

What is process design–analysis?

To 'design' is to conceive the looks, arrangement and workings of something *before it is constructed.* Process design should be treated at two levels–the broad, aggregated level and the more detailed level. The previous chapter took a broad approach by relating process design to the volume–variety position of the process. That will have identified the broad process type, and given some guidance as to the layout, process technology and job designs to be used within the process. This chapter takes a more detailed view. However, in working out the details of a process design it is sometimes necessary to revisit the overall broad assumptions under which it is being designed. This is why the detailed analysis of process design covered in the chapter should always be thought through in the context of the broader process positioning issues covered in Chapter 4. The following two examples illustrate processes whose detailed design is important in determining their effectiveness.

Example | ### Processes for even faster food[1]

The quick service restaurant (QSR) industry reckons that the very first drive-through dates back to 1928 when Royce Hailey first promoted the drive-through service at his Pig Stand restaurant in Los Angeles. Customers would simply drive by the back door of the restaurant where the chef would come out and deliver the restaurant's famous 'Barbequed Pig' sandwiches. Today, drive-through processes are slicker and faster. They are also more common: in 1975, McDonald's had no drive-

Source: Courtesy McDonald's Europe Limited

throughs, but now more than 90 per cent of its US restaurants incorporate a drive-through process. In fact 80 per cent of recent fast-food growth has come through the growing number of drive-throughs. Says one industry specialist, *'There are a growing number of customers for whom fast-food is not fast enough. They want to cut waiting time to the very minimum without even getting out of their car. Meeting their needs depends on how smooth we can get the process.'*

The competition to design the fastest and most reliable drive-through process is fierce. Starbucks' drive-throughs have strategically placed cameras at the order boards so that servers can recognize regular customers and start making their order even before it's placed. Burger King has experimented with sophisticated sound systems, simpler menu boards and see-through food bags to ensure greater accuracy (no point in being fast if you don't deliver what the customer ordered). These details matter. McDonald's reckon that their sales increase 1 per cent for every six seconds saved at a drive-through, while a single Burger King restaurant calculated that its takings increased by 15,000 dollars a year each time it reduced queuing time by one second. Menu items must be easy to read and understand. Designing 'combo meals' (burger, fries and a cola), for example, saves time at the ordering stage. But not everyone is thrilled by the boom in drive-throughs. People living in the vicinity may complain of the extra traffic they attract, and the unhealthy image of fast-food combined with a process that does not even make customers get out of their car is, for some, a step too far.

Example   Yamaha Corporation of Japan

The Yamaha Corporation of Japan, founded in 1887, has grown to become the world's largest manufacturer of musical instruments, as well as producing a whole variety of other goods, from semiconductors and robots through to sporting goods and furniture. In recent years it has developed a reputation for product diversification, an understanding of new markets and, especially, innovative manufacturing methods. For example, it was one of the first piano manufacturers to make up-market grand pianos using assembly line techniques. Traditionally, grand pianos (as opposed to the less expensive and better selling vertical pianos) were made using individual build methods which relied on craft skills. The main advantage of this was that skilled workers could accommodate individual variations in the (often inconsistent) materials from which the piano is made. Each individual piano would be constructed around the idiosyncrasies of the material to make a product unique in its tone and tuning. Not so with Yamaha, who, although making some of the highest quality pianos in the world, emphasize consistency and reliability, as well as richness of tone. When Yamaha announced their intention to produce grand pianos in this way, many thought it could not be done. The skill needed would be too subtle to codify, the variability in process times would be too great for this type of process to handle, and well, it just wasn't right to make a delicate instrument in this way. But Yamaha proved that through an emphasis on deepening the process knowledge and effective process design, they could maintain quality levels as well as reap all the benefits of a mass process.

What do these two examples have in common?

Both examples highlight a number of process design issues. The first is that the payback from good process design is clearly significant. Quick-service restaurant operations devote time and effort to the design process, assessing the performance of alternative process designs in terms of efficiency, quality, and above all, throughput time. The return for Yamaha is even more dramatic. For a product that competes primarily on quality, being able to achieve the cost benefits of slick process design without compromising quality gives the company a significant competitive advantage. Also it is difficult to separate the design of the process from the design of the product or service that it produces. The 'combo meal' is designed with the constraints and capabilities of the drive-through process in mind, and even the design of Yamaha's pianos will need to be adapted marginally to facilitate assembly. An important point here is that, in both cases, processes are designed to be appropriate for the market they are serving. Different market strategies may require different process designs. So a good starting point for any operation is to understand the direct relationship between strategic and process performance objectives. But, notwithstanding this relatively strategic starting point for process design, both examples illustrate the importance of not being afraid to analyze processes at a very detailed level. This may include thoroughly understanding current processes so that any improvement can be based on the reality of what happens in practice. It will certainly involve allocating the tasks and associated capacity very carefully to appropriate parts of the process. And, for most processes, it will also involve a design that is capable of taking into consideration the variability that exists in most human tasks. These are the topics covered in this chapter.

Operations principle
Processes should always be designed to reflect customer and/or market requirements.

Are process performance objectives understood?

Operations principle
A process' performance can be judged in terms of the levels of quality, speed, dependability, flexibility, and cost it achieves.

The whole point of process design is to make sure that the performance of the process is appropriate for whatever it is trying to achieve. For example, if an operation competed primarily on its ability to respond quickly to customer requests, its processes would need to be designed to give fast throughput times. This would minimize the time between customers requesting a product or service and their receiving it. Similarly, if an operation competed on low price, cost-related objectives are likely to dominate its process design. Some kind of logic should link what the operation as a whole is attempting to achieve, and the performance objectives of its individual processes. This is illustrated in Table 5.1.

Process flow objectives

All the strategic performance objectives translate directly to process design as shown in Table 5.1. But, because processes will be managed at a very operational level, process

Operations principle
Process flow objectives should include throughput rate, throughput time, work-in-process, and resource utilization; all of which are interrelated.

design also needs to consider a more 'micro' and detailed set of objectives. These are largely concerned with flow through the process. When whatever is being 'processed' (we shall refer to these as 'units' irrespective of what they are) enter a process they will progress through a series of activities where they are 'transformed' in some way. Between these activities the units may dwell for some time in inventories, waiting to be transformed by the next activity. This means that the time that a unit spends in the process (its throughput time) will be longer than the sum of all the transforming activities that it passes through. Also the resources that perform the process's activities may not be used all the time because not all units will necessarily require the same activities and the capacity of each resource may not match the demand placed upon it. So neither the units moving through the process nor the resources performing the activities may be fully utilized. Because of this, the way in which units leave the process is unlikely to be exactly the same as the way they arrive at the process. Figure 5.2 illustrates some of the 'micro' performance flow objectives that describe process flow performance and the process design factors that influence them. The flow objectives are:

FURTHER EXAMPLE

- Throughput rate (or flow rate) – the rate at which units emerge from the process, i.e. the number of units passing through the process per unit of time.
- Throughput time – the average elapsed time taken for inputs to move through the process and become outputs.
- The number of units in the process (also called the 'work in process', or in-process inventory), as an average over a period of time.
- The utilization of process resources – the proportion of available time for which the resources within the process are performing useful work.

Table 5.1 The impact of strategic performance objectives on process design objectives and performance

Strategic performance objective	Typical process design objectives	Some benefits of good process design
Quality	• Provide appropriate resources, capable of achieving the specification of product or service • Error-free processing	• Products and service produced 'on-specification' • Less recycling and wasted effort within the process
Speed	• Minimum throughput time • Output rate appropriate for demand	• Short customer waiting time • Low in-process inventory
Dependability	• Provide dependable process resources • Reliable process output timing and volume	• On-time deliveries of products and services • Less disruption, confusion and rescheduling within the process
Flexibility	• Provide resources with an appropriate range of capabilities • Change easily between processing states (what, how, or how much is being processed?)	• Ability to process a wide range of products and services • Low cost/fast product and service change • Low cost/fast volume and timing changes • Ability to cope with unexpected events (e.g. supply or a processing failure)
Cost	• Appropriate capacity to meet demand • Eliminate process waste in terms of: – excess capacity – excess process capability – in-process delays – in-process errors – inappropriate process inputs	• Low processing costs • Low resource costs (capital costs) • Low delay/inventory costs (working capital costs)

Figure 5.2 'Micro' process performance objectives and process design factors

The design factors that will influence the flow objectives are:

- The variability of input arrival to the process
- The configuration of the resources and activities within the process
- The capacity of the resources at each point in the process
- The variability of the activities within the process.

As we examine each of these design factors, we will be using a number of terms that, although commonly used within process design, need some explanation. These terms will be described in the course of the chapter, but for reference they are summarized in Table 5.2.

Table 5.2   Some common process design terms[2]

Term	Definition
Process task	The sum of all the activities that must be performed by the process.
Work content of the process task	The total amount of work within the process task measured in time units.
Activity	A discrete amount of work within the overall process task.
Work content of an activity	The amount of work within an activity measured in time units.
Precedence relationship	The relationship between activities expressed in terms of their dependencies, i.e. whether individual activities must be performed before other activities can be started.
Cycle time	The average time that the process takes between completions of units.
Throughput rate	The number of units completed by the process per unit of time (= 1/cycle time).
Process stage	A work area within the process through which units flow; it may be responsible for performing several activities.
Bottleneck	The capacity constraining stage in a process; it governs the output from the whole process.
Balancing	The act of allocating activities as equally as possible between stages in the process.
Utilization	The proportion of available time that the process, or part of the process, spends performing useful work.
Starving	Underutilization of a stage within a process caused by inadequate supply from the previous stage.
Blocking	The inability of a stage in the process to work because the inventory prior to the subsequent stage is full.
Throughput time	The elapsed time between a unit entering the process and it leaving the process.
Queue time	The time a unit spends waiting to be processed.

How are processes currently designed?

> **Operations principle**
> Process mapping is needed to expose the reality of process behaviour.

Existing processes are not always sufficiently well defined or described. Sometimes this is because they have developed over time without ever being formally recorded, or they may have been changed (perhaps improved) informally by the individuals who work in the process. But processes that are not formally defined can be interpreted in different ways, leading to confusion and inhibiting improvement. So, it is important to have some recorded visual descriptor of a process that can be agreed by all those who are involved in it. This is where process mapping comes in.

Process mapping

Process mapping (or process blueprinting as it is sometimes called) at its most basic level involves describing processes in terms of how the activities within the process relate to each other. There are many, broadly similar, techniques that can be used for process mapping. However, all the techniques have two main features:

- They identify the different types of activity that take place during the process.
- They show the flow of materials or people or information through the process (or, put another way, the sequence of activities that materials, people or information are subjected to).

Different process mapping symbols are sometimes used to represent different types of activity. They can be arranged in order, and in series or in parallel, to describe any process. And although there is no universal set of symbols used all over the world, some are relatively common. Most derive either from the early days of 'scientific' management around a century ago or, more recently, from information system flowcharting. Figure 5.3 shows some of these symbols.

PRACTICE NOTE

Example | **Theatre lighting operation**

Figure 5.4 shows one of the processes used in a theatre lighting operation. The company hires out lighting and stage effects equipment to theatrical companies and event organizers. Customers' calls are routed to the store technician. After discussing their requirements, the technician checks the equipment availability file to see whether the equipment can be supplied from the company's own stock on the required dates. If the equipment cannot be supplied in-house, customers may be asked whether they want the company to try and obtain it from other possible suppliers. This offer depends on how busy and how helpful individual technicians are. Sometimes customers decline the offer and a 'Guide to Customers' leaflet is sent to the customer. If the customer does want a search, the technician will call potential suppliers in an attempt to find available equipment. If this is not successful the customer is informed, but if suitable equipment is located it is reserved for delivery to the company's site. If equipment can be supplied from the company's own stores, it is reserved on the equipment availability file and the day before it is required a 'kit wagon' is taken

Figure 5.3   Some common process mapping symbols

to the store where all the required equipment is assembled, taken back to the workshop and checked, and if any equipment is faulty it is repaired at this point. After that it is packed in special cases and delivered to the customer.

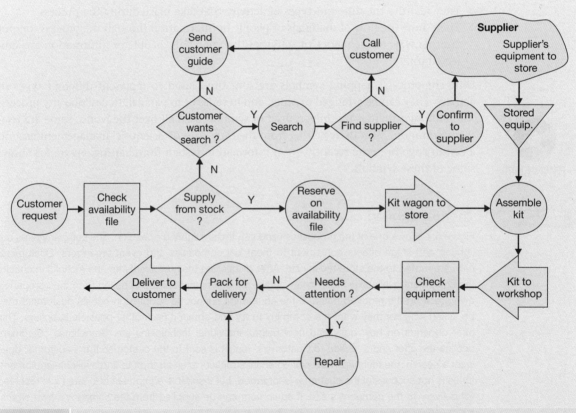

Figure 5.4   Process map for 'enquire to delivery' process at stage lighting operation

Different levels of process mapping

For a large process, drawing process maps at this level of detail can be complex. This is why processes are often mapped at a more aggregated level, called high-level process mapping, before more detailed maps are drawn. Figure 5.5 illustrates this for the total *'supply and install lighting'* process in the stage lighting operation. At the highest level the process can be drawn simply as an input–transformation–output process with materials and customers as its input resources and lighting services as outputs. No details of how inputs are transformed into outputs are included. At a slightly lower or more detailed level, what is sometimes called an outline process map (or chart) identifies the sequence of activities but only in a general way. So the process of *'enquire to delivery'* that is shown in detail in Figure 5.4 is here reduced to a single activity. At the more detailed level, all the activities are shown in a 'detailed process map' (the activities within the process 'install and test' are shown).

Although not shown in Figure 5.5 an even more micro set of process activities could be mapped within each of the detailed process activities. Such a micro detailed process map could specify every single motion involved in each activity. Some quick-service restaurants, for example, do exactly that. In the lighting hire company example most activities would not be mapped in any more detail than that shown in Figure 5.5. Some activities, such as 'return to base', are probably too straightforward to be worth mapping

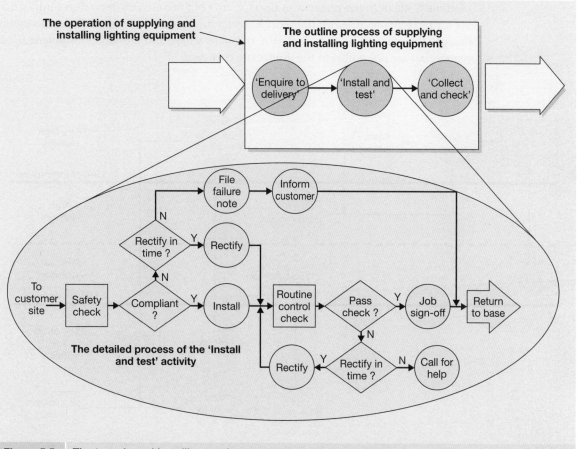

Figure 5.5   The 'supply and install' operations process mapped at three levels

any further. Other activities, such as 'rectify faulty equipment', may rely on the technician's skills and discretion to the extent that the activity has too much variation and is too complex to map in detail. Some activities, however, may need mapping in more detail to ensure quality or to protect the company's interests. For example, the activity of safety checking the customer's site to ensure that it is compliant with safety regulations will need specifying in some detail to ensure that the company can prove it exercised its legal responsibilities.

Process visibility

It is sometimes useful to map such processes in a way that makes the degree of visibility of each part of the process obvious.[3] This allows those parts of the process with high visibility to be designed so that they enhance the customer's perception of the process. Figure 5.6 shows yet another part of the lighting equipment company's operation: the 'collect and check' process. The process is mapped to show the visibility of each activity to the customer. Here four levels of visibility are used. There is no hard and fast rule about this; many processes simply distinguish between those activities that the customer *could* see and those that they couldn't. The boundary between these two categories is often called the 'line of visibility'. In Figure 5.6 three categories of visibility are shown. At the very highest level of visibility, above the 'line of interaction', are those activities that involve direct interaction between the lighting company's staff and the customer. Other activities take place at the customer's site or in the presence of the customer but involve less or no direct interaction. Yet further activities (the two transport activities in this case) have some degree of visibility because they take place away from the company's base and are visible to potential customers, but are not visible to the immediate customer.

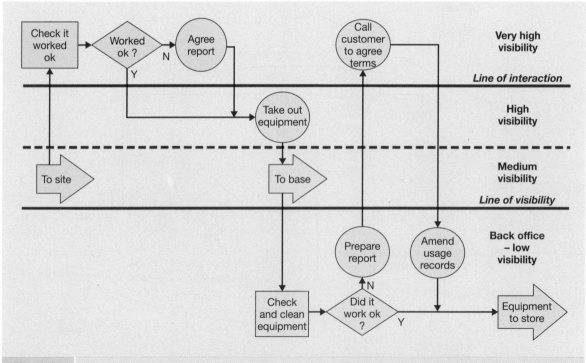

Figure 5.6   The 'collect and check' process mapped to show different levels of process visibility

Are process tasks and capacity configured appropriately?

Process maps show how the activities of any particular process are currently arranged and help to suggest how they can be reconfigured. But there are also some general issues that must be understood before processes can be analyzed. These relate to how the total task can be divided up within the process and determine how capacity is allocated. This, in turn, determines the flow through the process.

Getting to grips with process capacity means understanding the following issues:

- Task precedence
- Series and parallel configurations
- Cycle time and process flow
- Process balancing
- Throughput, cycle time and work in process.

Task precedence

> **Operations principle**
> Process design must respect task precedence.

Any process redesign needs to preserve the inherent precedence of activities within the overall task. Task 'precedence' defines which activities must occur before others, because of the nature of the task itself. At its simplest level task precedence is defined by:

- The individual activities that comprise the total process task
- The relationship between these individual activities.

Task precedence is usually described by using a 'precedence diagram', which, in addition to the above, also includes the following information:

- The time necessary to perform the total task (sometimes known as the 'work content' of the task)
- The time necessary to perform each of the individual activities within the task.

Example   Computer repair service centre

A repair service centre receives faulty or damaged computers sent in by customers, repairs them and dispatches them back to the customer. Each computer is subject to the same set of tests and repair activities, and although the time taken to repair each computer will depend on the results of the tests, there is relatively little variation between individual computers.

Table 5.3 defines the process task of testing and repairing the computers in terms of the seven activities that comprise the total task, the relationship between the activities in terms of each activity's 'immediate predecessor', and the time necessary to perform each activity. Figure 5.7 shows the relationship between the activities graphically. This kind of illustration is called the 'precedence diagram' for the process task. It is useful because it indicates how activities *cannot* be sequenced in the eventual process design. For example, the process cannot perform activity 'b' before activity 'a' is completed. However, it does not determine how a process *can* be designed. Yet once the task has been analyzed in this way, activities can be arranged to form the process's general configuration.

Table 5.3 Process task details for the 'computer test and repair' task

Activity code	Activity name	Immediate predecessor	Activity time (minutes)
a	Preliminary test 1	–	5
b	Preliminary test 2	a	6
c	Dismantle	b	4
d	Test and repair 1	c	8
e	Test and repair 2	c	6
f	Test and repair 3	c	4
g	Clean/replace casing elements	d, e, f	10

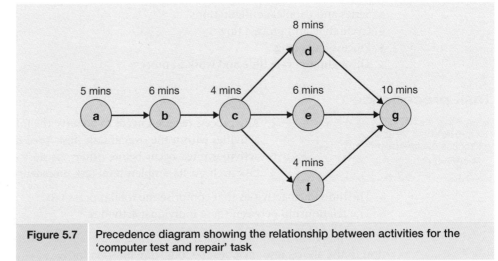

Figure 5.7 Precedence diagram showing the relationship between activities for the 'computer test and repair' task

Series and parallel configurations

FURTHER EXAMPLE

At its simplest level the general configuration of a process involves deciding the extent to which activities are arranged sequentially and the extent to which they are arranged in parallel.

For example, the task illustrated in Figure 5.7 involves seven activities that in total take 43 minutes. Demand is such that the process must be able to complete the test and repair task at the rate of one every 12 minutes in order to meet demand. One possible process design is to arrange the seven activities in a series arrangement of stages. The first question to address is 'How many stages would this type of series arrangement require?' This can be calculated by dividing the total work content of the task by the required cycle time. In this case, number of stages = 43 minutes / 12 minutes = 3.58 stages.

Given the practical difficulties of having a fraction of a stage, this effectively means that the process needs four stages. The next issue is to allocate activities to each stage. Because the output from the whole process will be limited by the stage with most work (the sum of its allocated activities), each stage can have activities allocated to it up to a maximum allocation of 12 minutes. Figure 5.8 illustrates how this could be achieved. The

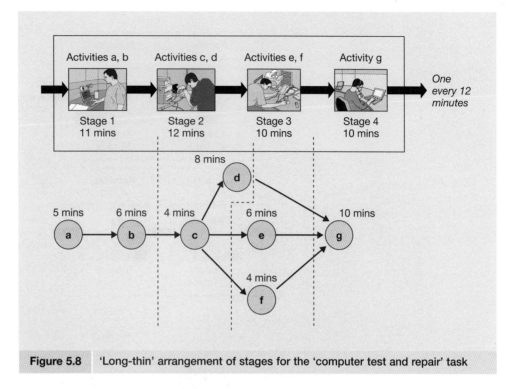

Figure 5.8 'Long-thin' arrangement of stages for the 'computer test and repair' task

longest stage (stage 2 in this case) will limit the output of the total process to one computer every 12 minutes and the other stages will be relatively underloaded.

However, there are other ways of allocating tasks to each stage, and involving the parallel arrangement of activities, that could achieve a similar output rate. For example, the four stages could be arranged as two parallel 'shorter' arrangements with each stage performing approximately half of the activities in the total tasks. This is illustrated in Figure 5.9. It involves two two-stage arrangements, with stage 1 being allocated four activities that amount to 21 minutes of work and the second stage being allocated three activities that amount to 22 minutes of work. So, each arrangement will produce one repaired computer every 22 minutes (governed by the stage with the most work). This means that the two arrangements together will produce two repaired computers every 22 minutes, an average of one repaired computer every 11 minutes.

Loading each stage with more work and arranging the stages in parallel can be taken further. Figure 5.10 illustrates an arrangement where the whole test and repair task is performed at individual stages, all of which are arranged in parallel. Here, each stage will produce one repaired computer every 43 minutes and so together will produce four repaired computers every 43 minutes, an average output rate of one repaired computer every 10.75 minutes.

This simple example represents an important process design issue. Should activities in a process be arranged predominantly in a single-series 'long–thin' configuration, or predominantly in several 'short-fat' parallel configurations, or somewhere in between? (Note that 'long' means the number of stages and 'fat' means the amount of work allocated to each stage.) Most processes will adopt a combination of series and parallel configurations, and in any particular situation there are usually technical constraints that limit either how 'long and thin' or how 'short and fat' the process can be. But there is usually a real choice to be made with a range of possible options. The advantages of each extreme of the long-thin to short-fat spectrum are very different and help to explain why different arrangements are adopted.

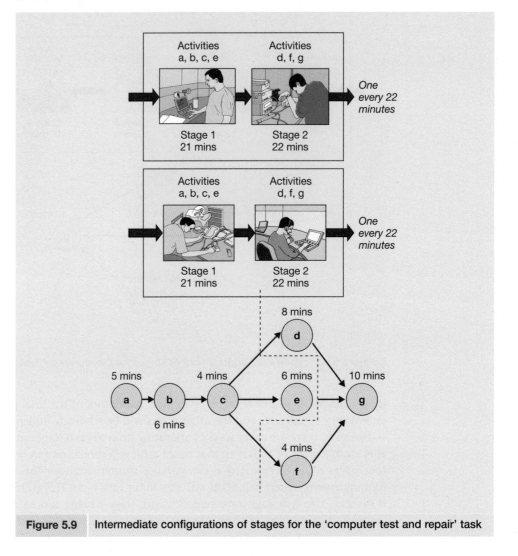

Figure 5.9   Intermediate configurations of stages for the 'computer test and repair' task

The advantages of the series-dominated (long-thin) configuration include:

- *A more controlled flow* through the process that is relatively easy to manage.
- *Simple materials handling* – especially if a product being manufactured is heavy, large or difficult to move.
- *Lower capital requirements.* If a specialist piece of equipment is needed for one element in the job, only one piece of equipment would need to be purchased; on short-fat arrangements every stage would need one.
- *More efficient operation.* If each stage is performing only a small part of the total job, the person at the stage may have a higher proportion of direct productive work as opposed to the non-productive parts of the job, such as picking up tools and materials.

The advantages of the parallel-dominated (short-fat) configuration include:

- *Higher mix flexibility.* If the process needs to produce several types of product or service, each stage could specialize in different types.
- *Higher volume flexibility.* As volume varies, stages can simply be closed down or started up as required.

Figure 5.10   'Short-fat' arrangement of stages for the 'computer test and repair' task

- *Higher robustness*. If one stage breaks down or ceases operation in some way, the other parallel stages are unaffected; a long-thin arrangement would cease operating completely.
- *Less monotonous work*. In the computer repair example, the staff in the short-fat arrangement are repeating their tasks only every 43 minutes; in the long-thin arrangement it is every 12 minutes.

Cycle time and process capacity

> **Operations principle**
> Process analysis derives from an understanding of the required process cycle time.

The cycle time of a process is the time between completed units emerging from it. Cycle time is a vital factor in process design and has a significant influence on most of the other detailed design decisions. It is usually one of the first things to be calculated because it can be used both to represent the demand placed on a process and the process's capacity. The cycle time also sets the pace or 'drum beat' of the process. However the process is designed it must be able to meet its required cycle time. It is calculated by considering the likely demand for the products or services over a period and the amount of production time available in that period.

Example   **Passport office**

Suppose the regional government office that deals with passport applications is designing a process that will check applications and issue the documents. The number of applications to be processed is 1600 per week and the time available to process the applications is 40 hours per week.

$$\text{Cycle time for the process} = \frac{\text{time available}}{\text{number to be processed}}$$

$$= \frac{40}{1600} = 0.025 \text{ hours}$$

$$= 1.5 \text{ minutes}$$

So the process must be capable of dealing with a completed application once every 1.5 minutes, or 40 per hour.

Process capacity

If the cycle time indicates the output that must be achieved by a process, the next decision must be how much capacity is needed by the process in order to meet the cycle time. To calculate this, a further piece of information is needed – the work content of the process task. The larger the work content of the process task and the smaller the required cycle time, the more capacity will be necessary if the process is to meet the demand placed upon it.

Example   **Passport office**

For the passport office, the total work content of all the activities that make up the total task of checking, processing and issuing a passport is, on average, 30 minutes. So, a process with one person would produce a passport every 30 minutes. That is, one person would achieve a cycle time of 30 minutes. Two people would achieve a cycle time of 30/2 = 15 minutes, and so on.

Therefore the general relationship between the number of people in the process (its capacity in this simple case) and the cycle time of the process is:

$$\frac{\text{Work content}}{N} = \text{cycle time}$$

where N is the number of people in the process. Therefore, in this case,

$$N = \frac{30}{\text{cycle time}} = \frac{30}{1.5} = 20 \text{ people}$$

So, the capacity that this process needs if it is to meet demand is 20 people.

Process balancing

Excel

Balancing a process involves attempting to allocate activities to each stage as equally as possible. Because the cycle time of the whole process is limited by the longest allocation of activity times to an individual stage, the more equally work is allocated, the less time will be 'wasted' at the other stages in the process. In practice it is nearly always impossible to achieve perfect balance, so some degree of imbalance in work allocation between stages will occur. The effectiveness of the balancing activity is measured by balancing loss.

Operations principle
Allocating work equally to each stage in a process (balancing) smoothes flow and avoids bottlenecks.

This is the time wasted through the unequal allocation of activities as a percentage of the total time invested in processing. This is illustrated in Figure 5.11. Here the computer test and repair task is used to illustrate balancing loss for the 'long-thin' arrangement of four sequential stages and the 'intermediate' arrangement of two parallel two-stage arrangements.

Figure 5.11(a) shows the ideal allocation of activities with each stage perfectly balanced. Here exactly a quarter of the total work content (10.75 minutes) has been allocated to each of the four stages. Every 10.75 minutes each stage performs its activities and passes a computer on to the next stage, or out of the process in the case of stage 4. No stage suffers any idle time and, because the stages are perfectly balanced, balancing loss = 0. In fact, because of the actual times of each activity, it is not possible to equally allocate work to each stage. Figure 5.11(b) shows the best allocation of activities. Most work is allocated to stage 2, so that stage will dictate the cycle time of the whole process. Stage 1 has only 11 minutes of work and so will be idle for (12–11) = 1 minute every cycle (or alternatively will keep processing one computer every 11 minutes and the build-up of inventory between stage 1 and stage 2 would grow indefinitely). Similarly, stages 3 and 4 have idle time, in both cases (12–10) = 2 minutes of idle time. They can process one computer only every 12 minutes because stage 2 will pass forward a computer to them only every 12 minutes. So, they are each being starved of work for 2 minutes in every 12 minutes. In practice, stages that are not the bottleneck stage may not actually be idle for a period of time in every cycle. Rather they will slow down the pace of work to match the time of the bottleneck stage. Nevertheless, this is still effective idle time because under conditions of perfect balance they could be performing useful work.

(a) An ideal balance where activities are allocated equally between stages

Cycle time = 10.75 mins

Stage 1, Stage 2, Stage 3, Stage 4

Idle time = 0
Balancing loss = 0

(b) The best achievable balance where activities are allocated between the stages of a four-stage arrangement

Cycle time = 12 mins

Stage 1, Stage 2, Stage 3, Stage 4

Idle time = (12 – 11)+
(12 – 10)+
(12 – 10) = 5 mins

Balancing loss = $\dfrac{5}{4 \times 12}$
= 0.104
= 10.4%

(c) The best achievable balance where activities are allocated between the stages of a two-stage arrangement

Cycle time = 22 mins

Stage 1, Stage 2

Idle time = (22 – 21) = 1 min

Balancing loss = $\dfrac{1}{2 \times 22}$
= 0.023
= 2.3%

Figure 5.11 Balancing loss is that proportion of the time invested in processing the product or service that is not used productively. For the 'computer test and repair' process, (a) is the theoretical perfect balance, (b) is the best balance for four stages, and (c) is the best balance for two stages

So, every cycle all four stages are investing an amount of time equivalent to the cycle time to produce one completed computer. The total amount of invested time, therefore, is the number of stages in the process multiplied by the cycle time. In this case, total invested time = 4 × 12 = 48 minutes.

The total idle time for every computer processed is the sum of the idle times at the non-bottleneck stages, in this case 5 minutes.

The balancing loss is the amount of idle time as a percentage of the total invested time. In this case, balancing loss = 5/(4 × 12) = 0.104 = 10.4%.

Figure 5.11(c) makes the same calculation for the intermediate process described earlier. Here too, two-stage arrangements are placed in parallel. Stage 2 has the greatest allocation of work at 22 minutes, and will therefore be the bottleneck of the process. Stage 1 has 21 minutes' worth of work and therefore one minute of idle time every cycle. Because the total invested time in the process in each cycle = 2 × 22 minutes, the balancing loss = 1/(2 × 22) = 0.023 = 2.3%.

Throughput, cycle time and work in process

The cycle time of a process is a function of its capacity. For a given amount of work content in the process task, the greater the capacity of the process, the smaller its cycle time. In fact, the capacity of a process is often measured in terms of its cycle time, or more commonly the reciprocal of cycle time that is called 'throughput rate'. So, for example, a theme park ride is described as having a capacity of 1000 customers per hour, or an automated bottling line would be described as having a capacity of 100 bottles a minute, and so on. However, a high level of capacity (short cycle time and fast throughput rate) does not necessarily mean that material, information or customers can move quickly through the process. This will depend on how many other units are contained within the process. If there is a large number of units within the process, they may have to wait in 'work in process' inventories for part of the time they are within the process (throughput time).

Little's law

The mathematical relationship that relates cycle time to work in process and throughput time is called Little's law. It is simple, but very useful, and it works for any stable process. Little's law can be stated as:

$$\text{Throughput time} = \text{work in process} \times \text{cycle time}$$

or

$$\text{Work in process} = \text{throughput time} \times (1/\text{cycle time})$$

That is,

$$\text{Work in process} = \text{throughput time} \times \text{throughput rate}$$

For example, in the case of the computer test and repair process with four stages,

$$\text{Cycle time} = 12 \text{ minutes (loading on the bottleneck station)}$$

$$\text{Work in process} = 4 \text{ units (one at each stage of the process,}$$
$$\text{assuming there is no space for inventory to}$$
$$\text{build up between stages)}$$

Therefore,

$$\text{Throughput time} = \text{work in process} \times \text{cycle time}$$
$$= 12 \times 4 = 48 \text{ minutes}$$

Similarly, for the example of the passport office, suppose the office has a 'clear desk' policy, which means that all desks must be clear of work by the end of the day. How many applications should be loaded onto the process in the morning in order to ensure that every one is completed and desks are clear by the end of the day?

From before,

$$\text{Cycle time} = 1.5 \text{ minutes}$$

From Little's law, assuming a 7.5-hour (450 minute) working day,

$$\text{Throughput time} = \text{work in process} \times \text{cycle time}$$

$$450 \text{ minutes} = \text{work in process} \times 1.5$$

Therefore,

$$\text{Work in process} = 450/1.5 = 300$$

FURTHER EXAMPLE

So, 300 applications can be loaded onto the process in the morning and be cleared by the end of the working day.

Example | Little's law at a seminar

Mike was totally confident in his judgement: *'You'll never get them back in time'*, he said. *'They aren't just wasting time, the process won't allow them to all have their coffee and get back for 11 o'clock.'* Looking outside the lecture theatre, Mike and his colleague Dick were watching the 20 businessmen who were attending the seminar queuing to be served coffee and biscuits. The time was 10.45 and Dick knew that unless they were all back in the lecture theatre at 11 o'clock there was no hope of finishing his presentation before lunch. *'I'm not sure why you're so pessimistic'*, said Dick. *'They seem to be interested in what I have to say and I think they will want to get back to hear how operations management will change their lives.'* Mike shook his head. *'I'm not questioning their motivation'*, he said, *'I'm questioning the ability of the process out there to get through them all in time. I have been timing how long it takes to serve the coffee and biscuits. Each coffee is being made fresh and the time between the server asking each customer what they want and them walking away with their coffee and biscuits is taking 48 seconds. Remember that, according to Little's Law, throughput equals work in process multiplied by cycle time. If the work in process is the 20 managers in the queue and cycle time is 48 seconds, the total throughput time is going to 20 multiplied by 0.8 minutes which equals 16 minutes. Add to that sufficient time for the last person to drink their coffee and you must expect a total throughput time of a bit over 20 minutes. You just haven't allowed long enough for the process.'* Dick was impressed. *'Err . . . what did you say that law was called again?'* *'Little's Law'*, said Mike.

Example | Little's law at an IT support unit

Every year it was the same. All the workstations in the building had to be renovated (tested, new software installed, etc.) and there was only one week in which to do it. The one week fell in the middle of the August vacation period when the renovation process would cause minimum disruption to normal working. Last year the company's 500 workstations had all been renovated within one working week (40 hours). Each renovation last year took on average 2 hours, and 25 technicians had completed the process within the week. This year there would be 530 workstations to renovate but the company's IT support unit had devised a faster testing and renovation routine that would take on average only $1\frac{1}{2}$ hours instead of 2 hours. How many technicians will be needed this year to complete the renovation processes within the week?

Last year:

$$\text{Work in progress (WIP)} = 500 \text{ workstations}$$
$$\text{Time available } (T_t) = 40 \text{ hours}$$
$$\text{Average time to renovate} = 2 \text{ hours}$$

Therefore:

$$\text{Throughput rate } (T_r) = 0.5 \text{ hour per technician}$$
$$= 0.5N$$

where N is the number of technicians. Applying Little's law:

$$\text{WIP} = T_t \times T_r$$
$$500 = 40 \times 0.5N$$
$$N = \frac{500}{40 \times 0.5}$$
$$= 25 \text{ technicians}$$

This year:

$$\text{Work in progress (WIP)} = 530 \text{ workstations}$$
$$\text{Time available } (T_t) = 40 \text{ hours}$$
$$\text{Average time to renovate} = 1.5 \text{ hours}$$
$$\text{Throughput rate } (T_r) = 1/1.5 \text{ hours per technician}$$
$$= 0.67N$$

where N is the number of technicians. Applying Little's law:

$$\text{WIP} = T_t \times T_r$$
$$530 = 40 \times 0.67N$$
$$N = \frac{530}{40 \times 0.67}$$
$$= 19.88 \text{ technicians}$$

DIAGNOSTIC QUESTION

Is process variability recognized?

So far in our treatment of process analysis we have assumed that there is no significant variability either in the demand to which the process is expected to respond, or
in the time taken for the process to perform its various activities. Clearly, this is not
the case in reality. So, it is important to look at the variability that can affect processes
and take account of it. However, do not dismiss the deterministic analysis we have
been examining up to this point. At worst it provides a good first approximation to
analyzing processes, while at best, the relationships that we have discussed do hold
for average performance values.

Sources of variability in processes

There are many reasons why variability occurs in processes. A few of these possible sources of variation are listed below.

- The late (or early) arrival of material, information or customers at a stage within the process.
- The temporary malfunction or breakdown of process technology within a stage of the process.
- The necessity for recycling 'misprocessed' materials, information or customers to an earlier stage in the process.
- The misrouting of material, information or customers within the process that then needs to be redirected.
- Each product or service being processed might be different, for example different models of automobile going down the same line.
- Products or services, although essentially the same, might require slightly different treatment. For instance, in the computer test and repair process, the time for some activities will vary depending on the results of the diagnostic checks.
- With any human activity there are slight variations in the physical coordination and effort on the part of the person performing the task that result in variation in activity times, even of routine activities.

All these sources of variation within a process will interact with each other, but result in two fundamental types of variability:

- Variability in the demand for processing at an individual stage within the process, usually expressed in terms of variation in the inter-arrival times of units to be processed.
- Variation in the time taken to perform the activities (i.e. process a unit) at each stage.

Activity time variability

Operations principle
Variability in a process acts to reduce its efficiency.

The effects of variability within a process will depend on whether the movements of units between stages, and hence the inter-arrival times of units at stages, are synchronized or not. For example, consider the computer test and repair process described previously. Figure 5.12 shows the average activity time at each stage of the process, but also the variability around the average time. Suppose that it was decided to

Figure 5.12   Processing time variability in a synchronized process. Cycle time will need to accommodate the longest activity time at any of the stages

synchronize the flow between the four stages by using an indexing conveyor or a simple traffic lights system that ensured all movement between the stages happened simultaneously. The interval between each synchronized movement would have to be set so as to allow all stages to have finished their activities irrespective of whether they had experienced a particularly fast or particularly slow activity time. In this case, from Figure 5.12 that synchronized indexing time would have to be set at 15 minutes. This then becomes the effective cycle time of the process. Note that the effective bottleneck stage is now stage 1 rather than stage 2. Although stage 2 has the longer average activity time (12 minutes), activity 1 with an average activity time of 11 minutes has a degree of variability that results in a maximum activity of 15 minutes. Note also that every stage will experience some degree of idle time, the average idle time at each station being the cycle time minus the average activity time at that station. This reduction in the efficiency of the process is only partly a result of its imbalance. The extra lost time is a result of activity time variability.

This type of effect is not at all uncommon. For example, automobiles are assembled using a moving belt assembly line whose speed is set to achieve a cycle time that can accommodate activity time variability. However, a more common arrangement, especially when processing information or customers, is to move units between stages as soon as the activities performed by each stage are complete. Here, units move through the process in an unsynchronized manner rather than having to wait for an imposed movement time. This means that each stage may spend less time waiting to move their unit forward, but it does introduce more variation in the demand placed on subsequent stations. When movement was synchronized the inter-arrival time of units at each stage was fixed at the cycle time. Without synchronization, the inter-arrival time at each stage will itself be variable.

Arrival time variability

To understand the effect of arrival variability on process performance, it is first useful to examine what happens to process performance in a very simple process as arrival time changes under conditions of no variability. For example, the simple process shown in Figure 5.13 is comprised of one stage that performs exactly 10 minutes of work. Units arrive at the process at a constant and predictable rate. If the arrival rate is one unit every 30 minutes, then the process will be utilized for only 33.33 per cent of the time, and the units will never have to wait to be processed. This is shown as point A on Figure 5.13. If the arrival rate increases to one arrival every 20 minutes, the utilization increases to 50 per cent, and again the units will not have to wait to be processed. This is point B on Figure 5.13. If the arrival rate increases to one arrival every 10 minutes, the process is now fully utilized, but, because a unit arrives just as the previous one has finished being processed, no unit has to wait. This is point C on Figure 5.13. However, if the arrival rate ever exceeded one unit every 10 minutes, the waiting line in front of the process activity would build up indefinitely, as is shown as point D in Figure 5.13. So, in a perfectly constant and predictable world, the relationship between process waiting time and utilization is a rectangular function as shown by the dotted line in Figure 5.13.

Operations principle
Process variability results in simultaneous waiting and resource under-utilization.

When arrival time is not constant but variable, then the process may have both units waiting to be processed and under-utilization of the process's resources over the same period. Figure 5.14 illustrates how this could happen for the same process as shown in Figure 5.13, with constant 10-minute activity times, but this time with variable arrival times. The table gives details of the arrival of each unit at the process and when it was processed, and the bar chart illustrates it graphically. Six units arrive with an average arrival time of 11 minutes, some of which can be processed as soon as they arrive (units A, D and F) while others have to wait for a short period. Over the same period the process has to wait for work three times.

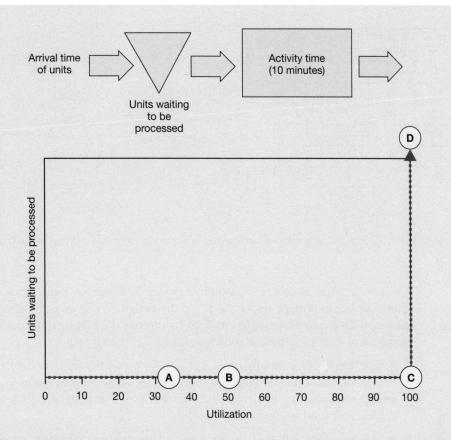

Figure 5.13   The relationship between process utilization and number of units waiting to be processed for no arrival time or activity time variability

During the observed period,

Time when a single unit was waiting = 3 minutes

Elapsed time for processing the six units = 65 minutes

Average number of units waiting = 3/65

= 0.046 units

Process idle time = 5 minutes

So, process idle percentage = 5 × 100/65

= 7.7%

Therefore, process utilization = 92.3%

This point is shown as point X in Figure 5.15. If the average arrival time were to be changed with the same variability, the dotted line in Figure 5.15 would show the relationship between average waiting time and process utilization. As the process moves closer to 100 per cent utilization the higher the average waiting time will become. To put it another way, the only way to guarantee very low waiting times for the units is to suffer low process utilization.

When both arrival times and activity times are variable, this effect is even more pronounced. And the greater the variability, the more the waiting time utilization deviates from the simple rectangular function of the 'no variability' conditions that was shown in

Unit	Arrival time	Start of activity	End of activity	Wait time
A	0	0	10	0
B	12	12	22	0
C	20	22	32	2
D	34	34	44	0
E	43	44	54	1
F	55	55	65	0

Figure 5.14 Units arriving at a process with variable arrival times and a constant activity time (10 minutes)

Figure 5.13. A set of curves for a typical process is shown in Figure 5.16(a). This phenomenon has important implications for the design of processes. In effect it presents three options to process designers wishing to improve the waiting time or utilization performance of their processes, as shown in Figure 5.16(b). Either:

- Accept long average waiting times and achieve high utilization (point X), or
- Accept low utilization and achieve short average waiting times (point Y), or
- Reduce the variability in arrival times, activity times, or both, and achieve higher utilization and short waiting times (point Z).

To analyze processes with both inter-arrival and activity time variability, queuing or 'waiting line' analysis can be used. This is treated in the supplement to this chapter. But, do not dismiss the relationship shown in Figures 5.15 and 5.16 as some minor technical phenomenon. It is far more than this. It identifies an important choice in process design that

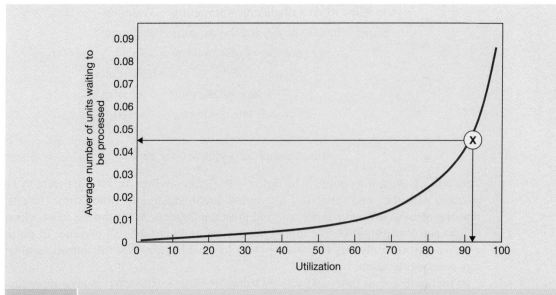

Figure 5.15 The relationship between process utilization and number of units waiting to be processed for the variable arrival times in the example

Figure 5.16 The relationship between process utilization and number of units waiting to be processed for variable arrival and activity times. (a) Decreasing variability allows higher utilization without long waiting times. (b) Managing capacity and/or variability

Operations principle
Process design involves some choice between utilization, waiting time, and variability reduction.

could have strategic implications. Which is more important to a business – fast throughput time or high utilization of its resources? The only way to have both of these simultaneously is to reduce variability in its processes, which may itself require strategic decisions such as limiting the degree of customization of products or services, or imposing stricter limits on how products or services can be delivered to customers, and so on. It also demonstrates an important point concerned with the day-to-day management of process – the only way to absolutely guarantee 100 per cent utilization of resources is to accept an infinite amount of work in progress and/or waiting time. We will take this point further in Chapter 8 when we deal with capacity management.

Critical commentary

Each chapter contains a short critical commentary on the main ideas covered in the chapter. Its purpose is not to undermine the issues discussed in the chapter, but to emphasize that, although we present a relatively orthodox view of operation, there are other perspectives.

■ There is not too much that would be considered contentious in this chapter. However, some practitioners would reject the idea of mapping processes as they exist currently. Rather, they would advocate a more radical 'clean sheet of paper' approach. Only by doing this, they would say, can one be sufficiently imaginative in the redesign of processes. The other potential point of contention would concern the viability of what we have called 'long-thin' process designs. As was discussed in the previous chapter, this assumes a degree of division of labour and systemization of work that is held by some to be 'dehumanizing'.

Summary checklist

This checklist comprises questions that can be usefully applied to any type of operations and reflect the major diagnostic questions used within the chapter.

☐ Have a clear set of performance objectives for each process been set?

☐ Do the process design objectives clearly relate to the business's strategic objectives?

☐ Is the following information known for all key processes in the operation?
- The throughput or flow rate of the process?
- The throughput time of the process?
- The number of units in the process (work-in-process)?
- The utilization of process resources?

☐ Are processes documented using process mapping techniques?

☐ Are formal process descriptions followed in practice?

☐ If not, should the process descriptions be changed or should existing process descriptions be enforced?

☐ Is it necessary for process descriptions to include the degree of visibility at each stage of the process?

☐ Are the details of task precedence known for each process?

☐ Have the advantages and disadvantages of series and parallel configurations been explored?

☐ Is the process balanced? If not, can the bottleneck stages be redesigned to achieve better balance?

☐ Is the relationships between throughput, cycle time and work-in-process understood (Little's law)?

☐ Are the sources of process variability recognized?

☐ Has the effect of variability been recognized in the design of the process?

Case study

North West Constructive Bank – The New Mortgage Centre 2

Andy Curtis, the Mortgage Operations Manager for North West Constructive Bank (NWCB), had launched a major investigation into his processes and how they might be redesigned (see Part 1 of this case study in Chapter 4). He had been prompted by the failure of his operation to improve after it had consolidated three separate sites into one location. The staff from the three old centres that covered the northern, southern and western areas of the bank's customer base had been kept largely intact in the new site. Andy and his team suspected that this may have contributed to their failure to improve performance, especially throughput time performance, immediately after the move.

Andy has initiated an investigation that would provide the basic data for a thorough examination of how the mortgage centre's processes could be redesigned. The results of this investigation are shown in Figure 5.17 and Table 5.4. These detail the activities contained within each stage of the overall process together with each activity's immediate predecessor, the type of skills necessary to carry out each activity, the allowed time for each activity (this had varied slightly between the three regional offices, so an average had been taken), and an estimate of the minimum and maximum times necessary to perform each activity.

Also shown for each activity is the percentage of applications that needed to be 'recycled' (applications that contained ambiguities, errors or omissions in the data supplied and therefore had to be returned to a previous activity) or 'rejected' (the mortgage was being refused for some reason). Two of the activities (activity b and activity h) were only necessary for approximately 40 per cent of applications. In addition, Andy had asked each section to make a 'spot check' on how many applications were currently being processed. To his surprise it emerged that around 5000 applications were in-process with most of them in the offer and completion parts of the process. '*I'm not surprised that offers spend a long time in the offer and completion parts of the process*', explained Andy. '*Those are the sections where we are waiting for the results of surveys or further information from legal representatives to arrive. Nevertheless, it's far too many applications to have just hanging around within the process.*'

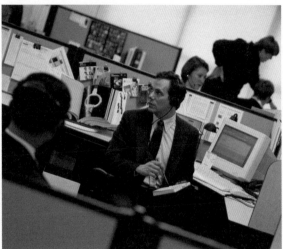

Source: © Getty Images

In addition 40 minutes is allowed for extra telephone calls, etc., that are not allocated to any specific stage or activity.

Skills required performing the task:

- Credit – Credit assessment skills
- U/R – Underwriting skills
- Local – Knowledge of local property market
- Legal – Knowledge of property law
- Rel. – Relationship skills

All the management team thought that going through the details of each part of the process had been useful. It had produced information that had not been collected before, such as the actual percentage of recycled and rejected applications at each stage. Also it had prompted an interesting debate around the appropriateness of the time allowances for each activity and the sequence of the activities. For example, the underwriting activities had always preceded the offer stage activities in all the centres. Yet there was no technical reason why the underwriting and offer activities could not be performed in parallel. '*When all applications were purely paper-based it would not have been possible to perform activities in parallel unless the documents had been physically copied and even then it would have led to confusion. Now, although there are paper-based files associated with each application, the information system allows real-time*

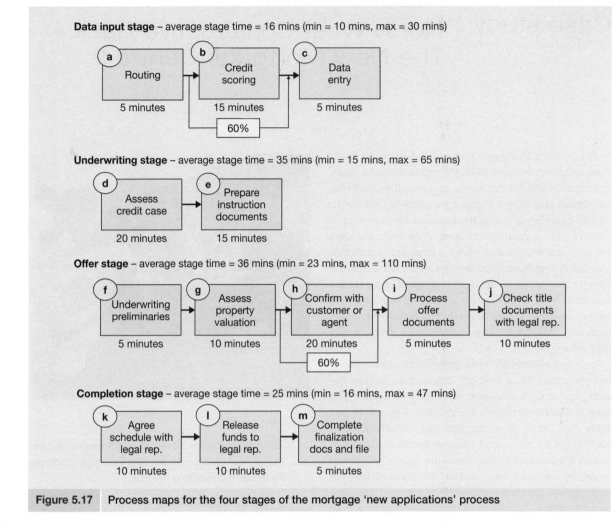

Figure 5.17   Process maps for the four stages of the mortgage 'new applications' process

updating of each application file. The only remaining argument in favour of making the underwriting and offer stages sequential is that work carried out on applications that are subsequently rejected or recycled may be wasted. I am also delighted that we have agreed on the time allowances for each activity as well as getting a sense of realistic minimum and maximum times. Even so, I doubt whether it is ever possible in this kind of job to give very precise times. There are just too many different situations that can occur. This is why we have had to incorporate the additional 40 minutes of unallocated time for the whole process. I guess that we could split this between the stages but I'm not sure it would be that helpful. We know that the majority of this extra allowed time is needed in the offer and completion stages rather than the first two stages, but I would rather not fall into the trap of spurious precision.'

Redesigning the process

Three separate options for the design of the process were being actively considered by the management team.

● *Option 1* – Keep the process as it is currently at the new centre, with a common data input stage serving all regions and with the three regions each having its own underwriting, offer and completion stages working in series. This arrangement had the advantage of not disrupting the existing way of working and of maintaining the organizational coherence of the three teams which were each already developing their own cultures.

● *Option 2* – Reorganize the whole process by abandoning the current regional structure and organizing four sequential teams around each of the four stages of data input, underwriting, offer and completion. This

Table 5.4   Total activities for all stages of the 'new applications' process

Stage	Activity code	Activity description	Immediate predecessor	Special skills needed?*	Percentage recycled and rejected	Allowed time	Approx. Min. time	Max. time
Data input	a	Routing	None	None	Recycled 2.2% Rejected 0.5%	5	5	5
	b	Credit scoring (40% of applications only)	a	None	Recycled 0 Rejected 0	15 (6 on average)	10	20
	c	Data entry	b	None	Recycled 0 Rejected 0	5	5	5
Underwriting	d	Assess credit case	c	Credit	Recycled 9.1% Rejected 5%	20	5	45
	e	Prepare instruction docs	d	Credit	Recycled 1.3% Rejected 0	15	10	20
Offer	f	Underwrite prelims	e?	U/R	Recycled 0 Rejected 0	5	5	5
	g	Assess property valuation	f	U/R Local	Recycled 7.7% Rejected 5%	10	8	30
	h	Confirm with customer or agent (40% of applications only)	g	U/R Local Rel.	Recycled 6.4% Rejected 3.2% (of all applications)	20 (8 on average)	10	40
	i	Process offer docs	h	U/R	Recycled 0 Rejected 0	5	5	5
	j	Check title docs with legal rep.	i	U/R Legal Rel.	Recycled 4.5% Rejected 2.8%	8	5	30
Completion	k	Agree schedule with legal rep.	j	Legal Rel.	Recycled 2.8%	10	5	20
	l	Release funds to legal rep.	k	Legal Rel.	Recycled 1.8% Rejected 0	10	8	15
	m	Complete finalization docs and file	l	Legal	Recycled 0.9% Rejected 0	5	3	12
					Total	112		

*See text for abbreviations.

arrangement was seen as being more appropriate for the higher volume that the new combined centre was processing. It would also allow some skills, such as underwriting skills and legal skills, to be developed because of the larger number of staff with these skills working together. However, the team saw two disadvantages of this arrangement. First, it would affect the morale of the existing regionally based teams, especially the southern team who had worked together for many years. Second, for some activities in the offer stage it was still an advantage to have some local knowledge of the regional property markets. Even if this option were adopted, the offer team would probably still have to retain some local 'cells' within the process.

- *Option 3* – In some ways this was the most radical design option being considered. It involved reorganizing into four teams around the four stages within the process, but operating the underwriting stage and offer stage in parallel. This was seen as risky, especially with such high levels of recycled applications, but offered the advantage of short throughput times.

The recycling problem

Andy had been aware of the problems that existed around the amount of 'rework' even prior to the reorganization. He had already requested an analysis of the reasons behind this recycling. In the previous year a total of 76,250 applications had been received and 60,921 offers were 'issued' (made) by the Mortgage Centre. In the same period a total of 21,735 of these required some recycling at least once during their processing. The majority of these were as a result of documents submitted with the application or information in the application being missing, incomplete, or inaccurate in some way. Some recycles were the result of the customers changing their mind about the details of the mortgage during the processing period; usually this was because they required to borrow a different amount. Some recycling was caused directly by errors made within the Mortgage Centre during earlier stages of the process. The largest single source of errors was those caused by inaccurate or incomplete data capture when initial customer and property information was taken. Agents were far worse at this than the Bank's own branches. Even those errors attributed to customers were often the result of their not being given appropriate guidance by staff at the agents' offices or at branches.

When an application needed recycling within the process, the application and accompanying documents were put in a yellow folder, the customer file on the data base was 'marked' with a yellow tag, and the application was reviewed by the team supervisor, who assessed how it should be treated. Usually this meant sending the application back to an earlier stage in the process. This resulted in a continual 'churn' of some applications being recycled through the process.

'Both rejected and recycled applications cause problems because they represent "wasted" work. Rejections are less serious in the sense that the whole purpose of this process is to "weed out" applications that we don't want to fund. Even so, I wonder whether we could screen these applications out earlier in the process. The recycled applications are more serious. One problem is that, although we know the percentage of applications recycled from each activity, we have no record of where in the process they are recycled to. One option we have is to redefine the very first "routing" activity at the data entry stage and make it an initial screening activity that would try to screen out the applications that were likely to be recycled later in the process. In other words, we should let through only those applications that were unlikely to be recycled. In effect, we would be making the initial routing activity the most important in the whole process. It would mean that we would have to staff the activity with people with a very wide range of skills and allow them sufficient time to do the initial screening, perhaps up to 20 minutes for each application. Whether it is worth doing this depends on the reduction in recycling. Some of the team feel that recycling could be cut down by at least 75 per cent if we did this.'

Staffing levels

The final issue being considered by the team was how many people the process should be employing. By pooling all data entry activity into one stage, the process had already saved 11 staff and there was a general feeling that similar savings could be made throughout the process if it were redesigned according to either Option 2 or Option 3 explained previously. In fact, irrespective of which design option was chosen, the agreed time allowances for the activities seemed to indicate that the process should be able to operate with few people.

Andy realized that his operation was facing a number of decisions. He also realized that none of them was straightforward. 'The real problem we face is that everything is interrelated. The process redesign options we have could affect our ability to reduce the time wasted on recycled applications as well as the number of staff we need. Yet by increasing the investment of staff time and effort in certain parts of the process we may be able to reduce recycling and even achieve an overall reduction in staff. In the long term that is what is important. We need to be able to drive down the cost of processing mortgage applications if we are to survive as an in-house operation. Ours is exactly the sort of process that could be outsourced if we don't provide an effective and efficient service to the business.'

QUESTIONS

1 Does it matter that Andy and his team cannot allocate all the time necessary to process a mortgage application to individual activities?

2 Should the process be redesigned, and if so, which option should be adopted?

3 How could the 'recycling' problem be reduced, and what benefits would this bring?

Active case study   Action Response

ACTIVE CASE

Action Response is a successful charity that provides fast responses to critical situations throughout the world. They are required to process requests for cash quickly and accurately in order to get the money to where it is needed, in time to make a difference. However, complaints about money not getting through quickly enough and rising operational costs are a concern for the charity.

● How would you assess and re-configure the processes employed to improve the responsiveness and efficiency of Action Response?

Please refer to the Active case on the CD accompanying this book to listen to the views of those involved.

Applying the principles

HINTS

Some of these exercises can be answered by reading the chapter. Others will require some general knowledge of business activity and some might require an element of investigation. All have hints on how they can be answered on the CD accompanying this book.

1 Choose a process with which you are familiar. For example, a process at work, registration for a university course, joining a video rental shop service, enrolling at a sports club or gym, registering at a library, obtaining a car parking permit, etc. Map the process that you went through from your perspective, using the process mapping symbols explained in this chapter. Try to map what the 'back-office' process might be (that is the part of the process that is vital to achieving its objective, but that you can't see). You may have to speculate on this but you could talk with someone who knows the process.

● How might the process be improved from your (the customer's) perspective and from the perspective of the operation itself?

2 *'It is a real problem for us'*, said Angnyeta Larson. *'We now have only 10 working days between all the expense claims coming from the departmental coordinators and authorizing payments on the next month's payroll. This really is not long enough and we are already having problems during peak times.'* Angnyeta was the department head of the internal financial control department of a metropolitan authority in southern Sweden. Part of her department's responsibilities included checking and processing expense claims from staff throughout the metropolitan authority and authorizing payment to the salaries payroll section. She had 12 staff who were trained to check expense claims and all of them were devoted full-time to processing the claims in the two weeks (10 working days) prior to the deadline for informing the salaries section. The number of claims submitted over the year averaged around 3200, but this could vary between 1000 during the quiet summer months up to 4300 in peak months. Processing claims involved checking receipts, checking that claims met with the strict financial allowances for different types of expenditure, checking all calculations, obtaining more data from the claimant if necessary, and (eventually) sending an approval notification to salaries. The total processing time was on average 20 minutes per claim.

● How many staff does the process need on average, for the lowest demand, and for the highest demand?

● If a more automated process involving electronic submission of claims could reduce the average processing time to 15 minutes, what effect would this have on the required staffing levels?

- If department coordinators could be persuaded to submit their batched claims earlier (not always possible for all departments) so that the average time between submission of the claims to the finance department and the deadline for informing salaries section was increased to 15 working days, what effect would this have?

3 The headquarters of a major creative agency offered a service to all its global subsidiaries that included the preparation of a budget estimate that was submitted to potential clients when making a 'pitch' for new work. This service had been offered previously to only a few of the group's subsidiary companies. Now that it was to be offered worldwide, it was deemed appropriate to organize the process of compiling budget estimates on a more systematic basis. It was estimated that the worldwide demand for this service would be around 20 budget estimates per week, and that, on average, the staff who would put together these estimates would be working a 35-hour week. The elements within the total task of compiling a budget estimate are shown in the following table.

Element	Time (mins)	What element(s) must be done prior to this one?
A – obtain time estimate from creatives	20	None
B – obtain account handler's deadlines	15	None
C – obtain production artwork estimate	80	None
D – preliminary budget calculations	65	A, B and C
E – check on client budget	20	D
F – check on resource availability and adjust estimate	80	D
G – complete final budget estimate	80	E and F

- What is the required cycle time for this process?
- How many people will the process require to meet the anticipated demand of 20 estimates per week?
- Assuming that the process is to be designed on a 'long-thin' basis, what elements would each stage be responsible for completing? And what would be the balancing loss for this process?
- Assuming that instead of the long-thin design, two parallel processes are to be designed, each with half the number of stations of the long-thin design, what now would be the balancing loss?

4 A company has decided to manufacture a general-purpose 'smoothing plane', a tool which smoothes and shapes wood. Its engineers estimated the time it would take to perform each element in the assembly process. The marketing department also estimated that the likely demand for the new product would be 98,000 units. The marketing department was not totally confident of its forecast; however, 'a substantial proportion of demand is likely to be export sales, which we find difficult to predict. But whatever demand does turn out to be, we will have to react quickly to meet it. The more we enter these parts of the market, the more we are into impulse buying and the more sales we lose if we don't supply.'

An idea of the assembly task can be gained from the following table which gives the 'standard time' for each element of the assembly task.

Standard times for each element of assembly task in standard minutes (SM)

Press elements	
Assemble poke	0.12 mins
Fit poke to front	0.10 mins
Rivet adjusting lever to front	0.15 mins
Press adjusting nut screw to front	0.08 mins

Bench elements	
Fit adjusting nut to front	0.15 mins
Fit frog screw to front	0.05 mins
Fit knob to base	0.15 mins
Fit handle to base	0.17 mins
Fit front assembly to base	0.15 mins
Assemble blade unit	0.08 mins
Final assembly	0.20 mins
Packing element	
Make box, wrap plane, pack	0.20 mins
Total time	**1.60 mins**

All elements must be performed sequentially in the order listed.

The standard costing system at the company involves adding a 150 per cent overhead charge to the direct labour cost of manufacturing the product, and the product would retail for the equivalent of around £35 in Europe where most retailers will sell this type of product for about 70–100 per cent more than they buy it from the manufacturer.

- How many people will be needed to assemble this product?
- Design a process for the assembly operation (to include the fly press work) including the tasks to be performed at each part of the system.
- How might the process design need to be adjusted as demand for this and similar products builds up?

Notes on chapter

1 Source: Horovitz, A. (2002) 'Fast food world ways drive-thru is the way to go', *USA Today*, 3 April.
2 Not everyone uses exactly the same terminology in this area. For example, some publications use the term 'cycle time' to refer to what we have called 'throughput rate'.
3 The concept of visibility is explained in Shostack, G.L. (1984) 'Designing services that deliver', *Harvard Business Review*, Jan.–Feb., pp. 133–9.
4 Little's law is best explained in Hopp, W.J. and Spearman, M.L. (2001) *Factory Physics* (2nd edn), McGraw-Hill, New York.

Taking it further

Anupindi, R., Chopra, S., Deshmukh, S.D., Van Mieghem, J.A. and Zemel, E. (1999) *Managing Business Process Flows,* Prentice Hall, New Jersey. An excellent, although mathematical, approach to process design in general.

Hammer, M. (1990) 'Reengineering work: don't automate, obliterate', *Harvard Business Review*, July–August. This is the paper that launched the whole idea of business processes and process management in general to a wider managerial audience. Slightly dated but worth reading.

Ramaswamy, R. (1996) *Design and Management of Service Processes*, Addison-Wesley Longman. A relatively technical approach to process design in a service environment.

Shostack, G.L. (1982) 'How to design a service', *European Journal of Marketing*, Vol. 16, No. 1. A far less technical and more experiential approach to design of service processes.

FURTHER RESOURCES

For further resources including examples, animated diagrams, self test questions, excel spreadsheets, active case studies and video materials please explore the CD accompanying this book.

Supplement to Chapter 5
Queuing analysis

Introduction

Queuing analysis (in many parts of the world it is called 'waiting line' analysis) is often explained purely in terms of customers being processed through service operations. This is misleading. Although queuing analysis can be particularly important in service operations, especially where customers really do 'queue' for service, the approach is useful in any kind of operation. Figure 5.18 shows the general form of queuing analysis.

The general form of queuing analysis

Customers arrive according to some probability distribution and wait to be processed (unless part of the operation is idle); when they have reached the front of the queue, they are processed by one of the n parallel 'servers' (their processing time also being described by a probability distribution), after which they leave the operation. There are many examples of this kind of system. Table 5.6 illustrates some of these. All of these examples can be described by a common set of elements that define their queuing behaviour.

- *The source of customers*, sometimes called the calling population, is the source of supply of customers. In queue management 'customers' are not always human. 'Customers' could for example be trucks arriving at a weighbridge, orders arriving to be processed, machines waiting to be serviced, etc.

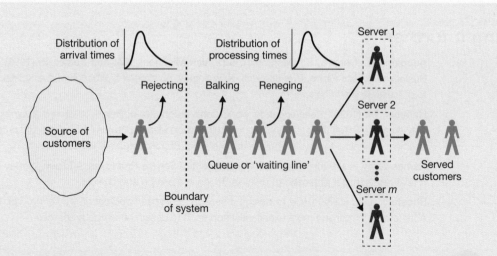

Figure 5.18   The general form of queuing analysis

Table 5.6	Examples of processes that can be analyzed using queuing analysis	
Operation	*Arrivals*	*Processing capacity*
Bank	Customers	Tellers
Supermarket	Shoppers	Checkouts
Hospital clinic	Patients	Doctors
Graphic artist	Commissions	Artists
Custom cake decorators	Orders	Cake decorators
Ambulance service	Emergencies	Ambulances with crews
Telephone switchboard	Calls	Telephonists
Maintenance department	Breakdowns	Maintenance staff

- *The arrival rate* is the rate at which customers needing to be served arrive at the server or servers. Rarely do customers arrive at a steady and predictable rate. Usually there is variability in their arrival rate. Because of this it is necessary to describe arrival rates in terms of probability distributions.
- *The queue.* Customers waiting to be served form the queue or waiting line itself. If there is relatively little limit on how many customers can queue at any time, we can assume that, for all practical purposes, an infinite queue is possible. Sometimes, however, there is a limit to how many customers can be in the queue at any one time.
- *Queue discipline* is the set of rules that determine the order in which customers waiting in the queue are served. Most simple queues, such as those in a shop, use a *first-come-first-served* queue discipline.
- *Servers.* A server is the facility that processes the customers in the queue. In any queuing system there may be any number of servers configured in different ways. In Figure 5.18 servers are configured in parallel, but some systems may have servers in a series arrangement. There is also likely to be variation in how long it takes to process each customer. Therefore processing time, like arrival time, is usually described by a probability distribution.

Calculating queue behaviour

Excel

Management scientists have developed formulae that can predict the steady-state behaviour of different types of queuing system. Unfortunately, many of these formulae are extremely complicated, especially for complex queuing systems, and are beyond the scope of this book. In practice, computer programs are almost always used to predict the behaviour of queuing systems. However, studying queuing formulae can illustrate some useful characteristics of the way queuing systems behave. Moreover, for relatively simple systems, using the formulae (even with some simplifying assumptions) can provide a useful approximation to process performance.

Notation

There are several different conventions for the notation used for different aspects of queuing system behaviour. It is always advisable to check the notation used by different authors before using their formulae. We shall use the following notation:

$$t_a = \text{average time between arrivals}$$
$$r_a = \text{arrival rate (items per unit time)} = 1/t_a$$
$$c_a = \text{coefficient of variation of arrival times}$$
$$m = \text{number of parallel servers at a station}$$

t_e = mean processing time

r_e = processing rate (items per unit time) = m/t_e

c_e = coefficient of variation of process time

u = utilization of station = r_a/r_e = $(r_a t_e)/m$

WIP = average work in progress (number of items) in the system

WIP_q = expected work in progress (number of items) in the queue

W_q = expected waiting time in the queue

W = expected waiting time in the system (queue time + processing time)

Variability

The concept of variability is central to understanding the behaviour of queues. If there were no variability there would be no need for queues to occur because the capacity of a process could be relatively easily adjusted to match demand. For example, suppose one member of staff (a server) serves customers at a bank counter who always arrive exactly every five minutes (i.e. 12 per hour). Also suppose that every customer takes exactly five minutes to be served, then because

(a) the arrival rate is less than or equal to the processing rate, and
(b) there is no variation,

no customer need ever wait because the next customer will arrive when, or before, the previous customer leaves. That is, WIP_q = 0.

Also, in this case, the server is working all the time, again because exactly as one customer leaves, the next one is arriving. That is, u = 1.

Even with more than one server, the same may apply. For example, if the arrival time at the counter is five minutes (12 per hour) and the processing time for each customer is now always exactly 10 minutes (6 per hour), the counter would need two servers (m = 2), and because

(a) the arrival rate is less than or equal to the processing rate $\times$ m, and
(b) there is no variation,

again, WIP_q = 0 and u = 1.

Of course, it is convenient (but unusual) if the arrival rate divided by the processing rate is a whole number. When this is not the case (for this simple example with no variation):

$$\text{Utilization} = \text{processing rate}/(\text{arrival rate} \times m)$$

For example, if arrival rate r_a = 5 minutes, processing rate r_e = 8 minutes, and number of servers m = 2, then:

$$\text{Utilization } u = 8/(5 \times 2) = 0.8 \text{ or } 80\%$$

Incorporating variability

The previous examples were not realistic because they assumed no variation in arrival or processing times. We also need to take into account the variation around these means. To do that, we need to use a probability distribution. Figure 5.19 contrasts two processes with different arrival distributions. The units arriving are shown as people, but they could be jobs arriving at a machine, trucks needing servicing or any other uncertain

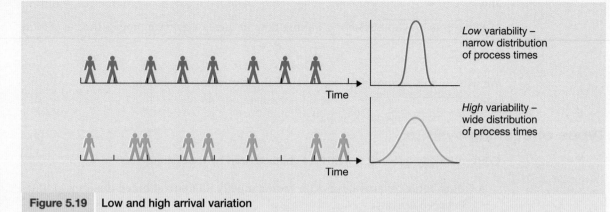

Figure 5.19   Low and high arrival variation

event. The top example shows low variation in arrival time where customers arrive in a relatively predictable manner. The bottom example has the same average number of customers arriving but this time they arrive unpredictably, with sometimes long gaps between arrivals and at other times two or three customers arriving close together. We could do a similar analysis to describe processing times.

In Figure 5.19 high arrival variation has a distribution with a wider spread (called 'dispersion') than the distribution describing lower variability. Statistically the usual measure for indicating the spread of a distribution is its standard deviation, σ. But variation depends not only on standard deviation. For example, a distribution of arrival times may have a standard deviation of 2 minutes. This could indicate very little variation when the average arrival time is 60 minutes. But it would mean a very high degree of variation when the average arrival time is 3 minutes. Therefore to normalize standard deviation, it is divided by the mean of its distribution. This measure is called the coefficient of variation of the distribution. So,

$$c_a = \text{coefficient of variation of arrival times} = \sigma_a/t_a$$

$$c_e = \text{coefficient of variation of processing times} = \sigma_e/t_e$$

Incorporating Little's law

Little's law (described earlier in the chapter) describes the relationship between the cycle time, the work in progress and the throughput time of the process. It was denoted by the following simple relationship:

$$\text{Throughput time} = \text{work in progress} \times \text{cycle time}$$

or

$$T = WIP \times C$$

Little's law can help to understand queuing behaviour. Consider the queue in front of the station.

Work in progress in queue = arrival rate at queue (equivalent to cycle time)
$\times$ waiting time in queue (equivalent to throughput time)

$$WIP_q = r_a \times W_q$$

and

Waiting time in whole system = waiting time in queue + average process time at station

$$W = W_q + t_e$$

We will use this relationship later to investigate queuing behaviour.

Types of queuing system

Conventionally queuing systems are characterized by four parameters:

A = distribution of arrival times (or more properly interarrival times, the elapsed times between arrivals)
B = distribution of process times
m = number of servers at each station
b = maximum number of items allowed in the system

The most common distributions used to describe A or B are:

● The exponential (or Markovian) distribution, denoted by M
● The general (for example, normal) distribution, denoted by G.

So, for example, an M/G/1/5 queuing system would indicate a system with exponentially distributed arrivals, process times described by a general distribution such as a normal distribution, with one server, and a maximum number of 5 items allowed in the system. This type of notation is called Kendall's Notation.

Queuing theory can help us investigate any type of queuing system, but in order to simplify the mathematics, we shall here deal only with the two most common situations, namely:

● M/M/m – the exponential arrival and processing times with m servers and no maximum limit to the queue
● G/G/m – general arrival and processing distributions with m servers and no limit to the queue.

First we will start by looking at the simple case when $m = 1$.

For M/M/1 queuing systems

The formulae for this type of system are as follows.

$$\text{WIP} = \frac{u}{1 - u}$$

Using Little's law,

$$\text{WIP} = \text{cycle time/throughput time}$$
$$\text{Throughput time} = \text{WIP} \times \text{cycle time}$$

Then

$$\text{Throughput time} = \frac{u}{1 - u} \times \frac{1}{r_a} = \frac{t_e}{1 - u}$$

and since throughput time in the queue = total throughput time – average processing time,

$$W_q = W - t_e$$

$$= \frac{t_e}{1-u} - t_e$$

$$= \frac{t_e - t_e(1-u)}{1-u} = \frac{t_e - t_e - ut_e}{1-u}$$

$$= \left(\frac{u}{1-u}\right) t_e$$

Again, using Little's law,

$$WIP_q = r_a \times W_q = \left(\frac{u}{1-u}\right) t_e r_a$$

and since

$$u = \frac{r_a}{r_e} = r_a t_e$$

$$r_a = \frac{u}{t_e}$$

then

$$WIP_q = \frac{u}{1-u} \times t_e \times \frac{u}{t_e}$$

$$= \frac{u^2}{1-u}$$

For M/M/m systems

When there are m servers at a station the formula for waiting time in the queue (and therefore all other formulae) needs to be modified. Again, we will not derive these formulae but just state them:

$$W_q = \frac{u^{\sqrt{2(m+1)}-1}}{m(1-u)} t_e$$

from which the other formulae can be derived as before.

For G/G/1 systems

The assumption of exponential arrival and processing times is convenient as far as the mathematical derivations of various formulae are concerned. However, in practice, process times in particular are rarely truly exponential. This is why it is important to have some idea of how G/G/1 and G/G/m queues behave. However, exact mathematical relationships are not possible with such distributions. Therefore some kind of approximation is needed. The one here is in common use, and although it is not always accurate, it is so for practical purposes. For G/G/1 systems the formula for waiting time in the queue is as follows:

$$W_q = \left(\frac{c_a^2 + c_e^2}{2}\right)\left(\frac{u}{1-u}\right) t_e$$

There are two points to make about this equation. The first is that it is exactly the same as the equivalent equation for an M/M/1 system but with a factor to take account of the variability of the arrival and process times. The second is that this formula is sometimes known as the VUT formula because it describes the waiting time in a queue as a function of:

V (the variability in the queuing system)
U (the utilization of the queuing system, that is, demand versus capacity), and
T (the processing times at the station).

In other words, we can reach the intuitive conclusion that queuing time will increase as variability, utilization or processing time increases.

For G/G/m systems

The same modification applies to queuing systems using general equations and m servers. The formula for waiting time in the queue is now as follows:

$$W_q = \left(\frac{c_a^2 + c_e^2}{2}\right)\left(\frac{u^{\sqrt{2(m+1)}-1}}{m(1-u)}\right) t_e$$

Example

'I can't understand it. We have worked out our capacity figures and I am sure that one member of staff should be able to cope with the demand. We know that customers arrive at a rate of around six per hour and we also know that any trained member of staff can process them at a rate of eight per hour. So why is the queue so large and the wait so long? Have at look at what is going on there, please.'

Sarah knew that it was probably the variation, both in customers arriving and in how long it took each of them to be processed, that was causing the problem. Over a two-day period when she was told that demand was more or less normal, she timed the exact arrival times and processing times of every customer. Her results were as follows.

Coefficient of variation of customer arrivals, c_a = 1
Coefficient of variation of processing time, c_e = 3.5
Average arrival rate of customers, r_a = 6 per hour
Therefore, average interarrival time = 10 minutes
Average processing rate, r_e = 8 per hour
Therefore, average processing time = 7.5 minutes

Therefore, utilization of the single server, u = 6/8 = 0.75

Using the waiting time formula for a G/G/1 queuing system,

$$W_q = \left(\frac{1 + 12.25}{2}\right)\left(\frac{0.75}{1 - 0.75}\right) \times 7.5$$

$$= 6.625 \times 3 \times 7.5 = 149.06 \text{ mins}$$

$$= 2.48 \text{ hours}$$

Also,

$$WIP_q = \text{cycle time/throughput time}$$

$$= 6 \times 2.48 = 14.88$$

So, Sarah had found out that the average wait that customers could expect was 2.48 hours and that there would be an average of 14.88 people in the queue.

'Ok, so I see that it's the very high variation in the processing time that is causing the queue to build up. How about investing in a new computer system that would standardize processing time to a greater degree? I have been talking with our technical people and they reckon that, if we invested in a new system, we could cut the coefficient of variation of processing time down to 1.5. What kind of a difference would this make?'

Under these conditions with $c_e = 1.5$

$$W_q = \left(\frac{1 + 2.25}{2}\right)\left(\frac{0.75}{1 - 0.75}\right) \times 7.5$$

$$= 1.625 \times 3 \times 7.5 = 36.56 \text{ mins}$$

$$= 0.61 \text{ hours}$$

Therefore,

$$WIP_q = 6 \times 0.61 = 3.66$$

In other words, reducing the variation of the process time has reduced average queuing time from 2.48 hours to 0.61 hours and has reduced the expected number of people in the queue from 14.88 to 3.66.

Example

A bank wishes to decide how many staff to schedule during its lunch period. During this period customers arrive at a rate of nine per hour and the enquiries that customers have (such as opening new accounts, arranging loans, etc.) take on average 15 minutes to deal with. The bank manager feels that four staff should be on duty during this period but wants to make sure that the customers do not wait more than 3 minutes on average before they are served. The manager has been told by his small daughter that the distributions that describe both arrival and processing times are likely to be exponential. Therefore, $r_a = 9$ per hour, so $t_a = 6.67$ minutes; and $r_e = 4$ per hour, so $t_e = 15$ minutes. The proposed number of servers, $m = 4$, therefore the utilization of the system, $u = 9/(4 \times 4) = 0.5625$.

From the formula for waiting time for an M/M/m system,

$$W_q = \frac{u^{\sqrt{2(m+1)}-1}}{m(1-u)}t_e$$

$$= \frac{0.5625^{\sqrt{10}-1}}{4(1-0.5625)} \times 0.25$$

$$= \frac{0.5625^{2.162}}{1.75} \times 0.25$$

$$= 0.042 \text{ hours}$$

$$= 2.52 \text{ minutes}$$

Therefore the average waiting time with four servers would be 2.52 minutes, that is well within the manager's acceptable waiting tolerance.

Notes on chapter supplement

1 Maister, D. (1983) 'The psychology of waiting lines', *Harvard Business Review*, Jan.–Feb.

Taking it further

Hopp, W.J. and Spearman, M.L. (2001) *Factory Physics* (2nd edn), McGraw-Hill, New York. Very technical so don't bother with it if you aren't prepared to get into the maths. However, some fascinating analysis, especially concerning Little's law.

6 PRODUCT AND SERVICE DESIGN PROCESSES

Introduction

The products and services produced by an operation are its 'public face'. They are how customers judge a business: good products and services equals a good company. Being good at the design of new products and services has always had a strategic impact. What has changed over the last few years is both the speed and scale of *design* changes. And it is now accepted that there is a connection between the design of design processes, and the success of those products and services in the marketplace. This is why the processes that design new products and services are so important. (See Figure 6.1.)

Source: courtesy BMW Group

Figure 6.1 Product/service design is the process of defining the specification of products and/or services in order to fulfil a specific market need

Executive summary

VIDEO
further detail

> What is product/service design?
>
> Are product/service design objectives specified?
>
> Is the product/service design process defined?
>
> Are the resources for developing products and services adequate?
>
> Are product/service design and process design simultaneous?

Decision logic chain for product and service design processes

Each chapter is structured around a set of diagnostic questions. These questions suggest what you should ask in order to gain an understanding of the important issues of a topic, and as a result, improve your decision making. An executive summary, addressing these questions, is provided below.

What is product/service design?

Product/service design is the process of defining the specification of products and/or services in order to fulfil a specific market need. It is (or should be) a cross-functional process that must both overcome the traditional communication barriers between functions while at the same time fostering the creativity and innovation that is often necessary in new product and service design. Product and service design is also a process in its own right that must itself be designed. This involves many of the same issues as the design of any other process. In particular, process objectives must be clear, the stages of the process must be defined, and the resources within the process need to be adequate.

Are product/service design objectives specified?

Product and service designs and the processes that produce them should be designed to satisfy market needs. The quality of the design process can be judged in terms of both conformance (no errors in the design) and specification (the effectiveness of the design in achieving its market requirements). Speed in the design process is often called 'time-to-market' (TTM). Short TTM implies that designs can be frequently introduced to the market, achieving strategic impact. Dependability in the design process means meeting launch delivery dates notwithstanding disruptions to the design process. This in turn often requires that the design process is sufficiently flexible to cope with disruptions. The cost of the design process can be thought of both as the amount of budget that is necessary to produce a design, and as the impact of the design on the produced cost of the product or service. As the design process progresses the impact on eventual costs rises faster than the rate at which the design budget is spent.

Is the product/service design process defined?

Although there is no universally agreed set of stages to the design process, almost all stage models start with a general idea or 'concept' and progress through to a fully defined product or service specification. Between these two states the design may pass through stages such as concept generation, concept screening, preliminary design (including consideration of standardization, commonality, modularization and mass customization), design evaluation and improvement, and prototyping and final design.

Are the resources for developing products and services adequate?

All processes, including design processes, need to be designed and resourced adequately. The design principles covered in Chapters 4 and 5 apply equally in product and service design. In particular, resourcing decisions concerning the capacity to devote to the design process, the extent to which the design process is performed in-house and the use of process technologies must be made so as to reflect strategic objectives.

Are product/service design and process design simultaneous?

At the end of the design process, the ongoing operations process that will produce the product or service must itself be designed. Often, it is best to think of designing the ongoing operations process as a continuation of product and service design. Considering all the stages of both product/service and process design together is often called simultaneous design. In recent years simultaneous (or concurrent) design has been used to reduce time-to-market. In particular, four simultaneous design factors can be identified that promote fast time-to-market. These are routinely integrating design process, overlapping design stages, early deployment of strategic decision making to resolve design conflict, and an organizational structure that reflects the nature of the design process.

What is product/service design?

Product/service design is the process of defining the specification of products and/or services in order for them to fulfil a specific market need. The outcome of the product/service design process is a fully detailed product or service that can be produced on an ongoing basis by the operation. This should be a cross-functional process. Contributions are needed from those who understand market requirements, those who understand the technical aspects of the product or service, those with access to cost and investment information, those who can protect the design's intellectual property, and most of all, the operations people who will have to produce the product or service on an ongoing basis. In addition to the usual process design issues that were treated in the previous two chapters, in this type of process there are almost always issues of cross-functional responsibility and communication. Product and service design is also an activity that depends upon imagination, innovation and creativity, attributes that are regarded as almost synonymous with design. And while accepting that design is essentially a creative process, it *is* also a process. And like any process, it must be well designed if it is to contribute to the overall competitiveness of the business.

The following two examples are both design processes. Even though we may not see software as having to be 'designed', the way in which it is specified is essentially a design process. In fact it is probably the most important process for companies like Microsoft. The actual mass production of the software is important, but not at all as important as designing (and redesigning) the software product itself. Similarly, we may not see pharmaceutical products as being 'designed'. Yet, again, they go through a long and rigorous process that leads to their final specification.

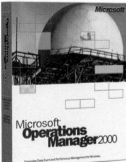

Source: Microsoft Corporation/Waggener Edstrom UK

| Example | **Product design at Microsoft[1]** |

Software products are complex and frighteningly interconnected in their internal structure. Both user requirements and the underlying technological possibilities are turbulent and difficult to predict. Furthermore, changing one part of a software product during the design process will almost certainly affect other parts, though exactly how, is again difficult to predict. Above all, software products are big and getting bigger. Some Microsoft products from the early 1980s had less than 100,000 lines of code. The first Windows NT in 1993 had about 4.5 million lines of code, now products can have tens of millions of lines of code. Similarly, teams of developers that once numbered 10 or 20 can now number many hundreds. Microsoft, the best known software company in the world, has developed two main clusters of ideas for coping with such difficult product design projects.

The first concerns the company's approach to conceptualizing the overall design task and allocating resources to its various stages. It includes the strict prioritization of individual features within the product, the most important being developed first. Without such prioritization design can drag on, always a tendency in software design, especially when customer requirements and technologies are moving rapidly. Brief vision statements for each part of the project help to define more detailed functional specifications needed to determine resources but not so detailed as to prevent the redefinition of design objectives as the project progresses. A modular product design also helps in making incremental changes. Microsoft likes to 'fix' project resources early in the design process, limiting the number of people and the time available for each part of the design process to encourage strict prioritization. It also focuses the team's creativity towards achieving a 'working' (if not perfect) version of the product which can be made ready for market testing. The second set of ideas concern the company's approach to managing day-by-day design. It is an attempt to ensure design discipline and order without inhibiting the developers' creativity. Big projects do need clearly defined design phases and task allocation, but over-specifying a project structure can discourage innovation. So Microsoft uses relatively small teams of 300–400 developers who synchronize their decisions very frequently. These synchronizations are called 'builds' and always occur at a fixed time, often every day. Developers submit their work at the fixed 'build' time. Frequent synchronization allows individual teams to be creative and to change their objectives in line with changing circumstances but, at the same time, ensures a shared discipline. Even so, it is necessary to stabilize the design periodically through the use of intermediate 'milestones'.

Example | ### Novartis[2]

There are few industries where new product or service design is more important than in pharmaceuticals. Designing new drugs needs budgets of several billion dollars. To Novartis, one of the most respected companies in the pharmaceutical sector, managing the design of new drugs is arguably its most important activity. *'We want to build the most competitive, most innovative research organization with the most promising pipeline in the industry to cure and help people around the world'*, says the company. *'We want to discover, develop and successfully market innovative products to cure diseases, to ease suffering and to enhance the quality of life.'* Of course the company also want to do this while being able to provide a return for their shareholders, and with R&D expenditures averaging around 20 per cent of sales revenue for most pharmaceutical companies, managing the design process is a 'make or break' activity. Drug design consists of several, sometimes overlapping stages. First is the 'drug discovery' phase. Naturally occurring or synthetic chemical compounds are investigated in the laboratory to explore their potential for further development. This process is no longer based on trial and error. Using a technique known as combinatorial chemistry, thousands of compounds are produced and tested automatically. When promising candidates for further design have been identified, 'preclinical' testing begins, where further laboratory tests investigate the pharmacological characteristics of potential new drugs. Issues such as efficacy and toxicity are investigated, and first thought is given to how the drug could be manufactured should it ever go into production. Of 10,000 candidates that are screened during the drug discovery stage, only about 250 will be selected to go through to the preclinical phase, which further cuts the number of candidates down to around five. These five go on to the first of three stages of 'clinical trials', a process that all drugs must undergo before they can be considered for market approval. Phase 1 of clinical trials starts by testing the drugs on healthy volunteers, then on patients who have the disease that the drug is intended to treat. Phase 2 attempts to establish appropriate scales for measuring the effectiveness of the drug, while phase 3 completes the process of quantifying the effectiveness of the drug and checks for any significant side effects. Generally, clinical trials are carefully regulated and monitored by government agencies, charged with giving approval (or not) for the drug to be marketed. Typically, for every five candidates entering the clinical testing phases only one is approved to be sold into the market. In total the whole process can easily take up to 15 years. This means that having plenty of potentially marketable drugs in the design pipeline is vital for any pharmaceutical company.

Source: © Getty Images/Digital Vision

What do these two examples have in common?

The nature of product and service design, to some extent, will be different in different types of operation; the technical issues will be different, as often will the time scales involved. For example, computing products made in volume now may not even exist in three or four years' time. There is also a difference between designing products and designing services, especially high-visibility services where the customer is inside the service, experiencing it. With products, customers judge the attributes of the product itself such as its functionality, its aesthetics, and so on. But with services customers will judge not only the functionality of what they receive, but also the process that they were put through in receiving it. For example, a retail bank may design the products that are available through its branches or its website, and the customer will make a judgement about the usefulness and value of these services. But they will also judge their experience in visiting the branch or using the website. So, whereas for products, the design of the product itself and the design of the process that produces it can be considered as two separate activities (although this may be a mistake, see later), the design of a service cannot be considered independently of the design of the process that creates it.

Yet notwithstanding these differences, the design *process* is essentially very similar irrespective of what is being designed. More importantly, it is a process that is seen as increasingly important. Poor design and development of new products in either Novartis or Microsoft would obviously have serious consequences for the company. Conversely, good design that incorporates innovation and creativity within a well-ordered design process can have a huge strategic impact. But the design activity is still a process that itself must be designed. It has stages that the design must go through. It must be clear about its process objectives and it must be structured and resourced in order to achieve those objectives. Figure 6.2 shows the design activity as a process, with inputs and outputs, as in any other process.

> **Operations principle**
> Product and service design is a process and can be managed using the same principles as any other process.

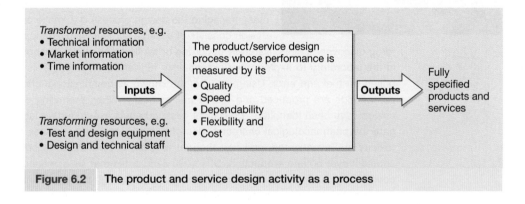

Transformed resources, e.g.
- Technical information
- Market information
- Time information

Inputs

The product/service design process whose performance is measured by its
- Quality
- Speed
- Dependability
- Flexibility and
- Cost

Outputs

Fully specified products and services

Transforming resources, e.g.
- Test and design equipment
- Design and technical staff

Figure 6.2   The product and service design activity as a process

Are product/service design objectives specified?

> **Operations principle**
> Product/service design processes can be judged in terms of their levels of quality, speed, dependability, flexibility and cost.

Products and services are designed to satisfy market needs, and the process that produces those designs should be assessed in terms of what the market will expect from any process, namely quality, speed, dependability, flexibility and cost. These performance objectives have just as much relevance for the production of new product and service designs as they do for their ongoing production once they are introduced to the market.

What is the quality of product/service design processes?

Design quality is not always easy to define precisely, especially if customers are relatively satisfied with existing products and services. Many software companies talk about the 'I don't know what I want but I'll know when I see it' syndrome, meaning that only when customers use the software are they in a position to articulate what they do or don't require. Nevertheless, it is possible to distinguish high and low quality designs (although this is easier to do in hindsight) by judging them in terms of their ability to meet market requirements. In doing this, the distinction between the specification quality and the conformance quality of designs is important. No business would want a design process that was indifferent to 'errors' in its designs, yet some are more tolerant than others. For example, neither Microsoft nor Novartis would want to produce products with errors in them. Both would suffer significant reputational damage if they did. Yet with Novartis the potential for harm is particularly high because their products directly affect our health. This is why the authorities insist on such a prolonged and thorough design process. Although withdrawing a drug from the market is unusual, it does occasionally occur. Far more frequent are the 'product recalls' that are relatively common in, say, the automotive industry. Many of these are design related and the result of 'conformance' failures in the design process. The 'specification' quality of design is different. It means the degree of functionality, or experience, or aesthetics, or whatever the product or service is primarily competing on. Some businesses require product or service designs that are relatively basic (although free from errors), while others require designs that are clearly special in terms of the customer response they hope to elicit.

What is the speed of product/service design processes?

Fast product and service design has become the norm in many industries, often because market competition has forced companies to capture the markets' imagination with the frequent introduction of new offerings. Sometimes this is the result of fast-changing consumer fashion. Sometimes it is forced by a rapidly changing technology base. Telecoms products need to be updated frequently because their underlying technology is constantly improving. Sometimes both of these pressures are evident, as in many Internet-based services. But no matter what the motivation, fast design brings a number of advantages.

- *Early market launch.* An ability to design products and services speedily means that they can be introduced to the market earlier and thus earn revenue for longer, and may command price premiums.
- *Starting design late.* Alternatively, starting the design process late rather than introducing a product or service early may have advantages, especially where either the nature of customer demand or the availability of technology is uncertain and dynamic, so fast design allows design decisions to be made closer to the time when they are introduced to the market.
- *Frequent market stimulation.* Fast design allows frequent new or updated product and service introductions.
- *More opportunities for innovation.* Where the underlying technology base is moving fast, short design times allow more windows of opportunity to introduce innovations.

What is the dependability of product/service design processes?

Fast product and service design processes that cannot be relied on to deliver innovations dependably are, in reality, not fast at all. Design schedule slippage can extend design times, but worse, a lack of dependability adds to the uncertainty surrounding the design process. Conversely, processes that are dependable minimize design uncertainty. Unexpected technical difficulties, such as suppliers who themselves do not deliver solutions on time, customers or markets that change during the design process itself, and so on, all contribute to an uncertain and ambiguous design environment. Professional project management (see Chapter 15) of the design process can help to reduce uncertainty and minimize the risk of internal disturbance to the design process and can prevent (or give early warning of) missed deadlines, process bottlenecks and resource shortages. External disturbances to the process will remain, however. These may be minimized through close liaison with suppliers and market or environmental monitoring. Nevertheless, unexpected disruptions will always occur and the more innovative the design, the more likely they are to occur. This is why flexibility within the design process is one of the most important ways in which dependable delivery of new products and services can be ensured.

What is the flexibility of product/service design processes?

Flexibility in product and service design is the ability of the design process to cope with external or internal change. The most common reason for external change is that markets, or specific customers, change their requirements. Although flexibility may not be needed in relatively predictable environments, it is clearly valuable in more fast-moving and volatile environments, where one's own customers and markets change, or where the designs of competitors' products or services dictate a matching or leapfrogging move. Internal changes include the emergence of superior technical solutions. In addition, the increasing complexity and interconnectedness of products and services may require flexibility. A bank, for example, may bundle together a number of separate services for one particular segment of its market. Privileged account holders may obtain special deposit rates, premium credit cards, insurance offers, travel facilities and so on together in the same 'product'. Changing one aspect of this bundle may require changes to be made in other elements. So extending the credit card benefits to include extra travel insurance may also mean the redesign of the separate insurance element of the package. One way of measuring design flexibility is to compare the cost of modifying a product or service design in response to such changes against the consequences to profitability if no changes are made. The higher the cost of modifying a product or service in response to a given change, the lower is the design flexibility.

What is the cost of product/service design processes?

The cost of designing products and services is usually analyzed in a similar way to the ongoing cost of producing the goods and services. In other words, cost factors are split up into three categories: the cost of buying the inputs to the process, the cost of providing the labour in the process, and the other general overhead costs of running the process. In most in-house design processes the latter two costs outweigh the former.

One way of thinking about the effect of the other design performance objectives on cost is shown in Figure 6.3. Whether through quality errors, intrinsically slow design processes, a lack of project dependability, or delays caused through inflexible design processes, the end result is that the design is late. Delayed completion of the design results in both more expenditure on the design and delayed (and probably reduced) revenue. The combination of both these effects usually means that the financial breakeven point for a new product or service is delayed by far more than the original delay in the product or service launch.

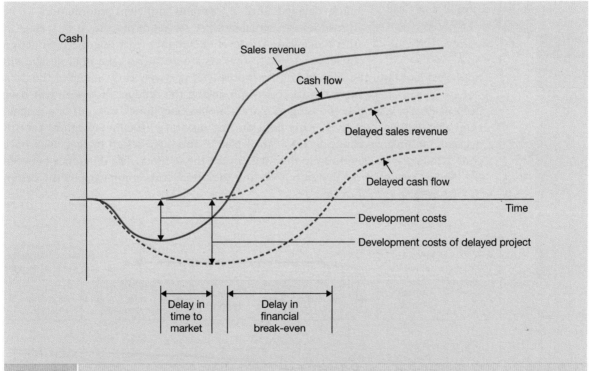

Figure 6.3   Delay in Time to Market of new products and services not only reduces and delays revenues; it also increases the costs of development. The combination of both of these effects usually delays the financial breakeven point far more than the delay in the Time to Market

Is the product/service design process defined?

To produce a fully specified product or service, a potential design must pass through several stages. These form an approximate sequence, although in practice designers will often recycle or backtrack through the stages. The stages in a typical design process are shown in Figure 6.4, although these exact stages are not used by all companies. Different processes are used by different companies. However, there is considerable similarity between the stages used and their sequence. Furthermore, they all have the same underlying principle: that over time an original idea, or 'concept', is refined and made progressively more detailed until it contains sufficient information to be turned into an actual product, service or process. At each stage in this progression the level of certainty regarding the final design increases as design options are discarded. The final design will not be evident until the very end of the process. Yet relatively early, many of the decisions that will affect the eventual cost of producing the product or service will have been made. For example, choosing to make a mobile telephone's case out of a magnesium alloy will be a relatively early decision that may take little investigation. Yet this decision, although accounting for a small part of the total design budget, may have gone a long way to determining the final cost of the product. The difference between the 'budget spend' of the design process and the actual costs committed by the design process are also shown in Figure 6.4.

> **Operations principle**
> Any product/service design process should involve a number of stages that move a design from a 'concept' to a fully specified state.

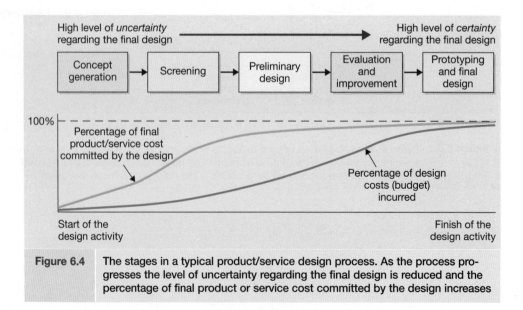

Figure 6.4   The stages in a typical product/service design process. As the process progresses the level of uncertainty regarding the final design is reduced and the percentage of final product or service cost committed by the design increases

Concept generation

Ideas for new products and services can come from anywhere. They are expected to emerge from the parts of the business that have that formal responsibility, such as research and development (R&D) or market research departments, but any business that restricts itself strictly to such internal sources is failing to exploit other, less formal but potentially useful sources. For example, although a business may use formal market research tools such as focus groups, questionnaires, etc., capturing the opinions of the staff who serve customers can often lead to deeper insights into customers' real preferences and opinions than more formal surveys. Similarly, customer complaints may be dealt with at a relatively operational level, whereas in fact they can be a rewarding source of customer opinion that should be making an impact at the more strategic level that sets objectives for product and service design. Closely analyzing competitors' designs (known as reverse engineering) may also help to isolate the key features of the design that are worth emulating. Some (more back office) aspects of services may be difficult to reverse engineer, but by consumer testing a service it may be possible to make educated guesses about how it has been created. Many service organizations employ 'testers' to check out the services provided by competitors.

Concept screening

Not all concepts will be capable of being developed into products and services. Designers need to be selective. The purpose of concept screening is to take the flow of concepts and evaluate them for their feasibility (can we do it?), acceptability (do we want to do it?) and 'vulnerability' (what are the risks of doing it?). Concepts may have to pass through many different screens, and several functions might be involved (for example marketing, operations and finance). Table 6.1 gives typical feasibility, acceptability and vulnerability questions for each of these three functional filters.

Preliminary design

Having generated one or more appropriate concepts, the next stage is to create preliminary designs. It is at this stage when opportunities arise for reducing the design complexity that can build cost into products and services when they are produced. The most elegant design solutions are often the simplest. However, when an operation produces a variety of products or services (as most do) the range, considered as a whole, can become

Table 6.1 Some typical evaluation questions for marketing, operations and finance

Evaluation criteria	Marketing	Operations	Finance
Feasibility	Is the market likely to be big enough?	Do we have the capabilities to produce it?	Do we have access to sufficient finance to develop and launch it?
Acceptability	How much market share could it gain?	How much will we have to reorganize our activities to produce it?	How much financial return will there be on our investment?
Vulnerability	What is the risk of it failing in the marketplace?	What is the risk of us being unable to produce it acceptably?	How much money could we lose if things do not go to plan?

complex, again increasing costs. Designers can adopt a number of approaches to reducing inherent design complexity.

Standardization

This is an attempt to overcome the cost of high variety by standardizing products and services, usually by restricting variety to that which has real value for the end customer. Examples include fast-food restaurants, discount supermarkets or telephone-based insurance companies. Similarly, although everybody's body shape is different, garment manufacturers produce clothes in only a limited number of sizes. The range of sizes is chosen to give a reasonable fit for most, but not all, body shapes. Controlling variety is an important issue for most businesses, who can all face the danger of allowing variety to grow excessively. Many organizations have significantly improved their profitability by careful variety reduction, often by assessing the real profit or contribution of each product or service.

Commonality

Common elements are used to simplify design complexity, for example by using the same components across a range of automobiles. Likewise, standardizing the format of information inputs to a process can be achieved by using appropriately designed forms or screen formats. The more that different products and services can be based on common components, the less complex it is to produce them. For example, the European aircraft maker Airbus designed its new generation of civil aircraft with a high degree of commonality with the introduction of fly-by-wire technology. This meant that 10 aircraft models featured virtually identical flight decks, common systems and similar handling characteristics. The advantages of commonality for the airline operators include a much shorter training time for pilots and engineers when they move from one aircraft to another. This offers pilots the possibility of flying a wide range of routes from short-haul to ultra-long-haul and leads to greater efficiencies because common maintenance procedures can be designed with maintenance teams capable of servicing any aircraft in the same family. Also, when up to 90 per cent of all parts are common within a range of aircraft, there is a reduced need to carry a wide range of spare parts.

> **Operations principle**
> A key design process objective should be to reduce the complexity of the design through standardization, commonality, and modularization.

Modularization

This involves designing standardized 'sub-components' of a product or service which can be put together in different ways. It is possible to create wide choice through the fully interchangeable assembly of various combinations of a smaller number of standard sub-assemblies; computers are designed in this way, for example. These standardized modules, or sub-assemblies, can be produced in higher volume, thereby reducing their cost. Similarly, the package holiday industry can assemble holidays to meet a specific customer requirement, from predesigned and purchased air travel, accommodation, insurance, and so on. In education also there is an increasing use of modular courses that allow 'customers' choice but permit each module to have economically viable numbers of students.

Mass customization[3]

Flexibility in design can allow the ability to offer different things to different customers. Normally, high variety means high cost, but some companies have developed their flexibility in such a way that products and services are customized for each individual customer, yet produced in a high-volume, mass production manner that keeps costs down. This approach is called mass customization. Sometimes this is achieved through flexibility in design. For example, Dell is the largest volume producer of personal computers in the world, yet allows each customer to 'design' (albeit in a limited sense) their own configuration. Sometimes flexible technology is used to achieve the same effect. For example Paris Miki, an up-market eyewear retailer that has the largest number of eyewear stores in the world, uses its own 'Mikissimes Design System' to capture a digital image of the customer and analyze facial characteristics. Together with a list of customers' personal preferences, the system then recommends a particular design and displays it on the image of the customer's face. In consultation with the optician the customer can adjust shapes and sizes until the final design is chosen. Within the store the frames are assembled from a range of pre-manufactured components and the lenses ground and fitted to the frames. The whole process takes around an hour.

Example | Customizing for kids[4]

Reducing design complexity is a principle that applies just as much to services as to products. For example, television programmes are made increasingly with a worldwide market in mind. However, most television audiences around the world have a distinct preference for programmes that respect their regional tastes, culture and of course language. The challenge facing global programme makers therefore is to try and achieve the economies which come as a result of high-volume production while allowing programmes to be customized for different markets. For example, take the programme 'Art Attack!' made for the Disney Channel, a children's TV channel shown around the world. Typically, over 200 episodes of the show are made in six different language versions. About 60 per cent of each show is common across all versions. Shots without speaking or where the presenter's face is not visible are shot separately. For example, if a simple cardboard model is being made, all versions will share the scenes where the presenter's hands only are visible. Commentary in the appropriate language is over-dubbed onto the scenes which are edited seamlessly with other shots of the appropriate presenter. The final product will have the head and shoulders of a Brazilian, French, Italian, German or Spanish presenter flawlessly mixed with the same pair of (British) hands constructing the model. The result is that local viewers in each market see the show as their own. Even though presenters are flown into the UK production studios, the cost of making each episode is only about one third of producing separate programmes for each market.

Design evaluation and improvement

The purpose of this stage in the design activity is to take the preliminary design and see whether it can be improved before the product or service is tested in the market. There are a number of techniques that can be employed at this stage to evaluate and improve the preliminary design. Perhaps the best known is quality function deployment (QFD). The key purpose of QFD is to try to ensure that the eventual design of a product or service actually meets the needs of its customers. Customers may not have been considered explicitly since the concept generation stage, and therefore it is appropriate to check that what is being proposed for the design of the product or service will meet their needs. It is a technique that was developed in Japan at Mitsubishi's Kobe shipyard and used extensively by Toyota, the motor vehicle manufacturer, and its suppliers. It is also known as the 'house of quality' (because of its shape) and the 'voice of the customer' (because of its purpose). The technique tries to capture what the customer needs and how it might be achieved. Figure 6.5 shows a simple QFD matrix used in the design of a promotional USB data storage pen (given away for promotion purposes). It is a formal articulation of how designers see the relationship between the requirements of the customer and the design characteristics of the new product or service.

PRACTICE NOTE

It is at this stage in the process when both creativity and persistence are needed to move from a potentially good idea to a workable design. One product has commemorated the persistence of its design engineers in its company name. Back in 1953 the Rocket Chemical Company set out to create a rust-prevention solvent and degreaser to be used in the aerospace

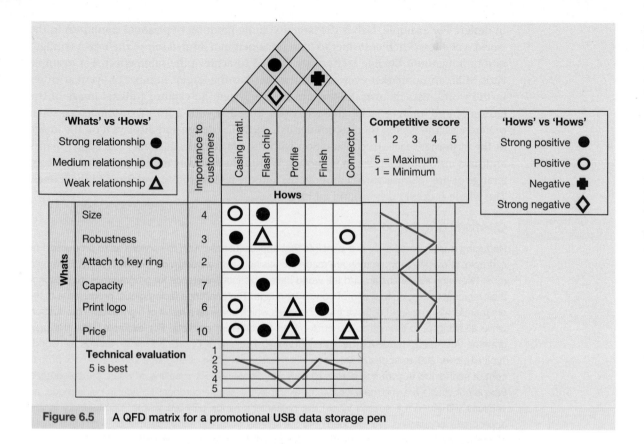

Figure 6.5 A QFD matrix for a promotional USB data storage pen

industry. Working in their lab in San Diego, California, it took them 40 attempts to get the water-displacing formula worked out. So that is what they called the product. WD-40 literally stands for Water Displacement, fortieth attempt. It was the name used in the lab book. Originally used to protect the outer skin of the Atlas Missile from rust and corrosion, the product worked so well that employees kept taking cans home to use for domestic purposes. Soon after, the product was launched with great success into the consumer market.

Prototyping and final design

At around this stage in the design activity it is necessary to turn the improved design into a prototype so that it can be tested. Product prototypes include everything from clay models to computer simulations. Service prototypes may also include computer simulations but also the actual implementation of the service on a pilot basis, for example, retailing organizations piloting new services in a small number of stores in order to test customers' reaction to them. It may also be possible to 'virtually' prototype in much the same way as a physical prototype. This is a familiar idea in some industries such as magazine publishing, where images and text can be rearranged and subjected to scrutiny prior to existing in any physical form, allowing them to be amended right up to the point of production. But, although the means of prototyping may vary, the principle is always the same: do whatever one can to test out the design before any possible errors in the design could damage the business's reputation or finances. This may be as simple as debating the new product or service thoroughly within the business and with customers and/or suppliers. Or, it could involve highly sophisticated mathematical modelling or simulation. The important point is that design should be tested in some way, and the results of those tests fed back into a refined and superior design.

EXAMPLE

Are the resources for developing products and services adequate?

For any process to operate effectively it must be appropriately designed and resourced. Design processes are no different. The detailed principles of process design that were discussed in Chapters 4 and 5 are as applicable here as they are for any other process in the business. But, in addition, because design processes are often an operation within the business in their own right, there are some more strategic aspects of organizing design processes that need managing. In particular there are the questions of how much capacity to devote to design, how much of the design activity to outsource, and how to organize design-related resources.[5]

> **Operations principle**
> For product/service design processes to be effective they must be adequately resourced.

Is there sufficient product and service design capacity?

As in any other process, the management of capacity involves deciding on the appropriate level of capacity needed by the process, and how capacity can be changed in order to respond to likely changes in demand. Demand in this case is the number of new designs needed by the business. The chief difficulty is that, even in very large companies, the rate of new service or product introduction is not constant. This means that product and service design processes are subjected to uneven internal 'demand' for designs, possibly with several new offerings being introduced to the market close together, while at other times little design is needed. This poses a resourcing problem because the capacity of a design process is often difficult to flex. The expertise necessary for design is embedded within designers, technologists, market analysts, and so on. Some expertise may be able to be hired in as and when it is needed, but much design resource is, in effect, fixed.

Such a combination of varying demand and relatively fixed design capacity leads some organizations to be reluctant to invest in design processes because they see them as an under-utilized resource. This may lead to a vicious cycle in which, although there is a short-term need for design resources, companies fail to invest in those resources because many of them (such as skilled design staff) cannot be hired in the short term, which leads to design projects being under-resourced with an increased chance of project overrun or failure to deliver appropriate technical solutions. This in turn may lead to the company losing business or otherwise suffering in the marketplace, which makes the company even less willing to invest in design resources. This issue relates to the relationship between capacity utilization and throughput time that was discussed in Chapter 4. Either the business must accept relatively low utilization of its design resources if it wants to maintain fast time to market, or, if it wants to maintain high levels of design resource utilization, it must accept longer design times, or it must try and reduce the variability in the process in some way. Reducing variability may mean introducing new designs at fixed periods, for example every year. See Figure 6.6.

| **Figure 6.6** | The relationship between design resource utilization, design process throughput time, and design process variability |

Should all design be done in-house?

Just as there are supply networks that produce products and services, there is also a supply network of design knowledge that connects suppliers and customers in the design process. This network of knowledge exchange is sometimes called the 'design (or development) network'. Design processes can adopt any position on a continuum of varying degrees of design engagement with suppliers, from retaining all the design capabilities in-house, to outsourcing all its design work. Between these extremes are varying degrees of internal and external design capability. Figure 6.7 shows some of the more important factors that will vary depending on where a design process is on the continuum. Design resources will be easy to control if they are kept in-house because they are closely aligned with the company's normal organizational structures, but control should be relatively loose because of the extra trust present in working with familiar colleagues. Outsourced design requires greater control and, because it has to be applied at a distance, contracts, often with penalty clauses for delay, may be needed.

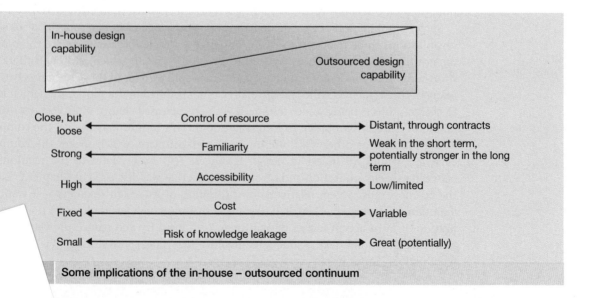

Some implications of the in-house – outsourced continuum

The overall cost of in-house versus outsourced design will vary, depending on the firm and the design project. An important difference, however, is that external designs tend to be regarded as a variable cost. The more external resources are used, the more the cost will be. In-house design is more of a fixed cost. Indeed a shift to outsourcing may occur because fixed design costs are viewed as too great. Also, a major driver of this decision can be the risk of knowledge leakage. Firms become concerned that experience gained through collaboration with a supplier of design expertise may be transferred to competitors. There is a paradox here. Businesses usually outsource design primarily because of the supplier's capabilities which are themselves an accumulation of specialist knowledge from working with a variety of customers. Without such knowledge 'leakage' the benefits of the supplier's accumulated design capabilities would not even exist.

Involving customers in design

Few people know the merits and limitations of products and services better than the customers who use them, which makes them an obvious source of feedback. Different types of customer have the potential to provide different types of information. New users can pinpoint more attractive product and service features; those who have switched to a competitor offering can reveal its problems. A particularly interesting group of customers are the so-called 'lead users', who have requirements of a product or service well ahead of the rest of the market, and who will benefit by finding a solution to their requirements. One reported example of lead user research concerns a new product design manager at Bose, the high quality hi-fi and speaker company. On visiting his local music store he noted the high quality of the background music. He found that the store manager was using Bose speakers designed for home use but had attached metal strips around the speaker boxes so that they could be suspended from the ceiling. Inspired by this, Bose built prototypes of speakers that would satisfy the need for quality in-store speakers. These were taken back to the music store for further testing and eventually led to the company successfully entering the market.

FURTHER EXAMPLE

Is product and service design technology being used?

Process technology has become important in product/service design processes. Simulation software, for example, is now common in the design of everything from transportation services through to chemical factories. These allow developers to make design decisions in advance of the actual product or service being created. They allow designers to work through the experience of using the service or product and learn more about how it might operate in practice. They can explore possibilities, gain insights and, most important, explore the consequences of their decisions.

Computer-aided design (CAD)

The best-known process technology in product design is computer-aided design (CAD). CAD systems store and categorize product and component information and allow designs to be built up on screen, often performing basic engineering calculations to test the appropriateness of proposed design solutions. They provide the computer-aided ability to create a modified product drawing and allow conventionally used shapes to be added swiftly to the computer-based representation of a product. Designs created on screen can be saved and retrieved for later use, enabling a library of standardized part and component designs to be built up. Not only can this dramatically increase the productivity of the design process but it also aids the standardization of parts in the design activity. Often CAD systems come with their own library of standard parts.

Knowledge management technologies

In many professional service firms, such as management consultancies, service design involves the evaluation of concepts and frameworks which can be used in client organizations to diagnose problems, analyze performance, and construct possible solutions. They may include ideas of industry best practice, benchmarks of performance within an industry, and ideas which can be transported across industry boundaries. However, the characteristics of management consulting firms are that they are geographically dispersed and rarely in their offices. The consultants are most of their time in client organizations acquiring knowledge day by day. Yet at the same time it is vital for such companies to avoid 'reinventing the wheel' continually. Any means of collectivizing the cumulative knowledge and experience within the organization must greatly assist the design of new concepts and frameworks. Most consultancy companies attempt to tackle this problem using knowledge management routines based on their intranet capabilities. This allows consultants to put their experience into a common pool, contact other staff within the company who have skills relevant to a current assignment, and identify previous similar assignments. In this way information is integrated into the ongoing knowledge design process within the company and can be tapped by those charged with developing new products.

FURTHER EXAMPLE

Design technologies are particularly useful when the design task is both uncertain and complex. Simulation technologies allow developers to reduce their own uncertainty of how products and services will work in practice. Similarly, knowledge management systems consolidate and juxtapose information on what is happening within the organization, thus presenting a more comprehensive vision and reducing uncertainty. CAD systems also help to deal with complexity by storing data on component details as they develop through various interactions. The absolute size and interrelatedness of some large products require sophisticated CAD systems if they are to be developed effectively. One of the most reported examples was the design of Boeing's 777 aircraft. The powerful CAD system used on this project was credited with Boeing's success in being able to involve its customers in the design process, allow more product configuration flexibility (such as the proportion of seats in each class, etc.), and still bring the huge project successfully to completion.

DIAGNOSTIC QUESTION

Are product/service design and process design simultaneous?

The outputs from the processes that design products and services (finished designs) become important inputs to the processes that produce these products and services on an ongoing basis. This is why it is a mistake to separate the design of products and services from the design of the processes that will produce them. Operations process managers should have some involvement from the initial evaluation of the concept right

> **Operations principle**
> Effective simultaneous design reduces time-to-market.

through to the production of the product or service and its introduction to the market. Merging the design of products/services and the processes that create them is sometimes called simultaneous or interactive design. Its benefits come from the elapsed time taken for the whole design activity, from concept through to market introduction – the design's time to market (TTM). Reducing time to market gives increased competitive advantage. For example, if it takes a business three years to develop a product from concept to market, with a given set of resources, it can introduce a new product only once every three years. If its rival can develop products in two years, it can introduce its (presumably) improved new product once every two years. So the rival does not have to make such radical improvements in performance each time it introduces a new product, because it is introducing its new products more frequently. Shorter TTM means that businesses get more opportunities to improve the performance of their products or services.

The factors that can significantly reduce time to market for a product or service include the following:

- Bringing 'product/service' and 'process' design together as one integrated process
- Overlapping (simultaneous) design of the stages in the combined design process
- Early deployment of strategic decision making and resolution of design conflict
- An organizational structure that reflects the nature of the design process.

Bringing product/service and process design together

What looks good as an elegant product or service design may be difficult to produce on an ongoing basis. Conversely, an operations process designed for one set of products and services may be incapable of producing new ones. It clearly makes sense to design products, services and operations processes together. However, the fact that many businesses do not do this is only partly a result of their ignorance or incompetence. There are real barriers to doing it. First, the time scales involved can be very different. Products and services may be modified, or even redesigned, relatively frequently. The processes that will be used to produce those products and services may be far too expensive to modify every time the product or service design changes. Second, the people involved with product or service designs on one hand, and ongoing process design on the other, are likely to be organizationally separate. Finally, it is sometimes not possible to design an ongoing process for the production of products and services until the product or service itself is fully defined.

Yet none of these barriers is insurmountable. Although ongoing processes may not be able to be changed every time there is a product or service design change, they can be designed to cope with a range of potential products and services. The fact that design staff and operations staff are often organizationally separate can also be overcome. Even if it is not sensible to merge the two functions, there are communication and organizational mechanisms to encourage the two functions to work together. Even the claim that ongoing processes cannot be designed until design staff know the nature of products and services they are going to produce is not entirely true. There can be sufficient clues emerging from product and service design for process design staff to be considering how they might modify ongoing processes. This is a fundamental principle of simultaneous design, considered next.

Encouraging simultaneous design

We have described the design process as a set of individual, predetermined stages, with one stage being completed before the next one commences. This step-by-step, or sequential, approach has traditionally been the typical form of product/service design processes.

It has some advantages. It is easy to manage and control design processes organized in this way because each stage is clearly defined. In addition, each stage is completed before the next stage is begun, so each stage can focus its skills and expertise on a limited set of tasks. The main problem of the sequential approach is that it is both time-consuming and costly. When each stage is separate, with a clearly defined set of tasks, any difficulties encountered during the design at one stage might necessitate the design being halted while responsibility moves back to the previous stage. This sequential approach is shown in Figure 6.8(a).

Often there is really little need to wait until the absolute finalization of one stage before starting the next.[6] For example, perhaps while generating the concept, the evaluation activity of screening and selection could be started. It is likely that some concepts could be judged as 'non-starters' relatively early in the process of ideas generation. Similarly, during the screening stage, it is likely that some aspects of the design will become obvious before the phase is finally complete. Therefore, the preliminary work on these parts of the design could be commenced at that point. This principle can be taken right through all the stages, one stage commencing before the previous one has finished, so there is simultaneous or concurrent work on the stages (see Figure 6.8(b)).

We can link this idea with the idea of uncertainty reduction, discussed earlier, when we made the point that uncertainty reduces as the design progresses. This also applies to each stage of the design. If this is so then there must be some degree of certainty which the next stage can take as its starting point prior to the end of the previous stage. In other

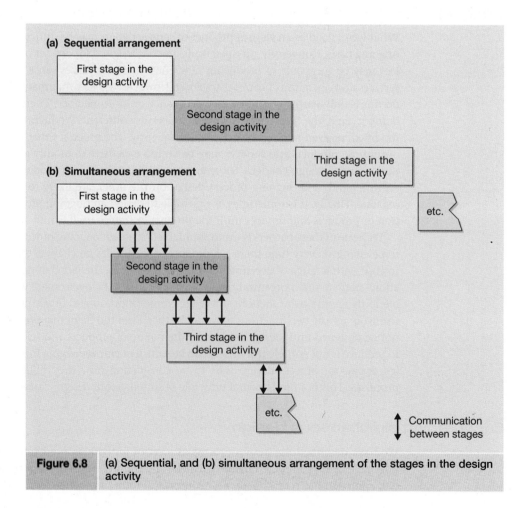

Figure 6.8   (a) Sequential, and (b) simultaneous arrangement of the stages in the design activity

words, designers can be continually reacting to a series of decisions and clues that are given to them by the designers working on the preceding stage. However, this can only work if there is effective communication between each pair of stages.

Deploying strategic intervention and resolving conflicts early

A design decision, once made, need not irrevocably shape the final design. All decisions can be changed, but it becomes increasingly hard to do so as the design process progresses. At the same time, early design decisions are often the most difficult to make because of the high level of uncertainty surrounding what may or may not work as a final design. This is why the level of debate, and even disagreement, over the characteristics of a design can be at its most heated in the early stages of the process. One approach is to delay decision making in the hope that an obvious 'answer' will emerge. The problem with this is that, if decisions are delayed and this causes changes to be made later in the design process, those changes will be more disruptive later in the process than they would have been earlier.

> **Operations principle**
> The product/service design process requires strategic attention early, when there is the most potential to affect design decisions.

The implications of this are, first, that it is worth trying to reach consensus in the early stages of the design process even if this seems to be delaying the total process in the short term, and second, that strategic intervention into the design process by senior management is particularly needed at these early stages in the process.

Unfortunately, there is a tendency for senior managers, after setting the initial objectives of the design process, to 'leave the details' to technical experts. They may only become engaged with the process again in the later stages as problems start to emerge that need reconciliation or extra resources. Figure 6.9 illustrates this in terms of the mismatch between senior management's ability to influence the design process and what, in some organizations, is the actual pattern of intervention.[7]

High level of *uncertainty* regarding the final design of product/service and operations process → High level of *certainty* regarding the final design of product/service and operations process

Concept generation → Screening → Preliminary design → Evaluation and improvement → Prototyping and final design → Finalize operations processes → Launch period

The ease with which designs can be changed

Degree of strategic intervention in the design process

Time

Figure 6.9 The degree of strategic intervention in the design process is often dictated by the need to resolve outstanding conflicts rather than the needs of the design process itself

Organizing design process in a way that reflects the nature of the design

The design process of developing concepts through to market will almost certainly involve people from several different areas of the business who will have some part in making the decisions shaping the final design. Yet any design project will also have an existence of its own. It will have a project name, an individual manager or group of staff who are championing the project, a budget and, hopefully, a clear strategic purpose in the organization. The organizational question is which of these two ideas – the various organizational functions that contribute to the design, or the design project itself – should dominate the way in which the design activity is managed?

There is a range of possible organizational structures – from pure functional to pure project forms. In a pure functional organization, all staff associated with the design project are based unambiguously in their functional groups. There is no project-based group at all. They may be working full-time on the project but all communication and liaison are carried out through their functional manager. The project exists because of agreement between these functional managers. At the other extreme, all the individual members of staff from each function involved in the project could be moved out of their functions and perhaps even co-located (working physically close to each other) in a task force dedicated solely to the project. The task force could be led by a project manager who might hold the entire budget allocated to the design project. Not all members of the task force necessarily have to stay in the team throughout the design period, but a substantial core might see the project through from start to finish. Some members of a design team may even be from other companies. Between these two extremes there are various types of matrix organization with varying emphasis on these two aspects of the organization[8] (see Figure 6.10).

Organization structures for design processes

- **Functional organization.** The project is divided into segments and assigned to relevant functional areas and/or groups within functional areas. The project is jointly coordinated by functional and senior management.
- **Functional matrix (or lightweight project manager).** A person is formally designated to oversee the project across different functional areas. This person may have limited authority over the functional staff involved and serves primarily to plan and coordinate the project. Functional managers retain primary responsibility for their specific segments of the project.
- **Balanced matrix.** A person is assigned to oversee the project and interacts on an equal basis with functional managers. This person and the functional managers jointly direct work flow segments and approve technical and operational decisions.
- **Project matrix (or *heavyweight* project manager).** A manager is assigned to oversee the project and is responsible for the completion of the project. Functional managers' involvement is limited to assigning personnel as needed and providing advisory expertise.
- **Project team (or *tiger* team).** A manager is given responsibility of a project team composed of a core group of personnel from several functional areas and/or groups, assigned on a full-time basis. The functional managers have no formal involvement.

Although there is no clear 'winner' among the alternative organizational structures, there is wide support for structures towards the project end rather than the functional end of the continuum. In one widely respected study, Professors Clark and Fujimoto argued that heavyweight project manager structures and dedicated project teams are the most efficient forms of organization for product competitiveness, shorter lead times and technical efficiency. Other studies, although sometimes more equivocal, have shown that, in terms of the best total outcome from the development process, structures from balanced matrix through to project teams can all give high success rates. Perhaps of more interest is the suitability of the alternative structures for different types of product or service development project. Matrix structures are generally deemed to be appropriate for both simple and highly complex projects. Dedicated project teams, on the other hand, are seen as appropriate for projects with a high degree of uncertainty, where their flexibility becomes valuable.

Functionally based design processes, with resources clustered around a functional specialism, help the development of technical knowledge. Some organizations manage to capture the deep technological and skills development advantages of functional structures, while at the same time coordinating between the functions so as to ensure satisfactory delivery of new product and service ideas. Perhaps the best known of these organizations is Toyota. They have a strong, functionally based organization to develop their products. It adopts highly formalized development procedures to communicate between functions and places strict limits on the use of cross-functional teams. But what is really different is their approach to devising an organizational structure for product development that is appropriate for them. The argument that most companies have adopted to justify cross-functional project teams goes something like this: *'Problems with communication between traditional functions have been the main reasons for, in the past, failing to deliver new product and service ideas to specification, on time and to budget. Therefore let us break down the walls between the functions and organize resources around the individual development projects. This will ensure good communication and a market-oriented culture.'* Toyota and similar companies, on the other hand, have taken a different approach. Their argument goes something like this: *'The problem with cross-functional teams is that they can dissipate the carefully nurtured knowledge that exists within specialist functions. The real problem is how to retain this knowledge on which our future product development depends, while overcoming some of the traditional functional barriers which have inhibited communicatio between the functions. The solution is not to destroy the function but to devise the organizational mechanisms to ensure close control and integrative leadership which will make the functional organization work.'[9]*

Critical commentary

Each chapter contains a short critical commentary on the main ideas covered in the chapter. Its purpose is not to undermine the issues discussed in the chapter, but to emphasize that, although we present a relatively orthodox view of operation, there are other perspectives.

■ The whole process-based approach to product and service design could be interpreted as implying that all new products and services are created in response to a clear and articulated customer need. While this is usually the case, especially for products and services that are similar to (but presumably better than) their predecessors, more radical innovations are often brought about by the innovation itself creating demand. Customers don't usually know that they need something radical. For example, in the late 1970s people were not asking for microprocessors – they did not even know what they were. They were improvised by an engineer in the USA for a Japanese customer who made calculators. Only later did they become the enabling technology for the PC and after that the innumerable devices that now dominate our lives.

■ Nor do all designers agree with the concept of the possible design options being progressively reduced stage by stage. For some it is just too neat and ordered an idea to reflect accurately the creativity, arguments and chaos that sometimes characterize the design activity. First, they argue, managers do not start out with an infinite number of options. No one could process that amount of information – and anyway, designers often have some set solutions in their mind, looking for an opportunity to be used. Second, the number of options being considered often increases as time goes by. This may actually be a good thing, especially if the activity was unimaginatively specified in the first place. Third, the real process of design often involves cycling back, often many times, as potential design solutions raise fresh questions or become dead ends. In summary, the idea of the design funnel does not describe what actually happens in the design activity. Nor does it necessarily even describe what should happen.

Summary checklist

DOWNLOADABLE

This checklist comprises questions that can be usefully applied to any type of operations and reflect the major diagnostic questions used within the chapter.

☐ Is the importance of product or service design as a contributor to achieving strategic impact fully understood?

☐ Are some functions of the business more committed to product/service design than others?

☐ If so, have the barriers to cross-functional commitment been identified and addressed?

☐ Is the design process really treated as a process?

☐ Is the design process itself designed with the same attention to detail as any other process?

☐ Are design objectives specified so as to give a clear priority between quality, speed, dependability, flexibility and cost?

☐ Are the stages in the product/service process clearly defined?

☐ Are ideas for new products and services captured from all appropriate sources (including employees)?

☐ Are potential designs screened in a systematic manner in terms of their feasibility, acceptability and vulnerability?

☐ Have all possibilities for design standardization been explored?

☐ Have all possibilities for design commonality been explored?

☐ Have all possibilities for modularization of design elements been explored?

☐ Has the concept of mass customization been linked to the design process?

☐ Are potential designs thoroughly evaluated and tested before they could expose the business to financial and/or reputational risk?

☐ Is sufficient capacity devoted to the design process?

☐ Have all options for outsourcing parts of the design process been explored?

☐ Has the possibility of involving customers formally in the design of new products and services been explored?

☐ Are design technologies such as CAD and knowledge management used in the design process?

☐ Are product/service design and process design considered together as one integrated process?

☐ Is overlapping (simultaneous) design of the stages in the process used?

☐ Is senior management effort deployed early enough to ensure early resolution of design conflict?

☐ Does the organizational structure of the design process reflect its nature?

Case study   Developing 'Savory Rosti-crisps' at Dreddo Dan's[10]

'Most people see the snack market as dynamic and innovative, but actually it is surprisingly conservative. Most of what passes for product innovation is in fact tinkering with our marketing approach, things like special offers, promotion tie-ins and so on. We occasionally put new packs round our existing products and even more occasionally we introduce new flavors in existing product ranges. Rarely though does anyone in this industry introduce something radically different. That is why project Orlando is both exciting and scary.'

Monica Allen, Technical Vice-President of PJT's snack division, was commenting on a new product to be marketed under PJT's best-known brand 'Dreddo Dan's Surfer Snacks'. The Dreddo Dan's brand made use of surfing and outdoor 'action-oriented youth' imagery, but in fact was aimed at a slightly older generation who, although aspiring to such a lifestyle, had more discretionary spend for the premium snacks in which the brand specialized. Current products marketed under the brand included both fried and baked snacks in a range of exotic flavours. The project, internally known as Project Orlando, was a baked product that had been 'in development' for almost three years but had hitherto been seen very much as a long-term development, with no guarantee of ever making it through to market launch. PJT had several of these long-term projects running at any one time. They were allocated a development budget, but usually no dedicated resources were associated with the project. Less than half of these long-term projects ever even reached the stage of being test marketed. Around 20 per cent never got past the concept stage, and fewer than 20 per cent ever went into production. However, the company viewed the development effort put into these 'failed' products as being worthwhile because it often led to 'spin-off' developments and ideas that could be used elsewhere. Up till this point 'Orlando' had been seen as unlikely ever to reach the test marketing stage, but that had now changed dramatically.

'Orlando' was a concept for a range of snack foods, described within the company as 'savory potato cookies'. Essentially they were one-and-a-half-inch discs of crisp, fried potato with a soft dairy cheese-like filling. The idea of incorporating dairy fillings in snacks had

Source: courtesy Christopher Bruno

been discussed within the industry for some time but the problems of manufacturing such a product were formidable. Keeping the product crisp on the outside yet soft in the middle, while at the same time ensuring microbiological safety, would not be easy. Moreover such a product would have to be capable of being stored at ambient temperatures, maintain its physical robustness and have a shelf life of at least three months.

Bringing Orlando products to market involved overcoming three types of technical problem. First, the formulation and ingredient mix for the product had to maintain the required texture yet be capable of being baked on the company's existing baking lines. The risk of developing an entirely new production technology for the product was considered too great. Second, extruding the mixture into baking moulds while maintaining microbiological integrity (dairy products are difficult to handle) would require new extrusion technology. Third, the product would need to be packaged in a material that both reflected its brand image but also kept the product fresh through its shelf life. Existing packaging materials were unlikely to provide sufficient shelf life. The first of these problems had, more or less, been solved in PJT's development laboratories. The second and third problems now seemed less formidable because of a number of recent technological breakthroughs made by equipment suppliers and packaging manufacturers. This had convinced the company that

Orlando was worth significant investment and it had been given priority development status by the company's board. Even so, it was not expected to come to the market for another two years and was seen by some as potentially the most important new product development in the company's history.

The project team

Immediately after the board's decision Monica had accepted responsibility to move the development forward. She decided to put together a dedicated project team to oversee the development. *'It is important to have representatives from all relevant parts of the company. Although the team will carry out much of the work themselves, they will still need the cooperation and the resources of their own departments. So, as well as being part of the team, they are also gateways to expertise around the company.'* The team consisted of representatives from Marketing, the development kitchens (laboratories), PJT's technology centre (a development facility that served the whole group, not just the snack division), packaging engineers, and representatives from the division's two manufacturing plants. All but the Manufacturing representatives were allocated to the project team on a full-time basis. Unfortunately, Manufacturing had no-one who had sufficient process knowledge and who could be spared from their day-to-day activities.

Development objectives

Monica had tried to set the objectives for the project in her opening remarks to the project team when they had first come together: *'We have a real chance here to develop a product that not only will have major market impact, but will also give us a sustainable competitive advantage. We need to make this project work in such a way that competitors will find it difficult to copy what we do. The product formulation is a real success for our development people, and as long as we get the hang of using the new extrusion method and packaging material, we should be difficult to beat. The success of Orlando in the marketplace will depend on our ability to operationalize and integrate the various technical solutions that we now have access to. The main problem with this type of product is that it will be expensive to develop and yet, once our competitors realize what we are doing, they will come in fast to try and out-innovate us. Whatever else we do we must ensure that there is sufficient flexibility in the project to allow us to respond quickly when competitors follow us into the market with their own 'me-too' products. We are not racing against the clock to get this to market, but once we do make a decision to launch we will have to move fast and hit the launch date reliably. Perhaps most important, we must*

ensure that the product is 200 per cent safe. We have no experience in dealing with the microbiological testing which dairy-based food manufacture requires. Other divisions of PJT do have this experience and I guess we will be relying heavily on them.'

Monica, who had been tasked with managing the now much expanded development process, had already drawn up a list of key decisions she would have to take.

- **How to resource the development project.** The division had a small development staff, some of whom had been working on Project Orlando, but a project of this size would require extra staff amounting to about twice the current number of people dedicated to product development.

- **Whether to invest in a pilot plant.** The process technology required for the new project would be unlike any of the division's current technology. Similar technology was used by some companies in the frozen food industry and one option would be to carry out trials at these (non-competitor) companies' sites. Alternatively, the Orlando team could build their own pilot plant, which would enable them to experiment in-house. As well as the significant expense involve, this would raise the problem of whether any process innovations would work when scaled up to full size. However, it would be far more convenient for the project team and allow them to 'make their mistakes' in private.

- **How much development to outsource.** Because of the size of the project, Monica had considered outsourcing some of the development activities. Other divisions within the company may be able to undertake some of the development work and there were also specialist consultancies that operated in the food processing industries. The division had never used any of these consultancies before but other divisions had occasionally done so.

- **How to organize the development.** Currently the small development function had been organized around loose functional specialisms. Monica wondered whether this project warranted the creation of a separate department independent of the current structure. This might signal the importance of this project to the whole division.

Fixing the budget

The budget to develop Project Orlando through to launch had been set at $30 million. This made provision to increase the size of the existing development team by 70 per cent over a 20-month period (for launch two years from now). It also included enough funding to build a pilot plant that would allow the team the flexibility to develop responses to potential competitor reaction after the launch. So, of the $30m around $12m was for extra staff and contracted-out product development, $5m for the pilot plant and $3m for one-off costs (such as the purchase of test equipment, etc.). Monica was unsure whether the budget would be big enough.

'I know everyone in my position wants more money, but it is important not to underfund a project like this. Increasing our development staff by 70% is not really enough. In my opinion we need an increase of at least 90% to make sure that we can launch when we want. This would need another $5m, spread over the next 20 months. We could get this by not building the pilot plant, I suppose, but I am reluctant to give that up. It would mean begging for test capacity on other companies' plants, which is never satisfactory from a knowledge-building viewpoint. Also it would compromise security. Knowledge of what we were doing could easily leak to competitors. Alternatively we could subcontract more of the research, which may be less expensive, especially in the long run, but I doubt if it would save the full $5m we need. More important, I am not sure that we should subcontract anything which would compromise safety, and increasing the amount of work we send out may do that. No, it's got to be the extra cash or the project could overrun. The profit projections for the Orlando products look great [see Table 6.2], but delay or our inability to respond to competitor pressures would depress those figures significantly. Our competitors could get into the market only a little after us. Word has it that Marketing's calculations indicate a delay of only six months

Table 6.2 Preliminary 'profit stream' projections for the Project Orlando range of products, assuming launch in 24 months' time

Time period*	1	2	3	4	5	6	7
Profit flow ($ million)	10	20	50	90	120	130	135

*Six-month periods.

could not only delay the profit stream by the six months but also cut it by up to 30%.'

Monica was keen to explain two issues to the management committee when it met to consider her request for extra funding. First, that there was a coherent and well thought-out strategy for the development of Project Orlando over the next two years. Second, that saving $5m on the development budget would be a false economy.

QUESTIONS

1 How would you rank the product development objectives for the project?

2 What are the key issues in resourcing this product development process?

3 What are the main factors influencing the resourcing decisions?

4 What advice would you give Monica?

Active case study   Getting Customer #1

ACTIVE CASE

Rellacast AG specializes in the precision die casting of zinc, magnesium and aluminium alloys. They have been asked to develop a component for a large telecoms and internet systems supplier known internally as Customer #1. In fact, Customer #1 is not yet a full customer. However, for some time they have been the most important target customer in the minds of Rellacast's marketing executives.

● How would you advise Rellacast over the development of the component and the dilemmas which emerge to ensure they win the business of Customer #1?

Please refer to the Active case on the CD accompanying this book to find out more about the company and the decisions they face in the development of the component.

Applying the principles

Some study activities can be answered by reading the chapter. Others will require some general knowledge of business activity and some might require an element of investigation. All have hints on how they can be answered on the CD accompanying this book.

HINTS

1   One product where a very wide range of product types is valued by customers is domestic paint. Most people like to express their creativity in the choice of paints and other decorating products that they use in their homes. Clearly, offering a wide range of paint must have serious cost implications for the companies that manufacture, distribute and sell the product. Visit a store that sells paint and get an idea of the range of products available on the market. How do you think paint manufacturers and retailers manage to design their products and services so as to maintain high variety but keep costs under control?

2   Design becomes particularly important at the interface between products or services and the people that use them. This is especially true for Internet-based services. Consider two types of website:

(a)   those that are trying to sell something such as Amazon.com, and

(b)   those that are primarily concerned with giving information, for example bbc.co.uk.

For each of these categories, what seems to constitute 'good design'? Find examples of particularly good and particularly poor Web design and explain what makes them good or bad.

3   Visit the website of the UK's Design Council (**www.design-council.org.uk**). There you will find examples of how design has provided innovation in many fields. Look through these examples and find one that you think represents excellence in design and one that you don't like (for example, because it seems trivial, or may not be practical, or for which there is no market, etc.). Prepare a case supporting your view of why one is good and the other bad. In doing this, derive a checklist of questions that could be used to assess the worth of any design idea.

4   How can the design of quick-service restaurant (fast-food) products and services be improved from the point of view of environmental sustainability? Visit two or three fast-food outlets and compare their approach to environmentally sensitive designs.

Notes on chapter

1   Sources: company website, and Cusumano, M.A. (1997) 'How Microsoft make large teams work like small teams', *Sloan Management Review,* Fall.

2   Sources: Novartis website, and Rowberg, R.E. (2001) 'Pharmaceutical research and design: A description and analysis of the process', *CRS Report for Congress,* 2 April.

3   Mass customization was first fully articulated in Pine, B.J. (1993) *Mass Customization: The new frontier in business competition,* Harvard Business School Press, Boston, MA.

4   Source: *The Economist* (2002) 'Think local', 13 April.

5   This section on resourcing is based on material from Slack, N. and Lewis, M.A. (2001) *Operations Strategy,* Financial Times Prentice Hall, Harlow, UK.

6   Wheelwright, S.C. and Clark, K.B. (1995) *Leading Product Development,* Free Press, New York.

7   This idea is based on one presented by Hayes, Wheelwright and Clark, in Hayes, R.H., Wheelwright, S.C. and Clark, K.B. (1988) *Dynamic Manufacturing,* Free Press, New York.

8   From an idea by Hayes, Wheelwright and Clark, *op. cit.*

9 Sobek, D.K. II, Liker, J.K. and Ward, A.K. (1998) 'Another look at how Toyota integrates product development', *Harvard Business Review,* July–August.

10 A more condensed version of this case was originally presented in Slack, N. and Lewis, M.A. (2001) *Operations Strategy,* Financial Times Prentice Hall, Harlow, UK.

Taking it further

Bangle, C. (2001) 'The ultimate creativity machine: How BMW turns art into profit', *Harvard Business Review,* January, pp. 47–55. A good description of how good aesthetic design translates into business success.

Baxter, M. (1995) *Product Design,* Chapman and Hall. Presents a structured framework for product design that will be of interest to practising managers.

Blackburn, J.D. (ed.) (1991) *Time Based Competition: The next battle ground in American manufacturing,* Irwin, Homewood, IL. A good summary of why interactive design gives fast time-to-market and why this is important.

Bruce, M. and Bessant, J. (2002) *Design In Business: Strategic innovation through design,* Financial Times Prentice Hall and The Design Council. Probably one of the best overviews of design in a business context available today.

Bruce, M. and Cooper, R. (2000) *Creative Product Design: A practical guide to requirements capture management,* Wiley, Chichester. Exactly what it says.

Cooper, R. and Chew, W.B. (1996) 'Control tomorrow's costs through today's designs', *Harvard Business Review,* Jan.–Feb., pp. 88–98. A really good description of why it is important to think about costs at the design stage.

Dyson, J. (1997) *Against the Odds: An autobiography,* Orion Business Books, London. One of Europe's most famous designers gives us his philosophy.

Lowe, A. and Ridgway, K. (2000) 'A user's guide to quality function deployment', *Engineering Management Journal,* June. A good overview of QFD explained in straightforward non-technical language.

Useful websites

www.cfsd.org.uk The Centre for Sustainable Design's site. Some useful resources, but obviously largely confined to sustainability issues.

www.conceptcar.co.uk A site devoted to automotive design. Fun if you like new car designs!

www.betterproductdesign.net A site that acts as a resource for good design practice. Set up by Cambridge University and the Royal College of Art. Some good material that supports all aspects of design.

www.ocw.mit.edu/OcwWeb/Sloan-School-of-Management Good source of open courseware from MIT.

www.design-council.org.uk Site of the UK's Design Council. One of the best sites in the world for design-related issues.

www.nathan.com/ed/glossary/#ED Glossary of design terms.

FURTHER RESOURCES

For further resources including examples, animated diagrams, self test questions, excel spreadsheets, active case studies and video materials please explore the CD accompanying this book.

SUPPLY CHAIN MANAGEMENT

Introduction

An operation's ability to deliver products or services to customers is fundamentally influenced by how its supply chains are managed. Chapter 3 treated the strategic design of supply networks. This chapter considers the planning and control activity for the individual supply chains in the network. Supply chain management is the overarching operations management activity that dictates an operation's *delivery* performance because it controls the flow of products and services from suppliers right through to the end customer. That is why it is the first chapter dealing with the planning and control of delivery. But planning and controlling delivery is a much larger topic, and includes capacity management (Chapter 8), inventory management (Chapter 9), resource planning and control (Chapter 10), and lean synchronization (Chapter 11). Figure 7.1 illustrates these 'delivery' topics treated in this chapter.

Source: Courtesy SAB Miller plc

Figure 7.1   Supply chain management is the management of the relationships and flows between operations and processes; it is the topic that integrates all the issues concerning the delivery of products and services

Executive summary

VIDEO
further detail

What is supply chain management?

↓

Are supply chain objectives clear?

↓

How should supply chain relationships be managed?

↓   ↓

How should the supply side be managed?   How should the demand side be managed?

↓   ↓

Are supply chain dynamics under control?

Decision logic chain for supply chain management

Each chapter is structured around a set of diagnostic questions. These questions suggest what you should ask in order to gain an understanding of the important issues of a topic, and as a result, improve your decision making. An executive summary, addressing these questions, is provided below.

What is supply chain management?

Supply chain management is the management of relationships and flows between operations and processes. Technically, it is different from supply network management, which looks at all the operations or processes in a network. Supply chain management refers to a string of operations or processes. However, the two terms are often used interchangeably. Many of the principles of managing external supply chains (flow between operations) are also applicable to internal supply chains (flow between processes).

Are supply chain objectives clear?

The central objective of supply chain management is to satisfy the needs of the end customer. So, each operation in the chain should contribute to whatever mix of quality, speed, dependability, flexibility and cost that the end customer requires. An individual operation's failure in any of these objectives can be multiplied throughout the chain. So, although each operation's performance may be adequate, the performance of the whole chain could be poor. An important distinction is between lean and agile supply chain performance. Broadly, lean (or efficient) supply chains are appropriate for stable 'functional' products and services, while agile (or responsive) supply chains are more appropriate for less predictable innovative products and services.

How should supply chain relationships be managed?

Supply chain relationships can be described on a spectrum from market-based, transactional, 'arms length' relationships, through to close and long-term partnership relationships. Each has its advantages and disadvantages. Developing relationships involves assessing which relationship will provide the best potential for developing overall performance. However, the types of relationships adopted may be dictated by the structure of the market itself. If the number of potential suppliers is small, there are few opportunities to use market mechanisms to gain any kind of advantage.

How should the supply side be managed?

Managing supply side relationships involves three main activities: selecting appropriate suppliers, planning and controlling ongoing supply activity, and supplier development. Supplier selection involves trading off different supplier attributes, often using scoring assessment methods. Managing ongoing supply involves clarifying supply expectations, often using service-level agreements to manage the supply relationships. Supplier development can benefit both suppliers and customers, especially in partnership relationships. Sometimes barriers to this are the mismatches in perception between customers and suppliers.

How should the demand side be managed?

This will depend partly on whether demand is dependent on some known factor and therefore predictable, or independent of any known factor and therefore less predictable. Approaches such as materials requirements planning (MRP) are used in the former case, while approaches such as inventory management are used in the latter case. The increasing outsourcing of physical distribution and the use of new tracking technologies, such as RFID, have brought efficiencies to the movement of physical goods and customer service. But customer service may be improved even more if suppliers take on responsibility for customer development, i.e. helping customers to help themselves.

Are supply chain dynamics under control?

Supply chains have a dynamic of their own that is often called the *bullwhip* effect. It means that relatively small changes at the demand end of the chain increasingly amplify into large disturbances as they move upstream. Three methods can be used to reduce this effect. Information sharing can prevent over-reaction to immediate stimuli and give a better view of the whole chain. Channel alignment through standardized planning and control methods allows for easier coordination of the whole chain. Improving the operational efficiency of each part of the chain prevents local errors multiplying to affect the whole chain.

DIAGNOSTIC QUESTION

What is supply chain management?

Supply chain management (SCM) is the management of the relationships and flows between the 'string' of operations and processes that produce value in the form of products and services to the ultimate consumer. It is a holistic approach to managing across the boundaries of companies and of processes. Technically, supply *chains* are different from supply *networks*. A supply network is *all* the operations that are linked together so as to provide goods and services through to end customers. In large supply networks there can be many hundreds of supply chains of linked operations passing through a single operation. The same distinction holds within operations. Internal supply network, and supply chain, management concerns flow between processes or departments. See Figure 7.2. Confusingly, the terms supply network and supply chain management are often used interchangeably.

> **Operations principle**
> The supply chain concept applies to the internal relationships between processes as well as the external relationships between operations.

It is worth emphasizing again that the supply chain concept applies to internal process networks as well as external supply networks. Many of the ideas discussed in the context of the 'operation-to-operation' supply chain also apply to the 'process-to-process' internal

Figure 7.2   Supply chain management is concerned with managing the flow of materials and information between a string of operations that form the strands or 'chains' of a supply network

- Long-term plans and requirements
- Market research information
- Individual orders
- Payment
- Potential new products and services

'Upstream' flow of customer requirements

Flow between processes

Flow between processes

Flow between processes

Consumer

- Products and services
- New products and services
- Delivery information
- Payment request/Credit

'Downstream' flow of products and services for customer fulfilment

Figure 7.3 Supply chain management is concerned with the flow of information as well as the flow of products and services

supply chain. It is also worth noting that the 'flows' in supply chains are not restricted to the downstream flow of products and services from suppliers through to customers. Although the most obvious failure in supply chain management occurs when downstream flow fails to meet customer requirements, the root cause may be a failure in the upstream flow of information. Modern supply chain management is as much concerned with managing information flows (upstream and downstream) as it is with managing the flow of products and services – see Figure 7.3.

The following two examples of supply chain management illustrate some of the issues that are discussed in this chapter.

Example

Seven-Eleven Japan's agile supply chain[1]

Seven-Eleven Japan (SEJ) is that country's largest and most successful retailer with higher sales per square metre or per store than any of its competitors. Perhaps most significantly, the average amount of stock in an SEJ store is between 7 and 8.4 days of demand, well below that of most other retailers. Industry analysts see SEJ's agile supply chain management as being the driving force behind its success. And this agility is supported by a fully integrated information system that provides visibility of the whole supply chain and ensures fast replenishment of goods in its stores, customized exactly to the needs of individual stores.

Source: Courtesy Masatoshi Ichimura

When a customer comes to the checkout counter the assistant first keys in the customer's gender and approximate age and then scans the bar codes of the purchased goods. This sales data is transmitted to the Seven-Eleven headquarters where it is recorded and analyzed so that store managers and headquarters have immediate point-of-sale information. This allows both store managers and headquarters, hour by hour, to analyze sales trends, potential stock-outs, types of customer buying certain products, and so on. The data is aggregated by region, product and time, so that all parts of the supply chain, from suppliers through to the stores, have the information by the next morning. Every Monday, top executives review all performance information for the previous week and develop plans for the coming week. These plans are presented on Tuesday morning to SEJ's 'operations field counsellors', each of whom is responsible for facilitating performance improvement in around eight stores. On Tuesday afternoon the field counsellors collectively decide how to implement the plans, fly back to their regions that night, and by next morning are visiting their stores to deliver the messages developed at headquarters. SEJ's agile physical distribution fleet maintains radio communications with all its drivers to keep track of all delivery activities. Delivery times and routes are planned in great detail and published in the form of a delivery timetable. On average each delivery takes only one and half minutes at each store and drivers are expected to make their deliveries within 10 minutes of scheduled time. If a delivery is late by more than 30 minutes the distribution company has to pay the store a fine equivalent to the gross profit on all the goods being delivered.

Example — Suppliers are vital to Lucent's success[2]

Lucent Technologies is one of the companies that provide the infrastructure equipment that runs the Internet. It must be both innovative in its product development and reliable in its delivery. But even a high-tech company such as Lucent cannot achieve this alone. It needs close working relationships with suppliers. *'It is vitally important for Lucent to be able to rely upon our suppliers to provide the materials and services we need'*, says the company, *'so that we can deliver the innovative solutions our customers need, when they need them, and at a price they can afford.'*

Lucent's 'Supply Chain Networks' function deals with supply chain issues throughout Lucent. One of its most significant mechanisms for managing its supply base is the Supplier Relationship Programme. *'Being a Lucent supplier is much more than being a reliable source for quality materials and services at a competitive price. We look to our suppliers to work beside us, from product design all the way through to the point of delivery to the customer and even beyond.'* The Supplier Relationship Programme's objective of managing the whole chain from suppliers through to customers (and customers' customers) includes the following functions:

- Evaluating suppliers to determine their qualification to be a supplier
- Providing suppliers with a single contact point within Lucent
- Providing a Web-based Supply Chain Portal for members of the supply chain network to receive a clear view of demand, availability and the state of delivery
- Organizing supplier forums to find ways of cutting costs, reducing time to market, and improving delivery and innovation.

Lucent's supply chain practices have paid off. Profit margins increased and inventory was cut from $7bn to $2.4bn, with component costs cut by between 35 and 55 per cent. *'When we looked at our supply chain situation'*, says Chief Operating Officer, Bob Holder, *'we recognized how fragmented it had become. We had decentralized manufacturing, inventory and purchasing. We had six different organizations buying the same memory chips. We said, this just doesn't make sense. So we created the supply chain networks.'* These organize and communicate through the company's supply chains. They tell suppliers of their future plans, allowing potential changes to be discussed openly so that the company retains more credibility, respect and a deeper relationship with its suppliers.

What do these two examples have in common?

The first lesson from these two companies is that they both take supply chain management seriously. They understand that, no matter how good individual operations or processes are, a business's overall performance is a function of the whole chain of which it is a part. That is why both of these companies put so much effort into managing the whole chain. This does not mean that both companies adopt the same, or even similar, approaches to supply chain management. Each has a slightly different set of priorities. SEJ needs agility from its supply chain, while Lucent places slightly more emphasis on innovation. The commonality between the two companies is that, although their supply chain objectives are different, both have a clear idea of what they are. Similarly, both companies understand the importance of managing relationships. Although the descriptions emphasized SEJ's downstream customer relationships and Lucent's upstream supplier relationships, the common theme is the importance of investing in relationships. In addition, both companies have invested in mechanisms for communicating along the supply chain and coordinating material and information flows. The rest of this chapter is structured around these three main issues: clarifying supply chain objectives; supply chain relationships, both with suppliers and with customers; and controlling and coordinating flow.

DIAGNOSTIC QUESTION

Are supply chain objectives clear?

All supply chain management shares one common, and central, objective – to satisfy the end customer. All stages in a chain must eventually include consideration of the final customer, no matter how far an individual operation is from the end customer. When a customer decides to make a purchase, he or she triggers action back along the whole chain. All the businesses in the supply chain pass on portions of that end customer's money to each other, each retaining a margin for the value it has added. Each operation in the chain should be satisfying its own customer, but also making sure that eventually the end customer is also satisfied.

For a demonstration of how end customer perceptions of supply satisfaction can be very different from that of a single operation, examine the customer 'decision tree' in Figure 7.4. It charts the hypothetical progress of 100 customers requiring service (or products) from a business (for example, a printer requiring paper from an industrial paper stockist). Supply performance, as seen by the core operation (the warehouse), is represented by the shaded part of the diagram. It has received 20 orders, 18 of which were 'produced' (shipped to customers) as promised (on time, and in full). However, originally 100 customers may have requested service, 20 of whom found the business did not have appropriate products (did not stock the right paper), 10 of whom could not be served because the products were not available (out of stock), and 50 of whom were not satisfied with the price and/or delivery (of whom 10 placed an order notwithstanding). Of the 20 orders received, 18 were produced as promised (shipped) but two were not received as promised (delayed or damaged in transport). So what seems a 90 per cent supply performance is in fact an 8 per cent performance from the customer's perspective.

> **Operations principle**
> The performance of an operation in a supply chain does not necessarily reflect the performance of the whole supply chain.

This is just one operation in a whole network. Include the cumulative effect of similar reductions in performance for all the operations in a chain, and the probability that the end customer is adequately served could become remote. The point here is not that all

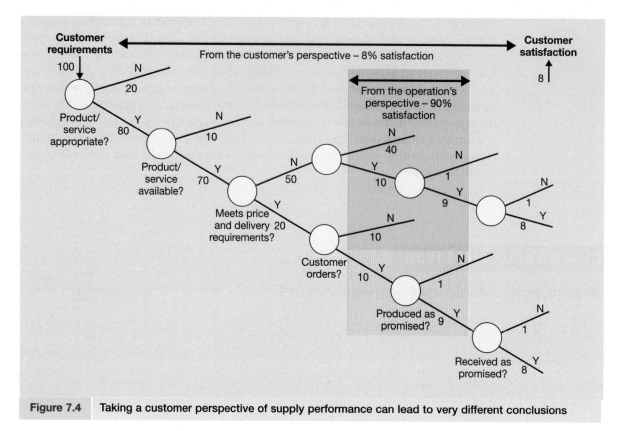

Figure 7.4   Taking a customer perspective of supply performance can lead to very different conclusions

supply chains have unsatisfactory supply performances (although most supply chains have considerable potential for improvement). Rather it is that the performance both of the supply chain as a whole, and of its constituent operations, should be judged in terms of how all end customer needs are satisfied.

Supply chain objectives

The objective of supply chain management is to meet the requirements of end customers by supplying appropriate products and services when they are needed, at a competitive cost. Doing this requires the supply chain to achieve appropriate levels of the five operations performance objectives – quality, speed, dependability, flexibility and cost.

Quality

The quality of a product or service when it reaches the customer is a function of the quality performance of every operation in the chain that supplied it. The implication of this is that errors in each stage of the chain can become multiplied in their effect on end customer service. For example, if each of seven stages in a supply chain has a 1 per cent error rate, only 93.2 per cent of products or services will be of good quality on reaching the end customer (i.e. 0.99). This is why only by every stage taking some responsibility for its own *and its suppliers'* performance, can a supply chain achieve high end customer quality.

Speed

This has two meanings in a supply chain context. The first is how fast customers can be served (the elapsed time between a customer requesting a product or service and receiving it in full), an important element in any business's ability to compete. However, fast customer response can be achieved simply by over-resourcing or over-stocking within the supply chain. For example, very large stocks in a retail operation can reduce the chances of stock-out to almost zero, so reducing customer waiting time virtually to zero. Similarly, an accounting firm may be able to respond quickly to customer demand by having a very large number of accountants on standby waiting for demand that may (or may not) occur. An alternative perspective on speed is the time taken for goods and services to move through the chain. So, for example, products that move quickly down a supply chain from raw material suppliers through to retailers will spend little time as inventory because, to achieve fast throughput time, material cannot dwell for significant periods as inventory. This in turn reduces the working capital requirements and other inventory costs in the supply chain, so reducing the overall cost of delivering to the end customer. Achieving a balance between speed as responsiveness to customers' demands and speed as fast throughput (although they are not incompatible) will depend on how the supply chain is choosing to compete.

Dependability

Dependability in a supply chain context is similar to speed in so much as one can almost guarantee 'on-time' delivery by keeping excessive resources, such as inventory, within the chain. However, dependability of throughput time is a much more desirable aim because it reduces uncertainty within the chain. If the individual operations in a chain do not deliver as promised on time, there will be a tendency for customers to over-order, or order early, so as to provide some kind of insurance against late delivery. The same argument applies if there is uncertainty regarding the *quantity* of products or services delivered. This is why delivery dependability is often measured as 'on time, in full' in supply chains.

Flexibility

In a supply chain context, this is usually taken to mean the chain's ability to cope with changes and disturbances. Very often this is referred to as supply chain agility. The concept of agility includes previously discussed issues such as focusing on the end customer and ensuring fast throughput and responsiveness to customer needs. But, in addition, agile supply chains are sufficiently flexible to cope with changes, either in the nature of customer demand or in the supply capabilities of operations within the chain.

Cost

In addition to the costs incurred within each operation to transform its inputs into outputs, the supply chain as a whole incurs additional costs that derive from each operation in a chain doing business with each other. These transaction costs may include such things as the costs of finding appropriate suppliers, setting up contractual agreements, monitoring supply performance, transporting products between operations, holding inventories, and so on. Many of the recent developments in supply chain management, such as partnership agreements or reducing the number of suppliers, are an attempt to minimize transaction costs.

FURTHER EXAMPLE

Should supply chains be lean or agile?

A distinction is often drawn between supply chains that are managed to emphasize supply chain efficiency (lean supply chains), and those that emphasize supply chain responsiveness and flexibility (agile supply chains). These two modes of managing supply chains are reflected in an idea proposed by Professor Marshall Fisher of Wharton Business School,[3] that supply chains serving different markets should be managed in different ways.

Even companies that have seemingly similar products or services, in fact, may compete in different ways with different products. For example, shoe manufacturers may produce classics that change little over the years, as well as fashion shoes that last only one season. Chocolate manufacturers have stable lines that have been sold for 50 years, but also product 'specials' associated with an event or film release, the latter selling only for a matter of months. Hospitals have routine 'standardized' surgical procedures such as cataract removal, but also have to provide emergency post-trauma surgery. Demand for the former products will be relatively stable and predictable, but demand for the latter will be far more uncertain. Also, the profit margin commanded by the innovative product will probably be higher than that of the more functional product. However, the price (and therefore the margin) of the innovative product may drop rapidly once it has become unfashionable in the market.

The supply chain policies that are seen to be appropriate for functional products and innovative products are termed efficient (or lean), and responsive (or agile) supply chain policies, respectively. Efficient supply chain policies include keeping inventories low, especially in the downstream parts of the network, so as to maintain fast throughput and reduce the amount of working capital tied up in the inventory. What inventory there is in the network is concentrated mainly

Operations principle
Supply chains with different end objectives need managing differently.

Figure 7.5   Matching the operations resources in the supply chain with market requirements

Source: Adapted from Fisher, M.C. (1997) 'What is the Right Supply Chain for Your Product?' *Harvard Business Review*, March–April, pp 105–116.

in the manufacturing operation, where it can keep utilization high and therefore manufacturing costs low. Information must flow quickly up and down the chain from retail outlets back up to the manufacturer so that schedules can be given the maximum amount of time to adjust efficiently. The chain is then managed to make sure that products flow as quickly as possible down the chain to replenish what few stocks are kept downstream.

> **Operations principle**
> 'Functional' products require lean supply chain management; 'innovative' products require agile supply chain management.

By contrast, responsive supply chain policy stresses high service levels and responsive supply to the end customer. The inventory in the network will be deployed as closely as possible to the customer. In this way, the chain can still supply even when dramatic changes occur in customer demand. Fast throughput from the upstream parts of the chain will still be needed to replenish downstream stocks. But those downstream stocks are needed to ensure high levels of availability to end customers. Figure 7.5 illustrates how the different supply chain policies match the different market requirements implied by functional and innovative products.

DIAGNOSTIC QUESTION

How should supply chain relationships be managed?

FURTHER EXAMPLE

The 'relationship' between operations in a supply chain is the basis on which the exchange of products, services, information and money is conducted. Managing supply chains is about managing relationships, because relationships influence the smooth flow between operations and processes. Different forms of relationship will be appropriate in different circumstances. An obvious but important factor in determining the importance of relationships to any operation is the extent to which they outsource their activities. In Chapter 3 we distinguished between non-vertically integrated operations that outsource almost all activities, and vertically integrated operations that outsource almost nothing. Only extremely vertically integrated businesses are able to ignore the question of how to manage customer–supplier relationships (because they do everything themselves). Initially, we can examine this question by describing two seemingly opposite approaches to managing relationships – arms-length, market-based, *transactional* relationships, and close, longer-term, *partnership* relationships.

Market-based 'transactional' relationships

Transactional relationships involve purchasing goods and services in a 'pure' market fashion, often seeking the 'best' supplier every time it is necessary to make a purchase. Each transaction effectively becomes a separate decision. The relationship may be short term, with no guarantee of further trading between the parties once the goods or services are delivered and payment is made.[4] The *advantages* of traditional market transactional relationships are usually seen as follows:

- They maintain competition between alternative suppliers. This promotes a constant drive between suppliers to provide best value.
- A supplier specializing in a small number of products or services, but supplying them to many customers, can gain natural economies of scale, enabling the supplier to offer the products and services at a lower price than if customers performed the activities themselves on a smaller scale.
- There is inherent flexibility in outsourced supplies. If demand changes, customers can simply change the number and type of suppliers – a faster and cheaper alternative to redirecting internal activities.
- Innovations can be exploited no matter where they originate. Specialist suppliers are more likely to come up with innovations that can be acquired faster and cheaper than by developing them in-house.

There are, however, *disadvantages* in buying in a totally 'free market' manner:

- Suppliers owe little loyalty to customers. If supply is difficult, there is no guarantee of receiving supply.
- Choosing who to buy from takes time and effort. Gathering sufficient information and making decisions continually are, in themselves, activities that need to be resourced.

Short-term market-based relationships of this type may be appropriate when new companies are being considered as more regular suppliers, or when purchases are one-off or very irregular. For example, the replacement of all the windows in a company's office block would typically involve this type of competitive-tendering market relationship.

Long-term 'partnership' relationships

Partnership relationships in supply chains are sometimes seen as a compromise between vertical integration on the one hand (owning the resources that supply you) and transactional relationships on the other. Partnership relationships are defined as:[5]

> . . . relatively enduring inter-firm cooperative agreements, involving flows and linkages that use resources and/or governance structures from autonomous organizations, for the joint accomplishment of individual goals linked to the corporate mission of each sponsoring firm.

This means that suppliers and customers are expected to cooperate, even to the extent of sharing skills and resources, to achieve joint benefits beyond those they could have achieved by acting alone. At the heart of the concept of partnership lies the issue of the *closeness* of the relationship. Partnerships are close relationships, the degree of which is influenced by a number of factors, as follows:

- *Sharing success* – both partners jointly benefit from the cooperation rather than manoeuvring to maximize their own individual contribution.
- *Long-term expectations* – relatively long-term commitments, but not necessarily permanent ones.
- *Multiple points of contact* – communication not restricted to formal channels, but may take place between many individuals in both organizations.
- *Joint learning* – a relationship commitment to learn from each other's experience.
- *Few relationships* – a commitment on the part of both parties to limit the number of customers or suppliers with whom they do business.

- *Joint coordination of activities* – fewer relationships allow joint coordination of activities such as the flow of materials or service, payment, and so on.
- *Information transparency* – confidence built through information exchange between the partners.
- *Joint problem solving* – jointly approaching problems can increase closeness over time.
- *Trust* – probably the key element in partnership relationships. In this context, trust means the willingness of one party to relate to the other on the understanding that the relationship will be beneficial to both, even though that cannot be guaranteed. Trust is widely held to be both the key issue in successful partnerships, but also, by far, the most difficult element to develop and maintain.

Which type of relationship?

It is very unlikely that any business will find it sensible to engage exclusively in one type of relationship or another. Most businesses will have a portfolio of, possibly, widely differing relationships. Also, there are degrees to which any particular relationship can be managed on a transactional or partnership basis. The real question is: Where, on the spectrum from transactional to partnership, should each relationship be positioned? And, while there is no simple formula for choosing the 'ideal' form of relationship in each case, there are some important factors that can sway the decision.

> **Operations principle**
> All supply chain relationships lie on a spectrum from 'transactional' to 'partnership'.

The most obvious issue will concern how a business intends to compete in its marketplace. If price is the main competitive factor then the relationship could be determined by which approach offers the highest potential savings. On one hand, market-based transactional relationships could minimize the actual price paid for purchased products and services, while partnerships could minimize the transaction costs of doing business. If a business is competing primarily on product or service innovation, the type of relationship may depend on where innovation is likely to happen. If innovation depends on close collaboration between supplier and customer, partnership relationships are needed. On the other hand, if suppliers are busily competing to out-do each other in terms of their innovations, and especially if the market is turbulent and fast growing (as with many software and Internet-based industries), then it may be preferable to retain the freedom to change suppliers quickly using market mechanisms. However, if markets are very turbulent, partnership relationships may reduce the risks of being unable to secure supply.

The main differences between the two ends of this relationship spectrum concern whether a customer sees advantage in long-term or short-term relationships. Transactional relationships can be either long or short term, but there is no guarantee of anything beyond the immediate transaction. They are appropriate when short-term benefits are important. Many relationships and many businesses are best served by concentrating on the short term (especially if, without short-term success, there is no long term).

> **Operations principle**
> True 'partnership' relationships involve mutual sacrifice as well as mutual benefit.

Partnership relationships are by definition long term. There is a commitment to work together over time to gain mutual advantage. The concept of mutuality is important here. A supplier does not become a 'partner' merely by being called one. True partnership implies mutual benefit, and often mutual sacrifice. Partnership means giving up some freedom of action in order to gain something more beneficial over the long term. If it is not in the culture of a business to give up some freedom of action, it is very unlikely to ever make a success of partnerships.

Opportunities to develop relationships can be limited by the structure of the market itself. If the number of potential suppliers is small, there may be few opportunities to use market mechanisms to gain any kind of supply advantage and it would probably be sensible to develop a close relationship with at least one supplier. On the other hand, if there are many potential suppliers, and especially if it is easy to judge the capabilities of the suppliers, transactional relationships are likely to be best.

DIAGNOSTIC QUESTION

How should the supply side be managed?

The ability of any process or operation to produce outputs is dependent on the inputs it receives. So good supply management is a necessary (but not sufficient) condition for effective operations management in general. It involves three main activities: selecting appropriate suppliers, planning and controlling the ongoing supply activity, and developing and improving suppliers' capabilities. All three activities are usually the responsibility of the purchasing or procurement function within the business. Purchasing should provide a vital link between the operation itself and its suppliers. They should understand the requirements of all the processes within their own operation and also the capabilities of the suppliers who could potentially provide products and services for the operation.

Supplier selection

Excel

Choosing appropriate suppliers should involve trading off alternative attributes. Rarely are potential suppliers so clearly superior to their competitors that the decision is self-evident. Most businesses find it best to adopt some kind of supplier 'scoring' or assessment procedure. This should be capable of rating alternative suppliers in terms of factors such as the following:

- Range of products or services provided
- Quality of products or services
- Responsiveness
- Dependability of supply
- Delivery and volume flexibility
- Total cost of being supplied
- Ability to supply in the required quantity.

In addition, there are likely to be less quantifiable or longer-term factors that will need taking into consideration. These may include the following:

- Potential for innovation
- Ease of doing business
- Willingness to share risk
- Long-term commitment to supply
- Ability to transfer knowledge as well as products and services.

Choosing suppliers should involve evaluating the relative importance of all these factors. So, for example, a business might choose a supplier who, although more expensive than alternative suppliers, has an excellent reputation for on-time delivery, because that is more appropriate to the way the business competes itself, or because the high level of supply dependability allows the business to hold lower stock levels, which may even save costs overall. Other trade-offs may be more difficult to calculate. For example, a potential supplier may have high levels of technical capability, but may be financially weak, with a small but finite risk of going out of business. Other suppliers may have little track record of supplying the products or services required, but show the managerial talent and energy for potential customers to view developing a supply relationship as an investment in future capability. But to make sensible trade-offs it is important to assess four basic capabilities:

Operations principle
Supplier selection should reflect overall supply chain objectives.

- *Technical capability* – the product or service knowledge to supply to high levels of specification.
- *Operations capability* – the process knowledge to ensure consistent, responsive, dependable and reasonable cost supply.
- *Financial capability* – the financial strength to fund the business in both the short term and the long term.
- *Managerial capability* – the management talent and energy to develop supply potential in the future.

Single- or multi-sourcing

A closely linked decision is whether to source each individual product or service from one, or more than one, supplier (single-sourcing or multi-sourcing). Some of the advantages and disadvantages of single- and multi-sourcing are shown in Table 7.1.

Table 7.1	Advantages and disadvantages of single- and multi-sourcing	
	Single-sourcing	*Multi-sourcing*
Advantages	• Potentially better quality because of more supplier quality assurance possibilities • Strong relationships that are more durable • Greater dependency encourages more commitment and effort • Better communication • Easier to cooperate on new product/service development • More economies of scale • Higher confidentiality	• Purchaser can drive price down by competitive tendering • Can switch sources in case of supply failure • Wide sources of knowledge and expertise to tap
Disadvantages	• More vulnerable to disruption if a failure to supply occurs • Individual supplier more affected by volume fluctuations • Supplier might exert upward pressure on prices if no alternative supplier is available	• Difficult to encourage commitment from suppliers • Less easy to develop effective supplier quality assurance • More effort needed to communicate • Suppliers less likely to invest in new processes • More difficult to obtain economies of scale

It may seem as though companies who multi-source do so exclusively for their own short-term benefit. However, this is not always the case: multi-sourcing can have an altruistic motive, or at least one that brings benefits to both supplier and purchaser in the long term. For example, Robert Bosch GmbH, the German automotive components manufacturer and distributor, at one time required that sub-contractors do no more than 20 per cent of their total business with them.[6] This was to prevent suppliers becoming too dependent on them. The purchasing organization could then change volumes up and down without pushing the supplier into bankruptcy. However, despite these perceived advantages, there has been a trend for purchasing functions to reduce their supplier base in terms of numbers of companies supplying any one part or service, mainly because it reduces the costs of transacting business.

Purchasing, the Internet and e-commerce

For some years, electronic means have been used by businesses to confirm purchased orders and ensure payment to suppliers. The rapid development of the Internet, however, opened up the potential for far more fundamental changes in purchasing behaviour. Partly this was as the result of supplier information made available through the Internet. Previously, a purchaser of industrial components may have been predisposed to return to suppliers who had been used before. There was inertia in the purchasing process because of the costs of seeking out new suppliers. By making it easier to search for alternative suppliers, the Internet changes the economics of the search process and offers the potential for wider searches. It also changed the economics of scale in purchasing. Purchasers requiring relatively low volumes find it easier to group together in order to create orders of sufficient size to warrant lower prices. In fact, the influence of the Internet on purchasing behaviour is not confined to *e-commerce*. Usually e-commerce is taken to mean the trade that actually takes place over the Internet. This is usually assumed to be a buyer visiting the seller's website, placing an order for parts and making a payment (also through the site). But the web is also an important source of purchasing information. For every 1 per cent of business transacted directly via the Internet, there may be 5 or 6 per cent of business that, at some point, involved the net, probably with potential buyers using it to compare prices or obtain technical information.

One increasingly common use of Internet technology in purchasing (or *e-procurement* as it is sometimes known) is for large companies, or groups of companies, to link their e-commerce systems into a common 'exchange'. In their more sophisticated form, such an exchange may be linked into the purchasing companies' own information systems (see the explanation of ERP in Chapter 10). Many of the large automotive, engineering and petrochemical companies, for example, have adopted such an approach. Typical of these companies' motives are those put forward by Shell Services International:[7] *'Procurement is an obvious first step in e-commerce. First, buying through the web is so slick and cheap compared to doing it almost any other way. Second, it allows you to aggregate, spend and ask: Why am I spending this money, or shouldn't I be getting a bigger discount? Third, it encourages new services like credit, insurance and accreditation to be built around it.'*

Managing ongoing supply

Managing supply relationships is not just a matter of choosing the right suppliers and then leaving them to get on with day-to-day supply. It is also about ensuring that suppliers are given the right information and encouragement to maintain smooth supply and that internal inconsistency does not negatively affect their ability to supply. A basic requirement is that some mechanism should be set up that ensures the two-way flow of information between customer and supplier. It is easy for both suppliers and customers simply to forget to inform each other of internal developments that could affect supply. Customers may see suppliers as having the responsibility for ensuring appropriate supply 'under any circumstances'. Or, suppliers themselves may be reluctant to inform customers of any potential problems with supply because they see it as risking the relationship. Yet, especially if customer and supplier see themselves as 'partners', the free flow of information, and a mutually supportive tolerance of occasional problems, is the best way to ensure smooth supply. Often day-to-day supplier relationships are damaged because of internal inconsistencies. For example, one part of a business may be asking a supplier for some special service beyond the strict nature of their agreement, whilst another part of the business is not paying suppliers on time.[8]

Service-level agreements

Some organizations bring a degree of formality to supplier relationships by encouraging (or requiring) all suppliers to agree service-level agreements (SLAs). SLAs are formal definitions of the dimensions of service and the relationship between suppliers and the organization. The type of issues covered by such an agreement could include response times, the range of services, dependability of service supply, and so on. Boundaries of responsibility and appropriate performance measures could also be agreed. For example, an SLA between an information systems support unit and a research unit in the laboratories of a large pharmaceutical company could define such performance measures as:

- The types of information network services that may be provided as 'standard'
- The range of special information services that may be available at different periods of the day
- The minimum 'up time', i.e. the proportion of time the system will be available at different periods of the day
- The maximum response time and average response time to get the system fully operational should it fail
- The maximum response time to provide 'special' services, and so on.

Although SLAs are described here as mechanisms for governing the ongoing relationship between suppliers and customers, they often prove inadequate because they are seen as being useful in setting up the terms of the relationship, but then are used only to resolve disputes. For SLAs to work effectively, they must be treated as working documents that establish the details of ongoing relationships *in the light of experience*. Used properly, they are a repository of the knowledge that both sides have gathered through working together. Any SLA that stays unchanged over time is, at the very least, failing to encourage improvement in supply.

How can suppliers be developed?

In any relationship other than pure market-based transactional relationships, it is in a customer's long-term interests to take some responsibility for developing supplier capabilities. Helping a supplier to improve not only enhances the service (and hopefully price) from the supplier; it may also lead to greater supplier loyalty and long-term commitment. This is why some particularly successful businesses (including Japanese automotive manufacturers) invest in supplier development teams whose responsibility is to help suppliers to improve their own operations processes. Of course, committing the resources to help suppliers is only worthwhile if it improves the effectiveness of the supply chain as a whole. Nevertheless, the potential for such enlightened self-interest can be significant.

How customers and suppliers see each other[9]

One of the major barriers to supplier development is the mismatch between how customers and suppliers perceive both what is required and how the relationship is performing. Exploring potential mismatches is often a revealing exercise, for both customers and suppliers. Figure 7.6 illustrates this. It shows that gaps may exist between four sets of ideas. As a customer you (presumably) have an idea about what you really want from a supplier. This may, or may not, be formalized in the form of a service level agreement. But no SLA can capture everything about what is required. There may be a gap between how you as a customer interpret what is required and how the supplier interprets it. This is the *requirements perception gap*. Similarly, as a customer, you (again presumably) have a view on how your supplier is performing in terms of fulfilling your requirements. That may not coincide with how your supplier believes it is performing. This is the *fulfilment perception gap*. Both these gaps are a function of the effectiveness of the communication between supplier and customer. But there are also two other gaps. The gap between what you want from your supplier and how they are performing indicates the type of development that, as a customer, you should be giving to your supplier. Similarly, the gap between your supplier's perceptions of your needs and its performance indicates how they should initially see themselves improving their own performance. Ultimately, of course, their responsibility for improvement should coincide with their customer's views of requirements and performance.

> **Operations principle**
> Unsatisfactory supplier relationships can be caused by requirements and fulfilment perception gaps.

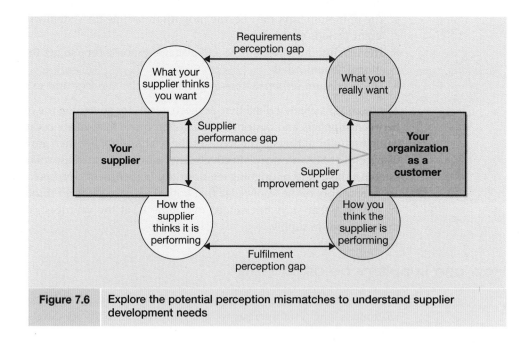

Figure 7.6   Explore the potential perception mismatches to understand supplier development needs

How should the demand side be managed?

The management of demand-side relationships will depend partly on the nature of demand, in particular how uncertain it is. Knowing the exact demands that customers are going to require allows a supplier to plan its own internal processes in a systematic manner. This type of demand is called 'dependent' demand; it is relatively predictable because it is dependent upon some factor which is itself predictable. For example, supplying tyres to an automobile factory involves examining the manufacturing schedules in the car plant and deriving the demand for tyres from these. If 200 cars are to be manufactured on a particular day, then it is simple to calculate that 1000 tyres will be demanded by the car plant (each car has five tyres). Because of this, the tyres can be ordered from the tyre manufacturer to a delivery schedule that is closely in line with the demand for tyres from the plant. In fact, the demand for every part of the car plant will be derived from the assembly schedule for the finished cars. Manufacturing instructions and purchasing requests will all be dependent upon this figure. Managing internal process networks when external demand is dependent is largely a matter of calculating, in as precise a way as possible, the internal consequences of demand. MRP, treated in Chapter 10, is the best-known dependent demand approach.

But not all operations have such predictable demand. Some operations are subject to independent demand. There is a random element in demand that is virtually independent of any obvious factors. Companies are often required to supply demand without having any firm forward visibility of customer orders. A drive-in tyre replacement service will need to manage a stock of tyres. In that sense it is exactly the same task that faced the supplier of tyres to the car plant, but demand is very different. The tyre service cannot predict either the volume or the specific needs of customers. It must make decisions on how many and what type of tyres to stock, based on demand forecasts and in the light of the risks it is prepared to run of being out of stock. Managing internal process networks when external demand is independent involves making 'best guesses' concerning future demand, attempting to put the resources in place to satisfy this demand, and attempting to respond quickly if actual demand does not match the forecast. Inventory planning and control, treated in Chapter 9, is a typical approach.

Logistics services

FURTHER EXAMPLE

Logistics means moving products to customers. Sometimes the term 'physical distribution management' or simply 'distribution' is used as being analogous to logistics. Logistics is now frequently outsourced to 'third party' logistics (or 3PL) providers, which vary in terms of the range and integration of their services. At the simplest level, the 'haulage' and 'storage' businesses either move goods around or store them in warehouses. Clients take responsibility for all planning. Physical distribution companies bring haulage and storage together, collecting clients' products, putting them into storage facilities and delivering them to the end customer as required. 'Contract' logistics service providers tend to have more sophisticated clients with more complex operations. Total 'supply chain management' (or 4PL) providers offer to manage supply chains from end to end, often for several customers simultaneously. Doing this requires a much greater degree of analytical and modelling capability, business process re-engineering and consultancy skills.

Logistics management and the Internet

Internet-based communication has had a significant impact on physical distribution management. Information can be made available more readily along the distribution chain, so that transport companies, warehouses, suppliers and customers can share knowledge of where goods are in the chain (and sometimes where they are going next). This allows the operations within the chain to coordinate their activities more readily. It also gives the potential for some significant cost savings. For example, an important issue for transportation companies is back-loading. When the company is contracted to transport goods from A to B, its vehicles may have to return from B to A empty. Back-loading means finding a potential customer who wants their goods transported from B to A in the right time-frame. With the increase in information availability through the Internet, the possibility of finding a back-load increases. Companies that can fill their vehicles on both the outward and return journeys will have significantly lower costs per distance travelled than those whose vehicles are empty for half the total journey. Similarly, Internet-based technology that allows customers visibility of the progress of distribution can be used to enhance the perception of customer service. 'Track-and-trace' technologies, for example, allow package distribution companies to inform and reassure customers that their service is being delivered as promised.

Automatic identification technologies

Tracing the progress of items through a supply chain has involved the use of bar codes to record progress. During manufacture bar codes are used to identify the number of products passing through a particular point in the process. In warehouses, bar codes are used to keep track of how many products are stored at particular locations. But bar codes have disadvantages. It is sometimes difficult to align the item so that the bar code can be read conveniently, items can only be scanned one by one, and the bar code identifies only the *type* of item, not a specific item itself. That is, the code identifies that an item is, say, a can of one type of drink rather than one specific can. These drawbacks can be overcome through the use of 'automated identification' or Auto-ID. Usually this involves Radio Frequency Identification (RFID). Here an Electronic Product Code (ePC) that is a unique number, 96 bits long, is embedded in a memory chip or smart tag. These tags are put on individual items so that each item has its own unique identifying code. At various points during its manufacture, distribution, storage and sale, each smart tag can be scanned by a wireless radio frequency 'reader'. This transmits the item's embedded identity code to a network such as the Internet, describing, for example, when and where it was made, where it has been stored, etc. This information can then be fed into control systems (see Figure 7.7). It is also controversial – see the critical commentary, later.

Customer development

Earlier in the chapter, Figure 7.6 illustrated some of the gaps in perception and performance that can occur between customers and suppliers. The purpose then was to demonstrate the nature of supplier development. The same approach can be used to analyze the nature of requirements and performance with customers. In this case the imperative is to understand customer perceptions, both of their requirements and of their view of your performance, and feed these into your own performance improvement plans. What is less

Figure 7.7 Using radio frequency identification for monitoring and control of operations processes

common, but can be equally valuable, is to use these gaps (shown in Figure 7.8) to examine the question of whether customer requirements and perceptions of performance are either accurate or reasonable. For example, customers may be placing demands on suppliers without fully considering their consequences. It may be that slight modifications in what is demanded would not inconvenience customers and yet would provide significant benefits to suppliers that could then be passed on to customers. Similarly, customers may be incompetent at measuring

Operations principle
Unsatisfactory customer relationships can be caused by requirement and fulfilment perception gaps.

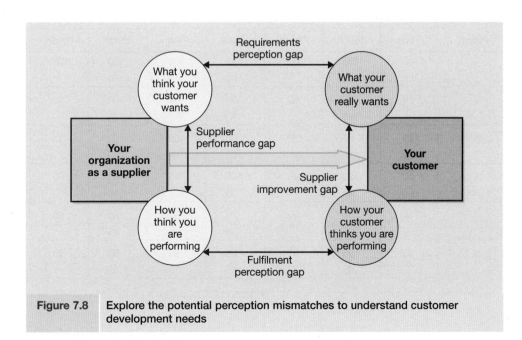

Figure 7.8 Explore the potential perception mismatches to understand customer development needs

supplier performance, in which case the benefits of excellent supplier service will not be recognized. So, just as customers have a responsibility to help develop their own supplier's performance, in their own as well as their supplier's interests, suppliers have a responsibility to develop their customer's understanding of how supply should be managed.

DIAGNOSTIC QUESTION

Are supply chain dynamics under control?

There are dynamics that exist between firms in supply chains that cause errors, inaccuracies and volatility, and these increase for operations further upstream in the supply chain. This effect is known as the Bullwhip Effect,[10] so called because a small disturbance at one end of the chain causes increasingly large disturbances as it works its way towards the end. Its main cause is a perfectly understandable and rational desire by the different links in the supply chain to manage their levels of activity and inventory sensibly. To demonstrate this, examine the production rate and stock levels for the supply chain shown in Table 7.2. This is a four-stage supply chain where an original equipment

Table 7.2 Fluctuations of production levels along the supply chain in response to a small change in end-customer demand

Period	Third-tier supplier Prodn.	Third-tier supplier Stock	Second-tier supplier Prodn.	Second-tier supplier Stock	First-tier supplier Prodn.	First-tier supplier Stock	Original equipment mfr. Prodn.	Original equipment mfr. Stock	Demand
1	100	100 / 100	100	100 / 100	100	100 / 100	100	100 / 100	100
2	20	100 / 60	60	100 / 80	80[b]	100[a] / 90[c]	90[d]	100 / 95	95
3	180	60 / 120	120	80 / 100	100	90 / 95	95	95 / 95	95
4	60	120 / 90	90	100 / 95	95	95 / 95	95	95 / 95	95
5	100	90 / 95	95	95 / 95	95	95 / 95	95	95 / 95	95
6	95	95 / 95	95	95 / 95	95	95 / 95	95	95 / 95	95

Starting stock (a) + production (b) = finishing stock (c) + demand, that is, production in previous tier down (d): see explanation in text.

All stages in the supply chain keep one period's inventory: c = d.

manufacturer (OEM) is served by three tiers of suppliers. The demand from the OEM's market has been running at a rate of 100 items per period, but in period 2, demand reduces to 95 items per period. All stages in the supply chain work on the principle that they will keep in stock one period's demand. This is a simplification but not a gross one. Many operations gear their inventory levels to their demand rate. The column headed 'stock' for each level of supply shows the starting stock at the beginning of the period and the finishing stock at the end of the period. At the beginning of period 2, the OEM has 100 units in stock (that being the rate of demand up to period 2). Demand in period 2 is 95 and so the OEM knows that it would need to produce sufficient items to finish up at the end of the period with 95 in stock (this being the new demand rate). To do this, it need only manufacture 90 items; these, together with five items taken out of the starting stock, will supply demand and leave a finishing stock of 95 items. The beginning of period 3 finds the OEM with 95 items in stock. Demand is also 95 items and therefore its production rate to maintain a stock level of 95 will be 95 items per period. The original equipment manufacturer now operates at a steady rate of producing 95 items per period. Note, however, that a change in demand of only five items has produced a fluctuation of 10 items in the OEM's production rate.

Carrying this same logic through to the first-tier supplier, at the beginning of period 2, the first-tier supplier has 100 items in stock. The demand that it has to supply in period 2 is derived from the production rate of the OEM. This has dropped down to 90 in period 2. The first-tier supplier therefore has to produce sufficient to supply the demand of 90 items (or the equivalent) and leave one month's demand (now 90 items) as its finishing stock. A production rate of 80 items per month will achieve this. It will therefore start period 3 with an opening stock of 90 items, but the demand from the OEM has now risen to 95 items. It therefore has to produce sufficient to fulfil this demand of 95 items and leave 95 items in stock. To do this, it must produce 100 items in period 3. After period 3 the first-tier supplier then resumes a steady state, producing 95 items per month. Note again, however, that the fluctuation has been even greater than that in the OEM's production rate, decreasing to 80 items a period, increasing to 100 items a period, and then achieving a steady rate of 95 items a period. Extending the logic back to the third-tier supplier, it is clear that the further back up the supply chain an operation is placed, the more drastic are the fluctuations.

Operations principle
Demand fluctuations become progressively amplified as their effects work back up the supply chain.

This relatively simple demonstration ignores any time lag in material and information flow between stages. In practice there will be such a lag, and this will make the fluctuations even more marked. Figure 7.9 shows the net result of all these effects in a typical supply chain. Note the increasing volatility further back in the chain.

Controlling supply chain dynamics

The first step in improving supply chain performance involves attempting to reduce the bullwhip effect. This usually means coordinating the activities of the operations in the chain in the following ways.[11]

Share information throughout the supply chain

Operations principle
The bullwhip effect can be reduced by information sharing, aligning planning and control decisions, improving flow efficiency, and better forecasting.

One reason for the bullwhip effect is that each operation in the chain reacts only to the orders placed by its *immediate* customer. They have little overview of what is happening throughout the chain. But if chain-wide information is shared throughout the chain, it is unlikely that such wild fluctuations will occur. With information transmitted throughout the chain, all the operations

Figure 7.9   Typical supply chain dynamics

can monitor true demand, free of distortions. So, for example, information regarding supply problems, or shortages, can be transmitted down the chain so that downstream customers can modify their schedules and sales plans accordingly. For example, the electronic point-of-sale (EPOS) systems, used by many retailers, make information on current demand downstream in the supply chain available to upstream operations. Sales data from checkouts or cash registers is consolidated and transmitted to the warehouses, transportation companies and supplier operations in the supply chain. This means that suppliers can be aware of the 'real' movements in the market.

Align all the channels of information and supply

Channel alignment means the adjustment of scheduling, material movements, stock levels, pricing and other sales strategies so as to bring all the operations in the chain into line with each other. This goes beyond the provision of information. It means that the systems and methods of planning and control decision making are harmonized through the chain. For example, even when using the same information, differences in forecasting methods or purchasing practices can lead to fluctuations in orders between operations in the chain. One way of avoiding this is to allow an upstream supplier to manage the inventories of its downstream customer. This is known as vendor-managed inventory (VMI). So, for example, a packaging supplier could take responsibility for the stocks of packaging materials held by a food manufacturing customer. In turn, the food manufacturer takes responsibility for the stocks of its products that are held in its customer's (the supermarket's) warehouses.

Increase operational efficiency throughout the chain

'Operational efficiency' in this context means the efforts that each operation in the chain makes to reduce its own complexity, the cost of doing business with other operations in the chain, and its throughput time. The cumulative effect of this is to simplify throughput in the whole chain. For example, imagine a chain of operations whose performance level is relatively poor: quality defects are frequent, the lead time to order products and services is long, delivery is unreliable and so on. The behaviour of the chain would be a continual sequence of errors and effort wasted in replanning to compensate for the errors. Poor quality would mean extra and unplanned orders being placed, and unreliable delivery and slow delivery lead times would mean high safety stocks. Just as important, most operations managers' time would be spent coping with the inefficiency. By contrast, a chain whose operations had high levels of operations performance would be more predictable and have faster throughput, both of which would help to minimize supply chain fluctuations.

Improve forecasts

Improved forecast accuracy also helps to reduce the bullwhip effect. Bullwhip is caused by the demand pattern, lead times, forecasting mechanisms and the replenishment decisions used to order product from production facilities or suppliers. Improving the accuracy of your forecasts directly reduces the inventory-holding requirements that will achieve customer service-level targets. Reducing lead times means that you need to forecast less far into the future and thus lead times have a large impact on bullwhip and inventory costs. The exact nature of how bullwhip propagates in a supply chain is also dependent on the nature of the demand pattern. Negatively correlated demands require less inventory in the supply chain than do positively correlated demand patterns, for example. But bullwhip is avoidable. By using sophisticated replenishment policies, designed using control engineering principles, many businesses have been able to eliminate bullwhip effects. Sometimes this comes at a cost. Extra inventory may be required in parts of the chain, or customer service levels reduce. But more often bullwhip avoidance creates a 'win–win' situation. It reduces inventory requirements and improves customer service.[12]

Critical commentary

Each chapter contains a short critical commentary on the main ideas covered in the chapter. Its purpose is not to undermine the issues discussed in the chapter, but to emphasize that, although we present a relatively orthodox view of operation, there are other perspectives.

■ This emphasis on understanding the end customer in a supply chain has led some authorities to object to the very term *supply* chain. Rather, they say, they should be referred to as *demand* chains. Their argument is based on the idea that the concept of 'supply' implies a 'push' mentality. Any emphasis on pushing goods through a supply chain should be avoided. It implies that customers should consume what suppliers see fit to produce. On the other hand, referring to 'demand chains' puts proper emphasis on the importance of seeing customers as pulling demand through the chain. Nevertheless, 'supply chain' is still the most commonly used term.

■ The use of technology in supply chain management is not always universally welcomed. Even e-procurement is seen by some as preventing closer partnership-type relationships that, in the long run, may be more beneficial. Similarly, track-and-trace technology is seen by some as a waste of time and money. *'What we need'*, they argue, *'is to know that we can trust the delivery to arrive on time; we do not need the capability to waste our time finding out where the delivery is.'*

■ The idea of Auto-ID also opens up many ethical issues. People see its potential and its dangers in very different ways. Take the following two statements:[13]

'We are on the brink of a revolution of "smart products" that will interconnect everyday objects, consumers and manufacturers in a dynamic cycle of world commerce. . . . The

vision of the Auto-ID centre is to create a universal environment in which computers under-
stand the world without help from human beings.'

'Supermarket cards and other retail surveillance devices are merely the opening volley of
the marketers' war against consumers. If consumers fail to oppose these practices now our
long term prospects may look like something from a dystopian science fiction novel. . . .
though many Auto-ID proponents appear focused on inventory and supply chain efficien-
cy, others are developing financial and consumer applications that, if adopted, will have
chilling effects on consumers' ability to escape the oppressive surveillance of manufactur-
ers, retailers, and marketers. Of course, government and law enforcement will be quick to
use the technology to keep tabs on citizens as well.'

It is this last issue that particularly scares some civil liberties activists. Keeping track of items
within a supply chain is a relatively uncontentious issue. Keeping track of items when those
items are identified with a particular individual going about their everyday lives is far more
problematic. So, beyond the checkout for every arguably beneficial application there is also
potential for misuse. For example, smart tags could drastically reduce theft because items
could automatically report when they are stolen; their tags serving as a homing device pinpoint their exact location. But, similar technology could be used to trace any citizen, honest
or not.

Summary checklist

This checklist comprises questions that can be usefully applied to any type of operations and reflect the major diagnostic questions used within the chapter.

- [ ] Is it understood that the performance of any one operation is partly a function of all the other operations in the supply chain?

- [ ] Are supply chain concepts applied internally as well as externally?

- [ ] Are supply chain objectives understood in the context of the whole chain rather than the single operation?

- [ ] Which product or service groups are 'functional' and which are 'innovative'?

- [ ] Therefore, which products or service groups need 'lean' and which need 'agile' supply chain management?

- [ ] Is the position on the 'transactional to partnership' spectrum understood for each customer and supplier relationship?

- [ ] Are customer and supplier relationships at an appropriate point on the 'transactional to partnership' spectrum?

- [ ] Are 'partnership' relationships *really* partnerships or are they just called that?

- [ ] Are suppliers and potential suppliers rigorously assessed using some scoring procedure?

- [ ] Are the trade-offs inherent in supplier selection understood?

- [ ] Is the approach to single- or multi-sourcing appropriate?

- [ ] Is the purchasing activity making full use of Internet-based mechanisms?

- [ ] Are service-level agreements used? And do they develop over time?

- [ ] Is sufficient effort put into supplier development?

- [ ] Are actual and potential mismatches of perception in the supplier relationships explored?

- [ ] Is the difference between dependent and independent demand understood?

- [ ] Is the potential for outsourcing logistics services regularly explored?

- [ ] Could new technologies such as RFID have any benefit?

- [ ] Has the idea of customer development been explored?

- [ ] Have mechanisms for reducing the impact of the bullwhip effect been explored?

- [ ] Has there been a risk assessment to assess supply chain vulnerability?

Case study   Supplying fast fashion[14]

Garment retailing has changed. No longer is there a standard look that all retailers adhere to for a whole season. Fashion is fast, complex and furious. Different trends overlap and fashion ideas that are not even on a store's radar screen can become 'must haves' within six months. Many retail businesses with their own brands such as H&M and Zara sell up-to-the-minute fashionability at low prices, in stores that are clearly focused on one particular market. In the world of fast fashion, catwalk designs speed their way into high street stores at prices anyone can afford. The quality of the garment means that it may last only one season, but fast fashion customers don't want yesterday's trends. As *Newsweek* puts it, '. . . *being a "quicker picker-upper" is what made fashion retailers H&M and Zara successful. [They] thrive by practicing the new science of "fast fashion"; compressing product development cycles as much as six times.*' But the retail operations that customers see are only the end part of the supply chain that feeds them. And these have also changed.

At its simplest level, the fast fashion supply chain has four stages. First, the garments are designed, after which they are manufactured and then distributed to the retail outlets where they are displayed and sold in retail operations designed to reflect the businesses' brand values. In this short case we examine two fast fashion operations, Hennes and Mauritz (known as H&M) and Zara, together with United Colors of Benetton (UCB), a similar chain but with a different market positioning.

Source: Courtesy H&M

Benetton

Almost 50 years ago Luciano Benetton took the world of fashion by storm by selling the bright, casual sweaters designed by his sister across Europe (and later the rest of the world), promoted by controversial advertising. By 2005 the Benetton Group was present in 120 countries throughout the world. Selling casual garments, mainly under its United Colors of Benetton (UCB) and its more fashion-oriented Sisley brands, it produces 110 million garments a year, over 90 per cent of them in Europe. Its retail network of over 5000 stores produces revenue of around €2 billion. Benetton products are seen as less 'high fashion' but higher quality and durability, with higher prices, than H&M and Zara.

H&M

Established in Sweden in 1947, H&M now sells clothes and cosmetics in over 1000 stores in 21 countries around the world. The business concept is 'fashion and quality at the best price'. With more than 45,000 employees, and revenues of around SEK 60,000 million, its biggest market is Germany, followed by Sweden and the UK. H&M is seen by many as the originator of the fast fashion concept. Certainly they have years of experience at driving down the price of up-to-the-minute fashions. '*We ensure the best price*', they say, '*by having few middlemen, buying large volumes, having extensive experience of the clothing industry, having a great knowledge of which goods should be bought from which markets, having efficient distribution systems, and being cost-conscious at every stage.*'

Zara

The first store opened almost by accident in 1975 when Amancio Ortega Gaona, a women's pajama manufacturer, was left with a large cancelled order. The shop he opened was intended only as an outlet for cancelled orders. Now Inditex, the holding group that includes the Zara brand, has over 1300 stores in 39 countries with sales of over €3 billion. The Zara brand accounts for over 75 per cent of the group's total retail sales, and is still based in north-west Spain. By 2003 it had become the world's fastest-growing volume garment retailer. The Inditex group also has several other branded chains, including Pull and Bear, and Massimo Dutti. In total it employs almost 40,000 people in a business that is known for a high degree of vertical integration compared with most fast fashion companies. The company believes that it is their integration along the supply chain that allows them to respond to customer demand quickly and flexibly while keeping stock to a minimum.

Design

All three businesses emphasize the importance of design in this market. Although not *haute couture,* capturing design trends is vital to success. Even the boundary between high and fast fashion is starting to blur. In 2004 H&M recruited high fashion designer Karl Lagerfeld, previously noted for his work with more exclusive brands. For H&M his designs were priced for value rather than exclusivity: *'Why do I work for H&M? Because I believe in inexpensive clothes, not "cheap" clothes',* said Lagerfeld. Yet most of H&M's products come from over 100 designers in Stockholm who work with a team of 50 pattern designers, around 100 buyers and a number of budget controllers. The department's task is to find the optimum balance between the three components comprising H&M's business concept – fashion, price and quality. Buying volumes and delivery dates are then decided.

Zara's design functions are organized in a different way from those of most similar companies. Conventionally, the design input comes from three *separate* functions: the designers themselves, market specialists, and buyers who place orders on to suppliers. At Zara the design stage is split into three product areas: women's, men's and children's garments. In each area, designers, market specialists and buyers are co-located in design halls that also contain small workshops for trying out prototype designs. The market specialists in all three design halls are in regular contact with Zara retail stores, discussing customer reaction to new designs. In this way, the retail stores are not the end of the whole supply chain but the beginning of the design stage of the chain. Zara's around 300 designers, whose average age is 26, produce approximately 40,000 items per year of which about 10,000 go into production.

Benetton also has around 300 designers, who not only design for all their brands, but also are engaged in researching new materials and clothing concepts. Since 2000 the company has moved to standardize their range globally. At one time more than 20 per cent of its ranges were customized to the specific needs of each country; now only between 5 and 10 per cent of garments are customized. This reduced the number of individual designs offered globally by over 30 per cent, strengthening the global brand image and reducing production costs.

Both H&M and Zara have moved away from the traditional industry practice of offering two 'collections' a year, for Spring/Summer and Autumn/Winter. Their 'seasonless cycle' involves the continual introduction of new products on a rolling basis throughout the year. This allows designers to learn from customers' reactions to their new products and incorporate them quickly into more new products. The most extreme version of this idea is practised by Zara. A garment is designed; a batch is manufactured and 'pulsed' through the supply chain. Often the design is never repeated; it may be modified and another batch produced, but there are no 'continuing' designs as such. Even Benetton has increased the proportion of what it calls 'flash' collections – small collections that are put into its stores during the season.

Manufacturing

At one time Benetton focused its production on its Italian plants. Then it significantly increased its production outside Italy to take advantage of lower labour costs. Non-Italian operations include factories in North Africa, Eastern Europe and Asia. Yet each location operates in a very similar manner. A central, Benetton-owned, operation performs some manufacturing operations (especially those requiring expensive technology) and coordinates the more labour-intensive production activities that are performed by a network of smaller contractors (often owned and managed by ex-Benetton employees). These contractors may in turn sub-contract some of their activities. The company's central facility in Italy allocates production to each of the non-Italian networks, deciding what and how much each is to produce. There is some specialization, for example jackets are made in Eastern Europe while T-shirts are made in Spain. Benetton also has a controlling share in its main supplier of raw materials, to ensure fast supply to its factories. Benetton is also known for the practice of dyeing garments after assembly rather than using dyed thread or fabric. This postpones decisions about colours until late in the supply process so that there is a greater chance of producing what is needed by the market.

H&M does not have any factories of its own, but instead works with around 750 suppliers. Around half of production takes place in Europe and the rest mainly in Asia. It has 21 production offices around the world that between them are responsible for coordinating the suppliers who produce over half a billion items a year for H&M. The relationship between production offices and suppliers is vital, because it allows fabrics to be bought in early. The actual dyeing and cutting of the garments can then be decided at a later stage in the production. The later an order can be placed on suppliers, the less the risk of buying the wrong thing. Average supply lead times vary from three weeks up to six months, depending on the nature of the goods. However, *'The most important thing'*, they say, *'is to find the optimal time to order each item. Short lead times are not always best. For some high-volume fashion basics, it is to our advantage to place orders far in advance. Trendier garments require considerably shorter lead times.'*

Zara's lead times are said to be the fastest in the industry, with a 'catwalk to rack' time as little as 15 days. According to one analyst, this is because they *'own most of the manufacturing capability used to make their products, which they use as a means of exciting and stimulating customer demand.'* About half of Zara's products are produced in its network of 20 Spanish factories, which, as at Benetton, tended to concentrate on the more capital-intensive operations such as cutting and dyeing. Sub-contractors are used for most of the labour-intensive operations such as sewing. Zara buys around 40 per cent of its fabric from its own wholly-owned subsidiary, most of which is in undyed form for dyeing after assembly. Most Zara factories and their sub-contractors work on a single-shift system to retain some volume flexibility.

Distribution

Both Benetton and Zara have invested in highly automated warehouses, close to their main production centres, that store, pack and assemble individual orders for their retail networks. These automated warehouses represent a major investment for both companies. In 2001, Zara caused some press comment by announcing that it would open a second automated warehouse even though, by its own calculations, it was only using about half its existing warehouse capacity.

More recently, Benetton caused some controversy by announcing that it was exploring the use of RFID tags to track its garments.

At H&M, while the stock management is primarily handled internally, physical distribution is sub-contracted. A large part of the flow of goods is routed from the production site to the retail country via H&M's transit terminal in Hamburg. Upon arrival the goods are inspected and allocated to the stores or to the centralized store stock room. The centralized store stock room, within H&M referred to as the 'Call-Off warehouse', replenishes stores on item level according to what is selling.

Retail

All H&M stores (average size, 1300 square metres) are owned and run solely by H&M. The aim is to *'create a comfortable and inspiring atmosphere in the store that makes it simple for customers to find what they want and to feel at home'*. This is similar to Zara stores, although they tend to be smaller (average size, 800 square metres). Perhaps the most remarkable characteristic of Zara stores is that garments rarely stay in the store for longer than two weeks. Because product designs are often not repeated and are produced in relatively small batches, the range of garments displayed in the store can change radically every two or three weeks. This encourages customers both to avoid delaying a purchase and to revisit the store frequently.

Since 2000 Benetton has been reshaping its retail operations. At one time the vast majority of Benetton retail outlets were small shops run by third parties. Now these small stores have been joined by several, Benetton-owned and operated, larger stores (1500 to 3000 square metres). These mega-stores can display the whole range of Benetton products and reinforce the Benetton shopping experience.

QUESTION

1 Compare and contrast the approaches taken by H&M, Benetton and Zara to managing their supply chain.

Active case study   NK Fleet Management

ACTIVE CASE

NK Fleet Management is looking to grow their business. Responsible for managing and servicing car fleets, the company's relationship with its main customer (the vehicle manufacturer) is governed by a set of service level agreements (SLAs). Whilst these agreements are comprehensive, they do not cover all eventualities. In the coming months the company have to respond to various more unusual requests from their customer.

● How would you react to each of the challenges to managing the relationship with their major customer?

Please refer to the Active case on the CD to work though the dilemmas faced by NK Fleet Management.

Applying the principles

Some of these exercises can be answered by reading the chapter. Others will require some general knowledge of business activity and some might require an element of investigation. All have hints on how they can be answered on the CD accompanying this book.

1 Read the description of Seven-Eleven Japan again and consider the following questions:

(a) SEJ stores typically carry around 3000 SKUs (Stock Keeping Units, that is types of different product) compared with a large supermarket that may have over 100,000 SKUs. How do you think this affects their ability to manage their supply chain in an agile manner?

(b) SEJ place a lot of emphasis on the use of their information system to achieve agility. How do you think the way in which an information system is used affects its value to a supply chain?

2 If you were the owner of a small local retail shop, what criteria would you use to select suppliers for the goods that you wish to stock in your shop? Visit three shops that are local to you and ask the owners how they select their suppliers. In what way were their answers different from what you thought they might be?

3 What is your purchasing strategy? How do you approach buying the products and services that you need (or want)? Classify the types and products and services that you buy and record the criteria you use to purchase each category. Discuss these categories and criteria with others. Why are their views different?

4 Visit a C2C (consumer-to-consumer) auction site (for example eBay) and analyze the function of the site in terms of the way it facilitates transactions. What does such a site have to get right to be successful?

5 The example of the bullwhip effect shown in Table 7.2 shows how a simple 5 per cent reduction in demand at the end of the supply chain causes fluctuations that increase in severity the further back an operation is placed in the chain.

(a) Using the same logic and the same rules (i.e. all operations keep one period's demand as inventory), what would the effect on the chain be if demand fluctuated period by period between 100 and 95? That is, period 1 has a demand of 100, period 2 has a demand of 95, period 3 of 100, period 4 of 95, and so on?

(b) What happens if all operations in the supply chain decide to keep only half of each period's demand as inventory?

(c) Find examples of how supply chains try to reduce this bullwhip effect.

6 Visit the websites of some distribution and logistics companies. For example, you might start with some of the following: **www.eddiestobart.co.uk, www.norbert-dentressangle.com, www.accenture.com** (under 'services' look for supply chain management), **www.logisticsonline.com.**

● What do you think are the market promises that these companies make to their clients and potential clients?
● What are the operations capabilities they need in order to fulfil these promises successfully?

Notes on chapter

1 Source: Slack, N. and Lewis, M.A. (2002) *Operations Strategy,* Financial Times Prentice Hall, Harlow, UK.

2 Source: Adam Grossberg and Mary Ward of Lucent Technologies, and Carbone, J. (2002) 'Lucent's supply chain flattens margins', *Purchasing Magazine,* 19 September.

3   Fisher, M.L. (1997) 'What is the right supply chain for your product', *Harvard Business Review,* March–April.

4   Kapour, V. and Gupta, A. (1997) 'Aggressive sourcing: a free-market approach', *Sloan Management Review,* Fall.

5   Parkhe, A. (1993) 'Strategic alliance structuring', *Academy of Management Journal,* Vol. 36, pp. 794–829.

6   Source: Grad, C. (2000) 'A network of supplies to be woven into the web', *Financial Times,* 9 February.

7   Harney, A. (2000) 'Up close but impersonal', *Financial Times,* 10 March.

8   Lee, L. and Dobler, D.W. (1977) *Purchasing and Materials Management,* McGraw-Hill.

9   Harland, C.M. (1996) 'Supply chain management relationships, chains and networks', *British Journal of Management,* Vol. 1, No. 7.

10 Lee, H.L., Padmanabhan, V. and Whang, S. (1997) 'The bull whip effect in supply chains', *Sloan Management Review,* Spring.

11 Lee *et al, op. cit.*

12 Thanks to Stephen Disney at Cardiff Business School, UK, for help with this section.

13 MIT Auto-ID website, and Albrecht, K. (2002) 'Supermarket cards: tip of the surveillance iceberg', *Denver University Law Review,* June.

14 All data from public sources and reflect period 2004–05.

Taking it further

Child, J. and Faulkner, D. (1998) *Strategies of Cooperation: Managing alliances, networks and joint ventures,* Oxford University Press. Very much a strategic view of supply networks, but insightful and readable.

Christopher, M. (1998) *Logistics and Supply Chain Management: Strategies for reducing cost and improving services* (2nd edn), Financial Times Prentice Hall. A comprehensive treatment on supply chain management from a distribution perspective by one of the gurus of supply chain management.

Fisher, M.L. (1997) 'What is the right supply chain for your product?', *Harvard Business Review,* Vol. 75, No. 2. A particularly influential article that explores the issue of how supply chains are not all the same.

Harland, C.M., Lamming, R.C. and Cousins, P. (1999) 'Developing the concept of supply strategy', *International Journal of Operations and Production Management,* Vol. 19, No. 7. An academic paper but one that gives a broad understanding of how supply chain ideas have developed and could develop.

Harrison, A. and van Hoek, R. (2002) *Logistics Management and Strategy,* Financial Times Prentice Hall. A short but readable book that explains many of the modern ideas in supply chain management, including lean supply chains and agile supply chains.

Hines, P. and Rich, N. (1997) 'The seven value stream mapping tools', *International Journal of Operations and Production Management,* Vol. 17, No. 1. Another academic paper, but one that explores some practical techniques that can be used to understand supply chains.

Macbeth, D.K. and Ferguson, N. (1994) *Partnership Sourcing: An integrated supply chain approach,* Financial Times, Pitman. A readable book that represents the arguments in favour of partnership sourcing.

Useful websites

www.cio.com/research/scm/edit/012202_scm Site of CIO's Supply Chain Management Research Center. Topics include procurement and fulfilment, with case studies.

www.stanford.edu/group/scforum/ Stanford University's supply chain forum. Interesting debate.

www.rfidc.com Site of the RFID Centre that contains RFID demonstrations and articles to download.

www.spychips.com Vehemently anti-RFID site. If you want to understand the nature of some activists' concerns over RFID, this site provides the arguments.

www.cips.org The Chartered Institute of Purchasing and Supply (CIPS) is an international organization, serving the purchasing and supply profession and dedicated to promoting best practice. Some good links.

FURTHER RESOURCES

For further resources including examples, animated diagrams, self test questions, excel spreadsheets, active case studies and video materials please explore the CD accompanying this book.

8

CAPACITY MANAGEMENT

Introduction

Providing the capability to satisfy current and future demand is a fundamental responsibility of operations management. It is at the heart of trade-offs between customer service and cost. Insufficient capacity leaves customers not served and excess capacity incurs increased costs. In this chapter we deal with *medium-term* capacity management, also sometimes referred to as *aggregate* capacity management. The essence of medium-term capacity management is to reconcile, at a general level, the aggregated supply of capacity with the aggregated level of demand. (See Figure 8.1.)

Source: © Catherine Karnow/Corbis

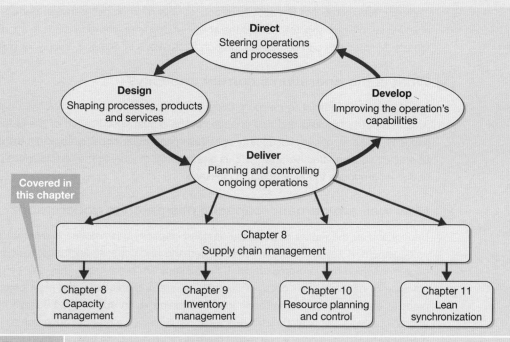

Covered in this chapter

Direct
Steering operations and processes

Design
Shaping processes, products and services

Develop
Improving the operation's capabilities

Deliver
Planning and controlling ongoing operations

Chapter 8
Supply chain management

| Chapter 8 Capacity management | Chapter 9 Inventory management | Chapter 10 Resource planning and control | Chapter 11 Lean synchronization |

Figure 8.1   Capacity management is the activity of coping with mismatches between demand and the ability to supply demand

Executive summary

VIDEO
further detail

Decision logic chain for capacity management

Each chapter is structured around a set of diagnostic questions. These questions suggest what you should ask in order to gain an understanding of the important issues of a topic, and as a result, improve your decision making. An executive summary, addressing these questions, is provided below.

What is capacity management?

Capacity management is the activity of coping with mismatches between demand and the ability to supply demand. Capacity is the ability an operation or process has to supply its customers. Mismatches can be caused through fluctuations in demand, supply, or both.

What is the operation's current capacity?

Capacity can be difficult to measure because it depends on activity mix, the duration over which output is required and any changes in the actual specification of the output. Often, capacity 'leakage' occurs because of scheduling and other constraints within the operation. Overall equipment effectiveness (OEE) is one method of judging the effectiveness of capacity that incorporates the idea of activity leakage.

How well are demand–capacity mismatches understood?

Understanding the nature of potential demand–capacity mismatches is central to capacity management. A key issue is the nature of demand and capacity fluctuations, especially the degree to which they are predictable. If fluctuations are predictable, they can be planned in advance to minimize their costs. If fluctuations are unpredictable, the main objective is to react to them quickly. Accurate, simple forecasting is an advantage because it converts unpredictable variation into predictable variation. However, a broader approach to enhancing market knowledge generally can reveal more about the options for managing mismatches.

What should be the operation's base capacity?

Capacity planning often involves setting a base level of capacity and then planning capacity fluctuations around it. The level at which base capacity is set depends on three main factors: the relative importance of the operation's performance objectives, the perishability of the operation's outputs, and the degree of variability in demand or supply. High service levels, high perishability of an operation's outputs and a high degree of variability in either demand or supply all indicate a relatively high level of base capacity.

How can demand–capacity mismatches be managed?

Demand–capacity mismatches usually call for some degree of capacity adjustment over time. There are three pure methods of achieving this, although in practice a mixture of all three may be used. A 'level capacity' plan involves no change in capacity and requires that the operation absorb demand–capacity mismatches, usually through under- or over-utilization of its resources, or the use of inventory. The 'chase demand' plan involves the changing of capacity through such methods as overtime, varying the size of the work force, sub-contracting, etc. The 'manage demand' plan involves an attempt to change demand through pricing or promotion methods, or changing product or service mix to reduce fluctuations in activity levels. Yield management is a common method of coping with mismatches when operations have relatively fixed capacities. Cumulative representations are sometimes used to plan capacity.

How should capacity be controlled?

In practice, capacity management is a dynamic process with decisions reviewed period by period. It is essential that capacity decisions made in one period reflect the knowledge accumulated from experiences in previous periods.

What is capacity management?

Capacity is the output that an operation (or a single process) can deliver in a defined unit of time. It reflects an 'ability to supply', at least in a quantitative sense. Capacity management is the activity of coping with mismatches between the demand on an operation and its ability to supply. Demand is the quantity of products or services that customers request from an operation or process at any point in time. A mismatch between demand and capacity can occur because demand fluctuates over time, or capacity fluctuates over time, or both.

Defining capacity as 'the ability to supply' is taking a broad view of the term. The ability to supply depends not only on the limitations of the previous stage in a supply network, operation or process, but on all the stages up to that point. So, for example, the capacity of an ice cream manufacturer is a function not only of how much ice cream its factories can produce at any point in time, but also of how much packaging material, raw material supplies, and so on, that its suppliers can provide. It may have the capacity to make 10,000 kilograms of ice cream a day, but if its suppliers of dairy produce can supply only 7000 kilos a day, then the effective capacity (in terms of 'ability to supply') is only 7000 kilos per day. Of course, if demand remains steady, any operation will attempt to make sure that its supply capacity does not limit its own ability to supply. But, capacity management is concerned with fluctuations in demand *and* supply. It involves coping with the dynamics of delivering products and services to customers. Balancing the individual capacities of each part of the network is therefore a more difficult, and ever changing, task.

> **Operations principle**
> Any measure of capacity should reflect the ability of an operation or process to supply demand.

It is worth noting that 'coping' with mismatches between demand and capacity may not mean that capacity should match demand. An operation could take the deliberate decision to fail to meet demand, or to fail to fully exploit its ability to supply. For example, a hotel may not make any effort to meet demand in peak periods because doing so would incur unwarranted capital costs. It is therefore content to leave some demand unsatisfied, although it may increase its prices to reflect this. Similarly, a flower grower may not supply the entirety of its potential supply (crop) if doing so would simply depress market prices and reduce its total revenue.

Levels of capacity management

The activity of coping with demand–capacity mismatches needs addressing over various time scales. In the long term, physical capacity needs adjusting to reflect the growth or decline in long-term demand. This task involves 'streaming on' or closing down relatively large units of physical capacity over a time period, possibly stretching into years. This activity was treated when we discussed the design of supply networks in Chapter 3. In addition, and within the physical constraints imposed by long-term capacity, most operations will need to cope with demand–capacity mismatches in the medium term, where 'medium term' may mean anything from one day to one year. It is this level that we discuss in this chapter. In an even shorter term, individual processes may need to cope with demand–capacity mismatches day-by-day or even minute-by-minute. This is an issue for 'resource planning and control', examined in Chapter 10.

The following two examples illustrate the nature of capacity management.

Example

The Penang Mutiara[1]

Source: courtesy Mutiara Beach Resort, Penang

One of the vacation regions of the world, South-East Asia has many luxurious hotels. One of the best is the Penang Mutiara, a top-of-the-market hotel which nestles in the lush greenery of Malaysia's Indian Ocean coast. Owned and managed by PERNAS, Malaysia's largest hotel group, the Mutiara has to cope with fluctuating demand, notwithstanding the region's relatively constant benign climate. *'Managing a hotel of this size is an immensely complicated task'*, says the hotel's manager. *'Our customers have every right to be demanding. Quality of service has to be impeccable. Staff must be courteous and yet also friendly towards our guests. And of course they must have the knowledge to be able to answer guests' questions. Most of all, though, great service means anticipating our guests' needs, thinking ahead so that you can identify what, and how much, they are likely to demand.'*

The hotel tries to anticipate guests' needs in a number of ways. If guests have been to the hotel before, their likely preferences will have been noted from their previous visit. *'A guest should not be kept waiting. This is not always easy but we do our best. For example, if every guest in the hotel tonight decided to call room service and request a meal instead of going to the restaurants, our room service department would obviously be grossly overloaded, and customers would have to wait an unacceptably long time before the meals were brought up to their rooms. We can predict this to some extent, but also we keep a close watch on how demand for room service is building up. If we think it's going to get above the level where response time to customers would become unacceptably long, we will call in staff from other restaurants in the hotel. Of course, to do this we have to make sure that our staff are multi-skilled. In fact we have a policy of making sure that restaurant staff can always do more than one job. It's this kind of flexibility which allows us to maintain fast response to the customer.'*

Although the hotel needs to respond to some short-term fluctuations in demand for individual services, it can predict likely demand relatively accurately because, each day, the actual number of guests is known. Most guests book their stay well in advance, so activity levels for the hotel's restaurants and other services can be planned ahead. Demand does vary throughout the year, peaking during holiday periods, and the hotel has to cope with these seasonal fluctuations. They do this partly by using temporary part-time staff. In the back-office parts of the hotel this isn't a major problem. In the laundry, for example, it is relatively easy to put on an extra shift in busy periods by increasing staffing levels. However, this is more of a problem in the parts of the hotel that have direct contact with the customer. New or temporary staff can't be expected to have the same customer contact skills as the regular staff. The solution to this is to keep the temporary staff as far in the background as possible and make sure that only skilled, well-trained staff interact with the customer. So, for example, a waiter who would normally take orders, serve the food and take away the dirty plates would in peak times restrict his or her activities to taking orders and serving the food. The less skilled part of the job, taking away the plates, could be left to temporary staff.

Example

Madame Tussaud's Amsterdam[2]

A short holiday in Amsterdam would not be complete without a visit to Madame Tussaud's located on four upper floors of the city's most prominent department store in Dam Square. With over 600,000 visitors each year, this is the third most popular tourist attraction in Amsterdam, after the flower market and canal trips. On busy days in the summer, the centre can just manage to handle 5000 visitors. On a wet day in January, however, there may only be 300 visitors throughout the whole day. But although *average* demand is predictable, the actual number of customers can fluctuate significantly. For example, unexpectedly poor weather when there are many visitors in Amsterdam can bring tourists flocking to the shelter and entertainment on offer.

Source: courtesy Madame Tussaud's

In the streets outside, orderly queues of expectant tourists snake along the pavement, looking in at the displays in the store windows. In this public open space, Tussaud's can do little to entertain the visitors, but entrepreneurial buskers and street artists are quick to capitalize on a captive market. On reaching the entrance lobby, individuals, families and groups purchase their admission tickets. The lobby is in the shape of a large horseshoe, with the ticket sales booth in the centre. On winter days or in quiet spells, there will be only one sales assistant, but on busier days, visitors can pay at either side of the ticket booth, to speed up the process. Having paid, the visitors assemble in the lobby outside the two lifts. While waiting in this area, a photographer wanders around offering to take photos of the visitors standing next to life-sized wax figures of famous people. They may also be entertained by living look-alikes of famous personalities who act as guides to groups of visitors in batches of around 25 customers (the capacity of each of the two lifts that take visitors up to the facility). The lifts arrive every four minutes and customers simultaneously disembark, forming one group of about 50 customers who stay together throughout the section.

What do these two examples have in common?

The obvious similarity between both these operations is that they have to cope with fluctuating customer demand. Also both operations have found ways to cope with these fluctuations, at least up to a point. This is good because both operations would suffer in the eyes of their customers and in terms of their own efficiency, if they could not cope. Yet in one important respect the two operations are different. Although both have to cope with variation in demand, and although the demand on both operations is a mixture of the predictable and the unpredictable, the balance between predictable variation in demand and unpredictable variation in demand is different. Demand at the Penang Mutiara is largely predictable. Seasonal fluctuations are related to known holiday periods and most customers book their stays well in advance. Madame Tussaud's, on the other hand, has to cope with demand that is unpredictable to a greater extent. Very short-term changes in the weather can significantly affect its demand.

In both these examples, mismatches between demand and capacity derive from predictable and unpredictable variation in demand. Although the mismatches that occur in most businesses result from demand fluctuations, some operations have to cope with predictable and unpredictable variation in capacity, if it is defined as 'the ability to supply'.

> **Operations principle**
> Capacity management decision should reflect both predictable and unpredictable variations in capacity and demand.

For example, Figure 8.2 shows the demand and capacity variation of two businesses. The first is a domestic appliance repair service. Both demand and capacity vary month by month. Capacity varies because the field service operatives in the business prefer to take their vacations at particular times of the year. Nevertheless, capacity is relatively stable throughout the year. Demand, by contrast, fluctuates more significantly. It would appear that there are two peaks of demand through the year, with peak demand being approximately twice the level of the low point in demand. The second business is a food manufacturer freezing spinach. The demand for this product is relatively constant throughout the year, but the capacity of the business (in terms not of the capacity of its factories, but of its ability to supply) varies significantly. During the growing and harvesting season capacity is high, but it falls off almost to zero for part of the year. Yet, although the mismatch between demand and capacity is driven primarily by fluctuations in demand in the first case, and by capacity in the second case, the essence of the capacity management activity is essentially similar for both.

FURTHER EXAMPLE

Figure 8.2 Demand–capacity mismatches for a domestic appliance repair service and a frozen spinach business

---

DIAGNOSTIC QUESTION

What is the operation's current capacity?

All operations and processes need to know their capacity because if they have too little they cannot meet demand and if they have too much they are paying for more capacity than they need. So a first step in managing capacity is being able to measure current capacity. This sounds simple, but often it is not. In fact, only when the operation is relatively standardized and repetitive is capacity easy to define unambiguously. Any measure of capacity will contain a number of assumptions, each of which may be necessary to give an estimate, but each of which obscures some aspect of reality. Again, taking capacity as 'the ability to supply', these assumptions relate to the mix of products or services supplied, the time over which they are supplied, and the specification of what is supplied.

> **Operations principle**
> Capacity is a function of product/service mix, duration, and product service specification.

Capacity depends on product or service mix

How much an operation can do depends on what it is being required to do. For example, a hospital has a problem in measuring its capacity, partly because there is not a clear relationship between its scale (in terms of the number of beds it has) and the number of patients it treats. If all its patients required relatively minor treatment with only short stays in hospital, it could treat many people per week. Alternatively, if most of its patients required long periods of observation or recuperation, it could treat far fewer. Output depends on the mix of activities in which the hospital is engaged and, because most hospitals perform many different types of activities, output is difficult to predict. Some of the problems caused by variation mix can be partially overcome by using aggregated capacity measures. 'Aggregated' means that different products and services are bundled together in order to get a broad view of demand and capacity. Medium-term capacity management is usually concerned with setting capacity levels in aggregated terms, rather than being concerned with the detail of individual products and services. Although this may mean some degree of approximation, especially if the mix of products or services being produced varies significantly, such approximation is usually acceptable and is a widely used practice in medium-term capacity management. For example, a hotel might think of demand and capacity in terms of 'room nights per month'; this ignores the number of guests in each room and their individual requirements, but it is a good first approximation. A computer manufacturer might measure demand and capacity in terms of the number of units it is capable of making per month, ignoring any variation in models.

Capacity depends on the duration over which output is required

Capacity is the output that an operation can deliver *in a defined unit of time*. The level of activity and output that may be achievable over short periods of time is not the same as the capacity that is sustainable on a regular basis. For example, a tax return processing office, during its peak periods at the end (or beginning) of the financial year, may be capable of processing 120,000 applications a week. It does this by extending the working hours of its staff, discouraging its staff from taking vacations during this period, avoiding any potential disruption to its IT systems (not allowing upgrades during this period, etc.), and maybe just by working hard and intensively. Nevertheless, staff do need vacations, nor can they work long hours continually, and eventually the information system will have to be upgraded. The capacity that is possible to cope with peak times is not sustainable over long periods. Often, capacity is taken to be the level of activity or output that can be sustained over an extended period of time.

Capacity depends on the specification of output

Some operations can increase their output by changing the specification of the product or service (although this is more likely to apply to a service). For example, a postal service may effectively reduce its delivery dependability at peak times. So, during the busy Christmas period, the number of letters delivered the day after being posted may drop from 95 per cent to 85 per cent. This may not always matter to the customer, who understands that the postal service is especially overloaded at this time. Similarly, accounting firms may avoid long 'relationship building' meetings with clients during busy periods. Important though these are, they can usually be deferred to less busy times. The important task is to distinguish between the 'must do' elements of the service that should not be sacrificed and the 'nice to do' parts of the service that can be omitted or delayed in order to increase capacity.

Capacity 'leakage'

Even after allowing for all the difficulties inherent in measuring capacity, the theoretical capacity of a process (the capacity that it was designed to have) is not always achieved in practice. Some reasons for this are, to some extent, predictable. Different products or services may have different requirements, so the process will need to be stopped while it is changed over. Maintenance will need to be performed. Scheduling difficulties could mean further lost time. Not all of these losses are necessarily avoidable; they may occur because of the market and technical demands on the process. However, some of the reduction in capacity can be the result of less predictable events. For example, labour shortages, quality problems, delays in the delivery of bought-in products and services, and machine or system breakdown, can all reduce capacity. This reduction in capacity is sometimes called 'capacity leakage'.

Overall equipment effectiveness[3]

The overall equipment effectiveness (OEE) measure is a popular method of judging the effectiveness of capacity that incorporates the concept of capacity leakage. It is based on three aspects of performance:

● The *time* for which equipment is available to operate
● The *speed,* or throughput rate, of the equipment
● The *quality* of the product or service it produces.

Overall equipment effectiveness is calculated by multiplying an availability rate by a performance (or speed) rate multiplied by a quality rate. Figure 8.3 illustrates this. Some of the reduction in available capacity of a piece of equipment (or any process) is caused by time losses such as setup and changeover losses (when the equipment or process is being prepared for its next activity), and breakdown failures (when the machine is being repaired). Some capacity is lost through speed losses such as when equipment is idling (for example, when it is temporarily waiting for work from another process) and when equipment is being run below its optimum work rate. Finally, not everything processed by a piece of equipment will be error free, so some capacity is lost through quality losses.

Taking the notation in Figure 8.3:

$$OEE = a \times p \times q$$

Figure 8.3   **Overall equipment effectiveness (OEE)**

For equipment to operate effectively, it needs to achieve high levels of performance against all three of these dimensions. Viewed in isolation, these individual metrics are important indicators of plant performance, but they do not give a complete picture of the machine's *overall* effectiveness. This can only be understood by looking at the combined effect of the three measures, calculated by multiplying the three individual metrics together. All these losses to the OEE performance can be expressed in terms of units of time – the design cycle time to produce one good part. So, a reject of one part has an equivalent time loss. In effect, this means that an OEE represents the valuable operating time as a percentage of the capacity something was designed to have.

OEE can be used for service operations and processes, but it is more difficult to do so. Of the three factors (time, speed, and quality) only time is straightforward. There is no direct equivalent of speed or throughput rate that is easy to measure objectively. Similarly with quality of output, softer factors such as 'relationship' may be important but, again, difficult to measure. Nevertheless, provided one can accept some degree of approximation, there is no theoretical reason why OEE cannot be used for services.

Worked example

In a typical 7-day period, the planning department programme a particular machine to work for 150 hours, its loading time. Changeovers and setups take an average of 10 hours, and breakdown failures average 5 hours every 7 days. The time when the machine cannot work because it is waiting for material to be delivered from other parts of the process is 5 hours on average, and during the period when the machine is running it averages 90 per cent of its rated speed. Three per cent of the parts processed by the machine are subsequently found to be defective in some way.

$$\text{Maximum time available} = 7 \times 24 \text{ hours}$$
$$= 168 \text{ hours}$$
$$\text{Loading time} = 150 \text{ hours}$$
$$\text{Availability losses} = 10 \text{ hours (setups)} + 5 \text{ hours (breakdowns)}$$
$$= 15 \text{ hours}$$

Therefore,

$$\text{Total operating time} = \text{loading time} - \text{availability}$$
$$= 150 \text{ hours} - 15 \text{ hours}$$
$$= 135 \text{ hours}$$

Speed losses while running amount to 10% (0.1) of rated speed, so

$$\text{Total speed losses} = 5 \text{ hours (idling)} + ((135 - 5) \times 0.1) \text{ hours (running)}$$
$$= 18 \text{ hours}$$

Therefore,

$$\text{Net operating time} = \text{total operating time} - \text{speed losses}$$
$$= 135 - 18$$
$$= 117 \text{ hours}$$
$$\text{Quality losses} = 117 \text{ (net operating time)} \times 0.03 \text{ (error rate)}$$
$$= 3.51 \text{ hours}$$

So,

$$\text{Valuable operating time} = \text{net operating time} - \text{quality losses}$$
$$= 117 - 3.51$$
$$= 113.49 \text{ hours}$$

Therefore,

$$\text{Availability rate} = a = \frac{\text{total operating time}}{\text{available operating time}}$$

$$= \frac{135}{150} = 90\%$$

$$\text{Performance rate} = p = \frac{\text{net operating time}}{\text{total operating time}}$$

$$= \frac{117}{135} = 86.67\%$$

$$\text{Quality rate} = q = \frac{\text{valuable operating time}}{\text{net operating time}}$$

$$= \frac{113.49}{117} = 97\%$$

$$\text{OEE } (a \times p \times q) = 75.6$$

DIAGNOSTIC QUESTION

How well are demand–capacity mismatches understood?

A sound understanding of the nature of potential mismatches between demand and capacity is necessary for effective capacity management. For most businesses, this equates to understanding how demand might vary (although the same logic would apply to variation in capacity). In particular, the balance between predictable and unpredictable variation in demand affects the nature of capacity management. When demand is predictable (usually under conditions of 'dependent demand' – see previous chapter), capacity may need adjusting, but the adjustments can be planned in advance, preferably to minimize the costs of making the change. With unpredictable variation in demand (usually under conditions of 'independent demand'), if an operation is to react to it at all, it must do so quickly; otherwise the change in capacity will have little effect on the operation's ability to cope with the changed demand. Figure 8.4 illustrates how the objective and tasks of capacity management vary depending on the balance between predictable and unpredictable variation.

Enhanced market knowledge makes capacity planning easier

Capacity planning has to cope with mismatches between capacity and demand. Therefore, a deep understanding of the market forces that will generate demand is, if not an absolute prerequisite, nevertheless particularly important. This goes beyond the idea of forecasting as the prediction of uncontrollable events. Enhanced market knowledge is a broader concept and is illustrated in Figure 8.5. When the main characteristic of demand–supply mismatch is unpredictable variation, then forecasting in its conventional sense is important because it converts unpredictable variation into predictable variation. But, when the main

Figure 8.4   The nature of capacity management depends on the mixture of predictable and unpredictable demand and capacity variation

Operations principle
The greater an operation's market knowledge, the more capacity management will focus on predictable demand-capacity mismatches.

capacity management is predictable variation, then better forecasting as such is of limited value because demand–supply mismatches are, by definition, already known. What is useful under these circumstances is not so much a knowledge of what demand–supply mismatches will be, but rather how they can be changed. So,

Figure 8.5   Enhanced demand and supply market knowledge can make capacity management easier for example, can a major customer be persuaded to move their demand to a quieter period? Will increasing prices at peak periods shift demand to off-peak periods? Can new storage techniques allow the supply of food ingredients throughout the year?

If capacity management is largely a matter of coping with significant, but predictable, mismatches between demand and supply, then knowledge about how markets can be changed is important. However, when unpredictable variation is high, the first task is to transform variation from unpredictable to predictable through better forecasting. Of course, forecasting cannot eliminate predictable variation, but it is a first step towards minimizing the negative effects of variation on capacity management.

Making forecasts useful for capacity management

Without some understanding of future demand and supply fluctuations, it is not possible to plan effectively for future events, only to react to them. This is why it is important to understand how forecasts are made. Forecasting was discussed in the supplement to Chapter 3, and it clearly helps the capacity management activity to have accurate forecasts. But, in addition to accuracy there are a number of other issues that make forecasts more (or less) useful as an input to capacity planning.

Forecasts can never be perfectly accurate all the time. Yet sometimes forecast errors are more damaging than at other times. For example, if a process is operating at a level close to its maximum capacity, over-optimistic forecasts could lead the process to committing itself to unnecessary capital expenditure to increase its capacity. Inaccurate forecasts for a process operating well below its capacity limit will also result in extra cost, but probably not to the same extent. So the effort put into forecasting should reflect the varying sensitivity to forecast error. Forecasts also need to be expressed in units that are useful for capacity planning. If forecasts are expressed only in money terms and give no indication of the demands that will be placed on an operation's capacity, they will need to be translated into realistic expectations of demand, expressed in the same units as the capacity (for example, machine hours per year, operatives required, space, etc.). Perhaps most importantly, forecasts should give an indication of relative uncertainty. Demand in some periods is more uncertain than others. The importance of this is that the operations managers need an understanding of when increased uncertainty makes it necessary to have reserve capacity. A probabilistic forecast allows this type of judgement between possible plans that would virtually guarantee the operation's ability to meet actual demand, and plans that minimize costs. Ideally, this judgement should be influenced by the nature of the way the business wins orders: price-sensitive markets may require a risk-avoiding cost minimization plan that does not always satisfy peak demand, whereas markets that value responsiveness and service quality may justify a more generous provision of operational capacity. Remember, though, the idea that 'better forecasting' is needed for effective capacity management is only partly true. A better approach would be to say that it is enhanced market knowledge (of both demand and supply) generally that is important.

Better forecasting or better operations responsiveness?

> **Operations principle**
> Attempting to increase market knowledge and attempting to increase operations flexibility, present alternative approaches to capacity management, but are not mutually exclusive.

The degree of effort (and cost) to devote to forecasting is often a source of heated debate within businesses. This often comes down to two opposing arguments. One goes something like this: *'Of course it is important for forecasts to be as accurate as possible; we cannot plan operations capacity otherwise. This invariably means we finish up with too much capacity (thereby increasing costs), or too little capacity (thereby losing revenue and dissatisfying customers).'* The counter-argument is very different: *'Demand will always be uncertain, that is the nature of demand. Get used to it. The only way to satisfy customers is to make the operation sufficiently responsive to cope with demand, almost irrespective of what it is.'* Both these arguments have some merit, but both are extreme positions. In practice, operations must find some balance between having better forecasts and being able to cope without perfect forecasts.

FURTHER EXAMPLE

Trying to get forecasts right has particular value where the operation finds it difficult or impossible to react to unexpected demand fluctuations in the short term. Internet-based retailers at some holiday times, for example, find it difficult to flex the quantity of goods they have in stock in the short term. Customers may not be willing to wait. On the other hand, other types of operation working in intrinsically uncertain markets may develop fast and flexible processes to compensate for the difficulty in obtaining accurate forecasts. For example, fashion garment manufacturers try to overcome the uncertainty in their market by shortening their response time to new fashion ideas (catwalk to rack time) and the time taken to replenish stocks in the stores (replenishment time). Similarly, when the cost of not meeting demand is very high, processes also have to rely on their responsiveness rather than accurate forecasts. For example, accident and emergency departments in hospitals must be responsive even if it means under-utilized resources at times.

DIAGNOSTIC QUESTION

What should be the operation's base capacity?

The most common way of planning capacity is to decide on a 'base level' of capacity and then adjust it periodically up or down to reflect fluctuations in demand. In fact, the concept of 'base' capacity is unusual because, although nominally it is the capacity level from which increases and decreases in capacity level are planned, in very unstable markets, where fluctuations are significant, it may never occur. Also, these two decisions of 'what should the base level of capacity be?' and 'how do we adjust capacity around that base to reflect demand?' are interrelated. An operation could set its base level of capacity at such a high level compared to demand that there is no need ever to adjust capacity levels because they will never exceed the base level of capacity. However, this is clearly wasteful, which is why most operations will adjust their capacity level over time. Nevertheless, although the two decisions are interrelated, it is usually worth setting a nominal base level of capacity before going on to consider how it can be adjusted.

> **Operations principle**
> The higher the base level of capacity, the less capacity fluctuation is needed to satisfy demand.

Setting base capacity

The base level of capacity in any operation is influenced by many factors, but should be clearly related to three in particular:

- The relative importance of the operation's performance objectives
- The perishability of the operation's outputs
- The degree of variability in demand or supply.

Factors tending to *increase* base level of capacity
- Low fixed costs
- Need for high levels of customer service
- High perishability (food, fashion, most services, etc.)
- Inexpensive fixed capacity

Base level of capacity

Demand

Factors tending to *decrease* base level of capacity
- High fixed costs
- Need for high capacity utilization
- Ability to store output
- Expensive fixed capacity

Time

Figure 8.6 **The base level of capacity should reflect the relative importance of the operation's performance objectives**

The operation's performance objectives

Base levels of capacity should be set primarily to reflect an operation's performance objectives: see Figure 8.6. For example, setting the base level of capacity high compared to average demand will result in relatively high levels of under-utilization of capacity and therefore high costs. This is especially true when an operation's fixed costs are high and therefore the consequences of under-utilization are also high. Conversely, high base levels of capacity result in a capacity 'cushion' for much of the time, so the ability to flex output to give responsive customer service will be enhanced. When the output from the operation is capable of being stored, there may also be a trade-off between fixed capital and working capital where base capacity level is set. A high level of base capacity can require considerable investment (unless the cost per unit of capacity is relatively low). Reducing the base level of capacity would reduce the need for capital investment but (where possible) may require inventory to be built up to satisfy future demand and therefore increased levels of working capital. For some operations, building up inventory is either risky because products have a short shelf life (for example perishable food, high performance computers, or fashion items) or impossible because the output cannot be stored at all (most services).

The perishability of the operation's outputs

When either supply or demand is perishable, base capacity will need to be set at a relatively high level because inputs to the operation or outputs from the operation cannot be stored for long periods. For example, a factory that produces frozen fruit will need sufficient freezing, packing and storage capacity to cope with the rate at which the fruit crop is being harvested during its harvesting season. Similarly, a hotel cannot store its accommodation services. If an individual hotel room remains unoccupied, the ability to sell for that night has 'perished'. In fact, unless a hotel is full every single night, its capacity is always going to be higher than the average demand for its services.

The degree of variability in demand or supply

Variability, in either demand or capacity (or processing rate), will reduce the ability of an operation to process its inputs. That is, it will reduce its effective capacity. This effect was

Figure 8.7   The effects of variability on the utilization of capacity

explained in Chapter 5 when the consequences of variability in individual processes were discussed. As a reminder, the greater the variability in arrival time or activity time at a process, the more the process will suffer both high throughput times and reduced utilization. This principle holds true for whole operations, and because long throughput times mean that queues will build up in the operation, high variability also affects inventory levels. This is illustrated in Figure 8.7. The implication of this is that the greater the variability, the more extra capacity will need to be provided to compensate for the reduced utilization of available capacity. Therefore, operations with high levels of variability will tend to set their base level of capacity relatively high in order to provide this extra capacity.

DIAGNOSTIC QUESTION

How can demand–capacity mismatches be managed?

Almost all operations have to cope with varying demand or supply; therefore they will need to consider adjusting capacity around its nominal base level. There are three 'pure' plans available for treating such variation, although in practice most organizations will use a mixture of all of them, even if one plan dominates.

- Ignore demand fluctuations and keep nominal capacity levels constant (level capacity plan)
- Adjust capacity to reflect the fluctuations in demand (chase demand plan)
- Attempt to change demand (demand management).

Level capacity plan

In a level capacity plan, the processing capacity is set at a uniform level throughout the planning period, regardless of the fluctuations in forecast demand. This means that the same number of staff operate the same processes and should therefore be capable of producing the same aggregate output in each period. Where non-perishable materials are processed, but not immediately sold, they can be transferred to finished goods inventory in anticipation of later sales. When inventory is not possible, as in most services, operations demand fluctuations are absorbed through under-utilization of the operation's resources and/or and failure to meet demand immediately (see Figure 8.8(a)). The more demand fluctuates, the higher is either inventory or under-utilization when using a level capacity plan. Both are expensive, but may be considered if the cost of building inventory is low compared with changing output levels, or in service operations if the opportunity cost of individual lost sales is very high: for example, in the high-margin retailing of jewellery and in (real-) estate agents. Setting capacity below the forecast peak demand level will reduce the degree of under-utilization, but, in the periods where demand is expected to exceed capacity, customer service may deteriorate.

Chase demand plan

Chase demand plans attempt to match capacity closely to the varying levels of forecast demand, as in Figure 8.8(b). This is much more difficult to achieve than a level capacity plan, as different numbers of staff, different working hours, and even different amounts of equipment may be necessary in each period. For this reason, pure chase demand plans are unlikely to appeal to operations producing standard, non-perishable products, especially where operations are capital-intensive. The chase demand policy would require a level of physical capacity (as opposed to effective capacity), all of which would be used only occasionally. A pure chase demand plan is more usually adopted by operations that cannot store their output, such as a call centre. It avoids the wasteful provision of excess staff that occurs with a level capacity plan, and yet should satisfy customer demand throughout the planned period. Where inventory is possible, a chase demand policy might be adopted in order to minimize it.

The chase demand approach requires that capacity is adjusted by some means. There are a number of different methods for achieving this, although they may not all be feasible for all types of operation. Some of these methods are shown in Table 8.1.

(a) Level capacity plan –
   absorb fluctuations

(b) Chase demand plan –
   change capacity to reflect
   demand fluctuations

(c) Manage demand plan –
   attempt to change demand
   to reduce fluctuations

Figure 8.8   Managing demand–capacity mismatches using 'level capacity', 'chase demand' and 'manage demand' plans

Table 8.1   Summary of advantages and disadvantages of some methods of adjusting capacity

Method of adjusting capacity	Advantages	Disadvantages
Overtime – staff working longer than their normal working times	Quickest and most convenient	Extra payment normally necessary, and agreement of staff to work can reduce productivity over long periods
Annualized hours – staff contracting to work a set number of hours per year rather than a set number of hours per week	Without many of the costs associated with overtime, the amount of staff time available to an organization can be varied throughout the year to reflect demand	When very large and unexpected fluctuations in demand are possible, all the negotiated annual working time flexibility can be used before the end of the year
Staff scheduling – arranging working times (start and finish times) to vary the aggregate number of staff available for working at any time	Staffing levels can be adjusted to meet demand without changing job responsibilities or hiring new staff	Providing start and finish (shift) times that both satisfy the need of staff for reasonable working times and shift patterns as well as providing appropriate capacity can be difficult
Varying the size of the workforce – hiring extra staff during periods of high demand and laying them off as demand falls, or 'hire and fire'	Reduces basic labour costs quickly	Hiring costs and possible low productivity while new staff go through the learning curve. Lay-offs may result in severance payments and possible loss of morale in the operation and loss of goodwill in the local labour market
Using part-time staff – recruit staff who work for less than the normal working day (at the busiest periods)	Good method of adjusting capacity to meet predictable short-term demand fluctuations	Expensive if the fixed costs of employment for each employee (irrespective of how long he or she works) are high
Skills flexibility – designing flexibility in job design and job demarcation so that staff can transfer across from less busy parts of the operation	Fast method of reacting to short-term demand fluctuations	Investment in skills training needed and may cause some internal disruption
Sub-contracting/outsourcing – buying, renting or sharing capacity or output from other operations	No disruption to the operation	Can be very expensive because of sub-contractor's margin, and sub-contractor may not be as motivated to give same service or quality. Also a risk of leakage of knowledge
Change output rate – expecting staff (and equipment) to work faster than normal	No need to provide extra resources	Can only be used as a temporary measure, and even then can cause staff dissatisfaction, a reduction in the quality of work, or both

Changing capacity when variation is unpredictable

Both the mix of methods used to change capacity and how they are implemented will depend on the balance between predictable and unpredictable variation. As we discussed earlier, the objective of capacity management when demand variation is predictable is to affect the changes as efficiently as possible, whereas, when demand fluctuations are unpredictable, the objective is usually to change capacity as fast as possible. In the latter case, it is necessary to understand the flexibility of the resources that may be used to increase capacity. In this case we are using flexibility to mean both how much capacity can be changed and how fast it can be changed. In fact, the degree of change and the response time required to make the change are almost always related. The relationship can be shown in what is termed a 'range–response' curve. Figure 8.9 shows one of these for a call centre. It shows that

Figure 8.9   The 'range–response' curve for increasing capacity at a call centre

FURTHER EXAMPLE

within a few minutes of demand for the call centre's services increasing, it has the ability to switch a proportion of its calls to the company's other call centres. However, not everyone in these other call centres is trained to take such calls, therefore any further increase in capacity must come from bringing in staff currently not on shift. Eventually, the call centre will hit its limits of physical capacity (computers, telephone lines, etc.). Any further capacity increase will have to wait until more physical capacity is added.

Manage demand plan

The objective of demand management is to change the pattern of demand to bring it closer to available capacity, usually by transferring customer demand from peak periods to quiet periods, as was shown in Figure 8.8(c). There are a number of methods for achieving this.

● *Constraining customer access* – allowing customers access to the operation's products or services only at particular times, for example reservation and appointment systems in hospitals.
● *Price differentials* – adjusting price to reflect demand. That is, increasing prices during periods of high demand and reducing prices during periods of low demand.
● *Scheduling promotion* – varying the degree of market stimulation through promotion and advertising in order to encourage demand during normally low periods.
● *Service differentials* – allowing service levels to reflect demand (implicitly or explicitly), allowing service to deteriorate in periods of high demand and increase in periods of low demand. If this strategy is used explicitly, customers are being educated to expect varying levels of service and hopefully move to periods of lower demand.

A more radical approach attempts to create alternative products or services to fill capacity in quiet periods. It can be an effective demand management method but, ideally, new products or services should meet three criteria: (a) they can be produced on the same processes, (b) they have different demand patterns from existing offerings, and (c) they are sold through similar marketing channels. For example, ski resorts may provide organized mountain activity holidays in the summer, and garden tractor companies may make snow movers in the autumn and winter. However, the apparent benefits of filling capacity in this way must be weighed against the risks of damaging the core product or service, and the operation must be fully capable of serving both markets.

Example	Hallmark Cards[4]

Companies that traditionally operate in seasonal markets can demonstrate some considerable ingenuity in their attempts to develop counter-seasonal products. One of the most successful industries in this respect has been the greetings card industry. Mothers' Day, Fathers' Day, Halloween, Valentine's Day and other occasions have all been promoted as times to send (and buy) appropriately designed cards. Now, having run out of occasions to promote, greetings card manufacturers have moved on to 'non-occasion' cards, which can be sent at any time. These have the considerable advantage of being less seasonal, thus making the companies' seasonality less marked. Hallmark Cards has been the pioneer in developing non-occasion cards. Their cards include those intended to be sent from a parent to a child with messages such as 'Would a hug help?', 'Sorry I made you feel bad', and 'You're perfectly wonderful – it's your room that's a mess'. Other cards deal with more serious adult themes such as friendship ('you're more than a friend, you're just like family') or even alcoholism ('this is hard to say, but I think you're a much neater person when you're not drinking'). Now Hallmark Cards have founded a 'loyalty marketing group' that 'helps companies communicate with their customers at an emotional level'. It promotes the use of greetings cards for corporate use, to show that customers and employees are valued.

Yield management

In operations which have relatively fixed capacities, such as airlines and hotels, it is important to use the capacity of the operation for generating revenue to its full potential. One approach used by such operations is called yield management.[5] This is really a collection of methods, some of which we have already discussed, that can be used to ensure that an operation maximizes its potential to generate profit. Yield management is especially useful where:

- Capacity is relatively fixed
- The market can be fairly clearly segmented
- The service cannot be stored in any way
- The services are sold in advance
- The marginal cost of making a sale is relatively low.

Airlines, for example, fit all these criteria. They adopt a collection of methods to try to maximize the yield (i.e. profit) from their capacity. Overbooking capacity may be used to compensate for passengers who do not show up for the flight. If the airline does not fill a seat it will lose the revenue from it, so airlines regularly book more passengers onto flights than the aircraft can cope with. However, if more passengers show up than expected, the airline will have a number of upset passengers (although they may be able to offer financial inducements for the passengers to take another flight). By studying past data on flight demand, airlines try to balance the risks of overbooking and underbooking. Operations may also use price discounting at quiet times, when demand is unlikely to fill capacity. Airlines also sell heavily discounted tickets to agents who then themselves take the risk of finding customers for them. This type of service may also be varied. For example, the relative demand for first-class, business-class, and economy-class seats varies throughout the year. There is no point discounting tickets in a class for which demand will be high. Yield management tries to adjust the availability of the different classes of seat to reflect their demand. They will also vary the number of seats available in each class by upgrading or even changing the configuration of airline seats.

Using cumulative representations to plan capacity

When an operation's output can be stored, a useful method of assessing the feasibility and consequences of adopting alternative capacity plans is the use of cumulative demand and supply curves. These plot (or calculate) both the cumulative demand on an operation,

Excel

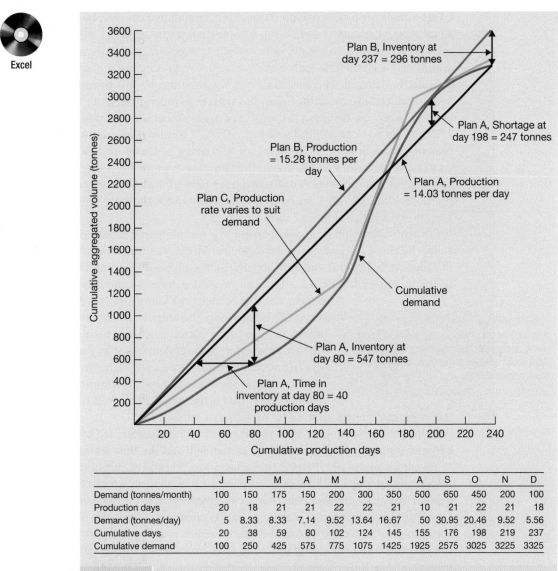

Figure 8.10 Cumulative representation of demand and three capacity plans

	J	F	M	A	M	J	J	A	S	O	N	D
Demand (tonnes/month)	100	150	175	150	200	300	350	500	650	450	200	100
Production days	20	18	21	21	22	22	21	10	21	22	21	18
Demand (tonnes/day)	5	8.33	8.33	7.14	9.52	13.64	16.67	50	30.95	20.46	9.52	5.56
Cumulative days	20	38	59	80	102	124	145	155	176	198	219	237
Cumulative demand	100	250	425	575	775	1075	1425	1925	2575	3025	3225	3325

and its cumulative ability to supply, over time. For example, Figure 8.10 shows the forecast aggregated demand for a chocolate factory that makes confectionery products. Demand for its products in the shops is greatest in December. To meet this demand and allow time for the products to work their way through the supply chain, the factory must supply a demand that peaks in September. But the cumulative representation of demand against available supply time (productive days) shown in Figure 8.10 reveals that, although total demand peaks in September, because of the restricted number of available productive days, the peak demand per productive day occurs a month earlier in August. It also shows that the effective fluctuation in demand over the year is even greater than it seemed. The ratio of monthly peak demand to monthly lowest demand is 6.5:1, but the ratio of peak to lowest demand per productive day is 10:1. Demand per productive day is more relevant to operations managers, because productive days represent the 'ability to supply'.

The feasibility and consequences of a capacity plan can be assessed on this basis. Figure 8.10 also shows a level capacity plan (A) that assumes production at a rate of

14.03 tonnes per productive day. This meets cumulative demand by the end of the year, so total over-capacity is equal to or greater than under-capacity. However, if one of the aims of the plan is to supply demand when it occurs, the plan is inadequate. Up to around day 168, the line representing cumulative production is above that representing cumulative demand. This means that at any time during this period, more product has been produced by the factory than has been demanded from it. In fact the vertical distance between the two lines is the level of inventory at that point in time. So by day 80, 1122 tonnes have been produced but only 575 tonnes have been demanded. The surplus of production above demand, or inventory, is therefore 547 tonnes. When the cumulative demand line lies above the cumulative production line, the reverse is true. The vertical distance between the two lines now indicates the shortage, or lack of supply. So by day 198, 3025 tonnes have been demanded but only 2778 tonnes produced. The shortage is therefore 247 tonnes.

For any capacity plan to meet demand as it occurs, its cumulative production line must always lie above the cumulative demand line. This makes it a straightforward task to judge the adequacy of a plan, simply by looking at its cumulative representation. An impression of the inventory implications can also be gained from a cumulative representation by judging the area between the cumulative production and demand curves. This represents the amount of inventory carried over the period. Level capacity plan B is feasible because it always ensures enough production to meet demand at any time throughout the year. However, inventory levels are high using this plan. It may even mean that the chocolate spends so much time in the factory's inventory, that it has insufficient shelf life when it arrives at the company's retail customers. Assuming a 'first-in-first-out' inventory management principle, the time product stays in inventory will be represented by the horizontal line between the demand at the time it is 'demanded' and the time it was produced.

> **Operations principle**
> For any capacity plan to meet demand as it occurs, its cumulative production line must always lie above its cumulative demand line.

Inventory levels (and therefore the time products spend as part of the inventory) can be reduced by adopting a chase demand plan, such as that shown as C in Figure 8.10. This reduces inventory-carrying costs, but incurs costs associated with changing capacity levels. Usually, the marginal cost of making a capacity change increases with the size of the change. For example, if the chocolate manufacturer wishes to increase capacity by 5 per cent, this can be achieved by requesting its staff to work overtime – a simple, fast and relatively inexpensive option. If the change is 15 per cent, overtime cannot provide sufficient extra capacity and temporary staff will need to be employed – a more expensive solution which also would take more time. Increases in capacity of above 15 per cent might only be achieved by sub-contracting some work out. This would be even more expensive.

DIAGNOSTIC QUESTION

How should capacity be controlled?

Although planning capacity levels in advance, and even planning how to respond to unexpected changes in demand, is an important part of capacity management, it does not fully reflect the dynamic nature of the activity. Capacity management must react to *actual* demand and *actual* capacity as it occurs. Period by period, operations management considers its forecasts of demand, its understanding of current capacity and, if outputs can be stocked, how much inventory has been carried forward from the previous period. Based on all this information, it makes plans for the following period's capacity. During the next period, demand might or might not be as forecast and the actual capacity of the operation might or might not turn out as planned (because of the capacity leakage discussed earlier). But whatever the actual conditions during that period, at the beginning of the next period the same types of decisions must be made, in the light of the new circumstances. Figure 8.11 shows how this works in practice. It shows the overall performance of an operation's capacity management as a function of the way it manages capacity and way it manages (or forecasts) demand.

The success of capacity management is generally measured by some combination of costs, revenue, working capital and customer satisfaction (which goes on to influence revenue). This is influenced by the actual capacity available to the operation in any period and the demand for that period. If capacity is in excess of demand, customer demands can be met, but under-utilized capacity and possibly inventory will increase costs. If capacity is less than demand, the operation's resources will be fully utilized, but at the expense of being unable to meet all demand. However, some operations are more able to cope than others with any mismatch between actual capacity and actual demand. If the underlying cost structure of the operation is such that fluctuations in output level have relatively little effect on costs, then the operation will be less sensitive to errors in capacity management.

Demand forecasting should always be an ongoing process that incorporates the general market factors which influence demand. In addition, the actual demand that occurs each month should be factored into each period's forecast. In fact, the whole process of capacity control is one of carrying forward, period by period, the decisions and the results of those decisions from one period to the next. In doing so the operation should

Figure 8.11　How should capacity be controlled – the dynamics of capacity management

be aiming to build up experience of managing demand, managing capacity, and adapting the operation to make it less sensitive to mismatches between the two.

Successful capacity control also requires businesses to learn from their handling of previous demand fluctuations. Period by period, operations managers are reacting to a set of stimuli as illustrated in Figure 8.11. Some of these stimuli may be ambiguous, such as the overall objectives of the operation and its approach to risk. Others will be uncertain, such as future demand and (to a lesser extent) future capacity. This is a complex decision-making process that depends on more than the availability and accuracy of information (although this is important). It also depends on the ability to refine decision-making behaviour through learning from past successes and mistakes. For example, some managers may tend to over-react to immediate stimuli by frequently increasing or decreasing capacity as forecasts of future demand are adjusted. If so, some mechanism will need to be put in place that smoothes both forecasts and the response to them.

> **Operations principle**
> The learning from managing capacity in practice should be captured and used to refine both demand forecasting and capacity planning.

Critical commentary

Each chapter contains a short critical commentary on the main ideas covered in the chapter. Its purpose is not to undermine the issues discussed in the chapter, but to emphasize that, although we present a relatively orthodox view of operation, there are other perspectives.

■ For such an important topic, there is surprisingly little standardization in how capacity is measured. Not only is a reasonably accurate measure of capacity needed for operations management, it is also needed to decide whether it is worth investing in extra physical capacity such as machines. Yet not all practitioners would agree with the way in which capacity has been defined or measured in this chapter (although it does represent orthodox practice). One school of thought is that whatever capacity efficiency measures are used, they should be useful as diagnostic measures that can highlight the root causes of inefficient use of capacity. The idea of overall equipment effectiveness (OEE) described earlier is often put forward as a useful way of measuring capacity efficiencies.

■ The other main point of controversy in capacity management concerns the use of varying staff levels. To many, the idea of fluctuating the workforce to match demand, either by using part-time staff or by hiring and firing, is more than just controversial, it is regarded as unethical. It is any business's responsibility, they argue, to engage in a set of activities that are capable of sustaining employment at a steady level. Hiring and firing merely for seasonal fluctuations, which can be predicted in advance, is treating human beings in a totally unacceptable manner. Even hiring people on a short-term contract, in practice, leads to them being offered poorer conditions of service and leads to a state of permanent anxiety as to whether they will keep their jobs. On a more practical note, it is pointed out that, in an increasingly global business world where companies may have sites in different countries, those countries that allow hiring and firing are more likely to have their plants 'downsized' than those where legislation makes this difficult.

Summary checklist

This checklist comprises questions that can be usefully applied to any type of operations and reflect the major diagnostic questions used within the chapter.

☐ Is the importance of effective capacity management fully understood?

☐ Is the operation's current capacity measured?

☐ If so, are all the assumptions inherent in the measurement of capacity made fully explicit?

☐ What capacity 'leakage' is normal, and have options for minimizing capacity leakage been explored?

☐ Is there scope for using the overall equipment effectiveness (OEE) measure of capacity?

☐ What is the balance between predictable variation and unpredictable variation in demand and capacity?

☐ Realistically, what potential is there for making unpredictable variability more predictable through better forecasting?

☐ Does an understanding of the market include the extent to which the behaviour of customers and/or suppliers can be influenced to reduce variability?

☐ Does the operations base capacity reflect all the factors that should be influencing its level?

☐ Have alternative methods of adjusting (or not) capacity been fully explored and assessed?

☐ If variation is unpredictable, have methods of speeding up the operation's reaction to demand–capacity mismatches been explored?

☐ Is there scope for using cumulative representations of demand and capacity for planning purposes?

☐ Is the method of deciding period-by-period capacity levels effective?

☐ How does the method of deciding period-by-period capacity levels reflect previous experience?

Case study   Blackberry Hill Farm

'Six years ago I had never heard of agri-tourism. As far as I was concerned, I had inherited the farm and I would be a farmer all my life.' (Jim Walker, Blackberry Hill Farm)

The 'agri-tourism' that Jim was referring to is 'a commercial enterprise at a working farm, or other agricultural centre, conducted for the enjoyment of visitors that generates supplemental income for the owner'. 'Farming has become a tough business', says Jim. 'Low world prices, a reduction in subsidies, and increasingly uncertain weather patterns have made it a far more risky business than when I first inherited the farm. Yet, because of our move into the tourist trade we are flourishing. Also . . . I've never had so much fun in my life.' But, Jim warns, agri-tourism isn't for everyone. 'You have to think carefully. Do you really want to do it? What kind of life style do you want? How open-minded are you to new ideas? How business-minded are you? Are you willing to put a lot of effort into marketing your business? Above all, do you like working with people? If you had rather be around cows than people, it isn't the business for you.'

History

Blackberry Hill Farm was a 200-hectare mixed farm in the south of England when Jim and Mandy Walker inherited it 15 years ago. It was primarily a cereal-growing operation with a small dairy herd, some fruit and vegetable growing and mixed woodland that was protected by local preservation laws. Six years ago it had become evident to Jim

and Mandy that they may have to rethink how the farm was being managed. 'We first started a pick-your-own (PYO) operation because our farm is close to several large centres of population. Also the quantities of fruit and vegetables that we were producing were not large enough to interest the commercial buyers. Entering the PYO market was a reasonable success and in spite of making some early mistakes, it turned our fruit and vegetable growing operation from making a small loss to making a small profit. Most importantly, it gave us some experience of how to deal with customers face-to-face and of how to cope with unpredictable demand. The biggest variable in PYO sales is weather. Most business occurs at the weekends between late spring and early autumn. If rain keeps customers away during part of those weekends, nearly all sales have to occur in just a few days.'

Within a year of opening up the PYO operation Jim and Mandy had decided to reduce the area devoted to cereals and increase their fruit and vegetable growing capability. At the same time they organized a Petting Zoo that allowed children to mix with, feed and touch various animals.

'We already had our own cattle and poultry but we extended the area and brought in pigs and goats. Later we also introduced some rabbits, ponies and donkeys, and even a small bee keeping operation.' At the same time the farm started building up its collection of 'farm heritage' exhibits. These were static displays of old farm implements

Source: courtesy Adrian Fisher Mazes Ltd, www.mazemaker.com

Source: courtesy Sue Williams

A maize maze of the type Blackberry Hill Farm are considering

and 'recreations' of farming processes together with information displays. This had always been a personal interest of Jim's and it allowed him to convert two existing farm outbuildings to create a 'Museum of Farming Heritage'.

The year after, they introduced tractor rides for visitors around the whole farm and extended the petting zoo and farming tradition exhibits further. But the most significant investment was in the 'Preserving Kitchen'. *'We had been looking for some way of using the surplus fruits and vegetables that we occasionally accumulated and also for some kind of products that we could sell in a farm shop. We started the Preserving Kitchen to make jams and fruit, vegetables and sauces preserved in jars. The venture was an immediate success. We started making just 50 kilograms of preserves a week; within three months that had grown to 300 kilograms a week and we are now producing around 1000 kilograms a week, all under the "Blackberry Hill Farm" label.'* The following year the preserving kitchen was extended and a viewing area added. *'It was a great attraction from the beginning'*, says Mandy. *'We employed ladies from the local village to make the preserves. They are all extrovert characters, so when we asked them to dress up in traditional "farmers wives" type clothing they were happy to do it. The visitors love it, especially the good-natured repartee with our ladies. The ladies also enjoy giving informal history lessons when we get school parties visiting us.'*

Within the last two years the farm had further extended its preserving kitchen, farm shop, exhibits and petting zoo. It had also introduced a small adventure playground for the children, a café serving drinks and its own produce, a picnic area and a small bakery. The bakery was also open to view by customers and staffed by bakers in traditional dress. *'It's a nice little visitor attraction'*, says Mandy, *'and it gives us another opportunity to squeeze more value out of our own products.'* Table 8.2a shows last year's visitor numbers, and Table 8.2b lists the farm's opening times.

Demand

The number of visitors to the farm was extremely seasonal. From a low point in January and February, when most people just visited the farm shop, the spring and summer months could be very busy, especially on public holidays.

Table 8.2a	Number of visitors last year		
Month	Total visitors	Month	Total visitors
January	1,006	August	15,023
February	971	September	12,938
March	2,874	October	6,687
April	6,622	November	2,505
May	8,905	December	3,777
June	12,304	Total	88,096
July	14,484	Average	7,341.33

Table 8.2b	Farm opening times*		
January to mid-March	Wed – Sun	10.00–16.00
Mid-March to May	Tues – Sun	9.00–18.00
May to September	All week	8.30–19.00
October to November	Tues – Sun	10.00–16.00
December	Tues – Sun	9.00–18.00

*Special evening events at Easter, summer weekends and Christmas.

The previous year Mandy had tracked the number of visitors arriving at the farm each day. *'It is easy to record the number of people visiting the farm attractions, because they pay the entrance charge. What we had not done before is include the people who just visited the farm shop and bakery that can be accessed both from within the farm and from the car park. We estimate that the number of people visiting the shop but not the farm ranges from 74 per cent in February down to around 15 per cent in August.'* Figure 8.12 shows the number of visitors in the previous year's August. *'What our figures do not include are those people who visit the shop but don't buy anything. This is unlikely to be a large number.'*

Mandy had also estimated the average stay at the farm and/or farm shop. She reckoned that in winter the average stay was 45 minutes, but in August it climbed to 3.1 hours (see also Figure 8.13).

Current issues

Both Jim and Mandy agreed that their lives had fundamentally changed over the last few years. Income from visitors and from the Blackberry Hill brand of preserves now accounted for 70 per cent of the farm's revenue. More importantly, the whole enterprise was significantly more profitable than it had ever been. Nevertheless, the farm faced a number of issues.

The first was the balance between its different activities. Jim was particularly concerned that the business remained a genuine farm. *'When you look at the revenue per hectare, visitor and production activities bring in far more revenue than conventional agricultural activities. However, if we push the agri-tourism too far we become no better than a theme park. We represent something more than this to our visitors. They come to us partly because of what we represent as well as what we actually do. I am not sure that we would want to grow much more. Anyway, more visitors would mean that we have to extend the car park. That would be expensive, and although it would be necessary, it does not directly bring in any more revenue. There are already parking problems during peak periods and we have had complaints from the police that our visitors park inappropriately on local roads.'*

'There is also the problem of complexity. Every time we introduce a new attraction, the whole business gets

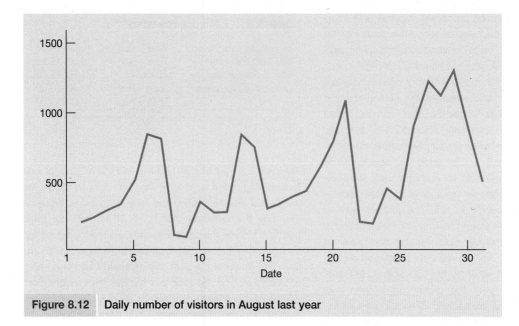

Figure 8.12 Daily number of visitors in August last year

that little bit more complex to manage. Although we enjoy it tremendously, both Mandy and I are spreading ourselves thinly over an ever widening range of activities.' Mandy was also concerned over this. 'I'm starting to feel that my time is being taken up in managing the day-to-day problems of the business. This does not leave time either for thinking about the overall direction in which we should be going, or spending time talking with the staff. That is why we both see this coming year as a time for consolidation and for smoothing out the day-to-day problems of managing the business, particularly the queuing, which is getting excessive at busy times. That is why this year we are limiting ourselves to just one new venture for the business.'

Staff management was also a concern for Mandy. The business had grown to over 80 (almost all part-time and seasonal) employees. 'We have become a significant employer in the area. Most of our employees are still local people working part-time for extra income but we are also now employing 20 students during the summer period and, last year, eight agricultural students from Eastern Europe. But now, labour is short in this part of the country and it is becoming more difficult to attract local people, especially to produce Blackberry Hill Farm Preserves. Half of the Preserving Kitchen staff work all year, with the other employed during the summer and autumn periods. But most of them would prefer guaranteed employment throughout the year.'

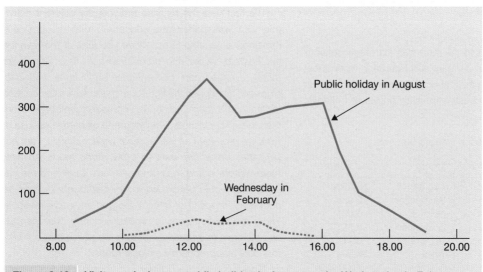

Figure 8.13 Visitor arrivals on a public holiday in August and a Wednesday in February

Table 8.3	The farm's main facilities and some of the issues concerned with managing them
Facility	**Issues**
Car park	85 car parking spaces, 4 × 40-seater tour bus spaces.
Fixed exhibits, etc. Recreation of old farmhouse kitchen, recreation of barnyard, old-fashioned milking parlour, various small exhibits on farming past and present, adventure playground, ice-cream and snack stands.	• Most exhibits in, or adjacent to, the farm museum. • At peak times helpers are dressed in period costume to entertain visitors. • Feedback indicates customers find exhibits more interesting than they thought they would. • Visitors free to look when they wish absorbs demand from busy facilities.
Tractor rides One tractor towing decorated covered cart with maximum capacity of 30 people, tour takes around 20 minutes on average (including stops). Waits 10 minutes between tours except at peak times when tractor circulates continuously.	• Tractor acts as both transport and entertainment; approximately 60 per cent of visitors stay on for the whole tour, 40 per cent use it as 'hop-on, hop-off' facility. • Overloaded at peak times, long queues building. • Feedback indicates it is popular, except for queuing. • Jim reluctant to invest in further cart and tractor.
Pick-your-own area Largest single facility on the farm. Use local press, dedicated telephone line (answering machine) and website to communicate availability of fruit and vegetables. Checkout and weighing area next to farm shop, also displays picked produce and preserves, etc, for sale.	• Very seasonal and weather dependent, for both supply and demand. • Farm plans for a surplus over visitor demand, uses surplus in preserves. • Six weighing/paying stations at undercover checkout area. Queues develop at peak times. Feedback indicates some dissatisfaction with this. • Can move staff from farm shop to help with checkout in busy periods, but farm shop also tends to be busy at the same time. • Considering using packers at pay stations to speed up the process.
Petting Zoo Accommodation for smaller animals including sheep and pigs. Large animals (cattle, horses) brought to viewing area daily. Visitors can view all animals and handle/stroke most animals under supervision.	• Approximately 50 per cent of visitors view Petting Zoo. • Number of staff in attendance varies between none (off-peak) and five (peak periods). • The area can get congested during peak periods. • Staff need to be skilled at managing children.
Preserving kitchen Boiling vats, mixing vats, jar sterilizing equipment, etc. Visitor viewing area can hold 15 people comfortably. Average length of stay 7 minutes in off-season, 14 minutes in peak season.	• Capacity of kitchen is theoretically 4500 kilograms per month on a 5-day week and 6000 kilograms on a 7-day week. • In practice, capacity varies with season because of interaction with visitors. Can be as low as 5000 kilograms on a 7-day week in summer, or up to 5000 kilograms on a 5-day week in winter. • Shelf-life of products is on average 12 months. • Current storage area can hold 16,000 kilograms.
Bakery Contains mixing and shaping equipment, commercial oven, cooling racks, display stand, etc. Just installed doughnut-making machine. All pastries contain farm's preserved fruit.	• Starting to become a bottleneck since doughnut-making machine installed, visitors like watching it. • Products also on sale at farm shop adjacent to bakery. • Would be difficult to expand this area because of building constraints.
Farm shop and café Started by selling farm's own products exclusively. Now sells a range of products from farms in the region and wider. Started selling frozen menu dishes (lasagne, goulash, etc.) produced off-peak in the preserving kitchen.	• The most profitable part of the whole enterprise, Jim and Mandy would like to extend the retailing and café operation. • Shop includes area for cooking displays, cake decoration, fruit dipping (in chocolate), etc. • Some congestion in shop at peak times but little visitor dissatisfaction. • More significant queuing for café in peak periods. • Considering allowing customers to place orders before they tour the farm's facilities and collect their purchases later. • Retailing more profitable per square metre than café.

Table 8.4   Preserve demand and production (previous year)

Month	Demand (kg)	Cumulative demand (kg)	Production (kg)	Cumulative product (kg)	Inventory (kg)
January	682	682	4,900	4,900	4,218
February	794	1,476	4,620	9,520	8,044
March	1,106	2,582	4,870	14,390	11,808
April	3,444	6,026	5,590	19,980	13,954
May	4,560	10,586	5,840	25,820	15,234
June	6,014	16,600	5,730	31,550	14,950
July	9,870	26,470	5,710	37,260	10,790
August	13,616	40,086	5,910	43,170	3,084
September	5,040	45,126	5,730	48,900	3,774
October	1,993	47,119	1,570*	50,470	3,351
November	2,652	49,771	2,770*	53,240	3,467
December	6,148	55,919	4,560	57,800	1,881
Average	**4,660**	–	–	–	**7,880**

*Technical problems reduced production level.

Table 8.3 gives more details of some of the issues of managing the facilities at the farm, and Table 8.4 shows the demand and production of preserves month by month through the previous year.

Where next?

By the 'consolidation' and improvement of 'day-to-day' activities Jim and Mandy meant that they wanted to increase their revenue, while at the same time reducing the occasional queues that they knew could irritate their visitors, preferably without any significant investment in extra capacity. They also were concerned to be able to offer more stable employment to the Preserving Kitchen 'ladies' throughout the year, who would produce at a near-constant rate. However, they were not sure whether this could be done without storing the products for so long that their shelf life would be seriously affected. There was no problem with the supply of produce to keep production level: less than 2 per cent of the fruit and vegetables that went into their preserves were actually grown on the farm. The remainder were bought at wholesale markets, although this was not generally understood by customers.

Of the many ideas being discussed as candidates for the 'one new venture' for next year, two were emerging as particularly attractive. Jim liked the idea of developing a Maize Maze, a type of attraction that had become increasingly popular in Europe and North America in the last five years. It involved planting a field of maize (corn) and, once grown, cutting through a complex series of paths in the form of a maze. Evidence from other farms indicated that a maze would be extremely attractive to visitors and Jim reckoned that it could account for up to an extra 10,000 visitors during the summer period. Designed as a separate activity with its own admission charge, it would require an investment of around £20,000, but generate more than twice that in admission charges as well as attracting more visitors to the farm itself.

Mandy favoured the alternative idea – that of building up their business in organized school visits. '*Last year we joined the National Association of Farms for Schools. Their advice is that we could easily become one of the top school attractions in this part of England. Educating visitors about farming tradition is already a major part of what we do. And many of our staff have developed the skills to communicate to children exactly what farm life used to be like. We would need to convert and extend one of our existing underused farm outbuildings to make a "school room" and that would cost between £30,000 and £35,000. And although we would need to discount our admission charge substantially, I think we could break even on the investment within around two years.*'

QUESTIONS

1 How could the farm's day-to-day operations be improved?

2 What advice would you give Jim and Mandy regarding this year's 'new venture'?

Active case study   Fresh Salads Ltd

ACTIVE CASE

Fresh Salads Ltd is an important division of a privately-owned farming company specializing in vegetable growing and distribution. Its most important customer group is the major UK supermarkets which require fresh produce to be delivered to them 364 days a year.

● Based on the information provided, how would you evaluate the capacity management of the company?

Please refer to the Active case on the CD to find out more about the processes involved in picking and ensuring the delivery of high quality vegetables to their customers.

Applying the principles

HINTS

Some of these exercises can be answered by reading the chapter. Others will require some general knowledge of business activity and some might require an element of investigation. All have hints on how they can be answered on the CD accompanying this book.

1   A pizza company has a demand forecast for the next 12 months that is shown in the table below. The current workforce of 100 staff can produce 1000 cases of pizzas per month.

(a) Prepare a production plan that keeps the output level. How much warehouse space would the company need for this plan?

(b) Prepare a 'chase demand' plan. What implications would this have for staffing levels, assuming that the maximum amount of overtime would result in production levels only 10 per cent greater than those achieved in normal working hours?

Pizza demand forecast

Month	Demand (cases per month)
January	600
February	800
March	1000
April	1500
May	2000
June	1700
July	1200
August	1100
September	900
October	2500
November	3200
December	900

2   Consider how airlines cope with balancing capacity and demand. In particular, consider the role of yield management. Do this by visiting the website of a low-cost airline, and for a number of flights price the fare that is being charged by the airline from tomorrow onwards. In other words, how much would it cost if you needed to fly tomorrow, how much if you needed to fly next week, how much if you needed to fly in 2 weeks, etc.? Plot the results for different flights and debate the findings.

3 Calculate the overall equipment efficiency (OEE) of the following facilities by investigating their use:

(a) A lecture theatre

(b) A cinema

(c) A coffee machine.

Discuss whether it is worth trying to increase the OEE of these facilities and, if it is, how you would go about it.

4 How should a business work out what it is prepared to pay for increasingly sophisticated weather forecasts?

5 What seem to be the advantages and disadvantages of the strategy adopted by Hallmark Cards described earlier in the chapter? What else could Hallmark do to cope with demand fluctuations?

Notes on chapter

1 Source: Interview with company staff.

2 Source: By kind permission of Dr Willem Bijleveld, Director, Madame Tussaud Scenerama BV, Amsterdam.

3 With special thanks to Philip Godfrey and Cormac Campbell of OEE Consulting Ltd (www.oeeconsulting.com).

4 Sources include Robinette, S. (2001) 'Get emotional', *Harvard Business Review,* May.

5 Kimes, S. (1989) 'Yield management: a tool for capacity-constrained service firms', *Journal of Operations Management,* Vol. 8, No. 4.

Taking it further

Brandimarte, P. and Villa, A. (1999) *Modelling Manufacturing Systems: From aggregate planning to real time control,* Springer, New York. *Very academic, although it does contain some interesting pieces if you need to get 'under the skin' of the subject.*

Buxey, G. (1993) 'Production planning and scheduling for seasonal demand', *International Journal of Operations and Production Management,* Vol. 13, No. 7. *Another academic paper but one that takes an understandable and systematic approach.*

Fisher, M.L., Hammond, J.H. and Obermeyer, W. (1994) 'Making supply meet demand in an uncertain world', *Harvard Business Review,* Vol. 72, No. 3, May–June.

Useful websites

www.dti.gov.uk/er/index Website of the Employment Relations Directorate, which has developed a framework for employers and employees that promotes a skilled and flexible labour market founded on principles of partnership.

www.worksmart.org.uk/index.php This site is from the Trades Union Congress. Its aim is 'to help today's working people get the best out of the world of work'.

www.eoc-law.org.uk This website aims to provide a resource for legal advisers and representatives who are conducting claims on behalf of applicants in sex discrimination and equal pay cases in England and Wales. This site covers employment-related sex discrimination only.

www.dol.gov/index.htm US Department of Labor's site with information regarding using part-time employees.

www.downtimecentral.com Lots of information on overall equipment efficiency (OEE).

FURTHER RESOURCES

For further resources including examples, animated diagrams, self test questions, excel spreadsheets, active case studies and video materials please explore the CD accompanying this book.

INVENTORY MANAGEMENT

Introduction

Operations managers often have an ambivalent attitude towards inventories. They can be costly, tying up working capital. They are also risky because items held in stock could deteriorate, become obsolete or just get lost. They can also take up valuable space in the operation. On the other hand, they can provide some security in an uncertain environment. Knowing that you have the items in stock is a comforting insurance against unexpected demand. This is the dilemma of inventory management: in spite of the cost and the other disadvantages associated with holding stocks, they do facilitate the smoothing of supply and demand. In fact they only exist because supply and demand are not exactly in harmony with each other. (See Figure 9.1).

Source: Courtesy Exel plc

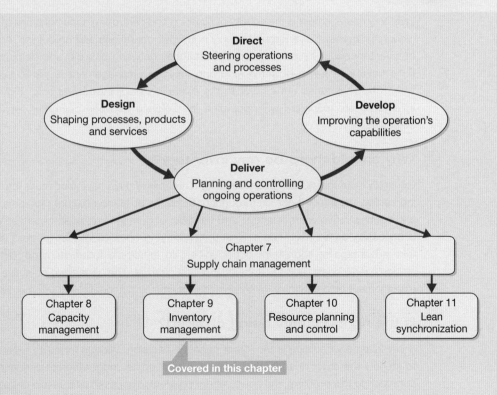

Figure 9.1   Inventory management is the activity of planning and controlling accumulations of transformed resources as they move through supply networks, operations and processes

Executive summary

VIDEO
further detail

What is inventory management?

↓

Why should there be any inventory?

↓

Is the right quantity being ordered?

↓

Are inventory orders being placed at the right time?

↓

Is inventory being controlled effectively?

Decision logic chain for inventory management

Each chapter is structured around a set of diagnostic questions. These questions suggest what you should ask in order to gain an understanding of the important issues of a topic, and as a result, improve your decision making. An executive summary, addressing these questions, is provided below.

What is inventory management?

Inventory management is the activity of planning and controlling accumulations of transformed resources as they move through supply networks, operations and processes. Accumulations of inventory occur because of local mismatches between supplier and demand. All operations have inventories of some kind and inventory management is particularly important where the inventories are central to the operation's objectives and/or of high value. How inventories are managed will determine the balance between customer service and cost objectives.

Why should there be any inventory?

Generally inventory is seen as negative for a number of reasons, including its impact on working capital, the effect it has on throughput times, its ability to obscure problems, the storage and administrative costs it incurs, and the risks of damage and obsolescence. Yet inventory is necessary as an insurance against uncertainty, to compensate for process inflexibility, to take advantage of short-term opportunities, to anticipate future demand, (sometimes) to reduce overall costs, and to fill the distribution pipeline. The underlying objective of inventory management is to minimize inventory while maintaining acceptable customer service.

Is the right quantity being ordered?

A key inventory decision is the 'order quantity' decision. Various formulae exist that attempt to identify the order quantity that minimizes total costs under different circumstances. One approach to this problem, the news vendor problem (discussed later in this chapter), includes the effects of probabilistic demand in determining order quantity.

Are inventory orders being placed at the right time?

Broadly, there are two approaches to this. The reorder point approach is to time reordering at the point in time where stock will fall to zero minus the order lead time. A variation of this is to reorder at the equivalent inventory level (the reorder level approach). Methods of reordering at a fixed point or level are termed continuous review methods because they require continuous monitoring of stock levels. A different approach, called the periodic review approach, places orders at predetermined times, but varies the order depending on the level of inventory at that time. Both continuous and periodic review can be calculated on a probabilistic basis to include safety stocks.

Is inventory being controlled effectively?

The most common inventory control approach is based on the Pareto (at 80:20) curve. It classifies stocked items by their usage value (usage rate multiplied by value). High usage value items are deemed A class and controlled carefully, whereas low usage value items (B and C class) are controlled less intensely. However, this approach often has to be modified to take account of slow-moving items. Inventory information systems are generally used to keep track of inventory, forecast demand, and place orders automatically.

DIAGNOSTIC QUESTION

What is inventory management?

Inventory is the stored accumulation of transformed resources such as materials, information, money, and sometimes customers. Occasionally the term is also used to describe transforming resource, such as rooms in a hotel, or cars in a vehicle-hire firm, but here we use the term exclusively for the accumulation of resources that flow through processes, operations or supply networks. Inventories of customers are normally referred to as 'queues' and were discussed in Chapter 5. Inventory management is the activity of planning and controlling accumulations of the resources that flow through supply networks, operations and processes.

All processes, operations and supply networks have inventories

All processes, operations and supply networks accumulate inventory. Table 9.1 gives some examples, but not all inventories have the same importance. Some in Table 9.1 are relatively trivial. For example, the cleaning materials in the computer assembly operation are of low value and relatively unimportant to the operation. By contrast, inventories of components for assembly are both high value and vital for continued operation. However, cleaning materials would be a far more important item of inventory for an industrial cleaning company, not only because it uses far more of this input, but also because its main operation would stop if it ran out.

Inventory can accumulate between the stages in a process, between the processes in an operation, and between the operations in a supply network. But, wherever inventory

Table 9.1	Examples of inventory held in processes, operations and supply networks
Process, operation or supply network	*Examples of inventory held*
Customer invoicing process	Money, customer and delivery information
Credit card application process	Customer's credit and personal details
Air conditioning systems service process	Spare parts, consumable materials
Hotel	Food items, drinks, toilet items, cleaning materials, customer information
Hospital	Wound dressings, disposable instruments, whole blood, food, drugs, cleaning materials, patient medical records
Computer manufacturer	Components for assembly, peripheral equipment for resale, packaging materials, cleaning materials
Automotive parts distribution network	Automotive parts in main depot, automotive parts at local distribution points
Supermarket supply network	Food and non-food items, packing materials

| Figure 9.2 | Inventory is created to compensate for the differences in timing between supply and demand |

accumulates, and whatever is being stored, it will be there because there is a difference in the timing or rate of supply and demand at that point. If the supply of any item occurred exactly when it was demanded, the item would never be stored. A common analogy is the water tank shown in Figure 9.2. If, over time, the rate of supply of water to the tank differs from the rate at which it is demanded, a tank of water (inventory) will be needed to maintain supply. When the rate of supply exceeds the rate of demand, inventory increases; when the rate of demand exceeds the rate of supply, inventory decreases. So if an operation or process can match supply and demand rates, it will also succeed in reducing its inventory levels.

But most organizations must cope with unequal supply and demand, at least at some points in their supply chain. Both organizations in the following examples depend on the ability to manage supply and demand inequality through their inventory management.

Example | ### The UK's National Blood Service[1]

No inventory manager likes to run out of stock. But for blood services, such as the UK's National Blood Service (NBS), the consequences of running out of stock can be particularly serious. Many

people owe their lives to transfusions that were made possible by the efficient management of blood, stocked in a supply network that stretches from donation centres through to hospital blood banks. The NBS supply chain has three main stages:

- *Collection,* that involves recruiting and retaining blood donors, encouraging them to attend donor sessions (at mobile or fixed locations) and transporting the donated blood to their local blood centre.
- *Processing,* that breaks blood down into its constituent parts (red cells, platelets, and plasma) as well over 20 other blood-based 'products'.
- *Distribution,* that transports blood from blood centres to hospitals in response to both routine and emergency requests. Of the Service's 200,000 deliveries a year, about 2500 are emergency deliveries.

Inventory accumulates at all three stages, and in individual hospitals' blood banks. Within the supply chain, around 11.5 per cent of donated red blood cells are lost. Much of this is due to losses in processing, but around 5 per cent is not used because it has 'become unavailable', mainly because it has been stored for too long. Part of the Service's inventory control task is to keep this 'time expired' loss to a minimum. In fact, only small losses occur within the NBS; most blood is lost when it is stored in hospital blood banks that are outside its direct control.

However, it does attempt to provide advice and support to hospitals to enable them to use blood efficiently.

Blood components and products need to be stored under a variety of conditions, but will deteriorate over time. This varies depending on the component; platelets have a shelf life of only five days and demand can fluctuate significantly. This makes stock control particularly difficult. Even red blood cells that have a shelf life of 35 days may not be acceptable to hospitals if they are close to their 'use by date'. Stock accuracy is crucial. Giving a patient the wrong type of blood can be fatal.

At a local level demand can be affected significantly by accidents. One serious accident involving a cyclist used 750 units of blood, which completely exhausted the available supply (miraculously, he survived). Large-scale accidents usually generate a surge of offers from donors wishing to make immediate donations. There is also a more predictable seasonality to the donating of blood, however, with a low period during the summer vacation. Yet there is always an unavoidable tension between maintaining sufficient stocks to provide a very high level of supply dependability to hospitals and minimizing wastage. Unless blood stocks are controlled carefully, they can easily go past the 'use by date' and be wasted. But avoiding outdated blood products is not the only inventory objective at NBS. It also measures the percentage of requests that it was able to meet in full, the percentage of emergency requests delivered within two hours, the percentage of units banked to donors bled, the number of new donors enrolled, and the number of donors waiting longer than 30 minutes before they are able to donate. The traceability of donated blood is also increasingly important. Should any problems with a blood product arise, its source can be traced back to the original donor.

Example   ## Howard Smith Paper Group[2]

The Howard Smith Paper Group operates the most advanced warehousing operation within the European paper merchanting sector, delivering over 120,000 tonnes of paper annually. The func-

tion of a paper merchant is to provide the link between the paper producers and the printers or converters who use large quantities of paper. It is a service-driven business, so the role of the operation function is to deliver whatever the salesperson has promised to the customer: the right product, at the right time, at the right place, and in the right quantity. This depends on professional inventory management. The company's operations are divided into two areas: 'logistics', which combines all warehousing and logistics tasks, and 'supply side', which includes inventory planning, and purchasing. Its main stocks are held at the national distribution centre, located in Northampton in central England. This location was chosen because it is at the centre of the company's main customer location and also because it has good access to motorways.

The key to any efficient merchanting operation lies in its ability to do two things well. It must be able to run a set of efficient processes that purchase, store, pick and distribute paper to customers. But also it must make the right decision on how much of each product to stock, how much to order, and when to replenish stocks at the company's 'dark warehouse' which is operational 24 hours per day, 5 days per week. All picking and movement within the dark warehouse is fully automatic and there is no need for any person to enter the high bay stores and picking area. A warehouse computer system (WCS) controls the whole operation without the need for human input. It manages pallet location and retrieval, robotic crane missions, automatic conveyors, bar code label production and scanning, and all picking routines and priorities. All products are identified by a unique bar code so that accuracy is guaranteed. The unique user log-on ensures that any picking errors can be traced back to the name of the picker, to ensure further errors do not occur. The WCS is linked to the company's Enterprise Resources Planning (ERP) system (we will deal with ERP in Chapter 12), such that once the order has been placed by a customer, the information systems manage the whole process from order placement to order dispatch. These systems also track demand trends and produce regularly updated forecasts, as well as controlling inventory levels and placing orders with paper manufacturers to ensure fast and accurate stock replenishment. This inventory control activity is at the heart of the company's success because it governs the amount of inventory held (a major element in the company's costs) and the service level to customers (which shapes customer satisfaction, and therefore the company's revenue).

What do these two examples have in common?

Both of these organizations depend on their ability to manage inventory. In doing so, both are attempting to manage the trade-off that lies at the heart of all inventory management – balancing the costs of holding stock against the customer service that comes from having appropriate stock levels. Too high stock levels have a cost. This may be simply working capital in the case of the paper merchants, or it could be the cost of blood becoming outdated and being wasted in the blood service. But without an appropriate level of inventory, customers go unserved. This means potentially losing revenue for the paper merchant. A failure to supply for the blood service may have even more drastic consequences. So, for both operations at each point in the inventory system, operations managers need to manage the day-to-day tasks of running the system. Orders will be received from internal or external customers; these will be dispatched and demand will gradually deplete the inventory. Orders will need to be placed for replenishment of the stocks; deliveries will arrive and require storing. In managing the system, three types of decision are needed:

- *How much to order.* Every time a replenishment order is placed, how big should it be? This is sometimes called the volume decision.
- *When to order.* At what point in time, or at what level of stock, should the replenishment order be placed? This is sometimes called the timing decision.
- *How to control the system.* What procedures and routines should be installed to help make these decisions? Should different priorities be allocated to different stock items? How should stock information be stored?

DIAGNOSTIC QUESTION

Why should there be any inventory?

There are plenty of reasons to avoid accumulating inventory where possible.

- Inventory (of products) ties up money, in the form of working capital, which is therefore unavailable for other uses, such as reducing borrowings or making investment in productive fixed assets (we shall expand on the idea of working capital later). In other words, it has an opportunity cost, and at the same time cannot be considered to directly add value.
- Inventory slows throughput in processes, operations and supply networks. While something is stored as inventory it is not progressing, or (usually) having value added to it. Low inventory levels mean that transformed resources move between stages,

processes or operations quickly, while high inventory levels mean that they spend time simply being stored. There is therefore a direct connection between high inventory and long throughput times.

- Inventory hides problems. High levels of inventory 'decouple' the activities of adjacent operations, processes or stages. This prevents problems being evident to anyone other than those immediately affected. This idea is central to the concept of lean synchronization and is treated further in Chapter 13.
- Inventory can become obsolete as alternatives become available.
- Inventory can be damaged, or deteriorate (age, rot, corrode, warp, shop-soil, etc.).
- Inventory can be totally lost, or be very expensive to retrieve, as it gets hidden amongst other inventory.
- Inventory might be hazardous to store (for example flammable solvents, explosives, chemicals, and drugs), requiring special facilities and systems.
- Inventory may take up excessive storage space compared to its value (for example packaging and insulation materials).
- Inventory could be duplicated at several different locations, possibly even being reordered at one, whilst excess inventory exists at others. This is not only a common dilemma for chains of retail shops or builders merchants, but also occurs in large hospitals.
- Inventory can involve high administrative and insurance costs.

So why have inventory?

> **Operations principle**
> Inventory should only accumulate when the advantages of having it outweigh its disadvantages.

All the negative effects of inventory, although very real, are only part of the inventory management activity. An equally powerful case can be based on the reasons why inventory is necessary. When a customer goes elsewhere because just one item is out of stock, or when a major project is waiting for just one small part, the value of inventories seems indisputable. The task of operations management is to allow inventory to accumulate only when its benefits outweigh its disadvantages. The following are some of the benefits of inventory.

FURTHER EXAMPLE

Inventory is an insurance against uncertainty

Inventory can act as a buffer against unexpected fluctuations in supply and demand. For example, a retail operation can never forecast demand perfectly over the lead time. It will order goods from its suppliers such that there is always a minimum level of inventory to cover against the possibility that demand will be greater than expected during the time taken to deliver the goods. This is buffer, or safety, inventory. It can also compensate for the uncertainties in the process of the supply of goods into the store. The same applies with the output inventories, which is why hospitals always have a supply of blood, sutures and bandages for immediate response to accident and emergency patients. Similarly, vehicle servicing services, factories and airlines may hold selected critical spare parts inventories so that maintenance staff can repair the most common faults without delay. Again, inventory is being used as an 'insurance' against unpredictable events.

Inventory can counteract a lack of flexibility

Where a wide range of customer options is offered, unless the operation is perfectly flexible, stock will be needed to ensure supply when it is engaged on other activities. This is sometimes called cycle inventory. For example, suppose a baker makes three types of bread. Because of the nature of the mixing and baking process, only one kind of bread can be produced at any time. The baker will have to produce each type of bread in batches large enough to satisfy the demand for each kind of bread between the times when each batch is ready for sale. So, even when demand is steady and predictable, there will always be some inventory to compensate for the intermittent supply of each type of bread.

Inventory allows operations to take advantage of short-term opportunities

Sometimes opportunities arise that necessitate accumulating inventory, even when there is no immediate demand for it. For example, a supplier may be offering a particularly good deal on selected items for a limited time period, perhaps because they want to reduce their own finished goods inventories. Under these circumstances a purchasing department may opportunistically take advantage of the short-term price advantage.

Inventory can be used to anticipate future demands

Medium-term capacity management (covered in Chapter 10) may use inventory to cope with demand–capacity fluctuations. Rather than trying to make a product (such as chocolate) only when it is needed, it is produced throughout the year ahead of demand and put into inventory until it is needed. This type of inventory is called anticipation inventory and is most commonly used when demand fluctuations are large but relatively predictable.

Inventory can reduce overall costs

Holding relatively large inventories may bring savings that are greater than the cost of holding the inventory. This may be when bulk-buying gets the lowest possible cost of inputs, or when large order quantities reduce both the number of orders placed and the associated costs of administration and material handling. This is the basis of the 'economic order quantity' (EOQ) approach that will be treated later in this chapter.

Inventory can increase in value

Sometimes the items held as inventory can increase in value and so become an investment. For example, dealers in fine wines are less reluctant to hold inventory than dealers in wine that does not get better with age. (However, it can be argued that keeping fine wines until they are at their peak is really part of the overall process rather than inventory as such.) A more obvious example is inventories of money. The many financial processes within most organizations will try to maximize the inventory of cash they hold because it is earning them interest.

Inventory fills the processing 'pipeline'

'Pipeline' inventory exists because transformed resources cannot be moved instantaneously between the point of supply and the point of demand. When a retail store places an order, its supplier will 'allocate' the stock to the retail store in its own warehouse, pack it, load it onto its truck, transport it to its destination, and unload it into the retailer's inventory. From the time that stock is allocated (and therefore unavailable to any other customer) to the time it becomes available for the retail store, it is pipeline inventory. Especially in geographically dispersed supply networks, pipeline inventory can be substantial.

Reducing inventory

The objective of most operations managers is to reduce the overall level (and/or cost) of inventory while maintaining an acceptable level of customer service. Table 9.2 identifies some of the ways in which inventory may be reduced.

Table 9.2 Some ways in which inventory may be reduced

Reason for holding inventory	Example	How inventory could be reduced
As an insurance against uncertainty	Safety stocks for when demand or supply is not perfectly predictable	• Improve demand forecasting • Tighten supply, e.g. through service-level penalties
To counteract a lack of flexibility	Cycle stock to maintain supply when other products are being made	• Increase flexibility of processes, e.g. by reducing changeover times (see Chapter 11) • Using parallel processes producing output simultaneously (see Chapter 5)
To take advantage of relatively short-term opportunities	Suppliers offer 'time limited' special low-cost offers	• Persuade suppliers to adopt 'everyday low prices' (see Chapter 11)
To anticipate future demands	Build up stocks in low-demand periods for use in high-demand periods	• Increase volume flexibility by moving towards a 'chase demand' plan (see Chapter 8)
To reduce overall costs	Purchasing a batch of products in order to save delivery and administration costs	• Reduce administration costs through purchasing process efficiency gains • Investigate alternative delivery channels that reduce transport costs
To fill the processing 'pipeline'	Items being delivered to customer	• Reduce process time between customer request and dispatch of items • Reduce throughput time in the downstream supply chain (see Chapter 7)

DIAGNOSTIC QUESTION

Is the right quantity being ordered?

To illustrate this decision, consider how we manage our domestic inventory. We implicitly make decisions on order quantity, that is, how much to purchase at one time, by balancing two sets of costs: the costs associated with going out to purchase the food items and the costs associated with holding the stocks. The option of holding very little or no inventory of food and purchasing each item only when it is needed requires little money because purchases are made only when needed, but involves buying several times a day, which is inconvenient. Conversely, making one journey to the local superstore every few months and purchasing all the provisions we would need until our next visit reduces purchasing time and costs but requires a very large amount of money each time the trip is made – money that could otherwise be in the bank and earning interest. We might also have to invest in extra cupboard units and a very large freezer. Somewhere between these extremes lies an ordering strategy that will minimize the total costs and effort involved in purchasing food.

Inventory costs

A similar range of costs apply in commercial order-quantity decisions as in the domestic situation. These are costs of placing an order, including preparing the documentation, arranging for the delivery to be made, arranging to pay the supplier for the delivery, and the general costs of keeping all the information that allows us to do this. An 'internal order' on processes within an operation has equivalent costs. Price discount costs for large orders or extra costs for small orders may also influence how much to purchase. If inventory cannot supply demand, there will be costs to us incurred by failing to supply customers. External customers may take their business elsewhere. Internal stock-outs could lead to idle time at the next process, inefficiencies and eventually, again, dissatisfied external customers. There are the working capital costs of funding the lag between paying suppliers and receiving payment from customers. Storage costs are the costs associated with physically storing goods, such as renting, heating and lighting a warehouse, as well as insuring the inventory. While stored as inventory there is a risk of obsolescence costs if the inventory is superseded (in the case of a change in fashion) or deteriorates with age (in the case of most foodstuffs).

Some of these costs will decrease as order size is increased; the first three costs (cost of placing an order, price discount costs, and stockout costs) are like this. The other costs (working capital, storage and obsolescence costs) generally increase as order size is increased. But it may not be the same organization that incurs each cost. For example, sometimes suppliers agree to hold consignment stock. This means that they deliver large quantities of inventory to their customers to store but will charge for the goods only as and when they are used. In the meantime they remain the supplier's property so do not have to be financed by the customer, who does, however, provide storage facilities.

Inventory profiles

An inventory profile is a visual representation of the inventory level over time. Figure 9.3 shows a simplified inventory profile for one particular stock item in a retail operation. Every time an order is placed, Q items are ordered. The replenishment order arrives in one batch instantaneously. Demand for the item is then steady and perfectly predictable at a

Figure 9.3 Inventory profiles chart the variation in inventory level

rate of D units per month. When demand has depleted the stock of the items entirely, another order of Q items instantaneously arrives, and so on. Under these circumstances:

$$\text{Average inventory} = \frac{Q}{2} \text{ (because the two shaded areas in Figure 9.3 are equal)}$$

$$\text{Time interval between deliveries} = \frac{Q}{D}$$

$$\text{Frequency of deliveries} = \text{reciprocal of the time interval} = \frac{D}{Q}$$

The economic order quantity (EOQ) formula

Excel

The economic order quantity (EOQ) approach attempts to find the best balance between the advantages and disadvantages of holding stock. For example, Figure 9.4 shows two alternative order-quantity policies for an item. Plan A, represented by the blue line, involves ordering in quantities of 400 at a time. Demand in this case is running at 1000 units per year. Plan B, represented by the red line, uses smaller but more frequent replenishment orders. This time only 100 are ordered at a time, with orders being placed four times as often. However, the average inventory for plan B is one-quarter of that for plan A.

To find out whether either of these plans, or some other plan, minimizes the total cost of stocking the item, we need some further information, namely the total cost of holding one unit in stock for a period of time (C_h) and the total costs of placing an order (C_o). In this case the cost of holding stocks is calculated at £1 per item per year and the cost of placing an order is calculated at £20 per order.

We can now calculate total holding costs and ordering costs for any particular ordering plan as follows:

$$\text{Holding costs} = \text{holding cost/unit} \times \text{average inventory}$$

$$= C_h \times \frac{Q}{2}$$

$$\text{Ordering costs} = \text{ordering cost} \times \text{number of orders per period}$$

$$= C_o \times \frac{D}{Q}$$

So,

$$\text{Total cost, } C_t = \frac{C_h Q}{2} + \frac{C_o D}{Q}$$

We can now calculate the costs of adopting plans with different order quantities. These are illustrated in Table 9.3. As we would expect with low values of Q, holding costs are low but ordering costs are high, because orders have to be placed very frequently. As Q

Figure 9.4   Two alternative inventory plans with different order quantities (Q)

Table 9.3 Costs of adoption of plans with different order quantities

Demand *(D)* = 1000 units per year, holding costs (C_h) = £1 per item per year, order costs (C_o) = £20 per order

Order quantity Q	Holding costs $0.5Q \times C_h$	+	Order costs $(D/Q) \times C_o$	=	Total costs
50	25		$20 \times 20 = 400$		425
100	50		$10 \times 20 = 200$		250
150	75		$6.7 \times 20 = 134$		209
200	100		$5 \times 20 \ \ = 100$		200[a]
250	125		$4 \times 20 \ \ = \ \ 80$		205
300	150		$3.3 \times 20 = \ \ 66$		216
350	175		$2.9 \times 20 = \ \ 58$		233
400	200		$2.5 \times 20 = \ \ 50$		250

[a] Minimum total cost.

increases, the holding costs increase but the costs of placing orders decrease. In this case the order quantity, *Q*, which minimizes the sum of holding and order costs, is 200. This 'optimum' order quantity is called the *economic order quantity* (EOQ). This is illustrated graphically in Figure 9.5.

A more elegant method of finding the EOQ is to derive its general expression. This can be done using simple differential calculus as follows. From before:

$$\text{Total cost} = \text{holding cost} + \text{order cost}$$

$$C_t = \frac{C_h Q}{2} + \frac{C_o D}{Q}$$

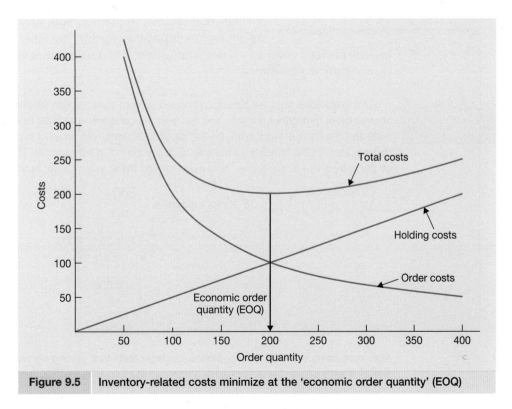

Figure 9.5 Inventory-related costs minimize at the 'economic order quantity' (EOQ)

The rate of change of total cost is given by the first differential of C_t with respect to Q:

$$\frac{dC_t}{dQ} = \frac{C_h}{2} - \frac{C_o D}{Q^2}$$

The lowest cost will occur when $\dfrac{dC_t}{dQ} = 0$, that is:

$$0 = \frac{C_h}{2} - \frac{C_o D}{Q_o^2}$$

where Q_o is the EOQ. Rearranging this expression gives:

$$Q_o = \text{EOQ} = \sqrt{\frac{2C_o D}{C_h}}$$

When using the EOQ:

$$\text{Time between orders} = \frac{\text{EOQ}}{D}$$

$$\text{Order frequency} = \frac{D}{\text{EOQ}} \text{ per period}$$

Sensitivity of the EOQ

The graphical representation of the total cost curve in Figure 9.5 shows that, although there is a single value of Q that minimizes total costs, any relatively small deviation from the EOQ will not increase total costs significantly. In other words, costs will be near-optimum provided a value of Q that is reasonably close to the EOQ is chosen. Put another way, small errors in estimating either holding costs or order costs will not result in a significant change in the EOQ. This is a particularly convenient phenomenon because, in practice, both holding and order costs are not easy to estimate accurately. The other implication is that, because the total cost curve is not symmetrical, it is usually better to have slightly more than slightly less inventory.

Operations principle
For any stock replenishment activity there is a theoretical 'optimum' order quantity that minimizes total inventory-related costs.

Worked example

A building materials supplier obtains its bagged cement from a single supplier. Demand is reasonably constant throughout the year, and last year the company sold 2000 tonnes of this product. It estimates the costs of placing an order at around £25 each time an order is placed, and calculates that the annual cost of holding inventory is 20 per cent of purchase cost. The company purchases the cement at £60 per tonne. How much should the company order at a time?

$$\text{EOQ for cement} = \sqrt{\frac{2C_o D}{C_h}}$$

$$= \sqrt{\frac{2 \times 25 \times 2000}{0.2 \times 60}}$$

$$= \sqrt{\frac{100{,}000}{12}}$$

$$= 91.287 \text{ tonnes}$$

After calculating the EOQ the operations manager feels that placing an order for 91.287 tonnes exactly seems somewhat over-precise. Why not order a convenient 100 tonnes?

Total cost of ordering plan for $Q = 91.287$:

$$= \frac{C_h Q}{2} + \frac{C_o D}{Q}$$

$$= \frac{(0.2 \times 60) \times 91.287}{2} + \frac{25 \times 2000}{91.287}$$

$$= £1095.45$$

Total cost of ordering plan for $Q = 100$:

$$= \frac{(0.2 \times 60) \times 100}{2} + \frac{25 \times 2000}{100}$$

$$= £1100$$

The extra cost of ordering 100 tonnes at a time is £1100 – £1095.45 = £4.55. The operations manager therefore should feel confident in using the more convenient order quantity.

Gradual replacement – the economic batch quantity (EBQ) model

The simple inventory profile shown in Figure 9.3 assumes that each complete replacement order arrives at one point in time. However, replenishment may occur over a time period rather than in one lot, for example where an internal order is placed for a batch of parts to be produced on a machine. The machine will start to produce items and ship them in a more or less continuous stream into inventory, but at the same time demand is removing items from the inventory. Provided the rate at which items are being supplied to the inventory (P) is higher than the demand rate (D), then the inventory will increase. After the batch has been completed the machine will be reset (to produce some other part), and demand will continue to deplete the inventory level until production of the next batch begins. The resulting profile is shown in Figure 9.6. This is typical for inventories supplied by batch processes, and the minimum-cost batch quantity for this profile is called the *economic batch quantity* (EBQ). It is derived as follows:

$$\text{Maximum stock level} = M$$

$$\text{Slope of inventory build-up} = P - D$$

Also, as is clear from Figure 9.6:

$$\text{Slope of inventory build-up} = M \div \frac{Q}{P}$$

$$= \frac{MP}{Q}$$

Figure 9.6 Inventory profile for gradual replacement of inventory

So,

$$\frac{MP}{Q} = P - D$$

$$M = \frac{Q(P - D)}{P}$$

$$\text{Average inventory level} = \frac{M}{2}$$

$$= \frac{Q(P - D)}{2P}$$

As before:

$$\text{Total cost} = \text{holding cost} + \text{order cost}$$

$$C_t = \frac{C_h Q(P - D)}{2P} + \frac{C_o D}{Q}$$

$$\frac{dC_t}{dQ} = \frac{C_h(P - D)}{2P} - \frac{C_o D}{Q^2}$$

Again, equating to zero and solving Q gives the minimum-cost order quantity, EBQ:

$$EBQ = \sqrt{\frac{2C_o D}{C_h(1 - (D/P))}}$$

Worked example

The manager of a bottle-filling plant that bottles soft drinks needs to decide how long a 'run' of each type of drink to process. Demand for each type of drink is reasonably constant at 80,000 per month (a month has 160 production hours). The bottling lines fill at a rate of 3000 bottles per hour, but take an hour to clean and reset between different drinks. The cost (of labour and lost production capacity) of each of these changeovers has been calculated at £100 per hour. Stock-holding costs are counted at £0.1 per bottle per month.

$$D = 80,000 \text{ per month}$$
$$= 500 \text{ per hour}$$

$$EBQ = \sqrt{\frac{2C_o D}{C_h(1 - (D/P))}}$$

$$= \sqrt{\frac{2 \times 100 \times 80000}{0.1(1 - (500/3000))}}$$

$$= 13,856$$

The staff who operate the lines have devised a method of reducing the changeover time from 1 hour to 30 minutes. How would that change the EBQ?

$$\text{New } C_o = £50$$

$$\text{New EBQ} = \sqrt{\frac{2 \times 50 \times 80000}{0.1(1 - (500/3000))}}$$

$$= 9798$$

If customers won't wait – the news vendor problem

A special case of the inventory order-quantity decision is when an order quantity is purchased for a specific event or time period, after which the items are unlikely to be sold. A simple example of this is the decision taken by a newspaper vendor of how many

Excel

newspapers to stock for the day. If the news vendor should run out of papers, customers will either go elsewhere or decide not to buy a paper that day. Newspapers left over at the end of the day are worthless and demand for the newspapers varies day by day. In deciding how many newspapers to carry, the news vendor is in effect balancing the risk and consequence of running out of newspapers against that of having newspapers left over at the end of the day. Retailers and manufacturers of high-class leisure products, such as some books and popular music CDs, face the same problem. For example, a concert promoter needs to decide how many concert T-shirts to order emblazoned with the logo of the main act. The profit on each T-shirt sold at the concert is £5 and any unsold T-shirts are returned to the company that supplies them, but at a loss to the promoter of £3 per T-shirt. Demand is uncertain but is estimated to be between 200 and 1000. The probabilities of different demand levels are as follows:

Demand level	200	400	600	800
Probability	0.2	0.3	0.4	0.1

How many T-shirts should the promoter order? Table 9.4 shows the profit that the promoter would make for different order quantities and different levels of demand. We can now calculate the *expected* profit that the promoter will make for each order quantity by weighting the outcomes by their probability of occurring.

If the promoter orders 200 T-shirts:

$$\text{Expected profit} = 1000 \times 0.2 + 1000 \times 0.3 + 1000 \times 0.4 + 1000 \times 0.1$$
$$= £1000$$

If the promoter orders 400 T-shirts:

$$\text{Expected profit} = 400 \times 0.2 + 2000 \times 0.3 + 2000 \times 0.4 + 2000 \times 0.1$$
$$= £1680$$

If the promoter orders 600 T-shirts:

$$\text{Expected profit} = -200 \times 0.2 + 1400 \times 0.3 + 3000 \times 0.4 + 3000 \times 0.1$$
$$= £1880$$

If the promoter orders 800 T-shirts:

$$\text{Expected profit} = -800 \times 0.2 + 800 \times 0.3 + 2400 \times 0.4 + 4000 \times 0.1$$
$$= £1440$$

The order quantity that gives the maximum profit is 600 T-shirts, which results in a profit of £1880.

The importance of this approach lies in the way it takes a probabilistic view of part of the inventory calculation (demand), something we shall use again in this chapter.

Table 9.4 Pay-off matrix for T-shirt order quantity (profit or loss in £s)

Demand level	200	400	600	800
Probability	0.2	0.3	0.4	0.1
Promoter orders 200	1000	1000	1000	1000
Promoter orders 400	400	2000	2000	2000
Promoter orders 600	−200	1400	3000	3000
Promoter orders 800	−800	800	2400	4000

DIAGNOSTIC QUESTION

Are inventory orders being placed at the right time?

When we assumed that orders arrived instantaneously and demand was steady and predictable, the decision on when to place a replenishment order was self-evident. An order would be placed as soon as the stock level reached zero; it would arrive instantaneously and prevent any stock-out occurring. When there is a lag between the order being placed and arriving in the inventory, we can still calculate the timing of a replacement order simply, as shown in Figure 9.7. The lead time for an order to arrive in this case is two weeks, so the reorder point (ROP) is the point at which stock will fall to zero minus the order lead time. Alternatively, we can define the point in terms of the level that the inventory will have reached when a replenishment order needs to be placed. In this case this occurs at a reorder level (ROL) of 200 items.

However, this assumes that both the demand and the order lead time are perfectly predictable. In most cases this is not so. Both demand and the order lead time are likely to vary to produce a profile that looks something like that in Figure 9.8. In these circumstances it is necessary to make the replenishment order somewhat earlier than would be the case in a purely deterministic situation. This will result in, on average, some 'safety' stock (s) still being in the inventory when the replenishment order arrives. The earlier the replenishment order is placed, the higher will be the expected level of safety stock when the replenishment order arrives.

> **Operations principle**
> For any stock replenishment activity, the timing of replenishment should reflect the effects of uncertain lead time and uncertain demand during that lead time.

But because of the variability of both lead time (t) and demand rate (d), the safety stock at the time of replenishment will vary. The main consideration in setting safety stock is the

Figure 9.7   Reorder level (ROL) and reorder point (ROP) are derived from the order lead time and demand **rate**

Figure 9.8   Safety stock (s) helps to avoid stock-outs when demand and/or order lead times are uncertain

probability that the stock will not have run out before the replenishment order arrives. This depends on the lead-time usage distribution. This is a combination of the distributions that describe lead-time variation and the demand rate during the lead time. If safety stock is set below the lower limit of this distribution then there will be shortages every single replenishment cycle. If safety stock is set above the upper limit of the distribution, there is no chance of stock-outs occurring. Usually, safety stock is set to give a predetermined likelihood that stock-outs will not occur. Figure 9.8 shows that, in this case, the first replenishment order arrived after t_1, resulting in a lead-time usage of d_1. The second replenishment order took longer, t_2, and demand rate was also higher, resulting in a lead-time usage of d_2. The third order cycle shows several possible inventory profiles for different conditions of lead-time usage and demand rate.

Worked example

An online retailer of running shoes can never be certain of how long, after placing an order, the delivery will take. Examination of previous orders reveals that out of 10 orders, one took one week, two took two weeks, four took three weeks, two took four weeks and one took five weeks. The rate of demand for the shoes also varies between 110 pairs per week and 140 pairs per week. There is a 0.2 probability of the demand rate being either 110 or 140 pairs per week, and a 0.3 chance of demand being either 120 or 130 pairs per week. The company needs to decide when it should place replenishment orders if the probability of a stock-out is to be less than 10 per cent.

Both lead time and the demand rate during the lead time will contribute to the lead-time usage. So the distributions that describe each will need to be combined. Figure 9.9 and Table 9.5 show how this can be done. Taking lead time to be either one, two, three, four or five weeks, and demand rate to be either 110, 120, 130 or 140 pairs per week, and also assuming the two variables to be independent, the distributions can be combined as shown in Table 9.5. Each element in the matrix shows a possible lead-time usage with the probability of its occurrence. So if the lead time is one week and the demand rate is 110 pairs per week, the actual lead-time usage will be $1 \times 110 = 110$ pairs. Since there is a 0.1 chance of the lead time being one week, and a 0.2 chance of demand rate being 110 pairs per week, the probability of both these events occurring is $0.1 \times 0.2 = 0.02$.

We can now classify the possible lead-time usages into histogram form. For example, summing the probabilities of all the lead-time usages that fall within the range 100–199 (all the first column) gives a combined probability of 0.1. Repeating this for subsequent intervals results in Table 9.6.

This shows the probability of each possible range of lead-time usage occurring, but it is the *cumulative* probabilities that are needed to predict the likelihood of stock-out (see Table 9.7).

Setting the reorder level at 600 would mean that there is only a 0.08 (8%) chance of usage being greater than available inventory during the lead time, i.e. there is a less than 10 per cent chance of a stock-out occurring.

Figure 9.9   The probability distributions for order lead time and demand rate combine to give the lead-time usage distribution

Table 9.5   Matrix of lead-time and demand-rate probabilities

			Lead-time probabilities				
			1	2	3	4	5
			0.1	0.2	0.4	0.2	0.1
	110	0.2	110 (0.02)	220 (0.04)	330 (0.08)	440 (0.04)	550 (0.02)
	120	0.3	120 (0.03)	240 (0.06)	360 (0.12)	480 (0.06)	600 (0.03)
Demand-rate *probabilities*	130	0.3	130 (0.03)	260 (0.06)	390 (0.12)	520 (0.06)	650 (0.03)
	140	0.2	140 (0.02)	280 (0.04)	420 (0.08)	560 (0.04)	700 (0.02)

Table 9.6   Combined probabilities

Lead-time usage	100–199	200–299	300–399	400–499	500–599	600–699	700–799
Probability	0.1	0.2	0.32	0.18	0.12	0.06	0.02

Table 9.7   Cumulative probabilities

Lead-time usage (x)	100	200	300	400	500	600	700	800
Probability of usage being greater than x	1.0	0.9	0.7	0.38	0.2	0.08	0.02	0

Continuous and periodic review

The approach we have described is often called the continuous review approach. To make the decision in this way the stock level of each item must be reviewed continuously and an order placed when the stock level reaches its reorder level. The virtue of this approach is that, although the timing of orders may be irregular (depending on the variation in demand rate), the order size (Q) is constant and can be set at the optimum economic order quantity. But continually checking inventory levels may be time-consuming. An alternative, and simpler, approach, but one which sacrifices the use of a fixed (and therefore possibly optimum) order quantity, is 'periodic review'. Here, rather than ordering at a predetermined reorder level, the periodic approach orders at a fixed and regular time interval. So the stock level of an item could be found, for example, at the end of every month and a replenishment order placed to bring the stock up to a predetermined level. This level is calculated to cover demand between the replenishment order being placed and the following replenishment order arriving. Safety stocks will also need to be calculated, in a similar manner as before, based on the distribution of usage over this period.

Two-bin and three-bin systems

Keeping track of inventory levels is especially important in continuous review approaches to reordering. A simple and obvious method of indicating when the reorder point has been reached is necessary, especially if there are a large number of items to be monitored. The simple two-bin system involves storing the reorder point quantity plus the safety inventory quantity in the second bin and using parts from the first bin. When the first bin empties, it is the signal to order the next reorder quantity. Different 'bins' are not always necessary to operate this type of system. For example, a common practice in retail operations is to store the second 'bin' quantity upside-down behind or under the first 'bin' quantity. Orders are then placed when the upside-down items are reached.

Is inventory being controlled effectively?

Even probabilistic models are still simplified compared with the complexity of real stock management. Coping with many thousands of stocked items, supplied by many hundreds of different suppliers, with possibly tens of thousands of individual customers, makes for a complex and dynamic operations task. Controlling such complexity requires an approach that discriminates between different items so that each has a degree of control that is appropriate to its importance. It also requires an information system to keep track of inventories.

Inventory priorities – the ABC system

Some stocked items are more important than others. Some might have a high usage rate, so if they ran out many customers would be disappointed. Others might be of particu-

larly high value, so excessively high inventory levels would be particularly expensive. One common way of discriminating between different stock items is to rank them by their usage value (usage rate multiplied by value). Items with a particularly high usage value are deemed to warrant the most careful control, whereas those with low usage values need not be controlled quite so rigorously. Generally, a relatively small proportion of the total range of items contained in an inventory will account for a large proportion of the total usage value. This phenomenon is known as the Pareto, or 80/20 rule. It is called this because, typically, 80 per cent of an operation's sales are accounted for by only 20 per cent of all stocked item types. (This idea is also used elsewhere in operations management, for example as described in Chapter 13.) Here the relationship is used to classify items into A, B or C categories, depending on their usage value.

- Class A items are those 20 per cent or so of high usage value items that account for around 80 per cent of the total usage value.
- Class B items are those of medium usage value, usually the next 30 per cent of items, which often account for around 10 per cent of the total usage value.
- Class C items are those low usage value items which, although comprising around 50 per cent of the total types of items stocked, probably only account for around 10 per cent of the total usage value of the operation.

Although annual usage and value are the two criteria most commonly used to determine a stock classification system, other criteria might also contribute towards the (higher) classification of an item. The consequence of stock-out might give higher priority to some items that would seriously delay or disrupt operations, if they were not in stock. Uncertainty of supply may also give some items priority, as might high obsolescence or deterioration risk.

Table 9.8 shows all the parts stored by an electrical wholesaler. The 20 different items stored vary in terms of both their usage per year and their cost per item as shown. However, the wholesaler has ranked the stock items by their usage value per year. The total usage value per year is £5,569,000. From this it is possible to calculate the usage value per year of each item as a percentage of the total usage value, and from that a running cumulative total of the usage value as shown. The wholesaler can then plot the cumulative percentage of all stocked items against the cumulative percentage of their value. So, for example, the part with stock number A/703 is the highest value part and accounts for 25.14 per cent of the total inventory value. As a part, however, it is only one-twentieth or 5 per cent of the total number of items stocked. This item together with the next highest value item (D/012) account for only 10 per cent of the total number of items stocked, yet account for 47.37 per cent of the value of the stock, and so on.

This is shown graphically in Figure 9.10. The first four part numbers (20 per cent of the range) are considered Class A whose usage will be monitored very closely. The six next part numbers (30 per cent of the range) are to be treated as Class B items with slightly less effort devoted to their control. All other items are classed as Class C items whose stocking policy is reviewed only occasionally.

Table 9.8 Warehouse items ranked by usage value

Stock no.	Usage (items/year)	Cost (£/item)	Usage value (£000/year)	% of total value	Cumulative % of total value
A/703	700	2.00	1,400	25.14	25.14
D/012	450	2.75	1238	22.23	47.37
A/135	1000	0.90	900	16.16	63.53
C/732	95	8.50	808	14.51	78.04
C/735	520	0.54	281	5.05	83.09
A/500	73	2.30	168	3.02	86.11
D/111	520	0.22	114	2.05	88.16
D/231	170	0.65	111	1.99	90.15
E/781	250	0.34	85	1.53	91.68
A/138	250	0.30	75	1.34	93.02
D/175	400	0.14	56	1.01	94.03
E/001	80	0.63	50	0.89	94.92
C/150	230	0.21	48	0.86	95.78
F/030	400	0.12	48	0.86	96.64
D/703	500	0.09	45	0.81	97.45
D/535	50	0.88	44	0.79	98.24
C/541	70	0.57	40	0.71	98.95
A/260	50	0.64	32	0.57	99.52
B/141	50	0.32	16	0.28	99.80
D/021	20	0.50	10	0.20	100.00
Total			5569	100.00	

Figure 9.10 Pareto curve for items in a warehouse

Inventory information systems

Most inventories of any significant size are managed by information systems. This is especially so since data capture has been made more convenient through the use of bar code readers, radio frequency identification (RFID) and the point-of-sale recording of sales transactions. Many commercial systems of stock control are available, although they tend to share certain common functions.

- **Updating stock records.** Every time an inventory transaction takes place the position, status and possibly value of the stock will have changed. This information must be recorded so that operations managers can determine their current inventory status at any time.
- **Generating orders.** Both the 'how much' and the 'when to order' decisions can be made by a stock control system. Originally almost all computer systems calculated order quantities by using the EOQ formulae. Now more sophisticated probabilistic algorithms are used, based on examining the marginal return on investing in stock. The system will hold all the information that goes into the ordering algorithm but might periodically check to see whether demand or order lead times, or any of the other parameters, have changed significantly, and recalculate accordingly. The decision on when to order, on the other hand, is a far more routine affair that computer systems make according to whatever decision rules operations managers have chosen to adopt: either continuous review or periodic review.
- **Generating inventory reports.** Inventory control systems can generate regular reports of stock value which can help management monitor its inventory control performance. Similarly, customer service performance, such as the number of stock-outs or the number of incomplete orders, can be regularly monitored. Some reports may be generated on an exception basis. That is, the report is only generated if some performance measure deviates from acceptable limits.
- **Forecasting.** Inventory replenishment decisions should ideally be made with a clear understanding of forecast future demand. Inventory control systems usually compare actual demand against forecast, and adjust forecasts in the light of actual levels of demand.

Common problems with inventory systems

Our description of inventory systems has been based on the assumption that operations

- have a reasonably accurate idea of costs such as holding cost, or order cost, and
- have accurate information that really does indicate the actual level of stock and sales.

In fact data inaccuracy often poses one of the most significant problems for inventory managers. This is because most computer-based inventory management systems are based on what is called the perpetual inventory principle. This is the simple idea that stock records are (or should be) automatically updated every time that items are recorded as having been received into an inventory or taken out of the inventory. So,

$$\text{Opening stock level} + \text{receipts in} - \text{dispatches out} = \text{new stock level}$$

Any errors in recording these transactions, and/or in handling the physical inventory, can lead to discrepancies between the recorded and actual inventory, and these errors are perpetuated until physical stock checks are made (usually quite infrequently). In practice there are many opportunities for errors to occur, if only because inventory transactions are numerous. This means that it is sur-

> **Operations principle**
> The maintenance of data accuracy is vital for the day-to-day effectiveness of inventory management systems.

prisingly common for the majority of inventory records to be inaccurate. The underlying causes of errors include:

- Keying errors: entering the wrong product code
- Quantity errors: a mis-count of items put into or taken from stock
- Damaged or deteriorated inventory not recorded as such, or not correctly deleted from the records when it is destroyed
- The wrong items being taken out of stock, but the records not being corrected when they are returned to stock
- Delays between the transactions being made and the records being updated
- Items stolen from inventory (common in retail environments, but also not unusual in industrial and commercial inventories).

Critical commentary

Each chapter contains a short critical commentary on the main ideas covered in the chapter. Its purpose is not to undermine the issues discussed in the chapter, but to emphasize that, although we present a relatively orthodox view of operation, there are other perspectives.

■ The approach to determining order quantity that involves optimizing costs of holding stock against costs of ordering stock, typified by the EOQ and EBQ models, has always been subject to criticisms. Originally these concerned the validity of some of the assumptions of the model; more recently they have involved the underlying rationale of the approach itself. Criticisms include that the assumptions included in the EOQ models are simplistic, that the real costs of stock in operations are not as assumed in EOQ models, and that cost minimization is not an appropriate objective for inventory management.

■ The last criticism is particularly significant. Many organizations (such as supermarkets and wholesalers) make most of their revenue and profits simply by holding and supplying inventory. Because their main investment is in the inventory it is critical that they make a good return on this capital, by ensuring that it has the highest possible 'stock turn' and/or gross profit margin. Alternatively, they may also be concerned to maximize the use of space by seeking to maximize the profit earned per square metre. The EOQ model does not address these objectives. Similarly for products that deteriorate or go out of fashion, the EOQ model can result in excess inventory of slower-moving items. In fact the EOQ model is rarely used in such organizations, and there is more likely to be a system of periodic review for regular ordering of replenishment inventory. For example, a typical builders' supply merchant might carry around 50,000 different items of stock (SKUs). However, most of these cluster into larger families of items such as paints, sanitary ware, or metal fixings. Single orders are placed at regular intervals for all the required replenishments in the supplier's range, and these are then delivered together at one time. If deliveries are made weekly then, on average, the individual item order quantities will be for only one week's usage. Less popular items, or those with erratic demand patterns, can be individually ordered at the same time, or (when urgent) can be delivered the next day by carrier.

■ The ABC approach to inventory classification is also regarded by some as misleading. Many professional inventory managers point out that it is the slow-moving (C category) items that often pose the greatest challenge in inventory management. Often these slow-moving items, although only accounting for 20 per cent of sales, require a large part (typically between one-half and two-thirds) of the total investment in stock. This is why slow-moving items are a real problem. Moreover, if errors in forecasting or ordering result in excess stock in 'A class' fast-moving items, it is relatively unimportant in the sense that excess stock can be sold quickly. However, excess stock in slow-moving C items will be there a long time. According to some inventory managers, it is the A items that can be left to look after themselves, and the B and even more the C items that need controlling.

Summary checklist

This checklist comprises questions that can be usefully applied to any type of operations and reflect the major diagnostic questions used within the chapter.

☐ Have all inventories been itemized and costed?

☐ Have all the costs and negative effects of inventory been assessed?

☐ What proportion of inventory is there:
  — as an insurance against uncertainty?
  — to counteract a lack of flexibility?
  — to allow operations to take advantage of short-term opportunities?
  — to anticipate future demand?
  — to reduce overall costs?
  — because it can increase in value?
  — because it is in the processing pipeline?

☐ Have methods of reducing inventory in these categories been explored?

☐ Have cost minimization methods been used to determine order quantity?

☐ Do these use a probabilistic estimate of demand?

☐ Have the relative merits of continuous and period inventory review been assessed?

☐ Are probabilistic estimates of demand and lead time used to determine safety stock levels?

☐ Are items controlled by their usage value?

☐ Does the inventory information system integrate all inventory decisions?

Case study   supplies4medics.com

Founded at the height of the 'dotcom bubble' of the late 1990s, **supplies4medics.com** has become one of Europe's most successful direct mail suppliers of medical hardware and consumables to hospitals, doctors' and dentists' surgeries, clinics, nursing homes and other medical-related organizations. Its physical and online catalogues list just over 4000 items, categorized by broad applications such as 'hygiene consumables' and 'surgeons' instruments'. Quoting their website:

'We are the pan-European distributors of wholesale medical and safety supplies . . . We aim to carry everything you might ever need; from nurses' scrubs to medical kits, consumables for operations, first aid kits, safety products, chemicals, fire-fighting equipment, nurse and physicians' supplies, etc. Everything is at affordable prices – and backed by our very superior customer service and support – supplies4medics is your ideal source for all medical supplies. Orders are normally despatched same-day, via our European distribution partner, the Brussels Hub of DHL. You should therefore receive your complete order within one week, but you can request next day delivery if required, for a small extra charge. You can order our printed catalogue on the link at the bottom of this page, or shop on our easy-to-use on-line store.'

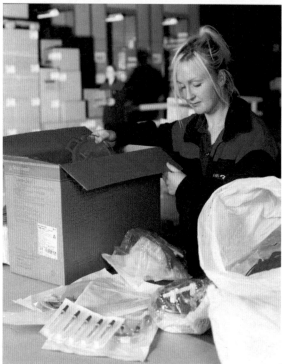

Source: Courtesy Exel plc

Last year turnover grew by over 25 per cent to about €120 million, a cause for considerable satisfaction in the company. However, profit growth was less spectacular; and market research suggested that customer satisfaction, although generally good, was slowly declining. Most worrying, inventory levels had grown faster than sales revenue, in percentage terms. This was putting a strain on cash flow, requiring the company to borrow more cash to fund the rapid growth planned for the next year. Inventory holding is estimated to be costing around 15 per cent per annum, taking account of the cost of borrowing, insurance, and all warehousing overheads.

Pierre Lamouche, the Head of Operations, summarized the situation faced by his department:

'As a matter of urgency, we are reviewing our purchasing and inventory management systems! Most of our existing re-order levels (ROL) and re-order quantities (ROQ) were set several years ago, and have never been recalculated.

Our focus has been on rapid growth through the introduction of new product lines. For more recently introduced items, the ROQs were based only on forecast sales, which actually can be quite misleading. We estimate that it costs us, on average, €50 to place and administer every purchase order, since most suppliers are still not able to take orders over the Internet or by EDI. In the meantime, sales of some products have grown fast, whilst others have declined. Our average inventory (stock) cover is about 10 weeks, but . . . amazingly . . . we still run out of critical items! In fact, on average, we are currently out of stock of about 500 SKUs (Stock Keeping Units) at any time. As you can imagine, our service level is not always satisfactory with this situation. We really need help to conduct a review of our system, so have employed a mature intern from the local business school to review our system. He has first asked my team to provide information on a random, representative sample of 20 items from the full catalogue range.' (This is reproduced in Table 9.9.)

Table 9.9   Representative sample of 20 catalogue items

Sample number	Catalogue reference number[a]	Sales unit description[b]	Sales unit cost (euro)	Last 12 months' sales (units)	Inventory as at last year end (units)	Reorder quantity (units)
1	11036	Disposable Aprons (10 pk)	2.40	100	0	10
2	11456	Ear-loop Masks (box)	3.60	6000	120	1000
3	11563	Drill Type 164	1.10	220	420	250
4	12054	Incontinence Pads Large	3.50	35400	8500	10000
5	12372	150 ml Syringe	11.30	430	120	100
6	12774	Rectal Speculum 3 Prong	17.40	65	20	20
7	12979	Pocket Organiser Blue	7.00	120	160	500
8	13063	Oxygen Trauma Kit	187.00	40	2	10
9	13236	Zinc Oxide Tape	1.50	1260	0	50
10	13454	Dual Head Stethoscope	6.25	10	16	25
11	13597	Disp. Latex Catheter	0.60	3560	12	20
12	13999	Roll-up Wheelchair Ramp	152.50	12	44	50
13	14068	WashClene Tube	1.40	22500	10500	8000
14	14242	Cervical Collar	12.00	140	24	20
15	14310	Head Wedge	89.00	44	2	10
16	14405	Three-Wheel Scooter	755.00	14	5	5
17	14456	Neonatal Trach. Tube	80.40	268	6	100
18	14675	Mouldable Strip Paste	10.20	1250	172	100
19	14854	Sequential Comp. Pump	430.00	430	40	50
20	24943	Toilet Safety Frame	25.60	560	18	20

[a]Reference numbers are allocated sequentially as new items are added to catalogue.
[b]All quantities are in sales units (e.g. item, box, case, pack).

QUESTIONS

1 Prepare a spreadsheet-based ABC analysis of usage value. Classify as follows:
   A items: top 20% of usage value
   B items: next 30% of usage value
   C items: remaining 50% of usage value.

2 Calculate the inventory weeks for each item, for each classification, and for all the items in total. Does this suggest that the OM's estimate of inventory weeks is correct? If so, what is your estimate of the overall inventory at the end of the base year, and how much might that have increased during the year?

3 Based on the sample, analyze the underlying causes of the availability problem described in the text.

4 Calculate the EOQs for the A items.

5 What recommendations would you give to the company?

Active case study   Rotterdam Serum

ACTIVE CASE

Anders works as a lab technician at Rotterdam Serum, one of the world's primary suppliers of antibody and other sera to the veterinarian and animal care sector. He faces the daunting task of operating the serum inventory. He must ensure that storage conditions are correct, stock is adequately controlled and costs are kept to a minimum.

● As the demand for serum varies, when are you going to place orders to replenish stocks and how much should you be ordering?

Please refer to the Active case on the CD accompanying this book to assess how Anders should manage serum stocks.

Applying the principles

HINTS

Some can be answered by reading the chapter. Others will require some general knowledge of business activity and some might require an element of investigation. All have hints on how they can be answered on the CD accompanying this book.

1 Read the example of the National Blood Service at the beginning of the chapter.

- What are the factors that constitute inventory holding costs, order costs and stock-out costs in a National Blood Service?
- What makes this particular inventory planning and control example so complex?
- How might the National Blood Service inventory management affect its ability to collect blood?

2 Estimate the annual usage value and average inventory level (or value) and space occupied by 20 representative items of food used within your household, or that of your family. Using Pareto analysis, categorize this into usage-value groups (e.g. A, B, C), and calculate the average stock turn for each group.

- Does this analysis indicate a sensible use of capital and space, and if not, what changes might you make to the household's shopping strategy?

3 Obtain the last few years' Annual Report and Accounts (you can usually download these from the company's web-site) for two materials-processing operations (as opposed to customer or information processing operations) within one industrial sector. Calculate each operation's stock–turnover ratio and the proportion of inventory to current assets over the last few years. Try to explain what you think are the reasons for any differences and trends you can identify, and discuss the likely advantages and disadvantages for the organizations concerned.

4 Visit a large petrol (gas) filling station to meet the manager. Discuss and analyze the inventory planning and control system used for fuel and other items in the shop, such as confectionery and lubricants. You should then obtain data to show how the system is working (for example, reorder points and quantities, use of forecasts to predict patterns of demand) and, if possible, prepare graphs showing fluctuations in inventory levels for the selected products.

5 Using product information obtained from Web searches, compare three inventory management systems (or software packages) that could be purchased by the General Manager of a large state-run hospital who wishes to gain control of inventory throughout the organization.

- What are the claimed benefits of each system, and how do they align to the theories presented in this chapter?
- What disadvantages might be experienced in using these approaches to inventory management, and what resistance might be presented by the hospital's staff, and why?

Notes on chapter

1 Source: NBS website and discussion with association staff.
2 With special thanks to John Mathews, Howard Smith Paper Group.

Taking it further

Flores, B.E. and Whybark, D.C. (1987) 'Implementing multiple criteria ABC analysis', *Journal of Operations Management*, Vol. 7, No. 1. An academic paper but one that gives some useful hints on the practicalities of ABC analysis.

Mather, H. (1984) *How to Really Manage Inventories,* McGraw-Hill. A practical guide by one of the more influential production management authors.

Viale, J.D. (1997) *The Basics of Inventory Management,* Crisp Publications. Very much 'the basics', but that is exactly what most people need.

Wild, T. (2002) *Best Practice in Inventory Management,* Butterworth-Heinemann. A straightforward and readable practice-based approach to the subject.

Useful websites

www.inventoryops.com/dictionary.htm A great source for information on inventory management and warehouse operations.

www.managementhelp.org/ops–mgnt/ops–mgnt.htm General 'private' site on operations management, but with some good content.

www.apics.org Site of APICS: a US 'educational society for resource managers'.

www.inventorymanagement.com Site of the Centre for Inventory Management. Cases and links.

FURTHER RESOURCES

For further resources including examples, animated diagrams, self test questions, excel spreadsheets, active case studies and video materials please explore the CD accompanying this book.

RESOURCE PLANNING AND CONTROL

Introduction

If materials or information or customers are to flow smoothly through processes, operations and supply networks, the value-adding resources at each stage must be managed to avoid unnecessary delay. But also resources must be used efficiently. Attempting to do this is the activity of resource planning and control (see Figure 10.1). It is a subject with many technical issues. We cover the best known of these, Materials Requirements Planning (MRP), in the supplement to this chapter.

Source: Courtesy Jonathan Natiuk

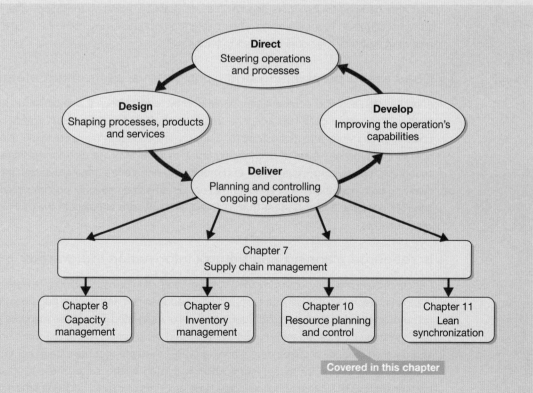

Direct
Steering operations and processes

Design
Shaping processes, products and services

Develop
Improving the operation's capabilities

Deliver
Planning and controlling ongoing operations

Chapter 7
Supply chain management

| Chapter 8 Capacity management | Chapter 9 Inventory management | Chapter 10 Resource planning and control | Chapter 11 Lean synchronization |

Covered in this chapter

| Figure 10.1 | Resource planning and control is concerned with managing the ongoing allocation of resources and activities to ensure that the operation's processes are efficient and reflect customer demand for products and services |

Executive summary

VIDEO
further detail

Decision logic chain for resource planning and control

Each chapter is structured around a set of diagnostic questions. These questions suggest what you should ask in order to gain an understanding of the important issues of a topic, and as a result, improve your decision making. An executive summary, addressing these questions, is provided below.

What is resource planning and control?

Resource planning and control is concerned with managing the ongoing allocation of resources and activities to ensure that the operation's processes are both efficient and reflect customer demand for products and services. In practice, planning (deciding what is intended to happen) and control (coping when things do not happen as intended) overlap to such an extent that they are usually treated together.

Does resource planning and control have all the right elements?

Although planning and control systems differ, they tend to have a number of common elements. These are a customer interface that forms a two-way information link between the operation's activities and its customers, a supply interface that does the same thing for the operation's suppliers, a set of overlapping 'core' mechanisms that perform basic tasks such as loading, sequencing, scheduling, and monitoring and control, and a decision mechanism involving both operations staff and information systems that makes or confirms planning and control decisions. It is important that all these elements are effective in their own right and work together.

Is resource planning and control information integrated?

Resource planning and control involves vast amounts of information. Unless all relevant information is integrated, it is difficult to make informed planning and control decisions. The most common method of doing this is through the use of integrated 'enterprise resource planning' (ERP) systems. These are information systems that have grown out of the more specialized and detailed material requirements planning (MRP) systems that have been common in the manufacturing sector for many years. MRP is treated in the supplement to this chapter. Investment in ERP systems often involves large amounts of capital and staff time. It may also mean a significant overhaul of the way the business organizes itself. Not all investments in ERP have proved successful.

Are core planning and control activities effective?

Unless the resource planning and control system makes appropriate decisions at a detailed level, it cannot be effective. These detailed decisions fall into four overlapping categories. Loading is the activity of allocating work to individual processes or stages in the operation. Sequencing is the activity of deciding the order or priority in which a number of jobs will be processed. Scheduling is the activity of producing a detailed timetable showing when activities should start and end. Monitoring and control is the activity of detecting any deviation from what has been planned and acting to cope and re-plan as necessary. The theory of constraints (TOC) is a useful concept in resource planning and control that emphasizes the role of bottleneck stages or processes in planning and control.

DIAGNOSTIC QUESTION

What is resource planning and control?

Resource planning and control is concerned with managing the ongoing allocation of resources and activities to ensure that the operation's processes are both efficient and reflect customer demand for products and services. Planning and control activities are distinct but often overlap. Formally, planning determines what is *intended* to happen at some time in the future, while control is the process of *coping* when things do not happen as intended. Control makes the adjustments that help the operation to achieve the objectives that the plan has set, even when the assumptions on which the plan was based do not hold true.

Look at the resource planning and control activities in the following two organizations. One, Air France, is a very large and very complex network of operations and processes. The other, the service section of a BMW automotive dealership, is far smaller. However, although the challenges are different, the task of planning and controlling each operation's resources is surprisingly similar.

Example ### Operations control at Air France[1]

'In many ways a major airline can be viewed as one large planning problem which is usually approached as many independent, smaller (but still difficult) planning problems. The list of things

Source: Courtesy Air France

which need planning seems endless: crews, reservation agents, luggage, flights, through trips, maintenance, gates, inventory, equipment purchases. Each planning problem has its own considerations, its own complexities, its own set of time horizons, its own objectives, but all are interrelated.'

Air France has 80 flight planners covering 24-hour operation in their flight planning office at Roissy, Charles de Gaulle. Their job is to establish the optimum flight routes, anticipate any problems such as weather changes, and minimize fuel consumption. Overall the goals of the flight planning activity are first, and most important, safety, followed by economy and passenger comfort. Increasingly powerful computer programs process the mountain of data necessary to plan the flights, but in the end many decisions still rely on human judgement. Even the most sophisticated expert systems only serve as support for the flight planners. Planning Air France's schedule is a massive job that includes the following.

- *Frequency.* For each airport how many separate services should the airline provide?
- *Fleet assignment.* Which type of plane should be used on each leg of a flight?
- *Banks.* At any airline hub where passengers arrive and may transfer to other flights to continue their journey, airlines like to organize flights into 'banks' of several planes which arrive close together, pause to let passengers change planes, and all depart close together.
- *Block times.* A block time is the elapsed time between a plane leaving the departure gate at an airport and arriving at its gate in the arrival airport. The longer the allowed block time the more likely a plane will keep to schedule even if it suffers minor delays, but the fewer flights can be scheduled.
- *Planned maintenance.* Any schedule must allow time for planes to have time at a maintenance base.

- *Crew planning.* Pilot and cabin crew must be scheduled to allocate pilots to fly planes on which they are licensed and to keep within the maximum 'on duty' allowances.
- *Gate plotting.* If many planes are on the ground at the same time there may be problems in loading and unloading them simultaneously.
- *Recovery.* Many things can cause deviations from any plan in the airline industry. Allowances must be built in that allow for recovery.

For flights within and between Air France's 12 geographic zones, the planners construct a flight plan that will form the basis of the actual flight only a few hours later. All planning documents need to be ready for the flight crew who arrive two hours before the scheduled departure time. Being responsible for passenger safety and comfort, the captain always has the final say and, when satisfied, co-signs the flight plan together with the planning officer.

Example   ### Joanne manages the schedule[2]

Joanne Cheung is the Senior Service Adviser at a premier BMW dealership. She and her team act as the interface between customers who want their cars serviced and repaired, and the 16 techni-

cians who carry out the work in their state-of-the-art workshop. *'There are three types of work that we have to organize'*, says Joanne. *'The first is performing repairs on customers' vehicles. They usually want this doing as soon as possible. The second type of job is routine servicing. It is usually not urgent so customers are generally willing to negotiate a time for this. The remainder of our work involves working on the pre-owned cars which our buyer has bought-in to sell on to customers. Before any of these cars can be sold they have to undergo extensive checks. To some extent we treat these categories of work slightly differently. We have to give good service to our internal car buyers, but there is some flexibility in planning these jobs. At the other extreme, emergency repair*

work for customers has to be fitted into our schedule as quickly as possible. If someone is desperate to have their car repaired at very short notice, we sometimes ask them to drop their car in as early as they can and pick it up as late as possible. This gives us the maximum amount of time to fit it into the schedule.'

'There are a number of service options open to customers. We can book short jobs in for a fixed time and do it while they wait. Most commonly, we ask the customer to leave the car with us and collect it later. To help customers we have ten loan cars which are booked out on a first-come first-served basis. Alternatively, the vehicle can be collected from the customer's home and delivered back there when it is ready. Our four drivers who do this are able to cope with up to twelve jobs a day.'

'Most days we deal with 50 to 80 jobs, taking from half-an-hour up to a whole day. To enter a job into our process all Service Advisers have access to the computer-based scheduling system. On-screen it shows the total capacity we have day-by-day, all the jobs that are booked in, the amount of free capacity still available, the number of loan cars available, and so on. We use this to see when we have the capacity to book a customer in, and then enter all the customer's details. BMW have issued "standard times" for all the major jobs. However, you have to modify these standard times a bit to take account of circumstances. That is where the Service Adviser's experience comes in.'

'We keep all the most commonly used parts in stock, but if a repair needs a part which is not in stock, we can usually get it from the BMW parts distributors within a day. Every evening our planning system prints out the jobs to be done the next day and the parts which are likely to be needed for each job. This allows the parts staff to pick out the parts for each job so that the technicians can collect them first thing the next morning without any delay.'

'Every day we have to cope with the unexpected. A technician may find that extra work is needed, customers may want extra work doing, and technicians are sometimes ill, which reduces our capacity. Occasionally parts may not be available so we have to arrange with the customer for the vehicle to be rebooked for a later time. Every day up to four or five customers just don't turn up. Usually they have just forgotten to bring their car in so we have to rebook them in at a later time. We can cope with most of these uncertainties because our technicians are flexible in terms of the

skills they have and also are willing to work overtime when needed. Also, it is important to manage customer's expectations. If there is a chance that the vehicle may not be ready for them, it shouldn't come as a surprise when they try and collect it.'

What do these two examples have in common?

The systems set up by Air France and the BMW dealership have a number of common elements. First, there is some kind of acknowledgement that there should be an effective *customer interface* that translates the needs of customers into their implications for the operation. This involved setting the timetable of flights (frequency, timing, etc.) and the interfaces between flights (banks) in Air France. On a more individual scale Joanne needed to judge the degree of urgency of each job and feed back to the customer, managing their expectations where appropriate. Both planning and control systems also have a *supply interface* that translates the operation's plans in terms of the supply of parts, fuel, ground services, crew availability, etc. At the heart of each company's activities is a set of *core mechanics* that load capacity, prioritize, schedule, monitor and control the operation. The aim of this decision making is to reconcile the needs of the customers and the operation's resources in some way. For Joanne this involves attempting to maximize the utilization of her workshop resources while keeping customers satisfied. Air France also has similar objectives with customer comfort and safety being paramount. Also each operation is attempting some *information integration* that involves both computer-assisted information handling and the skills and experience of planning and control staff.

DIAGNOSTIC QUESTION

Does resource planning and control have all the right elements?

Figure 10.2 illustrates the elements that should be present in all planning and control systems. In more sophisticated systems they may even be extended to include the integration of the core operations resource planning and control task with other functional areas of the firm such as finance, marketing and personnel. We deal with this cross-functional perspective when we discuss Enterprise Resource Planning (ERP) later.

How does the system interface with customers?

The part of the resource planning and control system that manages the way customers interact with the business on a day-to-day basis is called the 'customer interface' or sometimes 'demand management'. This is a set of activities that interface with both individual customers and the market more broadly. Depending on the business, these activities may include customer negotiation, order entry, demand forecasting, order promising, updating customers, keeping customer histories, post-delivery customer service and physical distribution.

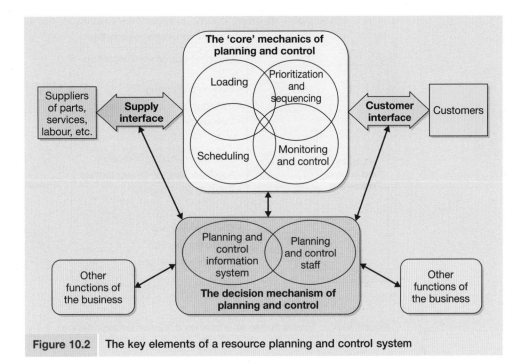

Figure 10.2 The key elements of a resource planning and control system

The customer interface defines the customer experience

The customer interface is important because it defines the nature of the customer experience. It is the public face of the operation (the 'line of visibility' as it was called in Chapter 8). Therefore, it needs to be managed like any other 'customer processing' process, where the quality of the service, as the customer sees it, is defined by the gap between customers' expectations and their perceptions of the service they receive. Figure 10.3 illustrates a typical customer experience of interacting with a planning and control customer interface. The experience itself will start before any customer contact is initiated. Customer expectations will have been influenced by the way the business presents itself through promotional activities, the ease with which channels of communication can be used (for example, design of the website), and so on. The question is: 'Does the communication channel give any indication of the kind of service response (for example, how long will we have to wait?) that the customer can expect?' At the first point of contact when an individual customer requests services or products, their request must be understood, delivery possibly negotiated, and a delivery promise made. Prior to the delivery of the service or product, the customer may or may not change their mind, which in turn may or may not involve renegotiating delivery promises. Similarly, customers may require or value feedback as to the progress of their request. At the point of delivery, not only are the products and services handed over to the customer, but there may also be an opportunity to explain the nature of the delivery and gauge customers' reactions. Following the completion of the delivery there may also be some sort of post-delivery action, such as a phone call to confirm that all is well.

As is usual with such customer experiences, the managing of customer expectations is particularly important in the early stages of the experience. For example, if there is a possibility that a delivery may be late (perhaps because of the nature of the service being requested) then that possibility is established as an element in the customer's

Operations principle
Customers' perceptions of an operation will partially be shaped by the customer interface of its planning and control system.

PRACTICE NOTE

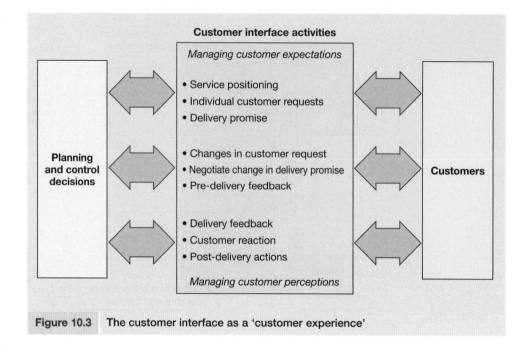

Figure 10.3 The customer interface as a 'customer experience'

expectations. As the experience continues, various interactions with the customer interface serve to build up customer perceptions of the level of support and care exhibited by the operation.

The customer interface should reflect the operation's objectives

In managing a customer's experience, the customer interface element of the planning and control system is, in effect, operationalizing the business's operations objectives. It may have to prioritize one type of customer over another. It may have to encourage some types of customer to transact business more than other (possibly less profitable) types of customer. It will almost certainly have to trade off elements of customer service against the efficiency and utilization of the operations resources. No matter how sophisticated the customer interface technology, or how skilled the customer interface staff, this part of the planning and control system cannot operate effectively without clear priorities derived from the operation's strategic objectives.

The customer interface acts as a trigger function

Acceptance of an order should prompt the customer interface to trigger the operation's processes. Exactly what is triggered will depend on the nature of the business. For example, some building and construction companies, because they are willing to build almost any kind of construction, will keep relatively few of their own resources within the business, but rather hire them in when the nature of the job becomes evident. This is a 'resource-to-order' operation where the customer interface triggers the task of hiring in the relevant equipment (and possibly labour) and purchasing the appropriate materials. If the construction company confined itself to a narrower range of construction tasks, thereby making the nature of demand slightly more predictable, it would be likely to have its own equipment and labour permanently within the operation. Here, accepting a job would only need to trigger the purchase of the materials to be used in the construction, and the business is a 'produce to order' operation. Some construction companies will construct pre-designed standard houses or apartments ahead of any firm demand for them. If demand is high, customers may place requests for houses before they are started or during their construction. In this case, the customer will form a backlog of demand and must wait. However, the company is also taking the risk of holding a stock of unsold houses. Operations of this type are called 'produce-ahead-of-order'.

How does the system interface with suppliers?

The supplier interface provides the link between the activities of the operation itself and those of its suppliers. The timing and level of activities within the operation or process will have implications for the supply of products and services to the operation. Suppliers need to be informed so that they can make products and services available when needed. In effect this is the mirror image of the customer interface. As such, the supplier interface is concerned with managing the supplier experience to ensure appropriate supply. Because the customer is not directly involved in this does not make it any less important. Ultimately, customer satisfaction will be influenced by supply effectiveness because that in turn influences delivery to customers.

> **Operations principle**
> An operation's planning and control system can enhance or inhibit the ability of its suppliers to support delivery effectiveness.

Using the expectations–perception gap to judge the quality of the supplier interface function may at first seem strange. After all, suppliers are not customers as such. Yet, it is important to be a 'quality customer' to suppliers because this increases the chances of receiving high-quality service from them. This means that suppliers fully understand one's expectations because they have been made clear and unambiguous.

PRACTICE NOTE

The supplier interface has both a long- and a short-term function. It must be able to cope with different types of long-term supplier relationship, and also handle individual transactions with suppliers. To do the former it must understand the requirements of all the processes within the operation and also the capabilities of the suppliers (in large operations, there could be thousands of suppliers). Figure 10.4 shows a simplified sequence of events in the management of a typical supplier–operation interaction which the supplier interface must facilitate. When the planning and control activity requests supply, the supplier interface must have identified potential suppliers and might also be able

Figure 10.4   The supplier interface as a 'customer experience'

to suggest alternative materials or services if necessary. Formal request for quotations may be sent to potential suppliers if no supply agreement exists. These requests might be sent to several suppliers or a smaller group, who may be 'preferred' suppliers. Just as it was important to manage customer expectations, it is important to manage supplier expectations, often prior to any formal supply of products or services. This issue was discussed in Chapter 7 as supplier development. To handle individual transactions, the supplier interface will need to issue formal purchase orders. These may be stand-alone documents or, more likely, electronic orders. Whatever the mechanisms, it is an important activity because it often forms the legal basis of the contractual relationship between the operation and its supplier. Delivery promises will need to be formally confirmed. Whilst waiting for delivery, it may be necessary to negotiate changes in supply, or to track progress to get early warning of potential changes to delivery. Also delivery supplier performance needs to be established and communicated, with follow-up as necessary.

How does the system perform basic planning and control calculations?

Resource planning and control requires the reconciliation of supply and demand in terms of the level and timing of activities within an operation or process. To do this, four overlapping activities are performed. These are loading, sequencing, scheduling, and monitoring and control. However, some caution is needed when using these terms. Different organizations may use them in different ways, and even textbooks in the area may adopt different definitions. Although these four activities are very closely interrelated, they do address different aspects of the resource planning and control task. Loading allocates tasks to resources in order to assess *what* level of activity will be expected of each part of the operation. Scheduling is more concerned with *when* the operation or process will do things. Sequencing is a more detailed set of decisions that determines *in what order* jobs pass through processes. Monitoring and control involves checking whether *activities are going to* plan by observing what is actually happing in practice, and making adjustments as necessary. See Figure 10.5. This part of the planning and control system can be regarded as the engine room of the whole system in so much as it calculates the consequences of planning and control decisions. Without understanding how these basic mechanisms work, it is difficult to understand how any operation is being planned and controlled. Because of their importance, we treat the four interrelated activities later in the chapter.

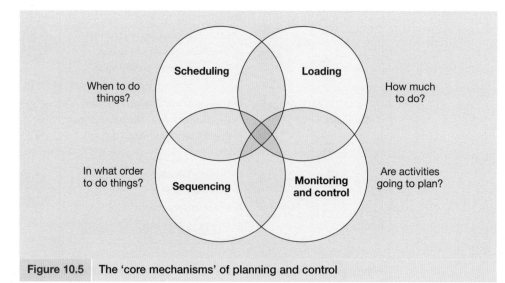

Figure 10.5   The 'core mechanisms' of planning and control

Does the system integrate human with 'automated' decision making?

Although computer-based resource planning and control systems are now widespread in many industries, much of the decision making is still carried out partially by people. This is always likely to be the case because some elements of the task, such as negotiating with customers and suppliers, are difficult to automate. Yet the benefits of computer-aided decision making are difficult to ignore. Unlike humans, computer-based planning and control can cope with immense complexity, both in terms of being able to model the interrelationship between decisions and in terms of being able to store large quantities of information. However, humans are generally better at many of the 'soft' qualitative tasks that can be important in planning and control. In particular, humans are good at the following.

- *Flexibility, adaptability and learning.* Humans can cope with ambiguous, incomplete, inconsistent and redundant goals and constraints. In particular they can deal with the fact that planning and control objectives and constraints may not be stable for longer than a few hours.
- *Communication and negotiation.* Humans are able to understand and sometimes influence the variability inherent in an operation. They can influence job priorities and sometimes processing times. They can negotiate between internal processes and communicate with customers and suppliers in a way that could minimize misunderstanding.
- *Intuition.* Humans can fill in the blanks of missing information that is required to plan and control. They can accumulate the tacit knowledge about what is, and what may be, really happening with the operation's processes.

These strengths of human decision making versus computer decision making provide a clue as to what should be the appropriate degree of automation built into decision making in this area. When planning and controlling stable and relatively straightforward processes that are well understood, decision making can be automated to a greater degree than processes that are complex, unstable and poorly understood.

Is resource planning and control information integrated?

One of the most important issues in resource planning and control is managing the sometimes vast amounts of information generated, not just from the operations function, but from almost every other function of the business. Unless all relevant information is brought together and integrated, it is difficult to make informed planning and control decisions. This is what Enterprise Resource Planning (ERP) is about. It has been defined as *'a complete enterprise wide business solution. The ERP system consists of software support modules such as: marketing and sales, field service, product design and development, production and inventory control, procurement, distribution, industrial facilities management, process design and development, manufacturing,*

> **Operations principle**
> Planning and control systems should integrate information from all relevant organizational functions.

quality, human resources, finance and accounting, and information services. Integration between the modules is stressed without the duplication of information.'[3]

The origins of ERP

Enterprise resource planning has spawned a huge industry devoted to developing the computer systems needed to drive it. The (now) large companies that have grown almost exclusively on the basis of providing ERP systems include SAP, Oracle and Baan. Yet ERP is the one of the latest (and most important) stages in a development that started with Materials Requirements Planning (MRP), an approach that became popular during the 1970s, although the planning and control logic that underlies it had been known for some time. It is a method (simple in principle but complex in execution) of translating a statement of required output into a plan for all the activities that must take place to achieve the required output. What popularized MRP was the availability of computer power to drive the basic planning and control mathematics in a fast, efficient, and most importantly, flexible manner. MRP is treated in the supplement to this chapter. Manufacturing Resource Planning (MRP II) expanded out of MRP during the 1980s. This extended concept has been described as a game plan for planning and monitoring all the resources of a manufacturing company: manufacturing, marketing, finance and engineering. Again, it was a technology innovation that allowed the development. Local Area Networks (LANs) together with increasingly powerful desktop computers allowed a much higher degree of processing power and communication between different parts of a business.

The strength of MRP and MRP II lay always in the fact that it could explore the *consequences* of any changes to what an operation was required to do. So, if demand changed, the MRP system would calculate all the 'knock-on' effects and issue instructions accordingly. The same principle applies to ERP, but on a much wider basis. ERP systems allow decisions and databases from all parts of the organization to be integrated so that the consequences of decisions in one part of the organization are reflected in the planning and control systems of the rest of the organization (see Figure 10.6).

ERP changes the way companies do business

Arguably the most significant issue in the decision by many companies to buy an off-the-shelf ERP system is its compatibility with the company's current business processes and practices. Experience of ERP installation suggests that it is extremely important to make sure that one's current way of doing business will fit (or can be changed to fit) with a standard ERP package. One of the most common reasons for not installing ERP is incompatibility between the assumptions in the software and the operating practice of core business processes. If a business's current processes do not fit, it can either change its processes to fit the ERP package, or modify the software within the ERP package to fit its processes.

> **Operations principle**
> ERP systems are only fully effective if the way a business organizes its processes is aligned with the underlying assumption of its ERP system.

Both of these options involve costs and risks. Changing business practices that are working well will involve reorganization costs as well introducing the potential for errors to creep into the processes. Adapting the software will both slow down the project and introduce potentially dangerous software 'bugs' into the system. It would also make it difficult to upgrade the software later on.

PRACTICE NOTE

ERP installation can be particularly expensive. Attempting to get new systems and databases to talk to old (sometimes called *legacy*) systems can be very problematic. Not surprisingly, many companies choose to replace most, if not all, their existing systems

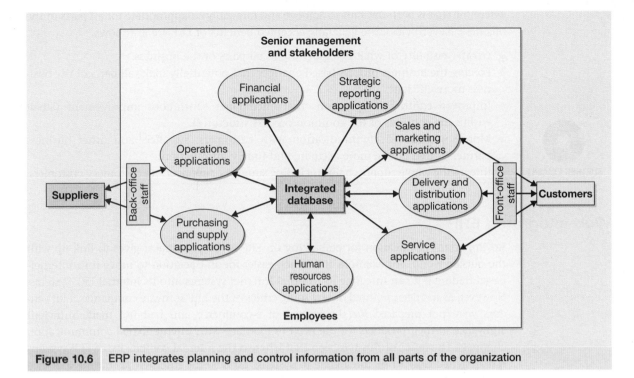

Figure 10.6 ERP integrates planning and control information from all parts of the organization

simultaneously. New common systems and relational databases help to ensure the smooth transfer of data between different parts of the organization. In addition to the integration of systems, ERP usually includes other features which make it a powerful planning and control tool:

- It is based on a client/server architecture; that is, access to the information systems is open to anyone whose computer is linked to central computers.
- It can include decision support facilities that enable operations decision makers to include the latest company information.
- It is often linked to external extranet systems, such as the electronic data interchange (EDI) systems, which are linked to the company's supply chain partners.
- It can be interfaced with standard applications programs which are in common use by most managers, such as spreadsheets, etc.
- Often, ERP systems are able to operate on most common platforms such as Windows NT, UNIX, or Linux.

The benefits of ERP

ERP is generally seen as having the potential to significantly improve the performance of many companies in many different sectors. This is partly because of the very much enhanced visibility that information integration gives, but it is also a function of the discipline that ERP demands. Yet this discipline is itself a double-edged sword. On one hand, it 'sharpens up' the management of every process within an organization, allowing best practice (or at least common practice) to be implemented uniformly through the business. No longer will individual idiosyncratic behaviour by one part of a company's operations cause disruption to all other processes. On the other hand, it is the rigidity of this discipline that is both difficult to achieve and (arguably) inappropriate for all parts of the business. Nevertheless, the generally accepted benefits of ERP are as follows.

● Greater visibility of what is happening in all parts of the business.
● Forcing the business process-based changes that potentially make all parts of the business more efficient.
● Improved control of operations that encourages continuous improvement (albeit within the confines of the common process structures).
● More sophisticated communication with customers, suppliers and other business partners, often giving more accurate and timely information.
● Integrating whole supply chains including suppliers' suppliers and customers' customers.

FURTHER EXAMPLE

Web-integrated ERP

An important justification for embarking on ERP is the potential it gives to link up with the outside world. For example, it is much easier for an operation to move into Internet-based trading if it can integrate its external Internet systems into its internal ERP systems. However, as has been pointed out by some critics of the ERP software companies, ERP vendors were not prepared for the impact of e-commerce and had not made sufficient allowance in their products for the need to interface with Internet-based communication channels. The result of this has been that whereas the internal complexity of ERP systems was designed only to be intelligible to systems experts, the Internet has meant that customers and suppliers (who are non-experts) are demanding access to the same information.

One problem is that different types of external company often need different types of information. Customers need to check the progress of their orders and invoicing, whereas suppliers and other partners want access to the details of operations planning and control. Not only that, but they want access all the time. The Internet is always there, but ERP systems are often complex and need periodic maintenance. This can mean that every time the ERP system is taken offline for routine maintenance or other changes, the website also goes offline. To combat this, some companies configure their ERP and e-commerce links in such a way that they can be decoupled so that ERP can be periodically shut down without affecting the company's Web presence.

Supply network ERP

The step beyond integrating internal ERP systems with immediate customers and suppliers is to integrate it with the systems of other businesses throughout the supply network. This is often exceptionally complicated. Not only do different ERP systems have to communicate together, they have to integrate with other types of system. For example, sales and marketing functions often use systems such as Customer Relationship Management (CRM) systems that manage the complexities of customer requirements, promises and transactions. Getting ERP and CRM systems to work together is itself often difficult. Nevertheless, such Web-integrated ERP or 'c-commerce' (Collaborative Commerce) applications are emerging and starting to make an impact on the way companies do business. Although a formidable task, the benefits are potentially great. The costs of communicating between supply network partners could be dramatically reduced and the potential for avoiding errors as information and products move between partners in the supply chain is significant. Yet such transparency also brings risks. If the ERP system of one operation within a supply chain fails for some reason, it may block the effective operation of the whole integrated information system throughout the network.

Are core planning and control activities effective?

All resource planning and control activity eventually relies on a set of calculations that guide how much work to load onto different parts of the operation, when different activities should be performed, in what order individual jobs should be done, and how processes can be adjusted if they have deviated from plan. These calculations can be thought of as the 'engine room' of the whole resource planning and control system. Although the algorithms that guide the calculations are often embedded within computer-based systems, it is worth understanding some of the core ideas on which they are based. These fall into four overlapping categories: loading, scheduling, sequencing, and monitoring and control.

Loading

Loading is the amount of work that is allocated to a process stage or the whole process. It is a capacity-related issue that attempts to reconcile how much the operation or the process is expected to do with how much the operation or process can do. Essentially the loading activity calculates the consequences on individual parts of the operation of the operation's overall workload. It may or may not assume realistic capacity limits on what can be loaded. If it does, it is called finite loading; if not, it is called infinite loading. Finite loading is an approach that allocates work to a work centre (a person, a machine, or perhaps a group of people or machines) only up to a set limit. This limit is the estimate of capacity for the work centre (based on the times available for loading). Work over and above this capacity is not accepted. Figure 10.7(a) shows that the load on the work centre is not allowed to exceed the capacity limit. Finite loading is particularly relevant for operations where:

> **Operations principle**
> For any given level of demand a planning and control system should be able to indicate the implications for the loading on any part of the operation.

- *it is possible to limit the load* – for example, it is possible to run an appointment system for a general medical practice or a hairdresser;
- *it is necessary to limit the load* – for example, for safety reasons only a finite number of people and weight of luggage are allowed on an aircraft;
- *the cost of limiting the load is not prohibitive* – for example, the cost of maintaining a finite order book at a specialist sports car manufacturer does not adversely affect demand, and may even enhance it.

Infinite loading is an approach to loading work which does not limit accepting work, but instead tries to cope with it. Figure 10.7(b) illustrates a loading pattern where capacity constraints have not been used to limit loading. Infinite loading is relevant for operations where:

- *it is not possible to limit the load* – for example, an accident and emergency department in a hospital should not turn away arrivals needing attention;

Figure 10.7   (a) Forward loading; (b) backward loading

- *it is not necessary to limit the load* – for example, fast-food outlets are designed to flex capacity up and down to cope with varying arrival rates of customers. During busy periods, customers accept that they must queue for some time before being served. Unless this is extreme, the customers might not go elsewhere;
- *the cost of limiting the load is prohibitive* – for example, if a retail bank turned away customers at the door because a set number were inside, customers would feel less than happy with the service.

In complex planning and control activities where there are multiple stages, each with different capacities and with a varying mix arriving at the facilities, such as a machine shop in an engineering company, the constraints imposed by finite loading make loading calculations complex and not worth the considerable computational power that would be needed.

Sequencing

After the 'loading' of work onto processes, the order or sequence in which it will be worked on needs to be determined. This task is called 'sequencing'. The priorities given to work in an operation are often determined by some predefined set of sequencing rules. Some of these are summarized below.

- **Customer priority**. This allows an important or aggrieved customer, or item, to be prioritized irrespective of their order of arrival. Some banks, for example, give priority to important customers. Accident and Emergency departments in hospitals must rapidly devise a schedule that prioritizes patients presenting symptoms of a serious illness. Hospitals have developed 'triage systems', whereby medical staff hurriedly sort through the patients to determine their relative urgency.
- **Due date (DD)**. Work is sequenced according to when it is 'due' for delivery, irrespective of the size of each job or the importance of each customer. For example, a support service in an office block, such as a reprographic unit, may sequence the work according to when the job is needed. Due date sequencing usually improves delivery reliability and average delivery speed, but may not provide optimal productivity.

- **Last in first out (LIFO)**. This is usually selected for practical reasons. For example, unloading an elevator is more convenient on a LIFO basis, as there is only one entrance and exit. LIFO has a very adverse effect on delivery speed and reliability.
- **First in first out (FIFO)**. Also called 'first come, first served' (FCFS), this is a simple and equitable rule, used especially when queues are evident to customers, as in theme parks.
- **Longest operation time first (LOT)**. Executing the longest job first has the advantage of utilizing work centres for long periods, but, although utilization may be high (therefore cost relatively low), this rule does not take into account delivery speed, delivery reliability or flexibility.
- **Shortest operation time first (SOT)**. This sends small jobs quickly through the process, so achieving output quickly, and enabling revenue to be generated quickly. Short-term delivery performance may be improved, but productivity and the throughput time of large jobs are likely to be poor.

PRACTICE NOTE

Scheduling

Scheduling is the activity of producing a detailed timetable showing when activities should start and end. Schedules are familiar in many consumer environments, for example a bus schedule that shows the time each bus is due to arrive at each stage of the route. But, although familiar, scheduling is one of the most complex tasks in operations and process management. Schedules may have to deal simultaneously with many activities and several different types of resource, probably with different capabilities and capacities. Also the number of possible schedules increases rapidly as the number of activities and resources increases. If one process has five different jobs to process, any of the five jobs could be processed first and, following that, any one of the remaining four jobs, and so on. This means that there are $5 \times 4 \times 3 \times 2 = 120$ different possible schedules. More generally, for n jobs there are $n!$ (factorial n, or $n \times (n - 1) \times (n - 2) \ldots \times 1$) different ways of scheduling the jobs through a single process or stage. If there is more than one process or stage, there are $(n!)^m$ possible schedules, where n is the number of jobs and m is the number of processes or stages. In practical terms, this means that there are often many millions of feasible schedules, even for relatively small operations. This is why scheduling rarely attempts to provide an 'optimal' solution but rather satisfies itself with an 'acceptable' feasible one.

> **Operations principle**
> An operation's planning and control system should allow for the effects of alternative schedules to be assessed.

Gantt charts

The most common method of scheduling is by use of the Gantt chart. This is a simple device which represents time as a bar, or channel, on a chart. The start and finish times for activities can be indicated on the chart and sometimes the actual progress of the job is also indicated. The advantages of Gantt charts are that they provide a simple visual representation both of what should be happening and of what actually is happening in the operation. Furthermore, they can be used to 'test out' alternative schedules. It is a relatively simple task to represent alternative schedules (even if it is a far from simple task to find a schedule that fits all the resources satisfactorily). Figure 10.8 illustrates a Gantt chart for a specialist software developer. It indicates the progress of several jobs as they are expected to progress through five stages of the process. Gantt charts are not an optimizing tool; they merely facilitate the development of alternative schedules by communicating them effectively.

FURTHER EXAMPLE

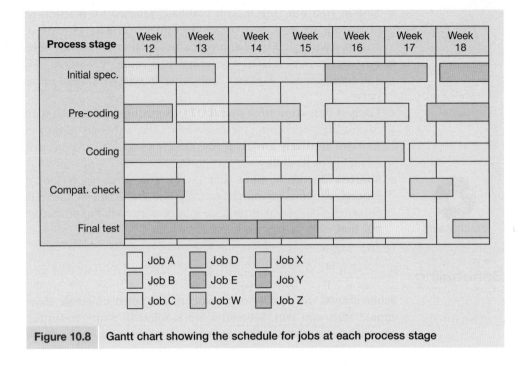

Figure 10.8   Gantt chart showing the schedule for jobs at each process stage

Scheduling work patterns

Where the dominant resource in an operation is its staff, then the schedule of work times effectively determines the capacity of the operation itself. Scheduling needs to make sure enough people are working at any time to provide a capacity appropriate for the level of demand. Operations such as call centres and hospitals, which must respond directly to customer demand, will need to schedule the working hours of their staff with demand in mind. For example, Figure 10.9 shows the scheduling of shifts for a small technical 'hotline' support service for the software company. Its service times are 4.00 hrs to 20.00 hrs on Monday, 4.00 hrs to 22.00 hrs Tuesday to Friday, 6.00 hrs to 22.00 hrs on Saturday, and 10.00 hrs to 20.00 hrs on Sunday. Demand is heaviest Tuesday to Thursday, starts to decrease on Friday, is low over the weekend and starts to increase

Figure 10.9   Shift allocation for the technical 'hotline' on (a) a daily basis, and (b) a weekly basis

again on Monday. The scheduling task for this kind of problem can be considered over different time scales, two of which are shown in Figure 10.9. During the day, working hours need to be agreed with individual staff members. During the week, days off need to be agreed. During the year, vacations, training periods, and other blocks of time where staff are unavailable need to be agreed. All this has to be scheduled such that:

- capacity matches demand;
- the length of each shift is neither excessively long nor too short to be attractive to staff;
- working at unsocial hours is minimized;
- days off match agreed staff conditions (in this example, staff prefer two consecutive days off every week);
- vacation and other 'time-off' blocks are accommodated;
- sufficient flexibility is built into the schedule to cover for unexpected changes in supply (staff illness) and demand (surge in customer calls).

Scheduling staff times is one of the most complex of scheduling problems. In the relatively simple example shown in Figure 10.9 we have assumed that all staff have the same level and type of skill. In very large operations with many types of skill to schedule and uncertain demand (for example, a large hospital) the scheduling problem becomes extremely complex. Some mathematical techniques are available but most scheduling of this type is, in practice, solved using heuristics (rules of thumb), some of which are incorporated into commercially available software packages.

Theory of constraints (TOC)

An important concept, closely related to scheduling, that recognizes the importance of planning to known capacity constraints, is the theory of constraints (TOC). It focuses scheduling effort on the bottleneck parts of the operation. By identifying the location of constraints, working to remove them, and then looking for the next constraint, an operation is always focusing on the part that critically determines the pace of output. The approach that uses this idea is called optimized production technology (OPT). Its development and its marketing as a proprietary software product were originated by Eliyahu Goldratt.[4] It helps to schedule production systems to the pace dictated by the most heavily loaded resources, that is, bottlenecks. If the rate of activity in any part of the system exceeds that of the bottleneck, then items are being produced that cannot be used. If the rate of working falls below the pace at the bottleneck, then the entire system is under-utilized. The 'principles' of underlying OPT demonstrate this focus on bottlenecks.

OPT principles

1 Balance flow, not capacity. It is more important to reduce throughput time rather than achieving a notional capacity balance between stages or processes.
2 The level of utilization of a non-bottleneck is determined by some other constraint in the system, not by its own capacity. This applies to stages in a process, processes in an operation, and operations in a supply network.
3 Utilization and activation of a resource are not the same. According to the TOC a resource is being *utilized* only if it contributes to the entire process or operation creating more output. A process or stage can be *activated* in the sense that it is working, but it may only be creating stock or performing other non-value added activity.
4 An hour lost (not used) at a bottleneck is an hour lost for ever out of the entire system. The bottleneck limits the output from the entire process or operation, therefore the under-utilization of a bottleneck affects the entire process or operation.

5 An hour saved at a non-bottleneck is a mirage. Non-bottlenecks have spare capacity anyway. Why bother making them even less utilized?

6 Bottlenecks govern both throughput and inventory in the system. If bottlenecks govern flow, then they govern throughput time, which in turn governs inventory.

7 You do not have to transfer batches in the same quantities as you produce them. Flow will probably be improved by dividing large production batches into smaller ones for moving through a process.

8 The size of the process batch should be variable, not fixed. Again, from the EBQ model, the circumstances that control batch size may vary between different products.

9 Fluctuations in connected and sequence-dependent processes add to each other rather than averaging out. So, if two parallel processes or stages are capable of a particular average output rate, in series they will never be able to achieve the same average output rate.

10 Schedules should be established by looking at all constraints simultaneously. Because of bottlenecks and constraints within complex systems, it is difficult to work out schedules according to a simple system of rules. Rather, all constraints need to be considered together.

Monitoring and control

Having created a plan for the operation through loading, sequencing and scheduling, each part of the operation has to be monitored to ensure that activities are happening as planned. Any deviation can be rectified through some kind of intervention in the operation, which itself will probably involve some re-planning. Figure 10.10 illustrates a simple view of control. The output from a work centre is monitored and compared with the plan which indicates what the work centre is supposed to be doing. Deviations from this plan are taken into account through a re-planning activity and the necessary interventions made (on a timely basis) to the work centre which will ensure that the new plan is carried out.

Operations principle
A planning and control system should be able to detect deviations from plans within a time scale that allows an appropriate response.

Eventually, however, some further deviation from planned activity will be detected and the cycle is repeated.

Push and pull control

An element of control is periodic intervention into processes and operations. A key distinction is between intervention signals that push work through processes and operations

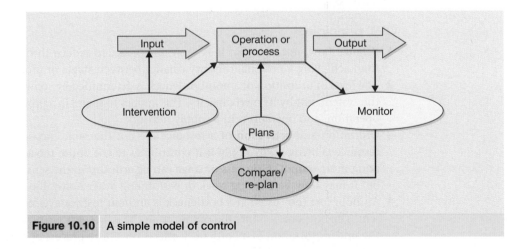

Figure 10.10 A simple model of control

and those that pull work only when it is required. In a *push* system of control, activities are scheduled by means of a central system and completed in line with central instructions, such as an MRP system (see the supplement to this chapter). Each work centre pushes out work without considering whether the succeeding work centre can make use of it. Deviations from plan are noted by the central operations planning and control system, and plans are adjusted as required. In a *pull* system of control, the pace and specification of what is done are set by the succeeding 'customer' workstation, which 'pulls' work from the preceding (supplier) workstation. The customer acts as the only 'trigger' for movement. If a request is not passed back from the customer to the supplier, the supplier cannot produce anything or move any materials. A request from a customer not only triggers production at the supplying stage, but also prompts the supplying stage to request a further delivery from its own suppliers. In this way, demand is transmitted back through the stages from the original point of demand by the original customer.

Push systems of control are more formal and require significant decision making or computing power when it is necessary to re-plan in the light of events. But push control can cope with very significant changes in circumstances such as major shifts in output level or product mix. By contrast, pull control is more self-adjusting in the sense that the more natural rules that govern the relationships between stages or processes can cope with deviations from plan without reference to any higher decision-making authority. But there are limits to the extent to which this can cope with major fluctuations in demand. Pull control works best when conditions are relatively

> **Operations principle**
> Pull control reduces the build-up of inventory between processes or stages.

stable. Understanding the differences between push and pull is also important because they have different effects in terms of their propensities to accumulate inventory. Pull systems are far less likely to result in inventory build-up and therefore have advantages in terms of the lean synchronization of flow (covered in Chapter 13).

Drum, buffer, rope control

The drum, buffer, rope concept comes from the Theory of Constraints (TOC) described earlier. It is an idea that helps to decide exactly *where* control should occur. Again, the TOC emphasizes the role of the bottleneck on work flow. If the bottleneck is the chief constraint, it should be the control point of the whole process. The bottleneck should be the *drum* because it sets the 'beat' for the rest of the process to follow. Because it does not have sufficient capacity, a bottleneck is (or should be) working all the time.

> **Operations principle**
> The constraints of bottleneck processes and activities should be a major input to the planning and control activity.

Therefore, it is sensible to keep a *buffer* of inventory in front of it to make sure that it always has something to work on. Also, because it constrains the output of the whole process, any time lost at the bottleneck will affect the output from the whole process. So it is not worthwhile for the parts of the process before the bottleneck to work to their full capacity. All they would do is produce work that would accumulate further along in the process up to the point where the bottleneck is constraining flow. Therefore, some form of communication between the bottleneck and the input to the process is needed to make sure that activities before the bottleneck do not overproduce. This is called the *rope* (see Figure 10.11).

The degree of difficulty in controlling operations

The simple monitoring control model in Figure 10.10 helps in understanding the basic functions of the monitoring and control activity. But it is a simplification. Some simple technology-dominated processes may approximate to it, but many other operations do not. In fact, the specific criticisms cited in the critical commentary below provide a

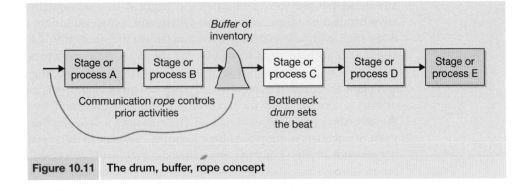

Figure 10.11 The drum, buffer, rope concept

useful set of questions that can be used to assess the degree of difficulty associated with control of any operation:

- Is there consensus over what the operation's objectives should be?
- How well can the output from the operation be measured?
- Are the effects of interventions into the operation predictable?
- Are the operation's activities largely repetitive?

Figure 10.12 illustrates how these four questions can form dimensions of 'controllability'. It shows three different operations. The food processing operation is relatively straightforward to control, while the child care service is particularly difficult. The tax advice service is somewhere in between.

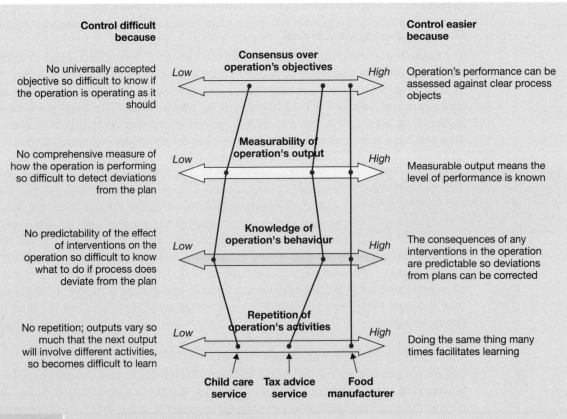

Figure 10.12 How easy is an operation to control?

Critical commentary

Each chapter contains a short critical commentary on the main ideas covered in the chapter. Its purpose is not to undermine the issues discussed in the chapter, but to emphasize that, although we present a relatively orthodox view of operation, there are other perspectives.

■ Far from being the magic ingredient which allows operations to fully integrate all their information, ERP is regarded by some as one of the most expensive ways of getting zero or even negative return on investment. For example, the American chemicals giant, Dow Chemical, spent almost half a billion dollars and seven years implementing an ERP system which became outdated almost as soon as it was implemented. One company, FoxMeyer Drug, claimed that the expense and problems which it encountered in implementing ERP eventually drove it into bankruptcy. One problem is that ERP implementation is expensive. This is partly because of the need to customize the system, understand its implications on the organization, and train staff to use it. Spending on what some call the *ERP ecosystem* (consulting, hardware, networking and complementary applications) has been estimated as being twice the spending on the software itself. But it is not only the expense which has disillusioned many companies, it is also the returns they have had for their investment. Some studies show that the vast majority of companies implementing ERP are disappointed with the effect it has had on their businesses. Certainly many companies find that they have to (sometimes fundamentally) change the way they organize their operations in order to fit in with ERP systems. This organizational impact of ERP (which has been described as the corporate equivalent of root-canal work) can have a significantly disruptive effect on the organization's operations.

■ If one accepts only some of the criticisms of ERP, it does pose the question as to why companies have invested such large amounts of money in it. Partly it was the attraction of turning the company's information systems into a 'smooth running and integrated machine'. The prospect of such organizational efficiency is attractive to most managers, even if it does presuppose a very simplistic model of how organizations work in practice. After a while, although organizations could now see the formidable problems in ERP implementation, the investments were justified on the basis that, 'even if we gain no significant advantage by investing in ERP, we will be placed at a disadvantage by *not* investing in it because all our competitors are doing so'. There is probably some truth in this; sometimes businesses have to invest just to stand still.

■ Most of the perspectives on control taken in this chapter are simplifications of a far more messy reality. They are based on models used to understand mechanical systems such as car engines. But anyone who has worked in real organizations knows that organizations are not machines. They are social systems, full of complex and ambiguous interactions. Simple models such as these assume that operations objectives are always clear and agreed, yet organizations are political entities where different and often conflicting objectives compete. Local government operations, for example, are overtly political. Furthermore, the outputs from operations are not always easily measured. A university may be able to measure the number and qualifications of its students, for example, but it cannot measure the full impact of its education on their future happiness. Also, even if it is possible to work out an appropriate intervention to bring an operation back into 'control', most operations cannot perfectly predict what effect the intervention will have. Even the largest of burger bar chains does not know *exactly* how a new shift allocation system will affect performance. Also, some operations never do the same thing more than once anyway. Most of the work done by construction operations are one-offs. If every output is different, how can 'controllers' ever know what is supposed to happen? Their plans themselves are mere speculation.

Summary checklist

This checklist comprises questions that can be usefully applied to any type of operations and reflect the major diagnostic questions used within the chapter.

☐ Is appropriate effort devoted to planning and controlling the operation's resources and activities?

☐ Have any recent failures in planning and control been used to reconsider how the planning and control system operates?

☐ Does the system interface with customers so as to encourage a positive customer experience?

☐ Does the planning and control system interface with suppliers so as to promote a supplier experience that is in the company's long-term interests?

☐ Does the system perform basic planning and control calculations in an appropriate and realistic manner?

☐ Is the balance between human and automated decision making understood and appropriate for the circumstances?

☐ How well is resource planning and control information integrated?

☐ Have the advantages and disadvantages of moving to a sophisticated (but expensive!) ERP system been investigated?

☐ If so, have the possibilities of Web integration and supply chain scope been investigated?

☐ Are bottlenecks accounted for in the way planning and control decisions are made?

☐ If not, have bottlenecks been identified and their effect on the smooth flow of items through the operation been evaluated?

Case study   *subText* Studios, Singapore

'C.K. One' was clearly upset. Since he had founded *subText* in the fast growing South East Asian computer generated imaging (CGI) market, three years ago, this was the first time that he had needed to apologize to his clients. In fact, it had been more than an apology; he had agreed to reduce his fee, though he knew that didn't make up for the delay. He admitted that, up to that point, he hadn't fully realized just how much risk there was, both reputational and financial, in failing to meet schedule dates. It wasn't that either he or his team was unaware of the importance of reliability. On the contrary. 'Imagination', 'expertise' and 'reliability' all figured prominently in their promotional literature, mission statements, and so on. It was just that the 'imagination' and 'expertise' parts had seemed to be the things that had been responsible for their success so far. Of course, it had been bad luck that, after more than a year of perfect reliability (not one late job), the two that had been late in the first quarter of 2004 had been particularly critical. *'They were both for new clients',* said CK, *'and neither of them indicated just how important the agreed delivery date was to them. We should have known, or found out, I admit. But it's always more difficult with new clients, because without a track record with them, you don't really like even to admit the possibility of being late.'*

The company

After studying computer science up to Masters level at the National University of Singapore, C.K. Ong had worked for four years in CGI workshops in and around the Los Angeles area of California and then taken his MBA at Stanford. It was there that his fellow students had named him CK One, partly because of his fondness for the fragrance and partly because his outgoing leadership talents usually left him as the leader of whatever group he was working in. After that, *'The name just kinda stuck',* even when he returned to Singapore to start *subText* Studios. While in California, CK had observed that a small but growing part of the market for computer-generated imaging services was in the advertising industry. *'Most CGI work is still connected with the movie industry',* admitted CK. *'However, two important factors have emerged over the last four or five years. First, the Ad agencies have realized that, with one or two notable exceptions, the majority of their output is visually less arresting than most of the*

public are used to seeing at the movies. Second, the cost of sophisticated CGI, once something of a barrier to most advertising budgets, is starting to fall rapidly. Partly this is because of cheaper computing power and partly because the scarcity of skilled CGI experts who also have creative talent is starting to rectify itself.' CK had decided to return to Singapore both for family reasons and because the market in the area was growing quickly and, unlike Hong Kong that had a large movie industry with its ancillary service industries, Singapore had few competitors.

The company was set up on a similar but slightly simpler basis to the companies CK had worked for in California. At the heart of the company were the three 'core' departments that dealt sequentially with each job taken on. These three departments were 'Pre-production', 'Production' and 'Post-production'.

● **Pre-production** was concerned with taking and refining the brief as specified by the client, checking with and liaising with the client to iron out any ambiguities in the brief, story-boarding the sequences, and obtaining outline approval of the brief from the client. In addition, pre-production also acted as account liaison with the client and were also responsible for estimating the resources and timing for each job. They also had nominal responsibility for monitoring the job through the remaining two stages, but generally they only did this if the client needed to be consulted during the production and post-production processes. The Supervising Artists in each department were responsible for the control of the jobs in their departments.

- **Production** involved the creation of the imagery itself. This could be a complex and time-consuming process involving the use of state-of-the-art workstations and CGI software. Around 80 per cent of all production work was carried out in-house, but for some jobs other specialist workshops were contracted. This was only done for work that subText either could not do, or would find difficult to do. Contracting was hardly ever used simply to increase capacity because the costs of doing so could drastically reduce margins.
- **Post-production** had two functions. The first was to integrate the visual image sequences produced by Production with other effects such as sound effects, music, voice-overs, etc. The second was to cut, edit and generally produce the finished 'product' in the format required by the client.

Each of the three departments employed teams of two people. *'It's a trick I learnt working for a workshop in L.A.'*, said CK. *'Two people working together both enhance the creative process (if you get the right two people!) and provide a discipline for each other. Also, it allows for some flexibility both in the mixing of different talents and in making sure that there is always at least one person from the team present at any time who knows the progress and status of any job.'* Pre-production had two teams, Production three teams, and Post-production two teams. In addition CK himself would sometimes work in the core departments, particularly in Pre-production, when he had the time, although this was becoming less common. His main role was in marketing the company's services and business development generally. *'I am the external face of the company and partly my job is to act as a cut-out, particularly for the Production and Post-production people. The last thing I want is them being disturbed by the clients all the time. I also try and help out around the place when I can, especially with the creative and storyboarding work. The problem with doing this is that, particularly for Pre-production and Post-production, a single extra person assisting does not always help to get the job done faster. In fact, it can sometimes confuse things and slow things down. This is why, for Pre-production and Post-production work, one team is always exclusively devoted to one job. We never allow either one team to be working on two jobs at the same time, or have both teams working on one job. It just doesn't work because of the confusion it creates. That doesn't apply to Production. Usually (but not always) the Production work can be parcelled up so that two or even all three of the teams could be working on different*

parts of it at the same time. Provided there is close coordination between the teams and provided that they are all committed to pulling it together at the end, there should be a more or less inverse relationship between the number of bodies working on the job and the length of time it takes. In fact, with the infamous 'fifty three slash F' job that's exactly what we had to do. However, not withstanding what I just said about shortening the time, we probably did lose some efficiency there by having all three teams working on it.'

'We pay our teams in the three core departments a salary based on their experience and a yearly bonus. For that they are expected to, within reason, work until the job is finished. It varies, but most of us work at least ten-hour days relatively frequently. That level of work is factored in to the time estimates we make for each stage of the process. And, although we can be a little inaccurate sometimes, I don't think it's anything to do with a lack of motivation or pace of work. It's just that this type of thing is sometimes difficult to estimate.'

The 'fifty three slash F' job

The 'fifty three slash F' job, recently finished (late) and delivered to the client (dissatisfied), had been the source of much chaos, confusion and recrimination over the last two or three weeks. Although the job was only three days late, it had caused the client (the Singapore office of a US Advertising agency) to postpone a presentation to its own client. Worse, subText had given only five days' notice of late delivery, trying until the last to pull back onto schedule.

The full name of the job that had given them so much trouble was 04/53/F. The 04 related to the year in which the job was started, the 53 was the client's reference number and the F the job identifier (at the start of the year the first job would be labelled A, then B, and so forth, with AA, BB, etc., being used subsequently). Table 10.1 shows the data for all the jobs started in 2004 up to the current time (day 58, every working day was numbered throughout the year). Figure 10.13 shows the schedule for this period. The job had been accepted on day 18 and had seemed relatively straightforward, although it was always clear that it would be a long production job. It was also clear that time was always going to be tight. There were 32 days in which to finish a job that was estimated to take 30 days.

'We had been negotiating for this job for two or three weeks and we were delighted to get it. It was important to us because the client, although small in Singapore, had interests all over the world. We saw it as a way into potentially some major business in the future. In hindsight we underestimated how much having three teams working on the production stage of this job at one point or other would increase its complexity. OK, it was not an easy piece of CGI to carry off, but we probably would have been OK if we had organized the CGI stage better. It was

Table 10.1   *subText* Studios Singapore – planning data for day 02 to day 58 2004

Job (04)	Day in	Estimated total time	Actual total time	Due date	Actual delivery	Pre-prod. Est.	Pre-prod. Actual	Prod. Est.	Prod. Actual	Post-prod. Est.	Post-prod. Actual
06/A	−4	29	30	40	34	6	8	11	10	12	12
11/B	−4	22	24	42	31	4	5.5	7	7.5	11	11
04/C	2	31	30.5	43	40	9	9.5	12	13	10	9
54/D	5	28	34	55	58	10	12	12	17	6	5
31/E	15	34	25	68	57	10	11	12	14	12	–
53/F	18	32	49	50	53	6	10	18	28	8	11
24/G	25	26	20	70	–	9	11	9	9	8	–
22/H	29	32	26	70	–	10	12	14	14	8	–
22/I	33	30	11	75	–	10	11	12	–	8	–
09/J	41	36	14	81	–	12	14	14	–	10	–
20/K	49	40	–	89	–	12	–	14	–	14	–

also real bad luck that, in our efforts to deliver the fifty three slash F job on time, we also disrupted the fifty four slash D job that turned out to be the only other new client we have had this year.' (C.K. Ong)

The job had proved difficult from the start. The pre-production stage took longer than estimated, mainly because the client's creative team changed just before the start of *subText* beginning the work. But it was the actual CGI itself that proved to be the major problem. Not only was the task intrinsically difficult, it was difficult to parcel it up into separate packages that could be coordinated for working on by the two teams allocated to the job. More

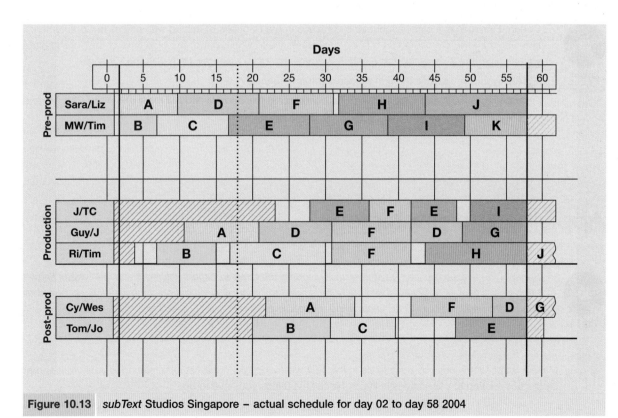

Figure 10.13   *subText* Studios Singapore – actual schedule for day 02 to day 58 2004

seriously, it became apparent, within two or three days of starting the production work, that they would need the help of another studio for some of the effects. Although the other studio was a regular supplier at short notice, this time they were too busy with their own work to help out. Help eventually came from a specialist studio in Hong Kong. *'The subcontracting delay was clearly a problem, but it was only half way through the production phase that we first realized just how much difficulty the fifty three slash F job was in. It was at that stage that we devoted all our production resources to finishing it. Unfortunately, even then, the job was late. The decision eventually to put all three teams on to the fifty three slash F job was not easy because we knew that it would both disrupt other jobs and potentially cause more coordination problems. However, when I accept jobs into Production I am accepting that I will try and do whatever it takes to pass it over to Post-production on the date agreed. We did miss out that time, but you can't say we didn't give it everything we've got and technically the job was brilliant, even the client admits that.'* ('TC' Ashwan, Supervising CGI Artist, Production Department)

'No way will we be doing that again'

'No way will we be doing that again', said CK to the core teams when they met to pick over what had gone wrong. *'We are desperately in need of a more professional approach to keeping track of our activities. There is no point in me telling everyone how good we are if we then let them down. The problem is that I don't want to encourage a "command and control" culture in the studio. We depend on all staff feeling that they have the freedom to explore seemingly crazy options that may just lead to something real special. We aren't a factory. But we do need to get a grip on our estimating so that we have a better idea of how long each job really will take. After that each of the core departments can be responsible for their own planning.'*

QUESTIONS

1 What went wrong with the fifty three slash F job and how could the company avoid making the same mistakes again?

2 What would you suggest that *subText* do to tighten up their planning and control procedures?

Active case study   Coburn Finnegan Accountants

ACTIVE CASE

Coburn Finnegan is a small accountancy practice in the Republic of Ireland with offices in Cork, Limerick and Galway. They are settled on a fairly busy week ahead when, out of the blue, one of their clients calls with an urgent request which forces Mark Williams, the team manager, to re-visit the schedule.

● How would you advise the firm to respond to the request?

Please refer to the Active case on the CD accompanying this book to find out more about the planning and control activities within the firm.

Applying the principles

HINTS

Some of these exercises can be answered by reading the chapter. Others will require some general knowledge of business activity and some might require an element of investigation. All have hints on how they can be answered on the CD accompanying this book.

---

1 (a) Make a list of all the jobs you have to do in the next week. Include in this list jobs relating to your work and/or study, jobs relating to your domestic life, in fact all the things you have to do.

(b) Prioritize all these jobs on a 'most important' to 'least important' basis.

(c) Draw up an outline schedule of exactly when you will do each of these jobs.

(d) At the end of the week compare what your schedule said you *would* do with what you actually *have* done. If there is a discrepancy, why did it occur?

(e) Draw up your own list of planning and control rules from your experience in this exercise in personal planning and control.

2 Revisit the example at the beginning of the chapter which explained how one car dealership planned and controlled its workshop activities. Try to visit a local car servicing operation and talk to them about their approach to planning and control. (Note that it may be less sophisticated than the operation described in the example, or if it is a franchised operation, it may have a different approach from the one described in the example.)

● What do you think the planning and control 'system' (which may or may not be computer-based) has to do well in order to ensure efficient and effective scheduling?

● What do you think are the ideal qualities for people with similar jobs to Joanne Cheung's?

3 From your own experience of making appointments at your General Practitioner's surgery, or by visiting whoever provides you with primary medical care, reflect on how patients are scheduled to see a doctor or nurse.

● What do you think planning and control objectives are for a General Practitioner's surgery?

● How could your own medical practice be improved?

Read the following descriptions of two cinemas, then answer the questions that follow.

Kinepolis in Brussels is one of the largest cinema complexes in the world, with 28 screens, a total of 8000 seats, and four showings of each film every day. It is equipped with the latest projection technology. All the film performances are scheduled to start at the same times every day: 4 pm, 6 pm, 8 pm and 10.30 pm. Most customers arrive in the 30 minutes before the start of the film. Each of the 18 ticket desks has a networked terminal and a ticket printer. For each customer, a screen code is entered to identify and confirm seat availability of the requested film. Then the number of seats required is entered, and the tickets are printed, though these do not allocate specific seat positions. The operator then takes payment by cash or credit card and issues the tickets. This takes an average of 19.5 seconds and a further 5 seconds is needed for the next customer to move forward. An average transaction involves the sale of approximately 1.7 tickets.

The UCI cinema in Birmingham has eight screens. The cinema incorporates many 'state-of-the-art' features, including the high-quality THX sound system, fully computerized ticketing and a video games arcade off the main hall. In total the eight screens can seat 1840 people; the capacity (seating) for each screen varies, so the cinema management can allocate the more popular films to the larger screens and use the smaller screens for the less popular films. The starting times of the eight films at UCI are usually staggered by 10 minutes, with the most popular film in each category (children's, drama, comedy, etc.) being scheduled to run first. Because the films are of different durations, and since the manager must try to maximize the utilization of the seating, the scheduling task is complex. Ticket staff are continually aware of the remaining capacity of each 'screen' through their terminals. There are up to four ticket desks open at any one time. The target time per overall transaction is 20 seconds. The average number of ticket sales per transaction is 1.8. All tickets indicate specific seat positions, and these are allocated on a first-come-first-served basis.

(a) Reflect on the main differences between the two cinemas from the perspectives of their operations managers. In other words, what are the advantages and disadvantages of the two different methods of scheduling the films onto the screens?

(b) Find out the running times and classification of eight popular films. Try to schedule these onto the UCI screens, taking account of what popularity you might expect at different times. Allow at least 20 minutes for emptying, cleaning, and admitting the next audience, and 15 minutes for advertising, before the start of the film.

(c) Visit your local cinema (meet the manager if you can). Compare the operations with those at Kinepolis and UCI, particularly in terms of scheduling.

Notes on chapter

1   Sources: Farman, J. (1999) 'Les Coulisses du Vol', Air France. Talk presented by Richard E. Stone, NorthWest Airlines, at the IMA Industrial Problems Seminar, 1998.

2   Source: Interview with Joanne Cheung, Steve Deeley and other staff at Godfrey Hall, BMW Dealership, Coventry.

3   Wallace, T.F. and Kretmar, M.K. (2001) *ERP: Making it happen,* Wiley, New York.

4   Goldratt, E.Y. and Cox, J. (1984) *The Goal,* North River Press.

Taking it further

Goldratt, E.Y. and Cox, J. (1984) *The Goal,* **North River Press.** Don't read this if you like good novels but do read this if you want an enjoyable way of understanding some of the complexities of scheduling. It particularly applies to the drum, buffer, rope concept described in this chapter and it also sets the scene for the discussion of OPT in Chapter 14.

Pinedo, M. and Chao, X. (1999) *Operations Scheduling with Applications in Manufacturing and Services,* **Irwin/McGraw-Hill, New York.** Specialist, comprehensive and detailed.

Sule, D.R. (1997) *Industrial Scheduling,* **PWSs Publishing Company.** Technical and detailed for those who like and/or need technical details.

Vollmann, T.E., Berry, W.L. and Whybark, D.C. (1992) *Manufacturing Planning and Control Systems* (3rd edn), **Irwin, Homewood, IL.** This is the bible of production planning and control. It deals with all the issues in this part of this textbook.

Useful websites

www.bpic.co.uk Some useful information on general planning and control topics.

www.cio.com/research/erp/edit/erpbasics.html Several descriptions and useful information on ERP-related topics.

www.erpfans.com Yes, even ERP has its own fan club! Debates and links for the enthusiast.

www.sap.com/index.epx *'Helping to build better businesses for more than three decades',* SAP has been the leading worldwide supplier of ERP systems for ages. They should know how to do it by now!

www.sapfans.com Another fan club, this one for SAP enthusiasts.

www.apics.org The American professional and education body that has its roots in planning and control activities.

FURTHER RESOURCES

For further resources including examples, animated diagrams, self test questions, excel spreadsheets, active case studies and video materials please explore the CD accompanying this book.

Supplement to Chapter 10
Materials Requirements Planning (MRP)

Introduction

Materials Requirements Planning (MRP) is an approach to calculating how many parts or materials of particular types are required and at what times they are required. This requires data files which, when the MRP program is run, can be checked and updated. Figure 10.14 shows how these files relate to each other. The first inputs to MRP are customer orders and forecast demand. MRP performs its calculations based on the combination of these two parts of future demand. All other requirements are derived from, and dependent on, this demand information.

Master production schedule

The master production schedule (MPS) forms the main input to materials requirements planning and contains a statement of the volume and timing of the end products to be made. It drives all the production and supply activities that eventually will come together to form the end products. It is the basis for the planning and utilization of labour and equipment, and it determines the provisioning of materials and cash. The MPS should include all sources of demand, such as spare parts, internal production promises, etc. For example, if a manufacturer of earth excavators plans an exhibition of its products and allows a project team to raid the stores so that it can build two pristine examples to be exhibited, this is likely to leave the factory short of parts. MPS can also be used in service organizations. For example, in a hospital theatre there is a master schedule that contains a statement of which operations are planned and when. This can be used to provision materials for the operations, such as the sterile instruments, blood and dressings. It may also govern the scheduling of staff for operations.

Figure 10.14   Materials requirements planning (MRP) schematic

The master production schedule record

Master production schedules are time-phased records of each end product, which contain a statement of demand and currently available stock of each finished item. Using this information, the available inventory is projected ahead in time. When there is insufficient inventory to satisfy forward demand, order quantities are entered on the master schedule line. Table 10.2 is a simplified example of part of a master production schedule for one item. In the first row the known sales orders and any forecast are combined to form 'Demand'. The second row, 'Available', shows how much inventory of this item is expected to be in stock at the end of each weekly period. The opening inventory balance, 'On hand', is shown separately at the bottom of the record. The third row is the master production schedule, or MPS; this shows how many finished items need to be completed and available in each week to satisfy demand.

'Chase demand' or level master production schedules

In the example in Table 10.2, the MPS increases as demand increases and aims to keep available inventory at 0. The master production schedule is 'chasing' demand (see Chapter 8) and so adjusting the provision of resources. An alternative 'levelled' MPS for this situation is shown in Table 10.3. Level scheduling involves averaging the amount required to be completed to smooth out peaks and troughs. It generates more inventory than the previous MPS.

'Available to promise' (ATP)

The master production schedule provides the information to the sales function on what can be promised to customers and when delivery can be promised. The sales function can load known sales orders against the master production schedule and keep track of what is 'available to promise' (ATP) (see Table 10.4). The ATP line in the master production schedule shows the maximum that is still available in any one week, against which sales orders can be loaded.

Table 10.2 Example of a master production schedule

				Week number					
	1	2	3	4	5	6	7	8	9
Demand	10	10	10	10	15	15	15	20	20
Available	20	10	0	0	0	0	0	0	0
MPS	0	0	10	10	15	15	15	20	20
On hand	30								

Table 10.3 Example of a 'level' master production schedule

				Week number					
	1	2	3	4	5	6	7	8	9
Demand	10	10	10	10	15	15	15	20	20
Available	31	32	33	34	30	26	22	13	4
MPS	11	11	11	11	11	11	11	11	11
On hand	30								

Table 10.4 Example of a level master production schedule including 'available to promise'

		Week number							
	1	**2**	**3**	**4**	**5**	**6**	**7**	**8**	**9**
Demand	10	10	10	10	15	15	15	20	20
Sales orders	10	10	10	8	4				
Available	31	32	33	34	30	26	22	13	4
ATP	31	1	1	3	7	11	11	11	11
MPS	11	11	11	11	11	11	11	11	11
On hand	30								

The bill of materials (BOM)

From the master schedule, MRP calculates the required volume and timing of assemblies, sub-assemblies and materials. To do this it needs information on what parts are required for each product. This is called the 'bill of materials'. Initially it is simplest to think about these as a product structure. The product structure in Figure 10.15 is a simplified structure showing the parts required to make a simple board game. Different 'levels of assembly' are shown with the finished product (the boxed game) at level 0, the parts and sub-assemblies that go into the boxed game at level 1, the parts that go into the sub-assemblies at level 2, and so on.

A more convenient form of the product structure is the 'indented bill of materials'. Table 10.5 shows the whole indented bill of materials for the board game. The term

Figure 10.15 Product structure for a simple board game

Table 10.5   Indented bill of materials for board game

Part number: 00289

Description: Board game

Level: 0

Level	Part number	Description	Quantity
0	00289	Board game	1
. 1	10077	Box lid	1
. 1	10089	Box base assembly	1
. . 2	20467	Box base	1
. . 2	10062	TV label	1
. . 2	23988	Inner tray	1
. 1	10023	Quest cards set	1
. 1	10045	Character set	1
. 1	10067	Die	2
. 1	10062	TV label	1
. 1	10033	Game board	1
. 1	10056	Rules booklet	1

'indented' refers to the indentation of the level of assembly, shown in the left-hand column. Multiples of some parts are required; this means that MRP has to know the required number of each part to be able to multiply up the requirements. Also, the same part (for example, the TV label, part number 10062) may be used in different parts of the product structure. This means that MRP has to cope with this commonality of parts and, at some stage, aggregate the requirements to check how many labels in total are required.

Inventory records

MRP calculations need to recognize that some required items may already be in stock. So, it is necessary, starting at level 0 of each bill, to check how much inventory is available of each finished product, sub-assembly and component, and then to calculate what is termed the 'net' requirements, that is the extra requirements needed to supplement the inventory so that demand can be met. This requires that three main inventory records are kept: the item master file, which contains the unique standard identification code for each part or component; the transaction file, which keeps a record of receipts into stock, issues from stock and a running balance; and the location file, which identifies where inventory is located.

The MRP netting process

The information needs of MRP are important, but it is not the 'heart' of the MRP procedure. At its core, MRP is a systematic process of taking this planning information and calculating the volume and timing requirements that will satisfy demand. The most important element of this is the MRP netting process.

Figure 10.16 illustrates the process that MRP performs to calculate the volumes of materials required. The master production schedule is 'exploded', examining the implications of the schedule through the bill of materials, checking how many sub-assemblies

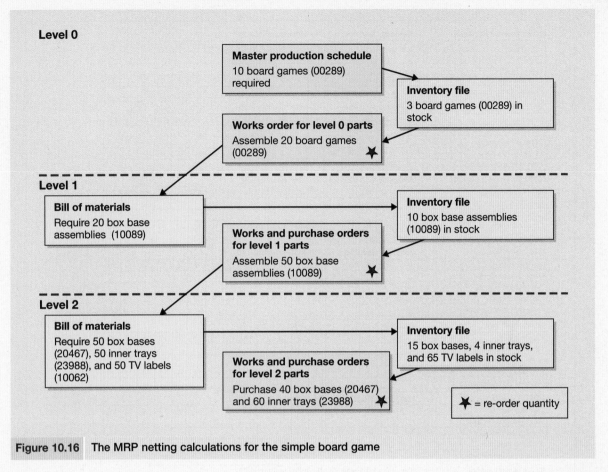

Figure 10.16   The MRP netting calculations for the simple board game

and parts are required. Before moving down the bill of materials to the next level, MRP checks how many of the required parts are already available in stock. It then generates 'works orders', or requests, for the net requirements of items. These form the schedule which is again exploded through the bill of materials at the next level down. This process continues until the bottom level of the bill of materials is reached.

Back-scheduling

In addition to calculating the volume of materials required, MRP also considers when each of these parts is required, that is, the timing and scheduling of materials. It does this by a process called back-scheduling which takes into account the lead time (the time allowed for completion of each stage of the process) at every level of assembly. Again using the example of the board game, assume that 10 board games are required to be finished by a notional planning day which we will term day 20. To determine when we need to start work on all the parts that make up the game, we need to know all the lead times that are stored in MRP files for each part (see Table 10.6).

Using the lead-time information, the programme is worked backwards to determine the tasks that have to be performed and the purchase orders that have to be placed. Given the lead times and inventory levels shown in Table 10.6, the MRP records shown in Figure 10.17 can be derived.

00289: Treasure Hunt game   Assembly lead time = 2   Re-order quantity = 20

Day Number:	0	1	2	3	4	5	6	7	8	9	10	11	12	13	14	15	16	17	18	19	20
Requirements Gross																					10
Scheduled Receipts																					
On hand Inventory	3	3	3	3	3	3	3	3	3	3	3	3	3	3	3	3	3	3	3	3	13
Planned Order Release																			20		

10077: Box lid   Purchase lead time = 8   Re-order quantity = 25

Day Number:	0	1	2	3	4	5	6	7	8	9	10	11	12	13	14	15	16	17	18	19	20
Requirements Gross																			20		
Scheduled Receipts																					
On hand Inventory	4	4	4	4	4	4	4	4	4	4	4	4	4	4	4	4	4	9	9	9	9
Planned Order Release											25										

10089: Box base assembly   Assembly lead time = 4   Re-order quantity = 50

Day Number:	0	1	2	3	4	5	6	7	8	9	10	11	12	13	14	15	16	17	18	19	20
Requirements Gross																			20		
Scheduled Receipts																					
On hand Inventory	10	10	10	10	10	10	10	10	10	10	10	10	10	10	10	10	10	10	40	40	40
Planned Order Release														50							

20467: Box base   Purchase lead time = 12   Re-order quantity = 40

Day Number:	0	1	2	3	4	5	6	7	8	9	10	11	12	13	14	15	16	17	18	19	20
Requirements Gross															50						
Scheduled Receipts																					
On hand Inventory	15	15	15	15	15	15	15	15	15	15	15	15	15	15	5	5	5	5	5	5	5
Planned Order Release			40																		

23988: Inner tray   Purchase lead time = 14   Re-order quantity = 60

Day Number:	0	1	2	3	4	5	6	7	8	9	10	11	12	13	14	15	16	17	18	19	20
Requirements Gross															50						
Scheduled Receipts																					
On hand Inventory	4	4	4	4	4	4	4	4	4	4	4	4	4	4	14	14	14	14	14	14	14
Planned Order Release	60																				

10062: TV label   Purchase lead time = 8   Re-order quantity = 100

Day Number:	0	1	2	3	4	5	6	7	8	9	10	11	12	13	14	15	16	17	18	19	20
Requirements Gross															50				20		
Scheduled Receipts																					
On hand Inventory	65	65	65	65	65	65	65	65	65	65	65	65	65	65	15	15	15	15	95	95	95
Planned Order Release											100										

10023: Quest card set   Purchase lead time = 3   Re-order quantity = 50

Day Number:	0	1	2	3	4	5	6	7	8	9	10	11	12	13	14	15	16	17	18	19	20
Requirements Gross																			20		
Scheduled Receipts																					
On hand Inventory	4	4	4	4	4	4	4	4	4	4	4	4	4	4	4	4	4	4	34	34	34
Planned Order Release																50					

10045: Character set   Purchase lead time = 3   Re-order quantity = 50

Day Number:	0	1	2	3	4	5	6	7	8	9	10	11	12	13	14	15	16	17	18	19	20
Requirements Gross																			20		
Scheduled Receipts																					
On hand Inventory	46	46	46	46	46	46	46	46	46	46	46	46	46	46	46	46	46	46	26	26	26
Planned Order Release																					

10067: Die   Purchase lead time = 5   Re-order quantity = 80

Day Number:	0	1	2	3	4	5	6	7	8	9	10	11	12	13	14	15	16	17	18	19	20
Requirements Gross																			40		
Scheduled Receipts																					
On hand Inventory	3	3	3	3	3	3	3	3	3	3	3	3	3	3	3	3	3	3	3	3	13
Planned Order Release														80							

10033: Game board   Purchase lead time = 15   Re-order quantity = 50

Day Number:	0	1	2	3	4	5	6	7	8	9	10	11	12	13	14	15	16	17	18	19	20
Requirements Gross																			20		
Scheduled Receipts																					
On hand Inventory	8	8	8	8	8	8	8	8	8	8	8	8	8	8	8	8	8	8	38	38	38
Planned Order Release			50																		

10056: Rules booklet   Purchase lead time = 3   Re-order quantity = 80

Day Number:	0	1	2	3	4	5	6	7	8	9	10	11	12	13	14	15	16	17	18	19	20
Requirements Gross																			20		
Scheduled Receipts																					
On hand Inventory	0	0	0	0	0	0	0	0	0	0	0	0	0	0	0	0	0	0	60	60	60
Planned Order Release														80							

Figure 10.17   Extract from the MRP records for the simple board game (lead times indicated by arrows ◄───►)

		Inventory on-hand at day 0	Lead time (days)	Reorder quantity
Table 10.6	**Back-scheduling of requirements in MRP**			
Part no.	*Description*			
00289	Board game	3	2	20
10077	Box lid	4	8	25
10089	Box base assembly	10	4	50
20467	Box base	15	12	40
23988	Inner tray	4	14	60
10062	TV label	65	8	100
10023	Quest cards set	4	3	50
10045	Character set	46	3	50
10067	Die	22	5	80
10033	Game board	8	15	50
10056	Rules booklet	0	3	80

MRP capacity checks

The MRP process needs a feedback loop to check whether a plan was achievable and whether it has actually been achieved. Closing this planning loop in MRP systems involves checking production plans against available capacity and, if the proposed plans are not achievable at any level, revising them. All but the simplest MRP systems are now closed-loop systems. They use three planning routines to check production plans against the operation's resources at three levels.

- *Resource requirements plans (RRPs)* involve looking forward in the long term to predict the requirements for large structural parts of the operation, such as the numbers, locations and sizes of new plants.
- *Rough-cut capacity plans (RCCPs)* are used in the medium to short term, to check the master production schedules against known capacity bottlenecks, in case capacity constraints are broken. The feedback loop at this level checks the MPS and key resources only.
- *Capacity requirements plans (CRPs)* are used to look at the day-to-day effects of the works orders issued from the MRP on the loading of individual process stages.

11 LEAN SYNCHRONIZATION

Introduction

Lean synchronization aims to meet demand instantaneously, with perfect quality and no waste. This involves supplying products and services in perfect synchronization with the demand for them, using 'lean' or 'just-in-time' (JIT) principles. These principles were once a radical departure from traditional operations practice, but have now become orthodox in promoting the synchronization of flow through processes, operations and supply networks. (See Figure 11.1.)

Source: © Flying Colours Ltd/Getty Images/Digital Vision

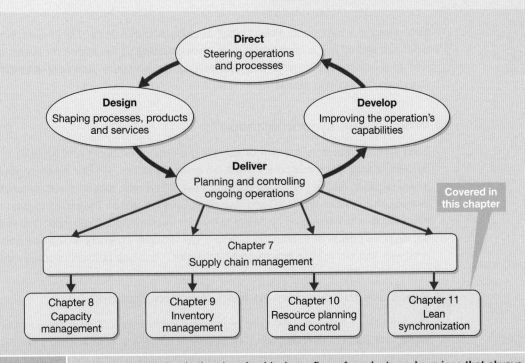

| **Figure 11.1** | Lean synchronization is the aim of achieving a flow of products and services that always delivers exactly what customers want, in exact quantities, exactly when needed, exactly where required, and at the lowest possible cost |

Executive summary

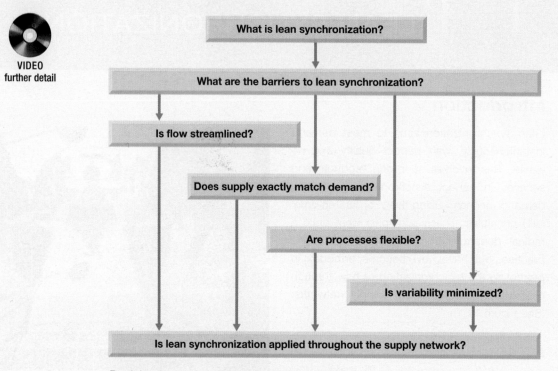

Decision logic chain for lean synchronization

Each chapter is structured around a set of diagnostic questions. These questions suggest what you should ask in order to gain an understanding of the important issues of a topic, and as a result, improve your decision making. An executive summary, addressing these questions, is provided below.

What is lean synchronization?

Lean synchronization is the aim of achieving a flow of products and services that always delivers exactly what customers want, in exact quantities, exactly when needed, exactly where required, and at the lowest possible cost. It is a term that is almost synonymous with terms such as 'just-in-time' (JIT) and 'lean operations principles'. The central idea is that if items flow smoothly, uninterrupted by delays in inventories, not only is throughput time reduced, but the negative effects of in-process inventory are avoided. Inventory is seen as obscuring the problems that exist within processes and therefore inhibiting process improvement.

What are the barriers to lean synchronization?

The aim of lean synchronization can be inhibited in three ways. First is the failure to eliminate waste in all parts of the operation. The causes of waste are more extensive than is generally understood. The second is a failure to involve all the people within the operation in the shared task of smoothing flow and eliminating waste. Japanese proponents of lean synchronization often use a set of 'basic working practices' to ensure involvement. Third is the failure to adopt continuous improvement principles. Because pure lean synchronization is an aim rather than something that can be implemented quickly, it requires the continual application of incremental improvement steps to reach it.

Is flow streamlined?

Long process routes are wasteful and cause delay and inventory build-up. Physically reconfiguring processes to reduce distance travelled and aid cooperation between staff can help to streamline flow. Similarly, ensuring flow visibility helps to make improvement to flow easier. Sometimes this can involve small-scale technologies that can reduce fluctuations in flow volume.

Does supply exactly match demand?

The aim of lean synchronization is to meet demand exactly: neither too much nor too little and only when it is needed. Achieving this often means pull control principles. The most common method of doing this is the use of kanbans, simple signalling devices that prevent the accumulation of excess inventory.

Are processes flexible?

Responding exactly to demand only when it is needed often requires a degree of flexibility in processes, both to cope with unexpected demand and to allow processes to change between different activities without excessive delay. This often means reducing changeover times in technologies.

Is variability minimized?

Variability in processes disrupts flow and prevents lean synchronization. Variability includes quality variability and schedule variability. Statistical process control (SPC) principles are useful in reducing quality variability. Levelled scheduling and mixed modelling can be used to reduce flow variability, and total productive maintenance (TPM) can reduce variability caused by breakdowns.

Is lean synchronization applied throughout the supply network?

The same benefits of lean synchronization that apply within operations can also apply between operations. Furthermore, the same principles that can be used to achieve lean synchronization within operations can be used to achieve it between operations. This is more difficult, partly because of the complexity of flow and partly because supply networks are prone to the type of unexpected fluctuations that are easier to control within operations.

What is lean synchronization?

Synchronization means that the flow of products and services always delivers exactly what customers want (perfect quality), in exact quantities (neither too much nor too little), exactly when needed (not too early nor too late), and exactly where required (not to the wrong location). *Lean* synchronization is to do all this at the lowest possible cost. It results in items flowing rapidly and smoothly through processes, operations and supply networks.

The benefits of synchronized flow

The best way to understand how lean synchronization differs from more traditional approaches to managing flow is to contrast the two simple processes in Figure 11.2. The traditional approach assumes that each stage in the process will place its output in an inventory that 'buffers' that stage from the next one downstream in the process. The next stage down will then (eventually) take outputs from the inventory, process them, and pass them through to the next buffer inventory. These buffers are there to 'insulate' each stage from its neighbours, making each stage relatively independent so that if, for example, stage A stops operating for some reason, stage B can continue, at least for a time.

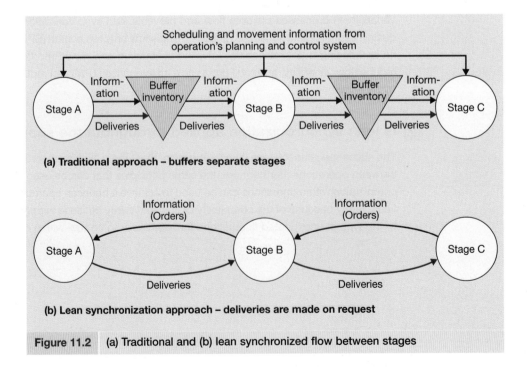

(a) Traditional approach – buffers separate stages

(b) Lean synchronization approach – deliveries are made on request

Figure 11.2   (a) Traditional and (b) lean synchronized flow between stages

The larger the buffer inventory, the greater the degree of insulation between the stages. This insulation has to be paid for in terms of inventory and slow throughput times, because items will spend time waiting in the buffer inventories.

The main 'learning' argument against this traditional approach lies in the very conditions it seeks to promote, namely the insulation of the stages from one another. When a problem occurs at one stage, the problem will not immediately be apparent elsewhere in the system. The responsibility for solving the problem will be centred largely on the people within that stage, and the consequences of the problem will be prevented from spreading to the whole system. Contrast this with the pure lean synchronized process illustrated in Figure 11.2. Here items are processed and then passed directly to the next stage 'just-in-time' for them to be processed further. Problems at any stage have a very different effect in such a system. Now if stage A stops processing, stage B will notice immediately and stage C very soon after. Stage A's problem is now quickly exposed to the whole process, which is immediately affected by the problem. This means that the responsibility for solving the problem is no longer confined to the staff at stage A. It is now shared by everyone, considerably improving the chances of the problem being solved, if only because it is now too important to be ignored. In other words, by preventing items accumulating between stages, the operation has increased the chances of the intrinsic efficiency of the plant being improved.

Non-synchronized approaches seek to encourage efficiency by protecting each part of the process from disruption. The lean synchronized approach takes the opposite view. Exposure of the system (although not suddenly, as in our simplified example) to problems can both make them more evident and change the 'motivation structure' of the whole system towards solving the problems. Lean synchronization sees accumulations of inventory as a 'blanket of obscurity' that lies over the production system and prevents problems being noticed. This same argument can be applied when, instead of queues of material, or information (inventory), an operation has to deal with queues of customers. Table 11.1 shows how certain aspects of inventory are analogous to certain aspects of queues.

Operations principle
When buffer inventory is used to insulate stages or processes it localizes the motivation to improve.

Table 11.1 Inventories of materials. Information or customers have similar characteristics

	Of material (queue of material)	Of information (queue of information)	Of customers (queue of people)
Cost	Ties up working capital	Less current information and so worth less	Wastes customers' time
Space	Needs storage space	Needs memory capacity	Needs waiting area
Quality	Defects hidden, possible damage	Defects hidden, possible data corruption	Gives negative perception
Decoupling	Makes stages independent	Makes stages independent	Promotes job specialization/ fragmentation
Utilization	Stages kept busy by work in progress	Stages kept busy by work in data queues	Servers kept busy by waiting customers
Coordination	Avoids need for synchronization	Avoids need for straight-through processing	Avoids having to match supply and demand

Source: Adapted from Fitzsimmons, J.A. (1990) 'Making continual improvement: a competitive strategy for service firms', in Bowen, D.E., Chase, R.B., Cummings, T.G. and Associates (eds), *Service Management Effectiveness*, Jossey-Bass, San Francisco.

Figure 11.3 Reducing the level of inventory (water) allows operations management (the ship) to see the problems in the operation (the rocks) and work to reduce them

The river and rocks analogy

The idea of obscuring effects of inventory is often illustrated diagrammatically, as in Figure 11.3. The many problems of the operation are shown as rocks in a river bed that cannot be seen because of the depth of the water. The water in this analogy represents the inventory in the operation. Yet, even though the rocks cannot be seen, they slow the progress of the river's flow and cause turbulence. Gradually reducing the depth of the water (inventory) exposes the worst of the problems which can be resolved, after which the water is lowered further, exposing more problems, and so on. The same argument will also apply for the flow between whole processes, or whole operations. For example, stages A, B and C in Figure 11.2 could be a supplier operation, a manufacturer and a customer's operation, respectively.

Synchronization, 'lean' and 'just-in-time'

Different terms are used to describe what here we call lean synchronization. Our shortened definition – *'lean synchronization aims to meet demand instantaneously, with perfect quality and no waste'* – could also be used to describe the general concept of 'lean', or 'just-in-time' (JIT). The concept of 'lean' stresses the elimination of waste, while 'just-in-time' emphasizes the idea of producing items only when they are needed. But all three concepts overlap to a large degree, and no definition fully conveys the full implications for operations practice. Here we use the term lean synchronization because it best describes the impact of these ideas on flow and delivery.

Two companies that have implemented lean synchronization are briefly described below. One is the company that is generally credited with doing most to develop the whole concept; the other is a far smaller craft-based company that nevertheless has derived benefits from adopting some of the principles.

Example | Toyota

Seen as the leading practitioner and the main originator of the lean approach, the Toyota Motor Company has progressively synchronized all its processes simultaneously to give high quality, fast throughput and exceptional productivity. It has done this by developing a set of practices that has largely shaped what we now call 'lean' or 'just-in-time' but which Toyota calls the Toyota Production System (TPS). The TPS has two themes, 'just-in-time' and 'jidoka'. Just-in-time is defined as the rapid and coordinated movement of parts throughout the production system and supply network

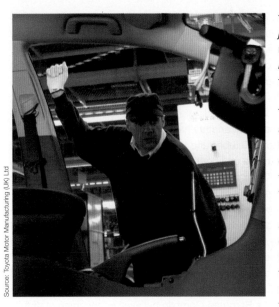

to meet customer demand. It is operationalized by means of *hei-junka* (levelling and smoothing the flow of items), *kanban* (signalling to the preceding process that more parts are needed) and *nagare* (laying out processes to achieve smoother flow of parts throughout the production process). *Jidoka* is described as 'humanizing the interface between operator and machine'. Toyota's philosophy is that the machine is there to serve the operator's purpose. The operator should be left free to exercise his or her judgement. Jidoka is operationalized by means of fail-safeing (or machine jidoka), line-stop authority (or human jidoka), and visual control (at-a-glance status of production processes and visibility of process standards).

Toyota believes that both just-in-time and jidoka should be applied ruthlessly to the elimination of waste, where waste is defined as 'anything other than the minimum amount of equipment, items, part and workers that are absolutely essential to production'. Fujio Cho of Toyota identified seven types of waste that must be eliminated from all operations processes. They are waste from overproduction, waste from waiting time, transportation waste, inventory waste, processing waste, waste of motion, and waste from product defects. Beyond this, authorities on Toyota claim that its strength lies in understanding the differences between the tools and practices used with Toyota operations and the overall philosophy of their approach to lean synchronization. This is what some have called the apparent paradox of the Toyota production system, 'namely, that activities, connections and production flows in a Toyota factory are rigidly scripted, yet at the same time Toyota's operations are enormously flexible and adaptable. Activities and processes are constantly being challenged and pushed to a higher level of performance, enabling the company to continually innovate and improve'.

One influential study of Toyota identified four rules that guide the design, delivery, and development activities within the company.[1]

1 All work shall be highly specified as to content, sequence, timing and outcome.
2 Every customer–supplier connection must be direct and there must be an unambiguous yes or no method of sending requests and receiving responses.
3 The route for every product and service must be simple and direct.
4 Any improvement must be made in accordance with the scientific method, under the guidance of a teacher, and at the lowest possible level in the organization.

| Example | Gamblin adopts just-in-time[2] |

Gamblin adopts just-in-time[2]

Gamblin Artists Colors is a small company with a growing reputation for making high-quality oil painting materials. Paints are made from formulas developed by Robert Gamblin over 20 years to

have the luscious working properties and permanence that artists particularly value. From its factory in Portland, Oregon, it makes paints for artists and restoration experts throughout the United States and the rest of the world. It is a company founded on high-quality craft skills and an appreciation of what artists really want from their materials. Not the type of company one would normally associate with the just-in-time and lean synchronization, yet not only did Martha Bergman-Gamblin, co-owner and General Manager of Gamblin, adopt the ideas, she has made a success of adapting them to the particular needs of the company. *'We started talking about making bigger and bigger batches of paint.*

Now, a 100 millilitre tube of titanium weighs close to half a kilo. You add that up, and it's a huge amount of weight. When someone started talking about putting over 200 kilos of paint on a rail above our heads, I knew I needed to talk to an engineer.'

Before its adoption of lean principles, the company made each colour in batches of 1200 tubes of paint at a time. The paint could then spend anything from three to six months in the company's finished goods inventory before being sold. By carefully scheduling colours in a sequence that keeps similar colours together (for example, different kinds of red all made on the same day) the cost and time involved in changing from one colour to another has shrunk to the point where colours can be made economically in batches of about 500 tubes and inventory is down to less than half of its previous level. This allowed the company to free up about $200,000 in cash, a bonus that is particularly important for any small company. *'Each colour turns over twice as fast'*, says Martha Bergman-Gamblin. *'Instead of putting three months of product on the shelf, it's now down to six weeks, so our cash returns twice as fast. Many small businesses don't realize that they need a manufacturing philosophy. Old style manufacturing works on a push system. The whole system is about putting a pig in a python. There is one huge bite that moves through the shop. Even though it is counter-intuitive at first, we have increased creativity and increased flexibility by reducing variation.'*

Quality and continuous improvement are also integral parts of the Gamblin approach. All staff are involved in problem solving and process improvement. The aim is for the production crew to solve one process problem every week. Martha Bergman-Gamblin believes in engaging staff fully in the improvement process. *'In each station we ask the question, "Am I making good stuff?". If the answer is no, the production process stops. The manager is called, and there is 20 minutes to make a decision. Adjust and fix, or pull. The decision gets made right at the station. People are not checking their minds at the door. We have better jobs, better teams, better management and a better environment for personal growth.'*

What do these two operations have in common?

Here are two companies separated by product, culture, size, location, and their route to adopting lean synchronization principles. Toyota took decades to develop a fully integrated and coherent philosophy to managing their operations and have become one of the world's leading and most profitable automotive companies as a result. Gamblin Paints adopted and adapted selected ideas from the lean synchronization philosophy and yet still gained some benefits. That is because, notwithstanding the differences between the two companies, the basic principles of lean synchronization remain the same, namely aiming to achieve perfect synchronization through smooth and even flow. But lean synchronization is an *aim*. It is not something that can simply be implemented overnight. Both these organizations have worked hard at overcoming the barriers to lean synchronization. These can be summarized as the elimination of all waste, the involvement of everyone in the business, and the adoption of a continuous improvement philosophy. The focus on eliminating waste uses four important methods: streamlining flow, making sure that supply matches demand exactly, increasing process flexibility, and reducing the effects of variability. And, although rooted in manufacturing, the techniques of lean or just-in-time philosophies are now being extended to service operations.

Before further discussion it is important to be clear on the distinction between the *aim* (lean synchronization), the *approach to overcoming the barriers* to achieving lean synchronization, the *methods of eliminating waste,* and the various *techniques* that can be used to help eliminate waste. The relationship between these elements is shown in Figure 11.4.

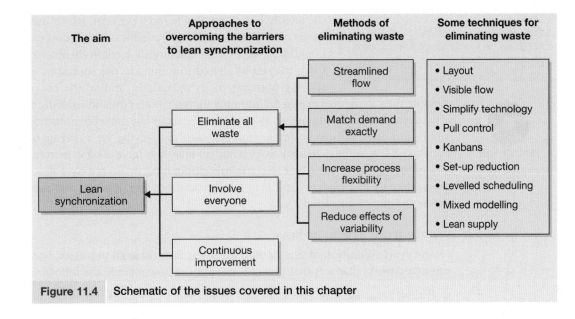

Figure 11.4 Schematic of the issues covered in this chapter

What are the barriers to lean synchronization?

The aim of pure lean synchronization represents an ideal of smooth, uninterrupted flow without delay, waste or imperfection of any kind. The supply and demand between stages in each process, between processes in each operation, and between operations in each supply network are all perfectly synchronized. It represents the ultimate in what customers are looking for from an operation. But first one must identify the barriers to achieving this ideal state. We group these under three headings:

- Failure to eliminate waste in all parts of the operation
- Failure to harness the contribution of all the people within the operation
- Failure to establish improvement as a continuous activity.

The waste elimination barrier

Arguably the most significant part of the lean philosophy is its focus on the elimination of all forms of waste. Waste can be defined as any activity that does not add value. For example, a study by Cummins Worldwide Fortune 500, the engine company, showed that, at best, an engine was being worked on for only 15 per cent of the time it was in the factory.[3] At worst, this fell to 9 per cent, which meant that for 91 per cent of its time, the operation was adding cost to the engine, not adding value. Although already a relatively efficient manufacturer, the results alerted Cummins to the enormous waste which still lay dormant in its operations, and which no performance measure then in use had exposed. Cummins shifted its objectives to reducing the wasteful activities and to enriching the value-added ones. Exactly the same phenomenon applies in service processes. Relatively simple requests, such as applying for a driving licence, may only take a few minutes to actually process, yet take days (or weeks) to be returned.

Identifying waste is the first step towards eliminating it. Toyota have described seven types. Here we consolidate these into four broad categories of waste that apply in many different types of operation.

Waste from irregular flow

Perfect synchronization means smooth and even flow through processes, operations and supply networks. Barriers that prevent streamlined flow include the following.

- *Waiting time.* Machine efficiency and labour efficiency are two popular measures that are widely used to measure machine and labour waiting time, respectively. Less obvious is the time for which items wait as inventory, there simply to keep operators busy.
- *Transport.* Moving items around the plant, together with double and triple handling, does not add value. Layout changes that bring processes closer together, improvements in transport methods and workplace organization can all reduce waste.
- *Process inefficiencies.* The process itself may be a source of waste. Some operations may exist only because of poor component design, or poor maintenance, and so could be eliminated.
- *Inventory.* All inventory should become a target for elimination. However, it is only by tackling the causes of inventory, such as irregular flow, that it can be reduced.
- *Wasted motions.* An operator may look busy but sometimes no value is being added by the work. Simplification of work is a rich source of reduction in the waste of motion.

Waste from inexact supply

Perfect synchronization supplies exactly what is wanted, exactly when it is needed. Any under- or oversupply and any early or late delivery will result in waste. Barriers to achieving an exact match between supply and demand include the following.

- *Overproduction or underproduction.* Supplying more than, or less than, the amount immediately needed by the next stage, process or operation. This is the greatest source of waste according to Toyota.
- *Early or late delivery.* Items should only arrive exactly when they are needed. Early delivery is as wasteful as late delivery.
- *Inventory.* Again, all inventories should become a target for elimination. However, it is only by tackling the causes of inventory, such as inexact supply, that it can be reduced.

Waste from inflexible response

Customer needs can vary, in terms of what they want, how much they want, and when they want it. However, processes usually find it more convenient to change what they do relatively infrequently, because every change implies some kind of cost. That is why hospitals schedule specialist clinics only at particular times, and why machines often make a batch of similar products together. Yet responding to customer demands exactly and instantaneously requires a high degree of process flexibility. Symptoms of inadequate flexibility include the following.

- *Large batches.* Sending a batch of items through a process inevitably increases inventory as the batch moves through the whole process (what the Gamblin Paints example at the beginning of the chapter referred to as the 'pig in a python').
- *Delays between activities.* The longer the time (and the cost) of changing over from one activity to another, the more difficult it is to synchronize flow to match customer demand instantaneously.
- *More variation in activity mix than in customer demand.* If the mix of activities in different time periods varies more than customer demand varies, then some 'batching' of activities must be taking place.

Waste from variability

Synchronization implies exact levels of quality. If there is variability in quality levels then customers will not consider themselves as being adequately supplied. Variability, therefore, is an important barrier to achieving synchronized supply. Symptoms of poor variability include the following.

- *Poor reliability of equipment.* Unreliable equipment usually indicates a lack of conformance in quality levels. It also means that there will be irregularity in supplying customers. Either way, it prevents synchronization of supply.
- *Defective products or services.* Waste caused by poor quality is significant in most operations. Service or product errors cause both customers and processes to waste time until they are corrected.

But capacity utilization may be sacrificed in the short term

A paradox in the lean synchronization concept is that adoption may mean some sacrifice of capacity utilization. In organizations that place a high value on the utilization of capacity this can prove particularly difficult to accept. But it is necessary. Return to the process shown in Figure 11.2. When stoppages occur in the traditional system, the buffers allow each stage to continue working and thus achieve high capacity utilization. The high utilization does not necessarily make the system as a whole produce more parts. Often the extra production goes into the large buffer inventories. In a synchronized lean process, any stoppage will affect the rest of the system, causing stoppages throughout the operation. This will necessarily lead to lower capacity utilization, at least in the short term. However, there is no point in producing output just for its own sake. Unless the output is useful and enables the operation as a whole to produce saleable output, there is no point in producing it anyway. In fact, producing just to keep utilization high is not only pointless, it is counter-productive, because the extra inventory produced merely serves to make improvements less likely. Figure 11.5 illustrates the two approaches to capacity utilization.

> **Operations principle**
> Focusing on lean synchronization can initially reduce resource utilization.

The involvement barrier

An organizational culture that supports lean synchronization must place a very significant emphasis on involving everyone in the organization. This approach to people management (sometimes called the 'respect-for-people' system, after a rough translation from the Japanese) is seen by some as the most controversial aspect of the lean philosophy. It encourages (and often requires) team-based problem-solving, job enrichment, job rotation and multi-skilling. The intention is to encourage a high degree of personal responsibility, engagement and 'ownership' of the job. Some Japanese companies refer to operationalizing the 'involvement of everyone' principle by adopting 'basic working practices'. They are held to be the basic preparation of the operation and its employees

(a) Traditional approach   (b) Lean synchronization approach

Figure 11.5   The different views of capacity utilization in (a) traditional and (b) lean synchronization approaches to planning and controlling flow

for implementing lean synchronization. They include the following.

- *Discipline.* Work standards that are critical for the safety of staff, the environment, and quality, must be followed by everyone all the time.
- *Flexibility.* It should be possible to expand responsibilities to the extent of people's capabilities. This applies as equally to managers as it does to shop-floor personnel. Barriers to flexibility, such as grading structures and restrictive practices, should be removed.
- *Equality.* Unfair and divisive personnel policies should be discarded. Many companies implement the egalitarian message through to company uniforms, consistent pay structures which do not differentiate between full-time staff and hourly-rated staff, and open-plan offices.
- *Autonomy.* Delegate responsibility to people involved in direct activities so that management's task becomes one of supporting processes. Delegation includes giving staff the responsibility for stopping processes in the event of problems, scheduling work, gathering performance monitoring data, and general problem solving.
- *Development of personnel.* Over time, the aim is to create more company members who can support the rigours of being competitive.
- *Quality of working life (QWL).* This may include, for example, involvement in decision making, security of employment, enjoyment and working area facilities.
- *Creativity.* This is one of the indispensable elements of motivation. Creativity in this context means not just doing a job, but also improving how it is done, and building the improvement into the process.
- *Total people involvement.* Staff take on more responsibility to use their abilities to the benefit of the company as a whole. They are expected to participate in activities such as the selection of new recruits, dealing directly with suppliers and customers over schedules, quality issues and delivery information, spending improvement budgets, and planning and reviewing work done each day through communication meetings.

The concept of continuous learning is also central to the 'involvement of everyone' principle. For example, Toyota's approach to involving its employees includes using a learning method that allows employees to discover the Toyota Production System rules through problem solving. So, while the job is being performed, a supervisor/trainer asks a series of questions that gives the employee deeper insights into the work.[4] These questions could be:

- How do you do this work?
- How do you know you are doing this work correctly?
- How do you know that the outcome is free of defects?
- What do you do if you have a problem?

The continuous improvement barrier

Lean synchronization objectives are often expressed as ideals, such as our previous definition: 'to meet demand instantaneously with perfect quality and no waste'. While any operation's current performance may be far removed from such ideals, a fundamental lean belief is that it is possible to get closer to them over time. Without such beliefs to drive progress, lean proponents claim improvement is more likely to be transitory than continuous. This is why the concept of continuous improvement is such an important part of the lean philosophy. If its aims are set in terms of ideals which individual organizations may never fully achieve, then the emphasis must be on the way in which an organization moves closer to the ideal state. The Japanese word that incorporates the idea of continuous improvement is 'kaizen'. It is one of the main pillars of process improvement and is explained fully in Chapter 13.

Techniques to address the four sources of waste

Of the three barriers to achieving lean synchronization (reduce waste, involve everyone, and adopt continuous improvement), the last two are addressed further in Chapter 13. Therefore the rest of this chapter is devoted to what could be called the 'core' of lean synchronization. These are a collection of 'just-in-time' tools and techniques that are the means of cutting out waste. Although many of these techniques are used to reduce waste generally within processes, operations and supply networks, we will group the approaches to reducing waste under four main headings: streamlining flow, matching demand exactly, increasing process flexibility, and reducing the effects of variability.

DIAGNOSTIC QUESTION

Is flow streamlined?

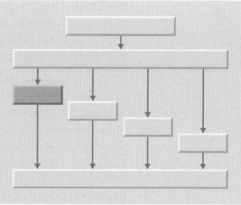

The smooth flow of materials, information and people in the operation is a central idea of lean synchronization. Long process routes provide opportunities for delay and inventory build-up, add no value, and slow down throughput time. So, the first contribution any operation can make to streamlining flow is to reconsider the basic layout of its processes. Primarily, reconfiguring the layout of a process to aid lean synchronization involves moving it down the 'natural diagonal' of process design that was discussed in

Chapter 4. Broadly speaking, this means moving from functional layouts towards cell-based layouts, or from cell-based layouts towards product layouts. Either way, it is necessary to move towards a layout that brings more systematization and control to the process flow. At a more detailed level, typical layout techniques include placing workstations close together so that inventory physically just cannot build up because there is no space for it to do so, and arranging workstations in such a way that all those who contribute to a common activity are in sight of each other and can provide mutual help, for example by facilitating movement between workstations to balance capacity.

> **Operations principle**
> Simple, transparent flow exposes sources of waste.

Examine the shape of process flow

The pattern that flow makes within or between processes is not a trivial issue. Processes that have adopted the practice of curving line arrangements into U-shaped or 'serpentine' arrangements can have a number of advantages (U shapes are usually used for shorter lines and serpentines for longer lines). One authority[5] sees the advantages of this type of flow pattern as *staffing flexibility and balance,* because the U shape enables one person to tend several jobs; *rework,* because it is easy to return faulty work to an earlier station; *free flow,* because long straight lines interfere with cross-travel in the rest of the operation; and *teamwork,* because the shape encourages a team feeling.

Ensure visibility

Appropriate layout also includes the extent to which all movement is transparent to everyone within the process. High visibility of flow makes it easier to recognize potential improvements to flow. It also promotes quality within a process because the more transparent the operation or process, the easier it is for all staff to share in its management and improvement. Problems are more easily detectable and information becomes simple, fast and visual. Visibility measures include the following.

- Clearly indicated process routes using signage
- Performance measures clearly displayed in the workplace
- Coloured lights used to indicate stoppages
- An area is devoted to displaying samples of one's own and competitors' process outputs, together with samples of good and defective output
- Visual control systems (e.g. kanbans, discussed later).

An important technique used to ensure flow visibility is the use of simple, but highly visual signals to indicate that a problem has occurred, together with operational authority to stop the process. For example, on an assembly line, if an employee detects some kind of quality problem, he or she could activate a signal that illuminates a light (called an 'andon' light) above the workstation and stops the line. Although this may seem to reduce the efficiency of the line, the idea is that this loss of efficiency in the short term is less than the accumulated losses of allowing defects to continue in the process. Unless problems are tackled immediately, they may never be corrected.

Use small-scale simple process technology

There may also be possibilities of encouraging smooth streamlined flow through the use of small-scale technologies, that is, using several small units of process technology (for example, machines) rather than one large unit. Small machines have several advantages over large ones. First, they can process different products and services simultaneously. For

Figure 11.6 Using several small machines rather than a single large one allows simultaneous processing, is more robust, and is more flexible

example, in Figure 11.6 one large machine produces a batch of A, followed by a batch of B, followed by a batch of C. However, if three smaller machines are used they can each produce A, B and/or C simultaneously. The system is also more robust. If one large machine breaks down, the whole system ceases to operate. If one of the three smaller machines breaks down, the system is still operating at two-thirds effectiveness. Small machines are also easily moved, so that layout flexibility is enhanced, and the risks of making errors in investment decisions are reduced. However, investment in capacity may increase in total because parallel facilities are needed, so utilization may be lower (see the earlier arguments).

Does supply exactly match demand?

The value of the supply of products or services is always time dependent. Something that is delivered early or late often has less value than something that is delivered exactly when it is needed. We can see many everyday examples of this. For example, parcel delivery companies charge more for guaranteed faster delivery. This is because our real need for the delivery is often for it to be as fast as possible. The closer to instantaneous delivery we can get, the more value the delivery has for us, and the more we are willing to pay for it. In fact delivery of information earlier than it is required can be even more harmful than late delivery because it results in information inventories that serve to confuse flow through the process. For example, an Australian tax office used to receive applications by mail, open the mail and send it through to the relevant department which, after processing it, sent it to the next department. This led to piles of unprocessed applications building up within its processes, causing problems in tracing applications, losing them, sorting through and prioritizing applications, and worst of all, long throughput times. Now they open mail only when the stages in front can process it. Each department requests more work only when they have processed previous work.

> **Operations principle**
> Delivering only and exactly, what is needed and when it is needed, smoothes flow and exposes waste.

Pull control

The exact matching of supply and demand is often best served by using 'pull control' wherever possible (discussed in Chapter 10). At its simplest, consider how some fast-food restaurants cook and assemble food and place it in the warm area only when the customer-facing server has sold an item. Production is being triggered only by real customer demand. Similarly supermarkets usually replenish their shelves only when customers have taken sufficient products off the shelf. The movement of goods from the 'back office' store to the shelf is triggered only by the 'empty-shelf' demand signal. Some construction companies make it a rule to call for material deliveries to their sites only the day before those items are actually needed. This not only reduces clutter and the chances of theft, it speeds up throughput time and reduces confusion and inventories. The essence of pull control is to let the downstream stage in a process, operation or supply network pull items through the system rather than have them 'pushed' to them by the supplying stage. As Richard Hall, an authority on lean operations put it, *'Don't send nothing nowhere, make 'em come and get it.'*[6]

Kanbans

The use of kanbans is one method of operationalizing pull control. Kanban is the Japanese for card or signal. It is sometimes called the 'invisible conveyor' that controls the transfer of items between the stages of an operation. In its simplest form, it is a card used by a customer stage to instruct its supplier stage to send more items. Kanbans can also take other forms. In some Japanese companies, they are solid plastic markers or even coloured ping-pong balls. Whichever kind of kanban is being used, the principle is always the same: the receipt of a kanban triggers the movement, production or supply of one unit or a standard container of units. If two kanbans are received, this triggers the movement, production or supply of two units or standard containers of units, and so on. Kanbans are the only means by which movement, production or supply can be authorized. Some companies use 'kanban squares'. These are marked spaces on the shop floor or bench that are drawn to fit one or more workpieces or containers. Only the existence of an empty square triggers production at the stage that supplies the square. As one would expect, at Toyota the key control tool is its kanban system. The kanban is seen as serving three purposes:

- It is an instruction for the preceding process to send more
- It is a visual control tool to show up areas of overproduction and lack of synchronization
- It is a tool for *kaizen* (continuous improvement). Toyota's rules state that 'the number of kanbans should be reduced over time'.

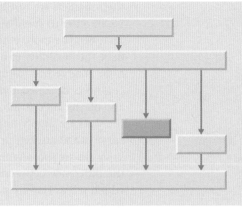

Are processes flexible?

Responding exactly and instantaneously to customer demand implies that operations resources need to be sufficiently flexible to change both what they do and how much they do of it without incurring high cost or long delays. In fact, flexible processes (often with flexible technologies) can significantly enhance smooth and synchronized flow. For example, new publishing technologies allow professors to assemble printed and e-learning course material customized to the needs of individual courses or even individual students. In this case flexibility is allowing customized, small batches to be delivered 'to order'. In another example, a firm of lawyers used to take 10 days to prepare its bills for customers.

> **Operations principle**
> Change-over flexibility reduces waste and smoothes flow.

This meant that customers were not asked to pay until 10 days after the work had been done. Now they use a system that, every day, updates each customer's account. So, when a bill is sent it includes all work up to the day before the billing date. The principle here is that process inflexibility also delays cash flow.

Reduce setup times

For many technologies, increasing process flexibility means reducing setup times, defined as the time taken to change the process over from one activity to the next. Compare the time it takes you to change the tyre on your car with the time taken by a Formula 1 team. Setup reduction can be achieved by a variety of methods such as cutting out time taken to search for tools and equipment, the pre-preparation of tasks that delay changeovers, and the constant practice of setup routines. Setup time reduction is also called single minute exchange of dies (SMED), because this was the objective in some manufacturing operations. The other common approach to setup time reduction is to convert work that was previously performed while the machine was stopped (called *internal* work) to work that is performed while the machine is running (called *external* work). There are three major methods of achieving the transfer of internal setup work to external work:[7]

- Pre-prepare equipment instead of having to do it while the process is stopped. Preferably, all adjustment should be carried out externally.
- Make equipment capable of performing all required tasks so that changeovers become a simple adjustment.
- Facilitate the change of equipment, for example by using simple devices such as roller conveyors.

Fast changeovers are particularly important for airlines because they cannot make money from aircraft that are sitting idle on the ground. It is called 'running the aircraft hot' in the industry. For many smaller airlines, the biggest barrier to running hot is that their markets are not large enough to justify passenger flights during the day *and* night. So, in order to avoid aircraft being idle overnight, they must be used in some other way. That was the motive behind Boeing's 737 'Quick Change' (QC) aircraft. With it, airlines have the flexibility to use it for passenger flights during the day and, with less than a one-hour changeover (setup) time, use it as a cargo airplane throughout the night. Boeing engineers designed frames that hold entire rows of seats that could smoothly glide on and off the aircraft, allowing 12 seats to be rolled into place at once. When used for cargo, the seats are simply rolled out and replaced by special cargo containers designed to fit the curve of the fuselage and prevent damage to the interior. Before reinstalling the seats the sidewalls are thoroughly cleaned so that, once the seats are in place, passengers cannot tell the difference between a QC aircraft and a normal 737. Airlines such as Aloha Airlines, which serves Hawaii, particularly value the aircraft's flexibility. It allows them to provide frequent reliable services in both passenger and cargo markets. So the aircraft that has been carrying passengers around the islands during the day can be used to ship fresh supplies overnight to the hotels that underpin the tourist industry.

DIAGNOSTIC QUESTION

Is variability minimized?

One of the biggest causes of the variability that will disrupt flow and prevent lean synchronization is variation in the quality of items. This is why a discussion of lean synchronization should always include an evaluation of how quality conformance is ensured within processes. In particular, the principles of statistical process control (SPC) can be used to understand quality variability. Chapter 12 and its supplement on SPC examine this subject, so in this section we shall focus on other causes of variability. The first of these is variability in the mix of products and services moving through processes, operations or supply networks.

> **Operations principle**
> Variability in product/service quality, or quantity, or timing, acts against smooth flow and waste elimination.

Level schedules as much as possible

Levelled scheduling (or *heijunka*) means keeping the mix and volume of flow between stages even over time. For example, instead of producing 500 parts in one batch, which would cover the needs for the next three months, levelled scheduling would require the process to make only one piece per hour regularly. Thus, the principle of levelled scheduling is very straightforward; however, the requirements to put it into practice are quite severe, although the benefits resulting from it can be substantial. The move from conventional to levelled scheduling is illustrated in Figure 11.7. Conventionally, if a mix of products were required in a time period (usually a month), a batch size would be calculated for

(a) Scheduling in large batches

(b) Levelled scheduling

Figure 11.7   Levelled scheduling equalizes the mix of products made each day

each product and the batches produced in some sequence. Figure 11.7(a) shows three products that are produced in a 20-day time period in a production unit.

Quantity of product A required = 3000
Quantity of product B required = 1000
Quantity of product C required = 1000
Batch size of product A = 600
Batch size of product B = 200
Batch size of product C = 200

Starting at day 1, the unit commences producing product A. During day 3, the batch of 600 of product A is finished and dispatched to the next stage. The batch of Bs is started but is not finished until day 4. The remainder of day 4 is spent making the batch of Cs and both batches are dispatched at the end of that day. The cycle then repeats itself. The consequences of using large batches are first, that relatively large amounts of inventory accumulate within and between the units, and second, that most days are different from one another in terms of what they are expected to produce (in more complex circumstances, no two days would be the same).

Now suppose that the flexibility of the unit could be increased to the point where the batch sizes for the products were reduced to a quarter of their previous levels without loss of capacity (see Figure 11.7(b)):

Batch size of product A = 150
Batch size of product B = 50
Batch size of product C = 50

A batch of each product can now be completed in a single day, at the end of which the three batches are dispatched to their next stage. Smaller batches of inventory are moving between each stage, which will reduce the overall level of work-in-progress in the operation. Just as significant, however, is the effect on the regularity and rhythm of production at the unit. Now every day in the month is the same in terms of what needs to be produced. This makes planning and control of each stage in the operation much easier. For example, if on day 1 of the month the daily batch of As was finished by 11.00 am, and all the batches were successfully completed in the day, then the following day the unit will know that, if it again completes all the As by 11.00 am, it is on schedule. When every day is different, the simple question 'Are we on schedule to complete our production today?' requires some investigation before it can be answered. However, when every day is the same, everyone in the unit can tell whether production is on target by looking at the clock. Control becomes visible and transparent to all, and the advantages of regular, daily schedules can be passed to upstream suppliers.

Level delivery schedules

A similar concept to levelled scheduling can be applied to many transportation processes. For example, a chain of convenience stores may need to make deliveries of all the different types of products it sells every week. Traditionally it may have dispatched a truck loaded with one particular product around all its stores so that each store received the appropriate amount of the product that would last them for one week. This is equivalent to the large batches discussed in the previous example. An alternative would be to dispatch smaller quantities of all products in a single truck more frequently. Then, each store would receive smaller deliveries more frequently, inventory levels would be lower and the system could respond to trends in demand more readily because more deliveries means more opportunity to change the quantity delivered to a store. This is illustrated in Figure 11.8.

Adopt mixed modelling where possible

The principle of levelled scheduling can be taken further to give mixed modelling; that is, a repeated mix of outputs. Suppose that the machines in the production unit can be made so flexible that they achieve the JIT ideal of a batch size of one. The sequence of individual products emerging from the unit could be reduced progressively as illustrated in Figure 11.9. This would produce a steady stream of each product flowing continuously from the unit. However, the sequence of products does not always fall as conveniently as in Figure 11.9. The unit production times for each product are not usually identical and the ratios of required volumes are less convenient. For example, if a process is required to produce products A, B and C in the ratio 8:5:4, it could produce 800 of A, followed by 500 of B, followed by 400 of C, or 80A, 50B and 40C. But ideally, to sequence the products as smoothly as possible, it would produce in the order . . . BACABACABACABACAB

Figure 11.8   Delivering smaller quantities more often can reduce inventory levels

Low	Degree of levelling	High

High	Setup times	Low

Low	System flexibility	High

Large batches, e.g.	Small batches, e.g.	Mixed modelling, e.g.
200 A 120 B 80 C	5 A 3 B 2 C	A A B A B C A B C A

Figure 11.9 Levelled scheduling and mixed modelling: mixed modelling becomes possible as the batch size approaches one

. . . repeated . . . repeated . . . etc. Doing this achieves relatively smooth flow (but does rely on significant process flexibility).

Adopt total productive maintenance (TPM)

Total productive maintenance aims to eliminate the variability in operations processes caused by the effect of breakdowns. This is achieved by involving everyone in the search for maintenance improvements. Process owners are encouraged to assume ownership of their machines and to undertake routine maintenance and simple repair tasks. By so doing, maintenance specialists can then be freed to develop higher-order skills for improved maintenance systems. TPM is treated in more detail in Chapter 14.

DIAGNOSTIC QUESTION

Is lean synchronization applied throughout the supply network?

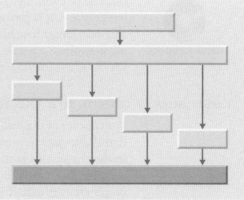

Although most of the concepts and techniques discussed in this chapter are devoted to the management of stages *within* processes and of processes *within* an operation, the same principles can apply to the whole supply chain. In this context, the stages in a process are the whole businesses, operations or processes between which products flow. And as any business starts to approach lean synchronization it will eventually come up against the constraints imposed by the lack of lean synchronization of the other operations in its supply chain. So, achieving further gains must involve trying to spread lean synchronization practice outward to its partners in the chain. Ensuring lean synchronization throughout an entire supply network is clearly a far more demanding task than doing the same within a single process. It is a complex task. And it becomes more complex as more of the supply chain embraces the lean philosophy. The nature of the interaction between whole operations is far more complex than between individual stages within a process. A far more complex mix of products and services is likely to be being provided and the whole network is likely to be subject to a less predictable set of potentially disruptive events. Making a supply chain adopt lean synchronization means more than making each operation in the chain lean. A collection of localized lean operations rarely leads to an overall lean chain. Rather one needs to apply the lean synchronization philosophy to the supply chain as a whole. Yet the advantages from truly lean chains can be significant.

> **Operations principle**
> The advantages of lean synchronization apply at the level of the process, the operation, and the supply network.

Essentially, the principles of lean synchronization are the same for a supply chain as they are for a process. Fast throughput throughout the whole supply network is still valuable and will save cost throughout the supply network. Lower levels of inventory will still make it easier to achieve lean synchronization. Waste is just as evident (and even larger) at the level of the supply network, and reducing waste is still a worthwhile task. Streamlined flow, exact matching of supply and demand, enhanced flexibility and minimal variability are all still tasks that will benefit the whole network. The principles of pull control can work between whole operations in the same way as they can between stages within a single process. In fact, the principles and the techniques of lean synchronization are essentially the same no matter what level of analysis is being used. And because lean synchronization is being implemented on a larger scale, the benefits will also be proportionally greater.

One of the weaknesses of lean synchronization principles is that it is difficult to achieve when conditions are subject to unexpected disturbance (see the critical commentary later). This is especially a problem with applying lean synchronization principles in the context of the whole supply network. Whereas unexpected fluctuations and disturbances do occur within operations, local management has a reasonable degree of control that it can exert in order to reduce them. Outside the operation, within the supply network, fluctuations can also be controlled to some extent (see Chapter 7), but it is far more difficult to do so. Nevertheless, it is generally held that, although the task is more difficult and although it may take longer to achieve, the aim of lean synchronization is just as valuable for the supply network as a whole as it is for an individual operation.

FURTHER EXAMPLE

Lean supply chains are like air traffic control systems[8]

The concept of the lean supply chain has been likened to an air traffic control system, in that it attempts to provide continuous, 'real-time visibility and control' to all elements in the chain. This is the secret of how the world's busiest airports handle thousands of departures and arrivals daily. All aircraft are given an identification number that shows up on a radar map. Aircraft approaching an airport are detected by the radar and contacted using radio. The control tower precisely positions the aircraft in an approach pattern which it coordinates. The radar detects any small adjustments that are necessary, which are communicated to the aircraft. This real-time visibility and control can optimize airport throughput while maintaining extremely high safety and reliability.

Contrast this to how most supply chains are coordinated. Information is captured only periodically, probably once a day, output levels at the various operations in the supply chain are adjusted, and plans are rearranged. But imagine what would happen if this was how the airport operated, with only a 'radar snapshot' once a day. Coordinating aircraft with sufficient tolerance to arrange take-offs and landings every two minutes would be out of the question. Aircraft would be jeopardized, or alternatively, if aircraft were spaced further apart to maintain safety, throughput would be drastically reduced. Yet this is how most supply chains have traditionally operated. They use a daily 'snapshot' from their ERP systems (see Chapter 10 for an explanation of ERP). This limited visibility means operations must either space their work out to avoid 'collisions' (i.e. missed customer orders), thereby reducing output, or they must 'fly blind', thereby jeopardizing reliability.

The concept of 'lean supply'

Professor Lamming of Southampton University has proposed a model of customer–supplier relationships that he calls 'lean supply'. Table 11.2 illustrates some of the characteristics of lean supply.

Table 11.2   Lamming's lean supply concept

Factor	Lean supply characteristics
Nature of competition	Global operation; local presence
	Dependent upon alliances/collaboration
How suppliers are selected by customers	Early involvement of established supplier
	Joint efforts in target costing/value analysis
	Single *and* dual sourcing
	Supplier provides global benefits
	Re-sourcing as a last resort after attempts to improve
Exchange of information between supplier and customer	True transparency: costs, etc.
	Two-way: discussion of costs and volumes
	Technical and commercial information
	Electronic data interchange
	Kanban system for production deliveries (see earlier in chapter)
Management of capacity	Regionally strategic investments discussed
	Synchronized capacity
	Flexibility to operate with fluctuations
Delivery practice	True just-in-time with kanban triggering deliveries
	Local, long-distance and international JIT
Dealing with price changes	Price reductions based upon cost reductions from the start of the relationship onwards, often pre-planned, and achieved from joint efforts of both supplier and customer
Attitude to quality	Supplier vetting schemes become redundant
	Mutual agreement on quality targets
	Continual interaction and kaizen (see Chapter 13)
	Perfect quality as goal

Source: Adapted from Lamming, R. (1993) *Beyond Partnership: Strategies for innovation and lean supply*, Prentice Hall.

At the time, Lamming saw lean supply as a step beyond the type of partnership relationships that were discussed in Chapter 7. And, although this view is not universally held, the concept of leanness in supply chains remains very influential, along with the concepts of agility and partnership. In particular, it is useful to note Lamming's emphasis on continual improvement in supply chain relationships. This concept of lean supply is not to be thought of as universally benign; in fact, the lean relationships essential for synchronized flow through the chain depend on a significant degree of rigour in relationships between operations. For example, consider how the prices charged by suppliers for products and services are handled over time. Often, in lean supply, price reductions in real terms are planned years in advance (e.g. over the next five years you will achieve a 3 per cent reduction in price, year by year). This then becomes the driver for equivalent reductions in the real cost of supply. The responsibility for reducing cost is shared in so much as customers are expected to cooperate in cost reduction. This may be by coordinating purchasing and planning activities so as to reduce the cost of each transaction, or more fundamentally, it may mean customers devoting resources such as 'supplier development engineers' to helping suppliers reduce their costs.

Although not an easy state to achieve, this concept of lean supply can bring advantages to both customers and suppliers. However, the idea of lean supply is often misinterpreted. One particularly common failing is for individual operations in a chain to reduce their inventories, and therefore throughput times, simply by moving stock elsewhere in the chain. Demanding instant delivery from a supplier, 'just-in-time' for when it is needed, could be achieved by a supplier holding excess resources and/or inventory. This may give the appearance of lean supply, but it certainly is not synchronized. The excessive resources and/or inventory in suppliers will add to their costs which will eventually be reflected in the price that is charged to the customer.

Critical commentary

Each chapter contains a short critical commentary on the main ideas covered in the chapter. Its purpose is not to undermine the issues discussed in the chapter, but to emphasize that, although we present a relatively orthodox view of operation, there are other perspectives.

■ Lean synchronization principles can be taken to an extreme. When just-in-time ideas first started to have an impact on operations practice in the West, some authorities advocated the reduction of between-process inventories to zero. While in the long term this provides the ultimate in motivation for operations managers to ensure the efficiency and reliability of each process stage, it does not admit the possibility of some processes always being intrinsically less than totally reliable. An alternative view is to allow inventories (albeit small ones) around process stages with higher than average uncertainty. This at least allows some protection for the rest of the system. The same ideas apply to just-in-time delivery between factories. The Toyota Motor Corporation, often seen as the epitome of modern JIT, has suffered from its low inter-plant inventory policies. Both the Kobe earthquake and fires in supplier plants have caused production at Toyota's main factories to close down for several days because of a shortage of key parts. Even in the best-regulated manufacturing networks, one cannot always account for such events.

■ One of the most counter-intuitive issues in lean synchronization is the way it appears to downplay the idea of capacity under-utilization. And it is true that, when moving towards lean

High

Process throughput time
(or inventory)

High utilization but long
throughput times

Low utilization but short
throughput times

Reduce
process
variability

Low

0   20%   40%   60%   80%   100%

Capacity utilization

Figure 11.10   Developing lean processes can mean accepting lower utilization in the short to medium term

synchronization, fast throughput time and smooth flow *are* more important than the high utilization that can result in inventory build-up. However, this criticism is not really valid in the long term. Remember the relationship between capacity utilization and process throughput time (or inventory), shown in Figure 11.10. The improvement path envisaged by adopting lean synchronization is shown as moving from the state that most businesses find themselves in (high utilization but long throughput times) towards the lean synchronization ideal (short throughput time). Although, inevitably, this means moving towards a position of lower capacity utilization, lean synchronization also stresses a reduction in all types of process variability. As this begins to become reality, the improvement path moves towards the point where throughput time is short and capacity utilization high. It manages to do this because of the reduction in process variability.

■ Not all commentators see lean synchronization-influenced people-management practices as entirely positive. The JIT approach to people management can be viewed as patronizing. It may be, to some extent, less autocratic than some Japanese management practices dating from earlier times. However, it is certainly not in line with some of the job design philosophies that place a high emphasis on contribution and commitment, described in Chapter 9. Even in Japan the JIT approach is not without its critics. Kamata wrote an autobiographical description of life as an employee at a Toyota plant, called *Japan in the Passing Lane*.[9] His account speaks of 'the inhumanity and the unquestioning adherence' of working under such a system. Similar criticisms have been voiced by some trade union representatives.

■ The major weakness of lean synchronization principles is that they can break down when fluctuations in supply or demand become extreme, especially when they are also unpredictable. The pull control of hamburgers in a fast-food restaurant works perfectly well when demand stays within predictable limits. However, when subjected to an unexpected large influx of customers, it leaves most of those customers waiting for their meal. Similarly, in very complex and interrelated processes, lean synchronization methods are sometimes difficult to apply. Generally, MRP is better at dealing with complexity, as measured by numbers of parts and finished products and demand fluctuations. It can handle detailed parts requirements, even for products that are made infrequently and in low volumes. Lean synchronization, and in particular pull scheduling, is less capable of responding instantaneously to changes in demand as product complexity and variety increase. In fact, there have been several successful attempts to blend MRP-based planning and control systems with lean synchronization principles. Often these involve using MRP (embedded within the ERP system) at a high level of planning and using lean synchronization to smooth flow at a more operational level.

Summary checklist

DOWNLOADABLE

This checklist comprises questions that can be usefully applied to any type of operations and reflect the major diagnostic questions used within the chapter.

☐ Are the benefits of attempting to achieve lean synchronization well understood within the business?

☐ Notwithstanding that the idea derives from manufacturing operations, have the principles been considered for non-manufacturing processes within the business?

☐ Is the extent of waste within operations and processes fully understood?

☐ Can flow of items through processes be made more regular?

☐ How much inventory of items is building up because of inexact supply?

☐ How much waste is caused because of inflexibility in the operation's processes?

☐ How much waste is caused because of variability (especially of quality) within the operation's processes?

☐ Are capacity utilization performance measures likely to prove a barrier to achieving lean synchronization?

☐ Does the culture of the organization encourage the involvement in the improvement process of all people in the organization?

☐ Are the ideas of continuous improvement understood?

☐ Are the ideas of continuous improvement used in practice?

☐ Are the various techniques used to promote lean synchronization understood and practised?

☐ Is the concept of lean synchronization applied throughout the supply network?

☐ Has the possibility of blending push (such as MRP) and pull (such as lean synchronization) been considered?

Case study   Boys and Boden (B&B)

'There **must** be a better way of running this place!' said Dean Hammond, recently recruited General Manager of B&B, as he finished a somewhat stressful conversation with a complaining customer, a large and loyal local building contractor.

'We had six weeks to make their special staircase, and we are still late. I'll have to persuade one of the joiners to work overtime this weekend to get everything ready for Monday. We never seem to get complaints about quality . . . our men always do an excellent job, but there is usually a big backlog of work, so how can we set priorities? We could do the most profitable work first, or the work for our biggest customers, or the jobs which are most behind. In practice, we try to satisfy everyone as best we can, but inevitably someone's order will be late. On paper, each job should be quite profitable, since we build in a big allowance for waste, and for timber defects. And we know the work content of almost any task we would have to do, and this is the basis of our estimating system. But, overall, the department isn't very profitable in comparison to our other operations, and most problems seem to end up with higher-than-anticipated costs and late deliveries!'

Boys and Boden was a small, successful, privately owned timber and building materials merchant based in a small town. Over the years it had established its large Joinery Department, which made doors, windows, staircases and other timber products, all to the exact special requirements of the customers, comprising numerous local and regional builders. In addition, the joiners would cut and prepare special orders of timber, such as non-standard sections, and special profiles including old designs of skirting board, sometimes at very short notice while the customers waited. Typically, for joinery items, the customer provided simple dimensioned sketches of the required products. These were then passed to the central Estimating/Quotations Department which, in conjunction with the Joinery Manager, calculated costs and prepared a written quotation which was faxed to the customer. This first stage was normally completed within two or three days, but on occasions could take a week or more. On receipt of an order, the original sketches and estimating details were passed back to the Joinery Manager across the yard, who roughly scheduled them into his plan, allocating them to individual craftsmen as

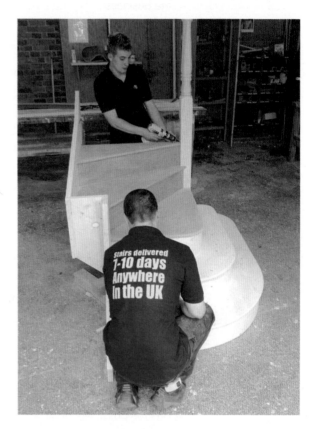

they became available. Most of the joiners were capable of making any product, and enjoyed the wide variety of challenging work.

The Joinery Department appeared congested and somewhat untidy, but everyone believed that this was acceptable and normal for job shops, since there was no single flow route for materials. Whatever the design of the item being made, or the quantity, it was normal for the joiner to select the required timber from the storage building across the yard. The timber was then prepared using a planer/thicknesser. After that, the joiner would use a variety of processes, depending on the product. The timber could be machined into different cross-sectional shapes, cut into component lengths using a radial arm saw, have joints formed by hand tools or using a mortise/tenon machine, and so on. Finally the products would be glued and assembled, sanded smooth by hand or machine, and treated with preservatives, stains or varnishes if required. All the large and more expensive machines were grouped together by type (for example, saws) or were single pieces of equipment shared by all 10 or so joiners. Dean described what one might observe on a random visit to the Joinery Department:

'One or two long staircases partly assembled, and crossing several work areas; large door frames on trestles being assembled; stacks of window components for a large contract being prepared and jointed, and so on. Off-cuts and wood shavings are scattered around the work area, but are cleared periodically when they get in the way or form a hazard. The joiners try to fit in with each other over the use of machinery, so are often working on several part-finished items at once. Varnishing or staining has to be done when it's quiet – for example, evenings or week-ends – or outside, to avoid dust contamination. Long off-cuts are stacked around the workshop, to be used up on any future occasion when these lengths or sections are required. However, it is often easier to take a new length of timber for each job, so the off-cuts do tend to build up over time. Unfortunately, everything I have described is getting worse as we get busier . . . our sales are increasing so the system is getting more congested. The joiners are almost climbing over each other to do their work. Unfortunately, despite having more orders, the department has remained stubbornly unprofitable.'

'Whilst analyzing in detail the lack of profit, we were hor-rified to find that, for the majority of orders, the actual times booked by the joiners exceeded the estimated times by up to 50 per cent. Sometimes this was attributable to new, inexperienced joiners. Although fully trained and qualified, they might lack the experience needed to complete a com-plex job in the time an estimator would expect, but there had been no feedback of this to the individual. We put one of these men on doors only; having overcome his initial reluctance, he has become our enthusiastic "door expert", and gets closely involved in quotations too, so he always does his work within the time estimates! However, the main time losses were found to be the result of general delays caused by congestion, interference, double handling and rework to rectify in-process damage. Moreover, we found that a joiner walked an average of nearly 5 km a day, usually carrying around bits of wood.'

'When I did my operations management course on my MBA, the professor described the application of cellular manufacturing and JIT. From what I can remember, the idea seemed to be to get better flow, reducing the times and distances in the process, and thus achieving quicker throughput times. That is just what we need, but these concepts were explained in the context of high-volume, repetitive production of bicycles, whereas everything we make is "one-offs". However, although we do make a lot of different staircases, they all use roughly the same process steps:

1 Cutting timber to width and length
2 Sanding
3 Machining
4 Tenoning
5 Manual assembly (glue and wedges).

We have a lot of unused factory floor-space, so it would be relatively easy to set up a self-contained staircase cell. There is huge demand for special stairs in this region, but also a lot of competing small joinery businesses which can beat us on price and lead time. So we go to a lot of trouble quoting for stairs, but only win about 20 per cent of the business. If we got the cell idea to work, we could be more competitive on price and delivery, hence winning more orders. I know we will need a lot more volume to justify establishing the cell, so it's really a case of "chicken and egg!".'

QUESTIONS

1 To what extent could (or should) Dean expect to apply the philosophies and techniques of JIT described in this chapter to the running of a staircase cell?

2 What are likely to be the main categories of costs and benefits in establishing the cell? Are there any non-financial benefits that should be taken into account?

3 At what stage, and how, should Dean sell his idea to the Joinery Manager and the workers?

4 How different would the cell work be to that in the main Joinery Department?

5 Should Dean differentiate the working environment by providing distinctive work-wear, such as T-shirts and distinctively painted machines, in order to reinforce a cultural change?

6 What risks are associated with Dean's proposal?

Active case study   Treating Ann

ACTIVE CASE

Ann is a self employed designer and decorator. As a result of some sanding work she takes on, she develops a painful lump in her forearm. Little does she realize the processes she will have to go through in order to get the right treatment.

- How would you assess and evaluate the two health systems that she encounters? How close is each to achieving lean synchronization?

Please refer to the Active case on the CD to follow her experience of the health system in the UK and Belgium and her quest to get the right diagnosis and treatment.

Applying the principles

HINTS

Some exercises can be answered by reading the chapter. Others will require some general knowledge of business activity and some might require an element of investigation. All have hints on how they can be answered on the CD accompanying this book.

1   Re-examine the description of the Toyota production system at the beginning of the chapter.

  (a) List all the different techniques and practices that Toyota adopts. Which of these would you call just-in-time philosophies and which are just-in-time techniques?

  (b) How are operations objectives (quality, speed, dependability, flexibility, cost) influenced by the practices that Toyota adopts?

2   Consider this record of an ordinary flight.

    'Breakfast was a little rushed but left the house at 6.15. Had to return a few minutes later, forgot my passport. Managed to find it and leave (again) by 6.30. Arrived at the airport 7.00, dropped Angela off with bags at terminal and went to the long-term car park. Eventually found a parking space after 10 minutes. Waited 8 minutes for the courtesy bus. Six-minute journey back to the terminal, we start queuing at the check-in counters by 7.24. Twenty-minute wait. Eventually get to check-in and find that we have been allocated seats at different ends of the plane. Staff helpful but takes 8 minutes to sort it out. Wait in queue for security checks for 10 minutes. Security decide I look suspicious and search bags for 3 minutes. Waiting in lounge by 8.05. Spend 1 hour and 5 minutes in lounge reading computer magazine and looking at small plastic souvenirs. Hurrah, flight is called 9.10, takes 2 minutes to rush to the gate and queue for further 5 minutes at gate. Through the gate and on to air bridge that is continuous queue going onto plane, takes 4 minutes but finally in seats by 9.21. Wait for plane to fill up with other passengers for 14 minutes. Plane starts to taxi to runway at 9.35. Plane queues to take-off for 10 minutes. Plane takes off 9.45. Smooth flight to Amsterdam, 55 minutes. Stacked in queue of planes waiting to land for 10 minutes. Touch down at Schiphol Airport 10.50. Taxi to terminal and wait 15 minutes to disembark. Disembark at 11.05 and walk to luggage collection (calling at lavatory on way), arrive luggage collection 11.15. Wait for luggage 8 minutes. Through customs (not searched by Netherlands security who decide I look trustworthy) and to taxi rank by 11.26. Wait for taxi 4 minutes. Into taxi by 11.30, 30 minutes ride into Amsterdam. Arrive at hotel 12.00.'

  (a) Analyze the journey in terms of value-added time (actually going somewhere) and non-value-added time (time spent queuing, etc.).

  (b) Visit the websites of two or three airlines and examine their business-class and first-class services to look for ideas that reduce the non-value-added time for customers who are willing to pay the premium.

  (c) Next time you go on a journey, time each part of the journey and perform a similar analysis.

3   Examine the value-added versus non-value-added times for some other services. For example:

(a) Handing an assignment in for marking if you are currently studying for a qualification (what is the typical elapsed time between handing the assignment in and receiving it back with comments?). How much of this elapsed time do you think is value-added time?

(b) Posting a letter (the elapsed time is between posting the letter in the box and it being delivered to the recipient).

(c) Taking a garment to be professionally dry cleaned.

4   Using an Internet search engine, enter 'kanban', and capture those who use such devices for planning and control. Contrast the ways in which they are used.

5   Consider how setup reduction principles can be used on the following.

(a) Changing a tyre at the side of the road (following a puncture).

(b) Cleaning out an aircraft and preparing it for the next flight between an aircraft on its inbound flight landing and disembarking its passengers, and the same aircraft being ready to take off on its outbound flight.

(c) The time between the finish of one surgical procedure in a hospital's operating theatre, and the start of the next one.

(d) The 'pitstop' activities during a Formula One race (how does this compare to (a) above?).

6   In the chapter the example of Boeing's success in enabling aircraft to convert between passenger and cargo operations was described.

(a) If the changeover between 'passengers' and 'cargo' took 2 hours instead of 1 hour, how much impact do you think it would have on the usefulness of the aircraft?

(b) For an aircraft that carries passengers all the time, what is the equivalent of setup reduction? Why might it be important?

Notes on chapter

1   Spears, S. and Bowen, H.K. (1999) 'Decoding the DNA of the Toyota production system', *Harvard Business Review*, October, pp 96–106.

2   Source: Applegate, J. (2001) 'A lean, mean manufacturing system means less inventory – and, often, more cash in your pocket', *The Entrepreneur*, 30 May, and thanks to Martha Bergman-Gamblin.

3   Lee, D.C. (1987) 'Set-up time reduction: making JIT work' *in* Voss, C.A. (ed.), *Just-in-Time Manufacture*, IFS/Springer-Verlag.

4   Spears and Bowen, *op. cit.*

5   Harrison, A. (1992) *Just-in-Time Manufacturing in Perspective*, Prentice Hall.

6   Hall R.W., (1983) *'Zero Inventories'*, McGraw-Hill, New York.

7   Yamashina, H. 'Reducing set-up times makes your company flexible and more competitive', unpublished, quoted in Harrison, *op. cit.*

8   This great metaphor seems to have originated from the consultancy '2think', www.2think.biz/index.htm

9   Kamata, S. (1983) *Japan in the Passing Lane: An insider's account of life in a Japanese auto factory*, Allen & Unwin.

Taking it further

Fiedler, K., Galletly, J.E. and Bicheno, J. (1993) 'Expert advice for JIT implementation', *International Journal of Operations and Production Management*, Vol. 13, No. 6. An academic paper but contains some good advice.

Schonberger, R.J. (1982) *Japanese Manufacturing Techniques: Nine hidden lessons in simplicity*, Free Press, New York. One of the really influential books that established JIT in the West. Now seen as over-simplistic but worth looking at to understand pure JIT.

Schonberger, R.J. (1986) *World Class Manufacturing: The lessons of simplicity applied,* Free Press, New York. As above, but developed further.

Schonberger, R.J. (1996) *World Class Manufacturing: The next decade*, Free Press, New York. As above (and above that) but more speculative.

Spear, S. and Bowen, H.K. (1999) 'Decoding the DNA of the Toyota Production System', *Harvard Business Review,* Sept.–Oct. Revisits the leading company in terms of JIT practice and re-evaluates the underlying philosophy behind the way it manages its operations. Recommended.

Womack, J.P., Jones, D.T. and Roos, D. (1990) *The Machine that Changed the World,* Rawson Associates. Arguably the most influential book on operations management practice of the last 50 years. Firmly rooted in the automotive sector but did much to establish JIT.

Womack, J.P. and Jones, D.T. (1996) Lean Thinking: Banish waste and create wealth in your corporation, Simon and Schuster. Some of the lessons from 'The Machine that Changed the World' but applied in a broader context.

Useful websites

www.lean.org Site of the Lean Enterprise Unit, set up by one of the founders of the Lean Thinking movement.

www.iee.org/index.cfm The site of the Institution of Electrical Engineers (which includes manufacturing engineers, surprisingly) has material on this and related topics as well as other issues covered in this book.

www.mfgeng.com The manufacturing engineering site.

FURTHER RESOURCES

For further resources including examples, animated diagrams, self test questions, excel spreadsheets, active case studies and video materials please explore the CD accompanying this book.

12 QUALITY MANAGEMENT

Introduction

All businesses are concerned with quality, usually because they have come to understand that high quality can give a significant competitive advantage. But 'quality management' has come to mean more than avoiding errors. It is also seen as an approach to the way processes should be managed and, more significantly, improved, generally. This is because quality management focuses on the very fundamental of operations and process management – the ability to produce and deliver the products and services that the market requires, in both the short and long term. A grasp of quality management principles is the foundation of any improvement activity. (See Figure 12.1.)

Source: courtesy BOC Group plc

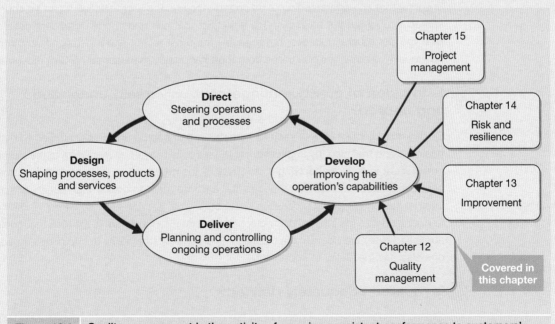

Figure 12.1 Quality management is the activity of ensuring consistent conformance to customers' expectations

Executive summary

VIDEO
further detail

Decision logic chain for quality management

Each chapter is structured around a set of diagnostic questions. These questions suggest what you should ask in order to gain an understanding of the important issues of a topic, and as a result, improve your decision making. An executive summary, addressing these questions, is provided below.

What is quality management?

Quality is consistent conformance to customers' expectations. Managing quality means ensuring that an understanding of its importance and the way in which it can be improved is spread throughout the business. It is a subject that has undergone significant development over the last several decades, but arguably the most recent and most significant impact on how quality is managed has come from the total quality management (TQM) movement.

Is the idea of quality management universally understood and applied?

Quality management is now seen as something that can be universally applied throughout a business and that also, by implication, is the responsibility of all managers in the business. In particular, it is seen as applying to all parts of the organization. The internal customer concept can be used to establish the idea that it is important to deliver high quality of service to internal customers (other processes in the business). Service-level agreements can be used to operationalize the internal customer concept. Just as important is the idea that quality also applies to every individual in the business. Everyone has the ability to impair quality, so everyone also has the ability to improve it.

Is 'quality' adequately defined?

Quality needs to be understood from the customer's point of view because it is defined by the customer's perceptions and expectations. One way of doing this is to use a quality gap model. This starts from the fundamental potential gap between customers' expectations and perceptions and deconstructs the various influences on perceptions and expectations. Gaps between these factors can then be used to diagnose possible root causes of quality problems. A further development is to define the quality characteristics of products or services in terms of their functionality, appearance, reliability, durability, recovery and contact.

Is 'quality' adequately measured?

Without measuring quality it is difficult to control it. The various attributes of quality can be measured either as a variable (measured on a continuously variable scale) or as an attribute (a binary, acceptable or not acceptable judgement). One approach to measuring quality is to express all quality-related issues in cost terms. Quality costs are usually categorized as prevention costs (incurred in trying to prevent errors), appraisal costs (associated with checking for errors), internal failure costs (errors that are corrected within the operation), and external failure costs (errors that are experienced by customers). Generally, it is held that increasing expenditure on prevention will bring a more than equivalent reduction in other quality-related costs.

Is 'quality' adequately controlled?

Control means monitoring and responding to any deviations from acceptable levels of quality. One of the most common ways of doing this is through statistical process control (SPC). This technique not only attempts to reduce the variation in quality performance, so as to enhance process knowledge, but also is used to detect deviations outside the 'normal' range of quality variation.

Does quality management always lead to improvement?

Very often quality improvements are not sustained because there is no set of systems and procedures to support and embed them within the operation's day-to-day routines. The best known system for doing this is the ISO 9000 approach adopted now throughout the world. Of the other systems, one of the most widely known is the EFQM excellence model. Once known only as the basis of the European Quality Award, it is now extensively used as a self-assessment tool that allows organizations to assess their own quality systems.

DIAGNOSTIC QUESTION

What is quality management?

There are many definitions of 'quality'–'conformance to specification', being 'fit for purpose', 'achieving appropriate specification', and so on. The one we use here is . . . *'quality is consistent conformance to customers' expectations'* because it includes both the idea of quality as *specification* (what the product or service can do) and the idea of quality as *conformance* (there are no errors, so it always does what it is supposed to do). Not surprisingly, for such an important topic, it has a history. Approaches to quality management have always been of interest to any business that aspired to satisfy its customers. Arguably, the most significant of the approaches to quality management was Total Quality Management (TQM) that became popular with all types of business in the late 1970s and 1980s, although it was based on earlier work by several management thinkers. Feigenbaum popularized the term 'total quality management' in 1957. After that it was developed through the work of several 'quality gurus' including Deming, Juran, Ishikawa, Taguchi and Crosby (see *Taking it further* at the end of the main part of the chapter).

TQM can be viewed as a logical extension of the way in which quality-related practice has progressed. Originally quality was achieved by inspection – screening out defects before customers noticed them. Then the 'quality control' (QC) concept developed a more systematic approach to not only detecting but also solving quality problems. 'Quality assurance' (QA) widened the responsibility for quality to include functions other than direct operations, such as Human Resources, Accounting and Marketing. It also made increasing use of more sophisticated statistical quality techniques. TQM included much of what went before but developed its own distinctive themes, especially in its adoption of a more 'all-embracing' approach. Since the fashionable peak of TQM, there has been some decline in its status, yet its ideas, many of which are included in this chapter, have become accepted quality practice. The two businesses described in the following examples both incorporate TQM ideas in their approach to quality, especially their inclusion of every employee.

| Example | ### The Four Seasons Hotel, Canary Wharf[1]

Source: courtesy, Four Seasons Hotels

The Four Seasons Hotel group has a chain of over 63 properties in 29 countries. Famed for its quality of service, the hotel group has won countless awards, including the prestigious Zagat survey ranking as 'top hotel chain' internationally. From its inception the group has had the same guiding principle, '*to make the quality of our service our competitive advantage*'. Its Golden Rule is 'do to others (guests and staff) as you would wish others to do to you'.

'*It may be a simple rule, but it guides the whole organization's approach to quality*', says Karen Earp, General Manager of the Four Seasons in London's Canary Wharf, who was recently voted Hotelier of the Year by one of the most popular trade journals. '*Quality of service is our distinguishing edge. The golden rule means treating your guests with courtesy and intelligence. It also means that treating your employees with humanity and respect encourages them to be equally sensitive to the needs and expectations of guests. When guests come to a Four Seasons Hotel they* need to have our assurance that they are going to get exceptional food, great service and a great night's sleep. We are not trading in service quality gimmicks. We focus on giving what we call "the exceptional basics". So we listen very carefully to our guests, give a lot of thought to their needs, and provide what they really need. For example, more than anything else, guests value a good night's sleep. We have invested time and research into obtaining the very best beds (they are made especially for us) and we have very strict linen requirements using the very finest cotton sheets. We have even developed a special fold at the end of the bed linen that means very tall people cannot push their feet out of the bottom of the bed. It's this attention to detail that counts in helping a good night's sleep.'

'There is no greater contribution than our staff in achieving such high quality of service. They respond to the culture of the organization that encourages three things – creativity, initiative and attitude. The most important of these is attitude. You can teach people the technical skills of the job but it is the attitude of our staff that sets us apart. We try and hire people who take great pride in delivering exceptional service. And attitude leads on to innovation and creativity. For example, we had a well-known person who was staying with us and speaking to a large gathering in the hotel in the evening. He was dressed casually and wearing bright green trainers. One of our staff escorted him to his room and carried his tuxedo for the evening's event. On arriving at the room the guest realized that he had forgotten to bring his formal shoes. Seeing that the guest's feet seemed to be around the same size as his own, our member of staff gave him his own shoes to wear. Not only was that guest delighted, he stood up at the event and told 200 very important people of his delight.'

All Four Seasons hotels use a 'guest history system' to track guests' preferences. If a guest likes particular types of flowers or fruit in their room, or if they like a particular type of wine, it is recorded and these items can be made available on the guest's next visit. Within the limits of privacy, all staff are empowered to make a record on the guest history file of anything that could improve the guest's stay next time.

'Many of our guests are senior managers of high quality businesses themselves, so they know about quality and their standards are very high', says Karen. 'Our objective is to exceed their expectations. And although **our** expectation is that we will achieve zero defects, you cannot always do that. Obviously we design our systems to try and prevent errors occurring but it is impossible to prevent all mistakes. We very rarely get formal complaints, but when we do I will always personally see to them myself by talking to the guest or answering any letters. The key is service recovery; this is why empowerment is so important. You have to make sure that all staff know they can turn around any negative experiences into positive ones before the guest leaves. It really is worth the effort. Giving exceptional service pays off in the long run because we get tremendous loyalty from our guests.'

| Example | Giordano |

Source: courtesy Jonathan Roberts

With a vision that explicitly states its ambition to be *'the best and the biggest world brand in apparel retailing',* Giordano is setting its sights high. Yet it is the company that changed the rules of clothes retailing in the fast-growing markets around Hong Kong, China, Malaysia and Singapore, so industry experts take its ambitions seriously. Before Giordano, up-market shops sold high-quality products and gave good service. Cheaper clothes were piled high and sold by sales assistants more concerned with taking the cash than smiling at customers. Jimmy Lai, founder and Chief Executive of Giordano Holdings, changed all that. He saw that unpredictable quality and low levels of service offered an opportunity in the casual clothes market. Why could not value and service, together with low prices, generate better profits? His methods were radical. Overnight he raised the wages of his salespeople by between 30 and 40 per cent, all employees were told they would receive at least 60 hours of training a year and new staff would be allocated a 'big brother' or 'big sister' from among experienced staff to help them develop their service quality skills. Even more startling by the standards of his competitors, Mr Lai brought in a 'no questions asked' exchange policy irrespective of how long ago the garment had been purchased. Staff were trained to talk to customers and seek their opinion on products and the type of service they would like. This information would be immediately fed back to the company's designers for incorporation into their new products. Now Giordano achieved the highest sales per square metre of almost any retailer in the region and its founding operations principles are summarized in its 'QKISS' list:

- **Quality** – do things right
- **Knowledge** – update experience and share knowledge
- **Innovation** – think 'outside of the box'
- **Simplicity** – less is more
- **Service** – exceed customers' expectations.

What do these two examples have in common?

The guests at the Four Seasons are paying for exceptional service at a top-range hotel and have high expectations. Giordano may not be 'top-range', but quality of service is just as important to its success. Both businesses define quality in terms of the expectations and perceptions of customers. This means seeing things *from a customer's point of view*. Customers are seen not as being *external* to the organization but as the most important *part* of it. Both see quality as multifaceted, not a single attribute but a combination of many different things, some of which are difficult to define (for example, a sense that the operation cares for its customers). There is also an emphasis on every part of the business and every individual having responsibility for ensuring quality. The root causes of quality errors may often be people related but so is excellent quality.

> **Operations principle**
> Quality is multifaceted, its individual elements differ for different operations.

DIAGNOSTIC QUESTION

Is the idea of quality management universally understood and applied?

FURTHER EXAMPLE

If an operation is to fully understand customers' expectations and to match or exceed them in a consistent manner, it needs to take a universal or *total* approach to quality. Adopting a universal approach means that an understanding of *why* quality is important and *how* quality can be improved permeates the entire organization. This idea was popularized by proponents of total quality management (TQM), who saw TQM as the ideal unifying philosophy that could unite the whole business behind customer-focused improvement. In particular, two questions are worth asking: first, does quality apply to all parts of the organization? And second, does every person in the organization contribute to quality?

Does quality apply to all parts of the organization?

If quality management is to be effective, every process must work properly together. This is because every process affects and in turn is affected by others. Called the *internal customer concept*, it is recognition that every part of an organization is both an internal customer and, at the same time, an internal supplier for other parts of the organization.

> **Operations principle**
> An appreciation of, involvement in, and commitment to quality should permeate the entire organization.

This means that errors in the service provided within an organization will eventually affect the product or service that reaches the external customer. So, one of the best ways of satisfying external customers is to satisfy internal customers. This means that each process has a responsibility to manage its own internal customer – supplier relationships by clearly defining their own and their customers' exact requirements. In fact the exercise replicates what should be going on for the whole operation and its external customers.

Service-level agreements

Some operations bring a degree of formality to the internal customer concept by requiring processes to agree service-level agreements (SLAs) with each other. SLAs are formal definitions of the service and the relationship between two processes. The type of issues that would be covered by such an agreement could include response times, the range of services, dependability of service supply, and so on. Boundaries of responsibility and appropriate performance measures could also be agreed. For example, an SLA between an information systems help desk and the processes that are its internal customers could define such performance measures as follows:

- The types of information network services that may be provided as 'standard'
- The range of special information services that may be available at different periods of the day
- The minimum 'up time', i.e. the proportion of time the system will be available at different periods of the day
- The maximum response time and average response time to get the system fully operational should it fail
- The maximum response time to provide 'special' services, and so on.

SLAs are best thought of as an approach to deciding service priorities between processes, and as a basis for improving process performance from the internal customers' perspective. At their best they can be the mechanism for clarifying exactly how processes can contribute to the operations as a whole. See the critical commentary at the end of the chapter for a more cynical view.

Does every person in the organization contribute to quality?

A total approach to quality should include every individual in the business. People are the source of both good and bad quality and it is everyone's personal responsibility to get quality right. This applies not only to those people who can affect quality directly and have the capability to make mistakes that are immediately obvious to customers, for example those who or serve customers face to face or physically make products. It also applies to those who are less directly involved in producing products and services. The keyboard operator who mis-keys data, or the product designer who fails to investigate thoroughly the conditions under which products will be used in practice, could also set in motion a chain of events that customers eventually see as poor quality.

It follows that, if everyone has the ability to impair quality, they also have the ability to improve it – if only by 'not making mistakes'. But their contribution is expected to go beyond a commitment not to make mistakes; they are expected to bring something positive to the way they perform their jobs. Everyone is capable of improving the way in which they do their own jobs and practically everyone is capable of helping the others in the organization to improve theirs. Neglecting the potential that is inherent in all people is neglecting a powerful source of improvement.

Is 'quality' adequately defined?

Quality is consistent conformance to customers' expectations. It needs to be understood from a customer's point of view because, to the customer, the quality of a particular product or service is whatever he or she perceives it to be. However, each individual customer's expectations may be different. Past experiences, individual knowledge and history will all shape a customer's individual expectations. Perceptions are not absolute. Exactly the same product or service may be perceived in different ways by different customers. Also, in some situations, customers may be unable to judge the 'technical' specification of the service or product. They may then use surrogate measures as a basis for their perception of quality. For example, after seeking financial advice from an adviser it might be difficult immediately to evaluate the technical quality of the advice, especially if no better solution presents itself. In reality a judgement of the quality of the advice may be based on perceptions of trustworthiness, relationship, the information that was provided, or the way in which it was provided.

> **Operations principle**
> Perceived quality is governed by the magnitude and direction of the gap between customers' expectations and their perceptions of a product or service.

Closing the gaps – alignment in quality

If the product or service experience was better than expected then the customer is satisfied and quality is perceived to be high. If the product or service was less than his or her expectations then quality is low and the customer may be dissatisfied. If the product or service matches expectations then the perceived quality of the product or service is seen to be acceptable. These relationships are summarized in Figure 12.2.

Both customers' expectations and perceptions are influenced by a number of factors, some of which cannot be controlled by the operation and some of which can, at least to

Figure 12.2   Perceived quality is governed by the magnitude and direction of the gap between customers' expectations and their perceptions of the product or service

a certain extent. Figure 12.3 shows some of the factors that influence the gap between expectations and perceptions and the potential gaps between some of these factors. This approach to defining quality is called a 'gap model' of quality. The model shown in Figure 12.3 is adapted from one developed by Zeithaml, Berry and Parasuraman,[2] primarily to understand how quality in service operations can be managed and to identify some of the problems in so doing. However, this approach is now also used in all types of operation.

Diagnosing quality problems

Describing perceived quality in this way allows a diagnosis of quality problems. If the perceived quality gap is such that customers' perceptions of the product or service fail to match their expectations of it, then the reason (or reasons) must lie in other gaps elsewhere in the model. Four other gaps could explain a perceived quality gap between customers' perceptions and expectations.

Gap 1: The customer's specification–operation's specification gap

Perceived quality could be poor because there may be a mismatch between the organization's own internal quality specification and the specification which is expected by the customer. For example, a car may be designed to need servicing every 10,000 kilometres but the customer may expect 15,000 kilometre service intervals. An airline may have a policy of charging for drinks during the flight whereas the customer's expectation may be that the drinks would be free.

Gap 2: The concept–specification gap

Perceived quality could be poor because there is a mismatch between the product or service concept and the way the organization has specified the quality of the product or service internally. For example, the concept of a car might have been for an inexpensive, energy-efficient means of transportation, but the inclusion of a catalytic converter may have both added to its cost and made it less energy-efficient.

Gap 3: The quality specification–actual quality gap

Perceived quality could be poor because there is a mismatch between the actual quality of the service or product provided by the operation and its internal quality specification.

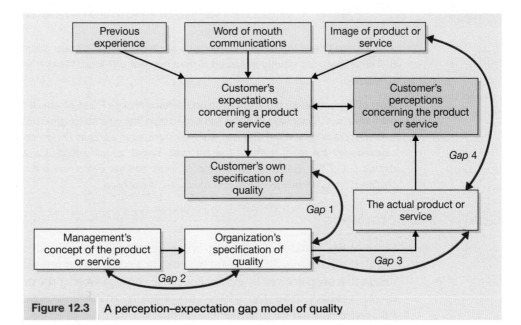

Figure 12.3   A perception–expectation gap model of quality

This may be the result, for example, of an inappropriate or unachievable specification, or of poorly trained or inexperienced personnel, or because effective control systems are not in place to ensure the provision of defined levels of quality. For example if, despite an airline's policy of charging for drinks, some flight crews provide free drinks, they add unexpected costs to the airline and influence customers' expectations for the next flight, when they may be disappointed.

Gap 4: The actual quality–communicated image gap

Perceived quality could also be poor because there is a gap between the organization's external communications or market image and the actual quality of the service or product delivered to the customer. This may be the result of either market positioning setting unachievable expectations in the minds of customers, or operations not providing the level of quality expected by the customer. The advertising campaign for an airline might show a cabin attendant offering to replace a customer's shirt on which food or drink has been spilt, but this service may not always be available.

Example   Tea and Sympathy[3]

Defining quality in terms of perception and expectation can sometimes reveal some surprising results. For example, Tea and Sympathy is a British restaurant and café in the heart of New York's West Village. Over the last 10 years it has become a fashionable landmark in a city with one of the broadest ranges of restaurants in the world. Yet it is tiny, around a dozen tables packed into an area little bigger than the average British sitting room. Not only expatriate Brits but also native New

Yorkers and celebrities queue to get in. As the only British restaurant in New York, it has a novelty factor, but also it has become famous for the unusual nature of its service. *'Everyone is treated in the same way'*, says Nicky Perry, one of the two ex-Londoners who run it. *'We have a firm policy that we don't take any shit.'* This robust attitude to the treatment of customers is reinforced by 'Nicky's Rules' that are printed on the menu.

1. Be pleasant to the waitresses – remember Tea and Sympathy girls are always right.
2. You will have to wait outside the restaurant until your entire party is present: no exceptions.
3. Occasionally, you may be asked to change tables so that we can accommodate all of you.
4. If we don't need the table you may stay all day, but if people are waiting it's time to naff off.
5. These rules are strictly enforced. Any argument will incur Nicky's wrath. You have been warned.

Most of the waitresses are also British and enforce Nicky's Rules strictly. If customers object they are thrown out. Nicky says that she has had to train 'her girls' to toughen up. *'I've taught them that when people cross the line they can tear their throats out as far as I'm concerned. What we've discovered over the years is that if you are really sweet, people see it as a weakness.'* People get thrown out of the restaurant about twice a week and yet customers still queue for the genuine shepherd's pie, a real cup of tea, and of course, the service.

Quality characteristics

Much of the 'quality' of a product or service will have been specified in its design. But not all the design details are useful in defining quality. Rather it is the *consequences* of the design that are perceived by customers. These consequences of the design are called *quality characteristics*. Table 12.1 shows a list of quality characteristics that are generally useful applied to a service (flight) and a product (car).

Table 12.1   Quality characteristics for a motor car and an air journey

Quality characteristics	Car	Flight
Functionality – how well the product or service does its job, including its performance and features	Speed, acceleration, fuel consumption, ride quality, road-holding, etc.	Safety and duration of journey, on-board meals and drinks, car and hotel booking services
Appearance – the sensory characteristics of the product or service: its aesthetic appeal, look, feel, sound and smell	Aesthetics, shape, finish, door gaps, etc.	Decor and cleanliness of aircraft, lounges and crew
Reliability – the consistency of the product's or service's performance over time, or the average time for which it performs within its tolerated band of performance	Mean time to failure	Keeping to the published flight times
Durability – the total useful life of the product or service, assuming occasional repair or modification	Useful life (with repair)	Keeping up with trends in the industry
Recovery – the ease with which problems with the product or service can be rectified or resolved	Ease of repair	Resolution of service failures
Contact – the nature of the person-to-person contact which might take place. It could include the courtesy, empathy, sensitivity and knowledge of contact staff	Knowledge and courtesy of sales and service staff	Knowledge, courtesy and sensitivity of airline staff

DIAGNOSTIC QUESTION

Is 'quality' adequately measured?

Some quality characteristics are relatively easy to measure. For example, is the gap between a car door and pillar less than 5 mm? Other more difficult-to-measure quality characteristics, such as 'appearance', need to be decomposed into their constituent elements such as 'colour match', 'surface finish' and 'the number of visible scratches', all of which are capable of being measured in a relatively objective manner. They may even be quantifiable. However, decomposing quality characteristics into their measurable subcomponents can result in some loss of meaning. A quantified list of 'colour match', the 'smoothness' of the surface finish and the 'number of visible scratches' does not cover factors such as 'aesthetics', a characteristic that is difficult to measure but nonetheless important. Some quality characteristics cannot themselves be measured at all. The 'courtesy' of airline staff, for example, has no objective quantified measure, yet airlines place a great deal of importance on the need to ensure courtesy in their staff. In cases like this, the operation will have to attempt to measure customer *perceptions* of courtesy.

Variables and attributes

The measures used to describe quality characteristics are of two types: variables and attributes. Variable measures are those that can be measured on a continuously variable scale (for example length, diameter, weight or time). Attributes are those that are assessed by judgement and have two states (for example right or wrong, works or does not work, looks OK or not OK). Table 12.2 categorizes some of the measures that might be used for the quality characteristics of the car and the flight.

Measuring the 'costs of quality'

One approach to measuring aggregated quality is to express all quality-related issues in cost terms. This is the 'cost of quality' approach (usually taken to refer to both costs and benefits of quality). These costs of quality are usually categorized as *prevention costs, appraisal costs, internal failure costs* and *external failure costs*. Table 12.3 illustrates the types of factors that are included in these categories.

Table 12.2　Variable and attribute measures for quality characteristics

Characteristic	Car		Flight	
	Variable	*Attribute*	*Variable*	*Attribute*
Functionality	Acceleration and braking characteristics from test bed	Is the ride quality satisfactory?	Number of journeys that actually arrived at the destination (i.e. didn't crash!)	Was the food acceptable?
Appearance	Number of blemishes visible on car	Is the colour to specification?	Number of seats not cleaned satisfactorily	Are the crew dressed smartly?
Reliability	Average time between faults	Is the reliability satisfactory?	Proportion of journeys that arrived on time	Were there any complaints?
Durability	Life of the car	Is the useful life as predicted?	Number of times service innovations lagged behind those of competitors	Generally, is the airline updating its services in a satisfactory manner?
Recovery	Time from fault discovered to fault repaired	Is the serviceability of the car acceptable?	Proportion of service failures resolved satisfactorily	Do customers feel that staff deal satisfactorily with complaints?
Contact	Level of help provided by sales staff (1 to 5 scale)	Did customers feel well served (yes or no)?	The extent to which customers feel well treated by staff (1 to 5 scale)	Did customers feel that the staff were helpful (yes or no)?

Table 12.3 Categories of quality-related costs

Category of quality-related cost	Examples in the category
Prevention costs – those costs incurred in trying to prevent problems, failures and errors from occurring in the first place	• Identifying potential problems and putting the process right before poor quality occurs • Designing and improving the design of products and services and processes to reduce quality problems • Training and development of personnel in the best way to perform their jobs • Process control
Appraisal costs – those costs associated with controlling quality to check whether problems or errors have occurred during and after the creation of the product or service	• The setting up of statistical acceptance sampling plans • The time and effort required to inspect inputs, processes and outputs • Obtaining processing inspection and test data • Investigating quality problems and providing quality reports • Conducting customer surveys and quality audits
Internal failure costs – failure costs that are associated with errors dealt with inside the operation	• The cost of scrapped parts and materials • The cost of reworking parts and materials • The lost production time as a result of coping with errors • Lack of concentration due to time spent troubleshooting rather than improvement
External failure costs – failure costs that are associated with errors being experienced by customers	• Loss of customer goodwill affecting future business • Aggrieved customers who may take up time • Litigation (or payments to avoid litigation) • Guarantee and warranty costs • The cost to the company of providing excessive capability (too much coffee in the pack and too much information to a client)

Understand the relationship between quality costs[4]

At one time it was assumed that failure costs were reduced as the money spent on appraisal and prevention was increased. There must be a point beyond which the cost of improving quality exceeds the benefits that it brings. Therefore there must be an optimum amount of quality effort to be applied in any situation that minimizes the total costs of quality. Figure 12.4(a) sums up this idea.

More recently the 'optimum quality effort' approach has been challenged. First, why should any operation accept the *inevitability* of errors? Some occupations seem to be able to accept a zero-defect standard (even if they do not always achieve it). No one accepts the inevitability of pilots crashing a certain proportion of their aircraft, or nurses dropping a certain number of babies. Second, failure costs are generally underestimated. They are usually taken to include the cost of 'reworking' defective products, 're-serving' customers, scrapping parts and materials, the loss of goodwill, warranty costs, etc. These are important, but in practice, the real cost of poor quality should include all the management time wasted in organizing rework and rectification and, more important, the loss of concentration and the erosion of confidence between processes within the operation. Third, it implies that prevention costs are inevitably high. But by stressing the importance of quality to every individual, preventing errors becomes an integral part of everyone's work. More quality is not only achieved by using more inspectors, we all have a

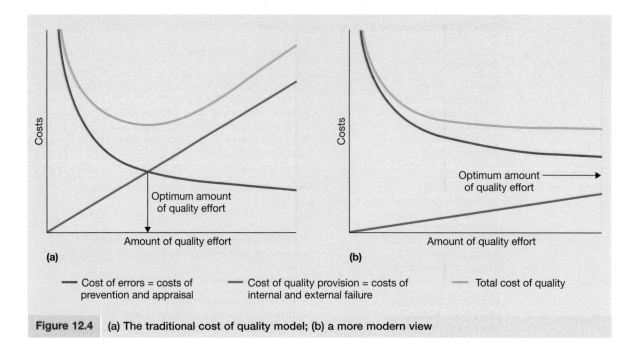

Figure 12.4   (a) The traditional cost of quality model; (b) a more modern view

responsibility for our own quality and all should be capable of 'doing things right first time'. This may incur some costs – training, automatic checks, anything which helps to prevent errors occurring in the first place – but not such a steeply inclined cost curve as in the 'optimum-quality' theory. Finally the 'optimum-quality level' approach, by accepting compromise, does little to challenge operations managers and staff to find ways of improving quality.

Put these corrections into the optimum-quality effort calculation and the picture looks very different (see Figure 12.4(b)). If there is an 'optimum', it is a lot further to the right, in the direction of putting more effort (but not necessarily cost) into quality.

The TQM-influenced quality cost model

TQM rejected the optimum-quality level concept. Rather, it concentrated on how to reduce all known and unknown failure costs. So, rather than placing most emphasis on appraisal (so that 'bad products and service don't get through to the customer'), it emphasized prevention (to stop errors happening in the first place). This has a significant, positive effect on internal failure costs, followed by reductions both in external failure costs and, once confidence has been firmly established, also in appraisal costs. Eventually even prevention costs can be stepped down in absolute terms, though prevention remains a significant cost in relative terms. Figure 12.5 illustrates this idea, showing how initially total quality costs may rise as investment in some aspects of prevention is increased. Once this relationship between categories of quality cost is accepted it shifts the emphasis from a reactive approach to quality (waiting for errors to happen, then screening them out), to a more proactive, 'getting it right first time' approach (doing something before errors happen).

Operations principle
Effective investment in preventing quality errors can significantly reduce appraisal and failure costs.

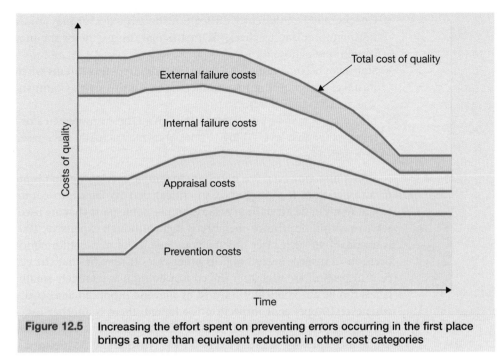

Figure 12.5 | Increasing the effort spent on preventing errors occurring in the first place brings a more than equivalent reduction in other cost categories

DIAGNOSTIC QUESTION

Is 'quality' adequately controlled?

After quality has been defined and measured, processes will need to check that their quality conforms to whatever quality standards are deemed appropriate. This does not necessarily mean checking everything – sampling may be more appropriate.

Check every product and service or take a sample?

There are several reasons why checking everything may not be sensible:

● It could be dangerous to check everything. A doctor, for example, checks just a small sample of blood rather than all of it. The characteristics of this sample are taken to represent those of the rest of the patient's blood.

● Checking of everything might destroy the product or interfere with the service. A lamp manufacturer cannot check the life of every single light bulb leaving the factory; they would all be destroyed. Nor would it be appropriate for a head waiter to check whether customers are enjoying the meal every 30 seconds.

● Checking everything may be too costly. For example, it just might not be feasible to check every single item from a high-volume plastic moulding machine or to check the feelings of every single bus passenger every day.

Even 100 per cent checking will not always guarantee that all defects or problems will be identified.

- Checks may be inherently difficult. Although a doctor may undertake all the correct testing procedures to check for a particular disease, he or she may not necessarily be certain to diagnose it.
- Staff may become fatigued when inspecting repetitive items where it is easy to make mistakes (try counting the number of 'e's on this page. Count them again and see if you get the same score).
- Information may be unreliable. Although all the customers in a restaurant may tell the head waiter that 'everything is fine', they may actually have reservations about their experience.

Sometimes, however, it is necessary to sample everything that is produced by a process or an operation. If a product is so critical that its failure to conform to specification would result in death or injury (for example, some parts that are used in aircraft, or some services within healthcare operations) then, although expensive, 100 per cent inspection is necessary. In such cases it is the consequence of non-conformance that is driving the decision to inspect everything. In other cases it may be that the economics of 100 per cent inspection are such that the cost of doing it is relatively small. For example, some labels can be automatically scanned as they are produced at virtually no extra cost. Yet, whenever 100 per cent inspection is adopted, there is another risk – that of classifying something as an error when, in fact, it conforms to specification. This distinction is summarized in what is often referred to as type I and type II errors.

Type I and type II errors

FURTHER EXAMPLE

Checking quality by sampling, although requiring less time than checking everything, does have its own problems. Take the example of someone waiting to cross a street. There are two main options: cross (take some action), or continue waiting (take no action). If there is a break in the traffic and the person crosses, or if that person continues to wait because the traffic is too dense, then a correct decision has been made (the action was appropriate for the circumstances). There are two types of incorrect decisions, or errors. One would be a decision to cross (take some action) when there is not an adequate break in the traffic, resulting in an accident – this is referred to as a type I error. Another would be a decision not to cross even though there was an adequate gap in the traffic – this is called a type II error. Type I errors are those which occur when a decision was made to do something and the situation did not warrant it. Type II errors are those which occur when nothing was done, yet a decision to do something should have been taken as the situation did indeed warrant it. So, there are four outcomes, summarized in Table 12.4.

Statistical process control (SPC)

Excel

The most common method of checking the quality of a sampled product or service so as to make inferences about all the output from a process is called statistical process control (SPC). SPC is concerned with sampling the process during the production of the goods or the delivery of service. Based on this sample, decisions are made as to whether the

Table 12.4 Type I and type II errors for a pedestrian crossing the road

Decision	Road conditions	
	Safe (action was appropriate)	Unsafe (action was not appropriate)
Cross (take some action)	Correct decision	**Type I error**
Wait (take no action)	**Type II error**	Correct decision

process is 'in control', that is, operating as it should be. If there seems to be a problem with the process, then it can be stopped (if possible and appropriate) and the problem identified and rectified. For example, an international airport may regularly ask a sample of customers if the cleanliness of its restaurants is satisfactory. If an unacceptable number of customers in one sample are found to be unhappy, airport managers may have to consider improving the procedures that are in place for cleaning tables.

Control charts

The value of SPC is not just to make checks of a single sample but to monitor the results of many samples over a period of time. It does this by using control charts. Control charts record some aspect of quality (or performance generally) over time to see whether the process seems to be performing as it should (called *in control*), or not (called *out of control*). If the process does seem to be going out of control, then steps can be taken *before* there is a problem.

FURTHER EXAMPLE

Figure 12.6 shows typical control charts. Charts that look something like these can be found in almost any operation. They could, for example, represent the percentage of customers in a sample of 1000 who, each week, were dissatisfied with the service they received from two call centres. In chart (a), measured customer dissatisfaction has been steadily increasing over time. There is evidence of a clear (negative) trend that management may wish to investigate. In chart (b), although there is little evidence of any trend in average dissatisfaction, the variability in performance seems to be increasing. Again the operation may want to investigate the causes.

Looking for *trends* is an important use of control charts. If the trend suggests the process is getting steadily worse, then it will be worth investigating the process. If the trend is steadily improving, it may still be worthy of investigation to try to identify what is happening that is making the process better. An even more important use of control charts is to investigate the *variation* in performance.

Why variation is a bad thing

> **Operations principle**
> High levels of variation reduce the ability to detect changes in process performance.

Although a trend such as that shown in Figure 12.6(a) clearly indicates deteriorating performance, the variation shown in Figure 12.6(b) can be just as serious. Variation is a problem because it masks any changes in process behaviour. Figure 12.7 shows the performance of two processes both of which change their behaviour

(a) (b)

Figure 12.6   Control charting – any aspect of the performance of a process is measured over time and may show trends in average performance and/or changes in the variation of performance over time

Figure 12.7   Low process variation allows changes in process performance to be readily detected

at the same time. The process on the left has such a wide natural variation that it is not immediately apparent that any change has taken place. Eventually it will become apparent, but it may take some time. By contrast, the performance of the process represented by the chart on the right has a far narrower band of variation, so the same change in average performance is more easily noticed. The narrower the variation of a process, the more obvious are any changes that might occur, and the easier it is to make a decision to intervene. SPC is discussed much further in the supplement to this chapter. It is also one of the core ideas in the Six-Sigma improvement approach that is discussed in the next chapter.

Process control, learning and knowledge

> **Operations principle**
> Statistical-based control gives the potential to enhance process knowledge.

In recent years the role of process control and SPC in particular has changed. Increasingly, it is seen not just as a convenient method of keeping processes in control, but also as an activity that is fundamental to the acquisition of competitive advantage. This is a remarkable shift in the status of SPC. Traditionally it was seen as one of the most *operational*, immediate and 'hands-on' operations management techniques. Yet it is now seen as contributing to an operation's *strategic* capabilities. This is how the logic of the argument goes:

1 SPC is based on the idea that process variability indicates whether a process is in control or not.
2 Processes are brought into *control* and improved by progressively reducing process variability. This involves eliminating the assignable causes of variation.
3 One cannot eliminate assignable causes of variation without gaining a better understanding of how the process operates. This involves *learning* about the process, where its nature is revealed at an increasingly detailed level.
4 This learning means that *process knowledge* is enhanced, which in turn means that operations managers are able to predict how the process will perform under different circumstances. It also means that the process has a greater capability to carry out its tasks at a higher level of performance.
5 This increased *process capability* is particularly difficult for competitors to copy. It cannot be bought 'off-the-shelf'. It only comes from time and effort being invested in controlling operations processes. Therefore, process capability leads to strategic advantage.

In this way, process control leads to learning which enhances process knowledge and builds difficult-to-imitate process capability.

Does quality management always lead to improvement?

No amount of effort put into quality initiatives can guarantee improvement in process performance. In fact some surveys show that up to half of all quality programmes provide only disappointing, if any, permanent improvement. Improving quality is not something that happens simply by getting everyone in an organization to 'think quality'. Very often improvements do not stick because there is no set of systems and procedures to support and embed them into the operation's day-to-day routines. 'Quality systems' are needed.

A quality system is *'the organizational structure, responsibilities, procedures, processes and resources for implementing quality management'*.[5] It should cover all facets of a business's operations and processes, and define the responsibilities, procedures and processes that ensure the implementation of quality improvement. The best-known quality system is ISO 9000.

The ISO 9000 approach

The ISO 9000 series is a set of international standards that establishes requirements for companies' quality management systems. It is being used worldwide to provide a framework for quality assurance. By 2000, ISO 9000 had been adopted by more than a quarter of a million organizations in 143 countries. Originally its purpose was to provide an assurance to the purchasers of products or services by defining the procedures, standards and characteristics of the control system that governed the process that produced them. In 2000, ISO 9000 was substantially revised. Rather than using different standards for different functions within a business, it took a 'process' approach and focused on the outputs from any operation's process, rather than the detailed procedures that had dominated the previous version. This process orientation requires operations to define and record core processes and sub-processes. ISO 9000 (2000) also stresses four other principles.

- Quality management should be customer focused, and customer satisfaction measured using surveys and focus groups. Improvement against customer standards should be documented.
- Quality performance should be measured, and relate to products and services themselves, the processes that created them, and customer satisfaction. Furthermore, measured data should always be analyzed.
- Quality management should be improvement driven. Improvement must be demonstrated in both process performance and customer satisfaction.
- Top management must demonstrate their commitment to maintaining and continually improving management systems. This commitment should include communicating the importance of meeting customer and other requirements, establishing a quality policy and quality objectives, conducting management reviews to ensure the adherence to quality policies, and ensuring the availability of the necessary resources to maintain quality systems.

The Deming Prize

The Deming Prize was instituted by the Union of Japanese Scientists and Engineers in 1951 and is awarded to those companies, initially in Japan, but more recently opened to overseas companies, which have successfully applied 'company-wide quality control' based upon statistical quality control. There are 10 major assessment categories: policy and objectives, organization and its operation, education and its extension, assembling and disseminating of information, analysis, standardization, control, quality assurance, effects, and future plans. The applicants are required to submit a detailed description of quality practices. This is a significant activity in itself and some companies claim a great deal of benefit from having done so.

The Malcolm Baldrige National Quality Award

In the early 1980s the American Productivity and Quality Center recommended that an annual prize, similar to the Deming Prize, should be awarded in America. The purpose of the awards was to stimulate American companies to improve quality and productivity, to recognize achievements, to establish criteria for a wider quality effort and to provide guidance on quality improvement. The main examination categories are leadership, information and analysis, strategic quality planning, human resource utilization, quality assurance of products and services, quality results and customer satisfaction. The process, like that of the Deming Prize, includes a detailed application and site visits.

The EFQM Excellence Model[6]

In 1988, 14 leading Western European companies formed the European Foundation for Quality Management (EFQM). An important objective of the EFQM is to recognize quality achievement. Because of this, it launched the European Quality Award (EQA), awarded to the most successful exponent of total quality management in Europe each year. To receive a prize, companies must demonstrate that their approach to total quality management has contributed significantly to satisfying the expectations of customers, employees and others with an interest in the company for the past few years. In 1999, the model on which the European Quality Award was based was modified and renamed

Leadership – how leaders develop and facilitate the achievement of the mission and vision, develop values required for long-term success and implement these through appropriate actions and behaviour, and are personally involved in ensuring that the organization's management system is developed and implemented.

People – how the organization manages, develops and releases the knowledge and full potential of its people.

Policy and strategy – how the organization implements its mission and vision through a clear stakeholder-focused strategy, supported by relevant policies, plans, objectives, targets and processes.

Partnerships and resources – how the organization plans and manages its external partnerships and internal resources to support its policy and strategy and the effective operation of its processes.

Processes – how the organization designs, manages and improves its processes in order to support its policy and strategy and fully satisfy, and generate increasing value for, its customers and other stakeholders.

People results – this covers employees' motivation, satisfaction, performance and the services the organization provides for its people.

Customer results – this includes customers' loyalty and their perceptions of the organization's image, product and services, sales and after-sales support.

Society results – this relates to the organization's performance as a responsible citizen, its involvement in the community in which it operates, and any recognition it might have received.

Key performance results – this shows the financial and non-financial outcomes of the organization's planned performance, including such things as cash flow, profit, meeting budgets, success rates and the value of intellectual property.

Figure 12.8   The EFQM Excellence Model

'The EFQM Excellence Model'. The changes made were not fundamental but did attempt to reflect some new areas of management and quality thinking (for example, partnerships and innovation) and placed more emphasis on customer and market focus. The model is based on the idea that the outcomes of quality management in terms of what it calls 'people results', 'customer results', 'society results' and 'key performance results' are achieved through a number of 'enablers'. These enablers are leadership and constancy of purpose, policy and strategy, how the organization develops its people, partnerships and resources, and the way it organizes its processes. These ideas are incorporated as shown in Figure 12.8. The five 'enablers' are concerned with how results are being achieved, while the four 'results' are concerned with what the company has achieved and is achieving.

Self-assessment

The EFQM defines *self-assessment* as 'a comprehensive, systematic, and regular review of an organization's activities and results referenced against a model of business excellence'. The main advantage of using such models for self-assessment seems to be that companies find it easier to understand some of the more philosophical concepts of quality management when they are translated into specific areas, questions and percentages. Self-assessment also allows organizations to measure their progress in achieving the benefits of quality management.

Critical commentary

Each chapter contains a short critical commentary on the main ideas covered in the chapter. Its purpose is not to undermine the issues discussed in the chapter, but to emphasize that, although we present a relatively orthodox view of operation, there are other perspectives.

■ Quality management has been one of the hottest topics in operations management and one of the most controversial. Much of the debate has centred on the people focus of quality management, especially the rhetoric of employee empowerment central to several modern approaches to quality. In many cases, it can be little more than an increase in employee discretion over minor details of their working practice. Some industrial relations academics argue that TQM rarely affects the fundamental imbalance between managerial control and employees' influence over organizational direction. For example, '. . . *there is little evidence that employee influence over corporate decisions which affect them has been, or can ever be, enhanced through contemporary configuration of involvement. In other words, whilst involvement might increase individual task discretion, or open up channels for communication, the involvement programme is not designed to offer opportunities for employees to gain or consolidate control over the broader environment in which their work is located.*'[7]

Other criticisms concern the appropriateness of some mechanisms such as service-level agreements (SLAs). Some see the strength of SLAs as the degree of formality they bring to customer–supplier relationships, but there also drawbacks. The first is that the 'pseudo-contractual' nature of the formal relationship can work against building partnerships. This is especially true if the SLA includes penalties for deviation from service standards. The effect can sometimes be to inhibit rather than encourage joint improvement. The second is that SLAs tend to emphasize the 'hard' and measurable aspects of performance rather than the 'softer' but often more important aspects. So a telephone may be answered within four rings, but how the caller is treated in terms of 'friendliness' may be far more important.

■   Similarly, and notwithstanding its widespread adoption (and its revision to take into account some of its perceived failing), ISO 9000 is not seen as beneficial by all authorities. Criticisms include the following.

- The whole process of documenting processes, writing procedures, training staff and conducting internal audits is expensive and time-consuming.
- Similarly, the time and cost of achieving and maintaining ISO 9000 registration are excessive.
- It is too formulaic. It encourages operations to 'manage by manual', substituting a 'recipe' for a more customized and creative approach to managing operations improvement.

Summary checklist

This checklist comprises questions that can be usefully applied to any type of operations and reflect the major diagnostic questions used within the chapter.

- [ ] Does everyone in the business really believe in the importance of quality, or is it just one of those things that people say without really believing it?

- [ ] Is there an accepted definition of quality used within the business?

- [ ] Do people understand that there are many different definitions and approaches to quality, and do they understand why the business has chosen its own particular approach?

- [ ] Do all parts of the organization understand their contribution to maintaining and improving quality?

- [ ] Are service-level agreements used to establish concepts of internal customer service?

- [ ] Is some form of gap model used to diagnose quality problems?

- [ ] Is quality defined in terms of a series of quality characteristics?

- [ ] Is quality measured using all relevant quality characteristics?

- [ ] Is the cost of quality measured?

- [ ] Are quality costs categorized as prevention, appraisal, internal failure, and external failure costs?

- [ ] Is quality adequately controlled?

- [ ] Has the idea of statistical process control (SPC) been explored as a mechanism for controlling quality?

- [ ] Do individual processes have any idea of their own variability of quality performance?

- [ ] Have quality systems been explored, such as ISO 9000 and the EFQM excellence model?

Case study   Turnround at the Preston plant

'Before the crisis the quality department was just for looks, we certainly weren't used much for problem solving, the most we did was inspection. Data from the quality department was brought to the production meeting and they would all look at it, but no one was looking behind it.' (Quality Manager, Preston Plant)

The Preston plant of Rendall Graphics was located in Preston, Vancouver, across the continent from their headquarters in Massachusetts. The plant had been bought from the Georgetown Corporation by Rendall in March 2000. Precision-coated papers for inkjet printers accounted for the majority of the plant's output, especially paper for specialist uses. The plant used coating machines that allowed precise coatings to be applied. After coating, the conversion department cut the coated rolls to the final size and packed the sheets in small cartons.

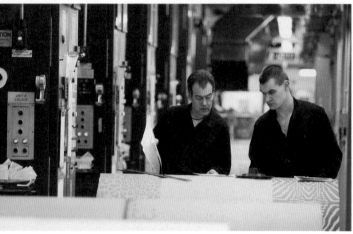

Source: © Getty Images/Digital Vision

The curl problem

In late 1998 Hewlett Packard (HP), the plant's main customer for inkjet paper, informed the plant of some problems it had encountered with paper curling under conditions of low humidity. There had been no customer complaints to HP, but their own personnel had noticed the problem, and they wanted it fixed. Over the next seven or eight months a team at the plant tried to solve the problem. Finally, in October 1999 the team made recommendations for a revised and considerably improved coating formulation. By January 2000 the process was producing acceptably. However, 1999 had not been a good year for the plant. Although sales were reasonably buoyant the plant was making a loss of around $2 million for the year. In October 1999, Tom Branton, previously accountant for the business, was appointed as Managing Director.

Slipping out of control

In the spring of 2000, productivity, scrap and rework levels continued to be poor. In response to this the operations management team increased the speed of the line and made a number of changes to operating practice in order to raise productivity.

*'Looking back, changes were made without any proper discipline, and there was no real concept of control. We were always meeting specification, yet we didn't fully understand how close we really were to not being able to make it. The culture here said, "If it's within specification then it's OK" and we were very diligent in making sure that the product which was shipped **was** in specification. However, Hewlett Packard gets "process charts" that enable them to see more or less exactly what is happening right inside your operation. We were also getting all the reports but none of them were being internalized, we were using them just to satisfy the customer. By contrast, HP have a statistically-based analytical mentality that says to itself, "You might be capable of making this product but we are thinking two or three product generations forward and asking ourselves, will you have the capability then, and do we want to invest in this relationship for the future?"'* (Tom Branton)

The spring of 2000 also saw two significant events. First, Hewlett Packard asked the plant to bid for the contract to supply a new inkjet platform, known as the Vector project, a contract that would secure healthy orders for several years. The second event was that the plant was acquired by Rendall. *'What did Rendall see when they bought us? They saw a small plant on the Pacific coast losing lots of money.'* (Finance Manager, Preston Plant)

Rendall were not impressed by what they found at the Preston plant. It was making a loss and had only just escaped from incurring a major customer's disapproval over the curl issue. If the plant did not get the Vector contract, its future looked bleak. Meanwhile the chief concern continued to be productivity. But also, once again, there were occasional complaints about quality levels. However, HP's attitude caused some bewilderment to the operations management team. *'When HP asked questions about our process the operations guys would say, "Look, we're making roll after roll of paper, it's within specification. What's the problem?" '* (Quality Manager, Preston Plant).

But it was not until summer that the full extent of HP's disquiet was made. *'I will never forget June of 2000. I was at a meeting with HP in Chicago. It was not even about quality. But during the meeting one of their engineers handed me a control chart, one that we supplied with every batch of product. He said "Here's your latest control chart. We think you're out of control and you don't know that you're out of control and we think that we are looking at this data more than you are." He was absolutely right, and I fully understood how serious the position was. We had our most important customer telling us we couldn't run our processes just at the time we were trying to persuade them to give us the Vector contract.'* (Tom Branton)

The crisis

Tom immediately set about the task of bringing the plant back under control. They first of all decided to go back to the conditions which prevailed in January, when the curl team's recommendations had been implemented. This was the state before productivity pressures had caused the process to be adjusted. At the same time the team worked on ways of implementing unambiguous 'shut-down rules' that would allow operators to decide under what conditions a line should be halted if they were in doubt about the quality of the product they were making.

'At one point in May of 2000 we had to throw away 64 jumbo rolls of out-of-specification product. That's over $100,000 of product scrapped in one run. Basically that was because they had been afraid to shut the line down. Either that or they had tried to tweak the line while it was running to get rid of the defect. The shut-down guidelines in effect say, "We are not going to operate when we are not in a state of control". Until then our operators just couldn't win. If they failed to keep the machines running we would say, "You've got to keep productivity up". If they kept the machines running but had quality problems as a result, we criticized them for making garbage. Now you get into far more trouble for violating process procedures than you do for not meeting productivity targets.' (Engineer, Preston Plant)

This new approach needed to be matched by changes in the way the communications were managed in the plant. *'We did two things that we had never done before. First, each production team started holding daily reviews of control chart data. Second, one day a month we took people away from production and debated the control chart data. Several people got nervous because we were not producing anything. But it was necessary. For the first time you got operators from the three shifts meeting together and talking about the control chart data and other quality issues. Just as significantly, we invited HP up to attend these meetings. Remember these weren't staged meetings, it was the first time these guys had met together and there was plenty of heated discussion, all of which the Hewlett Packard representatives witnessed.'* (Engineer, Preston Plant)

At last something positive was happening in the plant and morale on the shop floor was buoyant. By September 2000 the results of the plant's teams efforts were starting to show results. Process were coming under control, quality levels were improving and, most importantly, personnel both on the shop floor and in the management team were beginning to get into the 'quality mode' of thinking. Paradoxically, in spite of stopping the line periodically, the efficiency of the plant was also improving.

Yet the Preston team did not have time to enjoy their emerging success. In September 2000 the plant learned that it would not get the Vector project because of their recent quality problems. Then Rendall decided to close the plant. *'We were losing millions, we had lost the Vector project, and it was really no surprise. I told the senior management team and said that we would announce it probably in April of 2001. The real irony was that we knew that we had actually already turned the corner.'* (Tom Branton)

Notwithstanding the closure decision, the management team in Preston set about the task of convincing Rendall that the plant could be viable. They figured it would take three things. First, it was vital that they continue to improve quality. Progressing with their quality initiative involved establishing full statistical process control (SPC).

Second, costs had to be brought down. Working on cost reduction was inevitably going to be painful. The first task was to get an understanding of what should be an appropriate level of operating costs. *'We went through a zero-based assessment to decide what an ideal plant would look like, and the minimum number of people needed to run it.'* (Tom Branton)

By December 2000 there were 40 per cent fewer people in the plant than two months earlier. All departments were affected. The quality department shrank more than most, moving from 22 people down to six. *'When the plant was considering down-sizing they asked me, "How can we run a lab with six technicians?" I said, "Easy. We just make good paper in the first place, and then we don't have to inspect all the garbage. That alone would save an immense amount of time."* (Quality Manager, Preston Plant)

Third, the plant had to create a portfolio of new product ideas which could establish a greater confidence in future sales. Several new ideas were under active investigation, the most important of which was 'Protowrap', a wrap for newsprint that could be repulped. It was a product that was technically difficult. However, the plant's newly acquired capabilities allowed the product to be made economically.

Out of the crisis

In spite of their trauma, the plant's management team faced Christmas 2000 with increasing optimism. They had just made a profit for the first time for over two years. By spring 2001 even HP, at a corporate level, was starting to take notice. It was becoming obvious that the Preston plant really had made a major change. More significantly, HP had asked the plant to bid for a new product. April 2001 was a good month for the plant. It had chalked up three months of profitability and HP formally gave the new contract to Preston. Also in April, Rendall reversed their decision to close the plant.

QUESTIONS

1 What are the most significant events in the story of how the plant survived because of its adoption of quality-based principles?

2 The plant's processes eventually were brought under control. What were the main benefits of this?

3 SPC is an operational-level technique of ensuring quality conformance. How many of the benefits of bringing the plant under control would you class as strategic?

Active case study   'You have eight messages'

ACTIVE CASE

The De Noorman hotel prides and distinguishes itself on offering high-quality accommodation and service. After his day off, Andries Claessen, the hotel's General Manager, returns to work to discover a number of phone messages awaiting him. The messages cause him to question how quality is defined and managed in the hotel.

● How would you advise Andries on his questions of quality definition, measurement, control and management and how would you suggest he acts to ensure improvement?

Please refer to the Active case on the CD accompanying this book to listen to the messages and find out more about what Andries decides to do.

Applying the principles

HINTS

Some of these exercises can be answered by reading the chapter. Others will require some general knowledge of business activity and some might require an element of investigation. All have hints on how they can be answered on the CD accompanying this book.

1 Using the four categories of quality-related costs, make a list of the costs that fall within each category for the following operations:

(a) A university library
(b) A washing machine manufacturer
(c) A nuclear electricity generating station
(d) A church.

2 Consider how a service-level agreement could be devised for the following:

(a) The service between a library and its general customers

(b) The service given by a motor vehicle rescue service to its customers

(c) The service given by a university audiovisual aids department to both academic staff and students.

3 Using an Internet search engine (such as google.com), look at the consultancy organizations that are selling help and advice on quality management. How do they try to sell quality improvement approaches to prospective customers?

4 Visit the website of the European Foundation for Quality Management (**www.efqm.org**). Look at the companies that have won or been finalists in the European Quality Awards and try to identify the characteristics which make them 'excellent' in the opinion of the EFQM. Investigate how the EFQM promotes its model for self-assessment purposes.

5 Find two products, one a manufactured food item (for example, a pack of breakfast cereals, packet of biscuits, etc.) and the other a domestic electrical item (for example, electric toaster, coffee maker, etc.).

(a) Identify the important quality characteristics for these two products.

(b) How could each of these quality characteristics be specified?

(c) How could each of these quality characteristics be measured?

6 Many organizations check up on their own level of quality by using 'mystery shoppers'. This involves an employee of the company acting the role of a customer and recording how they are treated by the operation. Choose two or three high-visibility operations (for example, a cinema, a department store, the branch of a retail bank, etc.) and discuss how you would put together a mystery shopper approach to testing their quality. This may involve your determining the types of characteristics you would wish to observe, the way in which you would measure these characteristics, an appropriate sampling rate, and so on. Try out your mystery shopper plan by visiting these operations.

Notes on chapter

1 Source: Interview with Karen Earp, General Manager, Four Seasons Canary Wharf Hotel.
2 Parasuraman, A. *et al.* (1985) 'A conceptual model of service quality and implications for future research', *Journal of Marketing,* Vol. 49, Fall.
3 Mechling, L. (2002) 'Get ready for a storm in a tea shop', *The Independent,* 8 March, and company website.
4 Source: Plunkett, J.J. and Dale, B.S. (1987) 'A review of the literature in quality-related costs', *International Journal of Quality and Reliability Management,* Vol. 4, No. 1.
5 Dale, B.G. (ed.) (1999) *Managing Quality,* Blackwell, Oxford.
6 Source: the EFQM website (www.efqm.org).
7 Hyman, J. and Mason, B. (1995) *Management Employees Involvement and Participation,* Sage.

Taking it further

Bounds, G., Yorks, L., Adams, M. and Ranney, G. (1994) *Beyond Total Quality Management: Towards the emerging paradigm,* McGraw-Hill. A useful summary of the state of play in total quality management at about the time it was starting to lose its status as the only approach to managing quality.

Crosby, P.B. (1979) *Quality is Free,* McGraw-Hill. One of the gurus. It had a huge impact in its day. Read it if you want to know what all the fuss was about.

Dale, B.G. (ed.) (1999) *Managing Quality*, Blackwell, Oxford. This is the third edition of a book that has long been one of the best respected texts in the area. A comprehensive and balanced guide to the area.

Deming, W.E. (1986) *Out of the Crisis*, MIT Press. Another of the quality gurus, whose work had a similarly huge impact.

Feigenbaum, A.V. (1986) *Total Quality Control*, McGraw-Hill. A more comprehensive book than those by some of the other quality gurus.

Garvin, D.A. (1991) 'How the Baldridge Award really works', *Harvard Business Review*, Vol. 69, No. 6. A look behind the scenes at what counts in getting quality prizes.

Pande, P.S., Neuman, R.P. and Kavanagh, R.R. (2000) *The Six Sigma Way*, McGraw-Hill, New York. There are many books written by consultants for practising managers on the now fashionable Six Sigma Approach (see supplement to chapter). This one is readable and informative.

Useful websites

www.quality-foundation.co.uk The British Quality Foundation is a not-for-profit organization promoting business excellence.

www.juran.com The Juran Institute's mission statement is to provide clients with the concepts, methods and guidance for attaining leadership in quality.

www.asq.org The American Society for Quality site. Good professional insights.

www.quality.nist.gov American Quality Assurance Institute, a well-established institution for all types of business quality assurance.

www.gslis.utexas.edu/~rpollock/tqm.html Non-commercial site on Total Quality Management with some good links.

www.iso.org/iso/en/ISOOnline.frontpage Site of the International Standards Organization that runs the ISO 9000 and ISO 14000 families of standards. ISO 9000 has become an international reference for quality management requirements.

FURTHER RESOURCES

For further resources including examples, animated diagrams, self test questions, excel spreadsheets, active case studies and video materials please explore the CD accompanying this book.

Introduction

The purpose of statistical process control (SPC) is both to control process performance, keeping it within acceptable limits, and to improve process performance by reducing the variation in performance from its target level. It does this by applying statistical techniques to understand the nature of performance variation over time. For those who are anxious about the 'statistical' part of SPC, don't be. Essentially SPC is based on principles that are both practical and intuitive. The statistical element is there to help rather than complicate quality decisions.

Variation in process performance

The core instrument in SPC is the control chart. These were explained earlier in the chapter. They are an illustration of the dynamic performance of a process, measuring how some aspect of process performance varies over time. All processes vary to some extent. No machine will give precisely the same result each time it is used. All materials vary a little. People in the process differ marginally in how they do things each time they perform a task. Given this, it is not surprising that any measure of performance quality (whether attribute or variable) will also vary. Variations that derive from these *normal* or *common causes* of variation can never be entirely eliminated (although they can be reduced).

For example, at a call centre for a utility company, customer care operatives answer queries over accounts, service visits, and so on. The length of time of each call will vary depending on the nature of the enquiry and the customer's needs. There will be some variation around an average call time. When the process of answering and responding to customer enquiries is stable, the computer system that intercepts and allocates calls to customer care operatives could be asked to randomly sample the length of each call. As this data built up, the histogram showing call times could develop as is shown in Figure 12.9. The first calls could lie anywhere within the natural variation of the process but are more likely to be close to the average call length (Figure 12.9(a)). As more calls are measured they would clearly show a tendency to be close to the process average (see Figure 12.9(b) and (c)). Eventually the data will show a smooth histogram that can be drawn into a smoother distribution that will indicate the underlying process variation (the distribution shown in Figure 12.9(f)).

Excel

Often this type of variation can be described by a *normal distribution*. (Even if this raw data does not conform to a normal distribution, it can be manipulated to approximate to one by using sampling – see later.) It is a characteristic of normal distributions that 99.7 per cent of the measures will lie within ±3 standard deviations of the distribution (standard deviation is a measure of how widely the distribution is spread or *dispersed*).

The central limit theorem

Not all processes vary in their performance according to a normal distribution. However, if a sample is taken from any type of distribution, the distribution of the average of the sample (sample mean) *will* approximate to a normal distribution. For example, there is an equal probability of any number between one and six being thrown on a six-sided, unweighted

Figure 12.9   The natural variation of call times in a call centre can be described by a normal distribution

die. The distribution is rectangular with an average of 3.5 as shown in Figure 12.10(a). But if a die is thrown (say) six times repeatedly and the average of the six throws calculated, the sample average will also be 3.5, but the standard deviation of the distribution will be the standard deviation of the original rectangular distribution divided by the square of the

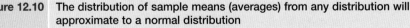

Figure 12.10   The distribution of sample means (averages) from any distribution will approximate to a normal distribution

sample size. More significantly, the shape of the distribution will be close to normal and so can be treated the same way as a normal distribution. This becomes important when control limits are calculated – see later.

Is the process 'in control'?

Not all variation in process performance is the result of common causes. There may be something wrong with the process that is assignable to an abnormal and preventable cause. Machinery may have worn or been set up badly. An untrained person may not be following the prescribed procedure for the process. The causes of such variation are called *assignable* or *abnormal causes*. The question for operations management is whether the results from any particular sample, when plotted on the control chart, simply represent the variation due to *common* causes or due to some specific and correctable *assignable* cause. Figure 12.11(a), for example, shows the control chart for the average call length of samples of customer calls in a utility's call centre. Like any process the results vary, but the last three points seem to be lower than usual. The question is whether this is natural variation or the symptom of some more serious cause. Is the variation the result of common causes, or does it indicate assignable causes (something abnormal) occurring in the process?

To help make this decision, control limits can be added to the control charts that indicate the expected extent of 'common-cause' variation. If any points lie outside these control limits then the process can be deemed *out of control* in the sense that variation is likely to be due to assignable causes. These can be set in a statistically revealing manner based on the probability that the mean of a particular sample will differ by more than a set amount from the mean of the population from which it is taken. Figure 12.11(b) shows the same control chart as Figure 12.11(a) with the addition of control limits put at ±3 standard deviations (of the population of sample means) away from the mean of sample averages. It shows that the probability of the final point on the chart being influenced by an assignable cause is very high indeed. When the process is exhibiting behaviour which is outside its normal 'common-cause' range, it is said to be 'out of control'.

However, we cannot be absolutely certain that the process is out of control. There is a small but finite chance that the point is a rare but natural result at the tail of its distribution. Stopping the process under these circumstances would represent a type I error because the process is actually in control. Alternatively, ignoring a result which in reality is due to an assignable cause is a type II error (see Table 12.5). Control limits that are set at three standard deviations either side of the population mean are called the upper control limit (UCL) and lower control limit (LCL). There is only a 0.3 per cent chance of any sample mean falling outside these limits by chance causes (that is, a chance of a type I error of 0.3 per cent).

Figure 12.11   Control chart for the average call length in a call centre: (a) without control limits; (b) with control limits derived from the natural variation of the process

Table 12.5   Type I and type II errors in SPC

	Actual process state	
Decision	In control	Out of control
Stop process	**Type I error**	Correct decision
Leave alone	Correct decision	**Type II error**

Process capability

Using control charts to assess whether the process is in control is an important internal benefit of SPC. An equally important question for any operations manager would be: 'Is the variation in the process performance acceptable to external customers?' The answer will depend on the acceptable range of performance that will be tolerated by the customers. This range is called the *specification range*. Returning to the boxed rice example, if the weight of rice in the box is too small then the organization might infringe labelling regulations; if it is too large, the organization is 'giving away' too much of its product for free.

Process capability is a measure of the acceptability of the variation of the process. The simplest measure of capability (C_p) is given by the ratio of the specification range to the 'natural' variation of the process (i.e. ±3 standard deviations):

$$C_p = \frac{\text{UTL} - \text{LTL}}{6s}$$

where UTL = the upper tolerance limit
LTL = the lower tolerance limit
s = the standard deviation of the process variability.

Generally, if the C_p of a process is greater than 1, it is taken to indicate that the process is 'capable', and a C_p of less than 1 indicates that the process is not 'capable', assuming that the distribution is normal (see Figure 12.12(a), (b) and (c)).

The simple C_p measure assumes that the average of the process variation is at the midpoint of the specification range. Often the process average is offset from the specification range, however (see Figure 12.12 (d)). In such cases, *one-sided* capability indices are required to understand the capability of the process:

$$\text{Upper one-sided index } C_{pu} = \frac{\text{UTL} - X}{3s}$$

$$\text{Lower one-sided index } C_{pl} = \frac{X - \text{LTL}}{3s}$$

where X = the process average.

Sometimes only the lower of the two one-sided indices for a process is used to indicate its capability (C_{pk}):

$$C_{pk} = \min(C_{pu}, C_{pl})$$

Worked example

In the case of the process filling boxes of rice, described previously, process capability can be calculated as follows:

$$\text{Specification range} = 214 - 198 = 16 \text{ g}$$

$$\text{Natural variation of process} = 6 \times \text{standard deviation}$$

$$= 6 \times 2 = 12 \text{ g}$$

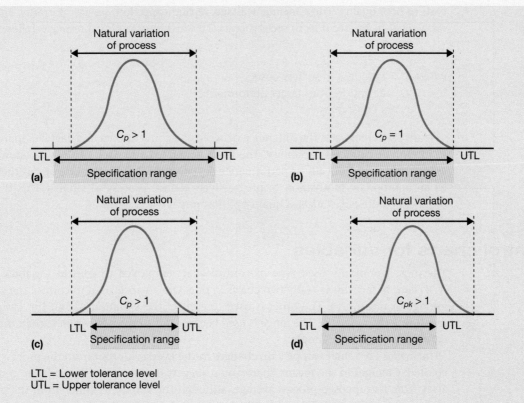

Figure 12.12 Process capability compares the natural variation of the process with the specification range that is required

$$C_p = \text{process capability}$$

$$= \frac{\text{UTL} - \text{LTL}}{6s}$$

$$= \frac{214 - 198}{6 \times 2} = \frac{16}{12}$$

$$= 1.333$$

If the natural variation of the filling process changed to have a process average of 210 grams but the standard deviation of the process remained at 2 grams:

$$C_{pu} = \frac{214 - 210}{3 \times 2} = \frac{4}{6} = 0.666$$

$$C_{pl} = \frac{210 - 198}{3 \times 2} = \frac{12}{6} = 2.0$$

$$C_{pk} = \min(0.666, 2.0)$$

$$= 0.666$$

The Taguchi loss function

Genichi Taguchi has criticized the concept of an acceptable range of variation.[1] He suggested that the consequences of being 'off-target' (that is, deviating from the required process average performance) were inadequately described by simple control limits. Instead, he proposed a quality loss function (QLF) – a mathematical function which includes all the costs of poor quality. These include wastage, repair, inspection, service, warranty, and generally what he termed 'loss to society' costs. This loss function is expressed as follows:

$$L = D^2C$$

where L = total loss to society costs
D = deviation from target performance
C = a constant.

Figure 12.13 illustrates the difference between the conventional and Taguchi approaches to interpreting process variability. The more graduated approach of the QLF shows losses increasing quadratically as performance deviates from target. Because of this there will be an appropriate motivation to progressively reduce process variability. This is sometimes called the *target-oriented* quality philosophy.

Control charts for variables

The most commonly used type of control chart employed to control variables is the $\overline{X}$–R *chart*. In fact this is really two charts in one. One chart is used to control the sample average or mean ($\overline{X}$). The other is used to control the variation within the sample by measuring the range (R). The range is used because it is simpler to calculate than the standard deviation of the sample.

The means ($\overline{X}$) chart can pick up changes in the average output from the process being charted. Changes in the means chart would suggest that the process is drifting generally away from its supposed process average, although the variability inherent in the process may not have changed. The range (R) chart plots the range of each sample, which is the difference between the largest and the smallest measurement in the samples. Monitoring sample range gives an indication of whether the variability of the process is changing, even when the process average remains constant.

Figure 12.13   The conventional and Taguchi views of the cost of variability

Control limits for variables control chart

As with attributes control charts, a statistical description of how the process operates under normal conditions (when there are no assignable causes) can be used to calculate control limits. The first task in calculating the control limits is to estimate the grand average or population mean $(\overline{\overline{X}})$ and average range $(\overline{R})$ using m samples each of sample size n. The population mean is estimated from the average of a large number (m) of sample means:

$$\overline{\overline{X}} = \frac{\overline{X}_1 + \overline{X}_2 + \cdots \overline{X}_m}{m}$$

The average range is estimated from the ranges of the large number of samples:

$$\overline{R} = \frac{R_1 + R_2 + \cdots R_m}{m}$$

The control limits for the sample means chart are:

$$\text{Upper control limit (LCL)} = \overline{\overline{X}} + A_2 \overline{R}$$

$$\text{Lower control limit (LCL)} = \overline{\overline{X}} - A_2 \overline{R}$$

The control limits for the range charts are:

$$\text{Upper control limit (UCL)} = D_4 \overline{R}$$

$$\text{Lower control limit (LCL)} = D_3 \overline{R}$$

The factors A_2, D_3 and D_4 vary with sample size and are shown in Table 12.6.

The LCL for the means chart may be negative (for example, temperature or profit may be less than zero) but it may not be negative for a range chart (or the smallest measurement in the sample would be larger than the largest). If the calculation indicates a negative LCL for a range chart then the LCL should be set to zero.

Worked example

GAM (Groupe À Maquillage) is a contract cosmetics company that manufactures and packs cosmetics and perfumes for other companies. One of its plants operates a filling line that automatically fills plastic bottles with skin cream and seals the bottles with a screw-top cap. The tightness with which the screw-top cap is fixed is an important aspect of quality. If the cap is screwed on too tightly, there is a danger that it will crack; if screwed on too loosely it might come loose. Either

Table 12.6   Factors for the calculation of control limits

Sample size n	A_2	D_3	D_4
2	1.880	0	3.267
3	1.023	0	2.575
4	0.729	0	2.282
5	0.577	0	2.115
6	0.483	0	2.004
7	0.419	0.076	1.924
8	0.373	0.136	1.864
9	0.337	0.184	1.816
10	0.308	0.223	1.777
12	0.266	0.284	1.716
14	0.235	0.329	1.671
16	0.212	0.364	1.636
18	0.194	0.392	1.608
20	0.180	0.414	1.586
22	0.167	0.434	1.566
24	0.157	0.452	1.548

outcome could cause leakage. The plant had received some complaints of product leakage, possibly caused by inconsistent fixing of the screw-tops. Tightness can be measured by the amount of turning force (torque) that is required to unfasten the tops. The company decided to take samples of the bottles coming out of the filling-line process, test them for their unfastening torque and plot the results on a control chart. Several samples of four bottles are taken during a period when the process is regarded as being in control.
The following data are calculated from this exercise:

$$\text{Grand average of all samples } \overline{\overline{X}} = 812 \text{ g/cm}^3$$
$$\text{Average range of the sample } \overline{R} = 6 \text{ g/cm}^3$$

Control limits for the means $(\overline{X})$ chart were calculated as follows:

$$UCL = \overline{\overline{X}} + A_2\overline{R}$$
$$= 812 + (A_2 \times 6)$$

From Table 12.6, we know that, for a sample size of four, $A_2 = 0.729$. Thus:

$$UCL = 812 + (0.729 \times 6)$$
$$= 816.37$$
$$LCL = \overline{\overline{X}} - (A_2\overline{R})$$
$$= 812 - (0.729 \times 6)$$
$$= 807.63$$

Control limits for the range (R) chart were calculated as follows:

$$UCL = D_4 \times \overline{R}$$
$$= 2.282 \times 6$$
$$= 13.69$$
$$LCL = D_3 \times \overline{R}$$
$$= 0 \times 6$$
$$= 0$$

After calculating these averages and limits for the control chart, the company regularly took samples of four bottles during production, recorded the measurements and plotted them as shown in Figure 12.14. This control chart reveals that only with difficulty could the process average be kept in control. Occasional operator interventions are required. Also the process range is moving towards (and once exceeds) the upper control limit. The process also seems to be becoming more variable. (After investigation it was discovered that, because of faulty maintenance of the line, skin cream was occasionally contaminating the part of the line that fitted the cap, resulting in erratic tightening of the caps.)

Control charts for attributes

Attributes have only two states – 'right' or 'wrong', for example – so the statistic calculated is the proportion of wrongs (p) in a sample. (This statistic follows a binomial distribution.) Control charts using p are called 'p-charts'. When calculating control limits, the population mean $(\overline{p})$ (the actual, normal or expected proportion of 'defectives') may not be known. Who knows, for example, the actual number of city commuters who are dissatisfied with their journey time? In such cases the population mean can be estimated from the average of the proportion of 'defectives' $(\overline{p})$, from m samples each of n items,

PART NO.	73/70328A									TOLERANCE	807–817							CHART		
PROCESS	Torque Cap #3		PRODUCT	Ski lan 707																
MACHINE	M732		OPERATOR	CH						UNITS	g/cm³									

Date	2/6																			
Time	6:00	6:30	7:00	7:30	8:00	8:30	9:00	9:30	10:00	10:30	11:00	11:30	12:00	12:30	13:00	13:30	14:00	14:30	15:00	15:30
Sample measurements 1	811	813	811	817	812	813	813	817	808	805	813	812	811	808	812	808	808	804	804	813
2	812	814	813	814	813	814	815	813	813	808	812	805	813	806	813	809	818	813	812	819
3	813	815	815	812	812	814	813	814	811	806	816	806	811	803	808	813	819	812	812	813
4	812	814	813	813	811	815	811	815	813	807	809	808	809	805	804	814	821	808	820	807
5																				
Sum	3248	3256	3252	3248	3248	3256	3252	3259	3245	3225	3250	3231	3244	3222	3237	3244	3266	3237	3248	3252
Mean, X	812	814	813	814	812	814	813	815	811	807	813	808	811	806	809	811	817	809	812	813
Range, R	2	2	4	5	2	2	4	4	5	3	7	7	4	5	9	6	13	9	16	12

Figure 12.14 The completed control form for GAM's torque machine showing the mean $(\overline{X})$ and range $(\overline{R})$ charts

where m should be at least 30 and n should be at least 100:

$$\overline{p} = \frac{p^1 + p^2 + p^3 \cdots p^n}{m}$$

One standard deviation can then be estimated from:

$$\sqrt{\frac{\overline{p}(1 - \overline{p})}{n}}$$

The upper and lower control limits can then be set as:

$$\text{UCL} = \overline{p} + 3 \text{ standard deviations}$$

$$\text{LCL} = \overline{p} - 3 \text{ standard deviations}$$

Of course, the LCL cannot be negative, so when it is calculated to be so it should be rounded up to zero.

Worked example

A credit card company deals with many hundreds of thousands of transactions every week. One of its measures of the quality of service it gives its customers is the dependability with which it mails customers' monthly accounts. The quality standard it sets itself is that accounts should be mailed within two days of the 'nominal post date' which is specified to the customer. Every week the company samples 1000 customer accounts and records the percentage not mailed within the standard time. When the process is working normally, only 2 per cent of accounts are mailed outside the specified period, that is, 2 per cent are 'defective'.

Control limits for the process can be calculated as follows:

$$\text{Mean proportion defective, } \bar{p} = 0.02$$

$$\text{Sample size } n = 1000$$

$$\text{Standard deviation } s = \sqrt{\frac{\bar{p}(1 - \bar{p})}{n}}$$

$$= \sqrt{\frac{0.02(0.98)}{1000}}$$

$$= 0.0044$$

With the control limits at $\bar{p} \pm 3s$:

$$\text{Upper control limit (UCL)} = 0.02 + 3(0.0044) = 0.0332$$

$$= 3.32\%$$

$$\text{Lower control limit (LCL)} = 0.02 - 3(0.0044) = 0.0068$$

$$= 0.68\%$$

Figure 12.15 shows the company's control chart for this measure of quality over the last few weeks, together with the calculated control limits. It also shows that the process is in control.

Sometimes it is more convenient to plot the actual number of defects (c) rather than the proportion (or percentage) of defectives, on what is known as a c-chart. This is very similar to the p-chart but the sample size must be constant and the process mean and control limits are calculated using the following formulae:

$$\text{Process mean } \bar{c} = \frac{c_1 + c_2 + c_3 \cdots c_m}{m}$$

$$\text{Control limits} = \bar{c} \pm 3\sqrt{c}$$

where c = number of defects
       m = number of samples.

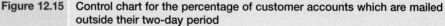

Figure 12.15   **Control chart for the percentage of customer accounts which are mailed outside their two-day period**

Note on chapter supplement

1. For more details of Taguchi's ideas, see Stuart, G. (1993) *Taguchi Methods: A hands-on approach,* Addison Wesley.
2. Taguchi, G. and Clausing, D. (1990) 'Robust quality', *Harvard Business Review,* Vol. 68, No. 1, pp. 65–75. For more details of the Taguchi approach, see Stuart, *op. cit.*

13

IMPROVEMENT

Introduction

All operations, no matter how well managed, are capable of improvement. In fact in recent years the emphasis has shifted markedly towards making improvement one of the main responsibilities of operations managers. And although the whole of this book is focused on improving the performance of individual processes, operations and whole supply networks, there are some issues that relate to the activity of improvement itself. In any operation, whatever is improved, and however it is done, the overall direction and approach to improvement needs to be addressed. (See Figure 13.1.)

Source: Courtesy LotusHead, http://www.pixelpusher.co.za

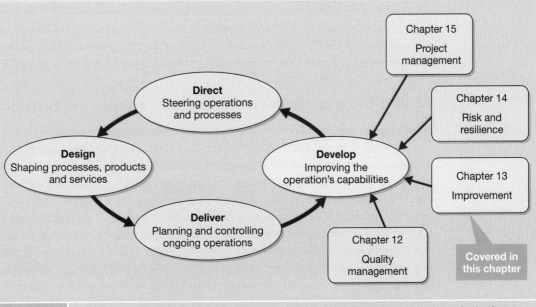

Figure 13.1   Improvement is the activity of closing the gap between the current and the desired performance of an operation or process

Executive summary

VIDEO
further detail

Decision logic chain for improvement

Each chapter is structured around a set of diagnostic questions. These questions suggest what you should ask in order to gain an understanding of the important issues of a topic, and as a result, improve your decision making. An executive summary, addressing these questions, is provided below.

What is improvement?

Improvement is the activity of closing the gap between the current and the desired perform-ance of an operation or process. It is increasingly seen as the ultimate objective for all opera-tions and process management activity. Furthermore, almost all popular operations initiatives in recent years, such as total quality management, lean operations, business process re-engineering and Six Sigma, have all focused on performance improvement. It involves assess-ing the gaps between current and required performance, balancing the use of continuous improvement and breakthrough improvement, adopting appropriate improvement techniques, and attempting to ensure that the momentum of improvement does not fade over time.

What is the gap between current and required performance?

Assessing the gap between actual and desired performance is the starting point for most improvement. This requires two sets of activities: first, assessing the operation's and each process's current performance; and second, deciding on an appropriate level of target per-formance. The first activity will depend on how performance is measured within the opera-tion. This involves deciding what aspects of performance to measure, which are the most important aspects of performance, and what detailed measures should be used to assess each factor. The balanced scorecard approach is an approach to performance measurement that is currently influential in many organizations. Setting targets for performance can be done in a number of ways. These include historically based targets, strategic targets that reflect strategic objectives, external performance targets that relate to external and/or competitor operations, and absolute performance targets based on the theoretical upper limit of per-formance. Benchmarking is an important input to this part of performance improvement.

What is the most appropriate improvement path?

Two improvement paths represent different philosophies of improvement, although both may be appropriate at different times. They are breakthrough improvement and continuous improvement. Breakthrough improvement focused on major and dramatic changes that are intended to result in dramatic increases in performance. The business process re-engineering approach is typical of breakthrough improvement. Continuous improvement focuses on small but never-ending improvements that become part of normal operations life. Its objective is to make improvement part of the culture of the organization. Often continuous improvement involves the use of multi-stage improvement cycles for regular problem solving. The Six Sigma approach to improvement brings many existing ideas together and can be seen as a combination of continuous and breakthrough improvement.

What techniques should be used to facilitate improvement?

Almost all techniques in operations management contribute directly or indirectly to performance improvement. However, some more general techniques have become popularly associated with improvement. These include scatter diagrams (correlation), cause–effect diagrams, Pareto analysis, and why–why analysis.

How can improvement be made to stick?

One of the biggest problems in improvement is to preserve improvement momentum over time. One factor that inhibits improvement becoming accepted as a regular part of operations activity is the emphasis on the fashionability of each new improvement approach. Most new improvement ideas contain some worthwhile elements but none will provide the ultimate answer. There must be some overall management of the improvement process that can absorb the best of each new idea. And, although authorities differ to some extent, most emphasize the importance of an improvement strategy, top management support, and training.

DIAGNOSTIC QUESTION

What is improvement?

Improvement comes from closing the gap between what you are and what you want to be. In a specifically operations context, it comes from closing the gap between current and desired performance. Performance improvement is the ultimate objective of operations and process management. It has also become the subject of innumerable ideas that have been put forward as particularly effective methods of ensuring improvement. These include many that are described in this book, for example, total quality management (TQM), 'lean' operations, business process re-engineering (BPR), Six Sigma, and so on. All of these, and other, ideas have something to contribute. What is important is that all managers develop an understanding of the underlying elements of improvement. The following two examples illustrate many of these.

> **Operations principle**
> Performance improvement is the ultimate objective of operations and process management.

Example   ### Improvement at Heineken[1]

Heineken International brews beer that is sold around the world and operates in over 170 countries with brands such as Heineken and Amstel. Its Zoeterwoude facility, a packaging plant that fills bottles and cans in The Netherlands, faced two challenges. First, it needed to improve its operations processes to reduce its costs. Second, it needed to improve the efficiency of its existing lines in order to increase their capacity, without which it would have to invest in a new packaging line. The goal of a 20 per cent improvement in operating efficiency was set because it was seen as challenging, yet achievable. It was also decided to focus the improvement project around two themes: (a) obtaining accurate operational data on which improvement decisions could be based, and (b) changing the culture of the operation to promote fast and effective decision making. Before the improvement, project staff at the Zoeterwoude plant had approached problem-solving as an *ad hoc* activity, only to be done when circumstances made it unavoidable. By contrast, the improvement initiative taught the staff to use various problem-solving techniques such as cause–effect and Pareto diagrams (discussed later in this chapter).

Source: courtesy Heineken International

'*Until we started using these techniques*', says Wilbert Raaijmakers, Heineken Netherlands Brewery Director, '*there was little consent regarding what was causing any problems. There was poor communication between the various departments and job grades. For example, maintenance staff believed that production stops were caused by operating errors, while operators were of the opinion that poor maintenance was the cause.*' The use of better information, analysis and improvement techniques helped the staff to identify and treat the root causes of problems. With many potential improvements to make, staff teams were encouraged to set priorities that would reflect the overall improvement target. There was also widespread use of benchmarking performance against targets to gauge progress.

Improvement teams had been 'empowered, organized, and motivated' before the improvement initiative, through the company's 'cultural change' programme. '*Its aim*', according to Wilbert Raaijmakers, '*was to move away from a command-and-control situation and evolve towards a more team-oriented organization.'* Fundamental to this was a programme to improve the skills and knowledge of individual operators through special training programmes. Nevertheless, the improvement initiative exposed a number of further challenges. For example, the improvement team discovered that people were more motivated to improve when the demand was high, but it was more difficult to motivate them when production pressures were lower. To overcome this, communication was improved so that staff were kept fully informed of future production levels and the upcoming schedule of training and maintenance activities that were planned during slumps in demand, the lesson being that it is difficult to convince people to change if they are not aware of the underlying reason for it. Even so, some staff much preferred to stick with their traditional methods, and some team leaders were more skilled at encouraging change than others. Many staff needed coaching, reassurance and formal training on how to take ownership of problems. But, at the end of 12 months, the improvement project had achieved its 20 per cent goal, allowing the plant to increase the volume of its exports and cut its costs significantly. Yet Wilbert Raaijmakers still sees room for improvement: *'The optimization of an organization is a never-ending process. If you sit back and do the same thing tomorrow as you did today, you'll never make it. We must remain alert to the latest developments and stretch the resulting information to its full potential.'*

Example   Taxing quality[2]

Source: © Keith Brofsky/Getty Images

Operations effectiveness is just as important an issue in public sector operations as it is for commercial companies. People have the right to expect that their taxes are not wasted on inefficient or inappropriate public processes. This is especially true of the tax collecting system, which is never a popular organization in any country, and taxpayers can be especially critical when the tax collection process is not well managed. This was very much on the minds of the Aarhus Region Customs and Tax unit (Aarhus CT) when they developed their improvement initiative. The Aarhus Region is the largest of Denmark's 29 local customs and tax offices. It acts as an agent for central government in collecting taxes while being able to respond to taxpayers' queries. Aarhus CT must *'keep the user (customer) in focus',* they say. *'Users must pay what is due – no more, no less and on time. But users are entitled to fair control and collection, fast and efficient case work, service and guidance, flexible employees, polite behaviour and a professional telephone service.'* The Aarhus CT approach to managing its performance initiative was built around a number of key points.

- A recognition that poorly designed and managed processes cause waste both internally and externally.
- A determination to adopt a practice of regularly surveying the satisfaction of its users. Employees were also surveyed, both to understand their views on quality and to check that their working environment would help to instil the principles of high performance service.
- Although a not-for-profit organization, performance measures included measuring the organization's adherence to financial targets as well as error reporting.
- Internal processes were redefined and redesigned to emphasize customer needs and internal staff requirements. For example, Aarhus CT was the only tax region in Denmark to develop an independent information process that was used to analyze customers' needs and 'prevent misunderstanding in users' perception of legislation'.
- Internal processes were designed to allow staff the time and opportunity to develop their own skills, exchange ideas with colleagues and take on greater responsibility for management of their own work processes.
- The organization set up what it called its 'Quality Organization' (QO) structure that spanned all divisions and processes. The idea of the QO was to foster staff commitment to continuous improvement and to encourage the development of ideas for improving process performance. Within the QO was the Quality Group (QG). This consisted of four managers and four process

staff, and reported directly to senior management. It also set up a number of improvement groups and suggestion groups consisting of managers as well as process staff. The role of the suggestion groups was to collect and process ideas for improvement which the improvement groups would then analyze and if appropriate implement.

- Aarhus CT were keen to stress that their Quality Groups would eventually become redundant if they were to be successful. In the short term they would maintain a stream of improvement ideas, but in the long term they should have fully integrated the idea of quality improvement into the day-to-day activities of all staff.

What do these two examples have in common?

The improvement initiatives at these two operations, and the way they managed them, is typical of improvement projects. Both measured performance and placed information gathering at the centre of their improvement initiative. Both had a view of improvement targets that related directly to strategic objectives. Both made efforts to collect information that would allow decisions based on evidence rather than opinion. Heineken also made extensive use of simple improvement techniques that would both analyze problems and help to channel its staff's creativity at all levels. Aarhus CT focused on their customers' perceptions, needs and requirements. This included what customers should not receive as well as what they should receive from the operation. Both companies had to foster an environment that allowed all staff to contribute to improvement, and both came to view improvement not as a 'one-off', but rather as the start of a never-ending cycle of improvement. Most importantly, both had to decide how to organize the whole improvement initiative. Different organizations with different objectives may choose to implement improvement initiatives in a different way. But all will face a similar set of issues to these two operations, even if they choose to make different decisions.

DIAGNOSTIC QUESTION

What is the gap between current and required performance?

The gap between how an operation or process is currently performing and how it wishes to perform is the key driver of any improvement initiative. The wider the gap, the more importance is likely to be given to improvement. But, in order to harness the gap as a driver of improvement, it must be addressed in some detail, in terms of both exactly what is failing to meet targets, and by how much. Answering these questions depends on the operation's ability to do three things: assess its current performance, derive a set of target levels of performance that the organization can subscribe to, and compare current against target performance in a systematic and graphic manner that demonstrates to everyone the need for improvement.

Assessing current performance – performance measurement

Some kind of *performance measurement* is a prerequisite for judging whether an operation is good, bad or indifferent, although this is not the only reason for investing in effective performance measurement. Without one, it would be impossible to exert any control over an operation on an ongoing basis. However, a performance measurement system that gives no help to ongoing improvement is only partially effective. Performance measurement, as we are treating it here, concerns three generic issues:

> **Operations principle**
> Performance measurement is a prerequisite for the assessment of operations performance.

- What factors to include as performance measures?
- Which are the most important performance measures?
- What detailed measures to use?

What factors to include as performance measures?

An obvious starting point for deciding which performance measures to adopt is to use the five generic performance objectives – quality, speed, dependability, flexibility and cost. These can be broken down into more detailed measures, or they can be aggregated into 'composite' measures, such as 'customer satisfaction', 'overall service level' or 'operations agility'. These composite measures may be further aggregated by using measures such as 'achieve market objectives', 'achieve financial objectives', 'achieve operations objectives' or even 'achieve overall strategic objectives'. The more aggregated performance measures have greater strategic relevance in so much as they help to draw a picture of the overall performance of the business, although by doing so they necessarily include many influences outside those that operations performance improvement would normally address. The more detailed performance measures are usually monitored more closely and more often, and although they provide a limited view of an operation's performance, they do provide a more descriptive and complete picture of what should be and what is happening within the operation. In practice, most organizations will choose to use performance targets from throughout the range. This idea is illustrated in Figure 13.2.

Choosing the important performance measures

One of the problems of devising a useful performance measurement system is trying to achieve some balance between having a few key measures on one hand (straightforward and simple, but may not reflect the full range of organizational objectives), or, on the other hand, having many detailed measures (complex and difficult to manage, but capable of conveying many nuances of performance). Broadly, a compromise is reached by making sure that there is a clear link between the operation's overall strategy, the most important (or 'key') performance indicators (KPIs) that reflect strategic objectives, and the bundle of detailed measures that are used to 'flesh out' each key performance indicator. Obviously, unless strategy is well defined then it is difficult to 'target' a narrow range of key performance indicators.

> **Operations principle**
> Without strategic clarity, key performance indicators cannot be appropriately targeted.

What detailed measures to use?

The five performance objectives – quality, speed, dependability, flexibility and cost – are really composites of many smaller measures. For example, an operation's cost is derived from many factors which could include the purchasing efficiency of the operation, the efficiency with which it converts materials, the productivity of its staff, the ratio of direct to indirect staff, and so on. All of these measures individually give a partial view of the operation's cost performance, and many of them overlap in terms of the information they include. However, each of them does give a perspective on the cost performance of

Figure 13.2   Performance measures can involve different levels of aggregation

an operation that could be useful either to identify areas for improvement or to monitor the extent of improvement. If an organization regards its 'cost' performance as unsatisfactory, disaggregating it into 'purchasing efficiency', 'operations efficiency', 'staff productivity', etc. might explain the root cause of the poor performance. Table 13.1 shows some of the partial measures which can be used to judge an operation's performance.

The balanced scorecard approach

The balanced scorecard retains traditional financial measures. But financial measures tell the story of past events, an adequate story for industrial age companies for which investments in long-term capabilities [and] customer relationships were not critical for success. These financial measures are inadequate, however, for guiding and evaluating the journey that information age companies must make to create future value through investment in customers, suppliers, employees, processes, technology, and innovation.[3]

Generally operations performance measures have been broadening in their scope. It is now generally accepted that the scope of measurement should, at some level, include external as well as internal, long-term as well as short-term, and 'soft' as well as 'hard' measures. The best-known manifestation of this trend is the 'Balanced Scorecard' approach taken by Kaplan and Norton.[4] As well as including financial measures of performance, in the same way as traditional performance measurement systems, the balanced scorecard approach also attempts to provide the important information that is required to allow the overall strategy of an organization to be reflected adequately in specific performance measures. In addition to financial measures of performance, it also includes more operational measures of customer satisfaction, internal processes, innovation and other improvement activities. In doing so it measures the factors behind financial performance which are seen as the key drivers of future financial success. In

Table 13.1	Some typical partial measures of performance
Performance objective	**Some typical measures**
Quality	Number of defects per unit Level of customer complaints Scrap level Warranty claims Mean time between failures Customer satisfaction score
Speed	Customer query time Order lead time Frequency of delivery Actual versus theoretical throughput time Cycle time
Dependability	Percentage of orders delivered late Average lateness of orders Proportion of products in stock Mean deviation from promised arrival Schedule adherence
Flexibility	Time needed to develop new products/services Range of products/services Machine changeover time Average batch size Time to increase activity rate Average/maximum capacity Time to change schedules
Cost	Minimum/average delivery time Variance against budget Utilization of resources Labour productivity Added value Efficiency Cost per operation hour

particular, it is argued that a balanced range of measures enables managers to address the following questions (see Figure 13.3):

- How do we look to our shareholders (financial perspective)?
- What must we excel at (internal process perspective)?
- How do our customers see us (the customer perspective)?
- How can we continue to improve and build capabilities (the learning and growth perspective)?

The balanced scorecard attempts to bring together the elements that reflect a business's strategic position, including product or service quality measures, product and service development times, customer complaints, labour productivity, and so on. At the same time it attempts to avoid performance reporting becoming unwieldy by restricting the number of measures and focusing especially on those seen to be essential. The advantages of the approach are that it presents an overall picture of the organization's performance in a single report, and by being comprehensive in the measures of performance it uses, encourages companies to take decisions in the interests of the whole organization rather than sub-optimizing around narrow measures. Developing a balanced scorecard is a complex process and is now the subject of considerable debate. One of the key questions that have to be considered is how specific measures of performance should be designed. Inadequately designed performance measures can result in dysfunctional behaviour, so teams of managers are often used to develop a scorecard which reflects their organization's specific needs.

Figure 13.3   The measures used in the balanced scorecard

Setting target performance

A performance measure means relatively little until it is compared against some kind of target. Knowing that only one document in 500 is sent out to customers containing an error tells us relatively little unless we know whether this is better or worse than we were achieving previously, and whether it is better or worse than other similar operations (especially competitors) are achieving. Setting performance targets transforms performance measures into performance 'judgements'. Several approaches to setting targets can be used, including the following.

- *Historically based targets* – targets that compare current against previous performance.
- *Strategic targets* – targets set to reflect the level of performance that is regarded as appropriate to achieve strategic objectives.
- *External performance-based targets* – targets set to reflect the performance that is achieved by similar, or competitor, external operations.
- *Absolute performance targets* – targets based on the theoretical upper limit of performance.

One of the problems in setting targets is that different targets can give very different messages regarding the improvement being achieved. So, for example, in Figure 13.4, one of an operation's performance measures is 'delivery' (in this case defined as the proportion of orders delivered on time). The performance for one month has been measured at 83 per cent, but any judgement regarding performance will be dependent on the performance targets. Using a *historical* target, when compared to last year's performance of 60 per cent, this month's performance of 83 per cent is good. But, if the operation's *strategy* calls for a 95 per cent delivery performance, the actual performance of 83 per cent looks decidedly poor. The company may also be concerned with how they perform against *competitors'* performance. If competitors are currently averaging delivery performances of around 80 per cent the company's performance looks rather good. Finally, the more ambitious managers within the company may wish to at least try and seek perfection. Why not, they argue, use an

Operations principle
Performance measures only have meaning when compared against targets.

Figure 13.4   Different standards of comparison give different messages

absolute performance standard of 100 per cent delivery on time? Against this standard the company's actual 83 per cent again looks disappointing.

Benchmarking

Benchmarking is 'the process of learning from others' and involves comparing one's own performance or methods against other comparable operations. It is a broader issue than setting performance targets, and includes investigating other organizations' operations practice in order to derive ideas that could contribute to performance improvement. Its rationale is based on the ideas that (a) problems in managing processes are almost certainly shared by processes elsewhere, and (b) there is probably another oper-

> **Operations principle**
> Improvement is aided by contextualizing processes and operations.

ation somewhere that has developed a better way of doing things. For example, a bank might learn some things from a supermarket about how it could cope with demand fluctuations during the day. Benchmarking is essentially about stimulating creativity in improvement practice.

Types of benchmarking

There are many different types of benchmarking (which are not necessarily mutually exclusive), some of which are listed below:

- *Internal benchmarking* is a comparison between operations or parts of operations which are within the same total organization. For example, a large motor vehicle manufacturer with several factories might choose to benchmark each factory against the others.
- *External benchmarking* is a comparison between an operation and other operations which are part of a different organization.
- *Non-competitive benchmarking* is benchmarking against external organizations which do not compete directly in the same markets.
- *Competitive benchmarking* is a comparison directly between competitors in the same, or similar, markets.
- *Performance benchmarking* is a comparison between the levels of achieved performance in different operations. For example, an operation might compare its own performance

in terms of some or all of our performance objectives – quality, speed, dependability, flexibility and cost – against other organizations' performance in the same dimensions.

● *Practice benchmarking* is a comparison between an organization's operations practices, or ways of doing things, and those adopted by another operation. For example, a large retail store might compare its systems and procedures for controlling stock levels with those used by another department store.

Benchmarking as an improvement tool

Although benchmarking has become popular, some businesses have failed to derive maximum benefit from it. Partly this may be because there are some misunderstandings as to what benchmarking actually entails. First, it is not a 'one-off' project. It is best practised as a continuous process of comparison. Second, it does not provide 'solutions'. Rather, it provides ideas and information that can lead to solutions. Third, it does not involve simply copying or imitating other operations. It is a process of learning and adapting in a pragmatic manner. Fourth, it means devoting resources to the activity. Benchmarking cannot be done without some investment, but this does not necessarily mean allocating exclusive responsibility to a set of highly paid managers. In fact, there can be advantages in organizing staff at all levels to investigate and collate information from benchmarking targets. There are also some basic rules about how benchmarking can be organized.

● A prerequisite for benchmarking success is to understand thoroughly your own processes. Without this it is difficult to compare your processes against those of other companies.

● Look at the information that is available in the public domain. Published accounts, journals, conferences and professional associations can all provide information that is useful for benchmarking purposes.

● Do not discard information because it seems irrelevant. Small pieces of information only make sense in the context of other pieces of information that may emerge subsequently.

● Be sensitive in asking for information from other companies. Don't ask any questions that we would not like to be asked ourselves.

PRACTICE NOTE

Assess the gap between actual and target performance

A comparison of actual and target performance should guide the relative priorities for improvement. A significant aspect of performance is the relative importance of the various performance measures. Because some factor of performance is relatively poor does not mean that it should be improved immediately if current performance as a whole exceeds target performance. In fact, both the relative importance of the various performance measures, and their performance against target, need to be brought together in order to prioritize for improvement. One way of doing this is through the importance–performance matrix.

The importance–performance matrix

As its name implies, the importance–performance matrix positions each aspect of performance on a matrix according to its scores or ratings on how important each aspect of relative performance is, and what performance it is currently achieving. Figure 13.5 shows an importance–performance matrix divided into zones of improvement priority. The first zone boundary is the 'lower bound of acceptability' shown as line AB in Figure 13.5.

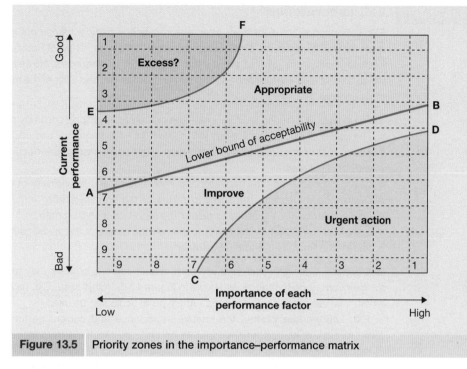

Figure 13.5 Priority zones in the importance–performance matrix

This is the boundary between acceptable and unacceptable current performance. When some aspect of performance is rated as relatively unimportant, this boundary will be low. Most operations are prepared to tolerate lower performance for relatively unimportant performance factors. However, for performance factors that are rated more important, they will be markedly less sanguine at poor or mediocre levels of current performance. Below this minimum bound of acceptability (AB) there is clearly a need for improvement; above this line there is no immediate urgency for any improvement. However, not all factors of performance that fall below the minimum line will be seen as having the same degree of improvement priority. A boundary approximately represented by line CD represents a distinction between an urgent priority zone and a less urgent improvement zone. Similarly, above the line AB, not all competitive factors are regarded as having the same priority. The line EF can be seen as the approximate boundary between performance levels which are regarded as 'good' or 'appropriate' on one hand and those regarded as 'too good' or 'excess' on the other. Segregating the matrix in this way results in four zones which imply very different priorities:

- *The 'appropriate' zone.* Performance factors in this area lie above the lower bound of acceptability and so should be considered satisfactory.
- *The 'improve' zone.* Lying below the lower bound of acceptability, any performance factors in this zone must be candidates for improvement.
- *The 'urgent-action' zone.* These performance factors are important to customers but current performance is unacceptable. They must be considered as candidates for immediate improvement.
- *The 'excess?' zone.* Performance factors in this area are 'high performing', but are not particularly important. The question must be asked, therefore, whether the resources devoted to achieving such a performance could be used better elsewhere.

PRACTICE NOTE

Example **EXL Laboratories**

EXL Laboratories is a subsidiary of an electronics company. It carries out research and development as well as technical problem-solving work for a wide range of companies. It is particularly keen to improve the level of service that it gives to its customers. However, it needs to decide which aspect of its performance to improve first. It has devised a list of the most important aspects of its service:

- *The quality of its technical solutions* – the perceived appropriateness by customers.
- *The quality of its communications with customers* – the frequency and usefulness of information.
- *The quality of post-project documentation* – the usefulness of the documentation which goes with the final report.
- *Delivery speed* – the time between customer request and the delivery of the final report.
- *Delivery dependability* – the ability to deliver on the promised date.
- *Delivery flexibility* – the ability to deliver the report on a revised date.
- *Specification flexibility* – the ability to change the nature of the investigation.
- *Price* – the total charge to the customer.

EXL assigns a rating to each of these performance factors, both for their relative importance and for their current performance, as shown in Figure 13.6. In this case, EXL have used a 1 to 9 scale, where 1 is 'very important', or 'good'. Any type of scale can be used.

EXL Laboratories plotted the relative importance and current performance ratings it had given to each of its performance factors on an importance–performance matrix. This is shown in Figure 13.7. It shows that the most important aspect of performance – the ability to deliver sound technical solutions to its customers – falls comfortably within the 'appropriate' zone. Specification flexibility and delivery flexibility are also in the 'appropriate' zone, although only just. Both delivery speed and delivery dependability seem to be in need of improvement as each is below the minimum level of acceptability for their respective importance positions. However, two competitive factors, communications and cost/price, are clearly in need of immediate improvement. These two factors should therefore be assigned the most urgent priority for improvement. The matrix also indicates that the company's documentation could almost be regarded as 'too good'.

Figure 13.6 Ratings of relative importance and current performance at EXL Laboratories

Figure 13.7   The importance–performance matrix for EXL Laboratories

The sandcone theory

As well as approaches that base improvement priority on an operation's specific circumstances, some authorities believe that there is also a generic 'best' sequence of improvement. The best-known theory is called *the sandcone theory*,[5] so called because the sand is analogous to management effort and resources. Building a stable sandcone needs a stable foundation of quality, upon which one can build layers of dependability, speed, flexibility and cost: see Figure 13.8. Building up improvement is thus a cumulative process, not a sequential one. Moving on to the second priority for improvement does not mean dropping the first, and so on. According to the sandcone theory, the first priority should be *quality*, since this is a precondition to all lasting improvement. Only when the operation has reached a minimally acceptable level of quality should it then tackle the next issue, that of internal *dependability*. Importantly, though, moving on to include dependability in the improvement process will actually require further improvement in quality. Once a critical level of dependability is reached, enough to provide some stability to the operation, the next stage is to improve the *speed* of internal throughput, but again only while continuing to improve quality and dependability further. Soon it will become evident that the most effective way to improve speed is through improvements in response *flexibility*, that is, changing things within the operation faster. Again, including flexibility in the improvement process should not divert attention from continuing to work further on quality, dependability and speed. Only now, according to the sandcone theory, should *cost* be tackled head on.

Figure 13.8　The sandcone model of improvement: cost reduction relies on a cumulative foundation of improvement in the other performance objectives

DIAGNOSTIC QUESTION

What is the most appropriate improvement path?

Once the priority of improvement has been determined, an operation must consider the approach or path it wishes to take to reaching its improvement goals. Two paths represent different, and to some extent opposing, philosophies – *breakthrough improvement* and *continuous improvement*. Although they represent different philosophies of improvement, they are not mutually exclusive. Few operations cannot benefit from improving their operations performance on a continuous basis, and few operations would reject investing in a major improvement breakthrough leap in performance if it represented good value. For most operations, both approaches are relevant to some extent, although possibly at different points in time. But to understand how and when each approach is appropriate one must understand their underlying philosophies.

> **Operations principle**
> Breakthrough and continuous improvement are not mutually exclusive.

Breakthrough improvement

Breakthrough (or 'innovation'-based) improvement assumes that the main vehicle of improvement is major and dramatic change in the way the operation works, for example the total reorganization of an operation's process structure, or the introduction of a fully integrated information system. The impact of these improvements represents a step change in practice (and hopefully performance). Such improvements can be expensive,

Figure 13.9   'Breakthrough' improvement may not provide the dramatic leaps in performance hoped for

often disrupting the ongoing workings of the operation, and frequently involving changes in the product/service or process technology. The red line in Figure 13.9 illustrates the intended pattern of performance with several breakthrough improvements. The improvement pattern illustrated by the blue line in Figure 13.9 is regarded by some as being more representative of what really occurs when operations rely on pure breakthrough improvement.

The business process re-engineering approach

Typical of the radical breakthrough way of tackling improvement is the business process re-engineering (BPR) approach. It is a blend of a number of ideas such as fast throughput, waste elimination through process flow charting, customer-focused operations, and so on. But it was the potential of information technologies to enable the fundamental redesign of processes that acted as the catalyst in bringing these ideas together. BPR has been defined as *'the fundamental rethinking and radical redesign of business processes to achieve dramatic improvements in critical, contemporary measures of performance, such as cost, quality, service and speed.'*[6]

Underlying the BPR approach is the belief that operations should be organized around the total process that adds value for customers, rather than the functions or activities that perform the various stages of the value-adding activity. (Figure 1.6 in Chapter 1 illustrated this idea.) The core of BPR is a redefinition of the processes within a total operation, to reflect the business processes that satisfy customer needs. Figure 13.10 illustrates this idea. The main principles of BPR have been summarized as follows:[7]

- Rethink business processes in a cross-functional manner that organizes work around the natural flow of information (or materials or customers). This means organizing around outcomes of a process rather than the tasks which go into it.
- Strive for dramatic improvements in the performance by radically rethinking and redesigning the process.
- Have those who use the output from a process perform the process. Check to see whether all internal customers can be their own supplier rather than depending on another function in the business to supply them (which takes longer and separates out the stages in the process).
- Put decision points where the work is performed. Do not separate those who do the work from those who control and manage the work. Control and action are just one more type of supplier–customer relationship that can be merged.

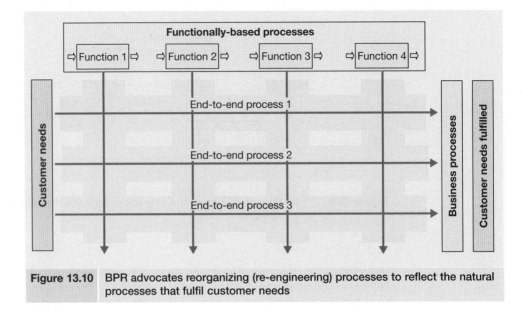

Figure 13.10   BPR advocates reorganizing (re-engineering) processes to reflect the natural processes that fulfil customer needs

Continuous improvement

Continuous improvement, as the name implies, adopts an approach to improving performance that assumes a never-ending series of small incremental improvement steps, for example modifying the way a product is fixed to a machine to reduce changeover time, or simplifying the question sequence when taking a hotel reservation. While there is no guarantee that such small steps towards better performance will be followed by other steps, the whole philosophy of continuous improvement attempts to ensure that they will be. It is also known as *kaizen,* defined by Masaaki Imai (who has been one of the main proponents of continuous improvement) as follows: '*Kaizen means improvement. Moreover, it means improvement in personal life, home life, social life and work life. When applied to the work place, kaizen means continuing improvement involving everyone – managers and workers alike.'*[8]

Continuous improvement is not concerned with promoting small improvements *per se,* but it does see small improvements as having one significant advantage over large ones – they can be followed relatively painlessly by others. It is not the *rate* of improvement which is important; it is the *momentum* of improvement. It does not matter if successive improvements are small; what does matter is that every month (or week, or quarter, or whatever period is appropriate) some kind of improvement has actually taken place. Continuous improvement does not always come naturally. There are specific abilities, behaviours and actions which need to be consciously developed if continuous improvement is to be sustained over the long term. Bessant and Caffyn[9] distinguish between what they call 'organizational abilities' (the ability to adopt a particular approach to continuous improvement),' constituent behaviours' (the behaviour that staff adopt) and 'enablers' (the techniques used to progress the continuous improvement effort). They identify six generic organizational abilities, each with its own set of constituent behaviours. These are identified in Table 13.2. Examples of enablers are the improvement techniques described later in this chapter.

FURTHER EXAMPLE

Table 13.2 Continuous improvement (CI) abilities and some associated behaviours

Organizational ability	Constituent behaviours
Getting the CI habit Developing the ability to generate sustained involvement in CI	• People use formal problem-finding and solving cycle • People use simple tools and techniques • People use simple measurement to shape the improvement process • Individuals and/or groups initiate and carry through CI activities – they participate in the process • Ideas are responded to in a timely fashion – either implemented or otherwise dealt with • Managers support the CI process through allocation of resources • Managers recognize in formal ways the contribution of employees to CI • Managers lead by example, becoming actively involved in design and implementation of CI • Managers support experiment not by punishing mistakes, but instead by encouraging learning from them
Focusing on CI Generating and sustaining the ability to link CI activities to the strategic goals of the company	• Individuals and groups use the organization's strategic objectives to prioritize improvements • Everyone is able to explain what the operation's strategy and objectives are • Individuals and groups assess their proposed changes against the operation's objectives • Individuals and groups monitor/measure the results of their improvement activity • CI activities are an integral part of the individual's or group's work, not a parallel activity
Spreading the word Generating the ability to move CI activity across organizational boundaries	• People cooperate in cross-functional groups • People understand and share a holistic view (process understanding and ownership) • People are oriented towards internal and external customers in their CI activity • Specific CI projects with outside agencies (customers, suppliers, etc.) take place • Relevant CI activities involve representatives from different organizational levels
CI on the CI system Generating the ability to manage strategically the development of CI	• The CI system is continually monitored and developed • There is a cyclical planning process whereby the CI system is regularly reviewed and amended • There is periodic review of the CI system in relation to the organization as a whole • Senior management make available sufficient resources (time, money, personnel) to support the development of the CI system • The CI system itself is designed to fit within the current structure and infrastructure • When a major organizational change is planned, its potential impact on the CI system is assessed
Walking the talk Generating the ability to articulate and demonstrate CI's values	• The 'management style' reflects commitment to CI values • When something goes wrong, people at all levels look for reasons why, rather than blame individuals • People at all levels demonstrate a shared belief in the value of small steps and that everyone can contribute, by themselves being actively involved in making and recognizing incremental improvements

continued overleaf

Table 13.2	Continuous improvement (CI) abilities and some associated behaviours (*continued*)
Organizational ability	*Constituent behaviours*
Building the learning organization Generating the ability to learn through CI activity	• Everyone learns from their experiences, both good and bad • Individuals seeks out opportunities for learning/personal development • Individuals and groups at all levels share their learning • The organization captures and shares the learning of individuals and groups • Managers accept and act on all the learning that takes place • Organizational mechanisms are used to deploy what has been learned across the organization

Source: Bessant, J. and Caffyn, S. (1997) 'High involvement innovation', *International Journal of Technology Management*, Vol. 14, No.1.

Improvement cycle models

An important element of continuous improvement is the idea that improvement can be represented by a never-ending process of repeatedly questioning and re-questioning the detailed working of a process. This is usually summarized by the idea of the *improvement cycle,* of which there are many, including some proprietary models owned by consultancy companies. Two of the more generally used models are the PDCA cycle (sometimes called the Deming Cycle, named after the famous quality 'guru', W.E. Deming), and the DMAIC cycle (made popular by the Six Sigma approach to improvement – see later).

> **Operations principle**
> Continuous improvement necessarily implies a never-ending cycle of analysis and action.

The PDCA cycle

The PDCA cycle model is shown in Figure 13.11(a). It starts with the P (for plan) stage, which involves an examination of the current method or the problem area being studied. This involves collecting and analyzing data so as to formulate a plan of action which is intended to improve performance. (Some of the techniques used to collect and analyze

(a)　　　　　　　　　(b)

Figure 13.11　(a) The plan–do–check–act, or 'Deming' improvement cycle;
(b) the define–measure–analyze–improve–control, or DMAIC Six Sigma improvement cycle

data are explained later.) The next step is the D (for do) stage. This is the implementation stage during which the plan is tried out in the operation. This stage may itself involve a mini-PDCA cycle as the problems of implementation are resolved. Next comes the C (for check) stage where the new implemented solution is evaluated to see whether it has resulted in the expected improvement. Finally, at least for this cycle, comes the A (for act) stage. During this stage the change is consolidated or standardized if it has been successful. Alternatively, if the change has not been successful, the lessons learned from the 'trial' are formalized before the cycle starts again.

The DMAIC cycle

In some ways this cycle is more intuitively obvious than the PDCA cycle in so much as it follows a more 'experimental' approach. The DMAIC cycle starts with defining the problem or problems, partly to understand the scope of what needs to be done and partly to define exactly the requirements of the process improvement. Often at this stage a formal goal or target for the improvement is set. After definition comes the measurement stage, important because the Six Sigma approach emphasizes the importance of working with hard evidence rather than opinion. It involves validating the problem (to make sure it is really worth solving), using data to refine the problem and measuring exactly what is happening. The analysis stage can be seen as an opportunity to develop hypotheses as to what the root causes of the problem really are. Such hypotheses are validated (or not) by the analysis and the main root causes of the problem identified. Once the causes of the problem are identified, work can begin on improving the process. Ideas are developed to remove the root causes of problems, solutions are tested and those solutions that seem to work are implemented, formalized and results measured. The improved process needs then to be continually monitored and controlled to check that the improved level of performance is sustaining. The then cycle starts again, defining the problems that are preventing further improvement.

The last point in both cycles is the most important – *'the cycle starts again'*. It is only by accepting that in a continuous improvement philosophy these cycles quite literally never stop that improvement becomes part of every person's job.

The differences between breakthrough and continuous improvement

Breakthrough improvement places a high value on creative solutions, and encourages free thinking and individualism. It is a radical philosophy in so much as it fosters an approach to improvement which does not accept many constraints on what is possible. 'Starting with a clean sheet of paper', 'going back to first principles' and 'completely rethinking the system' are all typical breakthrough improvement principles. Continuous improvement, on the other hand, is less ambitious, at least in the short term. It stresses adaptability, teamwork and attention to detail. It is not radical; rather it builds upon the wealth of accumulated experience within the operation itself, often relying primarily on the people who operate the system to improve it. One analogy used to explain this difference is the sprint versus the marathon. Breakthrough improvement is a series of explosive and impressive sprints. Continuous improvement, like marathon running, does not require the expertise and prowess required for sprinting; but it does require that the runner (or operations manager) keeps on going. Yet notwithstanding these differences, it is possible to use both approaches. Large and dramatic improvements can be implemented as and when they seem to promise significant improvement steps, but between such occasions the operation can continue making its quiet and less spectacular 'kaizen' improvements. Table 13.3 lists some of the differences between the two approaches.

Operations principle
Breakthrough improvement necessarily implies radical and/or extensive change.

Table 13.3   Some features of breakthrough and continuous improvement

	Breakthrough improvement	Continuous improvement
Effect	Short-term but dramatic	Long term and long-lasting but undramatic
Pace	Big steps	Small steps
Time-frame	Intermittent and non-incremental	Continuous and incremental
Change	Abrupt and volatile	Gradual and constant
Involvement	Select a few 'champions'	Everybody
Approach	Individualism, individual ideas and efforts	Collectivism, group efforts, systems approach
Stimulus	Technological breakthroughs, new inventions, new theories	Conventional know-how and state of the art
Risks	Concentrated – 'all eggs in one basket'	Spread – many projects simultaneously
Practical requirements	Requires large investment but little effort to maintain	Requires little investment but great effort to maintain it
Effort orientations	Technology	People
Evaluation criteria	Results for profit	Process and effects for better results

Source: based on Imai, M. (1986) *Kaizen – The Key to Japan's Competitive Success*, McGraw-Hill.

The Six Sigma approach to organizing improvement

One approach to improvement that combines breakthrough and continuous philosophies is *Six Sigma*. Although technically the 'Six Sigma' name derives from statistical process control (SPC), and more specifically the concept of process capability, it has now come to mean a much broader approach to improvement. The following definition gives a sense of its modern usage: *'Six Sigma is a comprehensive and flexible system for achieving, sustaining and maximizing business success. Six Sigma is uniquely driven by close understanding of customer needs, disciplined use of facts, data, and statistical analysis, and diligent attention to managing, improving, and reinventing business processes.'*[10]

The Six Sigma concept, therefore, includes many of the issues covered in this and other chapters of this book, for example process design and redesign, balanced scorecard measures, continuous improvement, statistical process control, ongoing process planning and control, and so on. However, at the heart of Six Sigma lies an understanding of the negative effects of variation in all types of business process. This aversion to variation was first popularized by Motorola, the electronics company, which set its objective as 'total customer satisfaction' in the 1980s, then decided that true customer satisfaction would only be achieved when its products were delivered when promised, with no defects, with no early-life failures and no excessive failure in service. To achieve this, they initially focused on removing manufacturing defects, but soon realized that many problems were caused by latent defects, hidden within the design of their products. The only way to eliminate these defects was to make sure that design specifications were tight (i.e. narrow tolerances) and their processes very capable.

FURTHER EXAMPLE

Motorola's Six Sigma quality concept was so named because it required that the natural variation of processes (±3 standard deviations) should be half their specification range. In other words, the specification range of any part of a product or service should be ±6 times the standard deviation of the process. The Greek letter sigma (σ) is often used to indicate the standard deviation of a process, hence the Six Sigma label. The Six Sigma approach also used the measure of 'defects per million *opportunities*' (DPMO). This is the number of defects that the process will produce if there were one million opportunities to do so. So difficult processes with many opportunities for defects can be compared with simple processes with few opportunities for defects.

The Six Sigma approach also holds that improvement initiatives can only be successful if significant resources and training are devoted to their management. It recommends a specially trained cadre of practitioners, many of whom should be dedicated full-time to improving processes as internal consultants. The terms that have become associated with this group of experts (and denote their level of expertise) are Master Black Belt, Black Belt, and Green Belt.

- *Master Black Belts* are experts in the use of Six Sigma tools and techniques as well as how such techniques can be used and implemented. They are seen as teachers who can not only guide improvement projects, but also coach and mentor Black Belts and Green Belts. Given their responsibilities, it is expected that Master Black Belts are employed full-time on their improvement activities.
- *Black Belts* take a direct hand in organizing improvement teams, and will usually have undertaken a minimum of 20 to 25 days training and carried out at least one major improvement project. Black Belts are expected to develop their quantitative analytical skills and also act as coaches for Green Belts. Like Master Black Belts, they are dedicated full-time to improvement, and although opinions vary, some organizations recommend one Black Belt for every 100 employees.
- *Green Belts* work within improvement teams, possibly as team leaders. They have less training than Black Belts – typically around 10 to 15 days. Green Belts are not full-time positions. They have normal day-to-day process responsibilities but are expected to spend at least 20 per cent of their time on improvement projects.

Devoting such a large amount of training and time to improvement is a significant investment, especially for small companies. Nevertheless, Six Sigma proponents argue that the improvement activity is generally neglected in most operations and if it is to be taken seriously, it deserves the significant investment implied by the Six Sigma approach. Furthermore, they argue, if operated well, Six Sigma improvement projects run by experienced practitioners can save far more than their cost.

DIAGNOSTIC QUESTION

What techniques should be used to facilitate improvement?

Operations principle
Improvement is facilitated by relatively simple analytical techniques.

All the techniques described in this book and its supplements can be regarded as 'improvement' techniques. However, some techniques are particularly useful for improving operations and processes generally. Here we select some techniques which either have not been described elsewhere or need to be reintroduced in their role of helping operations improvement particularly.

Scatter diagrams

Scatter diagrams provide a quick and simple method of identifying whether there is evidence of a connection between two sets of data: for example, the time at which you set off for work every morning and how long the journey to work takes. Plotting each journey on a graph with departure time on one axis and journey time on the other could give an indication of whether departure time and journey time are related, and if so, how. Scatter diagrams can be treated in a far more sophisticated manner by quantifying the strength of the relationship between the sets of data. But, however sophisticated the approach, this type of graph only identifies the existence of a relationship, not necessarily the existence of a cause–effect relationship. If the scatter diagram shows a very strong connection between the sets of data, it is important evidence of a cause–effect relationship, but not proof positive. It could be coincidence!

| Example | Kaston Pyral Services Ltd (1) |

Kaston Pyral Services Ltd (KPS) installs and maintains environmental control, heating and air conditioning systems. It has set up an improvement team to suggest ways in which it might improve its levels of customer service. The improvement team had completed its first customer satisfaction survey. The survey asked customers to score the service they received from KPS in several ways. For example, it asked customers to score services on a scale of 1 to 10 on promptness, friendliness, level of advice, etc. Scores were then summed to give a 'total satisfaction score' for each customer – the higher the score, the greater the satisfaction. The spread of satisfaction scores puzzled the team and they considered what factors might be causing such differences in the way their customers viewed them. Two factors were put forward to explain the differences.

1 The number of times in the past year the customer had received a preventive maintenance visit.
2 The number of times the customer had called for emergency service.

All this data was collected and plotted on scatter diagrams as shown in Figure 13.12. Figure 13.12(a) shows that there seems to be a clear relationship between a customer's satisfaction score and the number of times the customer was visited for regular servicing. The scatter diagram in Figure 13.12(b) is less clear. Although all customers who had very high satisfaction scores had made very few emergency calls, so had some customers with low satisfaction scores. As a result of this analysis, the team decided to survey customers' views on its emergency service.

Figure 13.12   Scatter diagrams for customer satisfaction versus (a) number of preventive maintenance calls and (b) number of emergency service calls

Cause–effect diagrams

FURTHER EXAMPLE

Cause–effect diagrams are a particularly effective method of helping to search for the root causes of problems. They do this by asking *what, when, where, how* and *why* questions, but also add some possible 'answers' in an explicit way. They can also be used to identify areas where further data is needed. Cause–effect diagrams (which are also known as Ishikawa diagrams) have become extensively used in improvement programmes. This is because they provide a way of structuring group brainstorming sessions. Often the structure involves identifying possible causes under the (rather old-fashioned) headings of machinery, manpower, materials, methods, and money. Yet in practice, any categorization that comprehensively covers all relevant possible causes could be used.

Example Kaston Pyral Services Ltd (2)

PRACTICE NOTE

The improvement team at KPS was working on a particular area which was proving a problem. Whenever service engineers were called out to perform emergency servicing for a customer, they took with them the spares and equipment which they thought would be necessary to repair the system. Although engineers could never be sure exactly what materials and equipment they would need for a job, they could guess what was likely to be needed and take a range of spares and equipment which would cover most eventualities. Too often, however, the engineers would find that they needed a spare that they had not brought with them. The cause–effect diagram for this particular problem, as drawn by the team, is shown in Figure 13.13.

Pareto diagrams

In any improvement process, it is worth distinguishing what is important and what is less so. The purpose of the Pareto diagram (first introduced in Chapter 9) is to distinguish between the 'vital few' issues and the 'trivial many'. It is a relatively straightforward technique which involves arranging items of information on the types of problem or causes of problem into their order of importance (usually measured by 'frequency of occurrence'). This can be used to highlight areas where further decision making will be

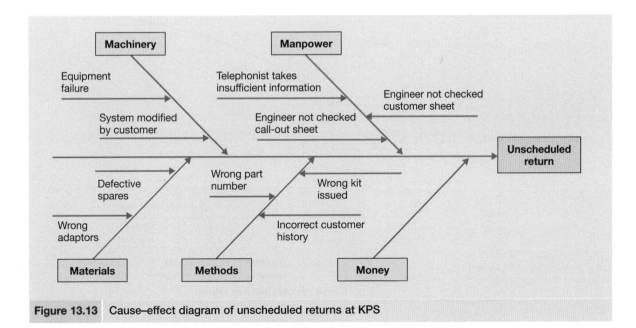

Figure 13.13 Cause–effect diagram of unscheduled returns at KPS

FURTHER EXAMPLE

useful. Pareto analysis is based on the phenomenon of relatively few causes explaining the majority of effects. For example, most revenue for any company is likely to come from relatively few of the company's customers. Similarly, relatively few of a doctor's patients will probably occupy most of his or her time.

Example

Kaston Pyral Services Ltd (3)

The KPS improvement team which was investigating unscheduled returns from emergency servicing (the issue which was described in the cause–effect diagram in Figure 13.13) examined all occasions over the previous 12 months on which an unscheduled return had been made. They categorized the reasons for unscheduled returns as follows:

1 The wrong part had been taken to a job because, although the information which the engineer received was sound, he or she had incorrectly predicted the nature of the fault.
2 The wrong part had been taken to the job because there was insufficient information given when the call was taken.
3 The wrong part had been taken to the job because the system had been modified in some way not recorded on KPS's records.
4 The wrong part had been taken to the job because the part had been incorrectly issued to the engineer by stores.
5 No part had been taken because the relevant part was out of stock.
6 The wrong equipment had been taken for whatever reason.
7 Any other reason.

The relative frequency of occurrence of these causes is shown in Figure 13.14. About a third of all unscheduled returns were due to the first category, and more than half the returns were accounted for by the first and second categories together. It was decided that the problem could best be tackled by concentrating on how to get more information to the engineers which would enable them to predict the causes of failure accurately.

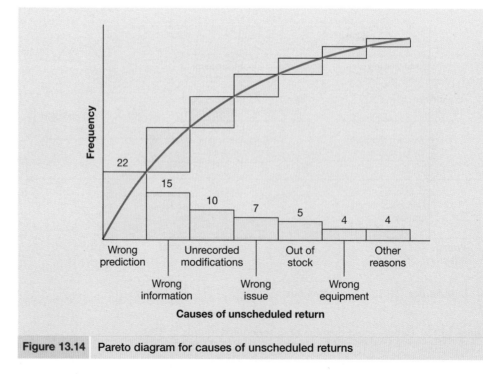

Figure 13.14   Pareto diagram for causes of unscheduled returns

Why–why analysis

Why–why analysis starts by stating the problem and asking *why* that problem has occurred. Once the major reasons for the problem occurring have been identified, each of the major reasons is taken in turn and again the question is asked *why* those reasons have occurred, and so on. This procedure is continued until either a cause seems sufficiently self-contained to be addressed by itself or no more answers to the question 'Why?' can be generated.

Example

Kaston Pyral Services Ltd (4)

The major cause of unscheduled returns at KPS was the incorrect prediction of reasons for the customer's system failure. This is stated as the 'problem' in the why–why analysis in Figure 13.15. The question is then asked, why was the failure wrongly predicted? Three answers are proposed: first, that the engineers were not trained correctly; second, that they had insufficient knowledge of the particular product installed in the customer's location; and third, that they had insufficient knowledge of the customer's particular system with its modifications. Each of these three reasons is taken in turn, and the questions are asked, why is there a lack of training, why is there a lack of product knowledge, why is there a lack of customer knowledge? And so on.

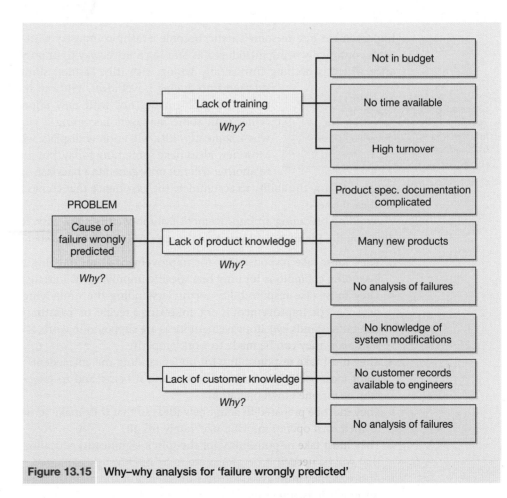

Figure 13.15   Why–why analysis for 'failure wrongly predicted'

How can improvement be made to stick?

Not all of the improvement initiatives (often launched with high expectations) will go on to fulfil their potential. Even those improvement initiatives that are successfully implemented may lose impetus over time. Sometimes this is because of managers' view of the nature of improvement; at other times it is because managers fail to manage the improvement process adequately.

Avoid becoming a victim of improvement 'fashion'

Improvement has, to some extent, become a fashion industry with new ideas and concepts continually being introduced as offering a novel way to improve business performance. There is nothing intrinsically wrong with this. Fashion stimulates and refreshes through introducing novel ideas. Without it, things would stagnate. The problem lies not with new improvement ideas, but rather with some managers becoming a victim of the process, where some new idea will entirely displace whatever went before. Most new ideas have something to say, but jumping from one fad to another will not only generate a backlash against any new idea, but also destroy the ability to accumulate the experience that comes from experimenting with each one.

> **Operations principle**
> The popularity of an improvement approach is not necessarily an indicator of its effectiveness.

Avoiding becoming an improvement fashion victim is not easy. It requires that those directing the improvement process take responsibility for a number of issues.

- They must take responsibility for improvement as an ongoing activity, rather than becoming champions for only one specific improvement initiative.
- They must take responsibility for understanding the underlying ideas behind each new concept. Improvement is not 'following a recipe' or 'painting by numbers'. Unless one understands *why* improvement ideas are supposed to work, it is difficult to understand *how* they can be made to work properly.
- They must take responsibility for understanding the antecedents to a 'new' improvement idea, because it helps to understand it better and to judge how appropriate it may be for one's own operation.
- They must be prepared to adapt new ideas so that they make sense within the context of their own operation. 'One size' rarely fits all.
- They must take responsibility for the (often significant) education and learning effort that will be needed if new ideas are to be intelligently exploited.
- Above all they must avoid the over-exaggeration and hype that many new ideas attract. Although it is sometimes tempting to exploit the motivational 'pull' of new ideas through slogans, posters and exhortations, carefully thought-out plans will always be superior in the long run, and will help avoid the inevitable backlash that follows 'overselling' a single approach.

Managing the improvement process

There is no absolute prescription for the way improvement should be managed. Any improvement process should reflect the uniqueness of each operation's characteristics.

> **Operations principle**
> There is no one universal approach to improvement.

What appears to be almost a guarantee of difficulty in managing improvement processes are attempts to squeeze improvement into a standard mould. Nevertheless, there are some aspects of any improvement process that appear to influence its eventual success, and should at least be debated.

Should an improvement *strategy* be defined?

Without thinking through the overall purpose and long-term goals of the improvement process, it is difficult for any operation to know where it is going. Specifically, an improvement strategy should have something to say about the following.

- The competitive priorities of the organization, and how the improvement process is expected to contribute to achieving increased strategic impact
- The roles and responsibilities of the various parts of the organization in the improvement process
- The resources which will be available for the improvement process
- The general approach to, and philosophy of, improvement in the organization.

Yet, too rigid a strategy can become inappropriate if the business's competitive circumstances change, or as the operation learns through experience. But, the careful modification of improvement strategy in the light of experience is not the same as making dramatic changes in improvement strategy as new improvement fashions appear.

What degree of top-management support is required?

For most authorities, the answer is unambiguous – a significant amount. Without top management support, improvement cannot succeed. It is the most crucial factor in almost all the studies of improvement process implementation. It also goes far beyond merely allocating senior resources to the process. Top-management support usually means that senior personnel must:

- understand and believe in the link between improvement and the business's overall strategy.
- understand the practicalities of the improvement process and be able to communicate its principles and techniques to the rest of the organization
- be able to participate in the total problem-solving process to improve performance
- formulate and maintain a clear idea of the operation's improvement philosophy.

Should the improvement process be formally supervised?

Some improvement processes fail because they develop an unwieldy 'bureaucracy' to run them. But any process needs to be managed, so all improvement processes will need some kind of group to design, plan and control its efforts. However, a worthwhile goal for many improvement processes is to make themselves 'self-governing' over time. In fact there are significant advantages in terms of people's commitment in giving them responsibility for managing the improvement process. However, even when improvement is driven primarily by self-managing improvement groups, there is a need for some sort of 'repository of knowledge' to ensure that the learning and experience accumulated from the improvement process is not lost.

To what extent should improvement be group-based?

No one can really know a process quite like the people who operate it. They have access to the informal as well as the formal information networks that contain the way processes really work. But, working alone, individuals cannot pool their experience or learn from one another. So improvement processes are almost always based on teams. The issue is how these teams should be formulated, which will depend on the circumstances of the operation, its context and its objectives. For example, *quality circles,* much used in Japan, encountered mixed success in the West. A very different type of team is the '*task force*', or what some US companies call a 'tiger team'. Compared with quality circles, this type of group is far more management directed and focused. Most improvement teams are between these two extremes (see Figure 13.16).

How should success be recognized?

If improvement is so important, it should be recognized, with success, effort and initiative being formally rewarded. The paradox is that, if improvement is to become part of everyday operational life, then why should improvement effort be especially rewarded? One compromise is to devise a recognition and rewards system that responds to improvement initiatives early in the improvement process, but then merges into the operation's normal reward procedures. In this way people are rewarded not just for the efficient and effective running of their processes on an ongoing basis, but also for improving their processes. Then improvement will become an everyday responsibility of all people in the operation.

How much training is required?

Training has two purposes in the development of improvement processes. The first is to provide the necessary skills that will allow staff to solve process problems and implement improvements. The second is to provide an understanding of the appropriate

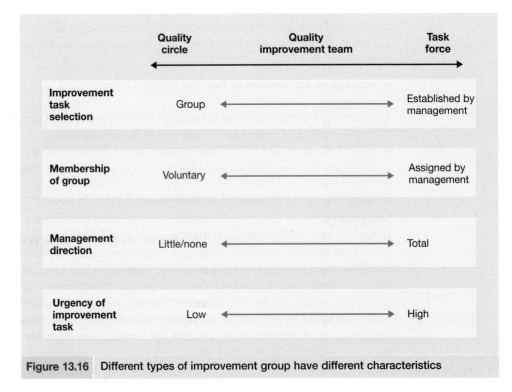

Figure 13.16   Different types of improvement group have different characteristics

interpersonal, group and organizational skills that are needed to 'lubricate' the improvement process. This second objective is more difficult than the first. Training and improvement techniques may take up significant time and effort, but none of this knowledge will be of much use if the organizational context for improvement mitigates against the techniques being used effectively. Although the nature of appropriate organizational development is beyond the scope of this book, it is worth noting that both technique-based skills and organizational skills are enhanced if staff have a basic understanding of the core ideas and principles of operations and process management.

Critical commentary

Each chapter contains a short critical commentary on the main ideas covered in the chapter. Its purpose is not to undermine the issues discussed in the chapter, but to emphasize that, although we present a relatively orthodox view of operation, there are other perspectives.

■ Many of the issues covered in this chapter are controversial, for different reasons. Some criticism concerns the effectiveness of improvement methods. For example, it can be argued that there is a fundamental flaw in the concept of benchmarking. Operations that rely on others to stimulate their creativity, especially those that are in search of 'best practice', are always limiting themselves to currently accepted methods of operating or currently accepted limits to performance. 'Best practice' is not 'best' in the sense that it cannot be bettered; it is only 'best' in the sense that it is the best one can currently find. And accepting what is currently defined as 'best' may prevent operations from ever making the radical breakthrough or improvement that takes the concept of 'best' to a new and fundamentally improved level. Furthermore, because one operation has a set of successful practices in the way it manages it process does not mean that adopting those same practices in another context will prove equally successful. It is possible that subtle differences in the resources within a process (such as staff skills or technical capabilities) or the strategic context of an operation (for example, the relative priorities of performance objectives) will be sufficiently different to make the adoption of seemingly successful practices inappropriate.

■ Other approaches are seen by some as too radical and too insensitive. For example, business process re-engineering has aroused considerable controversy. Most of its critics are academics, but some practical objections to BPR have also been raised, such as the fear that BPR looks only at work activities rather than at the people who perform the work. Because of this, people become 'cogs in a machine'. Also some see BPR as being too imprecise because its proponents cannot agree as to whether it has to be radical or whether it can be implemented gradually, or exactly what a process is, or whether it has to be top-down or bottom-up, or whether it has be supported by information technology or not. Perhaps most seriously, BPR is viewed as merely an excuse for getting rid of staff. Companies that wish to 'downsize' (that is, reduce numbers of staff within an operation) are using BPR as an excuse. This puts the short-term interests of the shareholders of the company above either their longer-term interests or the interests of the company's employees. Moreover, a combination of radical redesign together with downsizing can mean that the essential core of experience is lost from the operation. This leaves it vulnerable to any marked turbulence since it no longer has the knowledge and experience of how to cope with unexpected changes.

■ Even the more gentle approach of continuous improvement is not universally welcomed. Notwithstanding its implications of empowerment and liberal attitude towards shop-floor staff, it is regarded by some worker representatives as merely a further example of management exploiting workers. Relatively established ideas such as TQM have been defined by its critics as 'management by stress'. Or, even more radically, 'TQM is like putting a vacuum cleaner next to a worker's brain and sucking out ideas. They don't want to rent your knowledge anymore, they want to own it – in the end that makes you totally replaceable.'

Summary checklist

DOWNLOADABLE

This checklist comprises questions that can be usefully applied to any type of operations and reflect the major diagnostic questions used within the chapter.

☐ Is the importance of performance improvement fully recognized within the operation?

☐ Do all operations and process managers see performance improvement as an integral part of their job?

☐ Is the gap between current and desired performance clearly articulated in all areas?

☐ Is the current performance measurement system seen as forming a basis for improvement?

☐ Does performance measurement focus on factors that reflect the operation's strategic objectives?

☐ Do performance measures allow likely problem areas to be diagnosed?

☐ Is some kind of balanced scorecard approach used that includes financial, internal, customer and learning perspectives?

☐ Is target performance set using an appropriate balance between historical, strategic, external and absolute performance targets?

☐ Are both performance and process methods benchmarked against similar operations and/or processes externally?

☐ Is benchmarking done on a regular basis and seen as an important contribution to improvement?

☐ Is some formal method of comparing actual and desired performance (such as the importance–performance matrix) used?

☐ To what extent does the operation have a predisposition towards breakthrough or continuous improvement?

☐ Have breakthrough improvement approaches such as business process re-engineering been evaluated?

☐ Are continuous improvement methods and problem-solving cycles used within the operation?

☐ If they are, has continuous improvement become a part of everyone's' job?

☐ Which 'abilities' and 'associated behaviours' (see Table 13.2) are evident within the operation?

☐ Has the Six Sigma approach to improvement been evaluated?

☐ Are the more common improvement techniques used to facilitate improvement within the operations?

☐ Does the operation show any signs of becoming a fashion victim of the latest improvement approach?

☐ Does the operation have a well thought-through approach to managing improvement?

Case study   Geneva Construction and Risk (GCR)

'This is not going to be like last time. Then, we were adopting an improvement programme because we were told to. This time it's our idea and, if it's successful, it will be us that are telling the rest of the group how to do it.' (Tyko Mattson, Six Sigma Champion, GCR)

Tyko Mattson was speaking as the newly appointed 'Champion' at Geneva Construction and Risk Insurance. He had been charged with 'steering the Six Sigma programme until it is firmly established as part of our ongoing practice'. The previous improvement initiative that he was referring to dated back many years to when GCR's parent company, Wichita Mutual Insurance, had insisted on the adoption of total quality management (TQM) in all its businesses. The TQM initiative had never been pronounced a failure and had managed to make some improvements, especially in customers' perception of the company's levels of service. However, the initiative had 'faded out' during the 1990s and, even though all departments still had to formally report on their improvement projects, their number and impact was now relatively minor.

Source: © Getty Images/Digital Vision

History

The Geneva Construction Insurance Company was founded in 1922 to provide insurance for building contractors and construction companies, initially in German-speaking Europe and then, because of the emigration of some family members to the USA, in North America. The company had remained relatively small and had specialized in housing construction projects until the early 1950s when it had started to grow, partly because of geographical expansion and partly because it moved into larger (sometimes very large) construction insurance in the industrial, oil, petrochemical and power plant construction areas. In 1983 it had been bought by the Wichita Mutual Group and had absorbed the group's existing construction insurance businesses.

By 2000 it had established itself as one of the leading providers of insurance for construction projects, especially complex, high-risk projects, where contractual and other legal issues, physical exposure and design uncertainty needed 'customized' insurance responses. Providing such insurance needed particular knowledge and skills from specialists including construction underwriters, loss adjusters, engineers, international lawyers and specialist risk consultants. Typically, the company would insure losses resulting

from contractor failure, related public liability issues, delays in project completion, associated litigation, other litigation (such as ongoing asbestos risks) and negligence issues.

The company's headquarters were in Geneva and housed all major departments including sales and marketing, underwriting, risk analysis, claims and settlement, financial control, general administration, specialist and general legal advice, and business research. There were also 37 local offices around the world, organized into four regional areas: North America, South America, Europe Middle East and Africa, and Asia. These regional offices provided localized help and advice directly to clients and also to the 890 agents that GCR used worldwide.

The previous improvement initiative

When Wichita Mutual had insisted that GCR adopt a TQM initiative, it had gone as far as to specify exactly how it should do it and which consultants should be used to help establish the programme. Tyko Mattson shakes his head as he describes it. *'I was not with the company at that time but, looking back, it's amazing that it ever managed to do any good. You can't impose the structure of an improvement initiative from the top. It has to, at least partially, be shaped by the people who are going to be involved in it. But everything had to be done according to the handbook. The* cost of quality was measured for different departments according to the handbook. Everyone had to learn the improvement techniques that were described in the handbook. Everyone had be part of a quality circle that was organized according to the handbook. We even had to have annual award ceremonies where we gave out special "certificates of merit" to those quality circles that had achieved the type of improvement that the handbook said they should.' The TQM initiative had been run by the 'Quality Committee', a group of eight people with representatives from all the major departments at head office. Initially, it had spent much of its time setting up the improvement groups and organizing training in quality techniques. However, soon it had become swamped by the work needed to evaluate which improvement suggestions should be implemented. Soon the workload associated with assessing improvement ideas had become so great that the company decided to allocate small improvement budgets to each department on a quarterly basis that they could spend without reference to the quality committee. Projects requiring larger investment or that had a significant impact on other parts of the business still needed to be approved by the committee before they were implemented.

Department improvement budgets were still used within the business and improvement plans were still required from each department on an annual basis. However, the quality committee had stopped meeting by 1994 and the annual award ceremony had become a general communications meeting for all staff at the headquarters. 'Looking back', said Tyko, 'the TQM initiative faded away for three reasons. First, people just got tired of it. It was always seen as something extra rather than part of normal business life, so it was always seen as taking time away from doing your normal job. Second, many of the supervisory and middle management levels never really bought into it, I guess because they felt threatened. Third, only a very few of the local offices around the world ever adopted the TQM philosophy. Sometimes this was because they did not want the extra effort. Sometimes, however, they would argue that improvement initiatives of this type may be OK

for head office processes, but not for the more dynamic world of supporting clients in the field.'

The Six Sigma initiative

Early in 2005 Tyko Mattson, who for the last two years had been overseeing the outsourcing of some of GCR's claims processing to India, had attended a conference on 'Operations Excellence in Financial Services', and had heard several speakers detail the success they had achieved through using a Six Sigma approach to operations improvement. He had persuaded his immediate boss, Marie-Dominique Tomas, the head of claims for the company, to allow him to investigate its applicability to GCR. He had interviewed a number of other financial services that had implemented Six Sigma as well as a number of consultants, and in September 2005 had submitted a report entitled 'What is Six Sigma and how might it be applied in GCR?'. Extracts from this are included in the Appendix. Marie-Dominique Tomas was particularly concerned that they should avoid the mistakes of the TQM initiative. 'Looking back, it is almost embarrassing to see how naive we were. We really did think that it would change the whole way that we did business. And although it did produce some benefits, it absorbed a large amount of time at all levels in the organization. This time we want something that will deliver results without costing too much or distracting us from focusing on business performance. That is why I like Six Sigma. It starts with clarifying business objectives and works from there.'

By late 2005 Tyko's report had been approved both by GCR and by Wichita Mutual's main board. Tyko had been given the challenge of carrying out the recommendations in his report, reporting directly to GCR's executive board. Marie-Dominique Tomas was cautiously optimistic: 'It is quite a challenge for Tyko. Most of us on the executive board remember the TQM initiative and some are still sceptical concerning the value of such initiatives. However, Tyko's gradualist approach and his emphasis on the 'three pronged' attack on revenue, costs, and risk, impressed the board. We now have to see whether he can make it work.'

Appendix – Extract from *What is Six Sigma and how might it be applied in GCR?'*

Some pitfalls of Six Sigma

Six Sigma is not simple to implement, and is resource hungry. The focus on measurement implies that the process data is available and reasonably robust. If this is not the case it is possible to waste a lot of effort in obtaining process performance data. It may also over-complicate

things if advanced techniques are used on simple problems.

It is easier to apply Six Sigma to repetitive processes – characterized by high volume, low variety and low visibility to customers. It is more difficult to apply it to low volume, higher variety and high visibility processes where standardization is harder to achieve and the focus is on managing the variety.

Six Sigma is not a 'quick fix'. Companies that have implemented Six Sigma effectively have not treated it as just another new initiative but as an approach that requires the long-term systematic reduction of waste. Equally, it is not a panacea and should not be implemented as one.

Some benefits of Six Sigma

Companies have achieved significant benefits in reducing cost and improving customer service through implementing Six Sigma.

Six Sigma can reduce process variation, which will have a significant impact on operational risk. It is a tried and tested methodology, which combines the strongest parts of existing improvement methodologies. It lends itself to being customized to fit individual company's circumstances. For example, Mestech Assurance has extended their Six Sigma initiative to examine operational risk processes.

Six Sigma could leverage a number of current initiatives. The risk self-assessment methodology, Sarbanes Oxley, the process library, and our performance metrics work are all laying the foundations for better knowledge and measurement of process data.

Six Sigma – key conclusions for GCR

Six Sigma is a powerful improvement methodology. It is not all new but what it does do successfully is to combine some of the best parts of existing improvement methodologies, tools and techniques. Six Sigma has helped many companies achieve significant benefits. It could help GCR significantly improve risk management because it focuses on driving errors and exceptions out of processes.

Six Sigma has significant advantages over other process improvement methodologies. It engages senior management actively by establishing process ownership and linkage to strategic objectives. This is seen as integral to successful implementation in the literature and by all companies interviewed who had implemented it. It forces a rigorous approach to driving out variance in processes by analyzing the root cause of defects and errors and measuring improvement. It is an 'umbrella' approach, combining all the best parts of other improvement approaches.

Implementing Six Sigma across GCR is not the right approach

Companies that are widely quoted as having achieved the most significant headline benefits from Six Sigma were already relatively mature in terms of process management. Those companies that understood their process capability typically had achieved a degree of process standardization and had an established process improvement culture.

Six Sigma requires significant investment in performance metrics and process knowledge. GCR is probably not yet sufficiently advanced. However, we are working towards a position where key process data are measured and known and this will provide a foundation for Six Sigma.

Why is a targeted implementation recommended?
Full implementation is resource hungry. Dedicated resource and budget for implementation of improvements is required. Even if the approach is modified, resource and budget will still be needed, just to a lesser extent. However, the evidence is that the investment is well worth it and pays back relatively quickly.

There was strong evidence from companies interviewed that the best implementation approach was to pilot Six Sigma, and select failing processes for the pilot. In addition, previous internal piloting of implementations has been successful in GCR – we know this approach works within our culture.

Six Sigma would provide a platform for GCR to build on and evolve over time. It is a way of leveraging the ongoing work on processes, and the risk methodology (being developed by the Operational Risk Group). This diagnostic tool could be blended into Six Sigma, giving GCR a powerful model to drive reduction in process variation and improved operational risk management.

Recommendations

It is recommended that GCR management implement a Six Sigma pilot. The characteristics of the pilot would be as follows:

- A tailored approach to Six Sigma that would fit GCR's objectives and operating environment. Implementing Six Sigma in its entirety would not be appropriate.
- The use of an external partner: GCR does not have sufficient internal Six Sigma expertise, and external experience will be critical to tailoring the approach, and providing training.
- Establishing where GCR's sigma performance is now. Different tools and approaches will be required to advance from 2 to 3 Sigma than those required to move from 3 to 4 Sigma.
- Quantifying the potential benefits. Is the investment worth making? What would a 1 Sigma increase in performance vs. risk be worth to us?
- Keeping the methods simple, if simple will achieve our objectives. As a minimum for us that means Team Based Problem Solving and basic statistical techniques.

Next steps

1 Decide priority and confirm budget and resourcing for initial analysis to develop a Six Sigma risk improvement programme in 2006.

2 Select an external partner experienced in improvement and Six Sigma methodologies.

3 Assess GCR current state to confirm where to start in implementing Six Sigma.

4 Establish how much GCR is prepared to invest in Six Sigma and quantify the potential benefits.

5 Tailor Six Sigma to focus on risk management.

6 Identify potential pilot area(s) and criteria for assessing its suitability.

7 Develop a Six Sigma pilot plan.

8 Conduct and review the pilot programme.

QUESTIONS

1. How does the Six Sigma approach seem to differ from the TQM approach adopted by the company almost 20 years ago?

2. Is Six Sigma a better approach for this type of company?

3. Do you think Tyko can avoid the Six Sigma initiative suffering the same fate as the TQM initiative?

Active case study   Ferndale Sands Conference Centre

ACTIVE CASE

Ferndale Sands Conference Centre is a conference venue of 52 rooms in Victoria State, Australia. They pride themselves on offering supreme quality and service; the *'executive retreat'*. Mario Romano, the owner and General Manager, is furious and alarmed to read a review which threatens their excellent reputation. An urgent meeting is called to address the negative publicity.

● How would you assess the performance of the hotel within different aspects of its business and what path of improvement would you recommend?

Please refer to the Active case on the CD accompanying this book to listen to the views of different staff working for Mario.

Applying the principles

HINTS

Some of these exercises can be answered by reading the chapter. Others will require some general knowledge of business activity and some might require an element of investigation. All have hints on how they can be answered on the CD accompanying this book.

1   Visit a library (for example, a university library) and consider how it could start a performance measurement programme which would enable it to judge the effectiveness with which it organizes its operations. Probably the library lends books on both long-term and short-term loans, keeps an extensive stock of journals, will send off for specialist publications to specialist libraries, and has an extensive online database facility.

● What measures of performance do you think it would be appropriate to use in this kind of operation and what type of performance standards should the library adopt?

2   (a) Devise a benchmarking programme that will benefit the course or programme that you are currently taking (if appropriate). In doing so, decide whether you are going to benchmark against other courses at the same institution, competitor courses at other institutions, or some other point of comparison. Also decide whether you are more interested in the performance of these other courses or the way they organize their processes, or both.

(b) Identify the institutions and courses against which you are going to benchmark your own course.

(c) Collect data on these other courses (visit them, send off for literature, or visit their Internet site).

(d) Compare your own course against these others and draw up a list of implications for the way your course could be improved.

3 Think back to the last product or service failure that caused you some degree of inconvenience. Draw a cause–effect diagram that identifies all the main causes of why the failure could have occurred. Try to identify the frequency with which such causes happen. This could be done by talking with the staff of the operation that provided the service. Draw a Pareto diagram that indicates the relative frequency of each cause of failure. Suggest ways in which the operation could reduce the chances of failure.

4 (a) If you are working in a group, identify a 'high visibility' operation that you all are familiar with. This could be a type of quick-service restaurant, record stores, public transport systems, libraries, etc.

(b) Once you have identified the broad class of operation, visit a number of them and use your experience as customers to identify the main performance factors that are of importance to you as customers, and how each store rates against the others in terms of their performance on these same factors.

(c) Draw an importance–performance diagram for one of the operations that indicates the priority they should be giving to improving their performance.

(d) Discuss the ways in which such an operation might improve its performance and try to discuss your findings with the staff of the operation.

Notes on chapter

1 Source: Deaves, M. (2002) 'Bottoms up!', *Manufacturing Engineer,* Dec.

2 Source: the EFQM website (www.efqm.org).

3 See Kaplan, R.S. and Norton, D.P. (1996) *The Balanced Scorecard,* Harvard Business School Press, Boston, MA.

4 Kaplan and Norton, *op. cit.*

5 Ferdows, K. and de Meyer, A. (1990) 'Lasting improvement in manufacturing', *Journal of Operations Management,* Vol. 9, No. 2. However, research for this model is mixed. For example, Patricia Nemetz questions the validity of the model, finding more support for the idea that the sequence of improvement is generally dictated by technological (operations resource) or market (requirements) pressures: Nemetz, P. (2002) 'A longitudinal study of strategic choice, multiple advantage, cumulative model and order winner/qualifier view of manufacturing strategy', *Journal of Business and Management,* January.

6 Hammer, M. and Champy, J. (1993) *Re-engineering the Corporation,* Nicholas Brealey Publishing.

7 Hammer, M. (1990) 'Re-engineering work: don't automate, obliterate', *Harvard Business Review,* Vol. 68, No. 4.

8 Imai, M. (1986) *Kaizen – The Key to Japan's Competitive Success,* McGraw-Hill.

9 Bessant, J. and Caffyn, S. (1997) 'High involvement innovation', *International Journal of Technology Management,* Vol. 14, No. 1.

10 Pande, P.S., Neuman, R.P. and Cavanagh, R.R. (2000) *The Six Sigma Way,* McGraw-Hill, New York.

Taking it further

Chang, R.Y. (1995) *Continuous Process Improvement: A practical guide to improving processes for measurable results,* Kogan Page.

Leibfried, K.H.J. and McNair, C.J. (1992) *Benchmarking: A tool for continuous improvement,* HarperCollins. There are many books on benchmarking; this is a comprehensive and practical guide to the subject.

Pande, P.S., Neuman, R.P. and Cavanagh, R. (2002) *Six Sigma Way Team Field Book: An implementation guide for project improvement teams,* McGraw-Hill. Obviously based on the Six Sigma principle and related to the book by the same author team recommended in Chapter 12, this is an unashamedly practical guide to the Six Sigma approach.

Useful websites

www.processimprovement.com Commercial site but some content that could be useful.

www.kaizen-institute.com Professional institute for *kaizen*. Gives some insight into practitioner views.

www.imeche.org.uk/mx/index.asp The Manufacturing Excellence Awards site. Dedicated to rewarding excellence and best practice in UK manufacturing. Obviously manufacturing biased, but some good examples.

www.ebenchmarking.com Benchmarking information.

www.quality.nist.gov American Quality Assurance Institute. Well-established institution for all types of business quality assurance.

www.balancedscorecard.org Site of an American organization with plenty of useful links.

FURTHER RESOURCES

For further resources including examples, animated diagrams, self test questions, excel spreadsheets, active case studies and video materials please explore the CD accompanying this book.

14 RISK AND RESILIENCE

Introduction

One obvious way of improving operations performance is by reducing the risk of failure (or of failure causing disruption) within the operation. All operations are subject to the risk of failure of many types, for example technology failure, supplier failure, natural and man-made disasters, and many other causes. A 'resilient' operation or process is one that can prevent failures occurring, minimize their effects, and learn how to recover from them. In an increasingly risky economic, political and social environment, resilience has become an important part of operations and process management, and in some operations – aircraft in flight or electricity supplies to hospitals, or the emergency services where failure can be literally fatal – it is vital. (See Figure 14.1.)

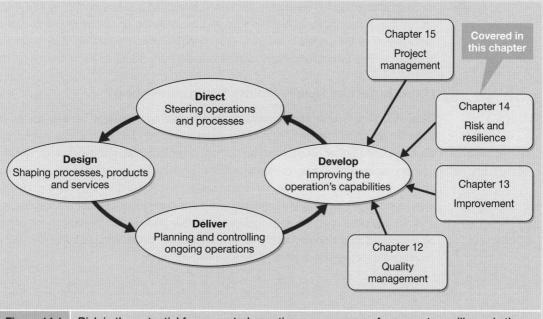

| Figure 14.1 | Risk is the potential for unwanted negative consequences from events; resilience is the ability to prevent, mitigate and recover from these events |

Executive summary

VIDEO
further detail

Decision logic chain for risk and resilience

Each chapter is structured around a set of diagnostic questions. These questions suggest what you should ask in order to gain an understanding of the important issues of a topic, and as a result, improve your decision making. An executive summary, addressing these questions, is provided below.

What are risk and resilience?

Risk is the potential for unwanted negative consequences from events. Resilience is the ability to prevent, withstand and recover from those events. Failures can be categorized in terms of the seriousness of their impact and the likelihood of their occurrence. Relatively low impact failures that happen relatively frequently are the province of quality management. Resilience involves attempting to reduce the combined effects of a failure occurring and the negative impact that it may have. It involves four sets of activities: understanding and assessing the seriousness of the potential failures, preventing failures, minimizing their negative consequences (called failure mitigation), and recovering from failure so as to reduce its impact.

Have potential failure points been assessed?

Resilience begins with understanding the possible sources and consequences of failure. Potential sources of failure can be categorized into supply failures, failures that happen inside the operation (further categorized as human, organizational, and technology failures), product/service design failures, customer failures, and the failures causes by environmental disruption such as weather, crime, terrorism, and so on. Understanding why such failures occur can be aided by post-failure analysis using accident investigation, traceability, complaint analysis, fault tree analysis, and other similar techniques. Judging the likelihood of failure may be relatively straightforward for some well-understood processes, but often has to be carried out on a subjective basis, which is rarely straightforward.

Have failure prevention measures been implemented?

Failure prevention is based on the assumption that it is generally better to avoid failures than suffer their consequences. The main approaches to failure prevention involve designing out the possibility of failure at key points in a process, providing extra but redundant resources that can provide back-up in the case of failure, installing fail-safeing mechanisms that prevent the mistakes which can cause failure, and maintaining processes so as to reduce the likelihood of failure. This last category is particularly important for many operations but can be approached in different ways such as preventive maintenance, condition-based maintenance, and total product maintenance.

Have failure mitigation measures been implemented?

Failure mitigation means isolating a failure from its negative consequences. It can involve a number of 'mitigation actions'. These include ensuring that planning procedures are installed that provide an overarching guide to mitigation as well as demonstrating that failure is taken seriously, economic mitigation using insurance, risk sharing and hedging, spatial or temporal containment that prevents the failure spreading geographically or over time, loss reduction that removes whatever might be harmed by a failure, and substitution that involves providing substitute resources to work on a failure before it becomes serious.

Have failure recovery measures been implemented?

Failure recovery is the set of actions that are taken after the negative effects of failure have occurred and that reduce the impact of the negative effects. Sometimes recovering well from a public failure can even enhance a business's reputation. However, recovery does need to be planned and procedures put in place that can discover when failures have occurred, guide appropriate action to keep everyone informed, capture the lessons learnt from the failure, and plan to absorb the lesson into any future recovery.

DIAGNOSTIC QUESTION

What are risk and resilience?

Risk is the potential for unwanted negative consequences from some event. Resilience is the ability to prevent, withstand and recover from those events. Things happen in operations, or to operations, that have negative consequences: this is failure. But accepting the fact that failure occurs is not the same thing as accepting failure itself, or ignoring it.

> **Operations principle**
> Failure will always occur in operations, recognizing this does not imply accepting or ignoring it.

Operations do generally attempt to minimize both the likelihood of failure and the effect it will have, although the method of coping with failure will depend on how serious are its negative consequences, and how likely it is to occur. At a minor level, every small error in the delivered product or service from the operation could be considered a failure. The whole area of quality management is concerned with reducing this type of 'failure'. Other failures will have more impact on the operation, even if they do not occur very frequently. A server failure can seriously affect service and therefore customers, which is why system reliability is such an important measure of performance for IT service providers. And, if we class a failure as something that has negative consequences, some are so serious we class them as disasters, such as freak weather conditions, air crashes, and acts of terrorism. These 'failures' are treated increasingly seriously by businesses, not necessarily because their likelihood of occurrence is high (although it may be at certain times and in certain places), but because their impact is so negative.

This chapter is concerned with all types of failure other than those with relatively minor consequences. This is illustrated in Figure 14.2. Some of these failures are irritating but relatively unimportant, especially those close to the bottom left-hand corner of the matrix in Figure 14.2. Other failures, especially those close to the top right-hand corner of the matrix, are normally avoided by all businesses because embracing such risks would be clearly foolish. In between these two extremes is where most operations-related risks occur. In this chapter will shall be treating various aspects of these types of failure, and in particular how they can be moved in the direction of the arrows in Figure 14.2. The two examples described next illustrate one organization that paid a high price for not achieving this and another that managed to minimize the effects of one particular failure.

Source: Pandis Media/Corbis Sygma

| Example | Barings Bank and Nick Leeson[1] |

On 3 March 1995 Nick Leeson, the Singapore-based 'rogue trader', was arrested immediately after his flight from the Far East touched down in Frankfurt. Since 27 February, the world's financial community had been in shock after Barings Bank collapsed following the discovery of massive debts. During the nine-month period Leeson spent in a German jail before finally being returned to Singapore to stand trial, auditors, regulators and legislators learnt that although most of the blame for the crash could be placed upon Leeson, whose increasingly risky and fraudulent deals eventually cost Barings $1.3 billion, it was also the bank's inadequate systems for monitoring their trading operations that were equally to blame.

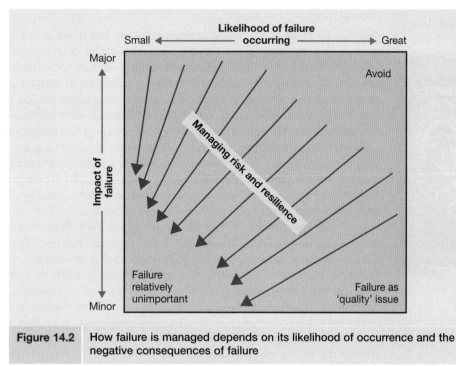

Figure 14.2 How failure is managed depends on its likelihood of occurrence and the negative consequences of failure

In March 1993 Barings Securities and Baring Brothers merged their operations (an action known as solo-consolidation) to form Baring Investment Bank (BIB). Although this had a financial logic, this action effectively created the operations structure that would allow Nick Leeson to get away with illicit dealing until the bank went bust. It enabled Barings to make large loans to its constituent parts without reference to the Bank of England, whose key principle was that no bank should ever risk more money than it can afford to lose. Large exposures (more than 10 per cent of a bank's capital) should be formally reported, yet by the end of 1993 Baring's exposure was nearly 45 per cent of its capital. In July 1992, Leeson opened the trading account 88888 as an 'error account' that is usually used to record sales pending their investigation and clearance. The volume of such trades is normally small and they are quickly cleared from the account. However, Leeson from the outset used account 88888 inappropriately. By the time of the collapse the size of the positions booked in this account was so large that, when market prices moved unfavourably, it caused the collapse of the Baring Group. Funding for positions in the form of cash or securities deposited with an exchange is known as margin. A margin call is a demand from an exchange or broker/dealer for additional cash or collateral to cover that position. In order to finance the SIMEX (Singapore's exchange) margin deposits for account 88888 transactions, Leeson needed funds from other Baring companies. In January 1995, Coopers & Lybrand's annual audit of Barings' Singapore office account picked up a discrepancy in the accounts, so that Barings' management knew that there was a problem, but not exactly where it lay or its size. However, Leeson managed to evade the auditors' questions. Around the same time, SIMEX auditors identified a problem with the 88888 account. By February 1995, Barings Securities was severely worried by events. Up until February 1995, the position might have been recoverable, but thereafter the market fell persistently and losses in account 88888 mounted almost exponentially. Barings' fate was sealed by the absence of either the people or the systems needed to stop the flow of funds to Singapore. By that time the bank was *'like a colander, leaking funds to Leeson through a variety of orifices'*. No checks were carried out when money was transferred from one part of Barings to another. Because no apparent risk was involved, the job was allocated to junior clerks. Also because no systems existed for detecting fraudulent activities, it was left up to individuals to pick up and interpret clues.

Source: courtesy Carlsberg

| Example |

Something in the beer[2]

Carlsberg UK is one of the biggest brewers in the UK, and shares the vision of its Danish parent company (the fifth largest global brewing group) of being 'probably the best beer company in the world'. The company's focus on quality dates back to what are known as the *golden words* of its founders. '*In working the Carlsberg Breweries it should be a constant purpose, regardless of immediate profit, to develop the art of making beer to the greatest possible degree of perfection in order that these breweries as well as their products may ever stand out as a model and so, through their example, assist in keeping beer brewing in Denmark on a high and honourable level.*' So, when it learned of the impending crisis late one Friday afternoon, with a public holiday the following Monday and on the eve of the Chairman's holiday, it was taken particularly seriously. Something appeared to have gone wrong with the 'widget' in one of its cans of beer (a widget is the device in the bottom of a can which gives some canned beer its creamy characteristic). One customer had taken a drink from a can of beer and found a piece of plastic in his mouth. He had complained to an environmental health official who had then taken it up with the company. The company's pre-planned crisis management procedure immediately swung into action. A crisis control group of 12 members, with experts on insurance, legal affairs, quality control and public relations, took control. This group always has everyone's telephone number, so any relevant person in the company can be contacted. It also has a control room at one of the company's sites with fax and telephone lines always available for the sole use of the crisis team. Over the weekend the team investigated the problem and by the following Tuesday had issued a press release, set up a hotline and taken out national advertising to announce the recall decision. Even though the problem had originated in only one of its six brands, the company decided to recall all of them – a total of one million cans. The hotline received 500 calls during its first week of operation, and all production using the suspect widget was halted. Linda Bain, the company spokeswoman, explained: '*We were very happy with our recall procedure and the effectiveness of the control group. It all went according to plan. In terms of public relations, the coverage we got from the media was positive, factual and up-front, and indicated the company had been as honest and truthful as it possibly could.*'

What do these two example have in common?

Both of these operations suffered failure, in the sense that failure means a disruption to normal operation. In Barings' case it was such a serious failure that the company did not survive. But both companies knew that they risked the type of failure that actually occurred and both companies had procedures in place that attempted to prevent failure occurring. Yet by the time that the extent of the failure at Barings did become evident, its impact had become too great and it could no longer recover. By contrast, Carlsberg, admittedly dealing with a less serious failure, did recover even to the extent of gaining some positive reaction.

Of course, some operations operate in a more risky environment than others. And, those operations with a high likelihood of failure and/or serious consequences deriving from that failure will need to give it more attention, but operations and process resilience is relevant to all businesses. They must all give attention to the four sets of activities which, in practical terms, resilience includes. The first is concerned with understanding what failures could potentially occur in the operation and assessing their seriousness. The second task is to examine ways of preventing failures occurring. The third is to minimize the negative consequences of failure (called failure or risk 'mitigation'). The final task is to devise plans and procedures that will help the operation to recover from failures when they do occur. The remainder of this chapter deals with these four tasks – see Figure 14.3.

> **Operations principle**
> Resilience is governed by the effectiveness of failure prevention, mitigation and recovery.

Figure 14.3 Operations and process resilience involves failure prevention, mitigating the negative consequences of failure, and failure recovery

Have potential failure points been assessed?

A prerequisite to achieving operations and process resilience is to understand where failure might occur and what the consequences of failure might be, by reviewing all possible causes of failure. Often it is the 'failure to understand failure' that leads to excessive disruption. Each cause of failure also needs to be assessed in terms of the impact it may have. Only then can measures be taken to prevent or minimize the effect of the more important potential failures. The classic approach to assessing potential failures is to inspect and audit operations activities. Unfortunately, inspection and audit cannot, on their own, provide complete assurance that undesirable events will be avoided. The content of the audit has to be appropriate, the checking process has to be sufficiently frequent and comprehensive, and the inspectors have to have sufficient knowledge and experience.

> **Operations principle**
> A 'failure to understand failure' is the root cause of a lack of resilience.

Identify the potential causes of failure

The causes of some failure are purely random, like lightning strikes, and are difficult, if not impossible, to predict. However, the vast majority of failures are not like this. They are caused by something that could have been avoided, which is why, as a minimum

Figure 14.4   The sources of potential failure in operations

starting point, a simple checklist of failure causes is useful. In fact the root cause of most failure is usually human failure of some type; nevertheless, identifying failure sources usually requires a more evident set, such as that illustrated in Figure 14.4. Here, failure sources are classified as failures of supply, internal failures such as those deriving from human organizational and technological sources, failures deriving from the design of products and services, failures deriving from customer failures, and general environmental failures.

Supply failure

Supply failure means any failure in the timing or quality of goods and services delivered into an operation, for example suppliers delivering the wrong or faulty components, outsourced call centres suffering a telecoms failure, disruption to power supplies, and so on. The more an operation relies on suppliers for materials or services, the more it is at risk from failure caused by missing or sub-standard inputs. This is an important source of failure because of increasing dependence on outsourced activities in most industries, and the emphasis on keeping supply chains 'lean' in order to cut costs. For example, in early 2002 Land Rover (a division of the Ford Motor Company) had to cope with a threat to the supply of chassis for its Discovery model when the single company to which it had sub-contracted its manufacture became insolvent. The receivers were demanding an up-front payment of around €60 million to continue supply, arguing that they were legally obliged to recover as much money as possible on behalf of creditors. And a single-supplier agreement was a valuable asset.

In this case the outsourcing of a component had made the supply chain more vulnerable. But there are also other factors which have, in recent years, increased the vulnerability of supply. For example, global sourcing usually means that parts are shipped around the world on their journey through the supply chain. Microchips manufactured in Taiwan could be assembled to printed circuit boards in Shanghai which are then finally assembled into a computer in Ireland. At the same time, many industries are suffering increased volatility in demand. Perhaps most significantly there tends to be far less inventory in supply chains that could buffer interruptions to supply. According to one authority on supply chain management, '*Potentially the risk of disruption has increased dramatically as the result of a too-narrow focus on supply chain efficiency at the expense of effectiveness.*'[3]

Human failures

There are two broad types of human failure. The first is where key personnel leave, become ill, die, or in some way cannot fulfil their role. The second is where people are actively doing their job but are making mistakes. Understanding risk in the first type of failure involves identifying the key people without whom operations would struggle to operate effectively. These are not always the most senior individuals, but rather those fulfilling crucial roles that require special skills or tacit knowledge. Human failure through 'mistakes' also comes in two types: errors and violations. 'Errors' are mistakes in judgement; with hindsight, a person should have done something different. For example, if the manager of a sports stadium fails to anticipate dangerous crowding during a championship event, this is an error of judgement. 'Violations' are acts which are clearly contrary to defined operating procedure. For example, if a maintenance engineer fails to clean a filter in the prescribed manner, it is eventually likely to cause failure. Catastrophic failures are often caused by a combination of errors and violations. For example, one kind of accident, where an aircraft appears to be under control and yet still flies into the ground, is very rare (once in two million flights).[4] For this type of failure to occur, first, the pilot has to be flying at the wrong altitude (error); second, the co-pilot would have to fail to cross-check the altitude (violation); third, air traffic controllers would have to miss the fact that the plane was at the wrong altitude (error); and finally, the pilot would have to ignore the ground proximity warning alarm in the aircraft, which can be prone to give false alarms (violation).

Organizational failure

Organizational failure is usually taken to mean failures of procedures and processes and failures that derive from a business's organizational structure and culture. This is a huge potential source of failure and includes almost all operations and process management. In particular, failure in the design of processes (such as bottlenecks causing system overloading) and failures in the resourcing of processes (such as insufficient capacity being provided at peak times) need to be investigated. But there are also many other procedures and processes within an organization that can make failure more likely. For example, remuneration policy may motivate staff to work in a way that, although increasing the financial performance of the organization, also increases its susceptibility to failure. Examples of this can range from salespeople being so incentivized that they make promises to customers that cannot be fulfilled, through to investment bankers being more concerned with profit than the risks of financial overexposure. This type of risk can derive from an organizational culture that minimizes consideration of risk, or it may come from a lack of clarity in reporting relationships; in fact, in the Barings Bank example at the beginning of the chapter, there was some evidence that both these types of failure contributed to its demise.

Technology/facilities failures

By 'technology and facilities' we mean all the IT systems, machines, equipment and buildings of an operation. All are liable to failure, or breakdown. The failure may be only partial, for example a machine that has an intermittent fault. Alternatively, it can be what we normally regard as a breakdown – a total and sudden cessation of operation. Either way, its effects could bring a large part of the operation to a halt. For example, a computer failure in a supermarket chain could paralyze several large stores until it is fixed.

Product/service design failures

In its design stage, a product or service might look fine on paper; only when it has to cope with real circumstances might inadequacies become evident. Of course, during the design process, potential risk of failure should have been identified and 'designed out'. But one only has to look at the number of 'product recalls' or service failures to understand that design failures are far from uncommon. Sometimes this is the result of a trade-off between fast time-to-market performance and the risk of the product or service failing in operation. And, while no reputable business would deliberately market flawed products or services, equally most businesses cannot delay a product or service launch indefinitely to eliminate every single small risk of failure.

Customer failures

Not all failures are (directly) caused by the operation or its suppliers. Customers may 'fail' in that they misuse products and services. For example, an IT system might have been well designed, yet the user could treat it in a way that causes it to fail. Customers are not 'always right'; they can be inattentive and incompetent. However, merely complaining about customers is unlikely to reduce the chances of this type of failure occurring. Most organizations will accept that they have a responsibility to educate and train customers, and to design their products and services so as to minimize the chances of failure.

Environmental disruption

Environmental disruption includes all the causes of failure that lie outside an operation's direct influence. This source of potential failure has risen to near the top of many firms' agenda since 11 September 2001. As operations become increasingly integrated (and increasingly dependent on integrated technologies such as information technologies), businesses are more aware of the critical events and malfunctions that have the potential to interrupt normal business activity and even stop the entire company. Typically, such disasters include the following:

- Hurricanes, floods, lightning, temperature extremes
- Fire
- Corporate crime, theft, fraud, sabotage
- Terrorism, bomb blast, bomb scare or other security attacks
- Contamination of product or processes.

Example   Slamming the door

On 25 January 2003 the 'SQL Slammer' worm, a rogue program, spread at frightening speed throughout the Internet. It disrupted computers around the world and, at the height of the attack, its effect was such that half the traffic over the Internet was being lost – see Figure 14.5. Thousands of cash dispensers in North America ceased operating and one police force was driven back to using pencils and paper when their dispatching system crashed. Yet security experts believe that

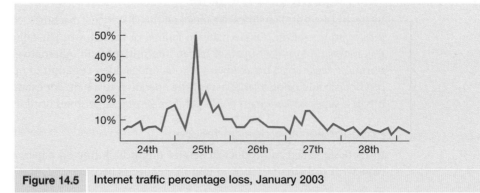

Figure 14.5   Internet traffic percentage loss, January 2003

the SQL Slammer did more good than harm because it highlighted weaknesses in Internet security processes. Like most rogue software, it exploited a flaw in a commonly used piece of software. Much commonly used software has security flaws that can be exploited in this way. Software producers issue 'patch' software to fix flaws but this can actually direct Internet terrorists to vulnerable areas in the software, and not all systems managers get around to implementing all patches. Nevertheless, every rogue program that penetrates Internet security systems teaches valuable lessons to those working to prevent security failures.

Detecting non-evident failure

Not all failures are immediately evident. Small failures may be accumulating for a while before they become evident. Purchasing officers encountering difficulties in using a website may cause them to abandon the purchase. Within an automated materials handling line, debris may periodically accumulate that, in itself, will not cause immediate failure, but could eventually lead to sudden and dramatic failure. Even when such failures are detected, they may not always receive the appropriate attention because there are inadequate failure identification systems, or a lack of managerial support or interest in making improvements. The mechanisms available to seek out failures in a proactive way include machine diagnostic checks, in-process checks, point-of-departure and phone interviews, and customer focus groups.

Post-failure analysis

One of the critical activities of operations and process resilience is to understand why a failure has occurred. This activity is called post-failure analysis. It is used to uncover the root cause of failures. Some techniques for this were described as 'improvement techniques' in Chapter 13. Others include the following.

- **Accident investigation.** Large-scale national disasters like oil tanker spillages and aeroplane accidents are usually investigated using accident investigation, where specifically trained staff analyze the causes of the accident.
- **Failure traceability.** Some businesses (either by choice or because of a legal requirement) adopt traceability procedures to ensure that all their failures (such as contaminated food products) are traceable. Any failures can be traced back to the process which produced them, the components from which they were produced, or the suppliers who provided them.
- **Complaint analysis.** Complaints (and compliments) are a potentially valuable source for detecting the root causes of failures of customer service. Two key advantages of complaints are that they come unsolicited and also they are often very timely pieces of information that can pinpoint problems quickly. Complaint analysis also involves tracking the actual number of complaints over time, which can in itself be indicative of developing problems. The prime function of complaint analysis involves analyzing the 'content' of the complaints to understand better the nature of the failure as it is perceived by the customer.
- **Fault-tree analysis.** This is a logical procedure that starts with a failure or a potential failure and works backwards to identify all the possible causes and therefore the origins of that failure. Fault-tree analysis is made up of branches connected by two types of nodes: AND nodes and OR nodes. The branches below an AND node all need to occur for the event above the node to occur. Only one of the branches below an OR node needs to occur for the event above the node to occur. Figure 14.6 shows a simple tree identifying the possible reasons for a filter in a heating system not being replaced when it should have been.

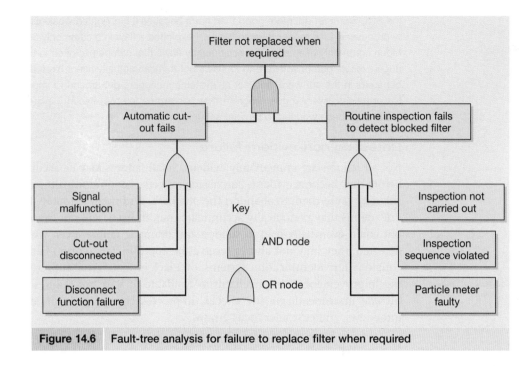

Figure 14.6 Fault-tree analysis for failure to replace filter when required

Likelihood of failure

The difficulty of estimating the chance of a failure occurring varies greatly. Some failures are the result of well-understood phenomena. A combination of rational causal analysis and historical performance data can lead to a relatively accurate estimate of failure occurring. For example, a mechanical component may fail between 10 and 17 months from its installation in 99 per cent of cases. Other types of failure are far more difficult to predict. The chances of a fire in a supplier's plant are (hopefully) low, but how low? There will be some data concerning fire hazards in this type of plant, and one may insist on regular hazard inspection reports from the supplier's insurance providers, but the estimated probability of failure will be both low and subjective.

'Objective' estimates

Estimates of failure based on historical performance can be measured in several ways, including:

● *Failure rates* – how often a failure occurs
● *Reliability* – the chances of a failure occurring
● *Availability* – the amount of available useful operating time.

PRACTICE NOTE

'Failure rate' and 'reliability' are different ways of measuring the same thing – the propensity of an operation, or part of an operation, to fail. Availability is one measure of the consequences of failure in the operation.

Sometimes failure is a function of time. For example, the probability of an electric lamp failing is relatively high when it is first used, but if it survives this initial stage, it could still fail at any point, and the longer it survives, the more likely its failure becomes. Most physical parts of an operation behave in a similar manner. The curve which describes failure probability of this type is called the bath-tub curve. It comprises three distinct stages:

● The 'infant-mortality' or 'early-life' stage where early failures occur caused by defective parts or improper use

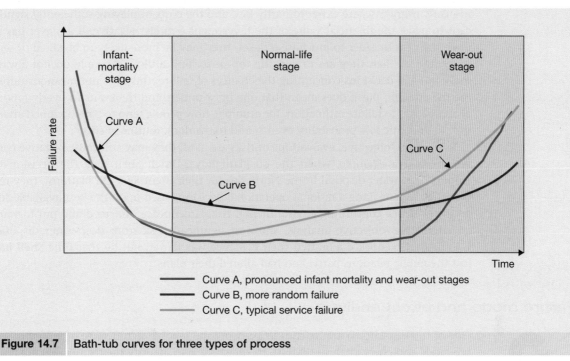

Figure 14.7　Bath-tub curves for three types of process

- The 'normal-life' stage when the failure rate is usually low and reasonably constant, and caused by normal random factors
- The 'wear-out' stage when the failure rate increases as the part approaches the end of its working life and failure is caused by the ageing and deterioration of parts.

Figure 14.7 illustrates three bath-tub curves with slightly different characteristics. Curve A shows a part of the operation which has a high initial infant-mortality failure but then a long, low-failure, normal life followed by the gradually increasing likelihood of failure as it approaches wear-out. Curve B, while having the same stages, is far less predictable. The distinction between the three stages is less clear, with infant-mortality failure subsiding only slowly and a gradually increasing chance of wear-out failure. Failure of the type shown in curve B is far more difficult to manage in a planned manner. The failure of operations which rely more on human resources than on technology, such as some services, can be closer to curve C of Figure 14.7. They may be less susceptible to component wear-out but more so to staff complacency. Without review and regeneration, the service may become tedious and repetitive, and after an initial stage of failure reduction, as problems in the service are ironed out, there can be a long period of increasing failure.

'Subjective' estimates

Failure assessment, even for subjective risks, is increasingly a formal exercise that is carried out using standard frameworks, often prompted by health and safety concerns, environmental regulations, and so on. These frameworks are similar to the formal quality inspection methods associated with quality standards like ISO 9000 (see Chapter 12) that often implicitly assume unbiased objectivity. However, individual attitudes to risk are complex and subject to a wide variety of influences. In fact many studies have demonstrated that people are generally very poor at making risk-related judgements. Consider the success of state and national lotteries. The chances of winning,

Operations principle
Subjective estimates of failure probability are better than no estimates at all.

in nearly every case, are extraordinarily low, and the costs of playing sufficiently significant to make the financial value of the investment entirely negative. If a player has to drive their car in order to purchase a ticket, they may be more likely to be killed or seriously injured than they are to win the top prize. But, although people do not always make rational decisions concerning the chances of failure, this does not mean abandoning the attempt. But it does mean that one must understand the limits to overly rational approaches to failure estimation, for example, how people tend to pay too much attention to dramatic low-probability events, and to overlook routine events.[5]

Even when 'objective' evaluations of risks are used, they may still cause negative consequences. For example, when the oil giant Royal-Dutch Shell took the decision to employ deep-water disposal in the North Sea for their Brent Spar Oil Platform, they felt that they were making a rational operational decision based upon the best available scientific evidence concerning environmental risk. Greenpeace disagreed and put forward an alternative 'objective analysis' showing significant risk from deep-water disposal. Eventually Greenpeace admitted their evidence was flawed but by that time Shell had lost the public relations battle and had altered their plans.

Failure mode and effect analysis

Excel

One of the best-known approaches to assessing the relative significance of failure is failure mode and effect analysis (FMEA). Its objective is to identify the factors that are critical to various types of failure as a means of identifying failures before they happen. It does this by providing a 'checklist' procedure built around three key questions for each possible cause of failure:

● What is the likelihood that failure will occur?
● What would the consequence of the failure be?
● How likely is such a failure to be detected before it affects the customer?

PRACTICE NOTE

Based on a quantitative evaluation of these three questions, a risk priority number (RPN) is calculated for each potential cause of failure. Corrective actions, aimed at preventing failure, are then applied to those causes whose RPN indicates that they warrant priority – see Figure 14.8.

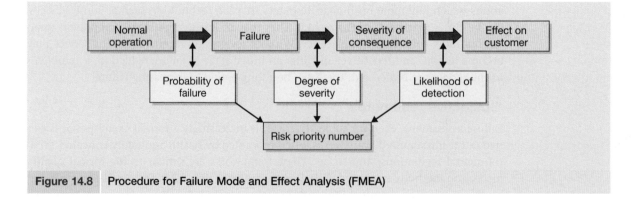

Figure 14.8   Procedure for Failure Mode and Effect Analysis (FMEA)

Have failure prevention measures been implemented?

It is almost always better to avoid failures and negative consequences than have to recover from them, which is why failure prevention is an important part of operations and process resilience. There are a number of approaches to this, including designing out failure points, deploying redundant resources, fail-safeing, and maintenance.

Designing out fail points

Process mapping, described in Chapter 5, can be used to 'engineer out' the potential fail points in operations. For example, Figure 14.9 shows a process map for an automobile repair process. The stages in the process that are particularly prone to failure and the stages that are critical to the success of the service have been marked. This will have been done by the staff of this operation metaphorically 'walking themselves through' the process and discussing each stage in turn.

Redundancy

Building in redundancy to an operation means having back-up processes or resources in case of failure. It can be an expensive solution to reduce the likelihood of failure and is generally used when breakdown could have a critical impact. Redundancy means doubling or even tripling some of the elements in a process so that these 'redundant' elements can come into action when one component fails. Nuclear power stations, hospitals and other public buildings have auxiliary or back-up electricity generators ready to operate in case the main electricity supply should fail. Some organizations also have back-up staff held in reserve in case someone does not turn up for work or is held up on one job and is unable to move on to the next. Spacecraft have several back-up computers on board that will not only monitor the main computer but also act as a back-up in case of failure. Human bodies contain two of some organs – kidneys and eyes, for example – both of which are used in 'normal operation' but the body can cope with a failure in one of them. One response to the threat of large failures, such as terrorist activity, has been a rise in the number of companies offering 'replacement office' operations, fully equipped with normal Internet and telephone communications links, and often with access to a company's current management information. Should a customer's main operation be affected by a disaster, business can continue in the replacement facility within days or even hours.

The effect of redundancy can be calculated by the sum of the reliability of the original process component and the likelihood that the back-up component will both be needed and be working.

$$R_{a+b} = R_a + (R_b \times P_{(\text{failure})})$$

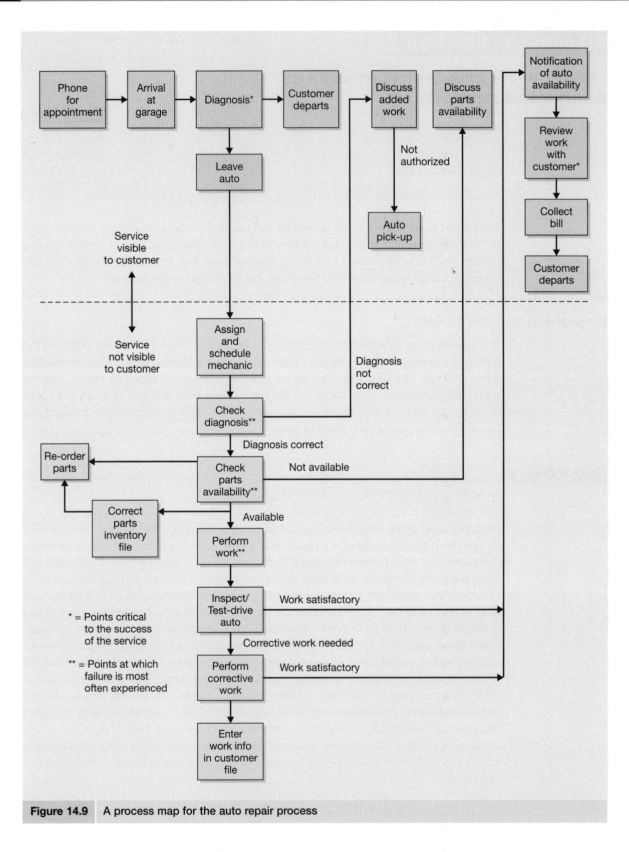

Figure 14.9   A process map for the auto repair process

where R_{a+b} = reliability of component *a* with its back-up component *b*

R_a = reliability of *a* alone

R_b = reliability of back-up component *b*

$P_{(failure)}$ = probability that component *a* will fail and therefore component *b* will be needed.

So, for example, a food manufacturer has two packing lines, one of which will come into action only if the first line fails. If each line has a reliability of 0.9, the lines working together (each with reliability = 0.9) will have a reliability of $0.9 + [0.9 \times (1 - 0.9)] = 0.99$.

Fail-safeing

The concept of fail-safeing has emerged since the introduction of Japanese methods of operations improvement. Called *poka-yoke* in Japan (from *yokeru* (to prevent) and *poka* (inadvertent errors)), the idea is based on the principle that human mistakes are to some extent inevitable. What is important is to prevent them becoming defects. Poka-yokes are simple (preferably inexpensive) devices or systems which are incorporated into a process to prevent inadvertent operator mistakes resulting in a defect.

> **Operations principle**
> Simple methods of fail-safeing can often be the most cost effective.

Typical poka-yokes are the following devices:

FURTHER EXAMPLE

- Limit switches on machines which allow the machine to operate only if the part is positioned correctly
- Gauges placed on machines through which a part has to pass in order to be loaded onto, or taken off, the machine – an incorrect size or orientation stops the process
- Digital counters on machines to ensure that the correct number of cuts, passes or holes have been machined
- Checklists which have to be filled in, either in preparation for, or on completion of, an activity
- Light beams which activate an alarm if a part is positioned incorrectly.

The same principle can also be applied to service operations, for example:

- Colour-coding cash register keys to prevent incorrect entry in retail operations
- The McDonald's french-fry scoop which picks up the right quantity of fries in the right orientation to be placed in the pack
- Trays used in hospitals with indentations shaped to each item needed for a surgical procedure – any item not back in place at the end of the procedure might have been left in the patient
- The paper strips placed round clean towels in hotels, the removal of which helps housekeepers to tell whether a towel has been used and therefore needs replacing
- The locks on aircraft lavatory doors, which must be turned to switch the light on
- Beepers on ATMs to ensure that customers remove their cards
- Height bars on amusement rides to ensure that customers do not exceed size limitations.

Maintenance

FURTHER EXAMPLE

Maintenance is the term used to cover the way operations and processes try to avoid failure by taking care of their physical facilities. It is particularly important when physical facilities play a central role in the operation, such as at power stations, airlines and petrochemical refineries. There are a number of approaches to maintenance, including the following.

Preventive maintenance (PM)

This attempts to eliminate or reduce the chances of failure by regularly servicing (cleaning, lubricating, replacing and checking) facilities. For example, the engines of passenger aircraft are checked, cleaned and calibrated according to a regular schedule after a set number of flying hours. Taking aircraft away from their regular duties for preventive maintenance is clearly an expensive option for any airline, but the consequences of failure while in service are considerably more serious.

Condition-based maintenance (CBM)

This attempts to perform maintenance only when the facilities require it. For example, continuous process equipment, such as that used in coating photographic paper, is run for long periods in order to achieve the high utilization necessary for cost-effective production. Stopping the machine when it is not strictly necessary to do so would take it out of action for long periods and reduce its utilization. Here condition-based maintenance might involve continuously monitoring the vibrations, or some other characteristic of the line. The results of this monitoring would then be used to decide whether the line should be stopped and the bearings replaced.

Total productive maintenance (TPM)

This is defined as '. . . *the productive maintenance carried out by all employees through small group activities*', where productive maintenance is '. . . *maintenance management which recognizes the importance of reliability, maintenance and economic efficiency in plant design.*'[6] TPM adopts team-working and empowerment principles, as well as a continuous improvement approach to failure prevention. It aims to establish good maintenance practice in operations through the pursuit of 'the five goals of TPM':[6]

1 Examine how the facilities are contributing to the effectiveness of the operation by examining all the losses which occur.
2 Achieve autonomous maintenance by allowing people to take responsibility for at least some of the maintenance tasks.
3 Plan maintenance by having a fully worked out approach to all maintenance activities, including the level of preventive maintenance which is required for each piece of equipment, the standards for condition-based maintenance and the respective responsibilities of operating staff and maintenance staff.
4 Train all staff in relevant maintenance skills so that staff have all the skills to carry out their roles.
5 Avoid maintenance altogether by 'maintenance prevention' (MP), that is, considering failure causes and the maintainability of equipment during its design stage, its manufacture, its installation and its commissioning.

How much maintenance?

Most operations plan their maintenance to include a level of regular preventive maintenance which gives a reasonably low but finite chance of breakdown. Usually the more frequent the preventive maintenance episodes, the less are the chances of a breakdown. Infrequent preventive maintenance will cost little to provide but will result in a high likelihood (and therefore cost) of breakdown. Conversely, very frequent preventive maintenance will be expensive to provide but will reduce the cost of having to provide breakdown maintenance, as shown in Figure 14.10(a). The total cost of maintenance appears to minimize at an 'optimum' level of preventive maintenance. However, this may not reflect reality. The cost of providing preventive maintenance in Figure 14.10(a) assumes that it is carried out by a separate set of people (skilled maintenance staff) whose time is scheduled

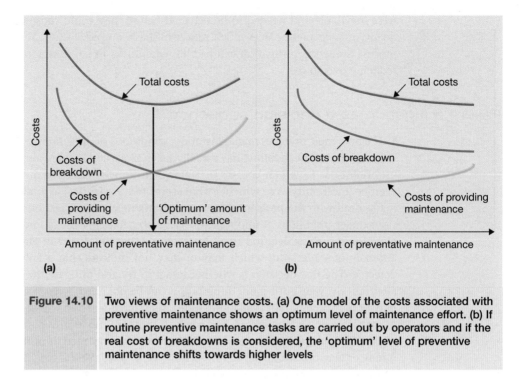

Figure 14.10 Two views of maintenance costs. (a) One model of the costs associated with preventive maintenance shows an optimum level of maintenance effort. (b) If routine preventive maintenance tasks are carried out by operators and if the real cost of breakdowns is considered, the 'optimum' level of preventive maintenance shifts towards higher levels

and accounted for separately from the 'operators' of the facilities. In many operations, however, at least some preventive maintenance can be performed by the operators themselves (which reduces the cost of providing it) and at times that are convenient for the operation (which minimizes the disruption to the operation). Furthermore, the cost of breakdowns could also be higher than is indicated in Figure 14.10(a) because unplanned downtime can take away stability from the operation, preventing it being able to improve itself. Put these two ideas together and the minimizing total curve and maintenance cost curve look more like Figure 14.10(b). The emphasis is shifted towards using more preventive maintenance than is generally thought appropriate.

Have failure mitigation measures been implemented?

Failure mitigation means isolating a failure from its negative consequences. It is an admission that not all failures can be avoided. However, in some areas of operations management, relying on mitigation, rather than prevention, is unfashionable. For example, 'inspection' practices in quality management were based on the assumption that failures were inevitable and needed to be detected before they could cause harm. Modern total quality management places much more emphasis on prevention. Yet, in operations and process resilience, mitigation can be vital when used in conjunction with prevention in reducing overall risk.

Failure mitigation as a decision sequence

This whole topic involves managing under conditions of uncertainty. There may be uncertainty as to whether a failure has actually taken place at all. There almost certainly will be uncertainty as to which courses of action will provide effective mitigation. There may even be uncertainty as to whether what seems to have worked as a mitigation action really has dealt with the problem. One way of thinking about mitigation is as a series of decisions under conditions of uncertainty. Doing so enables the use of formal decision analysis techniques such as decision trees, for example that illustrated in Figure 14.11. Here, an anomaly of some kind, which may or may not indicate that a failure has occurred, is detected. The first decision is whether to act to try and mitigate the supposed failure or, alternatively, wait until more information can be obtained. Even if mitigation is tried, it may or may not contain the failure. If not, then further action will be needed, which may or may not contain the failure, and so on. If more information is obtained prior to enacting mitigation, then the failure may or may not be confirmed. If mitigation is then tried, it may or may not work, and so on. Although the details of the specific mitigation actions will depend on circumstances, what is important in practical terms is that for all significant failures some kind of decision rules and mitigation planning has been established.

Failure mitigation actions

The nature of the action taken to mitigate failure will obviously depend on the nature of the failure. In most industries technical experts have established a classification of failure mitigation actions that are appropriate for the types of risk likely to be suffered. So, for example, in agriculture, government agencies and industry bodies have published mitigation strategies for such 'failures' as the outbreak of crop disease, contagious animal infections, and so on. Such documents will outline the various mitigation actions that can be taken under different circumstances and detail exactly who are responsible for

Figure 14.11   A decision tree for mitigation when failure is not immediately obvious

each action. Although these classifications tend to be industry specific, the following generic categorization gives a flavour of the types of mitigation actions that may be generally applicable.

- **Mitigation planning** is the activity of ensuring that all possible failure circumstances have been identified and the appropriate mitigation actions identified. It is the overarching activity that encompasses all subsequent mitigation actions, and may be described in the form of a decision tree or guide rules. Almost certainly there will be some form of escalation that will guide the extra mitigation effort should early actions not prove successful. It is worth noting that mitigation planning, as well an overarching action, also provides mitigation action in its own right. For example, if mitigation planning has identified appropriate training, job design, emergency procedures, and so on, then the financial liability of a business for any losses should a failure occur will be reduced. Certainly businesses that have not planned adequately for failures will be more liable in law for any subsequent losses.
- **Economic mitigation** includes actions such as insurance against losses from failure, spreading the financial consequences of failure, and 'hedging' against failure. Insurance is the best known of these actions and is widely adopted, although ensuring appropriate insurance and effective claims management is a specialized skill in itself. Spreading the financial consequences of failure could involve, for example, spreading the equity holding in supply companies to reduce the financial consequences of such companies failing. Hedging involves creating a portfolio of ventures whose outcomes happen to be correlated so as to reduce total variability. This often takes the form of financial instruments, for example a business may purchase a financial 'hedge' against the price risk of a vital raw material deviating significantly from a set price.
- **Containment (spatial)** means stopping the failure physically spreading to affect other parts of an internal or external supply network. Preventing contaminated food from spreading through the supply chain, for example, will depend on real-time information systems that provide traceability data.
- **Containment (temporal)** means containing the spread of a failure over time. It particularly applies when information about a failure or potential failure needs to be transmitted without undue delay. For example, systems that give advance warning of hazardous weather such as snowstorms must transmit such information to local agencies such as the police and road-clearing organizations in time for them to stop the problem causing excessive disruption.
- **Loss reduction** covers any action that reduces the catastrophic consequences of failure by removing the resources that are likely to suffer those consequences. For example, the road signs that indicate evacuation routes in the event of severe weather, or the fire drills that train employees in how to escape in the event of an emergency, may not reduce the consequences of failure on buildings or physical facilities, but can dramatically help in reducing loss of life or injury.
- **Substitution** means compensating for failure by providing other resources that can substitute for those rendered less effective by the failure. It is a little like the concept of redundancy that was described earlier, but does not always imply excess resources if a failure has not occurred. For example, in a construction project, the risk of encountering unexpected geological problems may be mitigated by the existence of a separate work plan that is invoked only if such problems are found. The resources may come from other parts of the construction project, which will in turn have plans to compensate for their loss.

Table 14.1 gives some examples of each type of failure mitigation action for three failures: the theft of money from one of a company's bank accounts, the failure of a new

Table 14.1   Failure mitigation actions for three failures

Failure mitigation actions	Type of failure		
	Financial failure – theft from company account	Development failure – new technology does not work	Emergency failure – fire at premises
Mitigation planning	Identify different types of theft that have been reported and devise mitigation actions including software to identify anomalous account behaviour	Identify possible types of technology failure and identify contingency technologies together with plans for accessing them	Identify fire hazards and methods of detecting, limiting and extinguishing fires
Economic mitigation	Insure against theft and possibly use several different accounts	Invest in, or form partnership with, supplier of alternative technology	Insure against fire and have more, smaller, premises
Containment (spatial)	'Ring fence' accounts so a deficit in one account cannot be made good from another account	Develop alternative technological solutions for different parts of the development project so that failure in one part does not affect the whole project	Install localized sprinkler systems and fire door barriers
Containment (temporal)	Invest in software that detects signs of possible unusual account behaviour	Build in project milestones that indicate the possibility of eventual development failure	Install alarm systems that indicate the occurrence of fire to everyone who may be affected (including in other premises)
Loss reduction	Build in transfer delays until approval for major withdrawals has been given, also institute plans for recovering stolen money	Ensure the development project can use old technology if new one does not work	Ensure means of egress and employee training are adequate
Substitution	Ensure that reserve funds and staff to manage the transfer can be speedily brought into play	Have fallback work package for devoting extra resources to overcome the new technology failure	Ensure back-up team that can take over from premises rendered inoperative by fire

product technology to work adequately during the new product development process, and the outbreak of fire at a business premises.

Example   Mitigating currency risk[7]

A multinational consumer goods firm was concerned at the way its operations in certain parts of the world were exposed to currency fluctuations. The company's Russian subsidiary sourced nearly all products from its parent's factories in France and Germany, while its main rivals had manufacturing facilities in Russia. Conscious of the potential volatility of the rouble, the firm needed to minimize its operating exposure to a devaluation of the currency that would leave the firm's cost structure at a serious disadvantage compared to its rivals, and without any real option but to increase their prices. In seeking to mitigate against the risk of devaluation, the firm could choose from among various financial and operations-based options. For example, financial tools were available to minimize currency exposure. Most of these allow the operation to reduce the risk of currency fluctuations but involve an 'up-front' cost. Usually, the higher the risk the greater the up-front cost. Alternatively the company may restructure its operations strategy in order to mitigate its currency risk. One option would be to develop its own production facilities within Russia. This may reduce, or even eliminate, the currency risk, although it may introduce other risks. A further option may be to form supply partnerships with other Russian companies. Again, this does not eliminate risks but can shift them to ones which the company feels more able to control. More generally the company may consider creating a portfolio of operations-based strategies, such as developing alternative suppliers in different currency zones, building up excess/flexible capacity in a global production network, and creating more differentiated products that are less price-sensitive.

DIAGNOSTIC QUESTION

Have failure recovery measures been implemented?

Failure recovery is the set of actions that are taken, after the negative effects of failure have occurred, that reduce the impact of the negative effects. All types of operation can benefit from well-planned recovery. For example, a construction company whose mechanical digger breaks down can have plans in place to arrange a replacement from a hire company. The breakdown might be disruptive, but not as much as it might have been if the operations manager had not worked out what to do. Recovery procedures will also shape customers' perceptions of failure. Even where the customer sees a failure, it may not necessarily lead to dissatisfaction; customers may even accept that things occasionally do go wrong. If there is a metre of snow on the train lines, or if the restaurant is particularly popular, we may accept the fact that something is wrong with the product or service. It is not necessarily the failure itself that leads to dissatisfaction but often the organization's response to the breakdown. Mistakes may be inevitable, but dissatisfied customers are not.

A failure may even be turned into a positive experience. If a flight is delayed by five hours, there is considerable potential for dissatisfaction. But if the airline informs passengers that the aircraft has been delayed by a cyclone at its previous destination, and that arrangements have been made for accommodation at a local hotel with a complimentary meal, passengers might then feel that they have been well treated and even recommend that airline to others. A good recovery can turn angry, frustrated customers into loyal ones. In fact one investigation[8] into customer satisfaction and customer loyalty used four scenarios to test the willingness of customers to use an operation's services again. The four scenarios were:

Operations principle
Successful failure recovery can yield more benefits than if the failure had not occurred.

1 The service is delivered to meet the customers' expectations and there is full satisfaction.
2 There are faults in the service delivery but the customer does not complain about them.
3 There are faults in the service delivery and the customer complains, but he or she has been fobbed off or mollified. There is no real satisfaction with the service provider.

4 There are faults in the service delivery and the customer complains and feels fully satisfied with the resulting action taken by the service providers.

Customers who are fully satisfied and do not experience any problems (1) are the most loyal, followed by complaining customers whose complaints are resolved successfully (4). Customers who experience problems but don't complain (2) are in third place and last of all come customers who do complain but are left with their problems unresolved and feelings of dissatisfaction (3).

The recovery process

Recovery needs to be a planned process. Organizations therefore need to design appropriate responses to failure, linked to the cost and the inconvenience caused by the failure to their customers. These must first meet the needs and expectations of customers. Such recovery processes need to be carried out either by empowered front-line staff or by trained personnel who are available to deal with recovery in a way which does not interfere with day-to-day service activities. Figure 14.12 illustrates a typical recovery sequence.

Discover

The first thing any manager needs to do when faced with a failure is to discover its exact nature. Three important pieces of information are needed: first of all, what exactly has happened; second, who will be affected by the failure; and third, why did the failure occur? This last point is not intended to be a detailed inquest into the causes of failure (that comes later), but it is often necessary to know something of the causes of failure in case it is necessary to determine what action to take.

Act

The discover stage could take only minutes or even seconds, depending on the severity of the failure. If the failure is a severe one with important consequences, we need to move on to doing something about it quickly. This means carrying out three actions, the first two of which could be carried out in reverse order, depending on the urgency of the situation. First, tell the significant people involved what you are proposing to do about the failure. In service operations this is especially important where the customers need to be kept informed, both for their peace of mind and to demonstrate that something is being done. In all operations, however, it is important to communicate what action is going to

Figure 14.12   Recovery sequence for minimizing the impact from failure

happen so that everyone can set their own recovery plans in motion. Second, the effects of the failure need to be contained in order to stop the consequences spreading and causing further failures. The precise containment actions will depend on the nature of the failure. Third, there needs to be some kind of follow-up to make sure that the containment actions really have contained the failure.

Learn

As discussed earlier in this chapter, the benefits of failure in providing learning opportunities should not be underestimated. In failure planning, learning involves revisiting the failure to find out its root cause and then engineering out the causes of the failure so that it will not happen again.

Plan

Learning the lessons from a failure is not the end of the procedure. Operations managers need formally to incorporate the lessons into their future reactions to failures. This is often done by working through 'in theory' how they would react to failures in the future. Specifically, this involves first identifying all the possible failures which might occur (in a similar way to the FMEA approach). Second, it means formally defining the procedures which the organization should follow in the case of each type of identified failure.

Critical commentary

Each chapter contains a short critical commentary on the main ideas covered in the chapter. Its purpose is not to undermine the issues discussed in the chapter, but to emphasize that, although we present a relatively orthodox view of operation, there are other perspectives.

■ The idea that failure can be detected through in-process inspection is increasingly seen as only partially true. Although inspecting for failures is an obvious first step in detecting them, it is not even close to being 100 per cent reliable. Accumulated evidence from research and practical examples consistently indicates that people, even when assisted by technology, are not good at detecting failure and errors. This applies even when special attention is being given to inspection. For example, airport security was significantly strengthened after 11 September 2001, yet one in ten lethal weapons that were entered into airports' security systems (in order to test them) were not detected. 'There is no such thing as 100 per cent security, we are all human beings', says Ian Hutcheson, the Director of Security at Airport Operator BAA. No one is advocating abandoning inspection as a failure detection mechanism. Rather it is seen as one of a range of methods of preventing failure.

■ Much of the previous discussion surrounding the prevention of failure has assumed a 'rational' approach. In other words, it is assumed that operations managers and customers alike will put more effort into preventing failures that are either more likely to occur or more serious in their consequences. Yet this assumption is based on a rational response to risk. In fact, being human, managers often respond to the perception of risk rather than its reality. For example, Table 14.2 shows the cost of each life saved by investment in various road and rail transportation safety (in other words, failure prevention) investments. The table shows that investing in improving road safety is very much more effective than investing in rail safety.

Table 14.2   The cost per life saved of various safety (failure prevention) investments

Safety investment	Cost per life (€m)
Advanced train protection system	30
Train protection warning systems	7.5
Implementing recommended guidelines on rail safety	4.7
Implementing recommended guidelines on road safety	1.6
Local authority spending on road safety	0.15

And while no one is arguing for abandoning efforts on rail safety, it is noted by some transportation authorities that actual investment reflects more the public perception of rail deaths (low) compared with road deaths (very high).

Summary checklist

This checklist comprises questions that can be usefully applied to any type of operations and reflect the major diagnostic questions used within the chapter.

- [ ] Does the business have an operations and process resilience policy?
- [ ] Have any possible changes in the business's vulnerability to failure been discussed and accommodated within its failure policy?
- [ ] Have all potential sources of failure been identified?
- [ ] Have any future changes in the sources of failure been identified?
- [ ] Have the impact of all potential sources of failure been assessed?
- [ ] Has the likelihood of each potential failure been assessed?
- [ ] Has the possibility of non-evident failures been addressed?
- [ ] Is post-failure analysis carried out when failure does occur?
- [ ] Are techniques such as failure mode and effect analysis (FMEA) used?
- [ ] Has due attention been paid to the possibility of designing out failure points?
- [ ] Is the concept of redundancy economically viable for any potential failures?
- [ ] Has the idea of fail-safeing (poka-yoke) been considered as a means of reducing the likelihood of failure?
- [ ] Have all approaches to process and technology maintenance been explored?
- [ ] Has the possibility that insufficient maintenance effort is being applied been investigated?
- [ ] Does the operation have a failure mitigation plan?
- [ ] Have the whole range of mitigation actions been thoroughly evaluated?
- [ ] Are specific plans in place for the use of each type of mitigation action?
- [ ] Is a well-planned recovery procedure in place?
- [ ] Does the recovery procedure cover all the steps of discover, act, learn and plan?

Case study   The Chernobyl failure[9]

At 1.24 in the early hours of Saturday morning on 26 April 1986, the worst accident in the history of commercial nuclear power generation occurred. Two explosions in quick succession blew off the 1000-tonne concrete sealing cap of the Chernobyl-4 nuclear reactor. Molten core fragments showered down on the immediate area and fission products were released into the atmosphere. The accident cost probably hundreds of lives and contaminated vast areas of land in the Ukraine.

Many reasons probably contributed to the disaster. Certainly the design of the reactor was not new – around 30 years old at the time of the accident – and had been conceived before the days of sophisticated computer-controlled safety systems. Because of this, the reactor's emergency-handling procedures relied heavily on the skill of the operators. This type of reactor also had a tendency to run 'out of control' when operated at low power. For this reason, the operating procedures for the reactor strictly prohibited it being operated below 20 per cent of its maximum power. It was mainly a combination of circumstance and human error which caused the failure, however. Ironically, the events which led up to the disaster were designed to make the reactor safer. Tests, devised by a specialist team of engineers, were being carried out to evaluate whether the emergency core cooling system (ECCS) could be operated during the 'free-wheeling' rundown of the turbine generator, should an off-site power failure occur. Although this safety device had been tested before, it had not worked satisfactorily and new tests of the modified device were to be carried out with the reactor operating at reduced power throughout the test period. The tests were scheduled for the afternoon of Friday, 25 April 1986 and the plant power reduction began at 1.00 pm. However, just after 2.00 pm, when the reactor was operating at about half its full power, the Kiev controller requested that the reactor should continue supplying the grid with electricity. In fact it was not released from the grid until 11.10 that night. The reactor was due to be shut down for its annual maintenance on the following Tuesday and the Kiev controller's request had in effect shrunk the 'window of opportunity' available for the tests.

The following is a chronological account of the hours up to the disaster, together with an analysis by James Reason, which was published in the Bulletin of the British Psychological Society the following year. Significant

Source: © Vladimir Repik/Reuters/Corbis

operator actions are italicized. These are of two kinds: errors (indicated by an 'E') and procedural violations (marked with a 'V').

25 April 1986

1.00 pm Power reduction started with the intention of achieving 25 per cent power for test conditions.
2.00 pm ECCS disconnected from primary circuit. (This was part of the test plan.)
2.05 pm Kiev controller asked the unit to continue supplying grid. *The ECCS was not reconnected (V).* (This particular violation is not thought to have contributed materially to the disaster, but it is indicative of a lax attitude on the part of the operators towards the observance of safety procedures.)
11.10 pm The unit was released from the grid and continued power reduction to achieve the 25 per cent power level planned for the test programme.

26 April 1986

12.28 am *Operator seriously undershot the intended power setting (E).* The power dipped to a dangerous 1 per cent. (The operator had switched off the 'auto-pilot' and had tried to achieve the desired level by manual control.)
1.00 am After a long struggle, the reactor power was finally stabilized at 7 per cent – well below the intended level and well into the low-power danger zone. At this point, the experiment should have been abandoned, but *it was not (E).* This was the most serious mistake (as opposed to violation): it meant that all subsequent activity would be conducted

within the reactor's zone of maximum instability. This was apparently not appreciated by the operators.

1.03 am All eight pumps were started (V). The safety regulations limited the maximum number of pumps in use at any one time to six. This showed a profound misunderstanding of the physics of the reactor. The consequence was that the increased water flow (and reduced steam fraction) absorbed more neutrons, causing more control rods to be withdrawn to sustain even this low level of power.

1.19 am The feedwater flow was increased threefold (V). The operators appear to have been attempting to cope with a falling steam-drum pressure and water level. The result of their actions, however, was to further reduce the amount of steam passing through the core, causing yet more control rods to be withdrawn. They also overrode the steam-drum automatic shut-down (V). The effect of this was to strip the reactor of one of its automatic safety systems.

1.22 am The shift supervisor requested printout to establish how many control rods were actually in the core. The printout indicated only six to eight rods remaining. It was strictly forbidden to operate the reactor with fewer than 12 rods. Yet the shift supervisor decided to continue with the tests (V). This was a fatal decision: the reactor was thereafter without 'brakes'.

1.23 am The steam line valves to No. 8 turbine generator were closed (V). The purpose of this was to establish the conditions necessary for repeated testing, but its consequence was to disconnect the automatic safety trips. This was perhaps the most serious violation of all.

1.24 am An attempt was made to 'scram' the reactor by driving in the emergency shut-off rods, but they jammed within the now warped tubes.

1.24 am Two explosions occurred in quick succession. The reactor roof was blown off and 30 fires started in the vicinity.

1.30 am Duty firemen were called out. Other units were summoned from Pripyat and Chernobyl.

5.00 am Exterior fires had been extinguished, but the graphite fire in the core continued for several days.

The subsequent investigation into the disaster highlighted a number of significant points which contributed to it:

- The test programme was poorly worked out and the section on safety measures was inadequate. Because the ECCS was shut off during the test period, the safety of the reactor was in effect substantially reduced.
- The test plan was put into effect before being approved by the design group who were responsible for the reactor.
- The operators and the technicians who were running the experiment had different and non-overlapping skills.
- The operators, although highly skilled, had probably been told that getting the test completed before the shut-down would enhance their reputation. They were proud of their ability to handle the reactor even in unusual conditions and were aware of the rapidly reducing window of opportunity within which they had to complete the test. They had also probably 'lost any feeling for the hazards involved' in operating the reactor.
- The technicians who had designed the test were electrical engineers from Moscow. Their objective was to solve a complex technical problem. In spite of having designed the test procedures, they probably would not know much about the operation of the nuclear power station itself.

Again, in the words of James Reason: *'Together, they made a dangerous mixture: a group of single-minded but non-nuclear engineers directing a team of dedicated but over-confident operators. Each group probably assumed that the other knew what it was doing. And both parties had little or no understanding of the dangers they were courting, or of the system they were abusing.'*

QUESTIONS

1 What were the root causes which contributed to the ultimate failure?

2 How could failure planning have helped prevent the disaster?

Active case study   Paterford Elevators

ACTIVE CASE

Elevators are one of the many products and services integral to our daily lives and whose smooth performance we take for granted. Yet their efficient operation really does depend on the type of maintenance services offered by companies like Paterford Elevators. Ensuring that elevators run smoothly depends upon an understanding of when they might fail, and for elevators, failure is not just irritating, but is potentially lethal.

- How would you recommend the company improve their maintenance service, whilst ensuring they do not place their customers at risk?

Please refer to the CD to work through the decisions that Paterford Elevators must make to ensure they offer the best service to their customers.

Applying the principles

HINTS

Some of these exercises can be answered by reading the chapter. Others will require some general knowledge of business activity and some might require an element of investigation. All have hints on how they can be answered on the CD accompanying this book.

1 Earlier in this chapter the failure of 'controlled flight into ground' was mentioned. Predominantly, the reason for this is not mechanical failure but human failure such as pilot fatigue. Boeing, which dominates the commercial airline business, has calculated that over 60 per cent of all the accidents which have occurred in the past 10 years had flight crew behaviour as their 'dominant cause'. For this type of failure to occur, a whole chain of minor failures must happen. First, the pilot at the controls has to be flying at the wrong altitude – there is only one chance in a thousand of this. Second, the co-pilot would have to fail to cross-check the altitude – only one chance in a hundred of this. The air traffic controllers would have to miss the fact that the plane was at the wrong altitude (which is not strictly part of their job) – a one-in-ten chance. Finally, the pilot would have to ignore the ground proximity warning alarm in the aircraft (which can be prone to give false alarms) – a one-in-two chance.

- What are your views on the quoted probabilities of each failure described above occurring?
- How would you try to prevent these failures occurring?
- If the probability of each failure occurring could be reduced by a half, what would be the effect on the likelihood of this type of crash occurring?

2 Conduct a survey amongst colleagues, friends and acquaintances of how they cope with the possibility that their computers might 'fail', in terms of either ceasing to operate effectively, or losing data. Discuss how the concept of redundancy applies in such failure.

3 Survey a range of people who own and/or are responsible for the performance of the following pieces of equipment. What is their approach to maintaining them and how is this influenced by the perceived seriousness of any failure?

(a) Motor cars

(b) Central heating systems or air conditioning systems

(c) Domestic appliances such as dishwashers and vacuum cleaners

(d) Furniture

(e) Lighting or lighting systems.

4 Visit the websites of some of the many companies that offer advice and consultancy to companies wishing to review their 'business continuity' plans. Based on your investigation of these sites, identify the key issues in any business continuity plan for the following types of operation:

(a) A university

(b) An airport

(c) A container port

(d) A chemicals manufacturing plant.

In terms of its effectiveness at managing the learning process, how does a university detect failures? What could it do to improve its failure detection processes?

Notes on chapter

1 Drawn primarily from Leeson's own book, *Rogue Trader* (1996), Warner Books, and (the more objective) *The Collapse of Barings: Panic, ignorance and greed* by Stephen Fay (1996), Arrow Books.
2 Source: 'How to cope in a crisis', *The Times,* 24 August 1995.
3 Christopher, M. (2002) 'Business is failing to manage supply chain vulnerability', *Odessey,* Issue 16, June.
4 Source: 'Air crashes, but surely . . .', *The Economist,* 4 June 1994.
5 Examples taken from Slack, N. and Lewis, M.A. (2002) *Operations Strategy,* Financial Times Prentice Hall, Harlow, UK.
6 Nakajima, S. (1988) *Total Productive Maintenance,* Productivity Press.
7 Example taken from Slack, N. and Lewis, M.A. (2002) *Operations Strategy,* Financial Times Prentice Hall, Harlow, UK.
8 Armistead, C.G. and Clark, G. (1992) *Customer Service and Support,* FT/Pitman Publishing.
9 Based on information from Read, P.P. (1994) *Ablaze: The story of Chernobyl,* Secker and Warburg; and Reason, J. (1987) 'The Chernobyl errors', *Bulletin of the British Psychological Society,* Vol. 4, pp. 201–6.

Taking it further

Dhillon, B.S. (2002) *Engineering Maintenance: A modern approach,* Technomic Publishing Company. A comprehensive book for the enthusiastic that stresses the 'cradle-to-grave' aspects of maintenance.

Heskett, J.L., Sasser, W.E. and Hart, C.W.L. (1990) *Service Breakthroughs: Changing the rules of the game,* Free Press, New York. A general book on managing service operations, but does contain some interesting points on service failure.

HMSO (1995) *An Introduction and a Guide to Business Continuity Management,* HMSO. One of the earliest technical guides to failure and disaster recovery.

Japan Institute (ed.) (1997) *Focused Equipment Improvement to TPM Teams,* Japan Institute of Plant Maintenance. Very much a simple and practical guide to an important element of total productive maintenance.

Löfsten, H. (1999) 'Management of industrial maintenance – Economic evaluation of maintenance policies', *International Journal of Operations and Production Management,* Vol. 19, No. 7. An academic paper, but provides a useful economic rationale for choosing alternative maintenance policies.

Mobley, K. (1999) *Root Cause Failure Analysis,* Butterworth-Heinemann. Root cause failure analysis is one of the more important techniques in reliability and maintenance. This book describes it in detail.

Smith, D.J. (2000) *Reliability, Maintainability and Risk,* Butterworth-Heinemann. A comprehensive and excellent guide to all aspects of maintenance and reliability.

Useful websites

www.smrp.org Site of the Society for Maintenance and Reliability Professionals. Gives an insight into practical issues.
www.sre.org American Society of Reliability Engineers. The newsletters give insights into reliability practice.
www.csob.berry.edu/faculty/jgrout/pokayoke.shtml The poka-yoke page of John Grout. Some great examples, tutorials, etc.
www.rspa.com/spi/SQA.html Lots of resources, involving reliability and poka-yoke.
www.sra.org Site of the Society for Risk Analysis. Very wide scope, but interesting.

**FURTHER
RESOURCES**

For further resources including examples, animated diagrams, self test questions, excel spreadsheets, active case studies and video materials please explore the CD accompanying this book.

15

PROJECT MANAGEMENT

Introduction

This chapter is concerned with managing 'projects'. Some projects are complex and large-scale, have activities involving diverse resources, and last for years. But other 'projects' are far smaller affairs, possibly limited to one part of a business, and may last only a few days. Yet, although the complexity and degree of difficulty involved in managing different types of projects will vary, the essential approach to the task does not. Whether projects are large or small, internal or external, long or short, they all require defining, planning and controlling. (See Figure 15.1.)

Source: © Getty Images/Digital Vision

Figure 15.1 Project management is the activity of defining, planning and controlling projects

Executive summary

What is project management?

Is the project environment understood?

Is the project well defined?

Is project management adequate?

Has the project been adequately planned?

Is the project adequately controlled?

Decision logic chain for project management

Each chapter is structured around a set of diagnostic questions. These questions suggest what you should ask in order to gain an understanding of the important issues of a topic, and as a result, improve your decision-making. An executive summary, addressing these questions, is provided below.

What is project management?

Project management is the activity of defining, planning and controlling projects. A project is a set of activities with a defined start point and defined end state, which pursues a defined goal and uses a defined set of resources. It is a very broad activity that almost all managers will become involved in at some time or other. Some projects are large-scale and complex, but most projects, such as implementation of a process improvement, will be far smaller. However, all projects are managed using a similar set of principles.

Is the project environment understood?

The project environment is the sum of all factors that may affect the project during its life. These include the geographical, social, economic, political and commercial environments, and on small projects also include the internal organizational environment. The project environment can also include the intrinsic difficulty of the project defined by its scale, degree of uncertainty, and complexity. Also included in a project's environment are the project stakeholders, those individuals or groups who have some kind of interest in the project. Stakeholder management can be particularly important both to avoid difficulties in the project and to maximize its chances of success. Stakeholders can be classified by their degree of interest in the project and their power to influence it.

Is the project well defined?

A project is defined by three elements: its objectives, its scope, and its overall strategy. Most projects can be defined by the relative importance of three objectives. These are cost (keeping the overall project to its original budget), time (finishing the project by the scheduled finish time), and quality (ensuring that the project outcome is as was originally specified). The project scope defines its work content and outcomes. More importantly, it should define what is not included in the project. The project strategy describes the general way in which the project is going to meet its objectives, including significant project milestones and 'stagegates'.

Is project management adequate?

Because of their complexity and the involvement of many different parties, projects need particularly careful managing. In fact, project management is seen as a particularly demanding role with a very diverse set of skills, including technical project management knowledge, interpersonal skills and leadership ability. Very often project managers need the ability to motivate staff who not only report to a manager other than themselves, but also divide their time between several different projects.

Has the project been adequately planned?

Project planning involves determining the cost and duration of the project and the level of resources that it will need. In more detail, it involves identifying the start and finish times of individual activities within the project. Generally, the five stages of project planning include identifying activities, estimating times and resources, identifying relationships and dependencies between activities, identifying time and resource schedule constraints, and fixing the final schedule. However, no amount of planning can prevent the need for replanning as circumstances dictate during the life of the project. Network planning techniques such as critical path analysis (CPA) are often used to aid the project planning process.

Is the project adequately controlled?

Project control involves monitoring the project in order to check its progress, assessing the performance of the project against the project plan, and, if necessary, intervening in order to bring the project back to plan. The process often involves continually assessing the progress of the project in terms of budgeted expenditure and progress towards meeting the project's final goal. It may also involve deciding when to devote extra resources to accelerating (also know as crashing) individual activities within the project. There are a number of proprietary computer-assisted project management packages on the market that range from relatively simple network planning programmes through to complex and integrated 'enterprise project management' (EPRM) systems.

What is project management?

A project is a set of activities with a defined start point and a defined end state, which pursues a defined goal and uses a defined set of resources. What can be defined as a 'project' can vary significantly from relatively small and local activities, through to very large 'put a man on the moon' enterprises. Project management is the activity of defining, planning and controlling projects of any type.

The activity of project management is very broad in so much as it could encompass almost all the operations and process management tasks described in this book. Partly because of this, it could have been treated almost anywhere within the direct, design, delivery, develop, structure of this book. We have chosen to place it in the context of operations and process development because most of the projects that most managers will be involved in are essentially improvement projects. Of course, many projects are vast enterprises with very high levels of resourcing, complexity and uncertainty that will extend over many years. Look around at the civil engineering, social, political and environmental successes (and failures) to see the evidence of major projects. Such projects require professional project management involving high levels of technical expertise and management skills. But so do the smaller, yet important, projects that implement the many and continuous improvements that will determine the strategic impact of operations development. This is why it is equally important to take a rigorous and systematic approach to managing improvement projects as it is to managing major projects.

At this point it is worth pointing out the distinction between 'projects' and 'programmes'. A programme, such as a continuous improvement programme, has no defined end point. Rather it is an ongoing process of change. Individual projects, such as the development of training processes, may be individual sub-sections of an overall programme, such as an integrated skills development programme. Programme management will overlay and integrate the individual projects. Generally, it is a more difficult task in the sense that it requires resource coordination, particularly when multiple projects share common resources, as emphasized in the following quotation: *'Managing projects is, it is said, like juggling three balls – cost, quality, and time. Programme management … is like organizing a troupe of jugglers all juggling three balls and swapping balls from time to time.'*[1]

The following two projects illustrate some of the issues in project management.

Example ## Popping the Millau cork[2]

For decades locals and French motorists had called the little bridge at Millau that was one of the few crossings on the river Tarn 'the Millau cork'. It held up all the traffic on what should have been one of the busiest north–south routes through France. No longer. In place of the little bridge is one of the most impressive and beautiful civil engineering successes of the last century. Lord Foster, the British architect who designed the bridge, described it as an attempt to enhance the natural beauty of the valley through a structure that had the 'delicacy of a butterfly', with the environment dominating the scene rather than the bridge. And although the bridge appears to float on the clouds, it has seven pillars and a roadway of $1^1/_2$ miles in length. It is also a remarkable technical achievement. At 300 metres it is the highest road bridge in the world, weighing 36,000 tonnes. The central pillar is higher than the Eiffel Tower, and took only three years to complete, notwithstanding the new engineering techniques that were needed.

Outline plans for the bridge were produced back in 1987. But, because of planning, funding and design considerations, construction did not begin until December 2001. It was completed in December 2004, on time and budget, having proved the effectiveness of its new construction technique. The traditional method of building this type of bridge (called a cable stay bridge) involves building sections of the roadway on the ground and using cranes to put them in position. Because of its height, 300 metres above the valley floor, a new technique had to be developed. First, the towers were built in the usual way, with steel-reinforced concrete. The roadway was built on the high ground at either side of the valley and then pushed forward into space as further sections were added, until it met with precision (to the nearest centimetre) in the centre. This technique had never been tried before and it carried engineering risks, which added to the complexity of the project management task.

It all began with a massive recruitment drive. *'People came from all over France for employment. We knew it would be a long job. We housed them in apartments and houses in and around Millau. Eiffel gave guarantees to all the tenants and a unit was set up to help everyone with the paperwork involved in this. It was not unusual for a worker to be recruited in the morning and have his apartment available the same evening with electricity and a telephone available.'* (Jean-Pierre Martin, Chief Engineer of Groupe Eiffage and director of building) Over 3000 workers – technicians, engineers, crane drivers, carpenters, welders, winchers, metal workers, painters, concrete specialists, and experts in the use of the stays and pylons that would support the bridge – contributed to the project. On the project site, 500 of them, positioned somewhere between the sky and the earth, worked in all weathers to complete the project on time. *'Everyday I would ask myself what was the intense force that united these men,'* said Jean-Pierre Martin. *'They had a very strong sense of pride and they belonged to a community that was to build the most beautiful construction in the world. It was never necessary to shout at them to get them to work. Life on a construction site has many ups and downs. Some days we were frozen. Other days we were subjected to a heatwave. But even on days of bad weather, one had to force them to stay indoors. Yet often they would leave their lodgings to return to work.'*

Many different businesses were involved in building the bridge – Arcelor, Eiffel, Lafarge, Freyssinet, Potain. All of them needed coordinating in such a way that they would cooperate towards the common goal, but yet avoid any loss of overall responsibility. Jean-Pierre Martin came up with the idea of nine autonomous work groups. One group was placed at the foot of each of the seven piles that would support the bridge and two others at either end. The motto adopted by the teams was *'rigueur et convivialité'*, rigorous quality and friendly cooperation. *'The difficulty with this type of project is keeping everyone enthusiastic throughout its duration. To make this easier we created these small groups. Each of the nine team's shifts were organized in relays between 7 and 14 hours, and 14 and 21 hours.'* So, to maintain the good atmosphere, no expense was spared to celebrate important events in the construction of the viaduct, for example a pile, or another piece of road completed. Sometimes, to boost the morale of the teams, and to celebrate these important events, Jean-Pierre would organize a *'méchouis'* – a spit roast of lamb, especially popular with the many workers who were of North African origin.

Example   Access HK[3]

Access HK is an independent non-profit organization that works to fight inequality and to provide underprivileged children with educational opportunities that are otherwise unaffordable by them. Every summer, Access HK's volunteers, mostly students studying at overseas universities, return to Hong Kong to give a free Summer School to children in need. It was set up in the summer of 2001 by a group of Hong Kong students at leading UK and US universities. Since then it has organized

Source: © Access HK

several large-scale events to help underprivileged children, including free four-week Summer Schools during which children are taught in interactive formats on subjects such as the English language, current affairs, speech and drama. Oxford student Ng Kwan-hung, Access HK's external secretary, said: *'We share a common belief that what distinguishes one child from another is not ability but access – access to opportunities, access to education, access to love. All of us realize the importance of a good learning environment for a child's development.'* Chung Tin-Wong, a law student at Oxford and sub-committee member, added: *'We are all dedicated to providing the best education for underprivileged children.'*

Project managing the summer schools is particularly important to Access HK because their opportunities to make a difference to the underprivileged are limited largely to the vacation periods when their student volunteers are available. Project failure would mean waiting until the next year to get another chance. Also, like many charities, the budget is limited with every dollar having to count. Because of this, the student volunteers soon learn some of the arts of the project management, including how to break the project down into four phases for ease of planning and control.

- *Conceptual phase*, during which the Access HK central committee agrees with the Summer School Committee, its direction, aim and goal.
- *Planning phase*, when the Summer School Committee sets the time and cost parameters for the project. The time frame for the Summer School is always tight. Student volunteers become available only after they have completed their summer exams, and the Summer School must be ready to run when the primary school students have their summer break.
- *Definition and design phase*, when the detailed implementation plans for the Summer School are finalized. Communication between the teams of volunteers is particularly important to ensure contributed smooth implementation later. Many of them, although enthusiastic, have little project management experience, and therefore need the support of detailed instructions as to how to carry out their part of the project.
- *Implementation phase*. Again, it is the relative inexperience of the volunteer force that dictates how the Summer School project is implemented. It is important to ensure that control mechanisms are in place that can detect any problems or deviations from the plan quickly, and help to bring it back on target.

'The success of these Summer School projects depends very much on including all our stakeholders in the process', says one Summer School coordinator. *'All our stakeholders are important but they have different interests. The students on the Summer Schools, even if they don't articulate their objectives, need to feel that are benefiting from the experience. Our volunteers are all bright and enthusiastic and are interested in helping to manage the process as well as taking part in it. Access HK wants to be sure that we are doing our best to fulfil their objectives and uphold their reputation. The Hong Kong government have an obvious interest in the success and integrity of the Summer Schools, and the sponsors need to be assured that their donations are being used wisely. In addition the schools who lend us their buildings and many other interested parties all need to be included, in different ways and to different extents, in our project management process.'*

What do these two example have in common?

Not all projects are as large or as complex as the Millau Bridge, but the same issues will occur. Because no single project exists in isolation, the social, political and operational environment must be taken into account. For the Access HK Summer School this means including many different community groups and organizations as well as sponsors. Each project's objectives and scope also need to be clarified with stakeholders. Detailed planning, however, will be the responsibility of those who act as project managers. They are the ones who determine the time and resource commitments that the project will need, as well as identifying the long list of things that could go wrong. Back-up plans will need to be made to minimize the impact of uncertainties. The project management teams for the two examples are very different – professional and experienced in one case, volunteer and inexperienced in the other. But both have elements in common. Both have an objective, a definable end result. Both are temporary in that they have a defined beginning and need a temporary concentration of resources that will be redeployed once their contribution has been completed. Both need to motivate the people involved in the project, both need planning, both need controlling. In other words, both need project managing.

DIAGNOSTIC QUESTION

Is the project environment understood?

The project environment comprises all the factors which may affect the project during its life. It is the context and circumstances in which the project takes place. Understanding the project environment is important because the environment affects the way in which a project will need to be managed and (just as important) the possible dangers that may cause the project to fail. Environmental factors can be considered under the following four headings.

- *Geo-social environment.* Geographical, climatic and cultural factors that may affect the project.
- *Econo-political environment.* The economic, governmental and regulatory factors in which the project takes place.
- *The business environment.* Industrial, competitive, supply network and customer expectation factors that shape the likely objectives of the project.
- *The internal environment.* The individual company's or group's strategy and culture, the resources available, and the interaction with other projects that will influence the project.

FURTHER EXAMPLE

Project difficulty

An important element in the project management environment is the degree of difficulty of the project itself. Three factors have been proposed as determining project difficulty. These are scale, uncertainty and complexity. This is illustrated in Figure 15.2. Large-scale projects involving many different types of resources with durations of many years will be more difficult to manage, both because the resources will need a high level of management effort, and because project management objectives must be maintained over a long time period. Uncertainty particularly affects project planning. Ground-breaking projects are likely to be especially uncertain, with ever-changing objectives leading to planning difficulties. When uncertainty is high, the whole project planning process needs to be sufficiently flexible to cope with the consequences of change. Projects with high levels of complexity, such as multi-organizational projects, often require considerable control effort. Their many separate

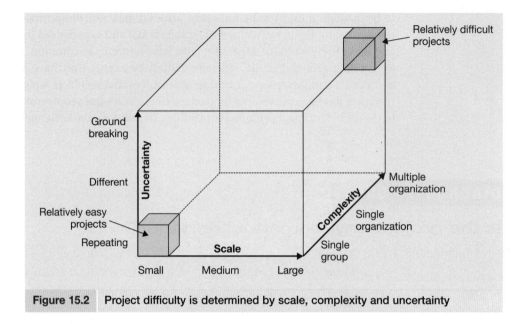

Figure 15.2   Project difficulty is determined by scale, complexity and uncertainty

> **Operations principle**
> The difficulty of managing a project is a function of its scale, complexity, and uncertainty.

activities, resources and groups of people involved increase the scope for things to go wrong. Furthermore, as the number of separate activities in a project increases, the ways in which they can impact on each other increase exponentially. This increases the effort involved in monitoring each activity. It also increases the chances of overlooking some part of the project which is deviating from the plan. Most significantly, it increases the 'knock-on' effect of any problem.

Stakeholders

One way of operationalizing the importance of understanding a project's environment is to consider the various 'stakeholders' who have some kind of interest in the project. The stakeholders in any project are the individuals and groups who have an interest in the project process or outcome. All projects will have stakeholders; complex projects will have many. They are likely to have different views on a project's objectives that may conflict with those of other stakeholders. At the very least, different stakeholders are likely

> **Operations principle**
> All projects have stakeholders with different interests and priorities.

to stress different aspects of a project. So, as well as an ethical imperative to include as many people as possible in a project from an early stage, it is often useful in preventing objections and problems later in the project. Moreover, there can be significant direct benefits from using a stakeholder-based approach. Project managers can use the opinions of powerful stakeholders to shape the project at an early stage. This makes it more likely that they will support the project, and also can improve its quality. Communicating with stakeholders early and frequently can ensure that they fully understand the project and understand potential benefits. Stakeholder support may even help to win more resources, making it more likely that projects will be successful. Perhaps most important, one can anticipate stakeholder reaction to various aspects of the project, and plan the actions that could prevent opposition, or build support.

> **Operations principle**
> Project stakeholders have responsibilities as well as rights.

Some (even relatively experienced) project managers are reluctant to include stakeholders in the project management process, preferring to 'manage them at a distance' rather than allowing them to interfere with the project. Others argue that the benefits

Table 15.1	The rights and responsibilities of project stakeholders in one IT company

Rights	Responsibilities
1 To expect developers to learn and speak their language	1 Provide resources (time, money, etc.) to the project team
2 To expect developers to identify and understand their requirements	2 Educate developers about their business
3 To receive explanations of artifacts that developers use as part of working with project stakeholders, such as models they create with them (e.g. user stories or essential prototypes), or artifacts that they present to them (e.g. deployment diagrams)	3 Spend the time to provide and clarify requirements
	4 Be specific and precise about requirements
	5 Make timely decisions
	6 Respect a developer's assessment of cost and feasibility
	7 Set requirement priorities
4 To expect developers to treat them with respect	8 Review and provide timely feedback regarding relevant work artifacts of developers
5 To hear ideas and alternatives for requirements	9 Promptly communicate changes to requirements
6 To describe characteristics that make the product easy to use	10 Own your organization's software processes: to both follow them and actively help to fix them when needed
7 To be presented with opportunities to adjust requirements to permit reuse, reduce development time, or reduce development costs	
8 To be given good-faith estimates	
9 To receive a system that meets their functional and quality needs	

of stakeholder management are too great to ignore and many of the risks can be moderated by emphasizing the responsibilities as well as the rights of project stakeholders. For example, one information technology company formally identifies the rights and responsibilities of project stakeholders as shown in Table 15.1.

Managing stakeholders

PRACTICE NOTE

Managing stakeholders can be a subtle and delicate task, requiring significant social and, sometimes, political skills. But it is based on three basic activities: identifying, prioritizing, and understanding the stakeholder group.

- *Identify stakeholders.* Think of all the people who are affected by your work, who have influence or power over it, or have an interest in its successful or unsuccessful conclusion. Although stakeholders may be both organizations and people, ultimately you must communicate with people. Make sure that you identify the correct individual stakeholders within a stakeholder organization.
- *Prioritize stakeholders.* Many people and organizations will be affected by a project. Some of these may have the power either to block or to advance the project. Some may be interested in what you are doing; others may not care. Map out stakeholders using the Power–Interest Grid (see later), and classify them by their power and by their interest in the project.
- *Understand key stakeholders.* It is important to know about key stakeholders. One needs to know how they are likely to feel about and react to the project. One also needs to know how best to engage them in the project and how best to communicate with them.

The power–interest grid

One approach to discriminating between different stakeholders, and more important, how they should be managed, is to distinguish between their power to influence the project and their interest in doing so. Stakeholders who have the power to exercise a major influence over the project should never be ignored. At the very least, the nature of their interest, and their motivation, should be well understood. But not all stakeholders who have the power to exercise influence over a project will be interested in doing so, and not everyone who is interested in the project has the power to influence it. The power–interest grid, shown in Figure 15.3, classifies stakeholders simply in terms of these two dimensions. Although there will be gradations between them, the two dimensions are useful in providing an indication of how stakeholders can be managed in terms of four categories.

Stakeholders' positions on the grid give an indication of how they might be managed. High-power, interested groups must be fully engaged, with the greatest efforts made to

> **Operations principle**
> Different stakeholder groups will need managing differently.

satisfy them. High-power, less interested groups require enough effort to keep them satisfied, but not so much that they become bored or irritated with the message. Low-power, interested groups need to be kept adequately informed, with checks to ensure that no major issues are arising. These groups may be very helpful with the detail of the project. Low-power, less interested groups need monitoring, but without excessive communication. Some key questions that can help in distinguishing high-priority stakeholders include the following.

- What financial or emotional interest do they have in the outcome of the project? Is it positive or negative?
- What motivates them most of all?
- What information do they need?
- What is the best way of communicating with them?
- What is their current opinion of the project?
- Who influences their opinions? Do some of these influencers therefore become important stakeholders in their own right?
- If they are not likely to be positive, what will win them round to support the project?
- If you don't think you will be able to win them round, how will you manage their opposition?

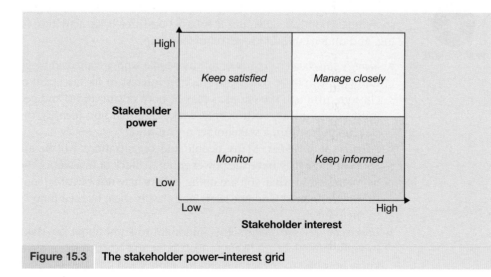

Figure 15.3   **The stakeholder power–interest grid**

Is the project well defined?

Before starting the complex task of planning and executing a project, it is necessary to be clear about exactly what the project is – its definition. This is not always straightforward, especially in projects with many stakeholders. Three different elements define a project:

- Its *objectives*: the end state that project management is trying to achieve
- Its *scope*: the exact range of the responsibilities taken on by project management
- Its *strategy*: how project management is going to meet its objectives.

Project objectives

PRACTICE NOTE

Objectives help to provide a definition of the end point which can be used to monitor progress and identify when success has been achieved. They can be judged in terms of the five performance objectives – quality, speed, dependability, flexibility and cost. However, flexibility is regarded as a 'given' in most projects which, by definition, are to some extent one-offs, and speed and dependability are compressed to one composite objective – 'time'. This results in what are known as the 'three objectives of project management' – cost, time and quality.

The relative importance of each objective will differ for different projects. Some aerospace projects, such as the development of a new aircraft, which impact on passenger safety, will place a very high emphasis on quality objectives. With other projects, for example a research project that is being funded by a fixed government grant, cost might predominate. Other projects emphasize time: for example, the organization of an open-air music festival has to happen on a particular date if the project is to meet its objectives. In each of these projects, although one objective might be particularly important, the other objectives can never be totally forgotten. Good objectives are those which are clear, measurable and, preferably, quantifiable. Clarifying objectives involves breaking down project objectives into three categories – the purpose, the end results, and the success criteria. For example, a project that is expressed in general terms as 'improve the budgeting process' could be broken down into:

> **Operations principle**
> Different projects will place different levels of emphasis on cost, time, and quality objectives.

- *Purpose* – to allow budgets to be agreed and confirmed prior to the annual financial meeting
- *End result* – a report that identifies the causes of budget delay, and which recommends new budgeting processes and systems
- *Success criteria* – the report should be completed by 30 June, meet all departments' needs, and enable integrated and dependable delivery of agreed budget statements. Cost of the recommendations should not exceed $200,000.

Project scope

The scope of a project identifies its work content and its products or outcomes. It is a boundary-setting exercise which attempts to define the dividing line between what each part of the project will do and what it won't do. Defining scope is particularly important when part of a project is being outsourced. A supplier's scope of supply will identify the legal boundaries within which the work must be done. Sometimes the scope of the project is articulated in a formal 'project specification'. This is the written, pictorial and graphical information used to define the output, and the accompanying terms and conditions.

Project strategy

The third part of a project's definition is the project strategy, which defines, in a general rather than a specific way, how the project is going to meets its objectives. It does this in two ways: by defining the phases of the project, and by setting milestones, and/or 'stagegates'. Milestones are important events during the project's life. Stagegates are the decision points that allow the project to move onto its next phase. A stagegate often launches further activities and therefore commits the project to additional costs, etc. Milestone is a more passive term, which may herald the review of a part-complete project or mark the completion of a stage, but does not necessarily have more significance than a measure of achievement or completeness. At this stage the actual dates for each milestone are not necessarily determined. It is useful, however, to at least identify the significant milestones and stagegates, either to define the boundary between phases or to help in discussions with the project's customer.

DIAGNOSTIC QUESTION

Is project management adequate?

In order to coordinate the efforts of many people in different parts of the organization (and often outside it as well), all projects need a project manager. Many of a project manager's activities are concerned with managing human resources. The people working in the project team need a clear understanding of their roles in the (usually temporary) organization. Controlling an uncertain project environment requires the rapid exchange of relevant information with the project stakeholders, both within and outside the organization. People, equipment and other resources must be identified and allocated to the various tasks. Undertaking these tasks successfully makes the management of a project a particularly challenging operations activity.

Project management skills

The project manager is the person responsible for delivering a project. He or she leads and manages the project team, with the responsibility, if not always the authority, to run the project on a day-to-day basis. They are special people. They must possess seemingly opposing skills. They must be able to influence without necessarily having authority, pay attention to details without losing sight of the big picture, establish an open, communicative environment while remaining wedded to project objectives, and be able to hope for the best but plan for the worst. It is a formidable role. Ideally it involves leading, communicating, organizing, negotiating, managing conflict, motivating, supporting, team building, planning, directing, problem solving, coaching and delegating.

> **Operations principle**
> The activity of project management requires interpersonal as well as technical skills.

PRACTICE NOTE

In more formal terms, typical project manager responsibilities include the following.

- Devising and applying an appropriate project management framework for the project
- Managing the production of the required deliverables
- Planning and monitoring the project
- Delegating project roles within agreed reporting structures
- Preparing and maintaining a project plan
- Managing project risks, including the development of contingency plans
- Liaison with programme management (if the project is part of a programme)
- Overall progress and use of resources, initiating corrective action where necessary
- Managing changes to project objectives or details
- Reporting through agreed reporting lines on project progress and stage assessments
- Liaison with senior management to assure the overall direction and integrity of the project
- Adopting technical and quality strategy
- Identifying and obtaining support and advice required for the management of the project
- Managing ongoing project administration
- Conducting post-project evaluation to assess how well the project was executed
- Preparing any follow-on action recommendations as required.

Five characteristics in particular are seen as important in an effective project manager:[4]

- Background and experience which are consistent with the needs of the project
- Leadership and strategic expertise, in order to maintain an understanding of the overall project and its environment, while at the same time working on the details of the project
- Technical expertise in the area of the project in order to make sound technical decisions
- Interpersonal competence and the people skills to take on such roles as project champion, motivator, communicator, facilitator and politician
- Proven managerial ability, in terms of a track record of getting things done.

Managing matrix tensions

In all but the simplest projects, project managers usually need to reconcile the interests of both the project itself and the departments contributing resources to the project. When calling on a variety of resources from various departments, projects are operating in a 'matrix management' environment, where projects cut across organizational boundaries and involve staff who are required to report to their own line manager as well as to the project manager. Figure 15.4 illustrates the type of reporting relationship that usually occurs in matrix management structures running multiple projects. A person in department 1, assigned part-time to projects A and B, will be reporting to three different managers all of whom will have some degree of authority over their activities. This is why matrix management requires a high degree of cooperation and communication between

Figure 15.4   Matrix management structures often result in staff reporting to more than one project manager as well as their own department

all individuals and departments. Although decision-making authority will formally rest with either the project or the departmental manager, most major decisions will need some degree of consensus. Arrangements need to be made that reconcile potential differences between project managers and departmental managers. To function effectively, matrix management structures should have the following characteristics.

- There should be effective channels of communication between all managers involved, with relevant departmental managers contributing to project planning and resourcing decisions.
- There should be formal procedures in place for resolving the management conflicts that do arise.
- Project staff should be encouraged to feel committed to their projects as well as to their own department.
- Project management should be seen as the central coordinating role, with sufficient time devoted to planning the project, securing the agreement of the line managers to deliver on time and within budget.

DIAGNOSTIC QUESTION

Has the project been adequately planned?

All projects, even the smallest, need some degree of planning. The planning process fulfils four distinct purposes. It determines the cost and duration of the project, it determines the level of resources that will be needed, it helps to allocate work and to monitor progress, and it helps to assess the impact of any changes to the project. It is a vital step

Figure 15.5   Stages in the project planning process

at the start of the project, but it could be repeated several times during the project's life as circumstances change. This is not a sign of project failure or mismanagement. In uncertain projects, in particular, it is a normal occurrence. In fact, later stage plans typically mean that more information is available, and that the project is becoming less uncertain. The process of project planning involves five steps, shown in Figure 15.5.

Identify activities – the work breakdown structure

Some projects are too complex to be planned and controlled effectively unless they are first broken down into manageable portions. This is achieved by structuring the project into a 'family tree' that specifies the major tasks or sub-projects. These in turn are divided up into smaller tasks until a defined, manageable series of tasks, called a work package, is arrived at. Each work package can be allocated its own objectives in terms of time, cost and quality. The output from this is called the work breakdown structure (WBS). The WBS brings clarity and definition to the project planning process. It shows 'how the jigsaw fits together'. It also provides a framework for building up information for reporting purposes.

For example, Figure 15.6 shows the work breakdown structure for a project to design a new information interface (a website screen) for a new sales knowledge management system that is being installed in an insurance company. The project requires cooperation between the company's IT systems department and its sales organization. Three types of activity will be necessary to complete the project: training, installation and testing. Each of these categories is further broken down into specific activities as shown in Figure 15.6.

Figure 15.6   Work breakdown structure for a project to design an information interface for a new sales knowledge management system in an insurance company

Table 15.2   Time and resource estimates and relationships for the sales system interface design project

Code	Activity	Immediate predecessor(s)	Duration (days)	Resources (developers)
a	Form and train user group	none	10	3
b	Install systems	none	17	5
c	Specify sales training	a	5	2
d	Design initial screen interface	a	5	3
e	Test interface in pilot area	b, d	25	2
f	Modify interface	c, e	15	3

Estimate times and resources

The next stage in planning is to identify the time and resource requirements of the work packages. Without some idea of how long each part of a project will take and how many resources it will need, it is impossible to define what should be happening at any time during the execution of the project. Estimates are just that, however – a systematic best guess, not a perfect forecast of reality. Estimates may never be perfect but they can be made with some idea of how accurate they might be. Table 15.2 includes time (in days) and resource (in terms of the number of IT developers needed) estimates for the sales system interface design project.

Probabilistic estimates

The amount of uncertainty in a project has a major bearing on the level of confidence which can be placed on an estimate. The impact of uncertainty on estimating times leads some project managers to use a probability curve to describe the estimate. In practice, this is usually a positively skewed distribution, as in Figure 15.7. More uncertainty increases the range of the distribution. The natural tendency of some people is to produce optimistic estimates, but these will have a relatively low probability of being correct because they represent the time which would be taken if everything went well. Most likely estimates have the highest probability of proving correct. Finally, pessimistic estimates assume that almost everything which could go wrong does go wrong. Because of the skewed nature of the distribution, the expected time for the activity will not be the same as the most likely time.

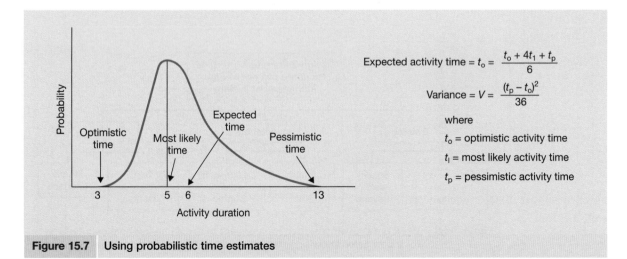

Expected activity time $= t_o = \dfrac{t_o + 4t_1 + t_p}{6}$

Variance $= V = \dfrac{(t_p - t_o)^2}{36}$

where

t_o = optimistic activity time

t_1 = most likely activity time

t_p = pessimistic activity time

Figure 15.7   Using probabilistic time estimates

Identify the relationships and dependencies between the activities

All the activities which are identified as comprising a project will have some relationship with one another that will depend on the logic of the project. Some activities will, by necessity, need to be executed in a particular order. For example, in the construction of a house, the foundations must be prepared before the walls are built, which in turn must be completed before the roof is put in place. These activities have a dependent or series relationship. Other activities do not have any such dependence on each other. The rear garden of the house could probably be prepared totally independently of the garage being built. These two activities have an independent or parallel relationship.

In the case of the sales system interface design, Table 15.2 provided the basic information that enables the relationships between activities in the project to be established. It did this by identifying the immediate predecessor (or predecessors) for each activity. So, for example, activities **a** and **b** can be started without any of the other activities being completed. Activity **c** cannot begin until activity **a** has been completed, nor can activity **d**. Activity **e** can start only when both activities **b** and **d** have been completed, and activity **f** can start only when activities **c** and **e** have been completed.

Planning tools

Project planning is greatly aided by the use of techniques that help to handle time, resource and relationships complexity. The simplest of these techniques is the *Gantt chart* (or bar chart) which we introduced in Chapter 10. Figure 15.8 shows a Gantt chart for the activities that form the sales system interface project. The bars indicate the start, duration and finish time for each activity. The length of the bar for each activity on a Gantt chart is directly proportional to the calendar time, and so indicates the relative duration of each activity. Gantt charts are the simplest way to exhibit an overall project plan, because they have excellent visual impact and are easy to understand. They are also useful for communicating project plans and status to senior managers as well as for day-to-day project control.

As project complexity increases, it becomes more necessary to identify clearly the relationships between activities, and show the logical sequence in which activities must take place. This is most commonly done by using the *critical path method* (CPM) to clarify the relationships between activities diagrammatically. The first way we can illustrate this is by using arrows to represent each activity in a project. Figure 15.9 shows this for the sales system interface design project. Each activity is represented by an arrow, in this case with the activity code and the duration in days shown next to it. The circles in Figure 15.9 represent

Figure 15.8   Gantt chart for the project to design an information interface for a new sales knowledge management system in an insurance company

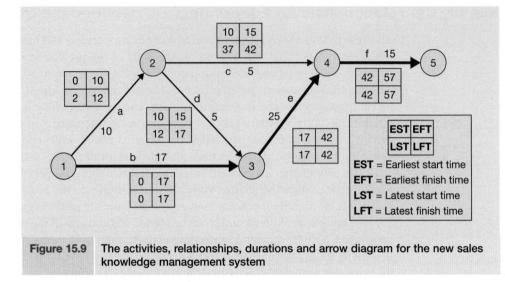

Figure 15.9 The activities, relationships, durations and arrow diagram for the new sales knowledge management system

PRACTICE NOTE

'events'. These are single points in time that have no duration but mark, for example, the start and finish of activities. So, in this case, event 2 represents the event 'activity **a** finishes'. Event 3 represents '*both* activities **b** and **d** finished', and so on.

The diagram shows that there are a number of chains of events that must be completed before the project can be considered as finished (event 5). In this case, activity chains **a–c–f**, **a–d–e–f** and **b–e–f** must all be completed before the project can be considered as finished. The longest of these chains of activities is called the 'critical path' because it represents the shortest time in which the project can be finished, and therefore dictates the project timing. In this case **b–e–f** is the longest path and the earliest the project can finish is after 57 days.

Figure 15.9 also includes information concerning the earliest and latest start and finish times for each activity. This can be derived by following the logic of the arrow diagram forwards by calculating the earliest times an event can take place, and backwards by calculating the latest time an event can take place. So, for example, the earliest the project can finish (event 5) is the sum of all the activities on the critical path, **b–e–f**, 57 days. If we then take 57 days as the latest that we wish the project to finish, the latest activity **f** can start is $57 - 15 = 42$, and so on. Activities that lie on the critical path will have the same earliest and latest start times and earliest and latest finish times. That is why these activities are critical. Non-critical activities, however, have some flexibility as to when they start and finish. This flexibility is quantified into a figure that is known as either 'float' or 'slack'. This can be shown diagrammatically, as in Figure 15.10. Here, the Gantt chart for the project has been revisited, but this time the time available to perform each activity (the duration between the earliest start time and the latest finish time for the activity) has been shown. So, combining the network diagram in Figure 15.9 and the Gantt chart in Figure 15.10, activity **c**, for example, is only of 5 days' duration, it can start any time after day 10 and must finish any time before day 42. Its 'float' is therefore $(42 - 10) - 5 = 27$ days. Obviously, activities on the critical path have no float; any change or delay in these activities would immediately affect the whole project.

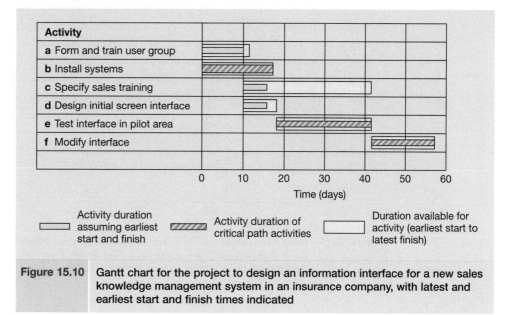

Figure 15.10 Gantt chart for the project to design an information interface for a new sales knowledge management system in an insurance company, with latest and earliest start and finish times indicated

Identify time and resource schedule constraints

Once estimates have been made of the time and effort involved in each activity, and their dependencies identified, it is possible to compare project requirements with the available resources. The finite nature of critical resources – such as staff with special skills – means that they should be taken into account in the planning process. This often has the effect of highlighting the need for more detailed replanning.

The logic that governs project relationships, as shown in the network diagram, is primarily derived from the technical details, but the availability of resources may also impose its own constraints, which can materially affect the relationships between activities. Return to the sales system interface design project. Figure 15.11 shows the resource profile under two different assumptions. The critical path activities (**b–e–f**) form the initial basis of the project's resource profile. These activities have no float and can only take place as shown. However, activities **a**, **c** and **d** are not on the critical path, so project managers have some flexibility as to when these activities occur, and therefore when the resources associated with these activities will be required. From Figure 15.11, if one schedules all activities to start as soon as possible, the resource profile peaks between days 10 and 15 when 10 IT development staff are required. However, if the project manager exploits the float that activity **c** possesses and delays its start until after activity **b** has been completed (day 17), the number of IT developers required by the project does not exceed 8. In this way, float can be used to smooth out resource requirements or make the project fit resource constraints. However, it does impose further resource-constrained logic on the relationship between the activities. So, for example, in this project moving activity **c** as shown in Figure 15.11 results in a further constraint of not starting activity **c** until activity **b** has been completed.

Fix the schedule

Project planners should ideally have a number of alternatives to choose from. The one which best fits project objectives can then be chosen or developed. However, it is not

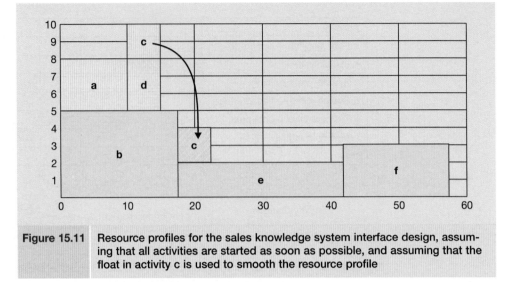

Figure 15.11 Resource profiles for the sales knowledge system interface design, assuming that all activities are started as soon as possible, and assuming that the float in activity c is used to smooth the resource profile

always possible to examine several alternative schedules, especially in very large or very uncertain projects, as the computation could be prohibitive. However, modern computer-based project management software is making the search for the best schedule more feasible.

Variations on simple network planning

There are several variations on the simple critical path method type of network that we have used to illustrate project planning thus far. While it is beyond the scope of this book to enter into much more detail of the various ways that simple network planning can be made more sophisticated, two variants are worth mentioning. The first, activity on node networks, is simply a different approach to drawing the network diagram. The second, programme evaluation and review technique (PERT), does represent an enrichment of the basic network approach.

Activity on node networks

The network we have described so far uses arrows to represent activities and circles at the junctions or nodes of the arrows to represent events. This method is called the activity on arrow (AoA) method. An alternative method of drawing networks is the activity on node (AoN) method. In the AoN representation, activities are drawn as boxes, and arrows are used to define the relationships between them. There are three advantages to the AoN method:

● It is often easier to move from the basic logic of a project's relationships to a network diagram using AoN rather than using the AoA method.
● AoN diagrams do not need dummy activities to maintain the logic of relationships.
● Most of the computer packages which are used in project planning and control use an AoN format.

Figure 15.12 shows the sales system interface design project drawn as an AoN diagram. In this case, we have kept a similar notation to the one used in the original AoA diagram. In addition, each activity box contains information on the description of the activity, its duration and its total float.

Figure 15.12 Activity on node network diagram for the sales system design project

Programme evaluation and review technique (PERT)

The programme evaluation and review technique, or PERT as it is universally known, had its origins in planning and controlling major defence projects in the US Navy. PERT had its most spectacular gains in the highly uncertain environment of space and defence projects. The technique recognizes that activity durations and costs in project management are not deterministic (fixed), and that probability theory can be applied to estimates, as was shown in Figure 15.7.

Operations principle
Probabilistic activity time estimates facilitate the assessment of a project being completed on time.

In this type of network each activity duration is estimated on an optimistic, a most likely and a pessimistic basis, and the mean and variance of the distribution that describes each activity can be estimated as was shown in Figure 15.7. The results are shown in Table 15.3.

In this case the sum of the expected times for each of the activities on the critical path (b–e–f) is 58.17 days, and the sum of the variances of these three activities is 6.07 days. From this, one could calculate the probability of the project overrunning by different amounts of time.

Table 15.3 PERT parameters for the sales system design project

Code	Activity	Optimistic estimate	Most likely estimate	Pessimistic estimate	Expected time	Variance
a	Form and train user group	8	10	14	10.33	1
b	Install systems	10	17	25	17.17	0.69
c	Specify sales training	4	5	6	5	0.11
d	Design initial screen interface	5	5	5	5	0
e	Test interface in pilot area	22	25	27	24.83	0.69
f	Modify interface	12	15	25	16.17	4.69

Is the project adequately controlled?

All the stages in project management described so far have all taken place before the actual project takes place. Project control deals with activities during the execution of the project. Project control is the essential link between planning and doing.

The process of project control involves three sets of decisions:

- How to monitor the project in order to check on its progress
- How to assess the performance of the project by comparing monitored observations of the project with the project plan
- How to intervene in the project in order to make the changes that will bring it back to plan.

Project monitoring

Project managers have first to decide what they should be looking for as the project progresses. Usually a variety of measures are monitored. To some extent, the measures used will depend on the nature of the project. However, common measures include current expenditure to date, supplier price changes, amount of overtime authorized, technical changes to project, inspection failures, number and length of delays, activities not started on time, missed milestones, etc. Some of these monitored measures affect mainly cost, some mainly time. However, when something affects the quality of the project, there are also time and cost implications. This is because quality problems in project planning and control usually have to be solved in a limited amount of time.

Assessing project performance

A typical planned cost profile of a project through its life is shown in Figure 15.13. At the beginning of a project some activities can be started, but most activities will be dependent on finishing. Eventually, only a few activities will remain to be completed. This pattern of a slow start followed by a faster pace with an eventual tail-off of activity holds true for almost all projects, which is why the rate of total expenditure follows an S-shaped pattern as shown in Figure 15.13, even when the cost curves for the individual activities are linear. It is against this curve that actual costs can be compared in order to check whether the project's costs are being incurred to plan. Figure 15.13 shows the planned and actual cost figures compared in this way. It shows that the project is incurring costs, on a cumulative basis, ahead of what was planned.

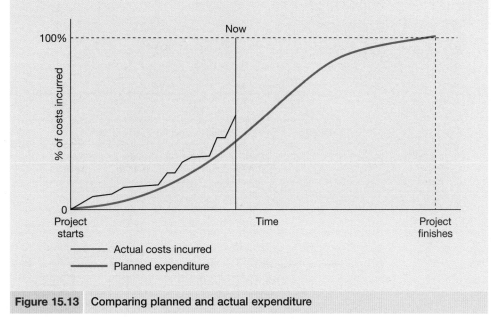

Figure 15.13   Comparing planned and actual expenditure

Intervening to change the project

If the project is obviously out of control in the sense that its costs, quality levels or times are significantly different from those planned, then some kind of intervention is almost certainly likely to be required. The exact nature of the intervention will depend on the technical characteristics of the project, but it is likely to need the advice of all the people who would be affected. Given the interconnected nature of projects – a change to one part of the project will have knock-on effects elsewhere – this means that interventions often require wide consultation. Sometimes intervention is needed even if the project looks to be proceeding according to plan. For example, the schedule and cost for a project may seem to be 'to plan', but when the project managers project activities and cost into the future, they see that problems are very likely to arise. In this case it is the trend of performance which is being used to trigger intervention.

Crashing, or accelerating, activities

Crashing activities is the process of reducing time spans on critical path activities so that the project is completed in less time. Usually, crashing activities incurs extra cost. This can be as a result of the following factors:

- Overtime working
- Additional resources, such as manpower
- Sub-contracting.

Figure 15.14 shows an example of crashing a simple network. For each activity the duration and normal cost are specified, together with the (reduced) duration and (increased)

> **Operations principle**
> Only accelerating activities on the critical path(s) will accelerate the whole project.

cost of crashing them. Not all activities are capable of being crashed; here activity **e** cannot be crashed. The critical path is the sequence of activities **a**, **b**, **c**, **e**. If the total project time is to be reduced, one of the activities on the critical path must be crashed. In order to decide which activity to crash, the 'cost slope' of each

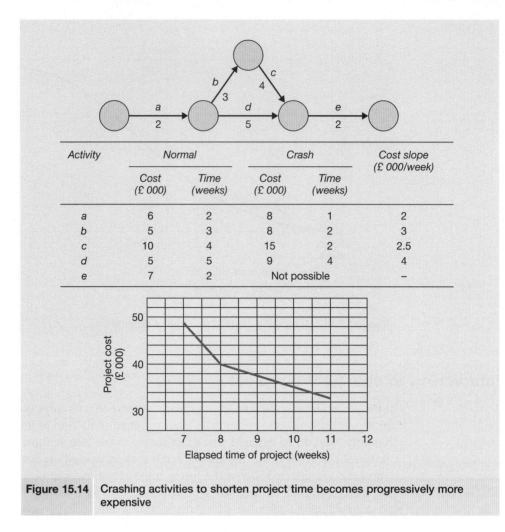

Activity	Normal		Crash		Cost slope (£ 000/week)
	Cost (£ 000)	Time (weeks)	Cost (£ 000)	Time (weeks)	
a	6	2	8	1	2
b	5	3	8	2	3
c	10	4	15	2	2.5
d	5	5	9	4	4
e	7	2	Not possible		–

Figure 15.14 Crashing activities to shorten project time becomes progressively more expensive

is calculated. This is the cost per time period of reducing durations. The most cost-effective way of shortening the whole project then is to crash the activity on the critical path which has the lowest cost slope. This is activity **a**, the crashing of which will cost an extra £2000 and will shorten the project by one week. After this, activity **c** can be crashed, saving a further two weeks and costing an extra £5000. At this point all the activities have become critical and further time savings can only be achieved by crashing two activities in parallel.

The shape of the time–cost curve in Figure 15.14 is entirely typical. Initial savings come relatively inexpensively if the activities with the lowest cost slope are chosen. Later in the crashing sequence the more expensive activities need to be crashed and eventually two or more paths become jointly critical. Inevitably by that point, savings in time can only come from crashing two or more activities on parallel paths.

Computer-assisted project management

For many years, since the emergence of computer-based modelling, increasingly sophisticated software for project planning and control has become available. The rather tedious computation necessary in network planning can be performed relatively easily by project planning models. All they need are the basic relationships between activities together with timing and resource requirements for each activity. Earliest and latest event times, float and other characteristics of a network can be presented, often in the form of a Gantt chart. More significantly, the speed of computation allows for frequent updates to project plans. Similarly, if updated information is both accurate and frequent, such computer-based systems can also provide effective project control data. More recently, the potential for using computer-based project management systems for communication within large and complex projects has been developed in so-called Enterprise Project Management (EPM) systems.

Figure 15.15 illustrates just some of the elements that are integrated within EPM systems. Most of these activities have been treated in this chapter. Project planning involves critical path analysis and scheduling, an understanding of float, and the sending of instructions on when to start activities. Resource scheduling looks at the resource implications of planning decisions and the way projects may have to be changed to accommodate resource constraints. Project control includes simple budgeting and cost management together with more sophisticated earned value control. However, EPM also includes other elements. Project modelling involves the use of project planning methods to explore alternative approaches to a project, identifying where failure might occur and exploring the changes to the project which may have to be made under alternative future scenarios. Project portfolio analysis acknowledges that, for many organizations, several projects have to be managed simultaneously. Usually these share common resources. Therefore, not only delays in one activity within a project affect other activities in that project, they may also have an impact on completely different projects which are relying on the same resource. Finally, integrated EPM systems can help to communicate, both within a project and to outside organizations which may be contributing to the project.

Figure 15.15   Some of the elements integrated in Enterprise Project Management Systems

Much of this communication facility is Web-based. Project portals can allow all stakeholders to transact activities and gain a clear view of the current status of a project. Automatic notification of significant milestones can be made by email. At a very basic level, the various documents that specify parts of the project can be stored in an online library. Some people argue that it is this last element of communication capabilities that is the most useful part of EPM systems.

Critical commentary

Each chapter contains a short critical commentary on the main ideas covered in the chapter. Its purpose is not to undermine the issues discussed in the chapter, but to emphasize that, although we present a relatively orthodox view of operation, there are other perspectives.

■ *When project managers talk of 'time estimates', they are really talking about guessing. By definition, planning a project happens in advance of the project itself. Therefore, no one really knows how long each activity will take. Of course, some kind of guess is needed for planning purposes. However, some project managers believe that too much faith is put in time estimates. The really important question, they claim, is not how long will something take, but how long could something take without delaying the whole project. Also, if a single most likely time estimate is difficult to estimate, then using three, as one does for probabilistic estimates, is merely over-analyzing what is highly dubious data in the first place.*

■ *The idea that all project activities can be identified as entities with a clear beginning and a clear end point and that these entities can be described in terms of their relationship with each other is an obvious simplification. Some activities are more or less continuous and evolve over time. For example, take a simple project such as digging a trench and laying a communications cable in it. The activity 'dig trench' does not have to be completed before the activity 'lay cable' is started. Only two or three metres of the trench needs to be dug before cable laying can commence – a simple relationship, but one that is difficult to illustrate on a network diagram. Also, if the trench is being dug in difficult terrain, the time taken to complete the activity, or even the activity itself, may change, to include rock drilling activities, for example. However, if the trench cannot be dug because of rock formations, it may be possible to dig more of the trench elsewhere – a contingency not allowed for in the original plan. So, even for this simple project, the original network diagram may reflect neither what will happen nor what could happen.*

Summary checklist

DOWNLOADABLE

This checklist comprises questions that can be usefully applied to any type of operations and reflect the major diagnostic questions used within the chapter.

☐ Have all the factors that could influence the project been identified?

☐ Do these factors include both external and internal influences?

☐ Has the project been assessed for its intrinsic difficulty by considering its relative scale, uncertainty and complexity, when compared to other projects?

☐ Is the importance of stakeholder management fully understood?

☐ Have the rights and responsibilities of project stakeholders been defined?

☐ Have all stakeholders been identified?

☐ Have all stakeholders been prioritized in terms of their relative power and interest?

☐ Has sufficient attention been paid to understanding the needs and motivation of key stakeholders?

☐ Has the project been well defined?

☐ Have the objectives of the project been defined, particularly in terms of the relative importance of cost, time and quality?

☐ Has the scope of the project been defined, including the areas that the project will not include?

☐ Has the overall strategy of the project been defined in terms of its overall approach, its significant milestones, and any decision gateways that may occur in the project?

☐ Have overall project management skills within the business been generally assessed?

☐ For this particular project, does the project manager have skills appropriate for the project's intrinsic degree of difficulty?

☐ Is sufficient effort being put into the project planning process?

☐ Have all activities been identified and expressed in the form of a work breakdown structure?

☐ Have all activity times and resources been estimated using the best possible information within the organization?

☐ Is there sufficient confidence in the time and resource estimates to make planning meaningful?

☐ Have the relationships and dependencies between activities been identified and summarized in the form of a simple network diagram?

☐ Have project planning tools, such as critical path analysis, been considered for the project?

☐ Have potential resource and time schedule constraints been built into the project plan?

☐ Are there mechanisms in place to monitor the progress of the project?

☐ Is there a formal mechanism to assess progress against project plans?

☐ Have mechanisms for intervening in the project to bring it back to plan been put in place?

☐ Is the level of computer-based project management support appropriate for the degree of difficulty of the project?

Case study   United Photonics Malaysia Sdn Bhd

Introduction

Anuar Kamaruddin, COO of United Photonics Malaysia (EPM), was conscious that the project in front of him was one of the most important he had handled for many years. The number and variety of the development projects underway within the company had risen sharply in the last few years, and although they had all seemed important at the time, this one – the 'Laz-skan' project – clearly justified the description given it by the President of United Photonics Corporation, the US parent of UPM: '. . . *the make or break opportunity to ensure the division's long term position in the global instrumentation industry.*'

The United Photonics Group

United Photonics Corporation had been founded in the 1920s (as the Detroit Gauge Company), a general instrument and gauge manufacturer for the engineering industry. By expanding its range into optical instruments in the early 1930s, it eventually moved also into the manufacture of high precision and speciality lenses, mainly for the photographic industry. Its reputation as a specialist lens manufacturer led to such a growth in sales that by 1969 the optical side of the company accounted for about 60 per cent of total business and it ranked as one of the top two or three optics companies of its type in the world. Although its reputation for skilled lens making had not diminished since then, the instrument side of the company had come to dominate sales once again in the 1980s and 1990s.

UPM product range

UPM's product range on the optical side included lenses for inspection systems which were used mainly in the manufacture of microchips. These lenses were sold both to the inspection system manufacturers and to the chip manufacturers themselves. They were very high precision lenses; however, most of the company's optical products were specialist photographic and cinema lenses. In addition about 15 per cent of the company's optical work was concerned with the development and manufacture of 'one or two off' extremely high precision lenses for defence contracts, specialist scientific instrumentation, and other optical companies. The Group's instrument product range consisted largely of electromechanical assemblies with an increasing emphasis on software-based recording, display

and diagnostic abilities. This move towards more software-based products had led the instrument side of the business towards accepting some customized orders. The growth of this part of the instrumentation had resulted in a special development unit being set up – the Customer Services Unit (CSU), which modified, customized or adapted products for those customers who required an unusual product. Often CSU's work involved incorporating the company's products into larger systems for a customer.

In 1995 United Photonics Corporation had set up its first non-North American facility just outside Kuala Lumpur in Malaysia. United Photonics Malaysia Sdn Bhd (UPM) had started by manufacturing sub-assemblies for Photonics instrumentation products, but soon had developed in a laboratory for the modification of United Photonics products for customers throughout the Asian region. This part of the Malaysian business was headed by T.S. Lim, a Malaysian engineer who had taken his postgraduate qualifications at Stanford and three years ago moved back to his native KL to head up the Malaysian outpost of the CSU, reporting directly to Bob Brierly, the Vice-President of Development, who ran the main CSU in Detroit. Over the last three years, T.S. Lim and his small team of engineers had gained quite a reputation for innovative development. Bob Brierly was delighted with their enthusiasm. '*Those guys really do know how to make things happen. They are giving us all a run for our money.*'

The Laz-skan project

The idea for Laz-skan had come out of a project which T.S. Lim's CSU had been involved with in 2004. At that time the CSU had successfully installed a high precision Photonics lens into a character recognition system for a large clearing bank. The enhanced capability which the lens and software modifications had given had enabled the bank to scan documents even when they were not correctly aligned. This had led to CSU proposing the development of a 'vision metrology' device that could optically scan a product at some point in the manufacturing process, and check the accuracy of up to 20 individual dimensions. The geometry of the product to be scanned, the dimensions to be gauged, and the tolerances to be allowed, could all be programmed into the control logic of the device. The T.S. Lim team were convinced that the idea could have considerable potential. The proposal, which the CSU team had called the Laz-skan project, was put to Bob Brierly in August 2004. Brierly both saw the potential value of the idea and was again impressed by the CSU team's enthusiasm. *'To be frank, it was their evident enthusiasm that influenced me as much as anything. Remember that the Malaysian CSU had only been existence for two years at this time – they were a group of keen but relatively young engineers. Yet their proposal was well thought out and, on reflection, seemed to have considerable potential.'*

In November 2004 Lim and his team were allocated funds (outside the normal budget cycle) to investigate the feasibility of the Laz-skan idea. Lim was given one further engineer and a technician, and a three-month deadline to report to the board. In this time he was expected to overcome any fundamental technical problems, assess the feasibility of successfully developing the concept into a working prototype, and plan the development task that would lead to the prototype stage.

The Lim investigation

T.S. Lim, even at the start of his investigation, had some firm views as to the appropriate 'architecture' for the Laz-skan project. By 'architecture' he meant the major elements of the system, their functions, and how they related to each other. The Laz-skan system architecture would consider five major sub-systems: the lens and lens mounting, the vision support system, the display system, the control logic software, and the documentation.

T.S. Lim's first task, once the system's overall architecture was set, was to decide whether the various components in the major sub-systems would be developed in-house, developed by outside specialist companies from UPM's specifications, or bought in as standard units and if necessary modified in-house. Lim and his colleagues made these decisions themselves, while recognizing that

a more consultative process might have been preferable. *'I am fully aware that ideally we should have made more use of the expertise within the company to decide how units were to be developed. But within the time available we just did not have the time to explain the product concept, explain the choices, and wait for already busy people to come up with a recommendation. Also there was the security aspect to think of. I'm sure our employees are to be trusted but the more people who know about the project, the more chance there is for leaks. Anyway, we did not see our decisions as final. For example, if we decided that a component was to be bought in and modified for the prototype building stage it does not mean that we can't change our minds and develop a better component in-house at a later stage.'* By February 2005, TS's small team had satisfied themselves that the system could be built to achieve their original technical performance targets. Their final task before reporting to Brierly would be to devise a feasible development plan.

Planning the Laz-skan development

As a planning aid the team drew up a network diagram for all the major activities within the project from its start through to completion, when the project would be handed over to Manufacturing Operations. This is shown in Figure 15.16 and the complete list of all events in the diagram is shown in Table 15.4. The durations of all the activities in the project were estimated either by T.S. Lim or (more often) by him consulting a more experienced engineer back in Detroit. While he was reasonably confident in the estimates, he was keen to stress that they were just that – estimates.

Two draughting conventions on these networks need explanation. The three figures in brackets by each activity arrow represent the 'optimistic', 'most likely' and 'pessimistic' times (in weeks) respectively. The figure in the left side of the event circles indicates the earliest time the event could take place, and the figure in the right side of the circles indicates the latest time the event could take place without delaying the whole project. Dotted lines represent 'dummy' activities. These are nominal activities which have no time associated with them and are there either to maintain the logic of the network or for drafting convenience.

(1) The lens (events 5–13–14–15)

The lens was particularly critical since the shape was complex and precision was vital if the system was to perform up to its intended design specification. T.S. Lim was relying heavily upon the skill of the Group's expert optics group in Pittsburgh to produce the lens to the required high tolerance. Since what in effect was a trial and error approach was involved in their manufacture, the exact

Table 15.4 Event listing for the Laz-skan project

Event number	Event description
1	Start systems engineering
2	Complete interface transient tests
3	Complete compatibility testing
4	Complete overall architecture block and simulation
5	Complete costing and purchasing tender planning
6	End alignment system design
7	Receive S/T/G, start synch mods
8	Receive Triscan/G, start synch mods
9	Complete B/A mods
10	Complete S/T/G mods
11	Complete Triscan/G mods
12	Start laser subsystem compatibility tests
13	Complete optic design and specification, start lens manufacture
14	Complete lens manufacture, start lens housing S/A
15	Lens S/A complete, start tests
16	Start technical specifications
17	Start help routine design
18	Update engineering mods
19	Complete doc sequence
20	Start vision routines
21	Start interface (tmsic) tests
22	Start system integration compatibility routines
23	Coordinate trinsic tests
24	End interface development
25	Complete alignment integration routine
26	Final alignment integration data consolidation
27	Start interface (tmnsic) programming
28	Complete alignment system routines
29	Start tmnsic comparator routines
30	Complete (interface) trinsic coding
31	Begin all logic system tests
32	Start cycle tests
33	Lens S/A complete
34	Start assembly of total system
35	Complete total system assembly
36	Complete final tests and dispatch

time to manufacture would be uncertain. T.S. Lim realized this: '*The lens is going to be a real problem. We just don't know how easy it will be to make the particular geometry and precision we need. The optics people won't commit themselves even though they are regarded as some of the best optics technicians in the world. It is a relief that lens development is not amongst the "critical path" activities.*'

(2) The vision support system (events 6–7–8–12, 9–5, 11)

The vision support system included many components which were commercially available, but considerable engineering effort would be required to modify them. Although the development design and testing of the vision support system was complicated, there was no great uncertainty in the individual activities, or therefore the schedule of completion. If more funds were allocated to their development, some tasks might even be completed ahead of time.

(3) The control software (events 20 to 26, 28)

The control software represented the most complex task, and the most difficult to plan and estimate. In fact, the software development unit had little experience of this type of work but (partly in anticipation of this type of development) had recently recruited a young software engineer with some experience of the type of work which would be needed for Laz-skan. He was confident that any technical problems could be solved even though the system needs were novel, but completion times would be difficult to predict with confidence.

(4) Documentation (events 5–16–17–18–19)

A relatively simple sub-system, 'documentation' included specifying and writing the technical manuals, maintenance routines, online diagnostics, and 'help desk' information. It was a relatively predictable activity, part of which was sub-contracted to technical writers and translation companies in Kuala Lumpur.

(5) The display system (events 29–27–30)

The simplest of the sub-systems to plan, the display system would need to be manufactured entirely outside the company and tested and calibrated on receipt.

Market prospects

In parallel with T.S. Lim's technical investigation, Sales and Marketing had been asked to estimate the market potential of Laz-skan. In a very short time, the Laz-skan

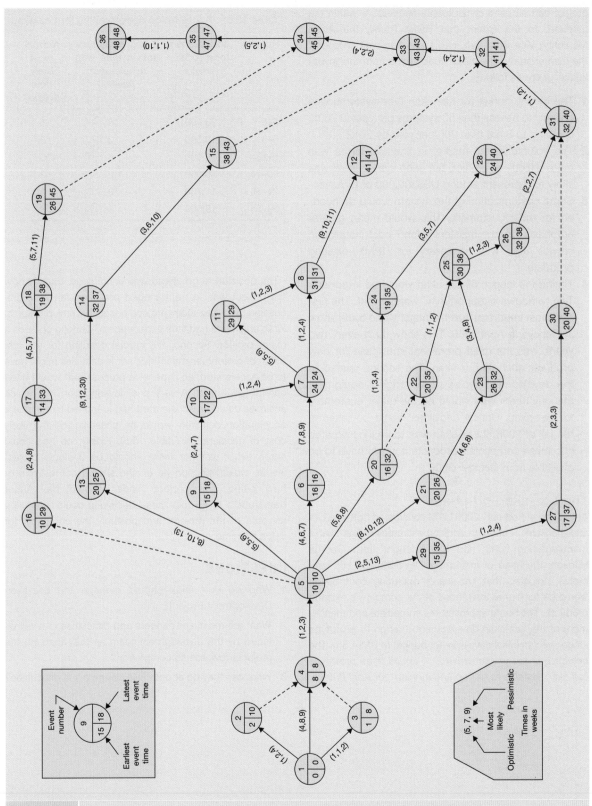

Figure 15.16

project had aroused considerable enthusiasm within the function, to the extent that Halim Ramli, the Asian Marketing Vice President, had taken personal charge of the market study. The major conclusions from this investigation were as follows.

1 The global market for Laz-skan type systems was unlikely to be less than 50 systems per year in 2008, climbing to more than 200 per year by 2012.
2 The volume of the market in financial terms was more difficult to predict, but each system sold was likely to represent around US$300,000 of turnover.
3 Some customization of the system would be needed for most customers. This would mean greater emphasis on commissioning and post-installation service than was necessary for UPM's existing products.
4 Timing the launch of Laz-skan would be important. Two 'windows of opportunity' were critical. The first and most important was the major world trade show in Geneva in April 2006. This show, held every two years, was the most prominent showcase for new products such as Laz-skan. The second related to the development cycles of the original equipment manufacturers who would be the major customers for Laz-skan. Critical decisions would be taken in the fall of 2006. If Laz-skan was to be incorporated into these companies' products it would have to be available from October 2006.

The Laz-skan go-ahead

At the end of February 2005 UPM considered both the Lim and the Ramli reports. In addition estimates of Laz-skan's manufacturing costs had been sought from George Hudson, the head of Instrument Development. His estimates indicated that Laz-skan's operating contribution would be far higher than those of the company's existing products. The board approved the immediate commencement of the Laz-skan development through to prototype stage, with an initial development budget of US$4.5m. The objective of the project was to '. . . *build three prototype Laz-skan systems to be "up and running" for April 2006'*.

Table 15.5 Acceleration opportunities for Laz-skan

Activity	Acceleration cost (US$/ week)	Likely maximum activity time, with acceleration (weeks)	Normal most likely time (weeks)
5–6	23,400	3	6
5–9	10,500	2	5
5–13	25,000	8	10
20–24	5,000	2	3
24–28	11,700	3	5
33–34	19,500	1	2

The decision to go ahead was unanimous. Exactly how the project was to be managed provoked far more discussion. The Laz-skan project posed several problems. First, engineers had little experience of working on such a major project. Second, the crucial deadline for the first batch of prototypes meant that some activities might have to be accelerated, an expensive process that would need careful judgement. A very brief investigation into which activities could be accelerated had identified those where acceleration definitely would be possible and the likely cost of acceleration (Table 15.5). Finally, no one could agree either whether there should be a single project leader, which function he or she should come from, or how senior the project leader should be. Anuar Kamaruddin knew that these decisions could affect the success of the project, and possibly the company, for years to come.

QUESTIONS

1 Who do you think should manage the Laz-skan Development Project?

2 What are the major dangers and difficulties that will be faced by the development team as they manage the projects towards its completion?

3 What can they do about these dangers and difficulties?

Active case study   National Trust

ACTIVE CASE

The National Trust of England, Wales and Northern Ireland was formed in 1895 with the objective to preserve places of historic interest or natural beauty for the nation to enjoy. When the local director and his project team take on 'The Workhouse' they know from the outset that it will be one of their more intriguing and challenging projects. Aware of the need for sensitive stakeholder management, the team draws up a list of stakeholders and set out to win them over with their enthusiasm for the project.

● How would you assess their plans for dealing with each one?

Please refer to the Active case on the CD accompanying this book to find out more about the stakeholder groups involved.

Applying the principles

HINTS

Some of these exercises can be answered by reading the chapter. Others will require some general knowledge of business activity and some might require an element of investigation. All have hints on how they can be answered on the CD accompanying this book.

1 The activities, their durations and precedences for designing, writing and installing a bespoke computer database are shown in the table below. Draw a Gantt chart and a network diagram for the project and calculate the fastest time in which the operation might be completed.

Bespoke computer database activities

Activity	Duration (weeks)	Activities that must be completed before it can start
1 Contract negotiation	1	–
2 Discussions with main users	2	1
3 Review of current documentation	5	1
4 Review of current systems	6	2
5 Systems analysis (A)	4	3, 4
6 Systems analysis (B)	7	5
7 Programming	12	5
8 Testing (prelim)	2	7
9 Existing system review report	1	3, 4
10 System proposal report	2	5, 9
11 Documentation preparation	19	5, 8
12 Implementation	7	7, 11
13 System test	3	12
14 Debugging	4	12
15 Manual preparation	5	11

2 Identify a project of which you have been part (for example moving apartments, a holiday, a dramatic production, revision for an examination, etc.).

- Who were the stakeholders in this project?
- What was the overall project objective (especially in terms of the relative importance of cost, quality and time)?
- Were there any resource constraints?
- Looking back, how could you have managed the project better?

3 The Channel Tunnel project was the largest construction project ever undertaken in Europe and the biggest single investment in transport anywhere in the world. The project, which was funded by the private sector, made provision for a 55-year concession for the owners to design, build and run the operation. The Eurotunnel Group awarded the contract to design and build the tunnel to TML (Trans-Manche Link), a consortium of 10 French and British construction companies. For the project managers it was a formidable undertaking. The sheer scale of the project was daunting in itself. The volume of rubble removed from the tunnel increased the size of Britain by the equivalent of 68 football fields. Two main railway tunnels, separated by a service/access tunnel, each 7.6 metres in diameter, run 40 metres below the sea bed. In total there are in excess of 150 kilometres of tunnel. The whole project was never going to be a straightforward management task. During the early negotiations, political uncertainty surrounded the commitment of both governments, and in the planning phase geological issues had to be investigated by a complex series of tests. Even the financing of the project was complex. It required investment by over 200 banks and finance houses, as well as over half a million shareholders. Furthermore, the technical problems posed by the drilling itself and, more importantly, in the commissioning of the tracks and systems within the tunnel needed to be overcome. Yet in spite of some delays and cost overruns, the project ranks as one of the most impressive of the twentieth century.

- What factors made the Channel Tunnel a particularly complex project and how might these have been dealt with?
- What factors contributed to 'uncertainty' in the project and how might these factors have been dealt with?
- Look on the Internet to see what has happened to the Channel Tunnel since it was built. How does this affect your view on the project of building it?

4 Identify your favourite sporting team (Manchester United, the Toulon rugby team, or if you are not a sporting person, choose any team you have heard of).

- What kind of projects do you think they need to manage? For example, merchandising, sponsorship, etc.
- What do you think are the key issues in making a success of managing each of these different types of project?

5 Visit the websites of some companies that have developed computer-based project management software (for example, **primavera.com**, **welcome.com**, **microsoft.com**, or just put 'project management software' in a search engine).

- What appear to be the common elements in the software packages on offer from these companies? Develop a method that could be used by any operation to choose different types of software.

Notes on chapter

1 Reiss, G. (1996) *Programme Management Demystified*, Spon, London.
2 Slack, A. (2005) 'Popping the Millau Cork', translated and adapted from *Le Figaro Entreprises*, 15 December 2004.
3 Source: Organization website.
4 Weiss, J.W. and Wysocki, R.K. (1992) *Five-Phase Project Management: A practical planning and implementation guide*, Addison-Wesley.

Taking it further

There are hundreds of books on project management. They range from the introductory to the very detailed, and from the managerial to the highly mathematical. Here are two general (as opposed to mathematical) books which are worth looking at.

Maylor, H. (2003) *Project Management* (3rd edn), Financial Times Prentice Hall.

Meredith, J.R. and Mantel, S. (1995) *Project Management:* A managerial approach (3rd edn), John Wiley.

Useful websites

www.apm.org.uk The UK Association for Project Management. Contains a description of what professionals consider to be the body of knowledge of project management.

www.pmi.org The Project Management Institute's home page. An American association for professionals. Insights into professional practice.

www.ipma.ch The International Project Management Association, based in Zürich. Some definitions and links.

www.comp.glam.ac.uk/pages/staff/dwfarth/projman.htm#automated A great site with lots of interesting stuff on software, project management and related issues, but also very good for general project management.

FURTHER RESOURCES

For further resources including examples, animated diagrams, self test questions, excel spreadsheets, active case studies and video materials please explore the CD accompanying this book.

Index

IMPORTANT: READ CAREFULLY
WARNING: BY OPENING THE PACKAGE YOU AGREE TO BE BOUND BY THE TERMS OF THE LICENCE AGREEMENT BELOW.

This is a legally binding agreement between You (the user or purchaser) and Pearson Education Limited. By retaining this licence, any software media or accompanying written materials or carrying out any of the permitted activities You agree to be bound by the terms of the licence agreement below.

If You do not agree to these terms then promptly return the entire publication (this licence and all software, written materials, packaging and any other components received with it) with Your sales receipt to Your supplier for a full refund.

SINGLE USER LICENCE AGREEMENT

❏ YOU ARE PERMITTED TO:

- Use (load into temporary memory or permanent storage) a single copy of the software on only one computer at a time. If this computer is linked to a network then the software may only be installed in a manner such that it is not accessible to other machines on the network.

- Make one copy of the software solely for backup purposes or copy it to a single hard disk, provided you keep the original solely for back up purposes.

- Transfer the software from one computer to another provided that you only use it on one computer at a time.

❏ YOU MAY NOT:

- Rent or lease the software or any part of the publication.

- Copy any part of the documentation, except where specifically indicated otherwise.

- Make copies of the software, other than for backup purposes.

- Reverse engineer, decompile or disassemble the software.

- Use the software on more than one computer at a time.

- Install the software on any networked computer in a way that could allow access to it from more than one machine on the network.

- Use the software in any way not specified above without the prior written consent of Pearson Education Limited.

ONE COPY ONLY
This licence is for a single user copy of the software
PEARSON EDUCATION LIMITED RESERVES THE RIGHT TO TERMINATE THIS LICENCE BY WRITTEN NOTICE AND TO TAKE ACTION TO RECOVER ANY DAMAGES SUFFERED BY PEARSON EDUCATION LIMITED IF YOU BREACH ANY PROVISION OF THIS AGREEMENT.

Pearson Education Limited owns the software You only own the disk on which the software is supplied.

LIMITED WARRANTY

Pearson Education Limited warrants that the diskette or CD rom on which the software is supplied are free from defects in materials and workmanship under normal use for ninety (90) days from the date You receive them. This warranty is limited to You and is not transferable. Pearson Education Limited does not warrant that the functions of the software meet Your requirements or that the media is compatible with any computer system on which it is used or that the operation of the software will be unlimited or error free.

You assume responsibility for selecting the software to achieve Your intended results and for the installation of, the use of and the results obtained from the software. The entire liability of Pearson Education Limited and its suppliers and your only remedy shall be replacement of the components that do not meet this warranty free of charge.

This limited warranty is void if any damage has resulted from accident, abuse, misapplication, service or modification by someone other than Pearson Education Limited. In no event shall Pearson Education Limited or its suppliers be liable for any damages whatsoever arising out of installation of the software, even if advised of the possibility of such damages. Pearson Education Limited will not be liable for any loss or damage of any nature suffered by any party as a result of reliance upon or reproduction of or any errors in the content of the publication.

Pearson Education Limited does not limit its liability for death or personal injury caused by its negligence.

This licence agreement shall be governed by and interpreted and construed in accordance with English law.